Jeff Mahlstedt

Houghton Mifflin English

# Grammar and Composition

**Fifth Course**

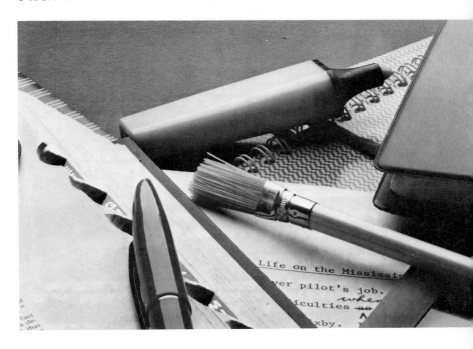

## Houghton Mifflin Company • Boston

Atlanta   Dallas   Geneva, Illinois
Lawrenceville, New Jersey   Palo Alto   Toronto

# Authors

**Ann Cole Brown** Former Lecturer in English composition and literature at Northern Virginia Community College in Alexandria, Virginia

**Jeffrey Nilson** Former teacher of English at the Wixon Middle School, South Dennis, Massachusetts, and independent computer software designer

**Fran Weber Shaw** Assistant Professor of English and Coordinator of the Writing Center at the University of Connecticut, Stamford

**Richard A. Weldon** Vice Principal, Associate Dean of Studies, and teacher of English at the Christian Brothers High School in Sacramento, California

# Editorial Advisers

**Edwin Newman** Veteran broadcast journalist, author, and chairman of the Usage Panel of the *American Heritage Dictionary of the English Language*

**Robert Cotton** Vice Principal, Curriculum Director, and former chairman of the English Department at Servite High School in Anaheim, California

# Consultant

**Nancy C. Millett** Professor of Language Arts Education at Wichita State University, Kansas, and co-author of *Houghton Mifflin English, K-8*

## Special Contributors

Ernestine Sewell, University of Texas at Arlington

Luella M. Wolff, Washburn University, Topeka, Kansas

# Acknowledgments

The Publisher gratefully acknowledges the cooperation of the National Council of Teachers of English for making available student writing from the Council's Achievement Awards in Writing Program.

(Acknowledgments continue on page 630.)

Printed in U.S.A.

ISBN: 0-395-38551-2

BCDEFGHIJ-RM-943210/89876

# Contents

**The English Language:** A Brief History of American English     viii

**Part One**    **Grammar, Usage, and Mechanics**    1

    **Unit 1**    **Parts of Speech**    2

       **1.1** Nouns    3
       **1.2** Pronouns    8
       **1.3** Verbs    13
       **1.4** Adjectives    18
       **1.5** Adverbs    23
       **1.6** Prepositions    27
       **1.7** Conjunctions    30
       **1.8** Interjections    35

    **Unit 2**    **Sentence Structure**    42

       **2.1** Four Sentence Purposes    43
       **2.2** Subjects and Predicates    45
       **2.3** Complements    51

    **Unit 3**    **Phrases and Clauses**    64

       **3.1** Phrases    65
       **3.2** Clauses    79
       **3.3** Sentences Classified by Structure    90
       **3.4** Writing Complete Sentences    93

**Unit 4   Usage**                                    106

    **4.1**  Correct Use of Verbs               107
    **4.2**  Subject-Verb Agreement            123
    **4.3**  Correct Use of Pronouns          134
    **4.4**  Correct Use of Modifiers          151
    **4.5**  Usage Notes                            156

**Unit 5   Mechanics**                               182

    **5.1**  Capitalization                        183
    **5.2**  Punctuation                           190
    **5.3**  Using Italics and Numbers
         in Writing                            211
    **5.4**  Preparing Your Manuscript         216

**Part Two   Composition**                         224

**Unit 6   Prewriting**                              226

    **6.1**  Finding Ideas for Writing          227
    **6.2**  Developing Your Ideas             233
    **6.3**  Focusing Your Ideas               238

**Unit 7   Writing Paragraphs**                    248

    **7.1**  Developing Paragraphs            249
    **7.2**  Organizing Coherent Paragraphs   261
    **7.3**  Combining Methods
         of Organization                   275

**Unit 8   Revising**                                284

    **8.1**  Revising: Unity and Coherence     285
    **8.2**  Revising: Consistency             289

**8.3** Revising: Combining Sentences 293
**8.4** Revising Sentences: Variety 306
**8.5** Revising Sentences:
    Parallel Structure 310
**8.6** Revising Sentences: Conciseness 313
**8.7** Revising and Proofreading 326

**Unit 9 Three Modes of Writing** 336

**9.1** Considering Your Purpose
    and Audience 337
**9.2** Expository Writing 340
**9.3** Descriptive Writing 348
**9.4** Narrative Writing 356

**Unit 10 Persuasive Writing** 372

**10.1** Selecting a Topic 373
**10.2** Preparing Support for Your Opinion 380
**10.3** Organizing and Writing
    an Argument 386
**10.4** Revising Your Argument 396

**Unit 11 Writing an Essay** 412

**11.1** Selecting and Limiting a Topic 413
**11.2** Determining Your Audience, Tone,
    and Style 417
**11.3** Planning Your Essay 424
**11.4** Writing Your First Draft 429
**11.5** Revising and Finishing Your Essay 437

**Unit 12 Writing About Literature** 448

**12.1** The Nature of the Literary Essay 449
**12.2** Preparing to Write a Literary Essay 453
**12.3** Taking Notes 457
**12.4** Organizing Your Ideas 461

**12.5** Writing the First Draft 465

**12.6** Revising and Finishing Your Essay 472

**Unit 13** Writing a Research Paper 482

**13.1** Planning Your Research Paper 483
**13.2** Doing the Research 489
**13.3** Taking Notes 498
**13.4** Organizing Your Information 505
**13.5** Drafting and Documenting
Your Paper 513
**13.6** Revising and Finishing Your Paper 519

**Unit 14** Writing Business Letters 542

**14.1** Standard Business Letters 543
**14.2** Applying for a Job 551
**14.3** Expressing an Opinion 556

# Part Three   Related Skills

566

**Unit 15** Spelling Skills 568

**15.1** How to Study Spelling Words 568
**15.2** Spelling Rules 568
**15.3** Spelling Patterns 573
**15.4** Pronunciation and Spelling 574
**15.5** Other Spelling Aids 575
**15.6** Frequently Misspelled Words 576

**Unit 16** Vocabulary Skills 578

**16.1** How to Learn New Words 578
**16.2** Using Context to Get Meaning 579
**16.3** Getting Meanings from Word Parts 579

**16.4** Word Origins — 583
**16.5** How to Choose the Best Word — 584
**16.6** Using the Dictionary — 585

**Unit 17 Public Speaking Skills** — 588

**17.1** Kinds of Speeches — 588
**17.2** Preparing Your Speech — 589
**17.3** Speeches to Inform — 591
**17.4** Speeches to Persuade — 597
**17.5** Delivering Informative and Persuasive Speeches — 603

**Unit 18 Test-Taking Skills** — 606

**18.1** Verbal Skills — 606
**18.2** Standard Written English — 614

**Index** — 618

**Acknowledgments** — 630

**Checklist for Revision** — 632

# The English Language

## A Brief History of American English

People who travel throughout the United States cannot help noticing the ways in which Americans in different regions of our country have made the English language their own. The differences in pronunciation between the South and the Midwest and between New England and the Southwest are obvious. More subtle are the variations in vocabulary from one region to another. In many parts of the country, one uses an earthworm as bait for fishing. However, in New England one is more likely to use an angleworm, in Delaware and Pennsylvania a fishworm, and along the Southern coast a fishing worm.

When we Americans travel to Britain, we must accustom ourselves to even greater differences in pronunciation and vocabulary. Even casual observers of British television programs on American television will notice that the English say *petrol* instead of *gasoline, lorry* instead of *truck,* and *chemist* instead of *pharmacist.*

*The Anglo-Saxon Chronicle is the earliest source of English history. This sample records the Danish invasion of A.D. 871; it is from a manuscript copied in the eleventh century. Later manuscripts show Old English developing into Middle English.*

However, considering the fact that English colonists established the first settlement at Jamestown almost four hundred years ago and that the U.S. is three thousand miles from Britain, it is perhaps surprising that British English and American English have remained so similar. The fact is that Americans and Britons have virtually no trouble understanding one another. The language is still English, and its native speakers number about three hundred million in Great Britain, the U.S., Canada, Australia, and New Zealand. Moreover, the importance of English exceeds its numbers of speakers, for English is used in international politics, science, and trade, leading people throughout the world to learn English as a second language. Almost one fourth of the population of the world speaks English.

The story of modern English really has two parts for Americans. There is the story of the English language itself, which goes back more than fifteen hundred years to the settlement of Britain by Germanic peoples. In addition, there is the evolution of American English, which is a complex story of colonization by people from different parts of Europe, of the development of regional dialects, and of the continuing absorption of words from science, technology, and other sources.

The history of English is fascinating in its own right. However, it also is worth learning because it gives us a historical perspective toward the problems that face us in using English well. When we travel back to the origins of English, we discover that it, like any language, is not an invention but rather a product of gradual evolution. People through the centuries have made adaptations to suit their needs, their lives, and their culture. To us, some of the adaptations may seem inconsistent. At the time, though, they made sense.

The process somewhat resembles a sculpture created not by one artist but by thousands of artists, each adding a bit of material here and changing a feature there. To our benefit, the sculpture remains malleable and awaits our own additions. Because the sculpture has evolved over a long period of time, it has blemishes that seem a bit out of place at first. However, the blemishes are part of the sculpture, and perhaps by learning how the sculpture developed, we can also learn to accept and admire the entire work of art.

# Origins of English

Along with most of the languages spoken in Europe and western Asia, English belongs to the Indo-European family of languages. Linguists believe that all of these languages developed from Proto-Indo-European, a tongue spoken by nomadic groups in Europe more than five thousand years ago. No written records of Proto-Indo-European exist, but linguists have reconstructed the language by comparing all the languages that developed from it.

As the original communities that spoke Proto-Indo-European dispersed, the language broke up into dialects, which are regional varieties of a language that differ from one another in terms of vocabulary, pronunciation, and grammar. The dialect spoken by people in northern Europe developed over a period of centuries into the Germanic group of Indo-European languages. Scholars divide this group into East Germanic, North Germanic, and West Germanic. All the East Germanic languages are extinct. Among the North Germanic languages are Icelandic, Norwegian, and Danish. English, German, and Dutch are some of the West Germanic languages.

English is closely related to German, although German has a more elaborate system of inflections, which are special endings attached to words to indicate such properties as case, number, and sometimes gender. English once had a similar system of inflections but lost many of them during its evolution.

# Development of Old English

During the A.D.400s and 500s, three groups of Germanic people—the Jutes, the Saxons, and the Angles—invaded Britain and settled there. Their settlement of Britain marks the beginning of the English language. The Germanic dialects of these people merged and gave birth to Old English.

Old English resembled German in having a complex system of inflections. Nouns, pronouns, verbs, and adjectives were all inflected. As a result, Old English had a much freer word order than does the English that we speak today. In modern English, word order indicates many of the grammatical elements that were indicated by inflections in Old English.

Old English seems like a foreign language to us, but some words from Old English are recognizable, such as *brothor* (brother), *faeder* (father), *modor* (mother), *monn* (man), and *sweostor* (sister). Our cardinal numbers come from Old English, as do most of our personal pronouns. In addition, many names for basic concepts come from Old English, including *day* and *night, heat* and *cold, heaven* and *earth, love* and *hate,* and *life* and *death.*

Some Scandinavian words entered Old English as a result of contact between the Anglo-Saxons and their Viking neighbors to the north. Such words include *anger, bull, dirt, leg, meek, seat, skill, tattered, trust,* and *ugly.*

## Development of Middle English

The English language changed after the Normans from Northern France invaded and conquered Britain in 1066. With this event, the French-speaking Normans began to introduce thousands of French words into the English vocabulary. This influx of French terms was especially great in certain categories, such as law and government (*court, judge, justice, parliament, council, tax, royal, prince, city, mayor, money*), military matters (*battle, siege, armor, fortress, assault*), and cooking (*sauce, boil, fry, roast*).

A number of the French words that entered Middle English came ultimately from Latin or Greek. For example, the Middle English word *theatre* came from Old French. But the Old French word came from the Latin word *theatrum,* which came from the Greek word *theatron,* which in turn was formed from *theasthai,* meaning "to watch." Similarly, our word *circle* comes from the Middle English word *cercle,* which came from Old French. The Old French word came from the Latin word *circulus,* a diminutive form of *circus,* which meant "ring." Our words *circle* and *circus,* which have different meanings, come from the same source.

By the 1400s, Middle English had developed to the point that many of the words were similar to those in modern English. The spelling of Middle English, however, was closely related to pronunciation. For example, the final *e* in many words, which is often silent today, was pronounced then. In addition, all consonants were pronounced, such as the *k* and *gh* in *knight* and the *g* in *gnaw* and *gnarl.*

# Rise of Modern English

The next major change in English came in about 1476, when William Caxton set up the first printing press in England. For the next century or so, English went through a period of upheaval distinguished primarily by important changes in the pronunciation of vowels. Linguists refer to these changes collectively as the Great Vowel Shift. It was during this period, for example, that *a, e,* and *i* came to be pronounced as they are in the modern English words *late, meet,* and *ride.* In Middle English these letters were pronounced, respectively, as we would pronounce *ah, a,* and *ee.*

The revival of classical learning during the English Renaissance in the sixteenth century had a major impact on Modern English. Many words were borrowed from the classical languages

*In 1480 William Caxton (left) printed* The Game and Playe of Chess. *A page from Chapter Three shows a philosopher teaching a king how to play. The mark below Caxton's portrait identifies him as the printer of the book.*

and from French. In some cases, Latin words that had already entered English through French were borrowed again directly from Latin. The entrance of the same words from several different, but related, languages produced a large store of synonyms. For example, English gained the words *blame* and *blaspheme, count* and *compute, frail* and *fragile, poor* and *pauper, ray* and *radius, sever* and *separate,* and *sure* and *secure.*

During this period many Middle English spellings were preserved, although the pronunciation of the words had changed. The advent of printing required some standardization in spelling. Before printed books became common, there was wide variation in the ways in which people spelled certain words. For example, *button* might be spelled as *button, butowne,* or *botheum.*

When Caxton set up his printing press, he decided to keep the spelling used by Middle English scribes rather than the spelling that followed the pronunciation of his day. He also hired Dutch printers who, not knowing English well, used their own language as a basis for some spellings. For example, they provided such spellings as *ghost* and *ghossip.* Some of these *gh* words, such as *gossip,* eventually were changed; but others, like *ghost,* kept the unnecessary *h.*

Although printing helped to standardize the spelling of Middle English, it also tended to freeze the spelling so that it no longer accommodated changes in pronunciation. However, there were other influences on spelling as well. The borrowing of words from the classical languages affected some spellings. For example, the silent *b* in *debt* was retained to indicate the Latin origin of the word *debitum.* Partly for these reasons, English spelling remains irregular or unphonetic today.

Elizabethan English—the language of the English poets William Shakespeare, John Donne, and Edmund Spenser—became the standard form of English during the reign of Queen Elizabeth from 1558 to 1603. This was the language of the educated classes of London.

In the 1700s Samuel Johnson published his *Dictionary of the English Language* in an attempt to standardize English spelling and usage. The publication of the first English grammar books took place at that time. English spelling has remained basically the same since then, in spite of frequent proposals for standardizing it.

*Samuel Johnson was the most eminent man of letters in England during the eighteenth century. His erudition is evident in his great dictionary, in which he boasts—not idly—that the definitions are based on the works of the best writers.*

## Beginnings of American English

When the British colonists came to America in the 1600s, the English language had been evolving for more than one thousand years. In the nearly four hundred years since then, American English has diverged slightly from British English in terms of pronunciation, vocabulary, and spelling. Radio and television have made all of us aware of the differences between the American and British pronunciation of many words. However, we may be less aware of differences in vocabulary and spelling. Americans do not call an elevator a *lift,* as Britons do. To a Briton, the word *lumber* means useless furniture; the word does not have this meaning to an American. Most of us recognize the spelling of the word *colour* as British and *color* as American. On one hand, these changes are minor and certainly do not affect communication between the two countries. On the other hand, they are proof that the experiences of Americans have required them to make certain additions to, and adaptations in, the language.

These adaptations were a natural result of encountering unfamiliar people, plants, animals, food, and other things in America. The colonists needed names for all that was new to them and frequently adopted words from the languages of the Native Americans whom they met. Native Americans gave us words for several trees, such as *hickory* and *persimmon,* and for many animals, such as *moose, opossum, raccoon, skunk,* and *woodchuck.* In addition, the names of numerous places, such as *Appalachia, Alleghenies, Mississippi, Missouri,* and *Michigan,* came from Native American languages. The Algonquians alone gave English more than one hundred words, including *hominy, papoose,* and *squash.* In most cases the colonists adapted the spelling of Native American words to English pronunciation. For example, to make the Native American word *otcheck* resemble familiar English, the colonists changed it to *woodchuck.*

The Native Americans were not the only people from whom the colonists borrowed words to describe their new experiences. Some Native American words, such as *caribou* and *toboggan,* entered English through Canadian French. Other words, including *barbecue* and *canoe,* came into the language from the West Indies through Spanish.

Besides borrowing words, the colonists also created new words on their own. They formed such compounds as *backwoods* and *bullfrog.* In other cases they gave new meanings to old words, including *corn* and *lumber.* (In British English, *corn* refers to any grain, especially wheat.)

American English also acquired new words from the early Dutch, French, and German settlers. These groups all contributed words from their languages to American English. The Dutch settlers of what is now New York gave us *boss, coleslaw, cookies, sleigh, stoop,* and *waffle.* Our American term *Santa Claus* comes from the Dutch term *Sinterklaas* for Saint Nicholas. The French missionaries, explorers, and settlers gave us *chowder, gopher, prairie, pumpkin,* and *sashay.* They also named many settlements, including *Cape Girardeau* and *Sault Sainte Marie.* The Germans who settled in Pennsylvania added the term *smearcase* (cottage cheese) to American English. They also gave us *rainworm* (earthworm) and *dunk* (immerse).

# American Changes in Spelling

When the colonists came to America, they brought with them a way of spelling that had not yet been systemized to be consistent. Consequently, on both sides of the Atlantic, authors used many spellings that are now obsolete. For example, in *The History of Plimoth Plantation*, William Bradford wrote *gifen* (given), *trible* (triple), *vacabund* (vagabond), and *woules* (wolves). He also used *rid* as the past form of *write*.

*Obsolete words and variant spellings are evident in a 1622 history of Plymouth, Massachusetts (left) and a* Boston News-letter *published in 1704. Notice the elongated s in both colonial-era documents.*

There were several attempts in America to make spelling regular. Some people, including Benjamin Franklin, proposed reforming the spelling of English to make it more phonetic. Franklin never pursued his proposal, however. Noah Webster, the first person to use the phrase *American English,* wrote a spelling book in the 1780s and published his first dictionary in 1806. In that dictionary he recommended many spellings that were different from British spellings. Some of his changes in spelling have survived, including the *-or* ending rather than the *-our* ending in such words as *color, honor,* and *labor;* the *-er* ending rather than the *-re* ending in such words as *center, meter,* and *theater;* and the single *l* in such words as *traveled* and *traveling.*

*Noah Webster, the American lexicographer and language reformer, helped to standardize spelling in the United States through his great work of 1828,* An American Dictionary of the English Language. *This illustration of the title page of an earlier work still shows the British spelling* traveller *for* traveler.

## Development of American Dialects

Throughout the 1600s and 1700s, American English was developing as a dialect with characteristics that differentiated it from those dialects in Britain. By the end of the eighteenth century, though, American English itself had developed three chief dialects, which originated in regions along the Atlantic coast. Each dialect has its own subdialects. The Northern dialect is spoken in New England and New York. The Midland dialect extends from New Jersey to Delaware and includes most of Pennsylvania. The Southern dialect ranges from southern Delaware to South Carolina. From these areas the various dialects spread west as people migrated across the country.

Distinctive pronunciations and some differences in vocabulary characterize the three dialect regions. The Northern terms *pail, stone wall,* and *teeter-totter* contrast with the Midland terms *bucket, stone fence,* and *seesaw. Brook, clapboard, eavestrough, johnnycake* (cornbread), and *whiffletree* are Northern words; *blinds, green beans, poke* (paper sack), *snake feeder* (dragonfly), and *skillet* are Midland terms. Southern words include *harp* (harmonica), *snap beans,* and *fritters.*

The speech of the West shows the blending of the Northern, Midland, and Southern dialects. In addition, throughout the West, Spanish has had a major influence on American English. Spanish-speaking people from Latin America gave the language such words as *canyon, chaparral, corral, lasso, mesa, mustang, patio, pronto, ranch,* and *rodeo.* Spanish names for places and geographic features, including *Montana, Rio Grande,* and *Santa Clara,* are numerous in the West.

Although regional varieties of American English exist, these dialectal differences are few in comparison with those in many European countries. Americans from different dialect regions can easily understand one another, but in Europe sharp divisions can exist between the standard language and a dialect. In fact, it is not uncommon that people from different regions of a country cannot understand one another. The United States has avoided this problem because of the high mobility of the population, which brings people from different regions into frequent contact.

## Immigrant Influences

The nineteenth century brought rich additions to American English as a result of the influx of immigrants from non-English-speaking countries. Before 1776 two thirds of the people who had come to settle in America were from England. However, during the following century, many Irish, German, Scandinavian, Slavic, and Italian immigrants came to the United States. From the Irish, American English gained the words *mammy* and *mountain dew*. Many new names of foods entered American English. The Germans contributed the word *pretzel*, while Italian immigrants added *antipasto* and *pizza* to our vocabulary. The Scandinavians gave us *lingonberries* and *smorgasbord*, and the Slavs added *kielbasa* and *kolacky*. From the African languages, American English gained *goober* (peanut), *gumbo, okra,* and *yam*.

Various ethnic groups have contributed still more new words to the English language. Hispanics have given us the word *macho,* and blacks have contributed the words *jazz* and *banjo*. Words from Yiddish include *kibitzer* and *chutzpah*.

## Slang in American English

Slang is the nonstandard use of language, and slang expressions are those that we use in everyday, informal communication. Each generation of Americans has added its own slang expressions to the language, both by giving new meanings to old words and by coining new words. Most slang words and expressions are popular for only a short time. However, some last for decades, and a number even become part of the standard language.

The exact origin of much slang is difficult to trace. *Okay*, a distinctly American word, first appeared in the early 1800s. The expression *cut the mustard,* meaning *to be of good quality* or *to be successful,* was popular among cowhands in the West during the late 1800s. The word *hairdo* originated in the 1920s as a slang term for *coiffure*. It became part of the standard language and is now more widely used than *coiffure*. In the 1930s Americans first used the term *malarkey* to describe meaningless or exaggerated talk. The word *hep*, meaning "aware," from the 1930s became *hip* after World War II. *Crazy*, meaning *wonderful,* was popular in the 1950s.

Professions and leisure pursuits in the United States have created their own slang. The world of baseball gave birth to such terms as *bean ball, clutch hitter, duster, in the hole, run down, shutout, southpaw,* and *switch hitter*. Journalism gave us *ghostwriter, scoop, potboiler,* and *hack writer,* and the music world gave us *blues* and *rock and roll*. Thus, Americans of all ages and occupations have added thousands of slang words to the vocabulary.

# Technical Words in American English

Since the time of Queen Elizabeth, the English language has grown from a vocabulary of 140,000 words to one of between 600,000 and 750,000 words. The greatest number of new words have been technical terms. The past century has witnessed a surge of developments in science and technology. As a result, technical terms, common to both British and American English, have entered our language.

Scientists have long used classical Greek as a source for creating new technical terms. In many cases, new words are formed by adding Greek words as prefixes or suffixes to existing words. For example, the term *telephotography* is a combination of the Greek word *tele,* meaning *distant,* and *photograph,* which is also of Greek origin. Other technical terms have been formed by blending words. Thus, *biology electronics* becomes *bionics,* a *pulsating star* is a *pulsar,* and a *binary unit* turns into a *bit.* In other cases, scientists have created new technical terms by joining the initial syllables or letters of long descriptive names. In this way, the word *Fortran* was formed from *formula translation; radar* was created from *radio detecting and ranging;* and *laser* became the name for *light amplification by stimulated emission of radiation.* The technical vocabulary of English can only continue to grow as new scientific and technological breakthroughs occur.

## Summary

The history of English is partly a survey of the many groups of people who have contributed to the language. An important feature of English has long been its openness to new vocabulary from many sources. The following list provides a glimpse into the diverse sources of words in our language.

| Origin | Word |
| --- | --- |
| Aboriginal Australian | boomerang |
| Algonquian | totem |
| Arabic | mosque |

| | |
|---|---|
| Basque | bizarre |
| Caribbean | hurricane |
| Chinese | tea |
| Cornish | gull |
| Czech | robot |
| Dutch | yacht |
| Eskimo | igloo |
| Finnish | sauna |
| French | residence |
| German | sauerbraten |
| Greek | metamorphosis |
| Hawaiian | ukelele |
| Hebrew | kosher |
| Hindi | jungle |
| Hungarian | goulash |
| Irish | shamrock |
| Italian | stanza |
| Japanese | tycoon |
| Latin | malnutrition |
| Malay | ketchup |
| Norwegian | ski |
| Persian | paradise |
| Portuguese | molasses |
| Polish | mazurka |
| Polynesian | taboo |
| Russian | mammoth |
| Scandinavian | birth |
| Spanish | mosquito |
| Tamil | pariah |
| Turkish | coffee |
| Welsh | flannel |

These additions to the language have resulted not only from its openness to new words from other languages but also from the inventiveness of its speakers. American English will undoubtedly continue to grow—and continue to change. Our language offers us an expanding resource for expressing ourselves.

# Assignments

### Assignment 1
Choose a word and list as many synonyms for the word as you can. Look up the word and its synonyms in a dictionary, and list the origin of each word. Tell whether any of the synonyms are derived from both a classical language and a modern foreign language. If the meaning of the word has changed, explain how it has changed.

### Assignment 2
Using the library, find the origin and meaning of your first name, your middle name, and last name. Write a paragraph describing your findings.

### Assignment 3
Make a list of ten words that are not spelled phonetically. Find the origin of each word in a dictionary. Then discuss the possible reason for the unphonetic spelling of each word. How would you make each spelling more phonetic?

### Assignment 4
Note some of the unusual place names or street names in the area in which you live. Find the origin of these names in a book on local history, and write the origin of each name. In addition, write an explanation of how each group of people in your area contributed to English.

### Assignment 5
Find out which Native American group originally lived in your area. List some place names that come from the language of these Native Americans. After doing research, write an explanation of what these place names mean in the language of that Native American group.

### Assignment 6
Using library resources, determine which American dialect people speak in the region where you live. List some distinctive features of this dialect and the major influences on the development of the

dialect. List some words or expressions that you ordinarily use that reflect this dialect.

## Assignment 7

Interview your parents or other people older than you to find out some slang expressions that were popular when they were your age. Make a list of these expressions and their definitions. Also, write slang expressions used by you and your friends that have approximately the same meaning. Below your list, write a paragraph in which you address the following questions: "What slang expressions seem to have lasted from one generation to another? What seems to be the most common source for slang—the media, sports, or some other source? Have any of the older generation's slang expressions become part of standard English?"

## Assignment 8

List ten technical words from one of your science courses. Some of the words should pertain to the latest developments in science and technology. Then use a dictionary or science book to find the origins of the words. Using the information that you locate, discuss how new technical terms are created.

## Assignment 9

Select one of the following fields of endeavor, and do research to find out what words and expressions from that field are commonly used by Americans. The expressions might have originally been slang or jargon, but now they should be an accepted part of standard English. The fields of endeavor are journalism, business, medicine, law, music, or sports. Write a report about your findings.

## Assignment 10

Write a two- or three-page persuasive essay in which you argue for or against setting up an authoritative body, such as the French Academy, for determining the correct spelling and usage of all words in our language. Support your position with pertinent facts, examples, and reasons.

# Part One

## Grammar, Usage, and Mechanics

Unit 1   Parts of Speech                    2
Unit 2   Sentence Structure                42
Unit 3   Phrases and Clauses               64
Unit 4   Usage                            106
Unit 5   Mechanics                        182

The rules of English grammar, usage, and mechanics are guides that will help you to express your thoughts in sentences that are precise and interesting. If you need to know how to join two sentences with a correlative conjunction, you can consult the rules of grammar. If you refer to the usage rules to check when to use the passive voice, you will also find an explanation of why it is better to use the active voice in most cases. You may refer to the rules of mechanics for ways to use correct punctuation to express your thoughts clearly.

As you study the units in Part One, you will observe that the rules work together to present a description of our language today. By applying this system of rules in your writing, you can accomplish an important goal: you can convey your ideas in sentences that your readers will easily understand.

# Unit 1

*Parts of Speech*

---

## Unit Preview

What makes one piece of writing clearer than another? Often the difference is in the way that each writer uses words. One writer settles for the first word that comes to mind, even if it is so general that it does not create a clear image for the reader. Another writer searches for the word that is just right, creating a specific image for the reader.

**For Analysis**   The two paragraphs that follow are descriptions of the same scene. As you read, ask yourself how the two paragraphs differ in word choice. Then answer the questions.

PARAGRAPH A

(1) He looked at the land on the bank of the body of water, saw the individual objects, the greenery and the lines in each piece of greenery—saw the very insects upon them. (2) He noted the prismatic colors on the ground. (3) The sound of the insects that danced above the water, the sound of the insects' wings, the movements of the insects' legs, like objects which had lifted their conveyance—all these made noise. (4) A creature slid along beneath his eyes and he heard the sound of its body parting the water.

PARAGRAPH B

(1) He looked at the forest on the bank of the stream, saw the individual trees, the leaves and the veining of each leaf —saw the very insects upon them: the locusts, the brilliant-bodied flies, the gray spiders stretching their webs from twig to

2

twig. (2) He noted the prismatic colors in all the dewdrops upon a million blades of grass. (3) The humming of the gnats that danced above the eddies of the stream, the beating of the dragonflies' wings, the strokes of the water-spiders' legs, like oars which had lifted their boat—all these made audible music. (4) A fish slid along beneath his eyes and he heard the rush of its body parting the water.

Ambrose Bierce, "An Occurrence at Owl Creek Bridge"

1. Reread the first sentence of both paragraphs. In Sentence 1 of Paragraph B, what nouns does Ambrose Bierce use instead of *land, body of water, objects, greenery,* and *lines,* which appear in Paragraph A?
2. In Sentence 1 in Paragraph B, what specific nouns does the author use to give examples of insects?
3. Reread the third sentence of each paragraph. What specific nouns does Bierce use instead of *sound, insects, water, movements,* and *objects*?
4. From the rest of Paragraph B, list several nouns that are more specific than the corresponding nouns in Paragraph A.

The description written by Ambrose Bierce abounds in vivid nouns: *veining, locusts, spiders, webs, twig, dewdrops,* and *blades.* You do not have to use complex or unusual words in order to be effective, but your words need to be specific. In your writing and speaking, you should be specific in using all the parts of speech. This unit helps you toward that goal by explaining how the different parts of speech function.

## 1.1   Nouns

A **noun** is a word that names a person, a place, a thing, or an idea.

PERSONS    athlete, grandfather, Queen Elizabeth II

PLACES     parlor, seashore, Venice

THINGS     painting, milk, atom

IDEAS      loneliness, harmony, capitalism

Dates and days of the week are also classified as nouns.

1492          Sunday          July 4, 1976

# 1.1a    Kinds of Nouns

## Common and Proper Nouns

A **common noun** refers to one of a class of people, places, things, or ideas. It does not begin with a capital letter unless it begins a sentence. A **proper noun** gives the name or title of a particular person, place, thing, or idea. It always begins with a capital letter.

COMMON NOUN      The sailors spotted an **island.**

PROPER NOUN       The largest state is **Alaska.**

## Compound Nouns

A **compound noun** consists of two or more words used together to form a single noun. There are four kinds of compound nouns. One kind is formed by joining two or more words: *wallpaper.* A second kind consists of words joined by hyphens: *dinner-dance.* A third kind consists of words that are often used together even though they are not joined: *bulletin board.* The fourth kind is a name that consists of more than one word: *Old Faithful.*

## Collective Nouns

A **collective noun** refers to a *group* of people, places, things, or ideas.

The **multitude** of people gathered in front of the stadium.
The museum has an excellent **collection** of Egyptian mummies.

## Concrete and Abstract Nouns

**Concrete nouns** refer to material things, to people, or to places. Some concrete nouns name things that you can perceive with your senses: *bell, odor, breeze.* Other concrete nouns name things that can be measured or perceived with the aid of technical devices. Although you may not be able to see helium, the noun *helium* is concrete because it names something that has a definite material existence. The nouns in boldface type in the following sentences are concrete.

> On his **face** was a large **smile**.
>
> The **explosion** of the **tank** could be heard two **miles** away.
>
> **Rudy** could smell the **fumes** of **gasoline** in the **air**.
>
> **People** need **oxygen** in order to live. [Even though you cannot see, hear, smell, or taste oxygen, it is a substance that can be measured.]

**Abstract nouns** name ideas, qualities, emotions, or attitudes. The nouns in boldface type in the following sentences are abstract.

> Thomas Jefferson named **liberty** and the **pursuit** of **happiness** as two of people's **rights**.
>
> Noreen's face showed great **concentration** as she awaited the start of the race.
>
> In a **meritocracy**, people assume **leadership** because of **ability** and **talent**.

**Exercise 1 Nouns** On your paper, write the nouns in each of the following sentences. Label each noun *Concrete* or *Abstract*. Write *Compound* next to the compound nouns and *Collective* next to the collective nouns.

> **SAMPLE**    Showing courage, Richardson led his platoon onto the battlefield.
>
> **ANSWER**    courage—Abstract; Richardson—Concrete; platoon —Concrete, Collective; battlefield—Concrete, Compound

1. Our admiration increased as the game progressed because players on both teams had made such outstanding plays.
2. When Dana started at the new school, he was surprised by the warmth and friendliness of the students.
3. The watchmaker made several repairs on my clock.
4. Al has little success in chess because he doesn't have the patience to develop strategy.

5. Despite its name, New College of Oxford University is actually more than six centuries old.
6. In *The Prince,* a book about political power, Machiavelli suggests that the end justifies the means.
7. Benjamin Franklin, who wrote *Poor Richard's Almanac,* also wrote an autobiography in which he described the reasons for his success.
8. Surprise, pleasure, and pride were all reflected in Jay's smile as he strode toward the podium to accept the award.
9. My mother and Uncle Henry can amuse us for hours with their delightful stories about the joy of a childhood spent on the farm.
10. During the colonial years, Massachusetts was a theocracy, or a state in which religious officials have the ruling power.

**Exercise 2  Kinds of Nouns**  On your paper, rewrite each of the following sentences, replacing the blank with a noun. Use the kind of noun indicated in parentheses. Underline the noun that you use.

> **SAMPLE**  A __?__ (*collective*) of geese flew over the salt marshes on the way south for the winter.
>
> **ANSWER**  A <u>flock</u> of geese flew over the salt marshes on the way south for the winter.

1. To the captain of a luxury liner, an important concern is the __?__ (*abstract*) of the passengers.
2. Ruth's family shared all of the chores of the __?__ (*common*) equally.
3. A large __?__ (*collective*) of students agreed to do volunteer work at the senior citizens' center.
4. The salaries of players in __?__ (*compound*) have increased dramatically in recent years!
5. __?__ (*proper*) attracted a great deal of attention when she became the first thirteen-year-old business executive in __?__ (*proper*).
6. Three __?__ (*common*), David, Michelle, and Jennifer, were awarded the Battin High School award for excellence in __?__ (*common*).
7. __?__ (*abstract*) and __?__ (*abstract*) are two elements that have made science-fiction films such popular attractions in our time.
8. __?__ (*common*) say that by studying __?__ (*abstract*), we can learn to avoid the mistakes of the past.

9. Acme Tire Company has arranged workers into seven __?__ (*collective*) that decide for themselves how to divide their __?__ (*abstract*).

10. __?__ (*proper*) has become a very popular vacation spot for people who want to escape the winters in __?__ (*proper*)

## 1.1b    Use of Effective Nouns

Every writer has a style, or a characteristic way of using words. Ernest Hemingway's style is concise and concrete. Nathaniel Hawthorne's style, on the other hand, is usually more complex and abstract than Hemingway's. An important part of your writing style is your choice of nouns. Good writers try to use nouns that are specific. As the following excerpt from Shakespeare's *Macbeth* shows, there are several specific synonyms for the general word *dog*.

FIRST
MURDERER:     We are men, my liege.

MACBETH:      Ay, in the catalogue ye go for men,
              As hounds and greyhounds, mongrels, spaniels, curs,
              Sloughs, water-rugs, and demi-wolves are clept
              All by the name of dogs. . . .

Act III, Scene 1, lines 92-95

In the excerpt, *hounds, greyhounds, mongrels, spaniels,* and *curs* create specific images. As you write, choose nouns that express your meaning most specifically.

**Exercise 3   Specific Nouns**   The following common nouns are general. On your paper, write each noun and then list at least three examples of the noun that are specific.

SAMPLE        leader
ANSWER        leader—president, tyrant, drill sergeant

1. dwelling      4. art        7. hobby
2. person        5. food       8. publication
3. vehicle       6. male       9. noise

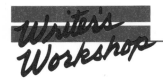

**Writing with Specific Nouns**

The four statements that follow contain nouns that are general. Rewrite the sentences so that they contain specific nouns. Then select one of your rewritten statements, and write a paragraph in which you develop that idea.

1. Some places have spectacular scenery.
2. Certain sports are difficult to learn.
3. Movies can be quite different from the books on which they are based.
4. Pets can be intelligent and well behaved.

# 1.2   Pronouns

A **pronoun** is a word that is used in place of a noun. Pronouns refer to persons, places, things, or ideas without renaming them.

> *Anne* is a person with a number of *goals*. Moreover, **she** is willing to work hard to develop **them**. [*She* is a pronoun replacing *Anne*. *Them* is a pronoun replacing *goals*.]

The noun that a pronoun replaces is the **antecedent** of that pronoun.

> *John* told **himself** that **he** should read the *book* and not stare at **it.** [*John* is the antecedent of the pronouns *himself* and *he*. *Book* is the antecedent of the pronoun *it*.]

There are seven kinds of pronouns: personal, demonstrative, reflexive, intensive, interrogative, relative, and indefinite.

## Personal Pronouns

**Personal pronouns** are pronouns that require different forms to express person, number, and gender. **Person** refers to the relationship between the speaker or writer and the person or thing being discussed. You use the first-person pronouns, *I, me, we,* and *us,* when you refer to yourself as the speaker or writer. You use the second-person pronoun, *you,* to refer to your audience. You use the third-person pronouns, *he, him, she, her, it, they,* and *them,* to refer to people or objects other than yourself or your audience.

The **number** of a personal pronoun indicates whether the antecedent is singular or plural. *I, she, he,* and *it* are some of the singular pronouns; *we, they,* and *us* are some of the plural pronouns; *you* can be either singular or plural.

The **gender** of a personal pronoun tells whether the antecedent is masculine, feminine, or neuter. *He, him,* and *his* indicate the masculine gender; *she, her,* and *hers* indicate the feminine gender; and *it* indicates the neuter gender.

**Possessive Pronouns.**    Personal pronouns that show ownership or belonging are called **possessive pronouns.**

If the books on the radiator are **yours,** you should remove them.

George went to get **his** calculator.

The following chart shows the personal pronouns, and the possessive pronouns are in parentheses.

|  | SINGULAR | PLURAL |
|---|---|---|
| FIRST PERSON | I, me (my, mine) | we, us (our, ours) |
| SECOND PERSON | you (your, yours) | you (your, yours) |
| THIRD PERSON | he, him (his) | they, them (their, theirs) |
|  | she, her (her, hers) |  |
|  | it (its) |  |

## Demonstrative Pronouns

**Demonstrative pronouns** specify the individual or the group that is being referred to. There are four demonstrative pronouns: *this, that, these,* and *those.*

**These** are cantaloupes, and **those** are honeydew melons.

Of the two cars, do you prefer **this** or **that**?

## Reflexive Pronouns

**Reflexive pronouns** indicate that people or things perform actions to, for, or on behalf of themselves. You form reflexive pronouns with the suffixes -*self* and -*selves*.

| | |
|---|---|
| FIRST PERSON | myself, ourselves |
| SECOND PERSON | yourself, yourselves |
| THIRD PERSON | himself, herself, itself, oneself, themselves |

The Chylaks gave **themselves** two weeks for a vacation. [**Think**: gave *to* themselves two weeks.]
Emma bought **herself** a record. [**Think**: bought *for* herself a record.]
The horse hurt **itself** during the jump. [The horse performed the action of hurting upon itself.]

## Intensive Pronouns

**Intensive pronouns** are the same words as the reflexive pronouns, but they draw special attention to a person or a thing mentioned in the sentence. Intensive pronouns usually follow the words that they intensify.

Shakespeare **himself** could not have said it better. [The pronoun *himself* draws special attention to the subject, *Shakespeare*.]
This book has been autographed by the author **herself.**[The pronoun *herself* draws special attention to *author*.]
The crowd expected the senator **himself** to show up at the rally. [*Himself* draws special attention to the direct object, *senator*.]
Albert's mother found the ring **itself** behind the sofa. [*Itself* draws special attention to the direct object, *ring*.]

## Interrogative Pronouns

**Interrogative pronouns** introduce questions. Here are the most frequently used interrogative pronouns: *who, whom, which, what,* and *whose*.

**Whose** is this scarf?
**Which** of the two sofas did you buy?
**What** did you receive from Ms. Taylor?

## Relative Pronouns

**Relative pronouns** introduce adjective clauses (*Unit 3*), which modify nouns and pronouns. Here are the relative pronouns:

who     whom     whose     which     that

The *aircraft* **that** Chuck Yeager used to break the sound barrier in 1947 was a Bell X-1 rocket airplane. [*Aircraft* is the antecedent of *that*.]

*People* **who** live by the sword die by the sword. [*People* is the antecedent of *who*.]

## Indefinite Pronouns

**Indefinite pronouns** refer to people, places, or things in general. You can often use these pronouns without antecedents. The following list contains commonly used indefinite pronouns:

| | | | |
|---|---|---|---|
| all | either | most | other |
| another | enough | much | others |
| any | everybody | neither | plenty |
| anybody | everyone | nobody | several |
| anyone | everything | none | some |
| anything | few | no one | somebody |
| both | many | nothing | someone |
| each | more | one | something |

Is **any** of the milk left?

**Either** of those three cyclists may win the bicycle race.

**Several** of the couples went out to dinner.

**Exercise  Pronouns**   On your paper, rewrite the following sentences, replacing the blanks with suitable pronouns. Use the kind of pronoun indicated in parentheses. Underline the pronouns that you use.

**SAMPLE**    __?__ (*interrogative*) was the face __?__ (*relative*) launched a thousand ships?

**ANSWER**    <u>Whose</u> was the face <u>that</u> launched a thousand ships?

1. Andy, __?__ (*relative*) has never lacked self-confidence, considers __?__ (*reflexive*) a talented artist.

**11**

2. Because Susan worked faster than __?__ (*indefinite*) of the other students, she was the first __?__ (*indefinite*) in the class to finish.

3. Today we remember Upton Sinclair primarily as the author __?__ (*relative*) exposed the meat-packing industry in his novel *The Jungle*.

4. Maria offered to pay for her lunch __?__ (*reflexive*), but Christina insisted on paying for __?__ (*personal*).

5. "__?__ (*interrogative*) knows the location of the fuse box?" Harold called. "Is it in this corner or __?__ (*demonstrative*)?"

6. __?__ (*indefinite*) of those __?__ (*relative*) visited the State House got to talk to the governor __?__ (*intensive*).

7. Jodie knew that __?__ (*personal*) could do a better job __?__ (*intensive*).

8. __?__ (*indefinite*) of the actors __?__ (*relative*) auditioned for the part of Hamlet were acceptable.

9. __?__ (*interrogative*) were the people __?__ (*relative*) left the peanut butter out after fixing __?__ (*reflexive*) sandwiches?

10. If Mary McGregor is chosen, __?__ (*personal*) will undoubtedly do her job and do __?__ (*personal*) well.

**Assignment  Using Pronouns in Writing**  The following paragraph needs pronouns to make it smoother and less repetitive. Rewrite the entire paragraph, replacing nouns with pronouns where suitable. Use any of the kinds of pronouns studied in this unit. Underline the pronouns in your rewritten paragraph.

> Many American writers got their start as newspaper reporters. Of these journalists-turned-authors, Samuel Clemens is one of the most eminent. Samuel Clemens is better known to us as Mark Twain. While Clemens was working for a newspaper in Sacramento, California, Clemens started to build Clemens a reputation by writing stories. Clemens published several stories, and one of the stories, "The Celebrated Jumping Frog of Calaveras County," reached numerous readers in the East. Clemens continued to challenge Clemens as a writer and published *Tom Sawyer* in 1876. Although *Tom Sawyer* does not have a great reputation for literary quality, *Tom Sawyer* has become a part of the folklore of the United States. Nine years later, Samuel Clemens published *Huckleberry Finn*, and *Huckleberry Finn* still stands as the best work by Clemens.

# 1.3 Verbs

A **verb** is a word that expresses an action or a state of being. There are three kinds of verbs: action verbs, linking verbs, and auxiliary verbs.

## 1.3a Kinds of Verbs

### Action Verbs

An **action verb** describes the behavior or action of someone or something. Action verbs may represent physical actions or mental activities.

Jim **ran** all the way home with the news.

The herd of cattle **thundered** toward us. [*Ran* and *thundered* refer to physical actions.]

Ida **studied** until late last night.

Most of the critics **admire** the new musical comedy. [*Studied* and *admire* refer to mental activities.]

### Linking Verbs

A **linking verb** connects a noun or a pronoun with a word or words that identify or describe that noun or pronoun. Many linking verbs are verbs of being, which are formed from the verb *be.*

Lucy Stone **was** an American reformer of the nineteenth century. [*Was* links *reformer* to *Lucy Stone.*]

The sofa along the far wall and the rocking chair in the corner **are** quite comfortable. [*Are* links the descriptive word *comfortable* to *sofa* and to *rocking chair.*]

There are several linking verbs in addition to *be.* To tell whether a word is a linking verb, you can substitute a form of *be* for it. A list of linking verbs follows:

| | | | |
|---|---|---|---|
| appear | grow | seem | stay |
| become | look | smell | taste |
| feel | remain | sound | |

**13**

Our hockey team **seems** ready for the game tonight. [**Think:** Our team *is* ready.]

The extinction of dinosaurs **remains** a mystery to scientists. [**Think:** Extinction *is* a mystery.]

Some verbs can be either action verbs or linking verbs, as in the following examples.

ACTION  Jeffrey **appeared** from nowhere when his mother called. [*Appeared* describes an action.]

LINKING  The department store **appears** rather crowded tonight. [**Think:** The store *is* crowded.]

## Auxiliary Verbs

Sometimes a verb needs the help of another verb, called an **auxiliary verb** or a **helping verb.** The verb that it helps is called the main verb. Together, a main verb and an auxiliary verb form a verb phrase. A verb phrase may have more than one auxiliary verb. Common auxiliary verbs appear in the following list:

am, are, be, been, is, was, were        may, might
can, could                              must
do, does, did                           shall, should
have, has, had                          will, would

In the following examples, the auxiliary verbs are in italic type, and the main verbs are in boldface type. *Not* and *never* are not part of the verb phrase.

The teachers of Central High School *have* **written** a handbook for new students.

The Kahns *will* not *be* **moving** to London after all.

How many satellites *does* the United States **launch** every year?

**Exercise 1  Verbs**  On your paper, write the verbs and verb phrases in the following sentences. After each one, write the label *Action verb* or *Linking verb* to describe its function in the sentence.

**SAMPLE**  How have you been spending your time since your vacation started?

**ANSWER**  have been spending—Action verb; started—Action verb

1. The solution to this problem will require a great deal of thought.
2. Larry picked Earl as his partner in the bridge competition because Earl had skill and experience.
3. The deer remained absolutely still as we approached it.
4. Those students who are attending vocational school after graduation will gain valuable expertise.
5. Robin can sell snowshoes even in summer, a fact that speaks well of her abilities as a salesperson.
6. The more spinach I eat, the fonder I grow of its taste.
7. I will not be going to the play this evening because my brother Neal will be arriving from Seattle sooner than I had expected.
8. Mr. Jenkins became somewhat upset when the nurse called and canceled his appointment for that afternoon.
9. Before you buy anything, ask yourself whether you need it.
10. This house has not changed much since the colonists built it more than three hundred years ago.

**Exercise 2 Using Action Verbs**  The following sentences have linking verbs. Rewrite each sentence, replacing each linking verb with an action verb. You may rephrase the rest of the sentence. Underline the action verbs that you supply.

**SAMPLE**  Maxwell seemed extremely happy when he learned that he had won the scholarship.

**ANSWER**  Maxwell grinned happily when he learned that he had won the scholarship.

1. All of the people in line were impatient while they waited for the ticket office to open.
2. The entire audience appeared impressed by the ballet performance.
3. Five-year-old Susan grew frightened when she could not find her parents in the department store.
4. The firefighters were courageous as they rushed into the burning building to save the top-floor tenants, who seemed panicky.

5. Waiting for his cue to walk onto the stage, Edgar seemed rather anxious.

6. To the observer standing at its base, Mount McKinley appears over-whelming.

7. The children were rather timid as they entered the front door of the deserted mansion.

8. Julia felt enthusiastic about the canoe trip that she was going on in another week.

# 1.3b   Characteristics of Verbs

## Transitive and Intransitive Verbs

All verbs are either transitive or intransitive. A verb is **transitive** when its action is directed toward someone or something, which is the object of the verb (*Unit 2*).

>        verb      obj.
> The attendant **filled** the tank with gasoline. [*Tank* is the object of the verb, *filled*. *Filled* is transitive.]

>     verb    obj.
> Ken **noticed** himself in the department store window. [*Himself* is the object of the verb, *noticed*. *Noticed* is transitive.]

A verb is **intransitive** when the performer of the action does not direct that action toward someone or something. In other words, an intransitive verb does not have a receiver of the action. Some action verbs, such as *lie,* are intransitive. All linking verbs are intransitive.

> On Sunday Mr. Marshall **relaxed** by going ice skating. [There is no object. *Relaxed* is intransitive.]

> From here the mountains **seem** quite far away. [*Seem* is a linking verb and is therefore intransitive.]

Many verbs can be either transitive or intransitive, depending on whether there is a receiver of the action.

>                                     obj.
> TRANSITIVE        The wind **slammed** the door shut with a loud bang. [The object of *slammed* is *door.*]

INTRANSITIVE    The door **slammed** shut with a loud bang. [*Slammed* has no object.]

## Changes in Verb Form

An important characteristic of verbs is that they change form according to how you use them. A verb form changes in order to agree in person and number with the noun or pronoun that is its subject. A verb form also changes to express tense and mood. For an explanation of how to use different verb forms, see Unit 4, "Usage."

**Exercise 3    Transitive and Intransitive Verbs**    On your paper, write the verbs and verb phrases in the following sentences. Label each verb or verb phrase *Transitive* or *Intransitive*.

SAMPLE    The invention of the wheel created a more comfortable way of life.

ANSWER    created—Transitive

(1) Before the invention of the wheel, people used sledges for carrying heavy loads.  (2) With the sledges, workers transported goods slowly from one place to another.  (3) Work animals dragged very heavy sledges, and by the end of the day, these animals were extremely tired.  (4) This arduous method of transportation became obsolete about five thousand years ago because of the invention of the wheel.  (5) The identity of the developer of the wheel is still unknown to scientists.  (6) However, archaeologists have found pictures of wheels on Mesopotamian tablets.  (7) Over the centuries the wheel has proven indispensable to the development of modern civilization.  (8) Vehicles with wheels carry us from one place to another, and machines with wheels produce consumer goods for all of us.

**Assignment    Action Verbs**    The following list contains six action verbs. For each verb list three words that are related in meaning. Then write an explanation of the specific meaning of each word. Use a dictionary as needed.

1. talk       3. move       5. fall
2. walk       4. eat        6. rise

## Using Action Verbs

Imagine that you are a radio or television broadcaster. For the evening news, you must write the script for a five-minute broadcast of the day's news. Write such a broadcast script by using news from the school that you attend. In writing this broadcast, use verbs that clearly and vividly describe and summarize the news. When you have finished writing, underline the action verbs in your script.

# 1.4   Adjectives

An **adjective** is a word that modifies a noun or a pronoun. To *modify* means to change; an adjective modifies a word by describing it or limiting it. In some sentences, nouns and certain pronouns are used as adjectives. In such cases, consider them adjectives. Adjectives answer *Which? What kind?* or *How many?*

> After looking at all the antiques, I prefer the **oak** *desk*. [Which desk? The *oak* desk.]
>
> A mortgage is actually a **long-term** *loan*. [What kind of loan? A *long-term* loan.]
>
> There are **one hundred** *houses* in the development. [How many houses? *One hundred* houses.]
>
> We did a **long, complex,** but **fascinating** *experiment* in chemistry. [*Long, complex,* and *fascinating* all modify *experiment*.]

**Articles.**   The most frequently used adjectives are the articles: *a, an,* and *the. A* and *an* are **indefinite articles** because they do not specify a particular person, place, thing, or idea. *The* is a **definite article** because it always points out a particular item.

INDEFINITE  For **an** *encore,* our band played its biggest hit. [There could be more than one encore.]

DEFINITE  Jay has been chosen to lead **the** *expedition.* [There will be only one expedition.]

## Placement of Adjectives

Adjectives usually appear directly before the nouns or pronouns that they modify. Sometimes a comma separates adjectives from the words that they modify.

The **nimble** *gymnast* was applauded by the **appreciative** *audience.*

**Lightweight** and **flexible,** *aluminum* is a very useful metal.

Adjectives may come after linking verbs and modify the subjects (*Unit 2*) of verbs.

The *mountain peak* did not look **awesome** from a distance,

but as we approached it, the *peak* was **overwhelming!**

Sometimes adjectives follow the words that they modify and are separated from them by a comma.

A *colt,* **energetic** and **friendly,** approached us at the corner of the pasture.

## Proper Adjectives

A **proper adjective** is an adjective formed from a proper noun. Proper adjectives are usually capitalized.

The **Kent** *residence* is always well kept.

**Yellowstone National Park** *campsites* are difficult to get.

To create many proper adjectives, you use the suffixes *-n, -an, -ian, -ese, -ish,* or *-al,* occasionally changing the spelling of the proper noun.

| PROPER NOUN | PROPER ADJECTIVE |
|---|---|
| Victoria | Victorian |
| Hungary | Hungarian |
| China | Chinese |
| Spain | Spanish |

## Nouns Used as Adjectives

Some nouns function as adjectives without changing form, as in the following examples.

A tour through a **newspaper** *office* is a fascinating experience.

It must be the season for **ragweed** *pollen* because Brenda has been sneezing quite a bit.

**Possessive Nouns.** Possessive nouns, which are nouns that show possession or ownership, function as adjectives because they modify nouns or pronouns. For the rules regarding the correct spelling of singular possessive nouns and plural possessive nouns, refer to Unit 15.

A **man's** *shadow* was on the opposite wall. [Which shadow? *Man's* shadow.]

Are the **vacationers'** *boats* tied securely to the pier? [Which boats? *Vacationers'* boats.]

## Pronouns Used as Adjectives

A pronoun functions as an adjective if it modifies a noun or a pronoun. Indefinite pronouns, demonstrative pronouns, interrogative pronouns, some of the possessive pronouns, and one of the relative pronouns (*page 11*) may all serve as adjectives. The possessive pronouns that can function as adjectives are in the following list:

|                | SINGULAR       | PLURAL |
|----------------|----------------|--------|
| FIRST PERSON   | my             | our    |
| SECOND PERSON  | your           | your   |
| THIRD PERSON   | his, her, its  | their  |

**Our** art *teacher* really admires **your** *sculpture* from last week's class. [Which teacher? *Our* teacher. Which sculpture? *Your* sculpture.]

The old coffee urn has certainly lost **its** *luster* over the years. [Which luster? *Its* luster. Note that you spell the possessive pronoun *its* without an apostrophe.]

The words in the preceding list are called *possessive pronouns* throughout this textbook, but some people call them *pronominal adjectives*. You should use the term that your teacher prefers.

The following list contains examples of the other kinds of pronouns that can function as adjectives.

| INDEFINITE     | few, many, much, other, several, some |
|----------------|---------------------------------------|
| DEMONSTRATIVE  | this, that, these, those              |
| INTERROGATIVE  | what, which, whose                    |
| RELATIVE       | whose                                 |

**Which** *map* did you use to locate **these** *cabins?*

**Several** *people* called, but **some** *callers* did not leave messages.

**Exercise 1** **Adjectives** Number your paper from 1 to 8. Next to each number, write the adjective or adjectives in the corresponding sentence from the following passage. Do not include articles. Next to each adjective, write the word or words that it modifies.

| SAMPLE | Imagine vine-covered trees, flying monkeys, and huge, colorful flowers, and you have formed an excellent image of a tropical forest. |
|--------|-------------------------------------------------------------------------------------------------------------------------------------|
| ANSWER | vine-covered—trees; flying—monkeys; huge—flowers; colorful—flowers; excellent—image; tropical—forest |

(1) The world's tropical forests are in equatorial regions. (2) These areas typically possess much lush vegetation, scarce sunlight, and considerable rainfall. (3) Perhaps the thickest plant growth and the greatest diversity of animal life exist in South American forests. (4) One hundred thousand species of plants and animals live under the trees' canopy near the Amazon River. (5) This Amazonian forest, which covers millions of square miles, contains valuable trees; their products include fruit, nuts, oils, rubber, and wood. (6) Some trees grow to the considerable height of two hundred feet, and they are homes for monkeys, bats, sloths, and other tree-dwelling creatures. (7) Day or night, the forest seems alive, although few humans can be found in it. (8) In the heart of the dense forest, a wandering explorer might detect the sounds of screaming parrots and dripping water.

**Exercise 2   Using Adjectives**   The following sentences need adjectives to make them more vivid and descriptive. Rewrite each sentence, adding adjectives to make the sentences more effective. Try to use words that are fresh and interesting. Underline the adjectives in your rewritten sentences.

> **SAMPLE**     The man walked through the fog.
>
> **ANSWER**     The <u>unknown</u>, <u>thickset</u> man walked through the <u>oppressive</u> fog.

1. The tiger growled at the hunters.
2. The rain pelted the golfers.
3. We went to a track meet yesterday.
4. A flock of geese flew over the field.
5. Before a breeze, the ships sailed into the harbor.
6. The group went to a film last evening.
7. An island lay ahead of the crew in the lifeboat.
8. A herd of buffalo stampeded through the town.
9. The singer gave a show.
10. The woman watched the children playing in the school yard.

**Assignment   Adjectives**   Attach a picture of an object to a sheet of paper. On another sheet, list ten adjectives that you think best describe the object. Read your list to your classmates, and ask them to guess what object you are describing.

## Adjectives in Advertisements

Examine several magazine advertisements and note how adjectives are used to make the products seem appealing. Then write a one-hundred-word advertisement for either the object that you described in the preceding assignment or for another object. Underline every adjective that you use. Be prepared to explain how each adjective helps to create product appeal.

# 1.5   Adverbs

Like adjectives, adverbs are modifiers. An **adverb** is a word that modifies a verb, an adjective, or another adverb. An adverb answers one of five questions about the word or phrase that it modifies: *How? When? Where? How often?* or *To what extent?*

| | |
|---|---|
| HOW | The excited woman *talked* **rapidly** on the telephone. [How did the woman talk? She talked *rapidly*.] |
| WHEN | Max *finished* the job **early.** |
| WHERE | As we climbed the hill, the children *ran* **ahead.** |
| HOW OFTEN | I **usually** *read* the newspaper from front page to back page. |
| TO WHAT EXTENT | I *was* **rather** *expecting* that we would go to the other restaurant. |

**23**

Adverbs such as *really, certainly, indeed,* and *truly* are adverbs of extent. You use them for emphasis.

Luis **really** *knows* how to fix a car, doesn't he? [*Really* emphasizes the fact that Luis is skilled at fixing cars.]

The words *not* and *never* are adverbs. They tell to what extent (*not at all*) and when (*never*).

Jean *will* **not** *pay* that price for pears. [*Not* modifies *will pay*.]

**Nouns Used as Adverbs.**    Some nouns function as adverbs, as in the following examples.

You *should have received* the package **Thursday.** [*Thursday* functions as an adverb telling when.]

**Today** city officials *expect* large crowds **downtown.** [*Today* functions as an adverb telling when and *downtown* as an adverb telling where.]

## Adverbs Used to Modify Verbs

Adverbs most frequently modify verbs. The adverb does not have to appear next to the verb that it modifies. Notice the different positions that the adverb *quickly* has in the following sentences.

BEGINNING    **Quickly,** the demolition crew *transformed* the old hotel into a pile of rubble.

MIDDLE    The demolition crew **quickly** *transformed* the old hotel into a pile of rubble.

## Adverbs Used to Modify Adjectives

Adverbs may modify adjectives. The adverb usually comes directly before the adjective that it modifies.

adv.    adj.
Gina is a **truly** *exceptional* swimmer. [To what extent is she exceptional? She is *truly* exceptional.]

adv.   adj.

Steve can hold his breath for **almost** *three* minutes. [*Almost* tells how close to three minutes Steve can hold his breath.]

adv.   adj.

The mystery left the playgoers **somewhat** *puzzled*. [*Somewhat* tells the extent to which the playgoers were puzzled.]

## Adverbs Used to Modify Adverbs

An adverb that modifies another adverb tells to what extent or degree. Such adverbs usually precede the adverbs that they modify.

adv.  adv.

Jimmy shouldn't worry **too** *much* about where the cat went because it always comes back. [*Too* emphasizes the fact that Jimmy should not worry much.]

adv.  adv.

The flu is spreading through the school **more** rapidly than the nurse had expected. [To what extent is the flu spreading rapidly? It is spreading *more* rapidly.]

**Exercise 1** **Adverbs** Number your paper from 1 to 8. Next to each number, write the adverbs in the corresponding sentences of the following paragraph. Next to each adverb, write the verb, adjective, or adverb that it modifies. There are twenty-one adverbs.

**SAMPLE**    In 1936 a handful of New Yorkers watched excitedly as the barely recognizable image of Felix the Cat came slowly onto the screens of their new television receivers.

**ANSWER**    excitedly—watched; barely—recognizable; slowly—came

(1) This cartoon was the culmination of nearly thirty years of efforts by scientists who worked doggedly to produce an electronic means of transmitting pictures. (2) A German scientist, Paul Gottlieb Nipkow, successfully transmitted pictures in 1884, but his device did not operate electronically. (3) The rather extraordinary efforts of scientists Philo T. Farnsworth, John Baird, and Vladimir Zworykin finally produced a relatively practical television system by the 1920s. (4) The initial telecasts began in the same decade, but

regular programs, shown primarily in the New York City area, started in 1939. (5) All programming was temporarily suspended during World War II; after the end of the war, the television boom started very quickly. (6) With increasingly successful technical advancements, television became widely accessible. (7) Quiz shows, professional wrestling, U.S. Senate hearings, and comedy or variety shows, seen on seven-inch screens, quickly attained popularity, and by 1950 nearly six million sets were in use. (8) This figure jumped dramatically to almost sixty million sets by 1960, when screens became wider, the quality of color programs improved significantly, national networks were firmly established, and the public became enchanted with the highly popular stars of television.

**Exercise 2   Adverbs in Writing**   Each of the following sentences needs adverbs to make it more specific. On your paper, rewrite each sentence, adding two adverbs that fulfill the function described in parentheses. Underline the adverbs.

> **SAMPLE**      The speaker paused, shook her head, and continued
> her speech, which outlined an economic policy for
> the future. (to modify verbs and tell *how*)
>
> **ANSWER**      The speaker paused <u>dramatically</u>, shook her head
> <u>gravely</u>, and continued her speech, which outlined an
> economic policy for the future.

1. When Andrea must write a composition, she goes to the library, where she finds the necessary resources. (to modify verbs and tell *how often*)

2. If you try to fix a television set quickly, the job may actually go slowly. (to modify adverbs and tell *to what extent*)

3. A lumpfish, which lives in ocean waters that are cold, is unattractive because it is covered with unappealing lumps instead of scales. (to modify adjectives and tell *to what extent*)

4. Did Julius deliver the equipment, or must we go to the warehouse to get it? (to modify verbs and tell *when*)

5. Historical novels have plots that are dramatic and entertaining; therefore, I have become a devoted fan. (to modify adjectives and tell *to what extent*)

6. The rainstorm soaked Stephanie and Wendy, who raced for a shelter nearby. (to modify verbs, the first telling *to what extent* and the second telling *how*)

7. When Lucy arrived at five o'clock in the evening, she looked for the gloves that she had lost. (to modify verbs and tell *where*)

8. Although Pat's scores on trigonometry exams had been good throughout the semester, he still felt anxious about the upcoming final. (to modify adjectives and tell *to what extent*)

**Assignment  Adverbs in Creative Writing**  In stories and novels, writers use adverbs to tell how a character performs an action. The adverbs are clues to the character's mood and personality. Find a passage in a story or a novel that describes actions performed by one of the characters in the work. On your paper, write the title of the work, the name of the author, and the page numbers of the passage. Select ten adverbs that contribute to the reader's understanding of the character. Write each adverb and the word or phrase that it modifies. After each adverb, explain in a sentence what that adverb reveals about the character's mood or personality.

# 1.6   Prepositions

A **preposition** is a word that expresses a relationship between a noun or a pronoun and another word in a sentence.

The sailors **in** a submarine must look **through** a periscope when they are **beneath** the surface. [The preposition *in* relates the noun *submarine* to the noun *sailors*. *Through* relates *periscope* to the verb phrase *must look*. *Beneath* relates *surface* to the verb *are*.]

The following list contains the prepositions that are used most frequently:

| | | | |
|---|---|---|---|
| along | between | off | to |
| among | beyond | on | toward |
| around | despite | onto | under |
| at | down | out | underneath |
| before | during | outside | until |
| behind | except | over | up |
| below | for | past | upon |
| beneath | from | since | with |
| beside | in | through | within |
| besides | near | till | without |

A **compound preposition** is a preposition that consists of more than one word.

**According to** the traffic report, the south expressway is completely jammed this morning.

Frequently used compound prepositions are in the list that follows:

| | |
|---|---|
| according to | in regard to |
| aside from | in respect to |
| as of | in spite of |
| as well as | instead of |
| because of | on account of |
| by means of | out of |
| in addition to | prior to |
| in front of | with regard to |
| in place of | with respect to |

A preposition is usually followed by a noun or a pronoun, which is called the **object of the preposition.** Together, the preposition, the object, and the modifiers of that object form a **prepositional phrase.**

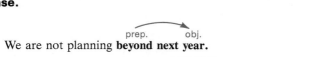

We are not planning **beyond next year.**

The Andersons were **behind a truck and a tractor.** [The prepositional phrase has a compound object, *truck* and *tractor.*]

The preposition sometimes comes after the object, as in the following sentence.

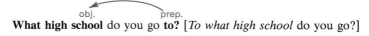

**What high school** do you go **to?** [*To what high school* do you go?]

A prepositional phrase functions as an adjective if it modifies a noun or a pronoun. A prepositional phrase functions as an adverb if it modifies a verb, an adjective, or an adverb.

USED AS AN ADJECTIVE

The first *street* **past the traffic light** is where you should turn.
[*Past the traffic light* tells which street.]

USED AS AN ADVERB

Bob *sprained* his ankle **during yesterday's football practice.**
[*During yesterday's football practice* tells when Bob sprained his ankle.]

The same word can be a preposition or an adverb, depending on its use in the sentence.

PREPOSITION     Did you find your pen **behind** the *sofa*?

ADVERB     Alex *fell* **behind** in the race.

**Exercise Prepositional Phrases** On your paper, list the prepositional phrases in the following sentences. Underline the prepositions once and the objects twice.

> **SAMPLE**     For nearly one hundred years, the Ferris wheel has been a source of entertainment for both children and adults.
>
> **ANSWER**     For nearly one hundred years; of entertainment; for both children and adults

1. Have you ever gazed at tiny houses, cars, and people as you sat suspended fifty feet above the ground?
2. If so, you have probably enjoyed a ride on the Ferris wheel at an amusement park.
3. Since 1893 the Ferris wheel has been a source of entertainment at most fairs and carnivals.
4. At that time the wheel was developed by G.W. Gale Ferris for the World's Columbian Exposition in Chicago.
5. This type of amusement ride, created to commemorate the fourth centennial of the discovery of America, was the largest as well as the first one built.
6. Although the wheel was used again during another fair held in St. Louis, it was eventually destroyed for scrap metal.

7. A Ferris wheel consists of two giant steel wheels mounted upon a sturdy base.
8. Between these wheels are secured swinging seats for two people.
9. The wheels turn by means of an engine that is powered by gasoline.
10. In spite of their size and widespread use, Ferris wheels have been the cause of remarkably few accidents.

# 1.7   Conjunctions

A **conjunction** is a word that connects words or groups of words. In fact, the word *conjunction* literally means "the act of joining" or "combination." There are three kinds of conjunctions: coordinating conjunctions, correlative conjunctions, and subordinating conjunctions.

## Coordinating Conjunctions

A **coordinating conjunction** connects individual words or groups of words that perform the same function in a sentence. The coordinating conjunctions are in the following list:

    and     but     for     nor     or     yet

A coordinating conjunction can connect individual nouns, pronouns, verbs, adjectives, adverbs, prepositions, or interjections.

During this autumn our weather has been *cool, crisp,* **and** *pleasant.*

A coordinating conjunction can also connect phrases or clauses *(Unit 3),* as in the following examples.

Rhonda plans *to take a bicycle tour* **and** *to visit her uncle's farm* during summer vacation.
If someone telephones me, you can *wake me up* **or** *take a message.*
*The streets of the city are arranged in a confusing pattern,* **but** *I confess that I have never become lost.*

## Correlative Conjunctions

A **correlative conjunction** is a conjunction that consists of two or more words that function together. Like coordinating conjunctions, correlative conjunctions connect words that perform equal functions in a sentence. The following list contains correlative conjunctions:

both . . . and          not only . . . but (also)
either . . . or          whether . . . or
neither . . . nor

You should take **either** *a raincoat* **or** *an umbrella* to school today.

By tomorrow Coach Jackson must decide **whether** *Debbie will swim in the freestyle competition* **or** *in the backstroke event* at the state meet.

## Subordinating Conjunctions

A **subordinating conjunction** introduces a subordinate clause (*Unit 3*), which is a clause that cannot stand by itself as a complete sentence. A subordinating conjunction connects a subordinate clause to an independent clause, which *can* stand by itself as a complete sentence.

┌──────────────── subordinate clause ────────────────┐
**Because** the biology class had to cancel its visit to the arboretum

┌──┐┌────────────independent clause ────────────┐
on account of rain, Ms. Boyle rescheduled the trip for next month.
[The subordinating conjunction, *because*, introduces the subordinating clause and connects the clause to the independent clause.]

Subordinating conjunctions usually express relationships of time, manner, cause, condition, comparison, or purpose.

| | |
|---|---|
| TIME | after, as, as long as, as soon as, before, since, until, when, whenever, while |
| MANNER | as, as if, as though |
| CAUSE | because |
| CONDITION | although, as long as, even if, even though, if, provided that, though, unless, while |

COMPARISON     as, than

PURPOSE        in order that, so that, that

We should leave for the beach **whenever** you are ready. [*Whenever* expresses time.]

Susan will be elected our new state representative **provided that** she carries the fourth precinct. [*Provided that* expresses condition.]

At the school's roller-skating party yesterday, Craig skated **as though** he were an expert instead of a beginner. [*As though* expresses manner.]

## Conjunctive Adverbs

A **conjunctive adverb** is an adverb that functions somewhat like a coordinating conjunction. Conjunctive adverbs usually connect independent clauses (*Unit 3*). A semicolon precedes the conjunctive adverb, and a comma usually follows it.

CONJUNCTIVE ADVERB
> The flight that we were planning to take to Denver had been canceled because of the weather; **consequently,** we waited all night in the airport for another flight.

COORDINATING CONJUNCTION
> We waited all night in the airport for another flight, **for** the one that we were planning to take to Denver had been canceled because of the weather.

The following list contains frequently used conjunctive adverbs:

| | | | |
|---|---|---|---|
| also | furthermore | later | still |
| besides | however | moreover | then |
| consequently | indeed | nevertheless | therefore |
| finally | instead | otherwise | thus |

**Exercise 1   Conjunctions and Conjunctive Adverbs**   On your paper, list the conjunctive adverbs and conjunctions in the following sentences. Identify the function of each in the sentence with the label *Coordinating conjunction, Correlative conjunction, Subordinating conjunction,* or *Conjunctive adverb.*

| SAMPLE | Because Jackson High is playing its biggest game in years this Saturday, a group of students is planning a special pep rally; moreover, the administration has given permission to hold the rally during the last period of school on Friday. |
| --- | --- |
| ANSWER | Because—Subordinating conjunction; moreover—Conjunctive adverb |

1. Turbines, which propel windmills and water wheels, are extremely simple machines; however, they have the ability to run generators and to power ocean liners.
2. Although Maurice does not swim or dive, he will take lessons this summer, and he hopes to become proficient in both activities.
3. Either Chicago or Dallas will be chosen as the next convention site unless another location appears more advantageous.
4. When the autumn foliage reached its peak, Claudette walked into the woods and gathered some leaves that she would press in a book.
5. Will you attend the art exhibit and the reception after work on Tuesday, or will you plan to see a play?
6. Not only were they lost, but they had also run out of gas, and rain showers began as soon as Chuck started walking to the gas station.
7. Both a loudspeaker and a megaphone were on the podium, yet Mr. Dworkin addressed the audience without using either.
8. Before her paper was finished, Maureen read some more about John Singleton Copley's life so that she would be sure that the paper was thorough.
9. The stationery store closed early; consequently, I purchased the cards elsewhere and mailed them promptly.
10. Mr. Friscia is indeed thrilled with the results; moreover, he will be praised for his diligent experiments in this field.

## Exercise 2   Conjunctions and Conjunctive Adverbs

Number your paper from 1 to 10. Beside each number, write a conjunction or a conjunctive adverb that fits in the corresponding blank in the following story.

| SAMPLE | Hearing about a blizzard __?__ experiencing one are two different things. |
| --- | --- |
| ANSWER | and |

__1__ I had seen blizzards on television, I had never personally experienced one __2__ a fierce one hit our area last year. __3__ it started snowing at three o'clock on Monday, my sisters __4__ I were excited. It was still snowing the next morning, __5__ strong winds made snow removal impossible. The wind and snow continued for another two days! The weather forecasters had predicted twelve inches; __6__, we got thirty-four.

The storm trapped thousands of people at work __7__ at stores. __8__ the police could not handle the emergency, the National Guard was called in to help. All efforts were directed toward delivering food to people. It took weeks __9__ the city returned to normal. __10__ the blizzard caused much inconvenience, it brought people closer together.

**Assignment** **Using Conjunctions** On your paper, rewrite the following paragraphs by using conjunctions and conjunctive adverbs whenever possible to connect ideas and to provide variety in sentence structure. Underline the conjunctions and conjunctive adverbs that you use. You may make other changes so that the passage reads smoothly.

The Underground Railroad played a unique part in American history. This was before the Civil War broke out. The members, or "railroaders," set up a system of hiding places for slaves. Many railroaders were former slaves. The former slaves had escaped from the South. The railroad was not a formal organization. The railroad worked well enough to help fifty thousand slaves. The slaves escaped to freedom from 1830 to 1860. There were Underground Railroad stations in the southern slave states. There were stations in the northern states. In the South, slaves gave food to runaway slaves. They gave clothing. They gave shelter. They gave directions. A fugitive slave law was passed in 1850. The law made it illegal to help runaway slaves. Blacks and white abolitionists continued to run the railroad. More slaves fled to Canada.

The most famous railroader was Harriet Tubman. Tubman herself had escaped from Maryland to Pennsylvania in 1849. She then returned to Maryland nineteen times. She helped other slaves to freedom. She even helped her own parents escape in 1857. Tubman was successful. Rewards for her arrest totaled forty thousand dollars at one point. However, she was never captured. She continued helping runaway slaves. So did others. Then the Civil War began. Their efforts were no longer necessary.

# 1.8    Interjections

An **interjection** is an exclamatory word or phrase that can stand by itself, although it may also appear in a sentence. Many interjections express strong emotions. They are followed by exclamation marks.

> **My goodness!**
> **Stop!** You're turning the wrong way.

When an interjection appears within a sentence, you should set it off with commas.

> **Heavens,** I never expected this to happen.
> **Hmmm,** I'm not really sure how to solve this problem.

**Exercise  Interjections**    On your paper, rewrite the following sentences. In place of each blank, use an interjection from the following list that suits the meaning of the sentence. You should use an interjection only once.

> **SAMPLE**        _ ? _! I got a splinter from that piece of wood.
> **ANSWER**        Ouch! I got a splinter from that piece of wood.

| | | | | |
|---|---|---|---|---|
| ugh | alas | oops | whew | good grief |
| great | oh, no | what | ah | hurrah |

1. _ ? _! That glass of orange juice really tasted good.
2. _ ? _! The train is pulling out of the station.
3. You mean that you forgot to return your library book? _ ? _!
4. _ ? _, we cannot expect continued growth in this region's economy this year.
5. _ ? _! We don't have to put a second coat of paint on the bedroom wall if we apply a thick first coat.
6. _ ? _! Don't trip on the corner of that rug.
7. Mark has set a new school record in the half-mile. _ ? _!
8. _ ? _! You think that you forgot to lock the front door before we left!

# Unit Practice

## Practice 1

**A. Nouns** (*pages 3–8*)  Rewrite each of the following sentences by replacing the blanks with nouns. Use the kind of noun indicated in parentheses.

1. The wild __?__ (*common*) that live near __?__ (*proper*) have survived the fierce winter storm.
2. __?__ (*common*) scientifically predict the weather, __?__ (*common*) forecast the weather on television, and __?__ (*common*) dress each day according to the weather.
3. My favorite city, __?__ (*proper*), is a place that is full of __?__ (*abstract*).
4. Have you seen the large __?__ (*collective*) waiting in front of the theater's __?__ (*common*)?
5. The __?__ (*concrete*) appointed a special __?__ (*collective*) to find a new __?__ (*abstract*) for the problem of traffic congestion downtown.

**B. Pronouns** (*pages 8–12*)  On your paper, list the pronouns in each of the following sentences.

6. The eyeglass case here is yours, and that is mine near the book on the tall bureau.
7. Few attended the outdoor ceremony; the temperature was almost too brisk for the graduates themselves.
8. Who will lower the flag, which can be seen from miles away, and then fold it to be stored overnight?
9. Blair, who is interested in aeronautics, bought himself a book about early monoplanes.
10. Either of the routes will be adequate, yet the one that winds past the reservoir may take longer.

**C. Verbs** (*pages 13–18*)  On your paper, rewrite each of the following sentences using the kind of verb listed in parentheses.

11. Melvil Dewey, a librarian, was the inventor of the Dewey Decimal Classification system. (*action*)
12. All summer I worked as a counselor at the day camp. (*linking*)

13. The passengers on the train were ready for the bumpy track ahead. (*action*)
14. Gorgeous leaves from the oak tree in our front yard covered the ground. (*linking*)
15. In Kansas her family was at the Eisenhower Library and Museum. (*action*)

**D. Adjectives and Adverbs** (*pages 18–27*)  On your paper, rewrite the following sentences by replacing each blank with an adjective or an adverb.

16. __?__ (*adjective*) applicants for the job typed their résumés __?__ (*adverb*).
17. Ray presents his ideas __?__ (*adverb*) clearly in __?__ (*adjective*) class.
18. Of all __?__ (*adjective*) tapes, I listen __?__ (*adverb*) to this one.
19. Will __?__ (*adjective*) report on ancient astronomy be presented at the college __?__ (*adverb*)?
20. The __?__ (*adjective*) mountains in the West provide a __?__ (*adverb*) remarkable view.

**E. Prepositions** (*pages 27–30*)  On your paper, list the prepositional phrases in the following sentences. Underline the preposition in each prepositional phrase.

21. The close-up photographs by Julia Margaret Cameron are noteworthy because of their vitality and character.
22. Although his favorite team was behind in the pennant race, Gary was optimistic in spite of the results.
23. Unfortunately, Jane's necklace is now lodged beyond her reach behind her bureau.
24. In which event did the cross-country team win that trophy?
25. The woman spoke loudly until she could be heard over the noise of the jackhammer.

**F. Conjunctions** (*pages 30–34*)  On your paper, write one sentence for each of the following words. Use the words as either

(Continue on the next page.)

conjunctions or conjunctive adverbs. At the end of the sentence, tell whether you used the word as a coordinating conjunction, a subordinating conjunction, a correlative conjunction, or a conjunctive adverb.

26. not only . . . but (also)
27. nor
28. as though

29. also
30. nevertheless

# Practice 2

Number your paper from 1 to 30. List the words and phrases in italics in the following passage. Label each word or phrase *Noun, Pronoun, Verb, Adjective, Adverb, Preposition, Conjunction,* or *Interjection* to identify its function in the sentence.

(1) *Although* little is known about the  (2) *very* early practice of medicine,  (3) *experts* believe that ancient civilization (4) *practiced* some surgery and treated illnesses  (5) *with* herbs and plants. For instance, written records  (6) *have revealed* the many (7) *medical* advancements of  (8) *Egyptian* civilization.  (9) *Imhotep* was the first physician  (10) *who* was named in an Egyptian document. Diseases, broken bones,  (11) *and* wounds were discussed in a  (12) *textbook* written  (13) *by* Egyptian surgeons. Medical specialization  (14) *eventually* began about 2500 B.C. when Egyptian physicians  (15) *became* diversified, and  (16) *each* treated (17) *only* certain ailments. An  (18) *important* figure in Greek medicine  (19) *was* Hippocrates. Hippocrates  (20) *himself* established a code of medical  (21) *ethics.* He asserted that medicine should be based on science  (22) *instead of* myths  (23) *or* superstition. Later, in approximately A.D. 100, Galen, who practiced in Rome, conducted  (24) *scientific·*experiments and developed (25) *some* knowledge of anatomy based on  (26) *his* observation of animals.  (27) *Alas,* Galen's observations led to erroneous assumptions  (28) *about* human anatomy,  (29) *but* his methods of inquiry were  (30) *still* an important step in the development of medicine.

# Unit Tests

## Test 1

**A. Nouns** (*pages 3–8*)   Rewrite the following sentences by replacing each blank with a noun. Use the kind of noun indicated in parentheses.

1. A long whistle from the __?__ (*compound*) told the __?__ (*collective*) that the voyage was over.
2. __?__ (*abstract*) is difficult to measure or to define; however, I feel it when I look at the __?__ (*concrete*).
3. His sister __?__ (*proper*) hiked up the craggy side of __?__ (*proper*) until she could view the entire __?__ (*common*).
4. Holding a piece of parchment, a __?__ (*common*) read a proclamation about __?__ (*abstract*) at the town square.
5. A __?__ (*collective*) gathered near the __?__ (*concrete*) to listen to the music of the __?__ (*common*).

**B. Pronouns** (*pages 8–12*)   On your paper, list the pronouns in each of the following sentences.

6. I taught myself how to make macramé plant holders that are decorative and useful.
7. The wicker chairs in the window will be auctioned, but those will remain at the shop.
8. What is the solution to the puzzle, which Dr. Jacobson himself has had difficulty answering?
9. Plenty of people spend vacations at the beach; however, Hal enjoys his at a cabin in the mountains.
10. Who invented vending machines, which are particularly convenient for those who are in a hurry?

**C. Verbs** (*pages 13–18*)   On your paper, rewrite each of the following sentences, using the kind of verb listed in parentheses.

11. Traffic slowed at the intersection because of construction work. (*linking*)
12. Steam was suddenly apparent at the top of the Kilauea volcano on Hawaii Island. (*action*)

(Continue on the next page.)

13. A group of aerobatic airplanes performing tricks was overhead. (*action*)
14. After a few lessons, operating a printing press became easy for Greg. (*action*)
15. Ticketholders anxious to go to the hit play were in the long line. (*action*)

**D. Adjectives and Adverbs** (*pages 18–27*)   On your paper, rewrite the following sentences by replacing each blank with an adjective or an adverb.

16. Joshua trees can __?__ (*adverb*) grow in the desert without __?__ (*adjective*) water.
17. Thursday is __?__ (*adverb*) busy because I have __?__ (*adjective*) lessons after school.
18. One __?__ (*adjective*) custom is to break a piñata that is __?__ (*adjective*).
19. After minor repairs, __?__ (*adjective*) motorbike is working __?__ (*adverb*).
20. Did Willy __?__ (*adverb*) attempt to make that __?__ (*adjective*) goal during the match?

**E. Prepositions** (*pages 27–30*)   On your paper, list the prepositional phrases in the following sentences. Underline the preposition in each prepositional phrase.

21. A tractor-trailer eased onto the highway, which' was slick after the first snowfall of the season.
22. Franco, please stand quietly beside your brother for this family portrait by the professional photographer.
23. Aside from a few minor delays, Del and Francesca had a smooth flight over the ocean to their grandparents' home.
24. Pick another topic in place of the one that has already been used in the past for this assignment.
25. Petrels are water birds that fly along the ocean's surface above the waves until they catch fish.

**F. Conjunctions** (*pages 30–34*)   On your paper, write one sentence for each of the following words. Use the words as either conjunctions or conjunctive adverbs. At the end of the sentence, tell whether you used the word as a coordinating conjunction, a subordinating conjunction, a correlative conjunction, or a conjunctive adverb.

26. but
27. therefore
28. because
29. so that
30. whether . . . or

## Test 2

Number your paper from 1 to 30. List the words and phrases in italics in the following passage. Label each word or phrase *Noun, Pronoun, Verb, Adjective, Adverb, Preposition,* or *Conjunction* to identify its function in the sentence.

(1) *Most* people depend upon a watch (2) *or* a clock. (3) *What* happens when a watch suddenly does not work (4) *properly*? Whether the (5) *timepiece* that (6) *has broken* is a (7) *grandfather* clock or a digital watch, (8) *someone* must repair (9) *it*. Fortunately, there are (10) *approximately* twelve thousand watch repairers (11) *in* the United States today. (12) *Their* job (13) *is* painstaking (14) *yet* rewarding. Watch (15) *repairers* generally (16) *fix* a watch (17) *by means of* magnifying glasses, tweezers, and tiny screwdrivers. (18) *With* these tools, a watch repairer can remove the entire watch movement from (19) *its* case in order to clean it and (20) *carefully* examine the parts. Broken or worn parts (21) *are replaced* (22) *before* the watch repairer reassembles the movement. (23) *Electronic* watches are (24) *always* tested with special electrical test (25) *equipment,* (26) *because* such watches have no moving parts. Of course, (27) *those* interested in obtaining a watch repair license for this profession must first pass the (28) *American Watchmakers Institute* exam after attending one of the schools (29) *around* the country or after working as an (30) *apprentice.*

# Unit 2

*Sentence*
*Structure*

---

## Unit Preview

When you put words in a certain order to communicate meaning, you create sentences, or units of thought. Some ways of organizing sentences are more effective than others. To understand what makes a sentence communicate clearly or not, you need to study its structure.

**For Analysis** The sentences in Paragraph A are structured differently from those in Paragraph B. Read both paragraphs, and on your paper answer the questions that follow.

PARAGRAPH A

(1) In 1873 a permanent name was given to a unique era in history by a novel entitled *The Gilded Age,* which was published by Mark Twain and Charles Dudley Warner. (2) During the last three decades of the 1800s, American life was changed in countless ways by industrialization. (3) Fortunes were made by the Vanderbilts, the Rockefellers, J.P. Morgan, and other industrialists, and their wealth was used for what was called "conspicuous consumption" by economist Thorstein Veblen. (4) Palace-style mansions were built by these multimillionaires, expensive works of art were purchased, and their mansions were filled with gaudy furnishings. (5) It was an age of unparalleled opulence, a Gilded Age in every sense of the term.

PARAGRAPH B

    (1) In 1873 Mark Twain and Charles Dudley Warner gave a permanent name to a unique era in history when they published a novel entitled *The Gilded Age*. (2) During the last three decades of the 1800s, industrialization changed American life in countless ways. (3) The Vanderbilts, the Rockefellers, J.P. Morgan, and other industrialists made fortunes, and they used their wealth for what economist Thorstein Veblen called "conspicuous consumption." (4) These multimillionaires built palace-style mansions, purchased expensive works of art, and filled their mansions with gaudy furnishings. (5) It was an age of unparalleled opulence, a Gilded Age in every sense of the term.

1. How is Sentence 1 of Paragraph B different from Sentence 1 of Paragraph A? What are the subject and the predicate of each sentence?
2. How is Sentence 2 of Paragraph B different from Sentence 2 of Paragraph A?
3. In your opinion, which paragraph is easier to understand? What makes it easier to understand?

    The subject of Sentence 1 in Paragraph A is *name*. However, in the corresponding sentence in Paragraph B, the subjects are *Mark Twain* and *Charles Dudley Warner*. The sentence in Paragraph B clarifies who performed the action. All of the sentences in Paragraph B are livelier and clearer than those in Paragraph A. As you can see from these two paragraphs, sentence structure has an important effect on your writing, and this unit will explain how.

## 2.1 Four Sentence Purposes

    A **sentence** is a group of words that has a subject and a predicate and expresses a complete thought. It describes an action or states a condition of a person, a place, a thing, or an idea. Depending on the purpose of a sentence, it may be classified into one of four categories: declarative, interrogative, imperative, or exclamatory.

A **declarative sentence** makes a statement and ends with a period. An **interrogative sentence** asks a question and ends with a question mark. An **exclamatory sentence** shows strong feeling and ends with an exclamation point. An **imperative sentence** gives an order or makes a request. A mild command or request ends with a period, but a strong command or request ends with an exclamation point. Some imperative sentences take the form of questions but are actually mild commands or polite requests. Such sentences end with periods.

| | |
|---|---|
| DECLARATIVE | Gwendolyn took the bus to school this morning. |
| INTERROGATIVE | When does your driver's license expire, Holly? |
| EXCLAMATORY | The barn is on fire! |
| IMPERATIVE | Pass the cauliflower to me, please. |
| | Get your football out of my garden immediately! |
| | Stan, will you please mail this letter when you go downtown. |

**Exercise    Sentence Purpose**    On your paper, write sentences in which you use the following groups of words, and add appropriate punctuation. Label each sentence *Declarative, Interrogative, Imperative,* or *Exclamatory.*

| | |
|---|---|
| **SAMPLE** | Have you seen |
| **ANSWER** | Have you seen my younger sister?—Interrogative |

1. do the attorneys
2. just between you and me
3. if you go to a World Series game
4. what a strong, proud woman
5. arguing about trivial things
6. remember to
7. is Aunt Sally planning to
8. how lucky
9. whether he should apply for a scholarship
10. move quickly from

**Assignment** **Sentence Purpose** Listen to three radio stations that feature three different kinds of programming. For example, one station might feature popular music, one might play classical music, and one might feature the news. As you listen to the announcers on the different stations, what differences do you notice in the kinds of sentences that they use? Does one use more exclamatory sentences than another? How is the choice of sentence purpose suitable to the style and purpose of the station's programming? Write one paragraph in which you contrast the different kinds of sentences used on the stations. Support the points that you make with representative quotations from the radio programs.

## 2.2   Subjects and Predicates

### Simple Subjects

Every sentence has a subject and a predicate. The **simple subject** is the noun or pronoun that names the person, place, thing, or idea that the sentence is about. The simple subject does not include modifiers. The complete subject (*page 47*) consists of the simple subject and its modifiers. In this book the term *subject* refers to the simple subject. In the following sentences, the simple subject is in boldface type.

> The **officer** directing traffic told us to move on.
> The **one** in the middle was the least expensive.
> Does a **victory** in the championship game mean that much to you?

The simple subject of an imperative sentence is always *you.* Often, *you* is understood rather than stated.

> Kevin, please practice your yodeling outside. [Think: Kevin, **you** please practice.]

**Compound Subjects.**   A compound subject is a simple subject that consists of two or more nouns or pronouns of equal rank. The term *compound subject* refers to a compound *simple* subject.

> Several white **hens**, a large **turkey**, and a **pheasant** with beautiful feathers wandered through the barnyard. [*Hens, turkey,* and *pheasant* form the compound subject.]

**45**

## Simple Predicates

The verb or verb phrase that describes the action or states the condition of the subject is the **simple predicate.** The simple predicate does not include modifiers and words that complete the meaning of the verb. The complete predicate (*page 47*) includes all such modifiers and complements (*page 51*). The simple predicate does not include the adverb *not* or *never,* but the complete predicate does. In this book the term *predicate* refers to the simple predicate. In the following sentences, the simple predicate is in boldface type.

subj.   pred.
Ellen **tried** hard to control her temper.

      subj.  ┌─── pred.──┐
Perhaps you **should adopt** a new strategy.

pred.            subj.  ┌─pred.─┐
**Have** Roberto's friends **been told** of his decision?

**Compound Predicates.**    A compound predicate is a simple predicate that consists of two or more verbs or verb phrases of equal rank. The term *compound predicate* refers to a compound *simple* predicate.

We **tilled** the earth, **planted** several kinds of seeds, and **watered** our new garden. [*Tilled, planted,* and *watered* form the compound predicate.]

**Exercise 1    Subjects and Predicates**    Number your paper from 1 to 8. Write the simple subject and the simple predicate of each numbered sentence in the following paragraph. Underline each simple subject once and each simple predicate twice.

SAMPLE     In 1936 Mary McLeod Bethune was appointed the director of the Division of Negro Affairs of the National Youth Administration.

ANSWER     <u>Mary McLeod Bethune</u> <u>was appointed</u>

    (1) Dr. Bethune's long career as an educator and as an adviser on minority concerns began in 1904.   (2) In that year Dr. Bethune founded the Daytona Normal and Industrial Institute for Girls in Daytona Beach, Florida.   (3) This school eventually merged with Cookman Institute for Men, forming the Bethune-Cookman

College.   (4) She served as president of the college until 1942, and again from 1946 to 1947.   (5) In addition to her other achievements, this dedicated educator acted as President Roosevelt's Special Adviser on Minority Affairs.   (6) In 1935 the National Council of Negro Women was founded by Dr. Bethune.   (7) In addition, she was elected vice president of the NAACP.   (8) For her efforts, Mary McLeod Bethune received the Spingarn Medal in 1935, the Thomas Jefferson Award in 1942, and the Haitian Medal of Honor and Merit.

## Complete Subjects and Complete Predicates

The **complete subject** consists of the simple subject and all of the words that modify it or identify it.

┌──complete subject──┐
**A large** *gust* **of wind** carried the flag away. [*A*, *large*, and *of wind* modify *gust*, which is the simple subject.]

┌──────── complete subject ────────┐
**Our favorite** *place* **for vacations, North Carolina,** has become quite popular. [*Our, favorite,* and *for vacations* modify *place*, the simple subject. *North Carolina* is an appositive (*page 68*) identifying *place*.]

┌──────────complete subject──────────┐
**The** *mayor* **and the star** *quarterback* **on the local football team** will help open the new mall. [The complete subject contains the compound simple subject, *mayor* and *quarterback*.]

The **complete predicate** consists of the simple predicate and all of the words that modify it or complete its meaning.

┌──────── complete predicate ────────┐
The first two runners ***crossed* the finish line simultaneously.** [*Finish line* is the direct object (*page 51*) of *crossed*, which is the simple predicate. *Simultaneously* modifies *crossed*.]

┌──────── complete predicate ────────┐
The sun ***resembled* a red disk as it went down beyond the horizon.** [The complete predicate includes an adverb clause (*Unit 3*), *as it went down beyond the horizon. A red disk* completes the meaning of *resembled*.]

┌──────complete predicate──────┐
People coming to the play this evening ***can* either** *make* **reservations by phone or** *buy* **a ticket at the box office.** [Included in the complete predicate is the compound simple predicate, *can make* and *buy*.]

## Placement of Subjects and Predicates

You will find subjects and predicates arranged in a variety of ways in sentences. The placement of the subject and the predicate often depends on the purpose of the sentence. In the sentences that follow, the complete subjects are underlined once and the complete predicates, twice.

DECLARATIVE SENTENCES

A flock of honking geese flew above us toward Canada. [The subject precedes the predicate. *Flock,* not *geese,* is the subject.]

There will be no exceptions to the rules. [The sentence has inverted word order, meaning that the subject follows the predicate.]

Across the bridge marched the soldiers. [The sentence has inverted word order.]

Although she had not been chosen to go to the state science fair, twelve-year-old Julie was proud of the science project that she had done. [The subject appears between the two parts of the predicate.]

INTERROGATIVE SENTENCE

Have you ever driven a tractor trailer down a narrow street? [**Think:** You have ever driven.]

IMPERATIVE SENTENCE

Lock the cellar door before you go to bed. [**Think:** *You* lock the cellar door. The entire imperative sentence is the complete predicate because the subject *you* is implied.]

EXCLAMATORY SENTENCES

The circus is coming to town!
What a great skater Bobby is!

**Exercise 2   Subjects and Predicates**   On your paper, write the following sentences. Underline the complete subjects once and the complete predicates twice. Write the label *subj.* over each simple subject and the label *pred.* over each simple predicate. If the subject is the understood pronoun, *you,* write it in parentheses, underline it, and label it.

SAMPLE     Into the stratosphere flew the space shuttle, which was carrying three astronauts.

ANSWER     Into the stratosphere flew <sub>pred.</sub> the space shuttle, which <sub>subj.</sub> was carrying three astronauts.

1. When she worked on her project for her design class, Marion, the best student, concentrated more than anybody else.
2. Up the side of the mountain lurched the ski lift, which did not feel too steady.
3. Can the people who are late find seats in the darkened auditorium?
4. In order to prevent overexposure to the sun's rays, wear some lotion.
5. Had the Knudsons arrived at the waterfront before the markets opened?
6. On my mantel is the pewter goblet that I noticed as I was going through an antique shop last week.
7. Should we repaint the faded walls of the living room with a bright color?
8. Because pins were scarce in the 1100s in England, they were sold only on January 1 and 2 of every year!
9. Until the fierce winds cease, do not go outside.
10. The cautious scientists had worn gloves during the top-secret experiment.

**Exercise 3**   **Subjects and Predicates**   In all of the following sentences, the subject precedes the predicate. *Step 1:* Rewrite the sentences so that they do not follow the subject-predicate pattern. You may do so by inverting the word order of a sentence, turning the sentence into a question, or putting the subject between two parts of the predicate. *Step 2:* Draw one line under the complete subjects and two lines under the complete predicates of your rewritten sentences.

SAMPLE     The cat climbed quickly up the telephone pole.

ANSWER     Quickly up the telephone pole climbed the cat.

OR

Did the cat climb quickly up the telephone pole?

OR

Quickly the cat climbed up the telephone pole.

1. Lemons and oranges grow in irrigated sections of the desert.
2. Clumsy Mr. Smythe stumbled along the muddy road.
3. A very strange event occurred without warning yesterday.
4. The anesthesia is working on the drowsy patient.
5. The experienced actors performed well in that television program.
6. A bag of flour fell from the top shelf in the pantry.
7. Grandmother will have arrived at the train station by noon.
8. Dozens of peonies are growing in the garden.

**Assignment**   **Sentence Variety**   Find an editorial in the local newspaper, cut it out, and attach it to a piece of paper. Examine the editorial closely for variety of sentence structure. Directly before each sentence of the editorial, write one of the following letters to identify the structure of the sentence.

> *A*—Declarative sentence in which the subject comes before the predicate
>
> *B*—Declarative sentence in which the subject follows the predicate
>
> *C*—Declarative sentence in which the subject appears between two parts of the predicate
>
> *D*—Imperative sentence
>
> *E*—Interrogative sentence
>
> *F*—Exclamatory sentence

On the paper to which you attached the editorial, write a paragraph in which you evaluate the effectiveness of the editorial. Is the editorial persuasive? Are the sentences sufficiently varied? Support your conclusions with examples from the editorial.

## Varying Sentence Structure

Suppose that you are the chief editorial writer for a newspaper. The editorial committee has decided to oppose a decision by the local government. Write the editorial opposing it. In your editorial do not rely exclusively on the subject-predicate sentence structure. Use questions, inverted word order, and other sentence structures to give sentence variety to the editorial. You may write about an actual decision in your community or one that you invent.

## 2.3  Complements

A **complement** is a word or a group of words that completes the meaning of the predicate. Complements are always part of the complete predicate.

> Larry became a **researcher** in a computer laboratory. [Larry became *what*? Researcher. *Researcher* is a complement.]
> We enjoyed the **hospitality** of the Tunneys this summer. [We enjoyed *what*? Hospitality. *Hospitality* is a complement.]

If the preceding sentences did not have complements, their meaning would be incomplete.

> Larry became [Became *what*?]
> We enjoyed [Enjoyed *what*?]

This unit covers three types of complements: objects, objective complements, and subject complements.

### 2.3a  Objects

**Objects** are nouns or pronouns that follow action verbs in the active voice (*Unit 4*). There are two kinds of objects: direct objects and indirect objects.

### Direct Objects

A **direct object** is a noun or a pronoun that follows an action verb in the active voice and receives the action of the verb. It answers the question *What?* or *Whom?* Verbs that take direct objects are called transitive verbs (*page 16*). Modifiers are not part of the object.

The new streetlights *sent* a **flood** of light over the expressway. [Sent *what?* Flood.]

Carrie *opened* the **door** to the closet, *grabbed* a **hanger**, and

*hung* her **coat** on it.

## Indirect Objects

An **indirect object** is a noun or a pronoun that names the person or thing *to* whom or *for* whom an action is performed. An indirect object follows an action verb in the active voice. In most cases an indirect object is used with a direct object. The indirect object comes immediately after the verb and before the direct object.

The tumble that Janie took gave **her** an ugly *bruise* on her knee. [**Think**: The tumble gave a bruise *to* her.]

To tell whether a noun or a pronoun is an indirect object, insert the word *to* or *for* before that noun or pronoun as you read the sentence. If the sentence makes sense, the word is an indirect object.

Mr. Harris made the **children** a *clubhouse* for the back yard. [**Think**: Mr. Harris made (*for*) the children a clubhouse.]

Peter's teamates awarded **him** the game *ball* for his good perform-ance in the game. [**Think**: His teammates awarded (*to*) him the game ball.]

**Compound Objects.**   Like subjects and verbs, objects may be compound. A **compound object** consists of two or more objects that complete the same predicate.

COMPOUND DIRECT OBJECT

          D.O.                     D.O.

I noticed a new **library** and a new **auditorium** on my trip through town.

COMPOUND INDIRECT OBJECT

          I.O.                I.O.

Have you written **Geraldine** and **Esther** a letter thanking them for your birthday presents?

**Exercise 1** **Subjects, Predicates, and Objects** On your paper, copy the following sentences. In each sentence underline the simple subject once and the simple predicate twice. Write *D.O.* over each direct object and *I.O.* over each indirect object.

| | |
|---|---|
| **SAMPLE** | Henry David Thoreau, the American writer and naturalist, left future generations a memorable literary work in *Walden*. |
| **ANSWER** | Henry David Thoreau, the American writer and naturalist, left future generations a memorable literary work in *Walden*. |

1. The young author desired simplicity and sought an alternative to his busy life in commerce.

2. In 1845 Ralph Waldo Emerson gave Thoreau the chance for an experiment in simple living.

3. Emerson offered his young friend some land near Walden Pond in Concord, Massachusetts.

4. In exchange for the use of the land, Thoreau left Emerson the cabin that he had built and the gardens that he had planted while living there.

5. Thoreau spent a total of two years and two months at Walden Pond, and that time alone afforded him the opportunity to observe, to reflect, and to write.

6. During Thoreau's self-sufficient and contemplative time there, he wrote *Walden*.

7. In *Walden*, Thoreau gives the reader a detailed account of his thoughts, his observations of nature, and his opinions about civilization.

8. Contemporary readers appreciate the informal style, the personal tone, and the often witty, insightful advice of *Walden*.
9. Throughout his book, Thoreau gives readers useful guidelines and descriptions of how he survived.
10. Many wise readers follow Thoreau's advice and find their own paths to happiness.

## 2.3b   Objective Complements

An **objective complement** is a noun or an adjective that follows a direct object and explains, identifies, or describes that object. Only certain verbs take an objective complement: *make, find, think, elect, choose, appoint, name, consider, call,* and synonyms of these verbs.

NOUN AS OBJECTIVE COMPLEMENT

D.O.              O.C.

The committee considered *Heather* the best **person** for editor of the newsletter. [*Person* is the objective complement of the verb, *considered*. It identifies the direct object, *Heather*.]

ADJECTIVE AS OBJECTIVE COMPLEMENT

D.O.              O.C.

Most critics thought the *play* quite **interesting**. [*Interesting* is the objective complement of the verb, *thought*. It describes the direct object, *play*.]

A sentence may have a compound objective complement, which consists of two or more objective complements, as is shown in the following example.

D.O.        O.C.

Visitors throughout the years have found *New Orleans* **varied,**

—O.C.—      O.C.

**tradition-filled,** and **colorful.** [The adjectives *varied, tradition-filled,* and *colorful* are objective complements.]

**54**

**Exercise 2 Objects and Objective Complements** On your paper, write the direct objects, indirect objects, and objective complements in the following sentences. Label each word that you write *Direct object, Indirect object,* or *Objective complement.*

SAMPLE    The trustees have appointed Michael the chairperson of the committee for this spring's fund-raising drive.

ANSWER    Michael—Direct object; chairperson—Objective complement

1. Ralph presented the dance-contest trophy to Betsy and Martin.
2. Sammy considered the horror movie very suspenseful because of its special effects.
3. Will Sarah take these cartons to the recycling center on Tuesday?
4. The owner considers this cabin, which does not have electricity, rustic and quaint.
5. Workers for the circus prepared the tent for the evening performance.
6. At the next practice, the coach will name Derek the team's new goalie.
7. Their grandparents have brought them exotic-looking shells from tropical seas.
8. Will the group appoint Anita or Marcus the leader of the discussion on hazardous waste?
9. My brother taught me the complicated rules of our new board game.
10. Jamie found the new ride at the carnival somewhat frightening.

## 2.3c   Subject Complements

A **subject complement** is a word that comes after a linking verb and identifies or describes the subject. Subject complements often follow forms of the verb *be.* Other verbs that may take subject complements are in the following list:

| | | |
|---|---|---|
| appear | look | sound |
| become | remain | stay |
| feel | seem | taste |
| grow | smell | |

There are two kinds of subject complements: predicate nominatives and predicate adjectives.

## Predicate Nominatives

A **predicate nominative** is a noun or a pronoun that follows a linking verb and identifies the subject of the sentence. The root of the word *nominative* is *nominate,* which means "to name." In a sense the predicate nominative renames the subject.

P.N.
For the last two summers, *Sandy* has been a **lifeguard** at the pool. [*Lifeguard* identifies the subject, *Sandy.*]

P.N.
*Betty* has remained a **force** of stability in the company. [*Force* identifies the subject, *Betty.*]

⌐——P.N.——⌐  ⌐—— P.N.——⌐   ⌐—— P.N.——⌐
This *field* will be a **playground,** a **tennis court,** or a **parking lot.** [The sentence has a compound predicate nominative: *playground, tennis court,* and *parking lot.*]

## Predicate Adjectives

A **predicate adjective** is an adjective that follows a linking verb and modifies the subject of the sentence.

P.A.
The Indiana sand *dunes* remain quite **beautiful** in spite of increasing numbers of visitors. [*Beautiful* modifies the subject, *dunes.*]

P.A.
The *air* near the factory smelled faintly **acrid.** [*Acrid* modifies the subject, *air.*]

P.A.      P.A.
The *tree* in the front yard has grown **tall** and **straight.** [The sentence has a compound predicate adjective: *tall* and *straight.*]

In some sentences the predicate adjective precedes the verb or verb phrase.

P.A. verb
**Eerie** was the *sound* that came from behind the door to the deserted mansion. [*Eerie* modifies the subject, *sound.*]

**Exercise 3  Subject Complements**  On your paper, list the subject complements in the following sentences. Label each complement *Predicate nominative* or *Predicate adjective.*

> **SAMPLE**     On the recording that Anthony bought, the orchestra sounded somewhat tinny.
>
> **ANSWER**     tinny—Predicate adjective

1. The woman that you met yesterday, Helga, is an excellent violinist.
2. Oh, the room that they just painted smells horrible!
3. Sarah seemed pleased by her performance at the audition.
4. David will become manager of the produce department in two weeks.
5. Curling, which probably originated in Scotland or in the Netherlands, is a game played on ice.
6. Although the geologists felt tired, they continued to collect rock samples.
7. Do you think that this note sounds flat when I play it on the tuba?
8. Bernard Courtois was the French chemist who discovered the element iodine.
9. The team members appeared optimistic; however, they could not put together a rally to win.
10. Darlene remained treasurer of the club for more than two years; her dedication is admirable.

**Exercise 4  Complements**  Next to each number that follows are a noun and a verb. *Step 1:* Using each noun as the subject and each verb in the predicate, write a sentence that has one or more complements. Add modifiers for some of the subjects, the verbs, and the complements. *Step 2:* Label each complement that you write *D.O.* for direct object, *I.O.* for indirect object, *O.C.* for objective complement, *P.N.* for predicate nominative, or *P.A.* for predicate adjective.

> **SAMPLE**     air show; gave
>
> **ANSWER**     Last Sunday's air show featuring the Thunderbirds
>                                    I.O.    D.O.
>                   gave Lance one of the greatest thrills of his life.

1. politics; seems
2. Roberta; supervised

3. factory workers; were
4. basketball; requires
5. Andrew; appointed
6. flowers; smell
7. critics; consider
8. dessert; tastes
9. day; brings
10. cousin; became

**Assignment**   **Complements in Directions**   Find a set of directions that explains how to do something. For instance, they could be directions explaining how to put a toy together or how to prepare a particular recipe. On your paper, write all of the complements that you can find in the set of directions. Label each complement *Direct object, Indirect object, Objective complement, Predicate nominative,* or *Predicate adjective.* Be sure to identify the source of the directions that you use.

## Using Objects and Complements

Assume that you are the proficient pilot of an unusual means of transportation, such as a hot-air balloon. A friend of yours has agreed to be a passenger with you on a voyage aboard the vehicle. First, though, the friend wants to read an account that will re-create the experience of traveling in the vehicle. Write such an account for your friend. In your narrative use complements. After you have finished writing, label each complement *D.O.* for direct object, *I.O.* for indirect object, *O.C.* for objective complement, *P.N.* for predicate nominative, or *P.A.* for predicate adjective.

# Unit Practice

## Practice 1

**A. Four Sentence Purposes** (*pages 43–45*)   On your paper, rewrite each sentence to fit the purpose indicated in parentheses.

1. The snowmobile must navigate the treacherous, icy slope. (Exclamatory)
2. Trevor threw the boomerang according to the instructions. (Imperative)
3. Sheila's acrobatic exercises are strenuous! (Interrogative)
4. Order the beige sofa and matching armchairs, Frieda. (Declarative)
5. Plants and animals do not live on the moon. (Interrogative)

**B. Subjects and Predicates** (*pages 45–51*)   On your paper, list the words or phrases in italic type. Label each word and phrase *Simple subject, Simple predicate, Compound subject, Compound predicate, Complete subject,* or *Complete predicate.*

6. *The two new employees* soon became familiar with the office routine.
7. Making a wide loop in the sky, the glider *circled* over the wheat field and the barn.
8. *How many different roles has* that veteran actor *played in his career*?
9. Our recently elected mayor, Rose Battista, *will choose* some new committee members and then *will appoint* a leader.
10. Before the race, the eager *teammates* practiced their rowing techniques.
11. *Tie* the square knot until the bundle is securely fastened.
12. Were glass *unicorns* and delicate paper *kites* in the window display?
13. *Tear* down that wire fence and *replace* it with a wooden one.
14. Has *our favorite German film maker* really received an award at the international film festival?
15. The tiny seeds *finally sprouted into small green shoots with leaves.*

**C. Complements** (*pages 51–58*)   On your paper, write all the complements in the following sentences. Label each complement *Direct object, Indirect object, Objective complement, Predicate nominative,* or *Predicate adjective.*

16. The eyes of bees contain thousands of connected lenses.
17. In Kentucky, farmers raise thoroughbred horses.

(Continue on the next page.)

18. Researchers consider these markings on the stone rather mysterious.
19. Grandfather told Barbara and me his amazing story about traveling throughout China.
20. Gazelles are graceful and can attain extremely high speeds.
21. Did Ernesto bring new statistics and an explanatory graph to the meeting?
22. Sports writers consider the latest heavyweight champion a truly great fighter.
23. The African violet is both beautiful and popular, but it is not really a member of the violet family.
24. Donna will give her brother several old albums; however, they sound quite old-fashioned and scratchy.
25. A visit by our class to a newspaper office was an informative trip.

# Practice 2

On your paper, list the words in italic type in the following passage. Label each *Simple subject, Simple predicate, Complete subject, Complete predicate, Direct object, Indirect object, Objective complement, Predicate nominative,* or *Predicate adjective.*

(1) *The mysterious underwater world of the sea* has always fascinated (2) *people.* Different devices have made (3) *divers* (4) *capable* of remaining under the surface for long periods of time. However, before such technology, (5) *divers* in ancient Greece held their (6) *breath* while diving for shells, pearls, and sponges. John Lethbridge was the (7) *inventor* of a leather and wooden diving suit in 1715. This suit gave (8) *divers* an extended opportunity to explore the sea. Eventually, advanced technology made extensive undersea (9) *exploration* (10) *possible.* The first major advance was the (11) *diving bell.* The diver (12) *sat inside the bell, which was open at the bottom.* Air pressure kept the (13) *water* from coming inside the bell. Other (14) *devices* for deep-sea diving were the (15) *bathysphere* and the benthoscope. Both (16) *had bell-shaped chambers with viewing windows.* Today, the most familiar underwater (17) *vehicle,* the submarine, is also the (18) *largest.* Such inventions for underwater exploration have certainly made this activity more (19) *common.* In the 1960s experimental, fully staffed stations (20) *permitted* divers to live and work on the floor of the ocean!

# Unit Tests

## Test 1

**A. Four Sentence Purposes** (*pages 43–45*)   On your paper, rewrite each sentence so that the purpose becomes that indicated in parentheses.

1. Polish this brass book end until it shines. (Exclamatory)
2. Was Hugh selected to portray King Claudius in the drama? (Imperative)
3. Flames raced through the woodland toward the firebreak! (Interrogative)
4. Take this announcement, Deborah, and tack it on the bulletin board. (Declarative)
5. Did you know that Grandma Moses began to paint at the age of seventy-six? (Exclamatory)

**B. Subjects and Predicates** (*pages 45–51*)   On your paper, list the words and phrases in italic type. Label each word or phrase *Simple subject, Simple predicate, Compound subject, Compound predicate, Complete subject,* or *Complete predicate.*

6. Cardinals and jays *screeched* and *chattered* while they perched near the newly built birdhouse.
7. *Were* you *able to send the heavy package to Minnesota by air freight*?
8. An early *frost* and a month-long *drought* caused crops to fail miserably last year.
9. *Turn* the old skeleton key in the trunk's rusty lock very cautiously.
10. *The slow-moving opossum* is often considered one of the least intelligent mammals.
11. How fortunate Dolores *was* to board the train just before it chugged away from the platform!
12. *Donate your bicentennial memorabilia to the annual town auction*!
13. Were the imaginative historical *costumes* and exotic *decorations* a huge success at the senior-high masquerade ball?
14. The gas gauge *showed* Lisa that the tank was still half full.
15. Bounding across the wooded lot and along the small creek were *two graceful deer.*

(Continue on the next page.)

**C. Complements** (*pages 51–58*)   On your paper, write all the complements in the following sentences. Label each complement *Direct object, Indirect object, Objective complement, Predicate nominative,* or *Predicate adjective.*

16. The economists called the proposal for a balanced budget very promising.
17. Doris's friends gave her a surprise birthday party and tickets to a concert.
18. From a distance the fog that had moved over the valley appeared damp and thick.
19. Annie Jump Cannon was an American astronomer and discovered more than three hundred variable stars, five new stars, and a double star.
20. A camel's thick eyebrows and curly eyelashes protect the animal's eyes from the desert sun and sandstorms.
21. Did the lawyer give the union and management a new proposal for the settlement of the strike?
22. Visitors to the Paris Exposition in 1900 saw the first escalator ever built.
23. Last year citizens named a local veteran the leader of the Memorial Day parade.
24. Toby felt extremely jubilant about the latest news.
25. The new computer company has brought the town hundreds of excellent jobs.

# Test 2

On your paper, list the words in italic type in the following passage. Label each *Simple subject, Simple predicate, Complete subject, Complete predicate, Direct object, Indirect object, Objective complement, Predicate nominative,* or *Predicate adjective.*

Venice   (1) *is* a   (2) *city* linked by canals and bridges. Gondolas ferry   (3) *travelers* from place to place, and cafes and Gothic architecture give   (4) *tourists* many things to visit. However, (5) *this particular Venice* is not in Italy. It   (6) *is located near Los Angeles, California*! In 1904 Abbot Kinney   (7) *developed*

(8) *Venice* based on a model of the Italian city. Kinney was a
wealthy (9) *industrialist* who considered Venice, Italy,
(10) *fascinating*, so he created a town of canals. Kinney considered
his (11) *Venice* primarily a commercial (12) *venture*. He
(13) *included* a long pier and three roller coasters. (14) *These commercial aspects* made Venice extremely (15) *prosperous* by 1920.
Kinney left his (16) *heirs* plans for future expansion in Venice, but
they abandoned Kinney's dream. The pier burned down, and the
canals became (17) *hazardous* because the water did not circulate
properly. Many (18) *canals* were filled in. Some, (19) *however,
have been left in residential areas.* Venice, California, (20) *has
changed* greatly since its heyday.

# Unit 3

## Phrases and Clauses

## Unit Preview

You may write for a variety of purposes—for example, to narrate, to persuade, to describe, or to explain. As a writer, you make your purpose clear through the sentences that you write. Phrases and clauses give you the flexibility that is needed to write sentences that make your purpose clear to your reader.

**For Analysis**   The purpose of the following paragraphs is to explain causes and effects. Read both paragraphs and decide which one makes the cause-and-effect relationships clearer. Use that paragraph to answer the questions that follow.

PARAGRAPH A

(1) Expressways began to connect suburbs and central cities in the 1950s. (2) Urban experts have studied the advantages and disadvantages of these ribbons of concrete. (3) City expressways were completed. (4) It became possible for more people to live in the more spacious suburbs. (5) Expressways also promoted the sale of automobiles. (6) Suburban life depends on the car. (7) The expressways were being built. (8) Many urban neighborhoods that had existed for decades were destroyed. (9) More and more people used the expressways. (10) The problem of air pollution became more common. (11) Urban experts will continue to debate whether the advantages of expressways outweigh the disadvantages.

PARAGRAPH B

(1) Since expressways began to connect suburbs and central cities in the 1950s, urban experts have studied the advantages and disadvantages of these ribbons of concrete. (2) When city expressways were completed, it became possible for more people to live in the more spacious suburbs. (3) Expressways also promoted the sale of automobiles because suburban life depends on the car. (4) However, as the expressways were being built, many urban neighborhoods that had existed for decades were destroyed. (5) Because more and more people used the expressways, the problem of air pollution became more common. (6) Urban experts will continue to debate whether the advantages of expressways outweigh the disadvantages.

1. What impact did expressways have on the suburbs?
2. How did expressways promote the sale of automobiles?
3. What impact did the building of expressways have on many city neighborhoods?
4. What is another negative consequence that expressways have had?
5. Which paragraph makes the relationship between causes and effects clearer?

By using clauses and phrases, Paragraph B makes the cause-and-effect relationships clearer than Paragraph A does. For example, Sentence 2 of Paragraph B explains clearly that the completion of expressways made it possible for more people to live in the suburbs. In this unit you will study clauses and phrases. Using such word groups will help you as a writer to clarify the relationships between ideas.

## 3.1   Phrases

A **phrase** is a group of related words that functions as a single part of speech and that lacks a subject, a predicate, or both. This unit deals with three common kinds of phrases: prepositional phrases, appositive phrases, and verbal phrases. Depending on which kind of phrase it is, a phrase may be used as an adjective, an adverb, or a noun.

## 3.1a   Prepositional Phrases

A **prepositional phrase** consists of a preposition and its object(s) (*pages 27–28*), including any modifiers of the object. In the following sentences, the prepositional phrases are in boldface type.

prep.       obj.

The congressional candidates **in next Tuesday's election**

prep.   obj.      obj.

will hold a debate **about taxes and expenditures**.

obj.          prep.

**Which downtown hotel** are your grandparents staying **in**? [**Think:** *In which downtown hotel* are your grandparents staying?]

## Prepositional Phrases Used as Adjectives

A prepositional phrase functions as an adjective when it modifies a noun or a pronoun. Such prepositional phrases are sometimes called **adjective phrases.**

MODIFIES NOUN

Who designed the *building* **across the street?**

MODIFIES PRONOUN

Dan has just given *one* **of his most powerful speeches.**

A prepositional phrase can modify the object in another prepositional phrase.

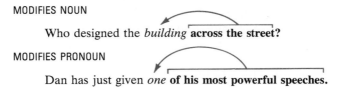

The *applause* **from one** *group* **in the lecture hall** quickly spread.

## Prepositional Phrases Used as Adverbs

A prepositional phrase functions as an adverb when it modifies a verb, an adjective, or another adverb. Such prepositional phrases are sometimes called **adverb phrases.**

MODIFIES VERB

Regional interests sometimes *conflict* with national interests.

MODIFIES ADJECTIVE

The service mechanic was *suspicious* of the sound.

MODIFIES ADVERB

You must look *further* behind the workbench to find the painting materials.

**Exercise 1   Prepositional Phrases**   *Step 1:* On your paper, write the prepositional phrases in the following sentences. *Step 2:* Next to each phrase, write the word or words that it modifies. *Step 3:* Label each phrase *Adjective phrase* or *Adverb phrase.*

**SAMPLE**      The American architect Frank Lloyd Wright (1869–1959) is famous for his influential ideas about buildings and the environment.

**ANSWER**      for his influential ideas, famous—Adverb phrase; about buildings and the environment, ideas—Adjective phrase

(1) Wright's philosophy of design has had a tremendous influence on modern architecture.   (2) In his philosophy Wright stressed the importance of harmony between a building and its surroundings.   (3) Houses that Wright built near Chicago were low, horizontal structures with open space inside.   (4) These were appropriate for the flat land of the Midwest.   (5) During his seventy-year career, Wright designed buildings for both residential and commercial use.   (6) The buildings fit well into their natural settings, and they were particularly useful for special functions.   (7) One of his best-known projects was the circular Guggenheim Museum in New York City, which features a spiral walkway that reaches from the ground floor

to the dome several stories above.    (8) Another famous Wright creation, the Imperial Hotel in Tokyo, was the only building that was still standing after an earthquake in 1923.

## 3.1b    Appositives and Appositive Phrases

An **appositive** is a noun or a pronoun placed near another noun or pronoun to explain or identify it.

*Edith Wharton,* **a novelist,** was a keen observer of wealthy society in the early twentieth century.

*We* **members** voted to increase the annual dues to ten dollars.

Three *topics,* **clubs, careers, and sports,** are covered regularly in Lorraine's column for the school newspaper.

**Appositive Phrases.**    An **appositive phrase** includes all the words or phrases that modify an appositive. Like an appositive, the appositive phrase explains or identifies a noun or a pronoun.

*Lake Placid,* **the site of the 1980 Winter Olympics,** is a popular resort in both summer and winter.

*You* **students with completed exams** may hand them in.

In some sentences the appositive precedes the word that it identifies.

**A man of courage and eloquence,** *Thomas Paine* expressed the sentiments of many colonists immediately before the Revolution.

**Essential and Nonessential Appositives.**    An essential appositive or an essential appositive phrase is one that is necessary to the meaning of the sentence. You should not use commas to separate this kind of appositive from the rest of the sentence.

Alfred Hitchcock's *film* **The 39 Steps** is widely regarded as a classic. [Hitchcock directed more than one film. The appositive is essential to identify which film.]

A **nonessential appositive** or a **nonessential appositive phrase** is one that is not necessary to the meaning of the sentence. You should use commas to separate such an appositive from the rest of the sentence.

Hitchcock also directed England's first sound *film*, **a 1929 release entitled *Blackmail*.** [Only one film could have been the first English film with sound. Thus, the appositive is not essential in identifying the film.]

**Exercise 2   Appositive Phrases**   The following sentences need appositives and appositive phrases to make them more specific. On your paper, rewrite the sentences, adding an appositive or an appositive phrase for at least one of the nouns or pronouns in each sentence. Then underline the appositives and appositive phrases.

SAMPLE      The patio furniture belongs to Bill.

ANSWER      The patio furniture belongs to Bill, <u>our neighbor who just moved here from Arkansas.</u>

1. The scientist was very pleased with the results of the research.
2. Albert saw the play performed by his friends in the school drama club last week.
3. My sister does well in several track events.
4. Have you seen my favorite film yet?
5. The two girls visited the tourist attraction.
6. The amazing dimensions of the new skyscraper were described to us by our guide.
7. The river is overflowing its banks and flooding the small town.
8. The architect drew a blueprint for the new shopping arcade.

## 3.1c   Verbals and Verbal Phrases

**Verbals** are verb forms that function as nouns, adjectives, or adverbs. Although verbals function as other parts of speech, they retain some of the properties of verbs; they express action or being, and they may take complements. There are three kinds of verbals: participles, gerunds, and infinitives.

## Participles

A **participle** is a verb form that can function as an adjective. Even when it functions as an adjective, a participle keeps some of the properties of a verb; it expresses action or being, and it may take a complement.

> **Fascinated,** the *children* watched the **grazing** *cattle.* [Both *fascinated* and *grazing* are participles.]

There are two kinds of participles: present participles and past participles. The present participle and the past participle are two of the four principal parts of a verb. (The other two principal parts are the infinitive and the past. For an explanation of the principal parts, see Section 4.1a of Unit 4.)

**Present Participles.**   You form a present participle by adding *-ing* to the infinitive form of a verb.

> That was certainly an **electrifying** *display* of fireworks! [*Electrifying* is a present participle that consists of the verb *electrify* and the ending *-ing.*]

**Past Participles.**   You form a past participle in one of two ways, depending on whether the verb is regular or irregular (*Unit 4*).

1. *Regular Verbs*. To form the past participle of a regular verb, add either *-d* or *-ed* to the infinitive form of the verb.

   | INFINITIVE | PAST PARTICIPLE |
   |------------|-----------------|
   | salute     | saluted         |
   | talk       | talked          |

2. *Irregular Verbs*. To form the past participle of an irregular verb, use a special form of the verb. You have to memorize the past participles of irregular verbs. See Unit 4 for a list of past participles of many common irregular verbs.

| INFINITIVE | PAST PARTICIPLE |
|------------|-----------------|
| break | broken |
| wear | worn |

Present participles and past participles do not always function as adjectives. They can also form part of a verb phrase in a sentence. When a participle functions as a verb, it is not a verbal. In this unit the emphasis is on present participles and past participles that function as adjectives. For an explanation of participles in verb phrases, see Unit 4.

**Participles with Auxiliary Verbs.** A participle used as an adjective may have one or more auxiliary verbs, which indicate the time of the action described. In most cases, participles with auxiliary verbs refer to actions that have already been completed.

**Having lost,** the *golfer* walked slowly back to the clubhouse. [*Having lost* indicates that the action of losing is completed.]

**Having been opened,** the *loaf* of bread was put into the refrigerator. [*Having been opened* indicates that the action of being opened is completed.]

## Participial Phrases

A **participial phrase** consists of a participle and its modifiers and complements. The participial phrase functions as an adjective to modify a noun or a pronoun. You may use either present participles or past participles to form participial phrases.

Who is the *person* **waving to us from across the river?**

**Accepted for a role in the play,** *Wayne* proceeded to learn his character's lines.

The Shepherd *family,* **having run out of gas,** walked two miles to the nearest service station.

In the preceding sentences, the participial phrases are near the words that they modify. To avoid misleading or awkward statements, always place a participial phrase near the word that it modifies. For more information about the correct placement of participial phrases, see Section 4.4b of Unit 4.

## Absolute Phrases

Another kind of phrase that is formed with participles is the absolute phrase. An **absolute phrase** modifies an entire sentence; it does not have a direct grammatical connection with any single word in the sentence. An absolute phrase contains both a participle and the noun or the pronoun that is modified by the participle.

absolute phrase

**A heavy rain having delayed the game for an hour,** fans started to leave the stadium. [The absolute phrase modifies the entire sentence by telling why fans started to leave the stadium.]

**Exercise 3   Participial and Absolute Phrases**   On your paper, combine each of the following pairs of sentences by rewriting one sentence as a participial phrase or an absolute phrase. Underline the participial phrases and absolute phrases in your sentences.

| SAMPLE | The furnace broke late Saturday night. We piled extra blankets on the bed. |
|---|---|
| ANSWER | <u>The furnace having broken late Saturday night</u>, we piled extra blankets on the bed. |

1. The first watches were invented in the 1500s by town watchmen. They consisted of nothing more than small clocks fastened to straps.
2. The fellowship is for travel and study in a foreign country. It has been given to a deserving student.
3. Teresa has been hired for another job. She has packed away her papers and cleaned out her files.
4. Helen and her brother finished their work. They stored canned fruit and vegetables on shelves in the basement.
5. All the managers left the store. Sumiko had to answer customers' questions by herself.
6. I discussed the issue with the guest lecturer. I disagreed with her position.

7. Our cousins were late for the wedding. A slow tractor held up all the traffic.

8. Hamlin Garland was interested in the prairie pioneers. He wrote about the problems of farm life.

## Gerunds

A **gerund** is a verbal that ends in -*ing* and functions only as a noun. Although it functions as a noun, a gerund has some of the properties of a verb. Like a verb, it expresses action or being, and it may take a direct object, an indirect object, a predicate nominative, or a predicate adjective. Like a noun, a gerund may function as a subject, a direct object, an indirect object, an object of a preposition, a predicate nominative, or an appositive in a sentence.

SUBJECT

**Surveying** was the occupation of Henry David Thoreau.

DIRECT OBJECT

An automatic transmission makes **driving** much easier.

INDIRECT OBJECT

Juanita will give **surfing** a try when she visits Hawaii.

OBJECT OF PREPOSITION

Please prepare this package for **mailing.**

PREDICATE NOMINATIVE

One of life's little pleasures is **conversing.**

APPOSITIVE

Albert's greatest interest, **singing,** may one day lead to a career in the entertainment field.

## Gerund Phrases

A **gerund phrase** consists of a gerund and its modifiers and complements. Like a gerund, a gerund phrase may perform all the functions of a noun.

SUBJECT

**Looking through the newspaper's classified ads** is one way to find a job.

DIRECT OBJECT

> I appreciate **your making the plans for Betty Foster's retirement party.**

INDIRECT OBJECT

> All of the candidates have given **fighting the high unemployment rate** their greatest priority.

OBJECT OF A PREPOSITION

> The trapeze artist received an ovation for **attempting the spectacular feat.**

PREDICATE NOMINATIVE

> The major project for the town this summer is **raising money for a new gazebo in which the local orchestra can play.**

APPOSITIVE

> Ned's hobby, **collecting license plates from all fifty states,** has turned out to be rather profitable.

**Exercise 4   Gerund Phrases**   On your paper, combine each of the following pairs of sentences by rewriting one sentence as a gerund phrase. Underline the gerund phrase in each of your rewritten sentences. Label each gerund phrase *Subject, Direct object, Indirect object, Object of a preposition, Predicate nominative,* or *Appositive.*

> **SAMPLE**   I rebuilt the engine of my twelve-year-old car. It was a difficult and time-consuming job.
>
> **ANSWER**   <u>Rebuilding the engine of my twelve-year-old car</u> was a difficult and time-consuming job.—Subject

1. We followed a "short cut" through the woods. It actually took us half an hour longer.
2. We heard something all the way across the lake. It was the dinner bell, which rang.
3. The roads will be resurfaced. It will make the drive to your house safer and more comfortable.
4. An architect named William Le Baron Jenney is credited with an achievement. He designed the first skyscraper in 1884.
5. The weather is predicted. That can sometimes be a thankless undertaking.

6. You should install a pump in the basement. That will help you keep the basement dry.

7. I practice gymnastics. It is my favorite after-school activity.

8. I will study hard for the final exam. I will have a good chance to earn above-average grades this semester.

## Infinitives

An **infinitive** is a verbal that consists of the first principal part, or dictionary form, of the verb. The word *to* usually, although not always, precedes the infinitive. Like a verb, an infinitive expresses action or being and may take a complement. In a sentence, an infinitive may function as a noun, an adjective, or an adverb.

NOUN

**To act** has always been Carl's dream. [subject]

The committee has decided **to vote.** [direct object]

Because the flight leaves early in the morning, our job tonight is **to pack**. [predicate nominative]

ADJECTIVE

If you have a *moment* **to spare,** will you help me? [What kind of moment? A moment *to spare.*]

ADVERB

We *go* to the beach **to swim.** [Why do we go? We go *to swim.*]

The professor's speech was *difficult* **to follow.** [How was the speech difficult? It was difficult *to follow.*]

You may form an infinitive by using one or more auxiliary verbs and a past participle. By using auxiliary verbs with the infinitive, you can express the time of the action.

You are *lucky* **to have won.** [*To have won* indicates that the act of winning was completed in the past.]

The *problems* **to be solved** are written on the blackboard. [*To be solved* indicates that the act of solving will occur in the future.]

## Infinitive Phrases

An **infinitive phrase** consists of an infinitive and its modifiers and complements. An infinitive phrase can function as a noun, an adjective, or an adverb.

NOUN

**To carry all these boxes without a two-wheeled cart** will be hard work. [subject of the sentence]

ADJECTIVE

The speaker's *request* **to listen quietly** was heeded by the audience. [Which request? The request *to listen quietly*.]

ADVERB

Claude felt too *tired* **to climb to the top of the mountain.** [To what extent was Claude tired? Too tired *to climb to the top of the mountain*.]

## Infinitive Clauses

Although the major types of clauses are covered in the next section of this unit, the infinitive clause has been included in the section on phrases because it is closely related to the infinitive phrase. An **infinitive clause** is an infinitive that has a subject. If the subject of the infinitive is a pronoun, that pronoun is in the objective case (*Section 4.3b, Unit 4*).

―――――― infinitive clause ――――――――
I asked **Loretta to call home when the game is over.** [*Loretta* is the subject of the infinitive.]

―― infinitive clause ――
Will you tell **him to give me a call?** [*Him* is the subject of the infinitive.]

―――――― infinitive clause ――――――
John expects **that to be a letter from Uncle Ned.** [*That* is the subject of the infinitive.]

Sometimes you use the infinitive without the word *to*, as in the following examples.

Feather pillows make **me sneeze.** [**Think:** make me *to* sneeze.]

―― infinitive clause ――
We watched **my sister ride her pony.** [**Think:** watched my sister *to* ride her pony.]

**Exercise 5  Infinitives**  On your paper, combine each of the following sets of sentences by rewriting at least one sentence as an infinitive phrase or an infinitive clause. Underline the infinitive phrases and infinitive clauses in your rewritten sentences.

> **SAMPLE**   Stan usually uses earphones. He listens to albums.
>
> **ANSWER**   Stan usually uses earphones <u>to listen to albums.</u>

1. Nick and Pamela bought a journal before their trip to England. They will record their experiences in the journal.
2. Did you lift the pan from the stove? You prevented the food from burning.
3. Rhonda, who is a poet, went to Windermere, the largest lake in England. She found inspiration there.
4. Harry should try pole vaulting. If you talk to him, perhaps you can persuade him.
5. Harriet took a trip on a steamboat to the mouth of the Mississippi River. She had always wanted this trip.
6. I must apply stain and lacquer. By doing so, I will finish the cabinet that I have been building.
7. The navigator William Baffin set sail toward Greenland in 1612. He would explore that land.
8. On their trip to Minneapolis and St. Paul, George and Fred watched for license plates from other states. Doing so made time pass quickly.

**Exercise 6  Verbal Phrases**  Copy the following sentences on your paper, and in place of each blank write a verbal phrase. The kind of verbal phrase required is indicated in parentheses. Underline the verbal phrases that you write.

> **SAMPLE**   For the end of August, Mr. Lockhart has rented a cabin __?__. (participial phrase)
>
> **ANSWER**   For the end of August, Mr. Lockhart has rented a cabin <u>facing a lake and a beautiful sandy beach.</u>

1. Certain birds that eat insects help farmers __?__. (infinitive phrase)
2. __?__ is an activity that I associate with most of our family gatherings for holidays. (gerund phrase)
3. A well-known sculptor created a monument __?__. (participial phrase)
4. In the autumn one of Alicia's favorite jobs is __?__. (gerund phrase)

5. Workers, __?__, finally left the fields at sunset. (participial phrase)
6. The passengers, who were forced __?__, remained very patient. (infinitive phrase)
7. The first thing that we saw after the slight earth tremor was the plates and cups __?__. (participial phrase)
8. __?__ is one of the goals of our company this year. (infinitive phrase)

**Assignment   Verbal Phrases**   The following poem, "A Noiseless Patient Spider," by Walt Whitman, contains several verbals and verbal phrases with descriptive details. Read the poem carefully. On your paper, write as many verbals and verbal phrases as you can find in the poem. For each verbal write a sentence explaining what that detail adds to your impression of the spider.

> A noiseless patient spider,
> I mark'd where on a little promontory it stood isolated,
> Mark'd how to explore the vacant vast surrounding,
> It launch'd forth filament, filament, filament, out of itself,
> Ever unreeling them, ever tirelessly speeding them.
> And you O my soul where you stand,
> Surrounded, detached, in measureless oceans of space,
> Ceaselessly musing, venturing, throwing, seeking the spheres
>     to connect them,
> Till the bridge you will need be form'd, till the ductile anchor
>     hold,
> Till the gossamer thread you fling catch somewhere, O my
>     soul.

## Phrases in Writing

A poem like "A Noiseless Patient Spider" in the preceding assignment is the product of close observation on the part of the poet. Select some action that you have noticed but have never watched closely. It might be an ant carrying something, a bird nibbling a piece of bread, or some similar scene in nature. Observe the action for half an hour, and write a paragraph describing what you observed. Use prepositional phrases, participial phrases, gerund phrases, and infinitive phrases that add descriptive details to your paragraph.

# 3.2 Clauses

A **clause** is a group of related words that contains both a subject and a predicate. There are two kinds of clauses: independent and subordinate.

## 3.2a Independent Clauses

An **independent clause** can stand by itself as a sentence. The example at the end of this paragraph contains two independent clauses, which are in boldface type. Notice that each clause has a subject and a predicate and that each clause could be a separate sentence. The simple subjects are underlined once, and the simple predicates are underlined twice.

> **<u>Surveyors</u> <u>are marking</u> the boundaries of the empty lot next door,** for **<u>someone</u> <u>has decided</u> to build a house there.**

A comma and the coordinating conjunction, *for,* join the clauses in the preceding example. *For* is not part of either clause. Rather, it coordinates, or connects, the independent clauses. Other coordinating conjunctions are *and, but, or, nor,* and *yet.*

You can also join independent clauses by using either a semicolon alone or a semicolon and a conjunctive adverb (*page 32*).

> The film has opened to excellent reviews; we are planning to see it as soon as possible. [semicolon alone]

The film has opened to excellent reviews; **consequently,** we are planning to see it as soon as possible. [semicolon and conjunctive adverb]

**Exercise 1   Independent Clauses**   Each of the following groups of words lacks either a subject or a predicate. Rewrite the group of words as an independent clause by adding a subject or a predicate. You should also add modifiers and complements.

> SAMPLE    that painting of a boy fishing
> ANSWER    That painting of a boy fishing has been in our family for generations.

1. one of the largest dams on this continent
2. will search the crowded closet
3. served the nation admirably for twelve years
4. the large machine in the corner of the factory
5. performs a generous task and takes no credit
6. relics and artifacts near the dusty cavern
7. had left the area weeks ago
8. spirals of smoke from chimneys

## 3.2b   Subordinate Clauses

A clause that cannot stand by itself is a **subordinate clause.** Such clauses are sometimes called **dependent clauses.** All of the clauses that follow have subjects, which are underlined once, and predicates, which are underlined twice. However, the clauses cannot stand by themselves because they do not express complete thoughts.

> which is interfering with the television reception
> if Larry brings his folk guitar
> since we saw you last year

Notice that the preceding subordinate clauses begin with the words *which, if,* and *since. Which* is a relative pronoun (*page 11*), and *if* and *since* are subordinating conjunctions (*pages 31–32*). Many subordinate clauses begin with either a relative pronoun or a subordinating conjunction. Such introductory words are part of the subordinate clause, and they join the subordinate clause to an independent clause.

```
┌─────────── indep. clause ──────────────┐
Somebody in the kitchen is operating the mixer,
┌──────────── sub. clause ───────────────┐
which is interfering with the television reception.
```

```
┌────── sub. clause ──────┐ ┌────────── indep. clause ──────────┐
If Larry brings his folk guitar, we can sing around the campfire.
```

```
┌──── indep. clause ────┐ ┌──────── sub. clause ────────┐
How have you been since we saw you last year?
```

**Exercise 2   Clauses**   On your paper, write the label *Independent* or *Subordinate* for each clause in italic type in the following sentences.

| | |
|---|---|
| **SAMPLE** | The receipt for the tune-up will be signed by *whoever worked on the car.* |
| **ANSWER** | Subordinate |

1. Will you return these history books *as long as you are going to the library*?
2. *The engine was leaking fluid,* and the car's starter would not work.
3. Ned spotted a green tree frog *that was nearly camouflaged by leaves and branches.*
4. *Remove the plastic covering* before you open the new jazz album that you bought today.
5. Mary Ann Evans was a British novelist *who wrote under the pseudonym George Eliot.*
6. *The review of the television special was generally favorable,* although the last segment of the show was criticized.
7. Wade asked *whose vintage car was being sold.*
8. The bridge between the two cities was closed, but *we followed an alternate route to reach our destination.*
9. Please call me *whenever you have a free moment in your hectic schedule.*
10. *While he was in China,* Marco Polo took numerous notes about the customs of the Chinese people.

## 3.2c   Kinds of Subordinate Clauses

### Clauses Used as Adjectives

A clause functions as an adjective if it modifies a noun or a pronoun. Such clauses are called **adjective clauses.** Most adjective clauses begin with a relative pronoun: *that, which, who, whom,* and *whose.*

|————— adj. clause —————|
One historical *figure* **whose** career was very interesting was Winston Churchill. [Which figure? The figure *whose career was very interesting.*]

|————— adj. clause —————|
Sally saw three *garter snakes*, **which** are really quite harmless. [What kind of snakes? Garter snakes, *which are really quite harmless.*]

You may also introduce adjective clauses with relative adverbs. Some of the relative adverbs are *after, before, since, when,* and *where.*

|————— adj. clause —————|
Can John remember any *places* **where** he might have left his wallet?

Sometimes the introductory word in an adjective clause is implied rather than stated.

|————— adj. clause —————|
The *ship* Uncle Leonard took to Europe was the *Queen Elizabeth II.* [**Think:** The ship *that* Uncle Leonard took.]

**Essential and Nonessential Clauses.**   An adjective clause that is necessary to the meaning of the sentence is an **essential clause.** You do not separate an essential clause from the rest of the sentence by commas.

ESSENTIAL CLAUSE

|————— adj. clause —————|
The *radio* **that** you gave me for my graduation has excellent tone. [The clause is essential in order to identify which radio is being discussed.]

A **nonessential clause** is an adjective clause that is not necessary to the meaning of a sentence. Use commas to set off a nonessential clause from the rest of the sentence.

NONESSENTIAL CLAUSE

adj. clause

Our vegetable *garden*, **which** we started as a hobby, will save us quite a bit of money. [The clause is nonessential because without it, the reader would still know which garden is being discussed.]

**Exercise 3 Adjective Clauses** On your paper, combine the following sets of sentences by writing one or more of the sentences as adjective clauses. Underline the adjective clauses in your rewritten sentences.

> SAMPLE Last week Leo and Brad went on a whale-watching trip. Leo and Brad were visiting us. The trip allowed them to view whales from a distance of only a few feet.
>
> ANSWER Last week Leo and Brad, who were visiting us, went on a whale-watching trip, which allowed them to view whales from a distance of only a few feet.

1. Rita recited her favorite folk tale. She has received recognition for her acting. The folk tale tells the story of a legendary cowboy.
2. The tourists arrived at the gorge to see the sunset. The sunset looks very dramatic from this spot.
3. Electricians wired the second floor of the split-level house. The electricians worked diligently. The house was being built for the Rodriguez family.
4. I cannot find my trigonometry textbook. I brought it home because I have an assignment.
5. As a short cut, we walked through the parking lot. We saw the lead actress in the parking lot.
6. Daphne gave Corinne a handmade ceramic vase. She has known Corinne for at least five years. The gift was a graduation present.
7. This morning Walter heard the howling of coyotes. The coyotes were probably miles away. Walter is always exceptionally cautious.

8. For our vacation we would like to stay at Van's seaside resort. Our vacation begins in three weeks. The resort is peaceful and interesting.

9. Did Chiyo finish her entry for the upcoming contest? The contest is for young composers. Chiyo won the prize for her last piece.

10. The father helped the child. The child's skate laces had become untied.

## Clauses Used as Adverbs

A subordinate clause functions as an adverb when it modifies a verb, an adjective, or an adverb. Such clauses are called **adverb clauses.**

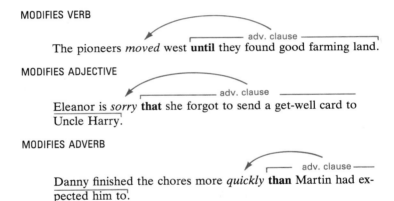

MODIFIES VERB

The pioneers *moved* west **until** they found good farming land.

MODIFIES ADJECTIVE

Eleanor is *sorry* **that** she forgot to send a get-well card to Uncle Harry.

MODIFIES ADVERB

Danny finished the chores more *quickly* **than** Martin had expected him to.

An adverb clause always begins with a subordinating conjunction (*pages 31–32*), which is a word that shows the relationship between the subordinate clause and the independent clause. The following list contains frequently used subordinating conjunctions:

| | | | |
|---|---|---|---|
| after | before | since | until |
| although | even if | so that | when |
| as | even though | than | whenever |
| as if | if | that | where |
| as soon as | in order that | though | wherever |
| as though | provided that | unless | while |
| because | | | |

Adverb clauses tell *how, when, where, to what extent,* and *why.* In the following examples, the subordinating conjunctions are in boldface type.

HOW

In his first debate, Silvio *performed* **as if** he were an experienced debater. [The clause modifies a verb.]

WHEN

The children *wanted* a pumpkin **as soon as** the first frost covered the ground. [The clause modifies a verb.]

WHERE

After the huge snowfall, drivers *went* **wherever** snowplows had cleared the streets. [The clause modifies a verb.]

TO WHAT EXTENT

The halfback ran so *quickly* **that** no defender could catch him. [The clause modifies an adverb.]

WHY

**Because** she wanted to play the role so much, Sheila *studied* the part of the main character in the play. [The clause modifies a verb.]

**Elliptical Clauses.** An elliptical clause is an adverb clause in which part of the clause is omitted. Even though the clause is incomplete, its meaning is clear, and it is still a clause.

The play obviously affected you *more* **than** me. [**Think:** affected you more than *it affected* me.]

**When** lifting a heavy box, *keep* your back straight. [**Think:** when *you are* lifting.]

**Exercise 4   Adverb Clauses**   On your paper, combine the following sets of sentences by rewriting one or more of the sentences as an adverb clause. Underline the adverb clauses in the sentences that you write.

> SAMPLE   You may take the sailboat out onto the lake. You must wear life jackets.
>
> ANSWER   You may take the sailboat out onto the lake <u>provided that you wear life jackets</u>.

1. Gas lamps were commonly used as the main source of light. Electric lamps replaced them in the late 1800s.
2. The guests looked pale and surprised. Jean-Pierre walked into the parlor after a long absence at sea.
3. Someone fixed the old bell in the tower of the town hall. It chimed loudly and beautifully.
4. At one time Cornelius Vanderbilt possessed a great number of steamboats. Other investors in the United States did not own as many.
5. I greatly enjoy camping. I will not be able to go on the trip. I sprained my ankle last week.
6. Will you help us put up the badminton net? We can play a game or two. It will get dark in a few hours.
7. Seth begins a garden each spring. He completely exhausts himself. There is so much work to do.
8. A family moves into the neighborhood. The family will feel more comfortable making the adjustment. There is often a welcoming committee to greet them.
9. A crowd of enthusiasts rushed backstage to catch a glimpse of the opera star. The final curtain call was over.
10. Greg and I floated along in our rubber raft. We viewed the forest on the banks of the river.

## Clauses Used as Nouns

Clauses that function as nouns in sentences are called **noun clauses.** A noun clause may function as a subject, a predicate nominative, a direct object, an indirect object, an object of a preposition, or an appositive.

SUBJECT

——————————— noun clause———————————

**How recent graduates can find successful careers** will be the subject of the seminar.

PREDICATE NOMINATIVE

—————————noun clause —————————

The lure of gold was **what brought prospectors to Alaska.**

DIRECT OBJECT

—————————noun clause—————————

We trust **that the train to Baltimore is on time.**

INDIRECT OBJECT

—————————noun clause—————————

Did you ask **whoever answered the telephone** his or her name?

OBJECT OF A PREPOSITION

—————————noun clause—————————

One should try to prepare for **whatever the future holds.**

APPOSITIVE

—— noun clause——

Mr. Hanson's advice, **whatever it was,** has had a good effect on Chip.

You may introduce a noun clause with various types of pronouns (including some used as adjectives) and adverbs. Among these words are the following.

| | | | |
|---|---|---|---|
| how | when | which | whom |
| that | where | whichever | whomever |
| what | wherever | who | whose |
| whatever | whether | whoever | why |

Sometimes you may omit the introductory word in a noun clause.

————— noun clause —————

The coach said **she had important news.** [**Think:** *that* she had important news.]

—————noun clause—————

Not until after the game did Karen learn **she had been selected as the most valuable player.** [**Think:** *that* she had been selected.]

**Exercise 5   Noun Clauses**   Make a complete sentence out of each of the following word groups by adding a noun clause. The noun clause should perform the sentence function indicated in parentheses. Write each sentence on your paper, and underline the noun clause.

> **SAMPLE**   most of the members of the school board wondered (direct object)
>
> **ANSWER**   Most of the members of the school board wondered <u>whether the school board president would agree to serve another term.</u>

1. can you explain (direct object)
2. at that time twelve sailing vessels left with (object of preposition)
3. the goal of owning her own business was (predicate nominative)
4. should go to the flower show at the botanical garden (subject)
5. in the county museum Terry discovered (direct object)
6. please raise your hands (subject)
7. the performance of the renowned actor gave a tremendous thrill (indirect object)
8. the community chorus fervently hoped (direct object)
9. the only remaining problem was (predicate nominative)
10. was lost amidst the clutter in the closet (subject)

**Assignment   Clauses in a Passage**   Alexis de Tocqueville was a French aristocrat who toured the United States in 1831 and wrote *Democracy in America,* one of the most penetrating books written about the political life and culture of the new nation. Tocqueville, like other good writers, uses subordinate clauses to make his ideas clear to the reader. Read the following paragraph adapted from *Democracy in America.* It is about one of the most important forces in American thought, individualism. On your paper, write all of the subordinate clauses that you find in the paragraph. Next to each clause, write the word or phrase that the clause modifies. Finally, write two sentences that summarize the main idea of the paragraph.

> *Individualism* is a novel expression to which a novel idea has given birth. Our fathers were acquainted only with *égoïsme* (selfishness). Selfishness is a passionate and exaggerated love of self, which

leads a man to connect everything with himself and to prefer himself to everything in the world. Individualism is a mature and calm feeling which disposes each member of the community to sever himself from the mass of his fellows and to draw apart with his family and his friends. After he has thus formed a little circle of his own, he willingly leaves society at large to itself.

## Subordinate Clauses in Writing

By using subordinate clauses, writers can make their ideas clear to their readers. For example, a writer who is explaining an idea often uses an adjective clause.

Economic growth, *which means an increase in the amount of goods and services,* is a sign of national strength.

The paragraph by Alexis de Tocqueville in the preceding assignment contains excellent examples of the use of subordinate clauses.

Select one of the following ideas, and write an essay in which you explain what role that idea plays in your school and community. You should use examples drawn from school and community life. Use subordinate clauses to make your explanation clear to the reader. Underline each subordinate clause in your essay.

| | |
|---|---|
| achievement | generosity |
| competition | materialism |
| equality | progress |

## 3.3   Sentences Classified by Structure

Sentences are classified according to the number and kinds of clauses that they contain. The four kinds of sentences are simple, compound, complex, and compound-complex.

### Simple Sentences

A **simple sentence** is a sentence that contains one independent clause and no subordinate clauses. It may have any number of phrases. It may have a compound subject, a compound predicate, or both. In the following two examples, the simple subject is underlined once and the simple predicate twice.

> The racing official waved the yellow flag.
> The novice and the expert skier jumped off the ski lift and then descended the slope. [compound subject and compound predicate]

### Compound Sentences

A **compound sentence** is a sentence that contains two or more independent clauses. A compound sentence never has a subordinate clause. You usually join the independent clauses with a comma and one of the coordinating conjunctions: *and, but, nor, or, for,* or *yet.*

> ┌─────────── indep. clause ───────────────┐
> We knocked at the door as hard as we could, **but**
> ┌─────── indep. clause ────────┐
> no one seemed to be at home.

You may also join the independent clauses with a semicolon or with a semicolon and a conjunctive adverb such as *therefore, nevertheless,* and *moreover* (*page 32*).

> ┌──────────────── indep. clause ────────────────┐
> The Florida Everglades cover an area of 2746 square
> ┌─────┐ ┌─────────── indep. clause ───────────┐
> miles; they consist of swampy grasslands.

> ┌──────────────── indep. clause────────────────┐
> Members of the chorus have practiced hard;
> ┌─────────────── indep. clause ───────────────┐
> **consequently,** they expect to give a good performance.

## Complex Sentences

A **complex sentence** is a sentence that contains one independent clause and one or more subordinate clauses.

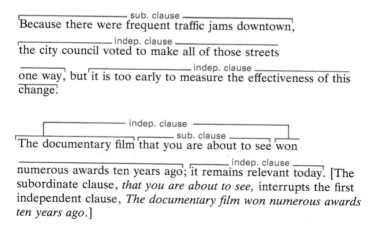

```
┌──────────────── sub. clause ──────────────────┐
Although the two sisters had not seen each other for
┌──────────┐ ┌──────── indep. clause ─────────┐ ┌─────────
ten years, they talked to each other as if they
┌──────────────── sub. clause ────────────────┐
had seen each other the day before.
```

```
┌────────────── sub. clause ────────────┐ ┌──────── indep. clause ──────
Before we plan our next meeting, we had better call the
┌──┐ ┌──── sub. clause ────┐
hall that we usually use.
```

## Compound-Complex Sentences

A **compound-complex** sentence is a sentence that contains two or more independent clauses and one or more subordinate clauses.

```
┌─────────────────── sub. clause ─────────────────────┐
Because there were frequent traffic jams downtown,
┌─────────────────── indep. clause ───────────────────┐
the city council voted to make all of those streets
┌──────────┐ ┌──────────────── indep. clause ────────────────────
one way, but it is too early to measure the effectiveness of this
change.
```

```
            ┌──────────────── indep. clause ──────────────────┐
            ┌──────── sub. clause ────────┐ ┌───┐
The documentary film that you are about to see won
┌──────────────────────────┐ ┌────────── indep. clause ─────────┐
numerous awards ten years ago; it remains relevant today.
```
[The subordinate clause, *that you are about to see,* interrupts the first independent clause, *The documentary film won numerous awards ten years ago.*]

**Exercise** **Sentence Classification** Each item contains a set of sentences. Combine each set to make one sentence, and write that sentence on your paper. Label the sentences that you write *Simple, Compound, Complex,* or *Compound-complex.*

> **SAMPLE**   Steve entered the personnel office. He saw the recep-
> tionist. The receptionist asked him to fill out an em-
> ployment application.
>
> **ANSWER**   As Steve entered the personnel office, he saw the
> receptionist, who asked him to fill out an employment
> application.—Complex

1. Kettledrums are the only drums that can be tuned. These drums are usually used in pairs. They are often used in orchestras.
2. The bananas were certainly not ripe. The colors of the pears, plums, and peaches were enticing.
3. Film producer Samuel Goldwyn was well known for mishandling the English language. He once said, "A verbal contract isn't worth the paper it's written on."
4. One of their hobbies is building models. Doug and Rick do not always have enough time or patience for it.
5. We have attended the meeting. We are concerned about this issue. We want to sign the petition.
6. Dominion Day is an important holiday. It is celebrated yearly in Canada on July 1. It commemorates the unification of the Canadian provinces under one government.
7. The Hudson River is the largest river in New York. It is still an important waterway for trade.
8. Geraldo and his sister searched the campgrounds. His sister had lost her glasses. They finally found them under a sleeping bag.
9. Miriam feels weary. She will complete her cello practice and run a few errands. She will then take a nap.
10. The weather prediction called for cloudy skies over the weekend. The soccer match took place as scheduled.

**Assignment   Sentence Variety**   To achieve sentence variety, effective writers use compound, complex, and compound-complex sentences in addition to simple sentences. The following paragraph contains only simple sentences. Rewrite the paragraph so that it is more varied in sentence structure.

Most people think of kites merely as toys. In the past, however, people used kites for many other purposes. During the 1800s, photographers used kites to take photographs from the air. The airplane had not been invented yet. Engineers used a kite to begin building a bridge across a river. The river flowed into Niagara Falls. They flew the kite across the river. The engineers then attached a heavy line to the kite line. They pulled the heavy line across the river. Probably the most famous use of a kite was by Benjamin Franklin. In 1752 he flew a kite during a thunderstorm. Franklin proved something. Lightning consists of electricity. He also ensured the place of the kite in history.

# 3.4 Writing Complete Sentences

A **complete sentence** is a group of words that has at least one subject and one predicate and that expresses a complete thought. In writing, you should use complete sentences. Writers often make two errors: they use either sentence fragments or run-on sentences. In this section you will learn how to recognize and correct both kinds of errors.

## 3.4a Avoiding Sentence Fragments

A **sentence fragment** is a group of words that either lacks a subject or a predicate or does not express a complete thought.

COMPLETE SENTENCE
>Jesse hurried to get to the store before it closed.

FRAGMENT
>Jesse hurried. **To get to the store before it closed.** [The second group of words lacks a subject.]

FRAGMENT
>Jesse hurrying to get to the store before it closed. [The group of words lacks a predicate.]

If the sentence fragment is a phrase, you can correct it by including it in a related sentence.

FRAGMENT

Our class had an excellent discussion. **About the issue of television advertising for children.**

COMPLETE SENTENCE

Our class had an excellent discussion **about the issue of**
——— prepositional phrase ———
**television advertising for children.**

FRAGMENT

Did you happen to watch the new television series? **An interesting blend of comedy and drama.**

COMPLETE SENTENCE

Did you happen to watch the new television series,
——— appositive phrase ———
**an interesting blend of comedy and drama?**

FRAGMENT

It is Diane's intention. **To leave the car at the garage for an oil change.**

COMPLETE SENTENCE

——— infinitive phrase ———
It is Diane's intention **to leave the car at the garage for an oil change.**

FRAGMENT

Do you recognize the man? **Walking on the other side of the street.**

COMPLETE SENTENCE

——— participial phrase ———
Do you recognize the man **walking on the other side of the street?**

FRAGMENT

**Clearing the snow off your car.** That is a good idea.

COMPLETE SENTENCE

——— gerund phrase ———
**Clearing the snow off your car** is a good idea.

If the sentence fragment is a subordinate clause used without an independent clause, you can correct it by combining it with a related sentence.

FRAGMENT

> Henry went to the library and took out several books about airplanes to prepare his report. **Which is due on Monday.**

COMPLETE SENTENCE

> Henry went to the library and took out several books about
>
> airplanes to prepare his report, $\overline{\text{sub. clause}}$ **which is due on Monday.**

FRAGMENT

> Will you please help me finish the dishes? **After you have finished reading the newspaper.**

COMPLETE SENTENCE

> $\overline{\text{sub. clause}}$
> **After you have finished reading the newspaper,** will you please help me finish the dishes?

To turn some sentence fragments into complete sentences, you must reword them.

FRAGMENT

> Clark, being stiff and sore after playing football all afternoon.

COMPLETE SENTENCE

> Clark was stiff and sore after playing football all afternoon.

FRAGMENT

> Kites, which were first used by the Greeks almost twenty-five hundred years ago.

COMPLETE SENTENCE

> Kites were first used by the Greeks almost twenty-five hundred years ago.

**Exercise 1  Eliminating Sentence Fragments**  The following paragraph contains numerous sentence fragments. On your paper, rewrite the paragraph, eliminating all the sentence fragments.

SAMPLE   Richard Trevithick, who was an English inventor. He built the first steam locomotive in 1804.

ANSWER   Richard Trevithick, who was an English inventor, built the first steam locomotive in 1804.

Ten tons of coal. That was how much weight Trevithick's locomotive could pull. Rather impressive for that time. A mere twenty-one years later. When the first public railroad in the world opened in England. Between the towns of Darlington and Stockton. That was where the railroad ran. Only freight trains, however. Until 1830, when another line started to carry passengers. John Stevens built a circular railway track in New Jersey in 1825. Which made his locomotive the first one in the United States. The future of the railroad was still uncertain. Even after the famous race between a horse and *Tom Thumb,* a locomotive. Peter Cooper, who owned *Tom Thumb.* He conceived the idea of the race. To advertise his locomotive to the owners of the Baltimore and Ohio Railroad. Although *Tom Thumb* broke down, and the horse won the race. In spite of the slow start. The railroad industry growing rapidly by the middle of the nineteenth century.

# 3.4b   Avoiding Run-On Sentences

A **run-on sentence** consists of two or more separate sentences written as if they were one sentence. In some run-on sentences, only a comma separates the two sentences. In other run-ons, the sentences are not separated at all.

RUN-ON   Engineers are working hard to extend the rapid transit line to the airport, they will not finish for two more years. [A comma by itself usually should not connect two independent clauses.]

RUN-ON   Engineers are working hard to extend the rapid transit line to the airport they will not finish for two more years. [The two sentences are written as one sentence.]

CORRECT   Engineers are working hard to extend the rapid transit line to the airport, **but** they will not finish for two more years. [A comma and the coordinating conjunction, *but*, connect the two clauses.]

You can correct run-on sentences in several ways. Read the following run-on sentence. Then study the five ways in which you can correct that sentence.

RUN-ON SENTENCE   On Saturday evening we are giving a dinner party, we hope that you can attend.

1. Separate the run-on sentence into two or more sentences.

    CORRECT      On Saturday evening we are giving a dinner party. **W**e hope that you can attend.

2. Join the independent clauses with a comma and a coordinating conjunction. The coordinating conjunctions are *and, but, or, for, nor,* and *yet.*

    CORRECT      We are giving a dinner party on Saturday evening, **and** we hope that you can attend.

3. Join the independent clauses with a semicolon.

    CORRECT      On Saturday evening we are giving a dinner party**;** we hope that you can attend.

4. Rewrite one of the independent clauses as a subordinate clause, and add a subordinating conjunction (*pages 31–32*) or a relative pronoun (*page 11*).

    CORRECT      On Saturday evening we are giving a dinner party, **which** we hope that you can attend.

5. Join the independent clauses with a semicolon and a conjunctive adverb such as *moreover, consequently,* or *furthermore* (*page 32*).

    CORRECT      On Saturday evening we are giving a dinner party**; furthermore,** we hope that you can attend.

**Exercise 2   Eliminating Run-On Sentences**   The following paragraph contains numerous run-on sentences. On your paper, rewrite the paragraph, correcting each of the run-on sentences.

SAMPLE   The field of advertising dates back to 3000 B.C., merchants in Babylonia hung signs outside the doors to their shops.

ANSWER   The field of advertising dates back to 3000 B.C., when merchants in Babylonia hung signs outside the doors to their shops.

The advertising techniques of merchants in ancient times were simple indeed when compared to today's complex strategies and techniques. Most people then could not read, merchants therefore carved symbols on the signs outside their shops, for instance, bootmakers put pictures of boots on their signs. The merchants of the Middle Ages hired town criers and the criers walked the streets and described the merchants' goods to the townspeople. Advertising took an important step forward with the invention of movable type by Johannes Gutenberg about 1440 in 1472 the Englishman William Caxton brought print advertising to England, he printed a poster to advertise a book. Another development in mass advertising was the newspaper ad *The Boston News-Letter* contained the first newspaper ad in the American colonies in 1704. By the end of the nineteenth century, advertisements had even become a form of popular art painters such as Henri de Toulouse-Lautrec created poster art that had inherent artistic value. The greatest boom in advertising has come with the development of radio and television in the twentieth century both media are able to reach audiences of millions. In fact, the amount of money spent on advertising each year in the United States is now more than $33 billion.

**Assignment   Run-Ons and Sentence Fragments**   Rewrite the following paragraph on your paper, eliminating all of the run-on sentences and the sentence fragments.

In literary history there have been many famous gatherings of writers and intellectuals, for example, influential critics, essayists, and artists gathered regularly at the Algonquin Hotel in New York City. Where they had many witty conversations throughout the

1920s. This literary gathering, which was known as the Algonquin Round Table. It greatly influenced the cultural atmosphere in New York City. The Bloomsbury group in England also discussed artistic and philosophical ideas regularly. At the homes of the novelist Virginia Woolf and her sister, who lived in London's Bloomsbury district. The group, consisting of Woolf, economist John Maynard Keynes, writer E. M. Forster, and many well-known sculptors, painters, and critics. For more than twenty years this highly talented group continued to meet and share their ideas. Another group in the United States actually established a home Fruitlands in Harvard, Massachusetts, was founded by Bronson Alcott and other writers. The members of Fruitlands held certain philosophical and educational beliefs. Which they attempted to put into practice. One of the major reasons for founding Fruitlands was to live in harmony with nature. As Ralph Waldo Emerson and Henry David Thoreau taught.

# Unit Practice

## Practice 1

**A. Phrases** (*pages 65–79*)   On your paper, write the phrases that are in italic type in the following sentences. Label each phrase *Prepositional phrase, Appositive phrase, Participial phrase, Gerund phrase,* or *Infinitive phrase.*

1. *Asking pertinent questions* is the foremost responsibility of a newspaper reporter.
2. The shop owner's reminder to be careful *near the glassware* was a cautious yet friendly suggestion.
3. *A member of the pine family,* the larch is a tree that loses its needles each fall.
4. *Having been given the house key,* Barney will feed his neighbors' pets and water their plants *for a week.*
5. Volunteers brought the island inhabitants safely *to the mainland* before the violent storm began.
6. The play resembles kabuki, which is a form of drama *originating in Japan.*
7. *During today's meeting* the board nominated him for the vacant position.
8. Remember *to use seasoned wood in the fireplace.*
9. Paula will make *mining in the western United States* her general topic when she begins her library research.
10. The weightlifter became too exhausted *to make another record-breaking attempt* during the competition.

**B. Clauses** (*pages 79–89*)   On your paper, write the clauses that are in italic type in the following sentences. Next to each clause, write the label *Independent clause, Adjective clause, Adverb clause,* or *Noun clause.*

11. Each year the uniforms *that the waiters wear* must be redesigned.
12. Because Cassie is able to swim long distances without tiring, *she is favored to win the ten-mile race this Saturday.*
13. Renata looked surprised *when she opened the large, bulky envelope.*
14. *Whichever road you take* will lead you to the appropriate destination.
15. Hang the oil painting *before someone accidentally damages it.*

**C. Classification of Sentences** (*pages 90–93*) On your paper, write the label *Simple, Compound, Complex,* or *Compound-complex* for each of the following sentences.

16. Frances would like to ride on a streetcar but has never visited a city that has one.
17. Dale is unable to attend today's rehearsal because of unforeseen circumstances.
18. The scientists were amazed by the discovery, and they did further tests that verified their findings.
19. The mayor, whom I met last year, has not announced that she is running for re-election.
20. The animals of the arctic are remarkably adapted to the climate, for they don't seem to mind the cold at all.

**D. Writing Complete Sentences** (*pages 93–99*) On your paper, rewrite each of the following word groups to eliminate sentence fragments and run-on sentences. Add words as needed.

21. Cartoons first began appearing regularly in 1841 in the magazine *Punch* they were often used to express political opinions.
22. Please repair this broken chair leg. With glue and a small piece of wood.
23. Painting a familiar scene on a large mural. Ted kept busy all day.
24. Check to see that you have all the spices that you need, the recipe requires several unusual ingredients.
25. To begin writing a novel about that particular intellectual movement in the 1800s.
26. Samantha became enchanted with Willa Cather's novel and she hopes to read more books by American authors this year.
27. Communication became possible by means of undersea cables that could transmit messages, these cable systems have been used for more than one hundred years.
28. The manager, who was answering requests throughout the busy week.
29. Participating in a fund-raising campaign for the restoration of the building.
30. The Allens purchased tickets for the Stanley Cup finals it should be an exhilarating and competitive tournament.

(Continue on the next page.)

# Practice 2

On your paper, write the following paragraph correctly so that all fragments and run-on sentences are eliminated.

Belva Lockwood was a remarkable woman. Of the nineteenth century. Born in 1830 in Royalton, New York, she was a reformer. And a leader of the women's suffrage movement she was also one of the few women to be nominated for President of the United States. After teaching school for several years. Belva became a lawyer in 1873. She struggled for women's rights her work paid off well. She won not only equal pay for women government employees. But also a law allowing women to appear as legal counsel. Before the Supreme Court. In addition, she successfully defended the land rights. Of the North Carolina Cherokee Indians. The Equal Rights party nominated Belva for President in 1884. And again in 1888.

# Unit Tests

## Test 1

**A. Phrases** (*pages 65–79*)   On your paper, write the phrases that are in italics in each of the following sentences. Label each phrase *Prepositional phrase, Appositive phrase, Participial phrase, Gerund phrase,* or *Infinitive phrase.*

1. Maxie Anderson, *a successful and daring hot-air balloonist,* made the first balloon flight across the Atlantic Ocean.
2. Parking meters were first used in Oklahoma City *to regulate parking time for vehicles.*
3. *For what commemorative event* will these festive decorations be used?
4. *Attracted by trading posts,* many pioneers lived in settlements that became today's large cities.
5. *To be a healthy individual* requires some exercise, adequate sleep, and a proper diet.
6. The classified section in our newspaper provides advertising *for most of the town's small businesses.*
7. The Pentagon, *the largest office building in the world,* was completed in 1943.
8. The group of scientists *observing the sun's activity* noted several solar flares.
9. One of the hardest tasks on a winter morning is *leaving the comfort of warm blankets.*
10. Judy was surprised *by the community's generous support.*

**B. Clauses** (*pages 79–89*)   On your paper, write the clauses that are in italic type in the following sentences. Next to each clause, write the label *Independent clause, Adjective clause, Adverb clause,* or *Noun clause.*

11. *Because the grocer has reduced the prices of many items this week,* we should go there.
12. *The race car drivers noisily started their vehicles* when the starter gave the signal.
13. Beth and I spent hours browsing in the rare book shop *that is on Main Street.*

(Continue on the next page.)

14. I cannot seem to remember *how we get to the miniature train museum.*

15. The pianist, *who has performed with many of the great orchestras of the world,* played gracefully and skillfully.

**C. Classification of Sentences** (*pages 90–93*) On your paper, write the label *Simple, Compound, Complex,* or *Compound-complex* for each of the following sentences.

16. Harold will appreciate whatever gift you choose for him.

17. Would you like to see the brand-new herbarium featuring rare dried plants?

18. As the fifth round began, the wrestler looked tired, but he had enough strength left to pin his opponent.

19. I went to the nearby skating rink, but it was closed because of the warm weather.

20. If you want to, you can do a research paper that surveys the history of writing from ancient times to the present.

**D. Writing Complete Sentences** (*pages 93–99*) On your paper, rewrite each of the following word groups to eliminate sentence fragments and run-on sentences. Add words as needed.

21. Working to meet a midnight deadline on the daily newspaper.

22. To be the captain of any team sport. You must have some patience and considerable ability.

23. A relative of the dodo bird called the solitaire existed until the 1790s yet it is known only through pictures.

24. Before the special exhibit closes next week.

25. I decided to audition for the musical my experience includes singing, acting, and dancing in a recent production.

26. Deadwood, South Dakota, became a boom town when gold was discovered there, the rich gold mines are still operating.

27. Claire's uncle plays the clarinet and oboe. A versatile and talented musician.

28. Is your camera focused properly you want to take a clear photograph of this spectacular sight.

29. Dan, becoming a better electrician with every day of training at school.

30. Electronic clocks make telling time easy, sundials were the earliest devices used to measure time.

# Test 2

On your paper, write the following paragraph correctly so that all fragments and run-on sentences are eliminated.

Calligraphy. That's the art of fine handwriting. Entirely different from ordinary handwriting. Who practices calligraphy is commonly called a calligrapher. When shaping letters, the calligrapher pays close attention. To such details as legibility, form, size, stroke, proportion, rhythm, spacing, character, and uniformity. Calligraphy is used in various ways in modern printing and publishing, it was also used by the ancient Persians and Chinese. Who considered it to be an art equal to, if not more important than, painting. Books and manuscripts were copied by hand. Before movable type was invented around 1440 the copyists of this period produced work of great calligraphic beauty and style, calligraphers of today often study the work of these early masters.

# Unit 4

## *Usage*

---

## Unit Preview

To communicate, you must be understood. By following the accepted standards of English usage, you will speak and write clearly, and others will understand you. You will also create a favorable impression of yourself and of your ideas.

In addition to the various kinds of usage problems covered in the unit, you should be aware of the appropriateness of the five categories of words that are considered here.

First, **idioms** are combinations of words that have a special meaning when used as a unit: *walk on air, walk of life.* Be careful to use correct idioms. Do not create an incorrect idiom instead of using a single word: write *this,* not *this here.*

Second, be aware of—and avoid—the pompous, confusing language sometimes known as **jargon**. Note, however, that the word *jargon* may also be used to mean occupational language, such as the theater and film terms *flats, props,* and *grip.* This kind of language is appropriate for an audience of specialists.

Third, be aware of levels of language. **Colloquial** language is informal, suitable in most speaking situations but not in formal writing and speaking. *Kind of,* meaning "rather," is a **colloquialism**—that is, a colloquial term.

Fourth, watch for **slang**, language that is even more colloquial. Slang is lively, but it is suitable only in casual speech, not in writing. *To do a number on* is slang.

The fifth category is **nonstandard** language: word choices and combinations that are incorrect in any speaking or writing situation. *Throwed* and *she suppose* are nonstandard.

**For Analysis** The following passage contains examples of all five of the types of language discussed on the previous page. Read the paragraph; then answer the questions.

(1) As you watched a film about the Old West, have you ever been real surprise to see tire tracks in the sand? (2) Have you ever saw a costume film and noticed that the women's dresses had zippers? (3) Such occurrences are call anachronisms, or things out of their proper time. (4) Sometimes authors or film makers make no bones about using anachronisms; they use them irregardless. (5) In other situations, however, anachronisms are a real boo-boo. (6) Persons in an audience frequently find entertainment value in examining plays and films for the purpose of making a personal determination with respect to the anachronism factor.

1. What is the idiom in Sentence 4?
2. Which sentence exemplifies jargon?
3. Identify the colloquial expression and the nonstandard expression in Sentence 1. What are the three additional nonstandard words in the passage?
4. What is the slang expression in the passage?

Now revise the entire passage to make it suitable for a formal situation. Responding to the questions has made you aware of the language that you use; in this unit you will review all the important details of correct usage.

# 4.1 Correct Use of Verbs

A verb shows tense, voice, and the number and person of its subject(s) through changes in its form. By knowing how to make these changes, you can use verbs correctly in sentences.

## 4.1a Principal Parts of Verbs

The four basic forms of a verb, called its **principal parts,** are the infinitive, the present participle, the past, and the past participle. You use these principal parts to form the various tenses of a verb.

The rules that govern the infinitive and the present participle are the same for all verbs. The infinitive—the basic verb form that appears in the dictionary—is usually preceded by the word *to*. In some sentences, however, *to* is understood but not stated. The present participle is always a combination of the infinitive and *-ing* with a form of the verb *be* as an auxiliary verb.

|  |  |
|---|---|
| INFINITIVE | Tomorrow Greg and Maria will have *to* **work**.     *(inf.)* |
|  | Tomorrow's assignment will make them **work**.     *(inf.)* |
| PRESENT PARTICIPLE | Greg and Maria *are* already **working** it.     *(aux.) (pres. part.)* |

You determine whether a verb is regular or irregular by the way in which its past and past participle forms are constructed.

## Regular Verbs

The past and past participle of any regular verb is formed by adding *-d* or *-ed* to the infinitive. The past participle of a regular verb takes a form of the verb *have* as an auxiliary verb.

|  |  |
|---|---|
| PAST | Maria **worked** on yesterday's assignment. |
| PAST PARTICIPLE | Maria *has* already **worked** on today's assignment.     *(aux.) (past part.)* |

The following list shows the principal parts of two regular verbs. The auxiliary verbs in parentheses remind you to use the correct form of the verb *be* (*am, is, are,* and so forth) with the present participle and the correct form of the verb *have* (*has, have, had,* and so forth) with the past participle.

| INFINITIVE | PRESENT PARTICIPLE | PAST | PAST PARTICIPLE |
|---|---|---|---|
| prepare | (is) preparing | prepared | (has) prepared |
| thank | (is) thanking | thanked | (has) thanked |

## Irregular Verbs

Irregular verbs do not follow the standard rules for forming the past and past participle. For this reason, you should memorize the principal parts of irregular verbs. Like regular verbs, irregular verbs use a form of the auxiliary verb *be* with the present participle and a form of the auxiliary verb *have* with the past participle. The following sentences show the correct use of the principal parts of the irregular verb *shrink*.

| | |
|---|---|
| INFINITIVE | inf.<br>Do you want your new dress to **shrink?** |
| PRESENT<br>PARTICIPLE | pres.<br>aux.  part.<br>Your new dress *is* **shrinking** in that hot water. |
| PAST | Your new dress **shrank** because you used hot water. |
| PAST<br>PARTICIPLE | past<br>aux. part.<br>Your new dress *has* **shrunk** in the hot water. |

Although no standard rules govern the formation of the past and the past participle of irregular verbs, you should have little trouble mastering their usage. You have probably already developed a good sense of what is correct by what sounds correct. The following list contains many common irregular verbs. Study this list and refer to it while doing the exercise that follows. Consult your dictionary for the principal parts of any irregular verbs that are not listed here.

| INFINITIVE | PRESENT<br>PARTICIPLE | PAST | PAST<br>PARTICIPLE |
|---|---|---|---|
| be | (is) being | was | (has) been |
| bear | (is) bearing | bore | (has) borne |
| become | (is) becoming | became | (has) become |
| begin | (is) beginning | began | (has) begun |
| bite | (is) biting | bit | (has) bitten |
| blow | (is) blowing | blew | (has) blown |
| break | (is) breaking | broke | (has) broken |
| burst | (is) bursting | burst | (has) burst |

| | | | |
|---|---|---|---|
| choose | (is) choosing | chose | (has) chosen |
| creep | (is) creeping | crept | (has) crept |
| do | (is) doing | did | (has) done |
| draw | (is) drawing | drew | (has) drawn |
| drink | (is) drinking | drank | (has) drunk |
| eat | (is) eating | ate | (has) eaten |
| fall | (is) falling | fell | (has) fallen |
| fight | (is) fighting | fought | (has) fought |
| fly | (is) flying | flew | (has) flown |
| forget | (is) forgetting | forgot | (has) forgotten |
| freeze | (is) freezing | froze | (has) frozen |
| get | (is) getting | got | (has) gotten |
| grow | (is) growing | grew | (has) grown |
| have | (is) having | had | (has) had |
| hang | (is) hanging | hung | (has) hung |
| know | (is) knowing | knew | (has) known |
| lay | (is) laying | laid | (has) laid |
| lead | (is) leading | led | (has) led |
| lie | (is) lying | lay | (has) lain |
| ring | (is) ringing | rang | (has) rung |
| rise | (is) rising | rose | (has) risen |
| set | (is) setting | set | (has) set |
| shake | (is) shaking | shook | (has) shaken |
| sing | (is) singing | sang | (has) sung |
| sink | (is) sinking | sank, sunk | (has) sunk, |
| sit | (is) sitting | sat | (has) sat |
| spin | (is) spinning | spun | (has) spun |
| spring | (is) springing | sprang | (has) sprung |
| steal | (is) stealing | stole | (has) stolen |
| sting | (is) stinging | stung | (has) stung |
| strike | (is) striking | struck | (has) struck, |
| | | | (has) stricken |
| swear | (is) swearing | swore | (has) sworn |
| swim | (is) swimming | swam | (has) swum |
| tear | (is) tearing | tore | (has) torn |
| tell | (is) telling | told | (has) told |
| throw | (is) throwing | threw | (has) thrown |
| wear | (is) wearing | wore | (has) worn |
| write | (is) writing | wrote | (has) written |

**Exercise 1**  **Principal Parts of Verbs**  On your paper, write the principal part of the verb in parentheses that correctly completes each sentence. Do not use auxiliary verbs other than those already given in the sentences.

> SAMPLE     Our team __?__ a good game today. (*play*)
>
> ANSWER     played

1. Both Bobby and Emma are __?__ ten warm-up pitches. (*throw*)
2. The pitcher __?__ off the catcher's first two signals. (*shake*)
3. The catcher __?__ five balls before Bobby threw a strike. (*catch*)
4. The fast ball had __?__ the catcher's hand (*sting*)
5. Joe __?__ five pitches, three balls and two strikes, before he decided to swing. (*see*)
6. Martha had __?__ second when no one was looking. (*steal*)
7. A fast ball had __?__ Gail's bat. (*break*)
8. Elaine finally __?__ a good pitch (*get*)
9. The ball seemed to __?__ in the air; then it __?__ (*hang, sink*)
10. The ball had __?__ into deep right field. (*soar*)
11. The wind has __?__ the ball over the fence. (*carry*)
12. The pitcher had __?__ to tire. (*begin*)
13. The umpire was __?__ impatient with the long conference at the mound. (*grow*)
14. After we beat the Jets, our team __?__ into first place. (*move*)
15. Coach Rigby __?__ all along that we could could win. (*believe*)

## 4.1b    Verb Tense

By using the various forms of a verb, you can show whether an action or a condition takes place in the present, the past, or the future. The forms of a verb that express time are called **tenses.** You form them by using the principal parts and auxiliary verbs. Verbs have six tenses: present, past, future, present perfect, past perfect, and future perfect.

A **conjugation of a verb** lists all the forms for the six tenses of a verb. It also shows how the verb form changes for the plural and for the first, second, and third persons in the singular.

**Conjugation of the Regular Verb** *Prepare*

| **Singular** | **Plural** |
|---|---|

*Present Tense*

| I prepare | we prepare |
| you prepare | you prepare |
| he/she/it prepares | they prepare |

*Past Tense*

| I prepared | we prepared |
| you prepared | you prepared |
| he/she/it prepared | they prepared |

*Future Tense*

| I will (shall) prepare | we will (shall) prepare |
| you will prepare | you will prepare |
| he/she/it will prepare | they will prepare |

*Present Perfect Tense*

| I have prepared | we have prepared |
| you have prepared | you have prepared |
| he/she/it has prepared | they have prepared |

*Past Perfect Tense*

| I had prepared | we had prepared |
| you had prepared | you had prepared |
| he/she/it had prepared | they had prepared |

*Future Perfect Tense*

| I will (shall) have prepared | we will (shall) have prepared |
| you will have prepared | you will have prepared |
| he/she/it will have prepared | they will have prepared |

## The Six Tenses of Verbs

**Present Tense.**   To form the present tense of a verb, use its infinitive. To form the third-person singular, you may have to add *-s* or *-es* to the infinitive.

**Rule**   Use the present tense to show an action that takes place now, to show an action that is repeated regularly, or to show a condition that is true at any time.

Pat **swims** in the lake.

Pat **swims** before breakfast every day.

Pat discovered that the water in the lake **is** cold. [The water is *always* cold.]

**Rule** Use the present tense in statements about literary works or other works of art.

In the play *The Miracle Worker*, Helen Keller **begins** to speak after touching water.

**Rule** Use the present tense to make past events seem fresh and alive. When the present tense is used in this way, it is called the **historical present**.

Henry VIII **appears** to have sent his friends to the Tower of London without a second thought.

When speaking or writing informally, you can use the present tense form to describe an action that will occur in the future. Be certain to include a word or phrase that indicates the future.

Next June Pat **swims** the English Channel.

**Past Tense.**  To form the past tense of a regular verb, add *-d* or *-ed* to the infinitive. As you know, you should memorize the principal parts of irregular verbs to be able to form their past tenses correctly.

**Rule** Use the past tense to describe an action that occurred and was completed entirely in the past.

Pat **wanted** to play football before he started swimming.

Pat **swam** indoors before spring arrived.

**Future Tense.**  To form the future tense, use the auxiliary verb *will* or *shall* with the infinitive form of the main verb.

**Rule** Use the future tense to describe action that will occur in the future.

Pat **will prepare** for the Olympics for the next year.

**Will** Pat **make** the Olympic team?

**Present Perfect Tense.**   To form the present perfect tense, use the auxiliary verb *has* or *have* with the past participle of the main verb.

**Rule**   Use the present perfect tense to describe action that was completed either in the recent past or at an indefinite time in the past.

> Pat **has** just **finished** ten lengths of the pool.
>
> I **have watched** Pat train outdoors many times.

**Past Perfect Tense.**   To form the past perfect tense, use the auxiliary verb *had* with the past participle of the main verb.

**Rule**   Use the past perfect tense to describe an action that was completed by a certain time in the past or before another action was completed.

> past perf.                                                                  past
> Pat **had finished** his daily workout by the time the coach *left*.
>
> past perf.                                                              past
> Pat already **had made** plans for the workout before he *discovered*
> that the swimming pool was closed.

**Future Perfect Tense.**   To form the future perfect tense, use the auxiliary verbs *will have* or *shall have* with the past participle of the main verb.

**Rule**   Use the future perfect tense to describe action that will be completed before another action will be completed in the future.

> fut. perf.                                                              fut.
> Pat **will have found** a new coach by the time I *return*.

**Exercise 2   Verb Tense**   On your paper, write a sentence using the given verb in the tense indicated in parentheses. Use the nouns that are listed, and add modifying words and phrases to complete the sentence.

> **SAMPLE**      arrive (past); *nouns:* friends, party, family
> **ANSWER**      My friends arrived for the party before my family.

1. describe (present); *nouns:* newspaper, election, candidates
2. finish (future perfect); *nouns:* books, homework, television
3. celebrate (future); *nouns:* birthday, present, friend
4. want (past); *nouns:* computer, parents, software
5. begin (present perfect); *nouns:* comics, cartoons, games
6. fly (past perfect); *nouns:* crew, airplane, flight
7. travel (future); *nouns:* parks, forest, campground
8. eat (past); *nouns:* restaurant, dinner, menu
9. hear (present perfect); *nouns:* band, drummer, guitarist
10. promise (present); *nouns: Romeo and Juliet,* loyalty, love

## The Progressive and Emphatic Forms

**The Progressive Form.** To make the progressive form, use the appropriate tense of the verb *be* with the present participle of the main verb.

**Rule** Use the progressive form of a verb to describe continuing action.

PRESENT PROGRESSIVE
> Pat **is swimming** now.

PAST PROGRESSIVE
> Pat **was swimming** two weeks ago. [This was a continuing action, but it is now completed.]

FUTURE PROGRESSIVE
> Pat **will be swimming** for the next two weeks.

PRESENT PERFECT PROGRESSIVE
> Pat **has been swimming** for hours.

PAST PERFECT PROGRESSIVE
> Pat **had been swimming** before we came. [This was a continuing action, but it is now completed.]

FUTURE PERFECT PROGRESSIVE
> Pat **will have been swimming** for four hours by the time the meet begins.

When speaking or writing informally, you can use the present progressive to show future action. Be sure to include a word or a phrase that indicates the future.

> I **am swimming** with Pat *next week.*
>
> Pat **is going** to see his coach *before the day is over.*

**The Emphatic Form.**   To form the emphatic, use the present or the past tense of the verb *do* with the infinitive of the main verb.

**Rule**   Use the emphatic form to add force or emphasis to the present and past tenses of a verb.

> PRESENT EMPHATIC   Pat **does swim** every day.
>
> PAST EMPHATIC   Pat **did swim** every day.

**Exercise 3   Progressive and Emphatic Forms**   On your paper, write the required tense of the verb in parentheses for each of the following sentences.

> SAMPLE   The women's caucus __?__ today. (*meet*—present progressive)
>
> ANSWER   is meeting

1. Michele __?__ her bicycle to work. (*ride*—future progressive)
2. When he can find the time, Robert __?__ beautiful poetry. (*write* —present emphatic)
3. The children in our family __?__ the dishes since they were very small. (*wash*—present perfect progressive)
4. Photography as a hobby __?__ in popularity for many years. (*increase* —present perfect progressive)
5. The weather vane on grandmother's barn __?__ north before the wind changed. (*point*—past perfect progressive)
6. Jim __?__ to the supermarket when we picked him up in our car. (*walk*—past progressive)
7. Mike and his father often __?__ duets at piano recitals. (*play*—present emphatic)
8. By next Saturday, we __?__ our garden for a week. (*plant*—future perfect progressive)

9. Geraldo __?__ to catch the earlier flight. (*want*—past emphatic)
10. Planning our vacation __?__ much more time than I thought it would. (*take*—present progressive)

## Sequence of Tenses

**Consistency of Tenses.** When two or more actions take place at the same time, use verbs that are in the same tense, particularly when you write compound sentences and sentences with compound predicates. Also, use the same verb tense throughout a paragraph unless the meaning of the paragraph requires that you shift tense.

INCORRECT
future
The mayor **will award** the trophy to the winners,
pres.
and the manager of the radio station **presents** the check.

CORRECT
future
The mayor **will award** the trophy to the winners,
future
and the manager of the radio station **will present** the check.

In the following examples, notice what happens to the meaning of the sentence when the verb tenses are not consistent.

pres.     pres.
Susan **says** that she **is** hungry. [Susan is reporting that she is hungry now.]

pres.          past
Susan **says** that she **was** hungry. [Susan is reporting that she was hungry earlier.]

past     pres.
Susan **said** that she **is** hungry. [Susan has reported that she is hungry now.]

past     past
Susan **said** that she **was** hungry. [Susan has reported that she was hungry earlier.]

None of these sentences is incorrect, but each conveys an entirely different message. Because verbs and their tenses can change your intended meaning, use them correctly to indicate the right period of time.

**Shifts in Tense.**   Sometimes in your writing you will need to show movement from one time period to another, even within the same sentence. You will be able to shift tenses correctly if you understand the relationships between the tenses.

**Rule**  If two actions occurred at different times in the past, use the past perfect tense for the earlier action and the past tense for the later one. Sometimes, however, you may want to emphasize the closeness in time of the two events; if so, use the past tense for both verbs.

<table>
<tr><td>1st action<br>past perf.</td><td>2nd action<br>past</td></tr>
</table>

Michael **had hiked** for several hours before he **reached** the mountain top. [The actions occurred at different times in the past.]

<table>
<tr><td>1st action<br>past</td><td>2nd action<br>past</td></tr>
</table>

When the famous tenor **received** a standing ovation, he **sang** an encore. [Past actions were close, almost simultaneous, in time.]

**Rule**  If two actions occur in the present but one began in the past, use the present perfect tense for the earlier action and the present tense for the later one.

<table>
<tr><td>1st action<br>pres. perf.</td><td>2nd action<br>pres.</td></tr>
</table>

We **have been waiting** since early morning, and now we **are** anxious to leave.

**Rule**  If two actions will occur in the future, use the future perfect tense for the action that will take place first and the future tense for the action that will happen later.

<table>
<tr><td>1st action<br>future perf.</td><td>2nd action<br>future</td></tr>
</table>

Michael **will have been** on the mountain nearly all day and **will want** to eat immediately.

**Exercise 4   Shifts in Tense**   Read the following passage from Abraham Lincoln's "Gettysburg Address." On your paper, list each verb and indicate its tense. In a short paragraph, explain why the shifts in verb tense in Sentences 3 and 4 are necessary and effective.

(1) But, in a larger sense, we cannot dedicate—we cannot consecrate—we cannot hallow—this ground.   (2) The brave men, living and dead, who struggled here, have consecrated it, far above our poor power to add or detract.   (3) The world will little note, nor long remember what we say here, but it can never forget what they did here.   (4) It is for us the living, rather, to be dedicated here to the unfinished work which they who fought here have thus far so nobly advanced.   (5) It is rather for us to be here dedicated to the great task remaining before us—that from these honored dead we take increased devotion to that cause for which they gave the last full measure of devotion; that we here highly resolve that these dead shall not have died in vain; that this nation, under God, shall have a new birth of freedom; and that government of the people, by the people, for the people, shall not perish from the earth.

## 4.1c   Active and Passive Voice

A verb is in the **active voice** when the subject performs the action of the verb. Generally, the active voice is a more straightforward and more effective way to express action.

The President **vetoed** the bill as soon as he received it.

A verb is in the **passive voice** when the subject *receives* the action of the verb. Because overuse of the passive voice quickly becomes tedious and weakens the impact of your message, you should use it only when you want to emphasize the receiver of the action, or when the person or thing performing the action is unknown, or occasionally when there is no other clear way to write the sentence.

The bill **was vetoed** by the President as soon as he received it. [Emphasizes the subject, *bill*.]

The bill **was drafted** without the approval of the committee. [Person performing the action is unknown.]

The bill **is used** as a bad example for new legislators. [There is no other clear way to write the sentence.]

Form the passive voice by using a form of the verb *be* and the past participle of the main verb. Only transitive verbs (*page 16*) can be written in the passive voice. Notice that when the active voice is changed to the passive voice, the direct object becomes the subject and the subject becomes the object of a preposition.

ACTIVE VOICE       *Joan* asked a *question.*

PASSIVE VOICE      A *question* was asked by *Joan.*

**Intransitive verbs** (*page 16*) cannot be in the passive voice because they do not take objects.

When writing about a series of events that are in sequence, avoid shifting from the active voice to the passive voice.

INCORRECT      Jerry **asked** to make a phone call, **was given** permission, and **left** before the fire drill.

CORRECT        Jerry **asked** to make a phone call, **received** permission, and **left** before the fire drill.

**Exercise 5   Active and Passive Voice**   For each verb listed, write a sentence using the verb in the active voice. Then rewrite the sentence, changing the verb to the passive voice.

SAMPLE      purchase
ANSWER      Andrea purchased a desk calendar.
            A desk calendar was purchased by Andrea.

1. shake
2. grow
3. freeze
4. motivate
5. write

6. dance
7. break
8. calculate
9. nominate
10. steal

# 4.1d   Mood

Verbs have yet another function; you can use them to express mood. Although nearly all of your communication is in the indicative mood, you can make good use of the imperative and the subjunctive moods as you increase your ability to speak and write.

## The Indicative Mood and the Imperative Mood

**Rule**  Use the indicative mood to make statements of fact or to ask questions.

> The crosswalk **provides** a safe place for pedestrians to cross the busy street.
>
> **Did** you **use** the crosswalk?

**Rule**  Use the imperative mood to make a request or to give a command.

This mood can add force to what you say. In the imperative mood, the subject, *you,* is usually understood but not expressed.

> **Use** the crosswalk every time you have

## The Subjunctive Mood

In the subjunctive mood, you change the form of the verb to make doubtful or wishful statements, to express something that is contrary to fact, or to ask or order in a respectful manner. Of the three moods, the subjunctive mood is the least frequently used in conversation. It is also used in formal communication, particularly in parliamentary procedure.

> If Sheldon **were** unhappy, he would find another job. [doubtful]
> I wish that I **were** as talented as you. [wishful]
> If I **were** you, I would enter the contest. [contrary to fact]
> The president asks that the committee **remain** seated when she enters the room. [after *asks*]
> I move that the meeting **be** adjourned. [parliamentary]

You can see the differences between the indicative mood and the subjunctive mood in the partial conjugation of the verb *be* that follows.

|  | INDICATIVE | | SUBJUNCTIVE | |
|---|---|---|---|---|
| PRESENT | I am | we are | (if) I be | (if) we be |
| | you are | you are | (if) you be | (if) you be |
| | he is | they are | (if) he be | (if) they be |
| PAST | I was | we were | (if) I were | (if) we were |
| | you were | you were | (if) you were | (if) you were |
| | he was | they were | (if) he were | (if) they were |

**Exercise 6   Mood**   For each sentence, write whether the verbs or verb phrases in italic type are in the indicative mood, the imperative mood, or the subjunctive mood.

> **SAMPLE**     If she *were going,* she would be ready by now.
>
> **ANSWER**     Subjunctive mood

1. When the English navy *defeated* the Spanish Armada in 1588, a new chapter in English naval history *was begun.*
2. Throughout history, people *have tried* to learn the secrets of nature.
3. The mastery of French *will reward* a student not only with fluency in another language but also with an introduction to another culture.
4. If you *were* British, you would refer to trucks as "lorries."
5. If Sam *were* more attentive, he would hear the class announcements.
6. Please *count* the ballots again.
7. *Do* not *look* too long at the sun, or you *will hurt* your eyes.
8. "*Beware* the Jabberwock, my son!
    The jaws that bite, the claws that catch!
    *Beware* the Jubjub bird, and *shun*
    The frumious Bandersnatch!"
9. Etiquette requires that you *respond* to all invitations.
10. Dan has used his credit card so often that he *has reached* his credit limit.

**Assignment   Mood**   Rewrite the stanza from Lewis Carroll's poem "Jabberwocky" given in Sentence 8 of Exercise 6. In the first rewriting, put the italicized words into the indicative mood. The second time, put these words into the subjunctive mood. Write a paragraph in which you compare the effect of the different moods.

## Using the Three Moods

You are the president of a large corporation. You have had an idea about how to improve working conditions. (Your idea might be something like staggering working hours or starting a day-care center. Think of your own idea.)

Write a memo to the members of that division letting them know what you want done, when, and how. Choose the mood and voice that will best present your idea. Be certain that any shift in time sequence of the verbs that you use is necessary and is consistent with your intended meaning. Your memo should have the details necessary to give adequate information and instructions to your employees.

# 4.2 Subject-Verb Agreement

## 4.2a Singular and Plural Subjects and Verbs

**Rule**  A subject and its verb must agree in number.

Nouns, pronouns, and verbs change form to reflect number —singular (one) and plural (more than one). If the subject is singular, use a singular verb form. If the subject is plural, use a plural verb form.

SINGULAR
subj. verb
The *horse* **eats** oats as well as hay.

subj. verb
My *ambition* **is** to go to work for my father.

PLURAL
subj. verb
The *horses* **eat** oats as well as hay.

subj. verb
My *ambitions* **are** to go to college and to be a writer.

**123**

Although nouns ending in *s* are usually plural, verb forms ending in *s* are usually singular. There are, however, exceptions. When using either *I* or the singular *you* as a subject, do not use an *s* for the singular present tense verb.

SINGULAR        *I* **sing** only in the shower.

                You **play** the guitar very well.

**Verb Phrases.**    To make a verb phrase agree with its subject, use an auxiliary verb that agrees in number with the subject.

                                    verb phrase
SINGULAR        The technician **has suggested** a new method.

                                    verb phrase
PLURAL          The technicians **have suggested** a new method.

**Intervening Words and Phrases.**    Sometimes words or phrases come between a subject and its verb. For example, a prepositional phrase or an adjective clause that modifies the subject usually follows the subject, separating the subject from the verb. Such words and phrases do not change the number of the subject. Be sure to make the verb agree in number with the subject, not with some word in the intervening phrase.

SINGULAR        The *President,* along with his wife and children, **is** leaving for Camp David. [**Think:** President **is.**]

PLURAL          The *trails* in the forest **are** hidden by undergrowth. [**Think:** trails **are.**]

**Exercise 1   Subject-Verb Agreement**    On your paper, write the verb form in each sentence that agrees in number with the subject. Indicate whether the subject is singular or plural.

**SAMPLE**        Uncle Nicky, aboard a boat owned by two friends, (go, goes) fishing every Saturday.

**ANSWER**        goes—Singular

1. The outcome of the elections (do, does) not surprise me.
2. The singers in Barbara's trio (is, are) very good.
3. When the light (go, goes) on, we are expected to applaud.
4. The flowers by the fence (is, are) called phlox.

5. Both candidates from the Democratic party (has, have) never run for office before.

6. A thick blanket of smoke and fog (hang, hangs) over the city.

7. Brutus, along with Cassius and Casca, (was, were) plotting Caesar's assassination.

8. The owners of the colonial house across the street (run, runs) an antique store in Westwood.

9. Jerry (doesn't, don't) want to learn to play backgammon.

10. The animals in the cage (is, are) fed twice daily.

## 4.2b  Determining the Number of the Subject

Some subjects, such as compound subjects and indefinite pronouns, require your special attention in order to use the correct verb form with them.

### Compound Subjects

A **compound subject** (*page 45*) is made up of two or more subjects that are connected by *and, or, nor, either . . . or,* or *neither . . . nor.* Two factors determine the form of the verb that agrees in number with a compound subject: (1) which conjunction is used in the subject; and (2) whether the words in the compound subject are singular or plural.

**Rule**  Use a plural verb with most compound subjects connected by *and.*

> PLURAL  Gary, Paul, *and* Stacy **sing** bass in the school chorus.

**Rule**  Use a singular verb with a compound subject that refers to one person or one thing or to something that is generally considered as a unit—that is, plural in form but singular in meaning.

> SINGULAR  *Ham and eggs* **makes** a filling breakfast. [*Ham and eggs* is considered to be one dish.]
>
> *The chairman and chief executive officer* **drives** his car to his office every day. [*Chairman* and *chief executive officer* refer to the same person.]

**125**

**Rule**  Use a singular verb with a compound subject that is made up of singular nouns or pronouns connected by *or* or *nor*. Use a plural verb with a compound subject that is made up of plural nouns or pronouns connected by *or* or *nor*.

SINGULAR    Either *Monday or Tuesday* **is** Carla's birthday.

PLURAL    Neither the *candidates nor* their *aides* **are prepared** to answer.

**Rule**  When a compound subject consists of a singular subject and a plural subject connected by *or* or *nor,* use a verb that agrees in number with the subject that is closer to the verb in the sentence.

    sing.           ⌐— pl. —⌐
Either *Chet* or his *brothers* **sing** at family weddings.
      pl.      ⌐sing.⌐
Neither *oranges* nor *milk* **is** on my shopping list.

Although correct, the sentences may sound awkward. You can eliminate the awkwardness by rephrasing the sentences.

     ⌐sing.⌐                          ⌐—pl.—⌐
Either *Chet* **sings** at family weddings, or his *brothers* **do.**

  ⌐—pl.—⌐                            ⌐ sing. ⌐
*Oranges* **are** not on my shopping list, and neither **is** milk.

**Rule**  When the subject is both affirmative and negative, use a verb form that agrees in number with the affirmative part of the subject.

    aff.   ⌐neg.⌐
*Robert*, not I, **is going** to the play.
    aff.  ⌐—neg.⌐
*I*, not Robert, **am going** to the play.

## Indefinite Pronouns as Subjects

**Indefinite pronouns** (*page 11*) are pronouns that refer to people or things in general. Some indefinite pronouns are always singular and, therefore, always take singular verbs. The following are examples of singular indefinite pronouns.

| anybody | either | neither | one |
| anyone | everybody | nobody | somebody |
| anything | everyone | no one | someone |
| each | everything | nothing | something |

SINGULAR      *Everyone* **is waiting** for the governor to arrive.

Some indefinite pronouns are always plural and, therefore, always take plural verbs. *Both, few, many,* and *several* are the most common.

PLURAL        *Both* **go** to every home basketball game.

The indefinite pronouns *all, any, enough, more, most, none, plenty,* and *some* may be singular or plural, depending upon their antecedents (*page 8*). They are singular when they refer to a single person, place, or thing. They are plural when they refer to two or more persons, places, or things that are considered individuals.

SINGULAR      *All* (*Some, Most*) of the concert **was** enjoyable. [The antecedent is singular.]

PLURAL        *All* (*Some, Most*) of the tickets **have been sold.** [The antecedent is plural.]

An indefinite pronoun sometimes refers to a word that is understood rather than stated and that does not appear in the sentence.

Although *some* **was eaten** by the guests, *most* **was left** for you. [Food is being referred to; the words *some* and *most* are therefore singular in this case.]

**Exercise 2  Subject-Verb Agreement**  On your paper, write a sentence using a verb in the present tense that agrees with each of the following subjects.

| **SAMPLE** | Neither of us |
|---|---|
| **ANSWER** | Neither of us is sure of the date of the first moon landing. |

1. None of the contestants
2. The children and Helen
3. Everyone
4. Margaret and Susan
5. Anything

6. Several reasons
7. Ellen and Jean, not I,
8. A few of the exercises
9. Either Jim or the twins
10. Part of the movie

## Collective Nouns as Subjects

A **collective noun** (*page 4*) names a group or a collection of people or objects. Examples include *team, crowd, fleet, class,* and *jury.* Although singular in form, a collective noun may take either a singular or a plural verb, depending on its meaning in a sentence.

**Rule**   If a collective noun refers to a group as a whole, use a singular verb.

The *team* **plays** well. [The team is thought of as a whole.]

**Rule**   If a collective noun refers to individual members or parts of a group acting individually, use a plural verb.

The *team* **disagree** about what to do. [The members of the team are acting as individuals.]

## Nouns Ending in *s*

Some nouns are plural in form but singular in meaning. Although such nouns end in *s,* they refer to a single thing or to a unit and, therefore, take a singular verb. (Notice that removing the *s* does not make a singular noun.) Examples include *news, economics, mathematics,* and *physics.*

SINGULAR   The *news* about next year's schedule **is** good.

Other nouns ending in *s* take a plural verb, even though they are understood to refer to one thing. Some examples are *scissors, pliers, trousers, pants, spectacles, clothes, thanks,* and *congratulations.*

PLURAL   Your *clothes* **have been sent** to the cleaners.

Some nouns ending in *s* may be singular or plural, depending on their meaning in the sentence. Some examples include *politics, athletics,* and *headquarters.* Use a dictionary to find out whether a noun that is plural in form takes a singular or a plural verb.

SINGULAR    *Headquarters* **has asked** that you be transferred. [one unit]

PLURAL    Many *headquarters* **have computerized** their office procedures. [more than one headquarters]

**Exercise 3   Collective Nouns and Nouns Ending in *s***   On your paper, write the verb that correctly completes each sentence.

**SAMPLE**    Politics (has, have) interested her since childhood.
**ANSWER**    has

1. These fancy scissors (was, were) given to me as a graduation gift.
2. The committee (was, were) divided and could not agree.
3. Economics (is, are) intriguing to me.
4. Our team (go, goes) to the finals every year.
5. Vast riches (was, were) on board the lost ship.
6. My glasses (was, were) lost during the football game.
7. The committee (is, are) having problems.
8. (Is, Are) measles still a common childhood illness?
9. The flock (huddle, huddles) close to one another for warmth.
10. School athletics (has, have) undergone many changes in recent years.

## Titles and Names as Subjects

Titles of individual books, stories, plays, movies, television programs, musical compositions, and magazines take the singular form of the verb, even though the titles may contain plural words. The name of a country or of an organization also takes a singular verb when it refers to an entire country or group. (See Unit 5, "Mechanics," for rules on capitalization and underlining, or italics, of titles.)

*The House of the Seven Gables* **was written** in 1851.
**Is** Honduras in Central America or South America?
When **was** the Organization of American States **formed**?

## Words of Amount and Time

**Rule**   Use a singular verb with words and phrases that refer to single units: fractions, measurements, amounts of money, weights, volumes, or specific intervals of time when the intervals refer to a specific unit.

> *Three fourths* of the pie **is** missing.
> *Two hundred yards* **is** the distance from here to the pool.
> *Five minutes* **is** all I can spare.

**Rule**   Use a plural verb when the amount or the time is considered to be a number of separate units.

> *Five years* **have passed** since I've seen my cousins in Florida.
> *Two dimes* **were left** in the telephone booth.

When you use the words *the number* as a subject, use a singular verb. When you use *a number* as a subject, use a plural verb. Use the same approach when *variety* is the subject; *the variety* is usually a singular subject, and *a variety* is usually a plural subject.

> SINGULAR   *The number* of automobiles in Los Angeles **is** increasing all the time.
>
> PLURAL   *A number* of automobiles on this lot **are** for sale.

**Exercise 4   Titles, Names, Amounts, and Time**   On your paper, write the verb that correctly completes each sentence.

> SAMPLE   *Romeo and Juliet* (was, were) recently shown on television.
>
> ANSWER   was

1. The United States (has, have) become more energy conscious.
2. The number of men, women, and children that watch the annual parade (is, are) amazing.
3. Six feet (is, are) equal to one fathom.
4. *Science Fiction Annals* always (has, have) many interesting stories.
5. A number of sailors (has, have) been shipwrecked on that reef.

6. Three weeks (has, have) passed and still there has been no answer to my letter.

7. (Isn't, Aren't) *Travels with Charley* by John Steinbeck the book you wanted?

8. Ten dollars (was, were) the price of the cheapest ticket for the basketball play-offs.

9. The *Manchester News* (has, have) published daily since 1917.

10. Twenty minutes (was, were) the time allotted for answering each essay question.

## 4.2c    Other Agreement Problems

**Inverted Word Order.**    In sentences with inverted word order and in questions that begin with *Here* or *There,* you may have difficulty locating the subject because the verb comes before the subject. Mentally rearrange the sentence into its normal subject-verb order, and then make the verb agree in number with its subject.

Near the head of the table **sits** Judge *Peters.* [**Think:** Judge Peters sits.]

There **are** two *sets* of twins in my family. [**Think:** sets are.]

Where **is** the *scarf* that I made? [**Think:** scarf is.]

Why **have** the *dates* for the auction **been changed**? [**Think:** dates have been changed.]

If a compound subject follows the verb, mentally rearrange the sentence into normal order, and then follow the rules for making the verb agree in number with a compound subject (*page 125*).

SINGULAR     **Is** either Fay *or* Kay Granger **coming**? [**Think:** Fay or Kay is coming.]

PLURAL     There **are** the book *and* the magazine that you wanted. [**Think:** book and magazine are.]

**Sentences with Predicate Nominatives.**   Sometimes, using a predicate nominative (*page 56*) makes subject-verb agreement confusing, when the subject is singular and the predicate nominative is plural or when the predicate nominative is singular and the subject is plural.

**Rule**   Use a verb that agrees in number with the subject, not with the predicate nominative.

|  |  |
|---|---|
| INCORRECT | The museum's greatest treasure are its rubies. |
| CORRECT | The museum's greatest *treasure* **is** its *rubies*. [The subject, *treasure*, is singular.] |
| INCORRECT | Its rubies is the museum's greatest treasure. |
| CORRECT | Its *rubies* **are** the museum's greatest *treasure*. [The subject, *rubies,* is plural.] |

**Agreement in Adjective Clauses.**   When the subject of an adjective clause (*page 82*) is a relative pronoun, such as *who, which,* or *that,* determine whether the verb of the adjective clause should be singular or plural by finding the antecedent (*page 8*) of the relative pronoun. If the antecedent is singular, the verb in the adjective clause should be singular; if the antecedent is plural, the verb should be plural.

|  |  |
|---|---|
| SINGULAR | Susan is the only *one* of the swimmers who **runs** on the track team. [*Who* refers to *one*. Susan is the swimmer who runs.] |
| PLURAL | Susan is one of the *swimmers* who **run** on the track team. [*Who* refers to *swimmers*. Several swimmers run.] |

***Every* and *Many a*.**   *Every* and *many a* (or *many an*) are adjectives that emphasize separateness when they modify subjects. *Every actor* means "every single actor" not "all actors"; *many an actor* means that each actor should be considered separately.

**Rule**   Use a singular verb with a single or a compound subject modified by *every, many a,* or *many an.*

*Many a climber* **has failed** to reach the top of Mount McKinley.
*Every player and coach* **attends** the post-season dinner.

***One of those.*** Because the phrase *one of those* is usually followed by an adjective clause, the verb of the clause should agree in number with the antecedent of the subject of the clause.

Carol is the only *one of those girls* who **enjoys** singing.

Carol is *one of those people* who **enjoy** hot, humid weather.

**Exercise 5  Subject-Verb Agreement**  On your paper, write the correct verb for each of the following sentences. Beside each verb, write its subject.

> **SAMPLE**  How (does, do) these plants survive in this cold room?
>
> **ANSWER**  do—plants

1. Here (is, are) the instructions for assembling the bookcase.
2. Dirk and Elinor are the only ones in the variety show who (needs, need) hand-held microphones.
3. Exaggerations (is, are) one characteristic of the tall tale.
4. Every athlete (benefits, benefit) from a good conditioning program.
5. There (has, have) been an hour's delay due to the weather.
6. Lauren is one of those people who (likes, like) to stay up late.
7. When (does, do) the committee plan to distribute the yearbooks?
8. The Portuguese man-of-war (is, are) really several organisms rather than a single animal.
9. Many an adolescent and adult (seems, seem) reluctant to take advice from someone older.
10. This is a copy of the guidelines that (was, were) written at the last meeting.

**Assignment  Subject-Verb Agreement**  On your paper, write ten interesting sentences, using one of the following phrases in each. If the subject and verb in each phrase agree, you can use the phrase as it appears in the list; if the subject and verb do not agree, you should correct the agreement problem before you use the phrase in a sentence.

1. Steven and Bill has found
2. politics are
3. holidays is
4. many a story is
5. several parts of the puzzle is
6. one of those friends who is
7. *Twice-told Tales* are
8. two dollars was
9. the latest news is
10. either Jim or Sara write

# 4.3   Correct Use of Pronouns

## 4.3a   Pronoun Antecedents

As you know, the antecedent of a pronoun is the word that it refers to or replaces in a sentence. A pronoun and its antecedent must agree in number, gender, and person (*page 9*).

### Agreement in Number

**Rule**   Use a singular pronoun to refer to or to replace a singular antecedent. Use a plural pronoun to refer to or to replace a plural antecedent.

| SINGULAR PRONOUNS | PLURAL PRONOUNS |
|---|---|
| I, me, my, mine | we, us, our, ours |
| you, your, yours | you, your, yours |
| he, him, his | they, them, their, theirs |
| she, her, hers | |
| it, its | |

SINGULAR   *Gwen* sent **her** brother a postcard from Miami.

PLURAL   The *boys* made **their** lunches before leaving home.

**Rule**   Use a plural pronoun to refer to or to replace two or more singular antecedents joined by *and*.

*Elaine and Morgan* are painting **their** house. **They** hope to finish by the end of the week.

**Rule**  Use a singular pronoun to refer to two or more singular antecedents joined by *or* or *nor*.

Neither *Leon nor Marty* remembered to bring **his** guitar.

**Indefinite Pronouns as Antecedents.**  The indefinite pronouns listed here are singular in meaning. When you use them as antecedents, use singular pronouns to refer to them or to replace them.

| | | | |
|---|---|---|---|
| anybody | everybody | nobody | somebody |
| anyone | everyone | no one | someone |
| anything | everything | nothing | something |
| each | much | one | |
| either | neither | other | |

SINGULAR  *Everyone* is supposed to buy **her** own track shoes.

Sometimes the intended meaning of a singular indefinite pronoun is clearly plural. In those cases, use a plural pronoun to refer to the antecedent or to replace it so that your sentence will be logical. For example, it does not make sense to use a singular pronoun in the following sentence.

UNCLEAR  When *everyone* saw Rita's sign, **he** yelled "Surprise!"

Because the antecedent *everyone* really means *all* and not *every single one,* you should make the pronoun plural or rewrite the sentence to avoid the awkward construction.

CLEAR  When *everyone* saw Rita's sign, **they** yelled "Surprise!"

BETTER  When *all* of the guests saw Rita's sign, **they** yelled "Surprise!"

Some indefinite pronouns, such as *several, both, few,* and *many,* are plural in meaning. When they are antecedents, use plural pronouns to refer to them or to replace them.

PLURAL  Because *both* tied for first place in the hundred-meter dash, **they** were each given a gold medal.

The following indefinite pronouns can be either singular or plural. When they are antecedents, use either singular or plural pronouns to refer to them or to replace them, depending on the meaning of the sentence.

| all | enough | most | plenty |
|-----|--------|------|--------|
| any | more | none | some |

SINGULAR   *Some* of my coin collection has lost **its** value. [*Some* refers to *collection,* which is singular; *its* is possessive and refers to *Some.*]

PLURAL   *Some* of these coins have lost **their** value. [*Some* refers to *coins*, which is plural; *their* refers to *Some.*]

**Collective Nouns as Antecedents.**   When a collective noun (*page 4*) is used as an antecedent, you must first determine whether its meaning is singular or plural in the sentence. If it is singular, use singular pronouns to refer to it or to replace it; if it is plural, use plural pronouns.

SINGULAR   The book *club* decided on **its** topics for future meetings. [The club is acting as a group.]

PLURAL   The book *club* obtained **their** books from several local stores and the library. [The club acted as individuals when buying books.]

## Agreement in Gender

Nouns and pronouns are masculine, feminine, or neuter in gender (*page 9*). The masculine pronouns are *he, him,* and *his;* the feminine pronouns are *she, her,* and *hers*; and the neuter pronouns —those referring to antecedents that are neither masculine nor feminine—are *it* and *its*.

**Rule**   Use a pronoun that agrees with its antecedent in gender.

FEMININE   *Janet* took **her** parents to the opera.

MASCULINE   *Mr. Feldman* closed **his** office early today.

NEUTER   The *house* was interesting because of **its** secret passageways.

When it is not clear whether a singular antecedent is masculine or feminine, you can often use the phrase *his or her* to show that the antecedent could be either.

> *Everyone* will recite **his or her** favorite poem.
> A *photographer* should take good care of **his or her** camera.

Sometimes, using two pronouns to refer to an antecedent is awkward. Instead, you can rewrite the sentence so that the antecedent and all words that refer to it or that replace it are plural; or, if it sounds all right, you can sometimes repeat the noun that is the antecedent.

| | |
|---|---|
| AWKWARD | A *teacher* should be sure to consult **his or her** handbook. |
| BETTER | *Teachers* should be sure to consult **their** handbooks. |
| BETTER | The *teacher* should be sure to consult the **teacher's** handbook. |

## Agreement in Person

Pronouns are in the first person, the second person, or the third person (*page 9*). First-person pronouns refer to or replace the speaker(s), second-person pronouns refer to or replace the person(s) being spoken to, and third-person pronouns refer to the person(s) or thing(s) being spoken about.

**Rule**   Use a pronoun that agrees in person with its antecedent.

| | |
|---|---|
| FIRST PERSON | *I* fed **my** dog before leaving. |
| SECOND PERSON | *Mother,* will **you** go with me to the doctor's office? |
| THIRD PERSON | *Henry* asked **his** boss for a raise. |

When the indefinite pronoun *one* is an antecedent, use third-person singular pronouns to refer to it or to replace it. You can also repeat the indefinite pronoun in some instances.

> *One should learn from* **his or her** mistakes. [not *their* mistakes or *your* mistakes.]
> When *one* goes out of the country, **one** must take a passport.

**Note:**   In general, do not use *he* to represent both *he* and *she*. Instead, repeat the noun or pronoun that is the antecedent or rewrite the sentence to make both the antecedent and the pronoun plural.

## Agreement of Reflexive and Intensive Pronouns

Reflexive and intensive pronouns (*page 10*) are formed by adding either *-self* or *-selves* to personal pronouns. Reflexive and intensive pronouns also must agree with their antecedents in number, gender, and person.

REFLEXIVE        *We* worked by **ourselves** until the rest of the class showed up.

INTENSIVE        The *pilot* **himself** greeted the passengers as they boarded the plane.

Reflexive and intensive pronouns must always be used with antecedents. Do not use them alone in place of a noun or a personal pronoun.

INCORRECT        *Harriet* and **myself** will meet you downtown.

CORRECT          *Harriet* and **I** will meet you downtown.

(For more information on the correct use of reflexive and intensive pronoun forms, see the Usage Notes on pages 167 and 170.)

**Exercise 1   Pronoun Antecedents**   On your paper, write the antecedent and the correct pronoun for each of the following sentences.

SAMPLE        Someone dropped (their, his, his or her) notebook.
ANSWER        Someone—his or her

1. I discovered that the car had a mysterious scratch on (his, her, its) left front fender.
2. When everyone heard that Jim had won, (they, he, he or she) cheered enthusiastically.

3. Each of the men drives (his, their) children to school.
4. Neither Sally nor Liz could remember (her, their) lines at dress rehearsal.
5. The President addressed the conference participants (itself, themselves).
6. Either Todd or Daniel can lend us (his, their) ladder over the weekend.
7. The members of the committee passed a resolution commending (itself, themselves).
8. Some of my friends can drive (himself, herself, themselves) to school.
9. When everyone heard the crash, (he, he or she, they) ran to the window.
10. Some of these old teaspoons have scratches on (its, their) handles.
11. One should learn from (your, their, one's) mistakes.
12. The ensemble gave a concert honoring (its, their) founder.
13. Both legislators represent (his or her, their) districts well.
14. No one had forgotten (his or her, their) assignment.
15. A few of the contestants needed to calm (his or her, their) nerves.

## 4.3b   Pronoun Case

A **pronoun** changes its form to show its grammatical use in a sentence. These changes in form divide pronouns into three groups, or **cases:** nominative, objective, and possessive.

|  | SINGULAR | PLURAL |
|---|---|---|
| NOMINATIVE CASE | I<br>you<br>he, she, it | we<br>you<br>they |
| OBJECTIVE CASE | me<br>you<br>him, her, it | us<br>you<br>them |
| POSSESSIVE CASE* | my, mine<br>your, yours<br>his, her, hers, its | our, ours<br>your, yours<br>their, theirs |

\* The words *my, your, his, her, its, our,* and *their* are sometimes called pronominal adjectives.

## Pronouns in the Nominative Case ▬▬▬▬▬▬▬

**Rule**  Use the nominative case when a pronoun acts as a subject or a predicate nominative (*page 56*).

SUBJECT

**She** asked Dr. Ferris to sit down.

Should **I** go with you now?

PREDICATE NOMINATIVE

It was **she** who answered the telephone.

The person chosen to greet the President was **I**.

**Rule**  Use the nominative case when a pronoun acts as an appositive to a subject or to a predicate nominative.

APPOSITIVE TO A SUBJECT

$$\underset{\text{subj.}}{} \quad \overset{\text{appos.}}{\rule{2cm}{0.4pt}}$$

The *winners*, **he and Peter**, both received trophies. [**Think:** He and Peter received trophies.]

APPOSITIVE TO A PREDICATE NOMINATIVE

$$\underset{\text{P.N.}}{} \quad \overset{\text{appos.}}{\rule{2cm}{0.4pt}}$$

The winners are *brothers*, **he and Peter**. [**Think:** The winners are he and Peter.]

## Pronouns in the Objective Case ▬▬▬▬▬▬▬

**Rule**  Use the objective case when a pronoun acts as a direct object (*page 51*), an indirect object (*page 52*), an object of a preposition (*page 28*), a subject of an infinitive clause (*page 76*), or an object of an infinitive clause.

DIRECT OBJECT

Carlton asked **me** about the game.

INDIRECT OBJECT

Please make **me** a cup of tea.

OBJECT OF A PREPOSITION

These seats are reserved for **us**.

SUBJECT OF AN INFINITIVE CLAUSE

┌─────inf. clause─────┐
Her coach wants **them** to go to the showers.

OBJECT OF AN INFINITIVE CLAUSE

┌────inf. clause────┐
John wanted to ask **them** for a ride.

**Rule** Use the objective case when a pronoun acts as an appositive to a direct or indirect object or to the object of a preposition.

D.O.   ┌────appos.────┐
Claire enjoys her two *brothers*, **Freddie and him**. [**Think:** Claire enjoys him.]

I.O.   ┌───appos.───┐
I gave my *friends*, **Peg and him**, a new record album. [**Think:** I gave him a new album.]

obj. of
prep.   ┌───appos.───┐
Mario rode home with his aunts, **Janet and her**. [**Think:** Mario rode with her.]

## Compound Constructions with Pronouns

Pronouns can be troublesome in a compound subject, in a compound direct or indirect object, or in a compound object of a preposition. You can determine which case to use by saying the sentence to yourself, leaving out the conjunction and the noun or the other pronoun in the compound construction. After determining how the pronoun functions alone, decide whether the nominative case or the objective case is correct.

She meant **you and me** to share the grapes. [**Think:** She meant me.]

Please stand over there with **Lily and her**. [**Think:** with her.]

Won't you join **my guests and me** in welcoming Senator Payne? [**Think:** join me.]

Weren't **you and he** supposed to present the awards? [**Think:** He was supposed to present the awards.]

**Exercise 2   Nominative Case and Objective Case**   On your paper, write the correct pronoun(s) for each of the following sentences. Beside each pronoun, write whether it is the nominative case or the objective case.

> **SAMPLE**      Frank and (I, me) went to the gym.
>
> **ANSWER**      I—Nominative case

1. Ms. Willis praised (she, her) for the perfection of her craftsmanship.
2. The catchers, (he, him) and Marcus, will be the co-captains.
3. It was (he, him) who won first prize.
4. Please hand (I, me) the scorecard from the last game.
5. Sheryl and (I, me) invited Megan to go to the concert with (we, us).
6. Standing over the grate in the middle of the sidewalk, (they, them) could feel the vibrations from the subway beneath (they, them).
7. The doctors were two surgeons, (she, her) and Keith, who stopped at the scene of the accident.
8. Mr. Dwyer asked (they, them) to work an additional four hours next week.
9. The movie gave (we, us), Roseann and (I, me), a creepy feeling.
10. Because Helen was well qualified, Carlotta was going to nominate (she, her) for class president.

## Pronouns in the Possessive Case

Possessive pronouns show to whom or to what something belongs. These pronouns do not need apostrophes to show possession.

**Rule**   Use the possessive pronouns *mine, yours, his, hers, its, ours,* and *theirs* to replace and to refer to nouns.

You can use possessive pronouns as either subjects, predicate nominatives, direct or indirect objects, objects of prepositions, or appositives. In other words, you can use them in any way that you would use a noun.

> SUBJECT                    **His** is the third *house* on the left.
>
> PREDICATE NOMINATIVE       These cowboy *boots* are **hers**.
>
> DIRECT OBJECT              Did you find **yours**?

| INDIRECT OBJECT | She gave her parents a check; I gave **mine** a gift certificate. |
| OBJECT OF A PREPOSITION | Charles is a friend of **mine**. |
| APPOSITIVE | I want these *books*, **hers and mine**, taken back to the library. |

**Rule**  Use the possessive pronouns* *my, your, his, her, its, our,* and *their* to modify nouns.

**My** dog lost its collar and license.

**Rule**  Use possessive pronouns to modify gerunds.

**Gerunds** are *-ing* verb forms that are used as nouns (*page 73*). Because they function as nouns, you should use the possessive forms of nouns and pronouns to modify them.

They have complained about **your** practicing the trumpet after nine o'clock. [*Your* is used instead of *you* because it is not *you* about whom they are complaining; it is the *practicing—your practicing.*]

I am sorry that **my** arriving late has caused problems for you. [*My* is used instead of *me* because it is not *me* about whom I am sorry; it is the *arriving—my arriving.*]

**Exercise 3  Possessive Pronouns**  On your paper, write the correct pronoun for each of the following sentences. Indicate the person, the number, and the case of each pronoun and tell how it is used in the sentence.

SAMPLE  (You, Your) leaving so soon was a surprise.

ANSWER  Your—second person; could be singular or plural; possessive case; used as an adjective to modify the gerund *leaving.*

1. My parents were surprised at (me, my) making breakfast.
2. Are (your, yours) the glasses with the black frames?
3. Did you know about (them, their) flying to Colorado?
4. He was pleased by (us, our) volunteering to shovel the snow.
5. The house on the corner of Jefferson and Pine is (our, ours).

* These possessive pronouns are sometimes called **pronominal adjectives**.

**143**

## *Who* and *Whom*

You can use the forms of the word *who* either as interrogative pronouns (*page 10*) or as relative pronouns (*page 11*). The way that you use the pronoun determines which form or case of the word you should choose. *Who* and *whoever* are in the nominative case; *whom* and *whomever* are in the objective case; *whose* is in the possessive case. You will probably have little difficulty using the possessive form, but you should pay special attention to the differences between *who* and *whom*.

**Who** and **Whom** as **Interrogative Pronouns.**   Who and *whom* are interrogative pronouns when they introduce questions. You can easily determine whether to use *who* (the nominative case) or *whom* (the objective case) by mentally turning the question into a statement.

**Rule**   When an interrogative pronoun acts as a subject or as a predicate nominative, use *who*. When it acts as a direct object or as an object of a preposition, use *whom*.

NOMINATIVE CASE

subj.

**Who** closed the window?

subj.

**Who** can name the capitals of all the states?

OBJECTIVE CASE

D.O.

**Whom** did you invite? [**Think:** You did invite *whom*.]

obj.
of prep.

To **whom** do you wish to speak? [**Think:** You wish to speak to *whom*.]

If the interrogative pronoun *who* or *whom* is followed by an interrupting phrase, such as *did she think,* mentally rearrange the sentence to eliminate the interrupting phrase. Then choose the correct form by determining the use of the interrogative pronoun in the sentence.

subj.
**Who** does she think is watching her dog? [**Think**: Who is watching?]

D.O.
**Whom** do you suppose she will invite to the party? [**Think**: She will invite whom.]

In informal writing and conversation, *who* is commonly used to ask a question, regardless of whether the nominative or the objective case is needed. In most formal conversation and writing, however, you should follow the rules for using the nominative case, *who,* and the objective case, *whom.*

INFORMAL     **Who** did you see at the office?

FORMAL       **Whom** will you accompany to the conference?

### *Who* and *Whom* as Relative Pronouns.

When a form of the word *who* introduces a subordinate clause (*page 80*), it is called a **relative pronoun**. Your choice of the form to use depends on the way that it is used in the subordinate clause only, not in the sentence as a whole.

**Rule**   If a relative pronoun serves as the subject of the subordinate clause, use *who* or *whoever*. If it serves as an object within the subordinate clause, use *whom* or *whomever*.

```
                    ┌──────────sub. clause──────────┐
                    │subj.   verb                    │
```
The man **who** *broke* the four-minute mile was Roger Bannister. [*Who* is the subject of the verb in the subordinate clause.]

```
                    ┌──────────sub. clause──────────┐
                    │  subj.     verb                │
```
There is room for **whoever** *wishes* to spend the night. [The subordinate clause is the object of the preposition *for*. *Whoever* is the subject of the verb *wishes* in the subordinate clause, not the object of the preposition *for*.]

```
                  ┌──────sub. clause ──────┐
                  │  obj. of                │
                  │  prep. subj. ┌──verb──┐ │
```
The person to **whom** you are referring does not live at this address. [**Think**: you are referring **to whom**. *Whom* is the object of the preposition *to* in the subordinate clause.]

```
                    ┌──────────── sub. clause ────────────┐
                    ┌ D.O. ┐
```
The Worths welcomed **whomever** their children brought home.
[**Think**: children brought **whomever**. *Whomever* is the object of the
verb *brought* in the clause.]

**Exercise 4   *Who* and *Whom***   On your paper, write the pronoun that is correct in formal usage. Then, tell how the pronoun is
used in the sentence.

> **SAMPLE**      To (who, whom) should I address the envelope?
>
> **ANSWER**      whom—Object of the preposition *to*

1. "(Who, Whom) can tell me the name of the first Secretary of State?"
   asked Ms. Drake.
2. There are several candidates (who, whom) I believe are qualified.
3. Give the message to (whoever, whomever) answers.
4. (Who, whom) do you think is this year's most outstanding senior?
5. Lester, (who, whom) had never been to Montana before, was delighted to receive an invitation from his aunt in Bozeman.
6. (Whoever, Whomever) wants to audition for the part should be at the
   theater this afternoon.
7. You'll never guess (who, whom) I saw in the market.
8. The man for (who, whom) this car was ordered no longer lives here.
9. I would be happy to interview (whoever, whomever) you recommend.
10. One of the persons (who, whom) I admire is Madame Curie.

## *We* and *Us* in Appositive Phrases

Often *we* and *us* are used in appositive phrases, such as *we
students* or *us actors*. Because an appositive explains or renames the
word with which it is in apposition, you must first determine how that
word, and therefore the phrase, functions in the sentence. If the
appositive phrase is the subject or the predicate nominative, use the
nominative case, *we*; if the phrase is an object, use the objective case,
*us*. In difficult instances, try saying the sentence to yourself without
the noun in the appositive phrase.

> **We students** want to take charge of the music festival. [**Think**: We
> want to take charge. *We*, as the subject, is in the nominative case;
> students is an appositive to *We*.]

The awards ceremony for **us actors** went very smoothly. [**Think**: The awards ceremony for us went. . . . *Us,* the object of the preposition *for,* is in the objective case; *actors* is an appositive to *us.*]

## Pronouns in Comparisons

In some comparisons using *than* or *as,* part of the phrase or clause is implied, not stated. To choose the correct pronoun case, mentally supply the missing words and determine how the pronoun is used.

Melanie swims much faster than I. [**Think**: faster *than I swim. I* is the subject of the clause *than I swim.*]

Because the correct pronoun for an incomplete comparison sometimes depends on your intention, make your choice carefully. Notice the change in meaning as the pronoun changes in the following examples:

NOMINATIVE     We visit Juan as often as they. [**Think**: *as often as they do; they* is the subject of the clause.]

OBJECTIVE     We visit Juan as often as them. [**Think**: *as often as we visit them; them* is the object of the clause.]

**Exercise 5**   **Pronoun Case: Comparisons**   On your paper, write the correct pronouns to complete the following sentences.

    **SAMPLE**      I have traveled more than (they, them).
    **ANSWER**      they

1. Kathleen has always played better than (he, him).
2. Do you think she fields the ball better than (I, me)?
3. I want to go to London as much as (she, her).
4. Alan exercises more than (we, us) or (they, them).
5. My father is as good a cook as (she, her).

**Exercise 6**   **Pronoun Case: Appositives**   On your paper, write five sentences, using each of the following appositive phrases in the way indicated. Be certain that the pronoun *we* or *us* is in the correct case according to its use in the sentence.

| | |
|---|---|
| **SAMPLE** | (*we, us*) *violinists* as a subject of the sentence |
| **ANSWER** | We violinists will be the first to rehearse. |

1. (*we, us*) *biologists* as an object of a preposition
2. (*we, us*) *motorcyclists* as a subject of a subordinate clause
3. (*we, us*) *politicians* as a subject of the sentence
4. (*we, us*) *patients* as a direct object
5. (*we, us*) *athletes* as an indirect object

## 4.3c   Correct Pronoun Reference

If a pronoun does not refer clearly to its antecedent, your reader or your listener may become confused. Rephrase any sentence that makes an unclear reference.

**Rule**   Avoid using a pronoun that could refer to more than one antecedent.

| | |
|---|---|
| UNCLEAR | When I tried to put a bulb in the lamp, **it** broke. [What broke? The antecedent of *it* is unclear.] |
| CLEAR | The bulb broke when I tried to put **it** in the lamp. |

**Rule**   Avoid using the pronoun *it, they, you,* or *your* without a clear antecedent.

The following examples show how to avoid an indefinite reference. You can usually replace the pronoun with a noun.

| | |
|---|---|
| UNCLEAR | In this article **it** says that dolphins have no sense of smell. [Who is *it*? The pronoun has no antecedent.] |
| CLEAR | This **article** says that dolphins have no sense of smell. |

If possession is not involved, do not use the pronoun *your* in place of the article *a, an,* or *the.*

| | |
|---|---|
| AVOID | Most of your hospital employees are protected by an insurance plan. |
| USE | Most hospital employees are protected by an insurance plan. |

**Rule**  Avoid using *which, it, this,* and *that* to refer to ideas that are not clearly stated.

The following example demonstrates how to avoid making such general references.

| | |
|---|---|
| UNCLEAR | The room was hot, and I was wearing a heavy sweater. This made me sleepy. [The pronoun *this* has no clear antecedent. Instead, *this* refers generally to the ideas in the previous sentence.] |
| CLEAR | The hot room and my heavy sweater made me sleepy. |
| CLEAR | Because the room was hot and I was wearing a heavy sweater, I became sleepy. |

**Exercise 7  Pronoun References**  On your paper, rewrite the following sentences, making each pronoun reference clear and accurate.

| | |
|---|---|
| **SAMPLE** | Next summer they are going to hire more lifeguards for this beach. |
| **ANSWER** | Next summer the parks commission will hire more lifeguards for this beach. |

1. Secretary of State Hillford bowed to Prime Minister Smythe when he was introduced to her.
2. Why don't they put a traffic light at that corner?
3. I like hiking and my sister likes scuba diving, which is why we take separate vacations.
4. On the radio it said that the game had been postponed because of the rain.
5. Take the curtains from the living room windows and wash them.
6. I had to change a tire on my bicycle; this made me late for school.
7. The law requires that your United States citizens report to the customs office.
8. I certainly hope that the bus won't be late because it will keep us from making our connections.

**Assignment   Pronoun Usage**   Read the following paragraph. Number your paper from 1–6. List the pronouns in each sentence and indicate their use, case, and person. If there are no pronouns in a sentence, write *None*.

(1) He used to go over to the schoolhouse after the children left, every afternoon, and the schoolteacher—a young man afraid of the big boys—would talk to him and show him books, books he would like Revere to read later on, books with colored bindings, with gold letters, in a glass case at the front of the room.   (2) Chalk dust would hang in the silent air.   (3) When Revere spoke it would be slowly and politely, not the way he bawled orders at home. (4) He could never understand why the young man did not laugh at him.   (5) He wanted to learn; he felt the young man's strange desire to teach him; but when it was time to speak or read—why, Revere would stare at the print and at his big thumbs on either page, and everything would get mixed up.   (6) Revere, filled with shame, could not look up at the teacher.

Joyce Carol Oates, "By the North Gate"

**Establishing Point of View**

You are the commander of a submarine on assignment under the ice near the North Pole. Write a one-page account of a day as if you were making an entry in the ship's log. Use third-person point of view. Then, write an account of the same day's events for your personal journal, using first-person point of view. Make sure that each pronoun that you use in the two accounts agrees with its antecedent and is consistent with the point of view from which you are writing.

# 4.4 Correct Use of Modifiers

## 4.4a Comparison of Modifiers

You can compare two or more persons or things by changing adjective and adverb forms. These forms make possible three degrees of comparison: positive, comparative, and superlative.

### The Three Degrees of Comparison

A modifier in the **positive degree** compares nothing; it merely assigns some quality to a person, a thing, an action, or an idea. A modifier in the **comparative degree** compares one thing with another. A modifier in the **superlative degree** compares one thing with two or more others.

| | ADJECTIVES |
|---|---|
| POSITIVE | This restaurant serves a **hearty** meal. |
| COMPARATIVE | This restaurant serves a **heartier** meal than the drive-in does. |
| SUPERLATIVE | This restaurant serves the **heartiest** meal in town. |

| | ADVERBS |
|---|---|
| POSITIVE | Gwen throws the ball **hard.** |
| COMPARATIVE | Gwen throws the ball **harder** than I do. |
| SUPERLATIVE | Gwen throws the ball **hardest** of all. |

### Using Comparisons Correctly

**Rule** Add the suffix *-er* to form the comparative and the suffix *-est* to form the superlative of modifiers of one or two syllables.

In some cases, in order to form the comparative modifier correctly, you must drop a final *e,* double a final consonant, or change a final *y* to *i* before adding the suffix. (See Unit 15, "Spelling Skills," pages 568–577.)

great, greater, greatest
late, later, latest
big, bigger, biggest

pretty, prettier, prettiest
cosy, cosier, cosiest

**Rule**   Use *more* to show the comparative and *most* to show the superlative for all three-syllable words, some two-syllable words that would otherwise be difficult to pronounce, and all adverbs ending in *ly*.

> curious, more curious, most curious
> peaceful, more peaceful, most peaceful
> softly, more softly, most softly

**Rule**   Use *less* and *least* to form the comparative and superlative degrees of comparisons showing less.

> physical, less physical, least physical
> difficult, less difficult, least difficult
> diplomatically, less diplomatically, least diplomatically

Some modifiers are irregular and do not form comparisons in a standard way. You should memorize them so that you can use them correctly.

| | |
|---|---|
| bad, worse, worst | little (adv.), less, least |
| far, farther, farthest | many, more, most |
| far, further, furthest | much, more, most |
| good, better, best | well, better, best |
| ill, worse, worst | |

**Rule**   Avoid double comparisons. Use either *more* or *most* with an adjective or adverb or use the appropriate suffix. Do not use both forms of comparison for the same word.

INCORRECT     He is the **most happiest** person I know.

CORRECT     He is the **happiest** person I know.

**Rule**   Avoid incomplete comparisons. Be careful to indicate clearly the persons, places, things, or ideas that you are comparing.

To avoid being unclear or misleading, use the comparative degree and the word *other* or *else* when you compare one member of a group with the rest of the group.

| UNCLEAR | Mandy is *faster* **than anyone** on the team. [This sentence says either that Mandy isn't on the team or that she is on the team and is faster than herself.] |
|---------|---|
| CLEAR   | Mandy is *faster* **than anyone else** on the team. [Mandy is on the team, and she is faster than any other member of the team.] |

**Rule**  In a compound comparison, use the words *as . . . as* or *as . . . as . . . than* to complete the comparison.

A **compound comparison** includes both the positive and the comparative degrees of a modifier and really makes two statements. The positive degree indicates that the things compared are at least equal or similar; the comparative degree indicates that they may, in fact, be different.

His aim is **as** good **as**, if not *better* **than**, Celia's.

Use commas to set off the second part of a compound comparison from the rest of the sentence. You still have a complete sentence if you remove the second, or parenthetical, part of the comparison.

| INCORRECT | I worked **as** *hard* if not *harder* **than** Jim did. |
|-----------|---|
| CORRECT   | I worked **as** *hard* **as**, if not *harder* **than**, Jim did. |
| CORRECT   | I worked **as** *hard* **as** Jim did, if not *harder*. |

**Rule**  Avoid making comparisons that are illogical because of missing or faulty elements.

An illogical comparison makes a comparison between things that cannot logically be compared. If there is a chance that your reader or listener will misunderstand your meaning, rephrase the comparison to include all of the important words.

| ILLOGICAL | His *talent* for drawing was almost **as impressive as** *Vincent van Gogh*. [Talent cannot be compared to a man.] |
|-----------|---|
| CLEAR     | His *talent* for drawing was almost **as impressive as** *Vincent van Gogh's*. [**Think:** His talent is almost as impressive as van Gogh's talent.] |

Certain adjectives have no comparative degree because they express an absolute condition, such as *perfect, unique, dead, round, full,* and *empty.* Logically, nothing can be "more perfect," "deadest," or "least empty." When you use these words in comparisons, use the forms *more nearly* or *most nearly.*

The circle that Chris drew is **more nearly round** than Joan's.

Greg's speech was the **most nearly perfect** of all the contestants'.

**Exercise 1   Correct Use of Comparisons**   On your paper, write the correct form in each of the following sentences.

SAMPLE       He is the (taller, tallest) of the two.

ANSWER        taller

1. Hardly anyone takes a car to the shopping center because riding the bus is (cheap, cheaper, cheapest).
2. The (good, better, best) debator in the group is always Dan.
3. That problem is easy, but this one is (easier, easiest).
4. Whatever you buy, always look for the (better, best) bargain.
5. I consider sincerity the (more, most) important characteristic to look for in a friend.
6. My test grade was the (high, highest) in the class.
7. Of all the musical acts, George's was the (less, least) entertaining.
8. Your idea is the (sillier, silliest) of the two.
9. Some consider self-sufficiency to be the (more, most) important goal in life.
10. I work (easier, more easily, easiest) in the morning than in the evening.

## 4.4b   Placement of Phrases and Clauses

**Rule**   To avoid unclear sentences, place modifying phrases and clauses as close as possible to the words that they modify.

Misplacement of phrases and clauses can lead to ridiculously unclear sentences, often with a humorous result. To revise a sentence that contains a misplaced modifier, first identify the word to be modified. Then move the modifying phrase or clause as close as possible to the word that it modifies, while maintaining the intended meaning of the sentence.

UNCLEAR    The small boy ate a hot dog **wearing a yellow shirt**.

CLEAR      The small *boy* **wearing a yellow shirt** ate a hot dog.

UNCLEAR    Mr. Wilson blamed Richard for the damage done to the lawn mower **last evening**. [What happened last evening?]

CLEAR      Mr. Wilson blamed Richard for the damage *done* **last evening** to the lawn mower. [The damage was done last evening.]

CLEAR      **Last evening**, Mr. Wilson *blamed* Richard for the damage done to the lawn mower. [Mr. Wilson blamed Richard last evening.]

Notice from the preceding examples that the way you revise a sentence can alter its meaning.

**Rule** Avoid dangling modifiers. Provide an antecedent for every modifying phrase or clause to modify.

A **dangling modifier** is a modifying phrase or clause that does not clearly or logically modify any word in the sentence. Dangling modifiers can also make sentences unclear or ridiculous.

UNCLEAR    **After looking through the keyhole,** the doorknob turned. [Who or what was looking through the keyhole? The doorknob?]

CLEAR      **After looking through the keyhole,** she turned the doorknob. [The adverb phrase modifies the verb *turned*.]

When the dangling modifier is an adverb phrase, you can also correct it by changing the phrase to a subordinate clause.

CLEAR      **After she looked through the keyhole,** she turned the doorknob.

There are, however, some dangling modifiers that have become accepted in idiomatic expressions. These are introduced by such present and past participles as *generally speaking, speaking of, provided, considering, judging, concerning, failing, given, granting, owing to, allowing for,* and so forth.

> **Generally speaking,** the club members like the idea.
> **Considering the needs of the community,** the meeting should be held soon.

To determine whether an expression is acceptable even though it is a dangling modifier, ask yourself, "Does the reader expect a noun for the phrase to modify? Is the phrase or clause common enough to be considered an idiom?"

**Exercise 2    Placement of Modifiers**   On your paper, write interesting sentences, using each of the following constructions as a modifier. Provide each with something to modify and place the modifiers close enough to avoid confusion.

1. roaring down the track
2. although fifty years old
3. riding home on my bike
4. at age twenty
5. with a broken leg
6. imitating my sister
7. considering all the options
8. without concern for others
9. to finish the project on time
10. peeking at the baby

**Assignment    Misplaced and Dangling Modifiers**   Write a one-page critique of your favorite television program. Your comments may be positive or negative or mixed. Each sentence in your essay must contain at least one modifying phrase or clause. Make certain that no sentence contains a misplaced or dangling modifier.

# 4.5    Usage Notes

The following pages contain an alphabetical list of words and phrases that often present usage problems. Each entry describes correct usage, and most entries include examples. Cross-references help you to locate related information.

**a lot, alot**   *A lot* means "a great number or amount" and is always two words; avoid it except in informal usage. *Alot* is not a word.

**a while, awhile**   *While* is a noun when it is preceded by *for a* or *in a* to make a prepositional phrase. *Awhile* is an adverb. Do not use *for* or *in* before *awhile*.

> My grandparents will be here *in* **a while**. [not *in awhile*]
> Aunt Beth asked us to stay **awhile**. [adverb]

**accept, except**   *Accept* is a verb meaning "to agree" or "to receive." *Except* is a preposition meaning "leaving out" or "but."

> Our neighbors will **accept** the package for us.
> We have finished all of our chores **except** cleaning the den.

**adapt, adopt**   *Adapt* means "to change" or "to adjust" or "to make more suitable." *Adopt* means "to take" or "to accept."

> The squirrel will not **adapt** to living in the house.
> You should not try to **adopt** wild animals.

**advice, advise**   *Advice* is a noun that means "helpful suggestion or opinion." *Advise* is a verb that means "to give or to offer counsel."

> I **advise** you to check your math homework.
> Your **advice** was useful; I had made two mistakes.

**affect, effect**   *Affect* is a verb that means "to influence." *Effect* can be a verb that means "to bring about" or "to achieve" or a noun that means "the result."

> The rules about basketball practice do not **affect** us because we are not on the team. [verb meaning "influence"]
> We **effected** a change in the rules. [verb meaning "brought about"]
> The **effects** of the storm were evident everywhere. [noun meaning "results"]

**ain't**   *Ain't* is nonstandard. Do not use it.

**all ready, already**   *All ready* is an adjective meaning "entirely ready or prepared." *Already* is an adverb that means "before some specified time" or "previously."

> Dr. Henderson is **all ready** to begin the lecture.
> When we arrived, the dance had **already** begun.

**all right, alright**   *All right* means "satisfactory," "unhurt," "correct," or "yes, very well." *Alright* is an incorrect spelling; do not use it.

> Despite last night's frost, the tomato plants are **all right.**

**all the farther, as far as**   In formal usage, phrases such as *all the farther* should not be used for *as far as.*

> Three times around the track is **as far as** Jim can run. [Not *all the farther*]

**all together, altogether**   *All together* means "in a group" or "collectively." *Altogether* is an adverb that means "completely" or "thoroughly."

> We wanted to sit **all together** in the restaurant.
> He is **altogether** too noisy.

**almost, most**   Do not confuse the adverb *almost* with the adjective *most.*

> adj.      adv.
> **Most** fish swim **almost** all the time.

**although, though**   Both of these conjunctions mean "in spite of the fact." In conversation, you can also use *though* as an adverb to mean "however." Avoid this usage in written English.

> Althea bought her brother a present, **although** [*or* **though**] she had little money. [conjunction]
> I didn't lose touch with my friends, **though,** when I moved here. [adverb used in informal conversation]

**among, between**   Use *among* when you are discussing groups of persons or things. Use *between* when only two items are being considered at a time.

> I had to choose **among** all of the courses offered.
> I had to choose **between** taking an algebra class and having another study hall.

**amount, number**   Use *amount* with nouns that name things that can be measured or weighed but not counted. Use *number* to refer to things that can be counted.

> Two pounds of steak will be the right **amount**.
> The **number** of people who swim here has decreased.

**and/or**   *And/or* is intended to mean "either *and* or *or*." It is confusing and should be avoided.

**anxious, eager**   Both words can mean "strongly desirous," but *anxious* suggests concern or worry.

> Although Mona was a good driver, she was **anxious** to avoid driving during the blizzard.
> We were **eager** for the program to begin.

**any more, anymore**   These terms are not interchangeable. The phrase *any more* describes quantity; *any* is an adverb modifying the adjective *more*. *Anymore* is an adverb meaning "at present" or "from now on."

> Do you have **any more** paper?
> I do not buy paper **anymore**.

**anywhere, everywhere, nowhere**   Do not use in a nonstandard plural form: *anywheres, everywheres, nowheres*.

> We went **everywhere** in search of our lost dog. [not *everywheres*]

**apt, liable, likely**   In informal usage, these words are often used interchangeably. In formal usage, only *apt* and *likely* are interchangeable, meaning "tending to" or "inclined to be." Use *liable* to suggest the probability of a harmful, unfortunate, or negative event or to show exposure to legal action.

INFORMAL          It's **apt** [*or* **likely**] **to be cold at the beach.**
                  Your car is **liable** to break down before we get there.

FORMAL            You will be **liable** for any damage done to her car.

**as, like**   In formal usage, *like* is most often used as a preposition to introduce a prepositional phrase. *As* is most often used as a conjunction to introduce a subordinate clause.

Flora speaks **like** her father. [prepositional phrase]
Flora speaks **as** her father does. [subordinate clause]

In informal usage, *like* is sometimes used as a conjunction; avoid using *like* as a conjunction in formal usage in place of *as if* or *as though.*

INFORMAL          The audience looked **like** they were bored.

FORMAL            The audience looked **as if** they were bored.

**as far as, all the farther**   See *all the farther, as far as.*

**author**   *Author* should not be used as a verb. Books are written, not authored.

Who **wrote** *Treasure Island*? [not *authored*]

**bad, badly**   *Bad* is always an adjective, and *badly* is always an adverb.

The **bad** guys wear black hats in old cowboy movies.
I play the trombone **badly**.

**because, on account of**   *On account of* means "because of" or "due to." It functions as a preposition and takes an object. Do not use *on account of* instead of *because* to introduce a subordinate clause.

I cannot come to your party **because** I have already accepted another invitation. [not *on account of*]

I can't come to your birthday party **on account of** [*or* **because of**] another engagement.

**being as, being as how, being that**   Do not use these expressions for *because* or *since*.

**Because** he was too young, he couldn't play on the basketball team. [not *being as* or *being as how*]

**beside, besides**   *Beside* means "next to." *Besides* means "in addition to."

My dog managed to walk **beside** me all the way home.
**Besides** typing, I have chemistry and German this afternoon.

**between, among**   See *among, between.*

**between you and me**   Never use the pronoun in the nominative case as the object of a preposition (*page 28*). *Between* is a preposition.

This argument is just **between you and me**. [not *between you and I*]

**both, either, neither**   When modifying compound elements, place *both, either,* and *neither* just before the compound construction. The elements in the compound construction should be parallel in form. (See Unit 8, "Revising," pages 310–312).

INCORRECT      You will find your glasses **either** under *the couch* or *the chair*.

CORRECT        You will find your glasses under **either** *the couch* or *the chair*.

**bring, take**   Use *bring* when you mean "to carry to." Use *take* when you mean "to carry away."

**Bring** your homework to my house so we can work together on our math assignment.
Don't forget to **take** your homework with you to Steve's house.

**bust, busted**    Do not use these words as nonstandard verbs to substitute for *burst* or *break*.

> Your basketball may **burst** if you put too much air in it. [not *bust*]
>
> I **broke** my favorite brush yesterday. [not *busted*]

**can't hardly, can't scarcely**    *Hardly* and *scarcely* are negative words. Do not form double negatives (*page 163*) by using *hardly* and *scarcely* with other negative words, such as *not, never,* or contractions with *-n't.*

> Wilhemina **can hardly** talk because of her sore throat. [not *can't hardly*]
>
> I **can scarcely** hear her. [not *can't scarcely*]

**compare to, compare with**    Use the idiom *compare to* when stating similarities. Use the idiom *compare with* when examining both similarities and differences.

> Who wrote, "Shall I **compare** thee to a summer's day?"
>
> I **compared** the work of Picasso **with** that of Braque for my report.

**consensus of opinion**    Because consensus means "general agreement" or "collective opinion," this phrase is redundant. Use only *consensus.*

> The **consensus** was that we should make a donation. [not *consensus of opinion*]

**credible, creditable, credulous**    *Credible* means "believable" or "worthy of belief." *Creditable* means "worthy of commendation." *Credulous* applies always to people and means "willing to believe" or "gullible."

> His story was not **credible**; the plot was too forced.
>
> Getting an *A* in every subject is a **creditable** achievement.
>
> Only a **credulous** person would be fooled by that advertisement.

**differ from, differ with**   These idioms have different meanings. Things (or persons) *differ from* each other if they are physically dissimilar. When persons *differ with* each other, they disagree.

> Goats **differ from** bears.
> I **differ with** David on this issue.

**different from, different than**   Use *different from*. One thing differs *from* another; it does not "differ than" something.

> My opinion is **different from** yours. [not *different than*]

**disinterested, uninterested**   *Disinterested* implies a lack of self-interest; it is synonymous with *unbiased* or *impartial*. *Uninterested* implies a lack of any interest.

> An umpire should be **disinterested** about a game's outcome.
> The dog seems to be **uninterested** in its food.

**dived, dove**   Both forms are correct as the past tense of the verb *dive*. The past participle is always *dived*.

> Jennifer **dived** from the fifteen-foot platform. [or *dove*]
> She **has dived** from it often. [not *has dove*]

**double negative**   A double negative is the use of two negative words when one is sufficient. Do not use *not* or contractions with *-n't* with words such as *no, none, never,* or *nothing*. See *can't hardly, can't scarcely*.

| INCORRECT | I **don't** have **no** change. |
| CORRECT | I **don't** have **any** change. |
| CORRECT | I have **no** change |

**double subject**   Do not use a noun and a pronoun together as a single subject.

| INCORRECT | My **father he** took me to the all-star game. |
| CORRECT | My **father** took me to the all-star game. |
| CORRECT | **He** took me to the all-star game. |

**dove, dived**   See *dived, dove.*

**each and every**   Use either *each* or *every*, not both.

> **Each** one of you is expected to be on time.
> **Every** one of you is expected to be on time.

**eager, anxious**   See *anxious, eager.*

**effect, affect**   See *affect, effect.*

**e.g., i.e.**   *E.g.* stands for the Latin words *exempli gratia* and means "for example." *I.e.* stands for the Latin words *id est,* meaning "that is." Use both devices sparingly.

**either, both, neither**   See *both, either, neither.*

**enthuse**   Do not use *enthuse* as a verb or *enthused* as an adjective.

> James was very **enthusiastic** about our plans to go to the concert. [not *enthused*]

**et al.**   This is the abbreviation for the Latin *et alii*; it means "and others" (persons, not things) or "and elsewhere." It is used most often in footnotes and bibliographies to refer to additional members of a team of authors.

**etc.**   This is the abbreviation for the Latin *et cetera*; it means "and other things" or "and so forth." Do not use *and* before *etc.* Avoid using *etc.* in formal writing; use *and so forth* instead.

**every day, everyday**   *Every day* means "each day." *Everyday* is an adjective meaning "ordinary."

> I practice the piano **every day**, even on weekends.
> For **everyday** use, these shoes are best.

**every one, everyone**   *Every one* refers to each person or each thing in a group and is usually followed by *of. Everyone* means "everybody, every person."

**Every one** of you did a good job.

**Everyone** will leave at the same time.

**everywhere, anywhere, nowhere**   See *anywhere, everywhere, nowhere.*

**except, accept**   See *accept, except.*

**explicit, implicit**   These adjectives are antonyms. *Explicit* refers to something that is directly stated; *implicit* is something that is not directly stated.

> Patricia was **explicit** about her liking for math; she frequently mentioned that it was her favorite subject.
>
> **Implicit** in his answer was that he resented being asked the question.

**farther, further**   These two words are not interchangeable. Use *farther* to refer to measurable distance. Use *further* to mean "greater in time, degree, or extent," or "additionally."

> Carmen walks **farther** than I do to get to school.
>
> The **further** you read in this text, the more you will learn.
>
> Burton **further** explained his tardiness.

**fewer, less**   Use *fewer* to refer to things that you can count. Use *less* to refer to quantities that you cannot count. *Less* can also refer to amounts of time, money, or distance when the amount is a single quantity.

> **Fewer** than a hundred people attended the performance.
>
> I have **less** musical ability than she has.
>
> I walk **less** than two miles to work.

**figuratively, literally**   *Figuratively* and *literally* are antonyms. An expression that uses a metaphor to represent a fact is figurative; an expression that states a fact is literal.

> Linda was speaking **figuratively** when she said, "I feel like a duck out of water."
>
> What she meant **literally** was that she felt uncomfortable.

**first, firstly; second, secondly**   Use *first* and *second,* not *firstly* and *secondly,* to mean "in the first (or second) place."

> **First,** sift two cups of buckwheat flour.

**formally, formerly**   *Formally* means "in a formal or official manner." *Formerly* means "previously" or "at an earlier time."

> Stuart **formally** introduced himself to the guests.
> He **formerly** lived in Duluth.

**former, latter**   Use *former* to refer to the first of two previously mentioned persons or things and *latter* to refer to the second of the two persons or things.

> Katherine and Laura both brought me presents. The **former** [Katherine] gave me a bracelet, and the **latter** [Laura] gave me a photograph album.

**further, farther**   See *farther, further.*

**good, well**   Always use *good* as an adjective. *Well* can be an adverb meaning "satisfactorily" or a predicate adjective meaning "satisfactory" or "in good health." The opposite of feeling sick is feeling *well.*

> Terry is a **good** mechanic. [adjective]
> I used to play the piano **well.** [adverb]
> Three o'clock, and all is **well.** [predicate adjective]

**got, have**   *Got* is the past tense of the verb *get.* It means "obtained." Avoid using *got* with or in place of *have.* Also avoid using *don't got* in place of *don't have.*

> I **have** to leave at 3:00 P.M. [not *have got*]
> We **got** his telephone number promptly. [obtained]
> I **don't have** the time to go with you. [not *don't got*]

**had ought, hadn't ought**   Avoid using *had ought* and *hadn't ought.* Instead, use *ought* or *ought not,* which is usually followed by the preposition *to.*

You **ought** to do your homework. [not *had ought*]
You **ought not** to wait until the last minute. [not *hadn't ought*]

**hanged, hung**   *Hanged* and *hung* are alternate forms of the past tense and past participle of the verb *hang*. Use *hanged* when referring to death by hanging. Use *hung* in all other cases.

> Henry VIII **hanged** several of his enemies.
> The shopkeeper **hung** the plants in the window.

**have, got**   See *got, have.*

**have, of**   *Have* and *of* sound similar in rapid speech, but they are different parts of speech. *Have* is a verb; *of* is a preposition. Be careful to say (and write) *have,* not *of,* when completing a verb phrase, especially after the helping verbs *should, would,* and *could.*

> You **should have** called me earlier. [not *should of*]

**hisself, theirselves**   *Hisself* and *theirselves* are both nonstandard forms; do not use them. *Himself* and *themselves* are the correct forms.

**hung, hanged**   See *hanged, hung.*

**i.e., e.g.**   See *e.g., i.e.*

**imply, infer**   *Imply* means "to hint at" or "to suggest." *Infer* means "to reach a conclusion based on evidence or deduction."

> Your questions seem to **imply** that you think I spilled your glass of juice on purpose.
> I can only **infer** that you don't believe me.

**in, into**   Use *in* to mean "within" and *into* to suggest movement toward the inside from the outside.

> William cautiously walked **into** the cave. [not *in*]
> When he was **in** the cave, he explored the rock formations that he found there.

**individual, person**   Use *individual* to distinguish one person from a larger group. Do not use *individual* in place of *person*.

> Each person on the team is rated as an **individual**.

**ingenious, ingenuous**   *Ingenious* means "clever"; *ingenuous* means "naive."

> It was **ingenious** of her to think of that riddle.
> On his first day at the factory, Frank seemed quite **ingenuous**.

**irregardless, regardless**   Do not use *irregardless;* it is nonstandard. Use *regardless* instead.

> The game will be played **regardless** of the weather. [not *irregardless*]

**just exactly**   Use either *just* or *exactly*, not both.

> It's **just** two miles more.
> It's **exactly** two miles more.

**kind of, sort of**   Do not use these colloquial terms to mean "somewhat" or "rather."

> It is **rather** hot today. [not *kind of* or *sort of*]

**latter, former**   See *former, latter*.

**lay, lie**   *Lay* is a transitive verb that means "to put or to place something somewhere." It always takes a direct object. *Lie* is an intransitive verb that means "to be in or to assume a reclining position." It does not take a direct object. (See page 000 for the principal parts of these irregular verbs.)

> **Lay** your books and coat down on the chair before you **lie** down for a nap.

**learn, teach**   Do not use these words interchangeably. *Learn* means "to receive knowledge" or "to acquire knowledge." *Teach* means "to give knowledge."

She **learned** to play the piano so well because Arthur Rubinstein **taught** her.

**leave, let**    *Leave* means "to go away" or "to abandon." *Let* means "to permit" or "to allow."

Please **let** me **leave** now.

**less, fewer**    See *fewer, less*.

**liable, apt, likely**    See *apt, liable, likely*.

**lie, lay**    See *lay, lie*.

**like, as**    See *as, like*.

**likely, apt, liable**    See *apt, liable, likely*.

**literally, figuratively**    See *figuratively, literally*.

**loose, lose**    *Loose* is an adjective that means "not tight," "not bound," or "free." *Lose* is a verb that means "to fail to find" or "to be deprived of."

The steering mechanism in the car seems very **loose**.
Be careful not to **lose** control of the car.

**many, much**    Use the adjective *many* to describe things that you can count (books, persons). Use the adjective *much* to describe things that you cannot count (water, work, strength). When used as indefinite pronouns, *much* is singular and *many* is plural.

You seem to have **much** strength but not **many** muscles.
**Much** *needs* to be done before we can open the shop tomorrow morning. [singular]
**Many** of us *want* to help. [plural]

**may be, maybe**   In the term *may be, may* is an auxiliary that indicates possibility. The adverb *maybe* means "perhaps."

> I **may be** able to go with you on Wednesday.
> **Maybe** we can go to a play on that day.

**most, almost**   See *almost, most.*

**much, many**   See *many, much.*

**myself, yourself**   Do not use a reflexive pronoun in place of *I, me,* or *you.*

> INCORRECT   Fred and **myself** like daffodils better than roses.
>
> CORRECT   Fred and **I** like daffodils better than roses.

**neither, both, either**   See *both, either, neither.*

**nohow, noway**   *Nohow* and *noway* are nonstandard English. Avoid using them. You can use *no way* correctly as two words.

> INCORRECT   **Noway** I'll be ready for school on time.
>
> CORRECT   There is **no way** that I will be ready for school on time.

**nowhere, anywhere, everywhere**   See *anywhere, everywhere, nowhere.*

**of, have**   See *have, of.*

**off, off of**   *Off of* is an incorrect idiom; the word *of* is unnecessary. Do not use *off* or *off of* in place of *from.*

> The lamp fell **off** the table. [not *off of*]
> Marilyn got her car **from** her uncle. [not *off*]
> I borrowed a pen **from** my brother. [not *off of*]

**on account of, because**   See *because, on account of.*

**only**   To avoid confusion, place *only* before the element that it modifies. The placement of *only* can dramatically affect the meaning of your sentence.

> **Only** Jerry spoke to her last night. [**Think:** No other person spoke to her.]
>
> Jerry **only** spoke to her last night. [**Think:** Jerry did nothing but speak.]
>
> Jerry spoke **only** to her last night. [**Think:** Jerry spoke to no one else.]
>
> Jerry spoke to her **only** last night. [**Think:** Jerry spoke to her on no other night.]

**on to, onto**   In the phrase *on to*, *on* is an adverb and *to* is a preposition. *Onto* is a preposition that means "in a position on or upon."

> When we leave Milwaukee, we will go **on to** San Francisco.
>
> Wilma stepped confidently **onto** the stage.

**outside, outside of**   Use the idiom *outside of* only when *outside* is a noun and *of* is a preposition.

> prep.
> We waited **outside** the building. [not *outside of*]
>
> noun   prep.
> The **outside of** the house needs painting.

**passed, past**   *Passed* is the past tense of the verb *pass*. *Past* can be one of four parts of speech: (1) an adjective that means "no longer current," "over, as in finished," or "before the present"; (2) a noun that means "a time earlier than the present"; (3) an adverb that means "so as to go beyond"; and (4) a preposition that means "beyond, after" or "later than."

> Judy **passed** near the lake on her hike. [verb]
>
> In **past** years, she has done a lot of hiking. [adjective]
>
> All of that is now in the **past**. [noun]
>
> The dog barked as I walked **past**. [adverb]
>
> Her teacher is afraid that Joan is **past** caring about her school assignments. [preposition]

**people, persons**   In normal usage, use *persons* when referring to a relatively small, specific group; use *people* when referring to a large group in a collective sense.

> Six **persons** have been invited to speak at the convention. [or *people*]
>
> **People** should begin arriving just before 8:00 P.M. [not *persons*]

**person, individual**   See *individual, person.*

**precede, proceed**   *Precede* means "to exist or come before in time." *Proceed* means "to go forward or onward."

> We **proceeded** toward Martha's house, knowing that she and Bob had **preceded** us and were already there.

**prophecy, prophesy**   *Prophecy* is a noun; it means "a prediction." *Prophesy* is a verb that means "to reveal" or "to predict." Their pronunciations differ.

> Was her **prophecy** correct?
>
> Can she **prophesy** what the future holds for us?

**raise, rise**   *Raise* is a regular transitive verb that means "to lift"; it always takes a direct object. *Rise* is an irregular intransitive verb that means "to move upward." (See page 110 for the principal parts of the verb *rise*.)

> Sally **raised** her arm to show us her cast.
>
> The stars appear to **rise** in the eastern sky.

**real, really**   *Real* is an adjective; *really* is an adverb.

> That is a *real* diamond.
>
> It is *really* too bad that he got lost. [not *real*]

**reason is because, reason is that, reason why**   *Reason is because* and *reason why* are redundant. Use *reason is that* or simply *because.*

| INCORRECT | The **reason** he left **is because** he had to go to work. |
|---|---|
| CORRECT | The **reason** he left **is that** he had to go to work. |
| CORRECT | He left **because** he had to go to work. |

**refer back**   *Refer back* is redundant. Use just *refer*.

**regardless, irregardless**   See *irregardless, regardless*.

**regretful, regrettable**   *Regretful* means "full of sorrow or regret." *Regrettable* means "deserving regret or sorrow."

> I was **regretful** over the **regrettable** loss of my pen.

**respectfully, respectively**   *Respectfully* means "showing respect." *Respectively* means "in the order indicated."

> I **respectfully** decline the nomination.
> My grandmother left her china and her silver to Kate and to Corinne **respectively**.

**rise, raise**   See *raise, rise*.

**said, says, goes, went**   *Said* is the past-tense form of the verb *say*; *says* is a present-tense form . Do not use *says* for *said*. Also, do not use *goes* or *went* for *said*.

> Greg called and **said**, "Did you get the job of mowing lawns for the summer?" [not *says, goes,* or *went*]

**second, secondly; first, firstly**   See *first, firstly*.

**seldom ever**   *Seldom ever* is redundant. Use only *seldom*.

> Martin **seldom** eats dessert. [not *seldom ever*]

**-self, -selves**   The suffix *-self* is singular; *-selves* is plural. Be sure to use the correct suffix to form a reflexive pronoun.

| SINGULAR | myself, yourself, himself, herself, itself |
|---|---|
| PLURAL | ourselves, yourselves, themselves |

**set, sit**   *Set* is a transitive verb that means "to place something." *Sit* is an intransitive verb that means "to rest in an upright position"; it does not take a direct object.

> **Set** your packages on that table.
> **Sit** beside me in English class.

**slow, slowly**   *Slow* is an adjective that can be used as an adverb in informal speech, especially in commands or for emphasis. *Slowly* is an adverb; it is preferred in formal usage.

> There is a **slow** train to Connecticut at six o'clock. [adjective]
> Bruce drank his juice **slowly,** enjoying every sip. [adverb]
> The floor is wet. Walk **slow.** [adverb; informal]

**some time, sometime, sometimes**   When two words are used, *some* is an adjective modifying *time*. *Sometime* can be either an adverb that means "at an indefinite time" or an adjective that means "occasional." *Sometimes* is an adverb that means "occasionally, now and then."

> adj.   noun
> I want **some time** to be alone.
>
> adv.
> I would like you to come with me **sometime**.
>
> adj.
> Irene is a **sometime** playwright.
>
> adv.
> **Sometimes** I walk down by the river.

**sort of, kind of**   See *kind of, sort of*.

**supposed to, used to**   Be sure to spell *supposed* and *used* with a final *-d*.

> Aren't you **supposed to** baby-sit with Mr. Jackson's children tonight? [not *suppose to*]

**sure, surely**   In most writing do not use the adjective *sure* to mean "certainly." Such usage is colloquial.

The muddy footprints on the floor were **sure** proof that it was raining.

We will **surely** arrive on time if we hurry.

**take, bring**   See *bring, take.*

**teach, learn**   See *learn, teach.*

**than, then**   Use *than* as a conjunction in a comparison. Use *then* as an adverb to show a sequence of time or events. Do not use *then* as a conjunction between two independent clauses.

conj.
This year's uniforms are more comfortable **than** last year's.

adv.
We were busy **then,** but we found time to take a vacation.

adv.
Finish your dinner promptly, and **then** you may borrow the car for an hour. [Note the needed conjunction *and*.]

**that, which, who**   Use *that* as a relative pronoun to introduce essential clauses (*page 82*) that refer to things or to collective nouns referring to people. Because it introduces an essential clause, do not use a comma before *that*.

The dog **that** I found did not have a collar.

Use *which* as a relative pronoun to introduce nonessential clauses (*page 83*) that refer to things or to groups of persons. Always use a comma before *which* when it introduces a nonessential clause.

This term paper, **which** is the longest one I've ever written, received a good grade.

Use *who* or *whom* as a relative pronoun to introduce essential or nonessential clauses that refer to persons. Use a comma before *who* or *whom* only when it introduces a nonessential clause.

The man **who** teaches mathematics at Wilson High is my uncle.

Alicia, **whom** I help to deliver papers after school, is a good friend of mine from Atlanta.

**that there, this here**   Do not use either construction. Use only *this* or *that*.

> Where should I put **this** package? [not *this here*]
> Sam wants **that** car. [not *that there*]

**theirselves, hisself**   See *hisself, theirselves.*

**then, than**   See *than, then.*

**these kinds, this kind**   Use *this* or *that* to modify the singular nouns *kind*, *sort*, and *type*. Use *these* and *those* to modify the plural nouns *kinds*, *sorts*, and *types*. Use the singular form of these nouns when the object of the preposition *of* is singular; use the plural form when the object of the preposition is plural.

> ┌────── sing.──────┐
> **This kind** of *cheese* is good for grating.

> ┌──────── pl.────────┐
> **These kinds** of *cheeses* are my favorites.

**though, although**   See *although, though.*

**till, until**   Both words are acceptable. *Until* is preferred as the first word in a sentence. Do not use *til* or *'til*.

> Don't stop swimming **till** you've done ten laps. [or *until*]
> **Until** next Monday, this store will be closed for repairs.

**toward, towards**   Both mean "in the direction of" or "approaching," but *toward* is preferred in American usage. *Towards* is the British form.

> Eager to meet the performers, we moved **toward** the stage.

**try and, try to**   Use *try to* instead of *try and*.

> Please **try to** be on time. [not *try and*]

**uninterested, disinterested**   See *disinterested, uninterested.*

**until, till**   See *till, until*.

**used to, supposed to**   See *supposed to, used to*.

**very**   Be certain that you use *very* only when it is needed. Overuse of the word *very* diminishes its effectiveness.

> OVERDONE    The band's performing was **very** outstanding. [*Outstanding* cannot be much more than outstanding.]

> OVERDONE    My sister is a **very** lovely young woman. [*Lovely* conveys the message sufficiently.]

**way, ways**   Do not use *ways* when referring to distance.

> It is only a short **way** from the school to the theater where the play is being produced. [not *ways*]

**well, good**   See *good, well*.

**where . . . at**   Do not use *at* after *where*.

> **Where** should we meet? [not *Where should we meet at?*]

**which, who, that**   See *that, which, who*.

**-wise**   Avoid using *-wise* on the end of a word to mean "with reference to" or "concerning."

> AVOID    I had a good semester **gradewise**.

> USE    My grades were good this semester.

**would have**   Do not use *would have* instead of *had* in clauses that begin with *if* or that express a wish.

> If you **had** called Jerry, he could have taken you to the airport. [not *would have*]
>
> I wish that I **had** known that you didn't receive an invitation. [not *would have*]

**yourself, myself**   See *myself, yourself*.

# Unit Practice

## Practice 1

**A. Correct Use of Verbs** (*pages 107–122*)   On your paper, copy each sentence, correcting all errors in the use of verbs.

1. Sea sponges gathered by the expert divers.
2. This umbrella would have kept them dry if they will use it.
3. The announcer asked that the awards are presented now.
4. The main character in "Bartleby the Scrivener" preferred not to work.
5. A small animal creeped silently out of the barn.
6. Wreckers are working at the site since last Tuesday.
7. The orchestra is practicing when we arrived at the concert hall.
8. By the time Dale packs everything, her baggage was quite heavy.
9. Mrs. Streeter volunteered, begins her training, and served well.
10. If Julius had brung his knapsack, he could have carried more gear.

**B. Subject-Verb Agreement** (*pages 123–133*)   On your paper, write the verb that correctly completes each sentence.

11. Members of that tribe still (live, lives) near their ancestral dwellings.
12. Somebody (lock, locks) the garage door each evening.
13. A willow tree, in addition to low bushes, (grows, grow) there.
14. Five seconds (was, were) remaining when the buzzer sounded.
15. Either gerbils or hamsters (play, plays) in that cage.
16. Crocheting is one of the hobbies that (interest, interests) me.
17. Intramural athletics (was, were) discussed at the meeting.
18. *Wuthering Heights* (belongs, belong) on the shelf at the public library.
19. The sun's temperature (is, are) highest at the core.
20. Under the pier (stands, stand) sandy wood pilings.

**C. Correct Use of Pronouns** (*pages 134–150*)   On your paper, write the pronoun that correctly completes each sentence.

21. It is (they, them) who will audition for the lead roles.
22. (Who, Whom) are the discoverers of the North Pole?
23. Informative pamphlets were distributed by (we, us) volunteers.
24. Most of the storytellers entertained (their, its) young audience.
25. Molly asked (whomever, whoever) was in charge about a summer internship.

26. Both Ted and Rosa are on time, but Rosa arrived earlier than (he, him).

27. Greta will show my cousin and (me, I) how to solve the equation.

28. Did you see the swarm of bees returning to (its, their) hive?

29. Coach Lee gave the newest players, Dana and (she, her), encouragement.

30. Was Sheila pleased by (me, my) sending her that humorous postcard?

**D. Correct Use of Modifiers** (*pages 151–156*)   On your paper, rewrite each sentence, correcting all errors in the use of modifiers.

31. The greyhound is faster than any breed of dog.

32. Flowers in the greenhouse were more abundant than the garden.

33. This year's crop was the best of the past two seasons.

34. The flying fish pushes up out of the water with a strong tail.

35. Sydney is older and larger than any city in Australia.

36. The Pacific Ocean is as active if not more active than any other ocean.

37. Reading the late edition, the newspaper headlines were fascinating.

38. The most brightest star in the constellation Gemini is Pollux.

39. Loren needs to practice lesser than her teammates.

40. Those canteens were most empty after the day's long journey.

# Practice 2

Rewrite the following passage, correcting all errors in the use of verbs, pronouns, and modifiers.

People have always use imagination to keep theirselves dry and warm. If it was raining, animal skins turned inside out would be weared. Liquid latex from rubber trees were also employed for waterproofing clothes. Many Europeans whom wore heavy wool coats stayed dry because of the natural oils in them. When fishermen rubbed linseed oil on canvas coats, it developed the first oilskin slickers. The need for more lighter and flexible rain gear arose during World War I. An Englishman, Thomas Burberry, treated gabardine coats with chemicals to make them waterproof. Known as trench coats, soldiers first wore these practical garments. The wearer today is one of those lucky people who receives excellent protection.

# Unit Tests

## Test 1

**A. Correct Use of Verbs** (*pages 107–122*)   On your paper, copy each sentence, correcting all errors in the use of verbs.

1. Has the old water pipe sprang a leak?
2. If the stadium was crowded, the spectators could not see.
3. By the time the assignment is done, I will do this sketch for hours.
4. The shutters open by the shopkeepers every day.
5. At this moment the group decided where to go.
6. Laura collected glass animals in the play *The Glass Menagerie*.
7. When Fran plants a garden tomorrow, she needed heavy gloves.
8. By the time registration began, Cal arranged his schedule.
9. Our moderator requests that questions are addressed to the panel.
10. Jill will jog for one mile by one o'clock, and then she will return.

**B. Subject-Verb Agreement** (*pages 123–133*)   On your paper, write the verb that correctly completes each sentence.

11. Neither a telegram nor any letters (were, was) delivered yesterday.
12. Few people (believe, believes) the legend of Pecos Bill.
13. Amber, valued by many people, (is, are) millions of years old.
14. The band plays each time the fleet (sail, sails) into the harbor.
15. Above the grassy hills (stands, stand) an old, faded billboard.
16. Swinging on a trapeze is one of those stunts that (is, are) dangerous.
17. After the successful campaign, congratulations (was, were) deserved.
18. Many a wild animal (has, have) protective coloring or camouflage.
19. The Netherlands (has, have) tulips that grow each spring.
20. The referee in charge of enforcing the rules (is, are) Mr. Manfredi.

**C. Correct Use of Pronouns** (*pages 134–150*)   On your paper, write the pronoun that correctly completes each sentence.

21. (We, Us) amateurs repaired these chairs.
22. The community will hold (its, their) annual rodeo.
23. Everyone takes (their, her) lessons at the music school.
24. The most relaxed passengers on the cruise were (they, them).
25. (Who, Whom) have the citizens elected by popular vote?

26. I hope that you do not mind (me, my) hammering those nails.
27. Pat has more work experience than (me, I).
28. Either Joel or Bret passed (his, their) driving test.
29. Two pilot whales managed to beach (itself, themselves) near shore.
30. Mr. Malone urged (we, us) to attend the showing of the documentary.

**D. Correct Use of Modifiers** (*pages 151–156*)   On your paper, rewrite each sentence, correcting all errors in the use of modifiers.

31. Her uncle returned with the most fine silk from the market.
32. Growing in the sand, he avoided stepping on the prickly thistle.
33. Martina's mistakes were less significant than all the players.
34. This beagle is as well trained if not better trained than that setter.
35. Have you seen the blackest sand of Kaimu Beach on Hawaii Island?
36. The athlete's behavior was like a spoiled child.
37. The old yellowed map was hard to read with fine print.
38. Sherene studied French longer than anyone in the program.
39. Dan attended the larger foreign trade fair that he had ever seen.
40. We were the most good dance team at the audition.

# Test 2

Rewrite the following passage, correcting all errors in the use of verbs, pronouns, and modifiers.

Henry Bergh, whom was a New York philanthropist, insisted that anticruelty laws for animals were reviewed. As a result of his intervention, a new law that protected work animals were passed in 1866. Then horses received some legal protection, that had pulled streetcars, carts, and carriages. To protect all creatures, the American Society for the Prevention of Cruelty to Animals founded by Henry Bergh. Him lecturing helped to inspire gooder conditions and the growth of other humane societies. For example, the first animal shelter is established in 1869 by the Women's Pennsylvania SPCA. Currently there do exist an ongoing need for further reforms. Despite the regulations passed to help them, our wildlife requires improved protection, shelters, and care. Supporting their efforts, humane societies depend on we citizens.

# Unit 5

## Mechanics

---

## Unit Preview

these i have loved white plates and cups clean gleaming
ringed with blue lines and feathery faery dust wet roofs beneath
the lamplight the strong crust of friendly bread and many
tasting food rainbows and the blue bitter smoke of wood and
radiant raindrops couching in cool flowers and flowers themselves that sway through sunny hours dreaming of moths that
drink them under the moon

The preceding passage may look almost like a simple list of
words with no other meaning, yet it is a part of a poem. As you
know, poets sometimes choose to leave out capital letters and
punctuation as a way of adding to the meaning of a poem. More
often, however, poets and all other people who write find that
**mechanics,** the use of punctuation marks, capitalization, and
italics in writing, helps to clarify meaning.

**For Analysis** Try to answer the following questions about the
passage at the beginning of this Unit Preview.

1. What is the poet writing about in this passage?
2. How many items has the poet loved?
3. What do the plates and cups look like?
4. Where are the wet roofs?
5. What specific kind of food does the poet mention?
6. What adjectives does the poet use to describe wood smoke?
7. Who or what sways through sunny hours?

Now look at the poem again, written in its proper form.

These I have loved:
    White plates and cups, clean-gleaming,
Ringed with blue lines; and feathery, faery dust;
Wet roofs, beneath the lamp-light; the strong crust
Of friendly bread; and many-tasting food;
Rainbows; and the blue, bitter smoke of wood;
And radiant raindrops couching in cool flowers;
And flowers themselves, that sway through sunny hours,
Dreaming of moths that drink them under the moon; . . .

Rupert Brooke, "The Great Lover"

You can see that the colon and the commas, semicolons, and hyphens all add greatly to your ability to read and appreciate the passage. This is the purpose of mechanics, which you will learn more about as you study this unit. Using the mechanics rules that you will learn will help you to make your writing clear to anyone who reads it.

# 5.1 Capitalization

In English, capital letters are generally used either to show the beginning of a sentence or to indicate that a word is a proper noun (*page 4*).

## Capitalization in Sentences

**Rule** Capitalize the first word in a sentence or in a direct quotation. If a quoted sentence is interrupted by an expression such as "Joshua asked" or "Grandmother replied," begin the second part of the quotation with a lower-case letter.

> **Blackbirds** nested in the eaves of the abandoned house.
> Rochelle exclaimed, "**Come** watch the sun setting over the ocean!"
> "I will begin work," Martin replied, "**when** the night shift has finished."

*New Sentence in a Quotation.* If the second part of the quotation is a new sentence, put a period after the interrupting expression, and begin the second part with a capital letter.

> "Will she run in the marathon?" asked Mr. Rourke. "**She** is certainly in good condition."

**Rule** Capitalize the first word in each line of a poem if that is how the poet wrote it.

> **Higher** still and higher
>    **From** the earth thou springest
> **Like** a cloud of fire;
>    **The** blue deep thou wingest,
> **And** singing still dost soar, and soaring ever singest.
>
>                   Percy Bysshe Shelley, "To a Skylark"

## Proper Nouns

**Rule** Capitalize the names and initials of people. If a last name begins with *Mc, O',* or *St.,* capitalize the next letter as well. If the last name begins with *Mac, de, D', la, le, van,* or *von,* capitalization varies. In such cases, capitalize the name as its owner does.

> Edward E. Curley            Cathleen St. James

*Family-Relationship Words.* Capitalize a word that shows family relationship when it is used as part of a person's name or as a substitute for a person's name. Do not capitalize a family-relationship word if it is used as a general term. Usually if the word is preceded by a possessive pronoun (*page 21*), it should not be capitalized. If the person's name follows the relationship word, and if that phrase is the name by which you call the person, capitalize both words. Otherwise, capitalize only the person's name.

> Grandfather Martin       Aunt Rosemary       Cousin June

> Rafael's **mother** designed this new wing for the museum.
> Her **uncle Paul** helped to evacuate residents before the volcano erupted. [She calls him *Paul.*]
> Her **Uncle Paul** helped to evacuate residents before the volcano erupted. [She calls him *Uncle Paul.*]

*Personal and Official Titles.* Capitalize personal or official titles or their abbreviations when you use them as names in direct address (*page 194*) or when you use them before people's names. Capitalize the names and abbreviations of academic degrees or honors that follow a person's name. Capitalize the abbreviations *Sr.* and *Jr.*

Edward Bouchet, **Ph.D.**           Frank Whitten, **Jr.**
**Ms.** Marta Gonzalez               **Ambassador** Chen
**Fr.** O'Casey                       **Empress** Josephine

Do not capitalize a title that follows or is a substitute for a person's name unless it is the title of a head of a national government or a head of state. Do not capitalize prepositions, conjunctions, and articles that are part of titles unless they begin a sentence.

TITLE BEFORE NAME                TITLE FOLLOWING NAME
**Mayor** Prague                  Jane Prague, **mayor**
**Professor** Tennenbaum          Jules Tennenbaum, **professor**
**Prince** Charles                Charles, **Prince of Wales**

Yes, **Governor,** I brought those statistics.
I told the **governor** that I had brought those statistics.

*Gods of Mythology.* Capitalize the names of the gods and goddesses of mythology, but do not capitalize the word *god* when it refers to one of them.

In Norse myths the **god Loki** was often portrayed as a trickster.

**Rule**   Capitalize the names of particular places, such as continents, cities, parks, and rivers.

Hungary        Bay of Bengal                South America
Nevada         Pacific Rim National Park    Palm Avenue

*Compass Points.* Capitalize compass points that refer to specific geographic regions or that form part of a place name. Do not capitalize a compass point that simply indicates direction.

Were you vacationing in the Pacific **Northwest**?
She enjoyed traveling through the **South.**
Drive **south** to the intersection, and then head **west.**

*Heavenly Bodies.* Capitalize the names of heavenly bodies except *sun* and *moon.* Capitalize *Earth* when referring to it as a planet. Do not capitalize *earth* when it is preceded by the word *the.*

Pluto                          Betelgeuse
the North Star                 Halley's Comet

The astronauts cheered as **Earth** came into view.

BUT     The first space traveler, Yuri A. Gagarin, orbited **the earth** in 1961.

**Rule**  Capitalize the names of nationalities, peoples, and languages.

Sudanese        Asian         Scandinavian
Micronesian     Seminole      Celtic

**Rule**  Capitalize the names of days, months, holidays, and special events. Do not capitalize the name of a season unless it is part of a proper noun.

Wednesday       Thanksgiving          summer
January         Autumn Sportsfest     winter

**Rule**  Capitalize the names of historical events and periods, awards, and documents.

the Hundred Years' War          the Articles of Confederation
the Industrial Revolution       the Golden Quill Award

**Rule**  Capitalize the first, last, and all other important words in the titles of books, newspapers, poems, television shows, musical and art works, movies, and so forth. (See also pages 201 and 211.) Capitalize a conjunction, an article, or a preposition when it is the first or last word in a title. Capitalize also in a title any preposition that has five or more letters.

*Tulsa Tribune*                "Ode to a Nightingale"
*To Kill a Mockingbird*        *Brandenburg Concertos*
*On the Waterfront*            "Among Schoolchildren"

**Rule** Capitalize the name of a school subject that is a language or a proper adjective (*page 19*) or is followed by a course number.

| | | |
|---|---|---|
| German | mathematics | British literature |
| Geometry II | physics | European history |

**Rule** Capitalize the names of structures and the names of organizations, such as businesses, religions, government bodies, clubs, and schools. Capitalize a word such as *school* or *club* only when it is part of a proper noun.

| | |
|---|---|
| the Alhambra | Parliament |
| Buddhism | Cafiero's Tire Shop |
| the League of Women Voters | the Asian-American Society |
| the Sierra **Club** | BUT a coin **club** |
| the Lee **School** | BUT a vocational **school** |

**Rule** Capitalize trade names. Do not capitalize a common noun that follows a trade name.

Rapido bug spray          Colorama paints

**Rule** Capitalize names of trains, ships, airplanes, rockets, and spacecraft. (See also page 211.)

the *San Francisco Zephyr*          *Gemini 7*

## Other Uses of Capitalization

**Rule** Capitalize most proper adjectives (*page 19*).

| CAPITALIZE THESE | BUT NOT THESE |
|---|---|
| **Venetian** glass | **morocco** leather |
| **Newtonian** physics | **manila** folder |
| **French** horn | **oriental** rug |

If you are unsure whether to capitalize a particular proper adjective, consult your dictionary.

**Rule** Capitalize the pronoun *I*.

After a nap **I** walked out into the country.

**Rule**   Capitalize both letters in the abbreviations *A.D., B.C., A.M.,* and *P.M.* and the two-letter Postal Service abbreviations of state names. Use Postal Service abbreviations only in addresses that include the ZIP code; do not use them in formal writing.

| | | |
|---|---|---|
| 1280 B.C. | A.D. 1980 | 3:20 P.M. |
| Colorado CO | Alaska AK | West Virginia WV |

**Note:**   A.D. precedes the year; B.C. follows the year.

**Exercise   Capitalization**   On your paper, write each sentence, making sure that you use capitals correctly. If you need help, use your dictionary.

> **SAMPLE**   Joe's grandfather tate lives north of miami.
> **ANSWER**   Joe's Grandfather Tate lives north of Miami.

1. if the sky is clear this evening at sunset, we should be able to see the planet mercury on the southwestern horizon.
2. in american history I, our class is studying the revolutionary war and the signing of the declaration of independence
3. in april 1912 the british steamship *titanic* sank after hitting an iceberg in the north atlantic.
4. steve purchased a thunderhead stapler and a box of ready-write typing paper at johnson's stationery shop.
5. "biographies are so interesting," remarked sheila to her friend. "i enjoy reading them in my spare time."
6. captain valdez, will admiral wellington be waiting for you?
7. according to greek mythology, helios was the god of light.
8. the writer and poet sophocles is thought to have been born in 496 b.c.
9. "are you ready," asked marissa, "for the french quiz tomorrow?"
10. in 1973 the southern writer eudora welty won the pulitzer prize for her novel *the optimist's daughter.*
11. "please join us at the yard sale on sunday afternoon," said ms. kromwell.
12. the scientists needed a geiger counter to conduct the experiment, but all they could find in the box was a bunsen burner.
13. the u.s.s. *constitution,* often called "old ironsides," was launched at boston harbor on september 20, 1797.

14. do you belong to either the wilkie chess club or the wilkie varsity swim team at the local university?

15. last year before thanksgiving i visited the metropolitan museum of art with my canadian cousin roger.

16. her first postcard was postmarked "amarillo, tx 79100," and the second one, "san francisco, ca 94100."

17. his paper began with lines from chaucer's *the canterbury tales:*

> hunting a hare or riding at a fence
> was all his fun; he spared for no expense.

18. this summer rosemont college will be offering these courses: italian, german, economics, and sociology II.

19. marcus matthews, ph.d., will give a talk in the auditorium of the science center at 7:00 p.m.

20. the hikers at snowcrest mountain park included mr. grimstead, t.d. tomaselli, and brenda s. bell.

**Assignment** **Capitalization** Make a list of twenty-five proper nouns. Include books, magazines, poems, people, places, holidays, school subjects, and so forth. Make sure that the items on your list are properly capitalized. When your list is complete, look at a magazine or a newspaper article for the same kinds of items and try to create a second list. For instance, if you have listed a mountain, try to find the name of another mountain in your magazine or newspaper. Check your second list for correct capitalization.

### Capital Letters

You are planning to write a screenplay for a short movie. Your movie will be about something that is important to you. To describe the plot to a friend, explain briefly in a paragraph or two what your movie will be about, who will be in it, and where the action will take place. If you wish, you may use one or more of the items that you listed in the preceding assignment. As you write your paragraph or paragraphs, include as many details as you can. Use proper nouns and dialogue. When you have completed the paragraph describing your short movie, check it to see that you have followed the rules of capitalization.

# 5.2   Punctuation

Punctuation shows your readers when you want them to stop, pause, or pay special attention to something. Without punctuation marks, it would be difficult for others to read what you write.

## 5.2a   Periods, Question Marks, and Exclamation Points

### The Period

**Rule**   Use a period at the end of a declarative sentence, a mild command, or a polite question.

> Bobbin lace made by hand comes from Belgium.
> Make a list of your favorite musicians.
> Cindy, will you please move your bicycle.

**Rule**   Use a period after most standard abbreviations, including initials that are used as part of people's names or titles. Do not use a period after abbreviations for units of weight, measure, or chemical elements, except the abbreviation *in.* for *inch* (to show that you are not writing the word *in*). Do not use periods when the abbreviation of a company or an organization uses all capital letters or when you are writing Postal Service abbreviations of state names.

| USE PERIODS | | DO NOT USE PERIODS | |
|---|---|---|---|
| **Maj. Gen. R.** Scott Vartuli | | **sec** | second |
| Percy Brown, **L.L.D.** | | **Al** | aluminum |
| **Dr.** | doctor | **cm** | centimeter |
| **Aug.** | August | **Xe** | xenon |
| **blvd.** | boulevard | **OH** | Ohio |
| **inc.** | incorporated | **BBC** | British Broadcasting |
| **Mont.** | Montana | | Corporation |

Do not confuse standard two-letter state abbreviations (which require periods) with Postal Service abbreviations (which require no periods). If the two abbreviations are spelled the same, do not use periods when the ZIP code is given, but do use periods when the ZIP code is not given.

| USE PERIODS | DO NOT USE PERIODS |
|---|---|
| Kittery, **Me.** [no ZIP code] | Moody, **ME** 04054 |
| Guayanilla, **P.R.** [no ZIP code] | Achiote, **PR** 00719 |

**Note:** Avoid using abbreviations in formal writing. Spell out words instead.

## The Question Mark

**Rule** Use a question mark at the end of an interrogative sentence.

Was the flooding very serious?
Did Rita tour with the road company of that musical?

## The Exclamation Point

**Rule** Use an exclamation point at the end of a sentence that expresses strong feeling or a forceful command, or after a strong interjection or other exclamatory expression.

Imagine the commotion!
Don't walk near the scaffolding!
Alas! The mirror smashed to the floor.
Oh! Don't forget the laundry basket!

**Exercise 1  End Punctuation and Abbreviations**  On your paper, copy each sentence. Supply the correct punctuation.

| | |
|---|---|
| **SAMPLE** | Were you speaking to Giles |
| **ANSWER** | Were you speaking to Giles? |

1. Wisconsin was the thirtieth state to enter the Union
2. The Stevenson Bulldogs won this crucial league victory
3. Come here this instant
4. Jack, will you please do your weekend chores
5. Hooray I correctly identified He as helium on the test
6. Ana wrote on the recipe card, "Add six oz of the mixture to the pan and bake for ten min"
7. The sign said, "Louisville Ky 12 km"
8. When was your uncle elected president of the PTA
9. Dr HF Stephens, will you come to the main desk immediately
10. Oh What a fantastic fireworks display we saw

## 5.2b  Commas

### Commas in Series

**Rule**  Use commas to separate items in a series. Use a comma after each item except the last. Do not use commas to separate pairs of nouns that are thought of as a unit.

> We discussed our project's goals, its **rules and regulations,** and its deadlines.

*Adjectives.* Use commas to separate two or more adjectives preceding a noun that they both modify.

> She left on a **clear, sunny** day.

If the last adjective before the noun is considered part of the noun, do not put a comma before it.

| | |
|---|---|
| INCORRECT | They want a **large, square, kitchen** table. |
| CORRECT | They want a **large, square kitchen** table. [no comma: It is not just a table, but a *kitchen table*.] |

If one of the words in the series modifies the next word, do not put a comma between them.

He wore a **light blue** tie. [It was the *blue* that was *light*, not the tie.]

To decide whether or not to put a comma between adjectives preceding a noun, ask yourself whether the sentence would still sound right if you reversed the adjectives or if you put *and* between them. If the sentence does not sound natural, you should not use a comma.

| | |
|---|---|
| SENTENCE | I want this summery cotton dress. |
| UNNATURAL | I want this **cotton summery** dress. |
| UNNATURAL | I want this summery **and** cotton dress. |
| NATURAL | I want this summery cotton dress. [no comma] |

*Other Modifiers.* Use commas to separate three or more modifiers in a series.

The sun set **majestically, gracefully,** and **slowly.**

*Phrases.* Use commas to separate three or more phrases in a series. Do *not* use commas to separate items or phrases in a series if all of them are joined by conjunctions.

Did she leave her book **at the library, in her locker,** or **on her desk?**
You can cook the meal **or** set the table **or** wash the dishes.

*Independent Clauses.* Use commas to separate three or more short independent clauses in a series.

**I picked up the receiver, I listened for the dial tone,** and then **I dialed the number.**

*Subordinate Clauses.* Use commas to separate three or more subordinate clauses in a series.

The newspaper article explained **how the fire began, when it was put out,** and **how much damage was done.**

## Commas to Separate Sentence Parts

**Rule**   At the beginning of a sentence, use a comma after prepositional phrases of four or more words, after participial phrases (*page 71*), and after adverb clauses (*page 84*).

> **At the conclusion of the seminar,** the class handed in their notebooks. [prepositional phrase]
>
> **Wondering if she had missed her appointment,** Carla raced to the elevator. [participial phrase]
>
> **Before the concert began,** the musicians tuned their instruments. [adverb clause]

**Rule**   Use a comma to separate *yes* and *no* and other interjections, such as *oh* and *well,* from the rest of the sentence. Use a comma also to separate sentence parts that might otherwise be read together in a confusing manner; if possible, rewrite such sentences.

> **No,** that purple rain slicker is not hers.
>
> **Well,** this detective story was not very captivating.
>
> **At last,** first place was determined by a photo finish.
>
> **True,** dogs can be devoted companions.
>
> **This time,** patio chairs were stored indoors before the storm.

**Rule**   Use a comma before a coordinating conjunction (*page 30*) when it joins the independent clauses of a compound sentence (*page 90*).

> Will those old oak trees be cut down, **or** can your community organization find a way to save them?
>
> The cassowary seems defenseless, **but** this flightless bird is able to sprint at speeds of up to forty miles per hour.

**Rule**   Use a comma or a pair of commas to set off words of direct address and parenthetical expressions within a sentence.

> To be honest, **Jeremy,** this color does not suit you.
>
> His performances in the past have, **after all,** been superb.

**Rule** Use a comma or a pair of commas to set off nonessential appositives (*page 68*), nonessential phrases, and nonessential clauses (*page 83*). Treat an abbreviated title or degree following a name as a nonessential appositive.

NONESSENTIAL

> Wanda, **my oldest cousin,** won the local diving championship.
>
> Her favorite hobby, **weaving,** requires skill and concentration. [She has only one favorite hobby.]
>
> Our speaker tonight is Monroe Barth, **M.D.,** who will discuss nutrition and health.

Do *not* set off essential appositives (*page 68*), essential phrases, or essential clauses.

ESSENTIAL

> The sweater **that Karen gave me last year** was packed in my suitcase. [I have more than one sweater.]
>
> The children **who entered this poster contest** are quite imaginative. [The writer is speaking only of those specific children.]
>
> The barbed-wire fences **crossing this field** will keep the horses from running away. [Only those specific fences are keeping the horses in the field.]

**Rule** Use commas to separate the items in a date or an address and to set off a date or an address from words that follow it. Do not use a comma if only the month and year are given. Do not use a comma between a state and its ZIP code.

> The pony express between **St. Joseph, Missouri,** and **Sacramento, California,** began on **April 3, 1860.**
>
> Jeanette received her diploma in **June 1983.**
>
> Will you please mail this music box to **145 Foxfire Lane, Ypsilanti, Michigan 48197.**

**Rule** Use a comma after the greeting, or salutation, of a social letter and after the closing of any letter.

> My dear Margaret,      Sincerely,      Best wishes,

**Exercise 2** **Commas** On your paper, write the following sentences, using commas where necessary.

> **SAMPLE** Listening to the radio he heard his favorite song.
> **ANSWER** Listening to the radio, he heard his favorite song.

1. Be sure to care for your begonia with plant food a moderate amount of water and sufficient sunlight.
2. Mr. Ellis can you explain what you mean?
3. Uncle Seth who likes deep-sea diving has gone to Bermuda.
4. The horse seemed docile well groomed and obedient.
5. No they did not say why they brought the package what it was or whom it was for.
6. The Empire State Building in New York New York was opened on May 1 1931.
7. After a day at the beach the exhausted small children slept during the ride home.
8. The Italian artist Gian Lorenzo Bernini created sculpture and portraits in the baroque style.
9. Chuck dug a large pit he planted the tree and he watered the base thoroughly.
10. It was Dominick I believe who was asked to be the group's leader.
11. Wes and his family live in New Brunswick a Canadian province.
12. While exploring the forest near her cottage Sarah saw wild plants and flowers and birds.
13. Chasing after the runaway wagon Pete nearly tripped over a fallen log that was in the road.
14. Airplanes buses and trains were delayed by the blizzard.
15. No Dad my best friend for six years did not write a letter to me last month.
16. Everyone who witnessed the accident gave the same details to the newspaper reporter.
17. At the antiques fair in Aurora Jack bought a vase that was made he was told in the eighteenth century.
18. A quilting bee which is a yearly event will be held in the town hall.
19. Richard who is an eager student finally piloted the airplane but he had the instructor right beside him.
20. Set three two-pronged forks which are used for special occasions on the banquet table.

## 5.2c  Semicolons

Semicolons are used to connect independent clauses and to substitute for commas in sentences that already have a number of commas.

**Rule**  Use a semicolon to connect independent clauses that are not joined by a coordinating conjunction.

> I caught up with Bertram on the ski trail; he is a fast and skillful skier.
>
> The town's hundredth anniversary will be celebrated next week; there will be parade floats, a circus, and a barbecue.

BUT    Fix the laces on your roller skate, or you may stumble.

**Rule**  Use a semicolon to connect independent clauses that are joined by a conjunctive adverb (*page 32*) or an explanatory expression. Use a comma after the conjunctive adverb or explanatory expression.

> Water vapor is constantly present in the atmosphere; **however,** it must undergo condensation to produce dew, rain, or snow.
>
> Greta diligently practices her leaps and pirouettes; **consequently,** her featured role in the ballet performance will be successful.

**Rule**  Use a semicolon to clarify meaning in a sentence that contains several commas. Use semicolons to separate independent clauses that have commas within them and to separate items in a series if those items have internal commas. The semicolons make clear how many items are in the series.

UNCLEAR The birds that the biologist had studied were the great blue heron, a wading bird, the bird of paradise, a bird from New Guinea, the ring-necked pheasant, a game bird, and the brightly colored quetzal, a bird from Central America. [seven birds?]

CLEAR    The birds that the biologist had studied were the great blue heron, a wading bird; the bird of paradise, a bird from New Guinea; the ring-necked pheasant, a game bird; and the brightly colored quetzal, a bird from Central America. [four birds]

**Exercise 3   Semicolons**   On your paper, write each sentence, adding semicolons where they are needed. You may need to replace commas with semicolons to make a sentence clearer.

> **SAMPLE**      It was below freezing we remained indoors.
> **ANSWER**      It was below freezing; we remained indoors.

1. The student representatives at the meeting were Francis, a freshman, Wally, a sophomore, Hank, a junior, and Janet, a senior.
2. Edna turned the key in the ignition the motor hummed.
3. I wanted to join the chorus however, I had a part-time job in the afternoon that occupied all of my free time.
4. The rain had soaked the grass, mud, and bleachers therefore, Derek could not schedule afternoon practice.
5. The runners lined up and positioned themselves the race was about to start.
6. The apartment was spacious, attractive, and just what Mr. Douglas had been looking for however, it would not be available until the spring.
7. My neighbor planted marigolds, petunias, and tulips, then I helped her to water them.
8. Cassandra hopes to pursue one of these sciences: geology, the study of the earth's surface, mineralogy, the identification of minerals, or astronomy, the observation of the stars.
9. The country music concert was crowded nevertheless, the Andersen family enjoyed the event.
10. Politicians must hold debates, give speeches, and answer questions consequently, political campaigns can be exhausting.

## 5.2d   Colons

**Rule**   Use a colon to introduce an explanatory phrase, a statement, or a list of items that completes a sentence. The part of the sentence before the list may contain a demonstrative word, such as *these* or *those,* or an expression such as *the following* or *as follows*.

Our guide gave us our instructions: **to wait by the reservoir.**

David and Cindy bought the following: **nails, sandpaper, and balsa wood.**

Bolivia's exports include these ores: **tin, copper, lead, and zinc.**

Do *not* use a colon to introduce a list that follows a verb or a preposition.

Gary and Olivia **saw** sharks, seals, and otters at the aquarium. [not *saw:*]

Phil's vacation pictures included shots **of** Mt. Rushmore, Old Faithful, and Glacier National Park. [not *of:*]

**Rule** Use a colon after a complete sentence that introduces a direct quotation or a formal statement if the sentence does not contain a verb that indicates speech.

One reviewer loved the play: **"The opening act was sheer joy."**

**Rule** Use a colon to separate the hour and minutes in an expression of time, the chapter and verse in a biblical reference, and the volume and page number of a book or magazine reference.

**8:55** A.M.      Genesis **43:2 – 10**      *National Geographic* **162:536**

**Rule** Use a colon after the salutation of a business letter.

Dear Senator Sandoz:          Dear Sir or Madam:

**Exercise 4  Colons**  Some of the sentences that follow need colons. On your paper, write the sentences, supplying colons where needed. If a sentence is correct as it is, write *Correct* on your paper.

**SAMPLE**     The bus will depart promptly at 810 A.M.
**ANSWER**     The bus will depart promptly at 8:10 A.M.

1. Dear Mr. Genesee
   I recently purchased an item from your mail-order catalogue.
2. The baseball scorecard listed the players' names, numbers, and batting averages.

3. Evelyn and Rodney baby-sat from 730 P.M. to 1030 P.M.

4. For the recipe you will need the following two pounds of cut-up chicken, bread crumbs, milk, and spices.

5. Joshua told Margie that he felt pleased and surprised to hear such wonderful news.

6. I could never have done the entire project without persistence, hard work, and determination.

7. Her favorite passage from the Bible is Ecclesiastes 3 1–9.

8. This is what Barney purchased for the camping trip a tent, a sleeping bag, and a compass.

9. Ned summed up our dilemma "No one can remember John's address or telephone number."

10. Bonnie telephoned two people her niece and her friend Jean.

11. I am trying to obtain a copy of an article that appeared in *Science News* (12 121).

12. The professor criticized Joshua's handwriting "Not even my youngest child writes so illegibly!"

## 5.2e  Quotation Marks

**Rule**  Use quotation marks to show that you are writing the exact words someone said, thought, or wrote. Use quotation marks at both the beginning and the end of the quotation. Do not use quotation marks around an indirect quotation: a report of what another person said, thought, or wrote.

> Martine said, "I plan to become an orchestra conductor."
>
> "The shopping mall is twelve miles from here," he said, "if you take Route 3."
>
> He told us that the mall is twelve miles from here.

**Rule**  When you are writing dialogue, begin a new paragraph and use a separate set of quotation marks each time the speaker changes.

> "Mr. Cabot, may I see your driver's license and your vehicle registration?" the officer inquired.
>
> "Certainly," came the sheepish reply. "I have them right here."

**Rule** If you are writing a brief quotation that continues for more than one paragraph, use an opening quotation mark at the beginning of each paragraph, but use an end quotation mark only at the end of the last paragraph.

> "My house was on the side of a steep hill, with a narrow road in front.
> "One winter when we had a blizzard, all the neighbors gathered on the hill for a sledding party."

**Rule** When you are copying a quotation of five or more lines, set it off from the rest of your paper by indenting it five spaces from the left and right margins. Single-space it if you are typing. Do not use quotation marks with a quotation that is set off in this way. (See also Unit 12.)

**Rule** Use quotation marks to set off the title of a short story, an essay, an article, a short poem, or a song. Use them also to set off the title of any piece that forms part of a larger work, such as a single television show that is part of a series, a chapter of a book, a section of a newspaper, or a feature in a magazine. (See also page 211.)

> Washington Irving wrote **"Rip Van Winkle."**
> My favorite song is **"Send in the Clowns."**
> Chapter Three was called **"The Missing File."**
> Her column, **"Cooking for Fun,"** appears in the Sunday paper.

**Rule** Use quotation marks to call attention to the special or unusual nature of some words: a nickname used with a person's full name, slang used in formal writing, technical terms, and odd expressions. Avoid this informal usage if possible.

> Lee laughed; we all knew he would say **"alunimum."**
> My favorite ballplayer was Lawrence **"Yogi"** Berra.

**Other Punctuation with Quotation Marks.** The following rules will help you to determine where and how to use single quotation marks, commas, periods, colons, semicolons, question marks, and exclamation points with quotation marks.

**Rule**   Put single quotation marks around a quotation or a title that occurs within a longer quoted passage.

> Michelle told me, "Today we read **'The Road Not Taken'** by Robert Frost."

**Rule**   Place a comma or a period *before* closing quotation marks.

> "The books were there," he said. "We put them there ourselves."

**Rule**   Place a semicolon or a colon *after* closing quotation marks.

> Hilary said, "You know how I feel about this"; however, none of us was sure.
>
> Here's what we'll do after we read "The Lake Isle of Innisfree": try to write nature poems of our own.

**Rule**   Place a question mark or an exclamation point *before* the closing quotation marks if only the quoted material is a question or an exclamation. If the entire sentence is a question or an exclamation, place the question mark or exclamation point *after* the closing quotation marks. If both the quotation and the sentence require a question mark or an exclamation point, put the end mark *before* the closing quotation marks.

> The teacher asked, "What day is this?"
>
> Did the coach say, "Run two laps"?
>
> When did you ask, "What are we doing here?"

**Exercise 5    Quotation Marks**   On your paper, write correctly the sentences that need single or double quotation marks. Be sure to use capitalization, other punctuation, and paragraphing correctly. If a sentence needs no quotation marks, write *Correct* on your paper.

> **SAMPLE**    That was a bright idea! she said.
> **ANSWER**    "That was a bright idea!" she said.

1. Wendy looked for the Help Wanted section of the newspaper.
2. Mel said that he wasn't sure whether the mail had arrived yet.

3. Greta told the others, Don't get too far behind; however, a few still got lost.

4. The jubilant members of the baseball team cheered wildly when Joseph Butch Swenson hit a grand slam.

5. Maureen remarked to Mr. Phillips, I enjoyed discussing the poem The Red Wheelbarrow by William Carlos Williams.

6. Mr. Greene asked, What time is it? Almost noon, Richard replied.

7. What did she say when she saw the cake and heard everyone singing Happy Birthday?

8. Mrs. Hyde explained to the gym class In tennis, the word *love* means a zero score.

9. We enjoy reading It Pays to Increase Your Word Power in *Reader's Digest* every month.

10. Paul said, The following people starred in the movie: Lloyd Bridges, Kurt Jurgens, and Judy Canova.

## 5.2f  Apostrophes

### Possessives

**Rule**  Use an apostrophe and an *s* (*'s*) to form the possessive of a singular noun whether or not it ends in *s*. Also use an apostrophe and an *s* (*'s*) to form the possessive of a plural noun that does not end in *s*. Use an apostrophe alone to form the possessive of a plural noun that ends in *s*.

The preceding rule applies to proper nouns as well as to common nouns.

| | |
|---|---|
| the **mice's** tails | the **women's** desks |
| **Rubens's** paintings | the **girls'** lockers |
| **Chris's** portfolio | the **Lawtons'** sailboat |

Do *not* add an apostrophe or *'s* to **possessive personal pronouns:** *mine, yours, his, hers, its, ours, theirs.* They already show ownership.

This summary is **yours.** [not *your's*]

These anthologies are **hers.** [not *her's*]

The tortoise buried **its** eggs. [not *it's*]

**Rule**  Form the possessive of a compound noun (*page 4*) by changing the last word of the compound to its possessive form.

the vice **president's** name          the school**children's** books

**Rule**  Use the possessive form of only the last person's name to show joint ownership of an item. Use the possessive form of each name to show that two or more persons each possess separate items.

**Wilbur** and **Orville's** aircraft.

**Elinor Wylie's** and **Sara Teasdale's** poetry.

## Contractions

**Rule**  Use an apostrophe in a contraction to replace letters or numbers that have been left out.

**We've** made our plans.

**She'd** never go with us.

I think that the **'70s** were interesting years.

## Plurals

**Rule**  Use an apostrophe and an *s* (*'s*) to form the plurals of letters, numbers, symbols, and words that you are referring to as words or symbols (*page 211*). Use underlining (italics) correctly in such cases. Do not underline the *'s*.

There are two *m*'s in *accommodate*.

I found six *%*'s and nine *#*'s in the printout.

If we get five more *no*'s, the election will be lost.

**Note:**  The plurals of abbreviations that do not include periods are formed by adding just -*s*.

There are two **YMCAs** in our town.

BUT          The *YMCA*'s on both signs were spelled out in bright red letters. [Referring to the letters]

Although names of years are written with numerals, they also usually function as words and should be treated as such, rather than as numbers.

> Everyone in the class was born in the **1970s.**

BUT The ink was so faded that we could barely read the *1982*'s on the books' copyright pages. [Referring to the numerals, not to the year.]

## Exercise 6 Apostrophes

On your paper, write correctly the sentences that need apostrophes. If a sentence needs no apostrophes, write *Correct.*

> SAMPLE Jills dog won first prize at the pet show.
>
> ANSWER Jill's dog won first prize at the pet show.

1. I found it difficult to read Hermans composition because his *is* look like *es.*
2. Sam shouldnt have borrowed Sue and Lisas dictionary without asking their permission first.
3. That dogs kennel is regularly cleaned by Alice Foxs cousin.
4. Jacks and Erins desks are rather cluttered.
5. Those arent the childrens favorite songs; theyre mine.
6. During the 1920s a quick and lively dance called the Charleston was very popular.
7. You should delete all of the %s and $s from the manuscript before submitting it.
8. Her uncle went to school in the '40s or '50s.
9. This speaker tends to use a great many *however*s and *therefore*s in his lectures.
10. We enjoyed looking at the Winstons photographs.

## 5.2g Hyphens, Dashes, and Ellipsis Points

### The Hyphen

**Rule** Use a hyphen to divide a word at the end of a line. Do not divide a word of one syllable, such as *washed* or *grieve.* Do not divide any word so that one letter stands by itself. Always divide a word between its syllables and in such a way that the reader will not be confused about its meaning or pronunciation.

> In the past few months, we did not have as much **communi-cation** with the Burtons.

**Rule**  Divide a word with a prefix after the prefix. Divide a word with a suffix before the suffix. Divide a compound word that is written as one word only between the base words. Divide a hyphenated compound word only at the hyphen.

> Benjamin, could you tell me where you found this **color-ful** puzzle? [not *col-orful*]
>
> Charlene remained at home on the morning of the **champion-ship** game. [not *champi-onship*]
>
> This year we will celebrate Thanksgiving with my **great-grandmother** at her home. [not *great-grand-mother*]

**Rule**  Use a hyphen after the prefixes *all-, ex-,* and *self-*. Use a hyphen to separate any prefix from a proper noun or a proper adjective.

| | | | |
|---|---|---|---|
| **all-**natural | **un-**American | BUT | **un**prepared |
| **ex-**ballplayer | **pre-**Raphaelite | BUT | **pre**arranged |
| **self-**conscious | **post-**Victorian | BUT | **post**script |

**Rule**  Hyphenate compound modifiers when they precede the noun that they modify, but not when they follow it. Do not hyphenate a compound modifier when its first part is an adverb that ends in *-ly*.

> Those are **well-polished** wood floors.
>
> BUT    Those wood floors are **well polished.**

> The costume collection at the museum features **turn-of-the century** clothing.
>
> BUT    The clothing featured in the costume collection at the museum is from the **turn of the century.**

The **rarely seen** snow leopard was carefully transported to the zoo.

Mr. Marshall said that the television program was **mildly satirical.**

*Fractions.* Use a hyphen in a fraction that is used as a modifier. Do not hyphenate a fraction that is used as a noun.

Her dance class will be **three-fourths** ballet.

BUT **Three fourths** of her dance class will be ballet.

**Rule** Use a hyphen to separate compound numbers from *twenty-one* through *ninety-nine*.

|       | seventy-two   | thirty-four      |
|-------|---------------|------------------|
| BUT   | six hundred   | seventy thousand |

## The Dash

**Rule** Use a dash to show an interrupted or unfinished thought or speech. Use a second dash to close the interruption if the sentence continues.

Someone—**it might have been Paul**—lost a set of keys during the confusion.

"Will you remember—**or have you already bought**—a few items at the bakery?" asked Nancy.

In typing, use two hyphens to represent a dash. Do not type a single hyphen to stand for a dash.

**Note:** Avoid using dashes in formal writing.

## Ellipsis Points

**Rule** Use **ellipsis points,** a set of three periods together ( . . . ), to show that you are leaving out part of a quotation. If what precedes the ellipsis points is a complete sentence, end the sentence with a period before you add the ellipsis points. If it is not a complete sentence, use only the ellipsis points.

> Abraham Lincoln said, "With malice toward none, with charify for all, . . . let us strive on to finish the work we are in."
>
> Thoreau proclaimed, "Our life is frittered away by detail. . . . Simplicity, simplicity, simplicity!"

**Exercise 7   Hyphens, Dashes, Ellipsis Points**   On your paper, write the following sentences. Add hyphens, dashes, and ellipsis points where necessary.

| | |
|---|---|
| **SAMPLE** | The over confident quarterback suddenly fumbled the football. |
| **ANSWER** | The over-confident quarterback suddenly fumbled the football. |

1. Four fifths of the twenty five people in my math class could not solve the problem.
2. "I believe but I am not sure that the twelfth of this month will fall on a Wednesday," said Jessica.
3. The neatly swept floor and the well polished furniture in the room were inviting.
4. We were asked to supply the missing words in the following quotation from our national anthem: "Oh, say, does that star-spangled banner yet wave / O'er the land of the brave?"
5. The all purpose glue that Josh bought worked on the broken vase.
6. All of my good news if I can remember it will fill three fourths of this letter!
7. The ex president of our club possessed good sense, self confidence, and years of experience.
8. The houses were covered with a layer of snow that day but that's not important.
9. Do you know the saying that begins "A penny saved"?
10. I watched a bird wheel around the cloud filled sky.
11. The blueprint for the house indicated that there should be a six foot space between beams.
12. Sometimes seemingly old fashioned ideas are quite modern.

## 5.2h   Parentheses and Brackets

### Parentheses

**Rule**   Use parentheses to enclose material that is not basic to the meaning of the sentence.

> The survey included some of the Middle Atlantic states (**Delaware, New Jersey, and Pennsylvania**) and Virginia.
>
> There will be a Mack Sennett (**1880–1960**) film festival here that includes his most famous silent comedies.

If the parenthetical material forms a complete sentence within another sentence, do not use a capital letter or a period to mark the sentence inside the parentheses. If a question mark or exclamation point is needed, include it.

> Claire has lived in rural areas (**she** once lived on a dairy farm!), but now she lives in a large town.

After the closing parenthesis, use the punctuation that would be needed if the parenthetical material were not in the sentence. If the parenthesis ends the sentence, put the period *outside* the parenthesis.

> The dawn redwood, discovered in China in a hidden valley (**1944**), was once thought to be extinct.
>
> Bert is fascinated by the theory that studying people's handwriting can reveal their personalities (**graphology**).

If the parenthetical material is not inside another sentence, use capitalization and punctuation within the parentheses just as if the parentheses were not there.

> The class examined some detailed photographs of Greek ruins. (**They** saw pictures of temples at Delphi.)

### Brackets

**Rule**   Put brackets around any explanatory words or other information that you are adding to a quotation.

> Tolstoi wrote, "The most powerful weapon of ignorance [is] the diffusion of printed matter." [In the original, a dash is used. The writer here inserted *is* to make a grammatically complete, clear sentence.]

**Exercise 8   Parentheses and Brackets**   On your paper, write the following sentences, using parentheses and brackets correctly.

> SAMPLE        *The Scarlet Letter* 1850 was Hawthorne's first novel.
> ANSWER        *The Scarlet Letter* (1850) was Hawthorne's first novel.

1. "In spite of the difficulty a shortage of water the pioneers settled there in the mid-1800s."
2. More than one American author notably Thoreau has written about people's need to simplify their lives.
3. "Let us meet again at the nobleman's *palazzo* palace near Venice to decide this crucial matter."
4. Shenandoah National Park approximately 190,000 acres is in the midst of Virginia's Blue Ridge Mountains.
5. "These two Michael Faraday and Alessandro Volta were the first scientists to experiment with electricity," the report stated.
6. One of the first globes created in Germany 1492 was made by Martin Behaim.
7. Carlos and Mike competed in the race both are stock-car drivers, and they had fair results.
8. "Toward glistening ridges the French Alps I glanced from the window of this convivial inn. . . ."
9. The ripe fruit probably mangoes fell from trees and into baskets.
10. In the 1800s a number of Utopian communities New Harmony, for example were founded in the United States.

**Assignment   Punctuation**   The following five word groups can be combined to make different sentences. Try to write at least ten sentences, each using different punctuation. Include question marks, exclamation points, commas, semicolons, colons, quotation marks, apostrophes, hyphens, dashes, ellipsis points, parentheses, and brackets. You may have to add or change some words in order to write complete sentences.

> SAMPLE        Waving his arms excitedly
>               Write to your aunt.
> ANSWER        Waving his arms excitedly, Maurice called, "Did you
>               write to your aunt?"

1. Counting out coins, jewels, and bills
2. Walk down the wide boulevard
3. She made the discovery accidentally
4. Philippa was the first one in the group
5. Whom did you see

# 5.3 Using Italics and Numbers in Writing

## 5.3a Italics

In printed material, certain words and figures are set in italic type (*slanted letters like these*). In handwriting and typing, this material should be underlined.

**Rule** Underline (italicize) the titles of books, book-length poems, newspapers, magazines, movies, works of art, television series, and so forth. Underline also the names of trains, ships, and spacecraft. Underline an article (*a, an, the*) that comes before the title only if it is part of the title. (See also page 201.)

| | |
|---|---|
| *Robinson Crusoe* | *Casablanca* |
| the *New Orleans Times-Picayune* | Rodin's *Orpheus* |
| *Modern Photography* | the U.S.S. *New Jersey* |

**Rule** Underline (italicize) letters, numbers, symbols, and words when you are calling special attention to them as words or symbols.

While typing his report, Daniel mistakenly capitalized the *g* in *geography.*

Please erase that *7* and replace it with a *9* to correct the chart.

**Rule** Underline (italicize) a word or a phrase that you wish to emphasize. Avoid overuse of this device.

Turn right at the *second* stoplight after Nevada Avenue.

**Rule**   Underline (italicize) words from other languages if those words are not commonly used in English.

> The man said that he was the *jefe de familia,* or head of the family.

BUT   We read about the coup d'état in that country. [*Coup d'état* has become commonly used in English.]

**Exercise 1   Italics**   Write the following sentences on your paper, supplying underlining wherever necessary.

SAMPLE   Theodore reads the Richmond Times-Dispatch regularly.

ANSWER   Theodore reads the <u>Richmond Times-Dispatch</u> regularly.

1. Homer's epic poem the Iliad describes the siege of Troy during the Trojan War.
2. Carrie looked up the spelling of millennium in her dictionary; then she double-checked the meaning of platitudinous.
3. Are the f and ? keys on your typewriter broken?
4. The satellite Sputnik I was the first spacecraft to circle the earth.
5. The word accidental was missing from the headline of an article I was reading in the Winnipeg Tribune.
6. The C in the sign advertising Casablanca did not light up like the other letters.
7. Does your little brother watch Sesame Street?
8. In Rome we loved watching the carabinieri dramatically directing the heavy traffic.
9. Place an X over the name of your choice for student-council treasurer.
10. Wally and his sister went to the art gallery to see Gainsborough's painting The Market Cart.

## 5.3b   Using Numbers in Writing

**Rule**   Spell out numbers of *one hundred* or less and all numbers that are rounded to even hundreds and can be written in two words or less (*twenty thousand*, but *22,100.*)

I counted **sixteen** dirigibles and **twenty-seven** hot-air balloons in the air show.

There are approximately **two hundred** species of monkeys in the world.

BUT    Colleen has bicycled **1050** miles in the past **two** years.

**Rule**  Use Arabic numerals for numbers greater than *one hundred* that are not rounded to even hundreds.

The highest recorded temperature was **134** degrees above zero.

**Rule**  Spell out any number at the beginning of a sentence, or rewrite the sentence.

The word *and* is unnecessary in writing numbers except those between *one hundred and one* and *one hundred and ten, two hundred and one* and *two hundred and ten,* and so forth.

INCORRECT    **205** pickers arrived at the apple orchards.

CORRECT    **Two hundred and five** pickers arrived at the apple orchards.

CORRECT    Early in the morning, **205** pickers arrived at the apple orchards.

**Rule**  When you write an expression of time, spell it out unless it is a specific time using *A.M.* or *P.M.* Use numerals and *A.M.* or *P.M.* in all technical writing.

Be at the crossroads at **five-thirty.**

BUT    The first alarm sounded at **8:42** P.M.

**Rule**  Use numerals to express dates, street numbers, room numbers, apartment numbers, telephone numbers, page numbers, and percentages. Spell out the word *percent*.

April **27, 1954**          **1-800-555-7840**
**139** Vista Canyon Road    pages **213 – 241**
Apartment **66** G           **85** percent

*Dates.* When you write a date, do not add *-st, -nd, -rd,* or *-th* to the numeral.

INCORRECT    November **12th**, 1967    March **9th**

CORRECT      November **12**, 1967    March **9**

**Exercise 2   Numbers in Writing**   On your paper, write the following sentences, correcting any errors in the writing of numbers.

SAMPLE    5 of us left for Oregon on June 22nd.

ANSWER    Five of us left for Oregon on June 22.

1. Mary Ellen now lives in Apartment Four in the large white building at thirty-nine Powell Street.
2. Close to forty % of Idaho's land area is covered with forests.
3. Approximately 500 students attended the pep rally.
4. Julius Caesar, Roman statesman and general, lived from one hundred to forty-four B.C.
5. Was this airplane scheduled to leave at four twenty P.M.?
6. The Canadian province of Manitoba covers an area of two hundred fifty-one thousand square miles.
7. Look on pages twenty-three and twenty-four to find 3 of Randy's poems in our literary magazine.
8. At the ceremony on December 10th, 14 grand-prize winners came to the podium to receive their tickets.
9. Please meet me at the shopping center at 2:30; I have about ten errands to finish.
10. 80% of the applicants must be taken to Room Eleven to fill out their 5 forms.

**Assignment 1   Italics**   Write ten sentences using three of the following topics. Try to include in each sentence titles, foreign words, letters, numbers, or symbols. Make sure that you check your sentences for correct underlining.

1. A shop on a street in a town or a city
2. A book about a well-known scientist
3. How to be a good friend

4. The magazines in your home
5. A courageous act that you have witnessed

**Assignment 2  Numbers in Writing**  Find information about the career of a well-known athlete. Your facts about this sports figure should answer some of the following questions:

1. What records did this athlete set or break?
2. Which years did his or her career span?
3. How many championships or awards did he or she win?
4. What other facts about this athlete are important?

Using the facts that you have gathered, write a short paragraph about the sports figure. Make sure that you correctly use numbers in your writing.

## Using Mechanics

You wish to persuade someone you know to take a trip. To do this, describe a place that you once visited or would like to visit. This place may be imaginary; however, be sure to include details in your description. Think of some of the attractions of this place: its physical features, its climate, its inhabitants, its culture, and so forth. Write a brief description, including some direct quotations about this location from other enthusiasts, some statistical information, some lists of its assets or products, and some historical points of interest. As you write your description, check to see that you correctly use mechanics: capitalization, punctuation, underlining (for italics), and numbers.

# 5.4   Preparing Your Manuscript

## 5.4a   Proofreading Symbols

The following symbols are commonly used to identify and correct errors in composition. Use them when you revise and proofread your writing.

| | | |
|---|---|---|
| ∧ | insert something | lost her ∧walking on stilts  *balance* |
| # | space | bought a red#balloon |
| ¶ | begin new paragraph | last of the heroes. ¶ In the next century |
| ∼ | transpose letter or words | this fabirc made has |
| ℓ | delete | a mountaintop ~~top~~ retreat |
| ◯ | close up letters | I am happ◯y to introduce |
| .... | let it stand (under something crossed out) | consisted of a ~~large~~ percentage |
| ≡ | capitalize | the Department of agriculture̲≡ |
| / | make lower case | Marlene gazed at the Portrait. |

## 5.4b  Manuscript Form

### Handwritten Manuscripts

**Paper.**  Write compositions on standard-size paper (8½ by 10 inches or 8½ by 11 inches). Write on one side only.

**Ink.**  Use black or blue ink.

**Margins.**  Leave margins of 1½ inches at the left side and 1 inch at the right side. The left margin must be even.

**Title.**  Write the title of your composition in the center of the top line. Skip at least one line between the title and the first paragraph. Do not put quotation marks around the title.

**Indentation.**  Indent the first line of every paragraph 1 inch.

### Typewritten Manuscripts

**Paper.**  Use standard-size white typing paper (8½ by 11 inches). Double-space, and use only one side of the paper.

**Ribbon.**  Use a black typewriter ribbon.

**Margins.**  Leave margins of 1½ inches at the left side and 1 inch at the right side. The left margin must be even. On all pages except the title page, place the first line at least 1 inch below the top of the page. Leave a margin of 1 inch at the bottom of all pages.

**Title.**  Center the title about 2 inches below the top of the page. Do not put quotation marks around the title. Begin the first paragraph four lines below the title.

**Indentation.**  Indent the first line of every paragraph five spaces.

### Labeling and Numbering Pages

Write your name, the subject, and the date (in that order) in the upper-right corner of the first page. On every page except the first page, put the page number in the upper-right corner unless your teacher gives you other instructions. Use Arabic numerals.

If your paper consists of more than one page, attach the pages at the upper-left corner with a staple or a paper clip.

# Unit Practice

## Practice 1

**A. Capitalization** (*pages 183–190*)  On your paper, write each of the following sentences, adding all necessary capital letters.

1. i like victorian architecture better than some of the colonial architecture that i saw in the east.
2. lars asked, "did you do a lesson on the pythagorean theorem in geometry I?"
3. uncle henry recited one of his favorite sonnets from elizabeth barrett browning's *sonnets from the portuguese.*
4. "come with us," said grandmother, "to the sudbury fair next sunday at 3 p.m."
5. f. scott fitzgerald wrote *the great gatsby* and *this side of paradise.*
6. in the middle ages, knights often wore armored gloves called gauntlets.
7. in roman myths the goddess of flowers and of spring is flora.
8. the crab nebula, an extensive cloud of dust and gases, probably resulted from the explosion of a very bright star.
9. "the annual tulip festival in may is an event that you should not miss," stated the feature writer. "it is held in holland, michigan."
10. her father, dr. gagliardi, saw the sphinx when he traveled to egypt with clarendon tours limited.

**B. Punctuation** (*pages 190–211*)  On your paper, write each of the following sentences, adding all necessary punctuation.

11. Maria responded Yes I have the papers that you wanted Andy and you may have them.
12. Before you close the garage door please bring in these items the lawn hose the barbecue grill and the bicycle
13. Did Marks oldest brother who was once a basketball captain participate in the all star tournament asked Stephanie
14. Beginning with the *J*s look in the telephone directory for a local jewelry shop and a good repair shop and a yarn store
15. The quotation began Seven long struggle filled years have passed and we are on the brink.
16. Yesterday I picked out two colors I chose an old fashioned pattern and I bought the yarn however I forgot my knitting needles

17. Yes Dr S J Shaw will be interviewed tonight however the time has been changed to 800 PM

18. A few of the items that I bought at the shopping mall were the following a spatula a utensil that is useful in cooking a garden hoe a necessary tool and wool socks which will keep me warm in winter

19. Is *Na* the symbol for sodium written correctly in the blank next to item twenty nine on the students tests

20. Larry hes moving from the neighborhood will hold a yard sale at 230 PM that will include books such as Frank Waterss story The Man Who Killed the Deer

## C. Italics and Numbers in Writing (*pages 211–215*)  As you write each sentence on your paper, underline the words that should be italicized, and use the correct number form.

21. Admiral George Dewey won an important victory with his ship, the U.S.S. Olympia, in Manila Bay on May (first, 1st, 1), 1898.

22. The capital of the Canadian province of Saskatchewan, which takes its name from the Latin word regina, meaning "queen," has more than (250, two hundred fifty) industrial plants.

23. Watch for the announcement of the opera La Traviata; it will be performed next Tuesday at (eight-thirty, 8:30, 8 thirty).

24. "Be considerate and always rinse out your beakers," said Professor Canetti, "because there are (one hundred twenty-eight, 128, one hundred and twenty-eight) students."

25. The tree with the Spanish name quebracho, or "ax-breaker," is valuable because the wood is (20%, 20 percent, twenty percent) tannin, which is used in tanning leather.

26. Brett forgot to paint the ! on the poster, but everyone read the important information about auditions for Hello, Dolly!

27. (1300, Thirteen hundred) homes will be built in the valley this year before December (2nd, second, 2).

28. Put an A for audit or a C for credit on the course-registration form.

29. Nearly (two hundred, 2 hundred, 200) trees were damaged in the storm that swept the area on May (22, 22nd, twenty-two), 1966.

30. I have (fifteen, 15) of the pieces for this board game, but I cannot find the piece with the 4 on it.

(Continue on the next page.)

# Practice 2

Rewrite the following passage, supplying the appropriate capitalization, punctuation, and underlining (for italics), and correcting the use of numbers.

chess a board game that traces its history to at least ad five hundred was first played in asia the game some believe was invented in india and its popularity eventually spread to other countries the basic elements of chess are the following a chessboard with 64 light and dark squares 32 carved pieces and 2 players the pieces 8 pawns 2 rooks 2 knights 2 bishops a queen and a king for each player may be carved out of rock stone or wood or made of metal porcelain or other materials according to established rules the players move these pieces in fixed directions each players goal is to move the pieces to force the opponents king into an inescapable position the word chess comes from the persian word for king

the first international chess tournament took place in london in 1851 such tournaments have become increasingly popular and competitive historically there are many well documented feats of chess champions who have played more than 100 concurrent games or those who have played blindfolded and with specific time limits perhaps the psychological nature of chess and the rules that govern its play are what contributed to thomas henry huxleys observation in his essay a liberal education The chessboard is the world

# Unit Tests

## Test 1

**A. Capitalization** (*pages 183–190*)   On your paper, write each of the following sentences, adding all necessary capital letters.

1. "will you be able to complete your piece of sculpture," asked ron, "before the art fair in november?"
2. the *seneca chief* was the first vessel to travel along the entire route of the erie canal.
3. on the island of crete, an archaeologist named sir arthur john evans discovered ancient greek writing on clay tablets.
4. hal stated, "wyoming was the first state in which women voted, held political office, and served on juries."
5. heimdall, who in norse mythology was the guardian of bridges, had such extraordinary senses that he could hear grass growing.
6. betty and cliff belong to the table tennis association, located in missouri.
7. in order to learn more about the atmosphere of venus, the space probe *mariner 5* went to the planet's dark side.
8. "try true blue ink," the store owner said. "it will not fade, and you can use it for your drawing class."
9. i enjoyed reading *across the plains,* a book by robert louis stevenson that describes a trip from new york to san francisco.
10. the north american treaty organization has its own flag.

**B. Punctuation** (*pages 190–211*)   On your paper, write each of the following sentences, adding all necessary punctuation.

11. Would you take record albums a tape recorder and extra tapes to the Lyles house asked Henry
12. His speech began All good deeds demand notice
13. What a beautiful night this is
14. Working all afternoon they completed the initial experiment however they still had to find information about helium He and hydrogen H
15. That ship set sail in fact on November 12 1757 with the following cargo spices silks and other fabrics teak and bamboo

(Continue on the next page.)

16. While visiting the new aquarium I enjoyed the trained seals act I learned about the habits of the penguin and I saw a sea turtle for the first time

17. Her mother who was an amateur gardener exclaimed Kate please do not trample those newly planted sweet smelling flowers

18. Charless source was *Bird Watcher Magazine* which is no longer being published

19. In Pella a town in Iowa the citizens have retained many Dutch customs and tourists visit during tulip time

20. Maxines report began The evidence includes data obtained by Mr S G Grassley the newspaper editor

**C. Italics and Numbers in Writing** (*pages 211–215*)    As you write each sentence on your paper, underline the words that should be italicized, and write the correct number form.

21. Arizona, which has (113,909; one hundred thirteen thousand nine hundred and nine; 113 thousand; 909) square miles of land, derived its name from the Native American word arizonac.

22. On a yacht called the Gipsy Moth IV, measuring (fifty-three, 53) feet, Sir Francis Chichester sailed alone from England to Australia.

23. (27, Twenty-seven) seats in (the twelfth, the 12th) row are filled for the opening of Chekhov's play Uncle Vanya.

24. On July (20th, 20, twenty), 1969, the historic first moonwalk took place after the lunar module called the Eagle landed.

25. Please meet Mr. Wertimer's bus promptly at (12:45, twelve forty-five) P.M.

26. When Cassie moved into the apartment complex on Applewood Lane, she was the first occupant of Apartment (Thirty-five, 35).

27. (Twelve hundred, 1200, 12 hundred) participants in the survey put a 7 instead of a 6 in the last blank.

28. Can you come to the seminar on April (4th, fourth, 4), when the art historian will give an analysis of El Greco's painting View of Toledo?

29. Remember to bring extra pencils and scratch paper, but do not write in the blank with the $ written beside it.

30. At the street fair, I heard bouzoukis (Greek stringed instruments), and I tasted the ethnic dishes from some of the (21, twenty-one) booths.

# Test 2

Rewrite the following passage, supplying the appropriate capitalization, punctuation, and underlining (for italics), and correcting the use of numbers.

by glancing at the combination of patterns and dyes of batik cloth said ms oates an art historian one can determine its specific history meaning and use she continued this traditional indonesian fabric tells a story to the knowledgeable observer all of the colors and designs are most likely pleasing to all 28 members of this group looking at this batik you can see white dots that crisscross the hand dyed material

in fact the term batik derives from the indonesian words mbat to play with and ntik to make a dot remarked ms oates after a design is traced on fabric with heated wax the material is dyed the wax is removed and decorative white motifs remain then the cloth is finished she exclaimed

this art has been practiced for at least 800 years but there have been many different uses for the fabric 1 of the uses is to convey beliefs for example if the god ratu kiduto is believed to be angry batik with a certain design is launched upon a raft into the indian ocean ms oates concluded whether from jogjakarta or solo on the island of java or from another island batik is beautiful even members of royalty wear their own special batik designs

# Part Two

## Composition

| | | | |
|---|---|---|---|
| Unit | 6 | **Prewriting** | **226** |
| Unit | 7 | **Writing Paragraphs** | **248** |
| Unit | 8 | **Revising** | **284** |
| Unit | 9 | **Three Modes of Writing** | **336** |
| Unit | 10 | **Persuasive Writing** | **372** |
| Unit | 11 | **Writing an Essay** | **412** |
| Unit | 12 | **Writing About Literature** | **448** |
| Unit | 13 | **Writing a Research Paper** | **482** |
| Unit | 14 | **Writing Business Letters** | **542** |

Writing paragraphs, essays, reports, and letters that present your ideas effectively requires more than simply applying the rules of grammar, usage, and mechanics. Writing well also requires the ability to focus your thoughts and to arrange them in a logical order. In Part Two, you will learn techniques of developing, organizing, and expressing your ideas in writing.

Units 6 through 8 explain the process of writing as a series of three steps: prewriting, writing, and revising. Units 9 and 10 demonstrate how you can adapt your writing for specific purposes: to explain, to describe, to narrate, and to persuade. Units 11 through 14 present additional techniques that you need in order to write effective essays, research papers, and letters.

# Unit 6

## Prewriting

---

## Unit Preview

The process of writing includes three stages: prewriting, writing, and revising. If you take the time to learn the skills in each stage, you will find that your writing is easier and the results better.

**Prewriting,** the first stage, is the planning and preparation that you do before you write. During the prewriting stage, you find subjects that interest you, you explore those subjects from many points of view, and you focus them according to the scope and purpose of your assignment. Careful and thoughtful prewriting will give your writing substance and direction.

The following example shows some prewriting notes by a writer who is interested in basketball.

Fast pace, exciting to watch or to play

Players need endurance.

Rules are easy.

Rim shots, dunk shots

Tall players

Passing, dribbling, shooting

Our team needs new uniforms.

"Foul Shot" by Edwin Hoey

How are professional games different from high school and college games?

What is the history of basketball?

Who are or were important players?

What are the different types of shots and fouls?

Can women join professional teams?

What are the characteristics of offensive and defensive play?

**For Analysis**   On your paper, answer these questions about the prewriting notes.

1. What are two additional questions that you would ask to help you to find out more about basketball?
2. What are two writing topics that come to mind when you look at the prewriting notes about basketball?
3. Which notes would be useful if you were planning to write about the different types of shots used in a basketball game?

In reviewing these notes and answering the questions about them, you have participated in prewriting. In this unit you will learn prewriting skills: how to find subjects to write about, how to explore those subjects, and how to use your prewriting material to help you write on specific topics.

# 6.1   Finding Ideas for Writing

Your first task as a writer is deciding what to write about. This decision becomes easier if you have an available source of writing ideas. You will discover many possible subjects for writing by continually observing and reflecting on your own activities and on the world around you.

## 6.1a   Keeping a Writer's Notebook

A **writer's notebook** is a record of your interests, observations, and experiences, together with your notes about those items. You may record these items in any form that makes sense to you—for example, words, phrases, sentences, questions, or lists. Beside each entry, you may jot down a related idea, a question, a comment about the item, or a note explaining why it interests you. These notes will help you find writing ideas whenever you need them.

The following strategies and examples will demonstrate ways to begin your writer's notebook.

## Strategies

1. *List your interests, hobbies, and ambitions.*

| EXAMPLES | NOTES |
|---|---|
| Swimming | Floating in Great Salt Lake |
| Coin collecting | Kinds of collections: series, type, topical, country |
| Careers in medicine | How can I become an emergency medical technician? |

2. *List your memorable experiences.*

| EXAMPLES | NOTES |
|---|---|
| Emergency appendectomy | Nurses' explanations made me feel less frightened. |
| Helped Ted build radio | How do radio signals work? |

3. *Note problems or issues that interest you.*

| EXAMPLE | NOTE |
|---|---|
| Should old city hall be razed for new one? | No; inconveniences of old building are less important than its beauty. |

4. *Note anything that you observe, think, or do that you want to remember.*

| EXAMPLES | NOTES |
|---|---|
| Dress rehearsal for dance program | Why do I perform better when I'm a bit nervous? |
| I've had twenty-four teachers since first grade. | What was it like in a one-room schoolhouse? |

5. *React to what you read.* Take notes on subjects or ideas that you would like to learn more about. Write down your questions or opinions about what you read.

| EXAMPLES | NOTES |
|---|---|
| A magazine article about UNICEF | How are donations used? |
| A negative review of a movie that I enjoyed | What criteria do I use for judging a movie? |
| A magazine quiz to determine my level of self-confidence | What are the attributes of a self-confident person? |
| A novel based on the history of a family | The Gordons are the most talented family I know. |

6. *Record your significant viewing and listening experiences.* Conversations, ceremonies, theatrical performances, radio, television, and movies are among the possible sources of ideas for writing.

| EXAMPLES | NOTES |
|---|---|
| Mayor Phelps addressing a group of supporters | How did the custom of applause originate? |
| The school production of *Twelve Angry Men* | Find someone who has served on a jury—what is it like? |
| A television special about the development of new medicines | Some ancient herbal medicines have actual therapeutic value—how were they discovered? |
| A performance of *The Nutcracker* | Offshoot of ballet: modern jazz dance |

**Exercise 1  Prewriting: Writer's Notebook**  On your paper, write a specific entry for six of the following items. Next to each entry, write a note in the form of a question, an observation, or a comment. Put your paper in your writer's notebook.

| SAMPLE | A meeting or an assembly at school |
|---|---|
| ANSWER | *Entry:* Student council candidates introduced |
| | *Note:* A good campaign slogan is an important publicity tool. |

1. A sports event
2. A book that you have enjoyed
3. A pleasant memory
4. A job or career that interests you
5. Something that you saw or heard that was funny
6. A news article about a local or national issue
7. A comic strip
8. One of your hobbies
9. An interview with a well-known person
10. A local problem or issue
11. An extracurricular activity that you are involved in
12. A ceremony that you have witnessed or taken part in
13. A letter to an advice column
14. A recording that you like
15. A stimulating idea from one of your textbooks

**Exercise 2   Prewriting: Writer's Notebook**   On your paper, list five of the following subjects. After each subject write a response in the form of a question or comment. Put your paper in your writer's notebook.

|  |  |
|---|---|
| **SAMPLE** | Friendship |
| **ANSWER** | Should a good friend be tactful or completely honest? |

1. An ambition
2. Animals
3. Health
4. Leisure time
5. Friendship

6. Music
7. Paid or volunteer work
8. Politics
9. Professional sports
10. Travel

## 6.1b   Finding Ideas in Data

Part of your prewriting to find ideas may consist of sifting through data that you encounter in charts and statistics. This information may not immediately suggest any ideas for writing; however, if you take the time to study and analyze it, you will often discover some ideas.

For example, you may have read in your school newspaper the following results of a survey of juniors and seniors:

Eighty-one percent are concerned about future work or careers.

Sixteen percent have definite career plans.

Twenty-five percent know the general career area in which they are interested.

Sixty-nine percent would like to get work experience while they are in high school.

Using the following strategies will help you to analyze data to find writing ideas.

### Strategies

1. *Look for trends in the information.* Try to draw the facts and ideas together to see if they point to a conclusion. Try to relate the information to a larger idea or issue.

2. *Look for problems to which you can suggest solutions.* A clear statement of a problem and your solution to the problem can be a good writing idea.

3. *List questions that might prompt further research.*

By using these strategies to analyze the data from the student survey, you might get the following notes:

*Trend:* Most students are concerned about what work they will do in the future.

*Problem:* Something needs to be done to help students learn about careers in order to make informed career decisions.

*Question:* When should students begin to plan careers?

You may include your data and your related notes in your writer's notebook.

### Exercise 3  Prewriting: Ideas in Data  On your paper, analyze the following sets of facts, using the preceding strategies. Write down trends, problems, and questions. Then briefly summarize the writing ideas that each set of data suggests.

1. The day after a local election in which the voter turnout was poor, you notice the following facts in your local newspaper:

   The weather was cold and stormy.

   Many voters did not have transportation to polling places or did not have child care.

   The heaviest voting took place before and after working hours.

2. A survey of young people in your community reveals the following statistics:

   Seventy-five percent would like to have a place for basketball, table tennis, weightlifting, exercising.

   Sixty-five percent feel that they do not have an appropriate place to socialize.

   Ten percent are not interested in socializing.

   Eighty percent meet friends in homes, parks, or on street corners.

   Twenty-five percent use the recreational center in a neighboring community.

**Assignment 1   Prewriting**   Keep your writer's notebook with you throughout one day. Record in your notebook the highlights of conversations and discussions of the people around you. Include at least three observations about what you have heard.

**Assignment 2   Prewriting**   Keep a log of your television viewing for one week. Note the programs, ideas, scenes, or dialogue that you particularly like or react to in some way. At the end of the week, review and summarize your notes. Add your log to your writer's notebook.

**Assignment 3   Prewriting**   Take a survey of at least ten people on one of the following subjects or on one of your own choice. Analyze your results and jot down possible writing subjects.

1. What would you do if you had $5000 to spend in one day?
2. If a day were thirty-six hours long, what would you do with the additional time?

3. What are the three most-needed inventions?

4. Make three predictions about life on Earth one hundred years from now.

**Continuing Assignment** **Prewriting** Select two subjects from your writer's notebook and one that you have discovered by analyzing data. Write each of them on a separate piece of paper. Save your papers.

### Assignment Checklist

Check your assignments for the following points:

☑ 1. In Assignment 1, did you include at least three observations about aspects of the conversations that you heard?

☑ 2. In Assignment 2, did you record and summarize your impressions of your television viewing?

☑ 3. In Assignment 3, did you analyze the results of your survey and note possible subjects for writing?

☑ 4. In the Continuing Assignment, did you select three items that you would like to develop?

## 6.2    Developing Your Ideas

Your writer's notebook will provide an extensive collection of subjects for you to write about. From this collection, select subjects that interest you or that fit your assignments. You can now develop these subjects by making lists and by exploring your subjects from many viewpoints.

### 6.2a    Making Lists

Begin to develop your subject by writing down all the ideas and facts about it that you know or need to learn and all the related ideas that you associate with it. Keep an open mind at this point. Do not be concerned if your thoughts are unconnected, overlapping, or even contradictory. Simply write down as many facts and ideas as you can.

Suppose, for example, that a television program about medical advances has sparked your interest in medicine and health care. You decide to write about some aspect of medicine and to list everything about medicine that you can think of. The following list of facts, ideas, impressions, and associations might be the result.

Hospitals—emergency rooms, green walls, patients, visitors with flowers and cards

Doctors in white coats, stethoscopes

Visits to Dr. Robey for checkups, vaccinations, broken arm when I fell out of a tree; she used to frighten me with strange instruments; "Say 'Aah'"

World Health Organization; health care in much of world is primitive

Many television shows about hospitals, doctors, nurses

Having my appendix out—ride in ambulance, paramedics, feeling frightened, relieved when it was over

Medical advances in past hundred years: anesthesia, X-rays, CAT scan, vaccines, new medicines

Before penicillin, many people died from infections.

What is preventive medicine?

People's faith in research; will there be a cure for the common cold?

**Exercise 1   Prewriting: Making Lists**   On your paper, make a list of at least ten facts, ideas, and associations for each of the following items.

| | | |
|---|---|---|
| **SAMPLE** | Hawaii | |
| **ANSWER** | Tropical islands | Beaches, surfing |
| | Waikiki, Honolulu | Pearl Harbor |
| | Vacations, tourists | Captain Cook |
| | Flowers, leis | East-West culture |
| | Aloha, luau | Active volcanoes |

1. Camping
2. Careers
3. Driving
4. Endangered species
5. Exercise
6. Job interviews
7. Industry
8. Machines
9. Self-confidence
10. Weather

## 6.2b    Exploring Your Subject

Another method of developing ideas about your subject is to ask and answer questions about it. The following list of general questions is designed to help you explore many aspects of your subject. Not all of these questions will be useful for every subject. When exploring your subject, use those questions that apply and that will produce useful information.

1. What are the characteristics of my subject?
2. What is the history of my subject?
3. What is the future of my subject?
4. What are categories within my subject?
5. What important books and people are connected with my subject?
6. What are comparisons or similarities within my subject or between my subject and another subject?
7. What are contrasts or opposites within my subject or between my subject and another subject?
8. What problems, controversies, or issues are involved in my subject?
9. What processes are involved in my subject?
10. What definitions are necessary to understand my subject?
11. What are examples of my subject?
12. What causes are involved in my subject?
13. What effects are involved in my subject?
14. What possibilities are related to my subject?
15. What personal experiences have I had with my subject?

When exploring a subject, you can generate additional questions that are appropriate to your subject. You may need to do research to answer your questions.

The following examples are a partial list of the notes that you might obtain by using some of these questions to explore the subject of medicine and health care.

*History:* Aesculapius, Hippocrates; discovery of blood circulation, bacteria, antibiotics, vaccines

*Future:* New cures; aging process will be slowed; computers will be used to diagnose and prescribe

*Comparison:* A doctor looking for the cause of an illness is like a detective looking for clues in a case.

*Contrast:* Home recuperation and hospital recuperation

*Categories:* General practitioners, specialists

*Examples of careers:* Doctor, nurse, paramedic, lab technician, dietitian, physical therapist

*Personal experiences:* Had tonsils and appendix removed

**Exercise 2 Prewriting: Exploring Subjects** On your paper, develop five of the following subjects by giving the information requested. You may do research first.

> SAMPLE    Advertising: two categories; one problem
>
> ANSWER    *Categories:* written advertising in magazines and newspapers; oral advertising on radio and television
> *Problem:* advertising directed at children

1. Plays: two examples; one contrast
2. Careers with computers: one cause; two future developments
3. Libraries: two characteristics; one issue; one possibility
4. Sculpture: two people connected with subject; two examples
5. Immigration: one definition; two causes; one problem
6. Electricity: history; one contrast; one person connected with subject
7. Maps: one contrast; two effects; one personal experience; two characteristics
8. Architecture: one process; two people connected with subject; one issue
9. Nutrition: one definition; one personal experience; one controversy
10. First aid: one definition; one cause; two examples

**Exercise 3 Prewriting: Exploring Subjects** On your paper, develop five of the following subjects. Use at least three of the questions on page 235 for each subject that you choose.

> SAMPLE    Cities
>
> ANSWER    *Characteristics:* large community; densely populated; city government; many cultural and recreational opportunities

*Contrasts:* city and small town life; advantages and disadvantages of city life

*Examples:* Atlanta, St. Louis, Seattle, Mexico City, Vancouver, Toronto, London, Tokyo, Peking

1. Fashions in clothing
2. Significant inventions
3. The United States Senate
4. Folk music
5. Consumerism

6. Stereo equipment
7. Horseback riding
8. Modern art
9. Spies
10. Censorship

**Assignment 1  Prewriting**  You have been asked to write about your town or city for a Chamber of Commerce pamphlet. To develop the subject, make a list of facts, ideas, and associations about your town or city. Then explore the subject by asking and answering at least four questions about it.

**Assignment 2  Prewriting**  Think of something that you do well, such as meeting new people, playing chess, wrestling, or playing an instrument. Develop notes for that subject by listing facts, ideas, and associations. Then write down questions and answers about at least three of the following: characteristics, processes, experiences, problems, causes, effects, examples, and definitions.

**Continuing Assignment  Prewriting**  In the Continuing Assignment on page 233, you selected three items that interest you. Develop each of the items as much as you can by making lists and by using questions to explore the subjects. Save your notes.

### Assignment Checklist

Check your assignments for the following points:

✔ 1. Did you list all of the facts, ideas, and associations that came to your mind?

✔ 2. Did you explore the subject further by asking and answering questions about it?

# 6.3    Focusing Your Ideas

## Finding Topics

When you have sufficiently developed a subject, your notes will cover many aspects of that subject. However, you are not yet ready to write. First you will need to focus on a **topic,** a specific aspect of a subject that is limited enough for you to cover in a paragraph or in a composition. From your extensive notes, you can probably derive several topics. The following procedure will help you to find specific topics for writing assignments.

### Procedure

1. *Review your prewriting notes on a subject and look for natural groupings of information.* For example, in the notes on medicine, you could group separately the notes on careers, personal experiences, and medical advances.

2. *Review each grouping and jot down ideas for topics that emerge.* For example, on the subject of medicine, a topic could be "How to give cardiopulmonary resuscitation." In addition, you may arrive at topics by combining, limiting, or expanding ideas in your notes. Under the grouping of careers in medicine and health care, for example, you might expand your ideas to arrive at the topic "The role of medical researchers in health care."

3. *From your list of ideas, choose a topic that suits your assignment or that strongly interests you.* It may be one about which you have much to say or one that you would like to learn more about.

## Determining Your Purpose

As you focus your topic, consider your **purpose**—what you intend to accomplish with your writing. The following list presents some common purposes for writing and sample topics that illustrate each purpose.

| PURPOSE | TOPIC |
|---|---|
| To inform | Recent developments in automobile safety devices |
| To explain | How a prism works |
| To entertain | A practical joke that backfired |
| To describe | My feelings after running ten miles |
| To express an opinion | Ice hockey players should be required to wear helmets. |
| To persuade | The benefits of joining a service club |
| To narrate | A challenge that I accepted |

## Identifying Your Audience

In order to decide what information to use in your writing, you must identify your **audience,** the reader or the group of readers to whom you address your writing. Knowing your audience will help you determine an appropriate topic and suitable details for it. For example, if your topic were "How to prepare for driving across the country," your readers could be anyone from experienced automobile travelers to people who have never left the state. The extent of your audience's experience would influence your selection and presentation of details. To understand the interests and needs of your audience, ask yourself the following questions:

1. What experience or knowledge of my subject does the audience have?
2. What would the audience want to know or need to know about my subject?
3. Might the audience have strong ideas or opinions on my subject? Would my ideas offend them or seem too obvious to them?

Use your answers to these questions to help you decide what information from your notes to include and what to omit.

Once you have identified your topic, your purpose, and your audience, you may need to repeat some of the techniques presented in this unit to develop additional information for your topic. Then you will be ready to organize your ideas and information for your writing assignment. In the subsequent composition units in this book, you will practice different ways to organize your writing.

**Exercise 1   Prewriting: Topics and Purposes**   On your paper, write three limited topics that could come from the following prewriting notes on the subject of automobiles. Then write a purpose for each topic.

"Horseless carriage"

Model T, Henry Ford, assembly lines

Convertibles

Engine, piston, rod, crankshaft, carburetor

Used for transportation, pleasure

Giant industry, important to economy

Changed way of life—suburbs, drive-in movies, banks, restaurants

Sports cars, foreign cars, luxury cars, antique cars

Diesels, gasoline engines

*History:* First invented in Europe, perfected in United States. Design for a steam-powered car in 1678, electric car in 1834, gasoline car in 1863

*Categories:* trucks, buses, motorcycles, military tanks

*Recent developments:* safety devices, improved gasoline mileage, pollution controls

*Issues:* Can automobiles be made safer? What is the proper speed limit on highways? When should a driver's license be revoked?

**Exercise 2   Prewriting: Audience**   On your paper, list the letters of the details that would be appropriate for each of the following topics and audiences.

1. *Topic:* Northern lights
   *Audience:* Children
   a. They are glowing or flickering lights seen in the night sky.
   b. Spectroscopy can be used to analyze their temperature and movement.
   c. They are most visible in Alaska, Canada, Scandinavia, and Russia.
   d. They are caused by flare activity on the sun.
   e. Scientists measure the particles that cause the lights to appear.

2. *Topic:* What happened to me during the marathon
   *Audience:* Other runners in the marathon
   a. A marathon course is just over twenty-six miles long.
   b. The day of the marathon was hot and sunny.
   c. Three miles before the end, I was too tired to go on.
   d. Because it was sunny, I developed a terrible sunburn.
   e. I developed blisters on my heels.

**Assignment 1  Prewriting**  Your local newspaper has offered to print an editorial by a high school student on a local issue. Develop a subject and select two possible topics that you could write an editorial about.

**Assignment 2  Prewriting**  Select an experience that you have had with friends or your family. Develop it by listing ideas, facts, and associations and by exploring your ideas. Identify one topic that you could use if your purpose were to entertain. Then identify a topic that you could use if your purpose were to describe.

**Continuing Assignment  Prewriting**  For each of the three subjects that you developed in the Continuing Assignment on page 237, select a topic that you would like to write about. Then write a purpose and an audience for each topic.

### Assignment Checklist

Check your assignments for the following points:

　✔ 1. Did you group the information in your prewriting notes and then review each group for topics?
　✔ 2. Did you combine, limit, or expand ideas, if necessary, to find a topic?
　✔ 3. Did you select topics that were suitable for your purposes?
　✔ 4. Did you identify your audience and determine what they need to know about your topics?

### Holidays: Planning a Radio Script

**Situation**: You are a scriptwriter for the radio series "The American Experience," and your focus this month is on holidays in North America. For one program, you want to contrast your childhood views and current views about a certain holiday. Keep in mind the following information as you do prewriting for your script.

**Writer**: you as a scriptwriter for "The American Experience"

**Audience**: families who listen to "The American Experience"

**Topic**: holidays in North America

**Purpose**: to develop two views of the topic

**Directions**: To develop your subject, follow these steps.

*Step 1.* Read the list of holidays. Choose the one that interests you most or that you remember most clearly. Try to choose a holiday that evokes childhood memories as well as present feelings.

*Step 2.* At the top of your paper, write the name of the holiday. Divide the paper into two columns, one labeled *Then* and one labeled *Now*.

*Step 3.* Under the heading *Then,* write everything that you can remember that made the holiday vivid to you as a child. In the *Now* column, list those things that you now associate with the holiday. Include people, experiences, ceremonies, and customs, as in the example on page 244.

(Continue on page 244.)

# HOLIDAYS

| | |
|---|---|
| New Year's Day | Native American Day |
| Martin Luther King Day | Mother's Day |
| Chinese New Year | Victoria Day |
| Lincoln's Birthday | Memorial Day |
| Valentine's Day | Flag Day |
| Washington's Birthday | Father's Day |
| St. Patrick's Day | Independence Day |
| April Fools' Day | Labor Day |
| Good Friday | Columbus Day |
| Easter | Halloween |
| Pan American Day | Veterans Day |
| Passover | Thanksgiving Day |
| Earth Day | Navidad |
| Arbor Day | Chanukah |
| May Day | Christmas |

```
                    Independence Day

  THEN                  NOW

  Fireworks             Middle of the summer
  Family picnics        Fireworks
  Swimming              History of the country
  Town Parade           Four-mile race
  Summer Vacation       Meaning of liberty
```

*Step 4.* Rearrange the notes on your lists so that corresponding items from each column are grouped
together to show comparisons and contrasts.
Then write ideas for topics as you review the
groups.

*Step 5.* Read your topic ideas and write one topic and a
purpose for your radio program.

# Unit Assignments

**Assignment 1**   Take a notebook to a place where you often go. Spend time making observations and then record your observations in your notebook. Choose a subject from your notes and develop it by listing ideas and by exploring it with at least three questions.

**Assignment 2**   Take a survey of at least ten people on one of the subjects below. Analyze the results of your survey and identify an idea for writing. Develop it with a list of ideas and associations.

1. What five items would you take with you for a year on a deserted island assuming that food and shelter were provided?
2. Describe the kind of person that you would most like to be.
3. What ten items would you place in a time capsule to be opened two hundred years from now?

**Assignment 3**   Make a list of ideas related to the subject of friendship. Explore your ideas by asking questions about examples, problems, contrasts, and personal experience. Identify a topic and a purpose for writing a composition.

**Assignment 4**   You are planning to write an advertisement for a summer vacation area. Select the place, and list five details that you would include if the advertisement were addressed to teen-agers and five if it were addressed to adults.

**Assignment 5**   Prepare to write an essay on the subject of breaking a bad habit. Develop your subject with lists and questions. Then choose a topic and identify a purpose for your writing. Finally, develop your topic for a specific audience.

**Assignment 6**   Prepare to write on the advantages of traveling by bus. First, list all your ideas related to the topic. Then ask and answer questions about the topic, doing research, if necessary. Determine an audience for your topic. Then, after asking questions about the audience, list the information from your notes that would be appropriate for your audience.

# Unit Tests

## Test 1

**A.** Number your paper from 1 to 5. Next to each number, write *True* if the sentence is true or *False* if it is false.

1. You may record items in your writer's notebook in any form—words, phrases, sentences, questions, or lists.
2. Charts and statistics are not useful sources of writing ideas.
3. When you develop a subject, list only important ideas and facts about it.
4. One way to develop a subject is to ask and answer questions about it.
5. Knowing your audience affects your choice of details for your writing.

**B.** Number your paper from 6 to 10. Next to each number, write the letter of the term that correctly completes the sentence. You will use all but one of the items.

a. purpose
b. writer's notebook
c. prewriting

d. audience
e. topic
f. list

6. __?__ is the planning and preparation that you do before you write.
7. Your __?__ is a record of your interests, observations, and activities, as well as your notes and comments.
8. A(n) __?__ is the specific aspect of a subject that you will write about in a paragraph or a composition.
9. Your __?__ is what you intend to accomplish with your writing.
10. Your __?__ is the reader or group of readers to whom your writing is directed.

**C.** Number your paper from 11 to 15. Next to each number, write the letter of the item that correctly answers the question.

11. Which one of the following do you *not* do in prewriting?
    a. Explore subjects from many points of view.
    b. Present subjects in a brief paragraph.
    c. Focus subjects according to the purpose of the assignment.
    d. Find subjects that interest you.

12. Which one of the following questions would *not* be useful for developing the subject of silent movies?
    a. How were silent movies made?
    b. What are examples of silent movies?
    c. Who were the stars of silent movies?
    d. How are videotapes processed?

13. Which one of the following is *not* a good way to analyze data in order to find ideas for writing?
    a. Look for similar data on another subject.
    b. Look for trends in the information.
    c. Look for problems to which you can suggest solutions.
    d. List questions that might prompt further research.

14. Which one of the following is a suitable purpose for a report on the topic "How irrigation was developed"?
    a. To explain          c. To describe
    b. To persuade         d. To express an opinion

15. Which one of the following steps will *not* help you to focus your prewriting notes for a specific assignment?
    a. Look for natural groupings of information in your notes.
    b. Ask and answer questions about a topic.
    c. Determine a purpose for your assignment.
    d. Decide which topics fit your assignment.

## Test 2

Choose one of the Unit Assignments or one that your teacher suggests. Complete the assignment as directed and hand it in to your teacher.

# Unit 7

# Writing Paragraphs

---

## Unit Preview

A **paragraph** is a group of sentences that develops a single idea or topic. The following group of sentences discusses a single topic—Emmy Noether's success as a mathematician—and, therefore, is a paragraph.

(1) Emmy Noether was one of the first women who successfully established a career as a mathematician. (2) She was fortunate in having advantages besides her mathematical ability. (3) For example, her father, who was a professor of mathematics, encouraged her study and allowed her to substitute for him at the university in Erlangen, Germany, after she received an advanced degree there. (4) However, despite her capability and experience, she, like all women, was not allowed an official university position. (5) Eventually, after 1919, when she began her best work in mathematics, Noether was allowed to teach at the University of Göttingen, but she received no salary. (6) In 1933 she left Germany for the United States, where she finally gained a full-time, paid professorship. (7) After her death in 1935, her friend Albert Einstein claimed that Noether was a mathematical genius. (8) Only because of her dedication and her financial independence during her years in Göttingen was Emmy Noether able to demonstrate her mathematical genius.

A topic sentence states the main idea of a paragraph. Supporting sentences develop, illustrate, or explain the topic. The paragraph on Emmy Noether contains six supporting sentences, each of which relates to her becoming a successful mathematician. A concluding sentence restates the topic sentence or presents the writer's thoughts about the topic.

A good paragraph is coherent. The use of transitional words and phrases, such as *after, however,* and *for example,* helps to make a paragraph coherent. You can use transitional words and phrases to connect ideas and to point out the relationship between them.

**For Analysis**   On your paper, follow these instructions about the model paragraph.

1. Write the topic sentence.
2. List the details given in the supporting sentences that explain the topic sentence.
3. Transitional words and phrases are used to show time, contrast, and examples. List by sentence number all the transitional words and phrases that are used in the paragraph.

By following the preceding instructions, you reviewed the structure and organization of a paragraph. In this unit you will study paragraphs. You will also practice effective methods of organizing paragraphs.

# 7.1   Developing Paragraphs

## 7.1a   Limiting a Topic

You are likely to write better paragraphs if you select topics that you find enjoyable and interesting. Choose topics that you are familiar with or are prepared to study.

After you select a general topic for a paragraph, you must limit it. Your goal is to arrive at a topic that you can develop thoroughly in the brief space of a paragraph. You can limit a topic by narrowing it to a specific time, place, instance, condition, or use. For example, rather than treat a broad topic like "Canoeing," concentrate on just one aspect of the topic, such as "How to enter a canoe."

A practical way to approach writing a paragraph is to list details about your topic as they occur to you or as you learn them. You can use your list to help you to limit your topic. The following list illustrates this process.

*General topic:* Sound

1. Sound intensity measured on decibel scale, named after the inventor of telephone, Alexander Graham Bell.
2. Zero on decibel scale represents power or force of softest sound that can be heard by human ear; one hundred indicates a sound ten billion times as strong as the zero sound.
3. Loud or shrill noises can inflict permanent injury on fragile parts of inner ear, such as ear drum.
4. According to the American Speech and Hearing Association, tens of millions of Americans hear dangerously loud sounds every day.
5. Dogs have more sensitive hearing than humans do.
6. Common noisemakers, such as jackhammers, power mowers, automobile horns, can impair hearing.
7. At extremes of decibel scale are sounds like rustle of leaves (10 decibels) and roar of a jet engine (130 decibels); hum of a vacuum cleaner is assigned a medium level (70 decibels).
8. Rock music is potentially one of most dangerous sounds imaginable, a fact demonstrated by high percentage of musicians and disc jockeys who are partially deaf.
9. People who work around airplanes or heavy machinery must wear ear protectors or risk losing hearing.
10. A dog will react to sounds that its owner is totally unaware of.

In the preceding list, the details fall into distinct groups. Details 5 and 10 contrast the hearing of humans with that of dogs. Details 1, 2, and 7 talk about the use of the decibel scale to measure sound intensity. A third group of details—3, 4, 6, 8, and 9—includes the dangers that loud noises present to human hearing. Using this breakdown of the details on the list, you can eliminate the two smaller groups and concentrate on the largest group. In this way you would narrow the paragraph topic from the general topic "Sound" to the limited topic "The connection between loud sounds and damage to human hearing."

**Exercise 1   Prewriting: Limiting Topics**   On your paper, separate the following items into groups by listing the numbers of those details that discuss each specific aspect of the general topic. Write the limited topic of each group.

*General topic:* Time

1. Research shows that in his or her lifetime the average American spends almost 9000 hours, or about one year, talking on the telephone.
2. In general, months and years seem to pass faster for adults than they do for children.
3. If it is true that "time flies when you're having fun," it is also true that time drags when you're miserable.
4. Eastern Standard Time is three hours ahead of Pacific Standard Time.
5. A typical American adult spends some time each day reading a newspaper.
6. Some periods of life seem to rush by; others seem as though they will never end.
7. North America has four major time zones: Eastern, Central, Mountain, and Pacific.
8. One hour separates each time zone from the next.
9. Science-fiction writers from H. G. Wells to Ray Bradbury have speculated about possibility of traveling backward in time.
10. As a rule, the more idle one is, the more time seems to drag.
11. Most American children and teen-agers spend as much time watching television as they do attending school.
12. According to Einstein's theory of time, if one could travel faster than the speed of light, which is essentially what going back in time means, it would be possible to witness the same event twice.

**Exercise 2   Prewriting: Limiting Topics**   On your paper, write a limited topic for each of the following general topics. If necessary, list details about each topic to help you limit the topic.

> SAMPLE    Medicine
>
> ANSWER    Responsibilities of an emergency medical technician

1. Sports
2. Weather
3. The environment
4. Games
5. Music
6. Computers
7. Driving
8. Careers in science
9. Summer work

## 7.1b   The Topic Sentence

### Writing a Topic Sentence

Most paragraphs require one sentence, called a **topic sentence,** that states the main idea of the paragraph and tells readers how the details of the paragraph are related. An effective topic sentence is neither too general nor too narrow. For example, consider the following statements as potential topic sentences for a paragraph based on details 3, 4, 6, 8, and 9 of the sample list on page 250:

> Human hearing can be lost or impaired in several ways.
> Many workers are exposed daily to loud sounds that can permanently damage their hearing.

The first statement is too general to be an effective topic sentence for the selected details. It promises to explore "several ways" that hearing can be lost or impaired, but the supporting details discuss only one way, exposure to loud noises. The second statement is also inappropriate because it is too narrow. It focuses on just one detail, the plight of workers exposed to loud noises. This sentence leaves no room for the information presented by the other details in the group.

An effective topic sentence for this paragraph would be "Human hearing can be severely damaged by exposure to loud sounds." It precisely states the limited topic and adequately accounts for all the details that would be included in the paragraph.

**Exercise 3  Prewriting: Topic Sentences**  On your paper, tell which topic sentence is too narrow, which is too broad, and which is appropriate for the paragraph that follows.

> In 1850 Levi Strauss went west to California with a load of brown canvas to sell in exchange for money to buy a gold claim. When Strauss discovered how quickly miners' pants wore out, he decided to use his tent canvas to make sturdy pants. The pants became popular, and Strauss decided to manufacture the pants instead of mining gold. Even though the pants were sturdy, the pockets still tore off easily because the miners put lumps of ore in their pockets. Strauss worked with Jacob Davis to use copper rivets to strengthen the pockets. Later, Strauss switched from canvas material to denim material and used indigo dye to achieve the blue color of jeans.

a. Copper rivets were an important addition to jeans.
b. Levi Strauss developed the blue jeans that are so popular today.
c. Jeans have become a popular item of clothing throughout the world.

**Exercise 4  Writing: Topic Sentences**  On your paper, write a topic sentence for each group of details that you separated in Exercise 1 on page 251.

## The Implied Topic Sentence

Not every paragraph requires a topic sentence. A topic sentence may be implied, rather than stated, if the pattern of a composition is very clear. For instance, if each paragraph on one item of a comparison is followed by a matching paragraph on the other item, the topics of some paragraphs may be so predictable that you need not state their topic sentences.

Implied topic sentences are especially common in narrative writing, where many of the paragraphs simply continue the description or story line of the preceding paragraphs. The topic sentences implied in most narrative paragraphs are "This is what happened next" or "The person (or place or object) looked like this."

In the following narrative paragraph taken from a novel, the topic sentence is implied, not stated.

**Model**

> And now a light truck approached, and as it came near, the driver saw the turtle and swerved. . . . His front wheel struck the edge of the shell, flipped the turtle like a tiddly-wink, spun it like a coin, and rolled it off the highway. The truck went to its course along the right side. Lying on its back, the turtle was tight in its shell for a long time. But at last its legs waved in the air, reaching for something to pull it over. Its front foot caught a piece of quartz and little by little the shell pulled over and flopped upright. The wild oat head fell out and three of the spearhead seeds stuck in the ground. And as the turtle crawled on down the embankment, its shell dragged dirt over the seeds. The turtle entered a dust road and jerked itself along, drawing a very shallow trench in the dust with its shell. The old humorous eyes looked ahead, and the horny beak opened a little. His yellow toe nails slipped a fraction in the dust.

> John Steinbeck, *The Grapes of Wrath*

In the preceding paragraph, the implied topic sentence is *Not even the impact of the truck could keep the determined turtle from its slow journey*. Although the author never states this sentence, it is the main idea that all the details in the paragraph combine to convey.

**Exercise 5   Prewriting: Topic Sentences**   Each of the following paragraphs has an implied topic sentence. On your paper, write the letter of the sentence that could serve as the topic sentence in each paragraph.

1.   Back at the house his mother bent over his rough hands, inspecting his fingers and nails. It did little good to start him clean to school for too many things could happen on the way. She sighed over the black cracks on his fingers, and then gave him his books and his lunch and started him on the mile walk to school. She noticed that his mouth was working a good deal this morning.

   John Steinbeck, "The Gift"

   a. The boy went to school as usual.

   b. The boy's mother observed him as she sent him off to school.

   c. The boy's mother worried over his inability to keep clean.

2.       Descending eastward, the highland meadows are a stairway to the plain. In July the inland slope of the Rockies is luxuriant with flax and buckwheat, stonecrop and larkspur. The earth unfolds and the limit of the land recedes. Clusters of trees, and animals grazing far in the distance, cause the vision to reach away and wonder to build upon the mind. The sun follows a longer course in the day, and the sky is immense beyond all comparison. The great billowing clouds that sail upon it are shadows that move upon the grain like water, dividing light.

N. Scott Momaday, The Way to Rainy Mountain

a. The juncture of the Rockies and the plains is awe-inspiring.

b. The eastward view is beautiful.

c. The inland slope of the Rockies meets the plains to the east.

## 7.1c   Developing the Body of a Paragraph

### Writing Supporting Sentences

The body of every effective paragraph consists of ideas or details that support and explain the topic sentence. The number of supporting details that you need in a paragraph depends on what you are trying to show. Always strive to treat your topic thoroughly and convincingly.

The most common types of supporting details are facts, examples, and reasons. A **fact** is something that is known with certainty. Factual statements consist of simple descriptions, statistics, historical or technical information—in short, knowledge that is either obvious or verifiable. Facts may serve both as examples and as reasons. An **example** is something representative of a group. It is a sample, a typical case, an instance, or an event, that illustrates and helps to clarify a larger idea. A **reason** is a statement that explains or justifies another statement. Reasons attempt to show causes or to answer questions beginning with *Why*.

The supporting sentences in most paragraphs use some combination of the three kinds of supporting details. In the following paragraph, for instance, the writer begins by stating the topic "How radio drama in the early 1920s led to the development of sound effects." The writer then supports the topic sentence with the three kinds of details: (1) reasons explaining the importance of sound effects, (2) facts about progress in the field of sound effects, and (3) examples of sound-effect techniques.

## Model

Topic sentence ———|    The appearance of radio drama was responsible for the great advancements made at this time in the field of sound effects. Without sound effects, drama

Reasons ———|    would have been little more than recitation. Since sound alone was the device that created the mental pictures in the mind of the listener, sound effects were as important to effective broadcasting as the words of the play. Sound effects "lend color and realism," wrote the radio producer and personality Samuel L. "Roxy" Rothafel. "A performance unaccompanied by noises that indicate actions on the part of the actors and actresses," he continued, "would result in a bare and somewhat unreal presentation."

Facts ———|    While sound effects would not be perfected until the 1930s, innovative engineers at this early date developed convincing ways to produce common noises.

Examples ———|    Forest fires were duplicated with the roar of a blowtorch and the breaking of wooden match sticks near the microphone. Rain on a roof was accomplished by rolling dried peas down a paper tube, and thunder was reproduced by waving a thin sheet of metal. Other standard devices included doorbells, alarms, telephone bells, locks, and dummy doors that could be opened and shut to indicate the coming and going of a character.

J. Fred MacDonald, *Don't Touch That Dial!*

## Writing a Concluding Sentence

A paragraph often needs a **concluding sentence** in which you restate the topic sentence or present your thoughts about the topic. If you present numerous facts or examples in a paragraph, for instance, your readers may forget by the end of the paragraph exactly what the facts or examples were intended to show. Adding a concluding sentence that restates the topic sentence can keep your purpose clear for your reader. Similarly, if you compose a paragraph mainly of reasons, you can conclude it with a sentence that draws a logical conclusion, raises a question, or reminds readers of what you have explained in the paragraph. Never leave your readers wondering about the meaning or the significance of the facts, examples, or reasons that you have included in your paragraph.

One of the following concluding sentences could be added to the paragraph on page 256 about radio drama and sound effects.

> All of these sound effects and many more came about with the advent of drama on radio. [Restates topic sentence]
>
> Clearly, the need to produce sound effects for realism in drama was a challenge to the creativity of the radio world. [Draws logical conclusion]
>
> The technicians of early radio drama were the true pioneers in the field of sound effects. [Summarizes writer's thoughts]

## Placement of the Topic Sentence

In general, a sensible plan is to tell readers what you intend to show before you show it. Thus, the common practice in writing a paragraph is to begin with the topic sentence and to follow it with supporting sentences. However, there are times when you may find it more effective to begin your paragraph with one or more supporting details, placing your topic sentence in the middle or even at the end of the paragraph. In the following paragraph, the writer's strategy is to begin with an observation and a statement of a problem that lead to the topic sentence, shown here in italic type, and then to give additional facts supporting the topic.

### Model

Wood is one practical alternative to oil and gas as heating fuels. However, wood leaves a flammable residue in chimneys and with it the danger of chimney fires. The use of wood as fuel has prepared the way for the return of the chimney sweep. *The chimney sweep, once an endangered species in North America, is now making a noticeable comeback.* A chimney sweep is not a bird but a person who cleans soot and residue from chimneys. Sweeps became scarce when homeowners began heating with oil and gas. Unlike wood, these fuels leave virtually no residue in chimneys. Because wood is increasingly replacing or supplementing oil and gas, sweeps are reappearing to clean chimneys, especially in northern regions where winters are colder and wood is readily available. If the trend continues, sweeps may perhaps become as common as they were in earlier centuries.

**Exercise 6  Prewriting: Topic Sentences**  The following sets of sentences include a topic sentence and supporting sentences for a paragraph. On your paper, arrange the sentences in a logical order. Write the sentences as a paragraph, placing the topic sentence of each paragraph somewhere other than at the beginning. Underline each topic sentence.

1. However, it took many years for dishwashers to become efficient.

   Modern dishwashers can save an average family many hours each year.

   The first motor-powered dishwasher was invented in 1911, but it, too, was unpleasant to use because it was cumbersome and noisy.

   The first dishwasher, which was invented in New York in 1850, was operated by a hand crank.

   A person had to turn the crank during the entire wash cycle.

   Later models were smaller and quieter, but they did not clean the dishes as well.

   Only recently have manufacturers developed heavy-duty machines that clean dishes as thoroughly as human dishwashers do.

2. In England in the sixteenth century, some coins would lose as much as a quarter of their metal within the first months of their circulation.

   When most coins were made from gold and silver, thieves would shave off some of the valuable metal from the coins.

   To stop the problem, coins were made with ridged edges.

   To prevent that problem, coin makers put an inscription, which could not be removed and replaced, around the sides of both faces of coins.

   Some thieves would still shave off metal from the edges and replace the grooves.

   These practices, persisting even after coins were no longer made of precious metals, explain why coins today have ridged edges and also mottoes on their faces.

**Exercise 7  Prewriting: Supporting Details**   Copy the following three topic sentences on your paper. Under each one, list the numbers of the supporting details that develop it.

*Topic sentences:*

A. Baseball fans collect many types of memorabilia.

B. Some people invest in baseball cards for their value.

C. Unusual and interesting mistakes appear in some baseball cards.

*Supporting details:*

1. Baseball cards most popular type of memorabilia.
2. Card from 1968 shows bat boy instead of Aurelio Rodriguez.
3. Old uniforms treasured by some collectors.
4. Complete sets for one year are worth most money.
5. Cards from early 1900s especially valuable.
6. Pitcher Lew Burdette shown as left-handed instead of right-handed.
7. Posters and team pictures decorate collectors' walls.
8. There are misspellings on cards.
9. One complete 1952 set is worth $10,000.
10. In 1910 Sherry Magee's name spelled "Magie."
11. Special pins and pennants sold at championship series.
12. Honus Wagner card of 1910 sold for almost $10,000.
13. Bats and signed baseballs popular.
14. Investors have paid $1200 for a 1933 set and expect price to double.
15. Players have been left out of a series, and special cards had to be issued for them.

**Exercise 8  Writing: Concluding Sentences**   On your paper, write a concluding sentence for each topic sentence and set of supporting details that you organized in Exercise 7.

**Exercise 9  Writing: The Paragraph**   On your paper, write a paragraph using one of the topic sentences from Exercise 7. Convert the details that you listed under that topic sentence to supporting sentences. You may change the wording and add transitional words as necessary. Add the appropriate concluding sentence that you wrote in Exercise 8. Place the topic sentence where it is most effective.

**Exercise 10   Writing: Developing Paragraphs**   The follow-ing paragraphs are insufficiently developed. *Step 1:* Copy each topic sentence on your paper, and beneath it list the supporting facts, examples, or reasons that are included in the paragraph. *Step 2:* Add at least three supporting details of your own to each list. Use any combination of facts, examples, and reasons that you think would best make the meaning or truth of the topic sentence clear to readers. *Step 3:* Write two new paragraphs using your expanded lists of supporting details.

1.   Every week my parents' softball team seems to figure out a new way of losing. The team is simply awful! It has a thirty-three-game losing streak that spans three years of play. My folks happen to be the best players on the team, but even they average five errors per game.

2.   Everyone should take a course in first aid. A doctor is not always available in an emergency. Many types of injury or illness require immediate, on-the-spot treatment. First aid includes reliable techniques for handling emergencies such as choking and snakebite.

**Assignment 1   Prewriting/Writing**   *Step 1:* Write the topic "People in my community" on the top of your paper. *Step 2:* Beneath it list ten or more thoughts that occur to you about people in your community. *Step 3:* Group the details according to the specific aspect of people in your community that the details discuss. *Step 4:* Use the two largest groups as the basis for two paragraphs. Make certain that each paragraph has an effective topic sentence.

**Assignment 2   Prewriting/Writing**   Choose one of the topics that you limited for Exercise 2 on page 252. Write a topic sentence for the limited topic, and list details that support it. Then write a paragraph using the topic sentence and the details. Carefully choose the placement of the topic sentence and the type of conclud-ing sentence that you use.

**Assignment 3   Writing**   From the paragraphs that you have written for previous exercises in this unit, select two with topic sentences at the beginning. Rewrite one of the paragraphs in such a way that the topic sentence appears in the middle; rewrite the other so that the topic sentence appears at the end. Change the wording of the remaining sentences in each paragraph as needed to ensure that the paragraph as a whole reads smoothly and naturally.

**Assignment 4** **Prewriting/Writing** Find two paragraphs that have implied topic sentences. Look for them in a short story or a novel or in a longer composition that you have written. Copy the paragraphs on your paper. Underneath each paragraph write the topic sentence that is implied.

### Assignment Checklist

Check your assignments for the following points:

1. Did you limit each topic enough to treat it adequately in a paragraph?
2. Did you write specific topic sentences?
3. Did you place the topic sentence in the most effective position in each paragraph?
4. Do your supporting sentences develop the topic sentences thoroughly?
5. Did you add a concluding sentence, if needed, either to restate the topic sentence or to summarize your thinking on the topic?
6. In Assignment 4, did you write the topic sentences implied by the paragraphs?
7. Did you check your paragraphs for correct grammar, usage, punctuation, and spelling?

## 7.2   Organizing Coherent Paragraphs

**Coherence** is the orderly presentation of ideas. You can make your paragraphs coherent by arranging the supporting details in an order that will be clear to your readers and by using transitional words and phrases to introduce and connect those details. Transitional words and phrases may be conjunctions, such as *and, but,* and *however,* or explanatory expressions, such as *for instance, on the other hand,* and so on. The common methods of organization and the transitional words suitable for each method will be discussed in this unit.

## 7.2a   Chronological Order

**Chronological order** is a way of arranging events according to the time at which they happen. You can use chronological order for relating a historical event, narrating a story, or explaining a process. Common transitional words and phrases used in chronologically arranged paragraphs are *after, at the same time, before, during, from that moment, in the beginning, in the end, meanwhile, next, now, since, subsequently, until, when,* and *while.*

The author of the following paragraph uses chronological order to describe an action. The transitional words are in italic type.

### Model

I stepped into the cabin and secured myself into the throne of command beneath the hodgepodge of dials, switches, gauges, and controls. A muffled roar grew and the great bird began to tremble *as* I switched on each of its eight mighty engines. As I increased the throttle, the aircraft crept forward. *Once* on the airstrip, I threw the eight turbine engines into full power. *At first* the weighted jet seemed to resist the tremendous thrust, but gradually it gained momentum. *At last* the jet was rolling at a steady clip and tilting gently from side to side. As optimum ground speed was achieved, I pulled up the flaps. The nose lightened, *then* lifted. The aircraft strained under the weight of our cargo, but *finally* the rear wheels left the ground, and we began to climb.

*Phill Powell, Asheboro High School*
*Asheboro, North Carolina*

### Exercise 1   Prewriting/Writing:   Chronological   Order

On your paper, arrange the following details in chronological order. Then use the details to write a paragraph arranged in chronological order. Write a topic sentence based on the limited topic. Use transitional words to highlight your use of chronological order.

*Limited topic:* Confusion in naming features on the moon

1. In 1645 a Belgian mathematician, Michael Florent Van Langren, named three hundred moon features after Spanish kings and nobles.
2. In 1921 International Astronomical Union formed to standardize naming of features on moon.

3. With beginning of space flights to moon, new features discovered (sometimes by two different countries) and named informally; caused confusion when names were submitted at meeting of the International Astronomical Union—which meets only once every three years.

4. At end of 1600s, twenty-five maps with differently named lunar features existed.

5. In 1610 Galileo mapped mountains, valleys, and craters of the moon.

6. In 1651 the Italian Riccioli began modern tradition of naming craters after scientists and plains after states of mind.

7. First official map produced by International Astronomical Union in 1932.

8. Improved methods of photographing the moon and continuing space flights will reveal new features to be named.

9. Because so many new features were found, namers ran out of scientists' names and began to use names of explorers, writers, and artists.

## 7.2b   Spatial Order

**Spatial order** is a way of arranging details according to their location in space. The most commonly used spatial arrangements are bottom to top, side to side, and foreground to background. The order that you use in a paragraph depends on whether you want to stress the height, the width, or the depth of your subject. You can emphasize spatial order by using words and phrases that indicate position. Transitional words useful for indicating spatial arrangement include *above, across, adjacent, alongside, around, behind, below, beneath, beside, between, beyond, by, in front of, in the middle, opposite, throughout, under, upon,* and *within.*

The writer of the following paragraph describes a scene from the foreground to the background. Notice how he gives a picture of the whole subject before describing the parts of the subject. The transitional words are in italic type.

### Model

I once took a picture from the window of a Spanish café during an otherwise uneventful day. This picture, an especially beautiful image of a late afternoon, sits *before* me now. The view is

*down* the hillside, *toward* the sea. A fog bank is rolling *in,* obscuring
the beach and beginning to climb *up* toward the town. As I
watched, the fog grew thicker and the view vanished, and, chilled,
I retreated into the café.

*Dan Staley, Woodrow Wilson High School*
*Long Beach, California*

**Exercise 2   Prewriting/Writing: Spatial Order**   On your
paper, write a paragraph organized in spatial order. Use the following
limited topic and supporting details. Your description should proceed
from the bottom to the top of the building. Write a topic sentence,
and use transitional words to emphasize the spatial order. You may
use more than one detail in a sentence.

*Limited topic:* Description of Empire State Building
1. There is an observation deck on 86th floor.
2. On top floors, people sometimes see rain below them even though
   they are in sun.
3. There is an observation deck on 102nd floor.
4. There is a 222-foot television tower on top of building.
5. The floors in middle of building contain offices.
6. First floor of building contains places to eat and shop.
7. Building is 102 stories tall.
8. Toward top, building begins to taper to a point.
9. Top of television tower is 1472 feet from ground.
10. Top of building itself is 1250 feet from ground.

**Exercise 3   Prewriting/Writing: Order**   The following passage mixes chronological and spatial details in a confusing manner.
*Step 1:* On your paper, make two lists of details, one including all of
the events or circumstances surrounding events discussed in the
paragraph and one including all of the physical details of the subject.
*Step 2:* Arrange the list of events in chronological order and the list of
physical details in spatial order. *Step 3:* Use the lists to write two
paragraphs. Decide where to begin and how to arrange the details
effectively. Use suitable transitional words to make clear your
organization in each paragraph. You may use more than one detail in
a sentence.

The largest airplane ever constructed was Howard Hughes's famous *Spruce Goose*. It had a wingspan of 320 feet. Mounted on the wings were eight piston-driven engines whose propellers were seventeen feet in diameter. Built during World War II by the eccentric millionaire pilot, aircraft designer, and film producer, the 213-ton craft was supposed to be the model for an entire fleet of "flying boats." Supporters of the project argued that the country needed the seaplanes because United States cargo ships were constantly being destroyed by German submarines. On the only flight that it ever made, the *Spruce Goose* achieved a height of seventy feet and a distance of one mile. The multmillion-dollar craft was then stored in a specially designed hangar for the rest of Hughes's life, at a maintenance cost of one million dollars per year.

Although personally doubtful about the project, Hughes contracted in November, 1942, to build the seaplane in just ten months. Unfortunately, the project took five years to complete. Everything about the plane was mammoth. The fuselage was thirty feet tall; the tail stood as high as an eight-story building. Millions of feet of layered spruce plywood went into the construction of the 219-foot craft. The wings were so thick that a person could stand inside them. Enormous pontoons were positioned outside the last engine on each wing. When the plane was finally completed, however, no one was certain that it could even fly. To calm the growing controversy over the cost and delay of the *Spruce Goose,* Hughes took the craft for a test flight in Long Beach Harbor on November 2, 1947.

## 7.2c   Order of Importance

**Order of importance** is a way of organizing ideas according to the degree of their value, power, authority, interest, or quality. You may begin a paragraph with the least important item and progress to the most important, thus building your reader's interest. Alternatively, you may use most-to-least-important order if you want to arouse your reader's attention immediately. You may emphasize order of importance with transitional words and expressions such as *first, in the first place, a second factor, equally important, furthermore, of major concern, of minor concern, best of all, finally, least important,* and *most important.*

The writer of the following paragraph uses least-to-most-important order to present the four effects. The transitional expressions are in italic type.

**Model**

> Today, as in certain other periods of United States history, it has become popular to disparage politicians. By doing so, however, we do severe damage to our ability to govern ourselves. *To begin with,* the criticism is demoralizing to the vast majority of political leaders, who are thoroughly honest and trustworthy. *Even more damaging* is the effect that our cynical attitude has on the young people who must lead the country in the future. Certainly the public's lack of respect for politicians is bound to discourage many qualified young men and women from pursuing political careers. *Worst of all,* though, is the mentality of helplessness and indifference that the notion of general corruption breeds. When citizens come to believe that, regardless of whom they vote for, the result is the same, then they either vote carelessly or do not vote at all. Disparaging politicians may be popular, but it is not wise.

**Exercise 4  Prewriting/Writing: Order of Importance**

On your paper, arrange the following supporting details in order of increasing importance. You may add more items to the list. Write a topic sentence. Then use the list to write a paragraph organized from least to most important. Include suitable transitional words in the paragraph.

*Limited topic:* Qualities of a good police officer

1. Enforces the law fairly; treats everyone the same.
2. Thoroughly understands the law and citizens' rights.
3. Routinely treats people with courtesy and respect.
4. Remains calm and steady in an emergency.

**Exercise 5  Prewriting/Writing: Order of Importance**

On your paper, arrange the following supporting details in order of decreasing importance. Write a topic sentence. Then use the list to write a paragraph organized from most to least important. Include transitional words as needed.

*Limited topic:* Duties of receptionists

1. Another important task for many receptionists is keeping a record on index cards or in a notebook of all visitors, their businesses, their addresses, and their telephone numbers.

2. When not otherwise occupied, receptionists make sure that the reception area is neat so that it makes a good impression on visitors.

3. The second most important duty of many receptionists is answering the telephone and directing calls to the appropriate person.

4. Good receptionists also watch their supervisors' schedules for delays and notify people with appointments about the delays.

5. Greeting visitors and directing them to their proper destinations is the most important duty of receptionists.

# 7.2d Classification

Anyone who has ever written a definition of a term has used **classification,** since part of a definition consists of the placement of the term in the larger class to which it belongs. Organizing a paragraph by classification works in a different way, however. When you organize a paragraph by classification, you start with a large group, which you divide into the smaller classes, or categories, that make up the group. You use a single principle to sort your topic into the smaller categories. For example, you might write a paragraph about the early settlers of Australia by dividing them into three groups according to the reason for their going to the country: the prisoners who were transported there, the soldiers who kept order, and the homesteaders. For another example, you might write a paragraph about the different kinds of jazz. In each case you would give names to the classes and provide information about each one. In the jazz paragraph, you would want to mention famous musicians who exemplified each type of jazz.

When you use classification, you need to choose a logical order for your groups, often one that is based on some kind of ranking. By using such transitional phrases as *one sort, another kind,* and *a third type,* you make the order of the classes clear to your reader. The transitional words in the following paragraph are italicized.

## Model

> Cloth is manufactured in three different ways. *The most common* manufacturing method is weaving: the over-and-under interlacing of two sets of yarns that are at right angles to each other. As you know, weaving is done on a frame called a loom, which is usually power-driven but may also be operated by hand. Denim, used for jeans and other sportswear, is a woven fabric. *The second* manufacturing method is knitting: the interlooping of loops of yarns. This process, too, is normally done by machine, but it can also be done by hand. Jersey and tricot are examples of knitted fabrics. *A less common* method of cloth manufacture is the process known as felting. Felted cloth is made by pressing together loose fibers of wool or fur. Moisture and heat cause the tiny scales on the fibers to hook together, or a gluelike substance is used to bond the fibers together. Felt is only one of the types of cloth made by the felting process. All three of these methods of manufacturing cloth are centuries old; over the years only the machinery has changed.

Notice that the writer has arranged the three categories in a sequence from the most common to the least common. She also has given examples of fabrics produced by each manufacturing method.

**Exercise 6  Prewriting/Writing: Classification**  Write a paragraph in which you use the following topic sentence and organize the supporting details by classification. Present the details in a logical order, using transitional words and phrases to make the progression of thought clear. Sometimes you will want to combine two details in one sentence.

*Topic sentence:*
The more than 800 species of trees in the continental United States may be roughly divided into three groups.

*Supporting details:*
1. Broadleaf group the largest
2. Conifer group: over 100 species
3. Conifer group next in size
4. Broadleaf group: 650 species
5. Palm group: over 15 species

6. Palm group last in size
7. Broadleaf group has flat leaves of varying size.
8. Conifers have scaly leaves shaped like needles.
9. Most conifers have cones.
10. Palm trees related to grasses, bamboo, and lilies
11. Palmettos and Washington palms common varieties of palm
12. Oaks, maples, cottonwoods in broadleaf family
13. Pines, hemlocks, firs in conifer family
14. *Conifer:* "cone-bearing"
15. Characteristic leaf shape of palms

## 7.2e   Comparison and Contrast

Comparison and contrast are useful methods for developing a topic that consists of two or more similar items. When you **compare,** you show how the items are alike. When you **contrast,** you show how the items differ. You may develop a paragraph through comparison, or contrast, or both.

There are two main ways to develop a paragraph by comparison or contrast. One way is to alternate details, following each point about one item with a corresponding point about the other. The pattern of this kind of development is AB AB AB. The second way is to present all of the details about one item before taking up the other. This pattern is AAA BBB. Whichever approach you use, make certain that your treatment is balanced—that every point of comparison or contrast is applied to both items.

You may use transitional expressions such as *equally, similarly, the same, in the same way, just as, however, on the other hand, despite,* and *otherwise* for emphasizing comparison or contrast.

The writer of the following paragraph uses both comparison and contrast, presenting corresponding details in alternating order. The transitional words are in italic type.

### Model

Two of the most celebrated major-league baseball players of the 1930s were a pair of brothers from Arkansas—Paul and Jerome

Dean, known *respectively* as "Daffy" and "Dizzy" because of their eccentric behavior both on and off the field. The Dean boys formed part of the St. Louis Cardinals' famed Gashouse Gang. *Both* brothers were pitchers—and feared ones at that. In his first year with the club, Daffy won nineteen games during the regular season and two more in World Series play. Daffy was a good pitcher, *but* his older brother Dizzy was a great one. The elder Dean recorded a fantastic thirty victories in the same year, and he, *too,* won a pair of games during the Series. Between them the brothers accounted for forty-nine of the Cardinals' ninety-five victories in the 1934 season. The next year they combined for forty-seven wins. *Only* Dizzy attained the necessary level of brilliance during his career to be elected to the Baseball Hall of Fame, *but* each brother was a talent to be reckoned with. Dizzy once pitched a three-hitter in the first game of a double-header, only to be outdone by Daffy's no-hit performance in the second game. "I wished I'd known Paul was going to pitch a no-hitter," remarked Dizzy after the game. "I'd have pitched one too."

**Exercise 7   Prewriting/Writing: Comparison**   The following lists contain details about astronauts and scuba divers. Match supporting details from the lists; then, on your paper, write a paragraph comparing their activities. Write a topic sentence, and include suitable transitional words and phrases.

ASTRONAUTS

1. Work in weightless environment.
2. Go into space to observe Earth, moon, planets, and stars.
3. Wear space suits for protection from radiation and heat.
4. Upon return to Earth, protected by special tile heat shields on craft.
5. Use oxygen systems of spacecraft or suit to breathe in outer space.
6. Can live in space labs for weeks or even months.

SCUBA DIVERS

1. Explore oceans for food sources and other natural resources.
2. Use air tanks to breathe under water.
3. Can live in underwater habitats for months.
4. Work in environment in which they weigh less than normal weight.
5. To return to surface, rise slowly to avoid rapid changes in pressure.
6. Wear rubber wet suits for protection against the cold.

**Exercise 8   Prewriting/Writing: Contrast**   On your paper, write a paragraph in which you contrast the activities of astronauts and scuba divers. Use the supporting details given in Exercise 7. Write a new topic sentence, and use transitional words and phrases that emphasize the contrast. You may make changes in the wording of the details to emphasize the contrast.

## 7.2f   Cause and Effect

When organizing a paragraph by cause and effect, you give an explanation. A **cause** produces a result; an **effect** is a result of a cause. To claim that one event or condition causes another is to say that the first brings about the second. Study the following examples.

| CAUSES | EFFECTS |
|---|---|
| Contact with poison ivy | Rash on skin |
| Invention of microchip | Reduction in size and cost of computers |

The cause-and-effect method is useful for explaining relationships. However, you must distinguish clearly between causes and effects. You must also be certain that one event or condition is actually a cause of another, not merely one that occurred or existed before the other. You can make the relationship clear by showing the process by which the cause produces the effect.

You can organize a paragraph by cause and effect in two ways: (1) Begin your paragraph with an effect and then follow with the causes of that effect. (2) Begin with a cause and follow with its effects. If you want to show why something exists or occurs, then effects-to-causes order is the better choice. If your goal is to show consequences —what results from something's existence or occurrence—then the causes-to-effects order is more appropriate.

When organizing a paragraph by cause and effect, you must present your material so that readers can easily distinguish the causes from the effects. You can achieve this clarity simply by using words and phrases that mean "cause" or "effect." Words particularly suited to writing about causes and effects are *affect, as a result, because, causes, consequently, effect, for, produces, results, therefore,* and *why.*

The writer of the following paragraph begins with a question about an effect. The rest of the paragraph explains the causes. The words that make clear the causes and effects are in italic type.

## Model

> What makes a bullwhip crack? The answer is probably not what you would expect. When a bullwhip is snapped, motion is conveyed from the handle to the tip with mounting speed. Studies have shown that even though the handle may move at just 40 feet per second, the tip moves as fast as 1400 feet per second. *Because* sound travels at an average speed of 1100 feet per second, at a point in its arc the tip of a bullwhip moves faster than the speed of sound. At the moment when it does so, the tip *creates* a shock wave. This shock wave *causes* a dramatic rise and fall in air pressure, which in turn *produces* a sharp cracking sound. A bullwhip cracks, then, *for the same reason* that a supersonic jet booms: it crashes through the sound barrier.

Sometimes causes and effects can be like a chain reaction. An effect of one cause can itself become a cause of other effects. For example, a dead battery may be the cause of your car's not starting; your car's not starting might be the cause of your missing an appointment, and so on.

**Exercise 9    Prewriting/Writing: Cause and Effect**    On your paper, write a paragraph using the following cause and effects. You may add further details. You may either begin with the cause and follow with the effects or present the effects first and then the cause. Include a topic sentence and transitional words that make clear the cause-and-effect relationship.

*Cause:* Air pollution
*Effects:*
1. Steel deteriorates up to thirty times faster than normal.
2. Building surfaces erode.
3. More than one hundred million dollars' worth of crops and livestock damaged each year.
4. Incidence of asthma and bronchitis increases.
5. Plants along highways die.

**Exercise 10   Prewriting/Writing: Cause and Effect**   On your paper, write a paragraph using the following causes and effect. You may either present the causes first and then the effect or begin with the effect and then present the causes. Include transitional words that make clear the cause-and-effect relationship.

*Effect:* Westward movement in the century after United States achieved independence
*Causes:*

1. Vast amounts of fertile land attracted farmers.
2. Discovery of gold and silver drew those who wanted to get rich quickly.
3. Homestead Act of 1862 guaranteed 160 acres of unclaimed land to anyone who would live on the land for five years.

**Exercise 11   Prewriting: Causes and Effects**   Each of the items listed can be both a cause and an effect. Select two and, on your paper, list causes and effects of each.

> **SAMPLE**    Disappearance of marshes
> **ANSWER**    *Causes:* Pollution
>               Drainage
>         *Effects:* Near extinction of whooping cranes
>                Creation of land for settlement

1. A power failure
2. Acid rain

3. Poor nutrition
4. Rising costs of goods and services

**Assignment 1   Prewriting/Writing**   *Step 1:* List from four to six events that have played a major role in helping you to grow up. List the events twice: first, in chronological order; second, in the order of their importance. *Step 2:* Construct a topic sentence for each list. *Step 3:* Use the topic sentences and lists to write two paragraphs, one arranged in chronological order, the other arranged in order of importance. Use suitable transitional words in each paragraph.

**Assignment 2   Prewriting/Writing**   *Step 1:* Visualize a person, place, or object that you think would make an interesting subject for a descriptive paragraph. On your paper, make a rough drawing of your chosen subject. *Step 2:* Next to key parts of your sketch, write notes describing the main features of your subject. *Step 3:* Use your notes to construct a paragraph organized in spatial order. Include appropriate transitional words.

**Assignment 3 Prewriting/Writing**   The   Indo-European language family includes languages spoken by roughly half of the people in the world today. At a library take notes on the classes of languages that constitute this language family and on examples of languages in each class. Then write a topic sentence for a paragraph organized by classification. Arrange the supporting details according to the number of speakers in each language class. As you write your paragraph, use transitional words to give it clarity. End the paragraph with a sentence that brings it to a definite conclusion.

**Assignment 4  Prewriting/Writing**   Write a paragraph in which you compare and contrast your way and a friend's way of handling the same situation, such as studying for a test or learning a new skill. Make two lists of details, one about your way and one about the other person's way. Use the lists to write your paragraph, presenting all of the information about one first and then all of the information about the other (AAA BBB order). In your concluding sentence, draw a conclusion about the two methods.

**Assignment 5  Prewriting/Writing**   A general topic and a list of potential supporting items are given at the top of page 275. Think of the topic as a cause and the supporting items as areas affected by the cause. *Step 1:* Make notes on the effects that the cause has had on one of the listed areas. You may need to do research. *Step 2:* Express the topic in a topic sentence, and use your notes to write supporting sentences. *Step 3:* Write a paragraph organized from cause to effect and with the effects arranged in order of importance. Be sure to include transitional words that help your reader distinguish the cause from the effects.

*General topic (cause):* Computer technology
*Supporting Items (areas affected by cause):*

1. Communications
2. Forms of entertainment
3. Business record keeping
4. Travel arrangements
5. Scientific research
6. Education

**Assignment Checklist**

Check your assignments for the following points:

1. Does each paragraph contain a precise topic sentence, supporting sentences, and a suitable concluding sentence?
2. In Assignment 1, did you organize the events first by chronological order and then by order of importance?
3. In Assignment 2, did you organize the supporting details by spatial order?
4. In Assignment 3, did you organize the supporting details by classification?
5. Did you provide examples of each class?
6. In Assignment 4, did you present all of your information about one method followed by all of the information about the other (AAA BBB order)?
7. In Assignment 5, did you make notes on the effects of the cause in one area?
8. Did you organize the paragraph from cause to effect?
9. Did you use suitable transitional words to highlight the organization of your paragraphs?
10. Did you check your paragraphs for correct grammar, usage, spelling, and punctuation?

# 7.3 Combining Methods of Organization

For some topics, you can most effectively develop your paragraph by combining two methods of organization. For example, if you are developing a paragraph by explaining an effect and then giving its causes, you can present the causes in the order of their importance. Similarly, if you are using comparison and contrast to develop a paragraph, you can arrange the corresponding points of comparison or contrast in spatial order or in order of importance.

The writer of the following paragraph begins with an effect, a dramatic change in baseball statistics, and then presents the causes of that effect. The causes are organized in chronological order.

**Model**

> What caused the explosion [in hitting and scoring]? The end of the war, Ruth, money, and the lively ball. Attendance in 1919 rose for every one of the sixteen major-league teams, in some instances doubling and even tripling. The release from war was largely responsible for the first burst of interest, and then Ruth's home run hitting came into focus. Babe was the most exciting aspect of the 1919 season, even more exciting than the pennant races. New fans bubbling into the ballparks . . . thrilled vicariously to the . . . power of the Ruthian home run. They wanted more. They wanted hits and they wanted runs, lots of hits and lots of runs. They wanted homers. The owners, delighted by the windfall at the ticket windows, were happy to give them what they wanted. They instituted legislation against the myriad trick pitches, like the spitball, that tended to befuddle batters, and they pepped up the ball.
>
> Robert W. Creamer
> "Babe Ruth Comes to New York"

The writer of the model paragraph moves from an effect to its causes to explain changes in baseball around 1920. One of the causes, the demand for more hits and runs, led to two additional causes: laws against trick pitches and the manufacture of a livelier ball. The writer follows a clear time sequence in his paragraph.

**Exercise 1   Prewriting: Methods of Organization**   On your paper, list two methods that you could combine to develop each of the following topics effectively.

SAMPLE          The movement of a glacier
ANSWER          Cause and effect, chronological order

1. An artist's sketch for a painting and the finished painting
2. Sources of energy
3. Sharks' supremacy in the ocean
4. Two strategies for playing a game

**Exercise 2  Prewriting/Writing: Organization**  On your paper, write a paragraph in which you compare and contrast the Arctic and Antarctica. First, match supporting details from the given lists. Then organize the lists from the most general information to the most specific. Write a topic sentence, and use transitional words to make clear the comparison and contrast.

ARCTIC

1. Average temperature goes from -30°F in winter to 45°F in summer.
2. Cold in winter; mild during summer
3. Warm period during July and August
4. During warm period, snow melts and some flowers bloom.

ANTARCTICA

1. During December, snow does not melt; only plant, lichen, grows in the warmest places.
2. Coldest region on Earth—continually cold.
3. Winter temperatures are between -40°F and -80°F; summer temperatures are always below freezing.
4. December is warmest month.

**Assignment  Prewriting/Writing**  Choose a topic that is suitable for a paragraph with more than one method of organization. List supporting details for the topic. If necessary, do research. Then organize the details according to the methods that seem most suitable for the topic. Write your paragraph.

## Assignment Checklist

Check your assignment for the following points:

1. Did you list enough supporting details to develop your chosen topic adequately?
2. Did you organize the supporting details in the most effective order for your topic?
3. Did you use transitional words and phrases to make clear the relationships between supporting details?
4. Did you check your paragraph for correct grammar, usage, spelling, and punctuation?

## Parrot Talk: Developing Paragraphs

**Situation:** The Children's Zoo in your town has just acquired Archie, a yellow-fronted Amazon parrot. The zoo administrators plan to feature Archie in their display of tropical birds. You have been asked to write a two-paragraph information sheet that will be placed beside Archie's cage in the aviary. The information sheet will consist of one paragraph about parrots in general and one paragraph specifically about the yellow-fronted parrot and Archie. Keep in mind the following information as you plan and write your paragraph.

**Writer:** you as assistant curator of the zoo

**Audience:** visitors to the zoo

**Topic:** parrots in general; the yellow-fronted Amazon parrot and Archie in particular

**Purpose:** to provide information

**Directions:** To write your paragraphs, follow these steps.

*Step 1.* Read the notes on the facing page. You will notice that some items deal with general information about parrots and some with specific facts about the new parrot.

*Step 2.* Divide a sheet of paper into two columns, one for your general paragraph and one for your specific paragraph. List the general details about parrots in the first column and specific details about the yellow-fronted Amazon parrot and Archie in the second column.

(Continue on page 280.)

                    Notes on Parrots

Named Archie

Already a popular favorite because of beautiful coloring and
friendly disposition; truly representative of the parrot family

Captured near Amazon River

Only the Carolina parakeet is native to United States, but
sailors and travelers to Africa, Asia, and South America
brought back birds from parrot family.

Life expectancy of yellow-fronted Amazon: thirty to fifty years

Archie's favorite foods: seeds, fresh green beans, corn, grapes

Popular because of tameness, ability to mimic human speech,
and comical ways

Archie likes to chew wood and to strip branches of leaves and bark.

Went through sixty days' quarantine before entering United States

Popular pets through the centuries

Archie is seven inches tall; will get fatter but not taller

Seven months old

Still a baby, not yet speaking words

Yellow-fronted Amazon, Archie, is iridescent green with yellow
crest on top of head and touch of red in wings.

Archie most active during daytime; sleeps at night on feet
on perch

General characteristics of species:
     Class: <u>Aves</u>
     Subclass: <u>Neornithes</u> (True Birds)
     Order: <u>Psittaciformes</u> (<u>psitta</u> means "parrot")
     Plumage: brilliant green, blue, yellow, or red
     Food: chiefly fruits
     Habitat: forests of tropics and subtropics
     Beak: stout, narrow, sharp-edged, hooked at tip
     Feet: adapted for grasping, two toes in front and two behind

*Step 3.* Read your list in Column 1. Put the letter *T* next to the item that can best be used in a topic sentence for a paragraph. Use numbers to arrange the other details so that your general information deals first with the history of parrots as pets and then with their characteristics as a species.

*Step 4.* Read your list in Column 2. Again, arrange the items so that the information about Archie covers first his history and then his individual characteristics. Put the letter *C* next to the item to be used in your concluding sentence.

*Step 5.* Using complete sentences, write drafts of your paragraphs. You may use more than one detail in each supporting sentence. Begin your first paragraph, the one on parrots in general, with a topic sentence using item marked *T*. For the second paragraph, in which you discuss the yellow-fronted Amazon parrot, write a topic sentence that introduces Archie and provides a transition between the two paragraphs. In both paragraphs, arrange the details in a logical order. Conclude with a sentence in which you use the item marked *C*.

# Unit Assignments

**Assignment 1**   Compare and contrast your expectations for an event with the way that the event actually happened. Using either chronological order or order of importance, write a paragraph. Use transitional words to emphasize the relationship between the details in your paragraph. Place the topic sentence somewhere other than at the beginning.

**Assignment 2**   Write two paragraphs about the dangers of overexposure to extreme temperatures. In the first paragraph, use cause and effect to explain the dangers of staying in the cold too long. Present the dangers in order of importance. In the second paragraph, compare and contrast the dangers of overexposure to cold with those of overexposure to heat.

**Assignment 3**   Write a paragraph on the topic of stalagmites and stalactites. Use both comparison and contrast and cause and effect to organize the paragraph. Discuss both the cause and the appearance of each type of formation and the similarities and differences between the two.

**Assignment 4**   Imagine that you are a reporter for a local newspaper and have been instructed to cover a recent flood. Your assignment is to write a three-paragraph article on the flood. In your first paragraph, use spatial order to describe the scene of the recent flood. In your second paragraph, use chronological order to recount the events leading to the present flood. Finally, in your last paragraph, use order of importance to itemize the plans for improved precautions to be taken by civil agencies against similar disasters in the future. Be sure to include suitable transitional words in each paragraph.

## Revising Your Assignments

For help in revising a paragraph, consult the Checklist for Revision on the last page of this book.

# Unit Tests

## Test 1

**A.** Number your paper from 1 to 5. Next to each number, write *True* if the sentence is true or *False* if the sentence is false.

1. Every paragraph must contain a topic sentence.
2. Every paragraph should contain three kinds of supporting details.
3. Facts may serve both as examples and as reasons.
4. A topic sentence may appear anywhere in a paragraph.
5. Transitional words emphasize the relationship between ideas in a paragraph.

**B.** Number your paper from 6 to 10. Next to each number, write the letter of the term that correctly completes the sentence. You will use all but one of the terms.

    a. reason          d. fact

    b. coherence    e. paragraph

    c. concluding sentence    f. classification

6. A(n) __?__ is a group of sentences that develops a single idea or topic.
7. A(n) __?__ restates the topic sentence or presents your thoughts about the topic.
8. A(n) __?__ is a statement that explains or justifies another statement.
9. __?__ is the clear and orderly presentation of ideas.
10. __?__ is a way of dividing an idea into smaller categories.

**C.** Number your paper from 11 to 15. Read the following paragraph. Next to each number, write the letter of the item that correctly answers the question.

      (1) Lasers, devices that strengthen light, have been developed to perform many useful tasks. (2) One common use for lasers is to scan price codes on packages in supermarket check-out counters and transmit the information to the cash register. (3) Furthermore, because they transmit great amounts of information less expensively, lasers can replace copper telephone wires. (4) Another use is in manufacturing, where lasers can be used to cut thick piles of cloth and to weld metal parts. (5) Most important, lasers can be used to

perform surgery that is too delicate to attempt with scalpels. (6) Because of their multiple uses, lasers are one of the most valuable inventions of this century.

11. Which one of the following is the limited topic of the paragraph?
    a. Uses of light
    b. Invention of lasers
    c. Medical uses of lasers
    d. Uses of lasers

12. Which one of the following describes Sentence 2?
    a. Topic sentence
    b. Concluding sentence
    c. Supporting sentence
    d. Introductory sentence

13. Which one of the following is the method of organization used in the paragraph?
    a. Chronological order
    b. Order of importance
    c. Classification
    d. Comparison and contrast

14. Which one of the following contains a transitional word that emphasizes the order of the paragraph?
    a. Sentence 1
    b. Sentence 2
    c. Sentence 5
    d. Sentence 6

15. Which one of the following describes Sentence 5?
    a. Example
    b. Reason
    c. Cause
    d. Event

# Test 2

Choose one of the Unit Assignments or one that your teacher suggests. Write the assignment as directed and hand it in to your teacher.

# Unit 8

## Revising

---

## Unit Preview

Once you have completed a first draft, you begin another part of the writing process: revision. In **revising** you look at your work again, reorganizing and rewriting it so that your finished paragraph expresses exactly what you want to communicate to your reader.

The following paragraph is a writer's first draft. As you read the draft, consider how you might improve it.

(1) Although steamboats almost disappeared during the period after the Civil War, they are once again sailing on the Mississippi, Ohio, and Missouri rivers. (2) The first commercially successful steam-powered vessel was launched in 1807, and within ten years, hundreds of them were moving cargo and passengers up and down the rivers, but steamboating was dangerous because boilers often exploded and boats often collided. (3) Also, the depths and curves of the rivers changed, causing many boats to run aground. (4) Steamboating never fully recovered from the time when no boats traveled on the river. (5) During the Civil War, steamboats stopped running because of the fact that shooting from nearby battles made the rivers too dangerous for travel. (6) The business that steamboats had handled was eventually taken over by the newly invented trains, cars, and trucks, which moved freight and people more quickly than the boats. (7) Today, the new steamboats are not used to move freight or to carry passengers who are eager to reach a destination quickly; they are used by vacationers who want to spend a leisurely evening, day, or week cruising on a river. (8) Most travelers who are in a hurry take an airplane.

**For Analysis**   On your paper, answer the following questions about the writer's first-draft paragraph.

1. Which sentence would be improved by dividing it into two sentences?
2. Sentence 5 would be more effective if placed somewhere else in the paragraph. Which sentence should it follow?
3. What words should be removed from Sentence 5 to make it more concise?
4. Which sentence is not closely related to the topic sentence and should be removed?

By answering these questions, you have made decisions about revising. Often, you may find it difficult to revise a draft that you consider finished. As you gain experience in writing and revising, you will develop methods that work best for you. This unit will give you practice in techniques for revising that you can use in your own writing.

## 8.1   Revising: Unity and Coherence

If possible, set your first draft aside for a time. Then start your revising by reading the draft to see whether it is clear: that is, unified and coherent (*page 261*). You can begin to revise any paragraph by following these steps.

**Procedure**

1. *Check for unity.* Be sure that your topic sentence is specific enough to make your purpose clear. Read each sentence to be sure that it is about the topic. If you find any supporting sentences that are not clearly related to the topic, discard them, rewrite them, or broaden the topic sentence to include them.

2. *Check to see that your paragraph is fully developed.* Look for gaps in your discussion of the topic. If you are lacking any facts, examples, or reasons, do the necessary research

to find them. Be sure that your supporting information is both clear and suitable for your audience. Add a concluding sentence if your paragraph seems incomplete.

3. *Be sure that your paragraph is coherent and clear.* Check to see that all the information is in the right order. Each idea and each sentence should lead logically to the next. If you have used chronological order, spatial order, or order of importance, be sure that no details violate that order. If any details or sentences seem out of place, move them. You can put them in the proper place when you rewrite, or you can cut up your rough draft (if you have written on only one side) and tape it together with the sentences in the right order.

4. *Check to be sure that your ideas are connected logically and smoothly.* Use transitional words to show how your ideas are related, to make clear your arrangement of details, and to help your paragraph flow smoothly from one sentence to the next.

Here is a first draft of a paragraph. To the left of the paragraph are the writer's notes on needed revisions. After you have read the first draft and the notes, compare the draft with the revised version that follows it.

FIRST DRAFT

Details needed

Unrelated
sentence

Sentences out
of order

A Pollyanna is a person who is cheerful and optimistic to the point of being irritating. The term *Pollyanna* comes from the title of a novel by Eleanor Porter. Porter was in her forties when she wrote the novel. The behavior of a Pollyanna is totally divorced from reality. In actuality, situations do not always have happy endings, and Pollyannas, who claim that they do, are generally regarded as either insincere or foolish. However gloomy things look in the novel, Pollyanna sees only their bright sides. However miserably some of the people whom she meets behave, Pollyanna sees only their good sides.

REVISED VERSION

Sentence removed
Details added

Sentences moved

Transitional
word added

A Pollyanna is a person who is cheerful and optimistic to the point of being irritating. The term *Pollyanna* comes from the title of a novel by Eleanor Porter. Published in 1913, it relates the adventures of a young girl named Pollyanna. However gloomy things look in the novel, Pollyanna sees only their bright sides. However miserably some of the people whom she meets behave, Pollyanna sees only their good sides. Consequently, the behavior of a Pollyanna is divorced from reality. In actuality, situations do not always have happy endings, and Pollyannas, who claim that they do, are generally regarded as either insincere or foolish.

**Exercise 1  Revising: Unity and Coherence**  On your paper, revise the following paragraphs. Rewrite each paragraph, organizing the sentences in the correct order. Remove any details that do not support the topic sentence. Add transitional words and phrases where they are needed.

1.     The federal government of the United States has three branches: the legislative, the executive, and the judicial. The legislature is made up of the Senate and the House of Representatives. Their chief responsibilities are to pass laws and to approve government spending. The main function of the judicial branch is to rule on legal matters involving the Constitution and federal laws. The federal judiciary consists of the United States Supreme Court and a system of lower courts. The Supreme Court consists of nine justices. The executive branch consists of the President and numerous executive departments and agencies. It is the President's responsibility to put into effect the laws of the land. Another major task of the federal judiciary is to settle disputes between individual states. It is also the duty of the President to serve as commander in chief of the armed forces.

2.     Because pain and risk of shock made surgery on a conscious patient dangerous, very little surgery was done before anesthetics were brought into use. In 1842 Crawford W. Long, an American doctor, was the first to use ether as an anesthetic during an operation. In 1800 the British chemist Humphry Davy suggested that nitrous oxide be used to deaden pain during operations. Nitrous oxide is also

known as laughing gas. No one at that time had used the gas on a patient during an operation. Long, who had already tried ether on himself, used it on a patient during the removal of a neck tumor. However, because Long did not make public his use of ether, he received no credit for it. Dr. W.T.G. Morton, who used ether during an operation and published his results, received the credit for it. As the nineteenth century progressed, the use of anesthesia became widespread. Every year millions of operations are performed with the aid of anesthetics.

**Exercise 2   Revising: Unity and Coherence**   The following paragraph is developed by comparison. On your paper, revise the paragraph to make it complete, unified, and well organized. Add necessary details and transitional words.

Being a member of a basketball team is a lot like being part of a symphony orchestra. In each case a group of people must work together to achieve success. An orchestra gets its direction from the conductor. If just one performer fails to follow the conductor's guidance, then the whole effect will be ruined. If one player on a basketball team does not do exactly what the coach says, then the game could be lost. That's the problem with the team I'm on.

**Assignment   Revising**   On your paper, revise the following paragraph. Make sure that the revised paragraph has unity and coherence.

Probably the most successful stagecoach robber of all time, and certainly the most interesting, was Black Bart. Between 1877 and 1883, Bart pulled off twenty-eight holdups. Wearing a duster and covering his head with a flour sack out of which he had cut holes for seeing, Bart always waited for his victims at a spot in their run where they would have to halt. Armed with a shotgun, he would waltz out on foot and politely ask the driver to throw down the strongbox. Black Bart left poems, which he signed "Black Bart, the PO8 (po-ate)," at the scenes of some of his robberies. Bart was apprehended when he dropped his handkerchief while fleeing from a holdup. Investigators traced the laundry mark to a San Francisco laundry and from the laundry to the customer. The notorious Black Bart turned out to be one of San Francisco's most illustrious citizens, a mild-mannered, dapper fellow named Charles Bolton. He was a fellow with a taste for high living, which he supported by robbing stagecoaches. San Francisco was the West Coast's leading city at the time. It was later discovered that Black Bart's shotgun was never loaded, and he had no way to defend himself. He was never violent.

## Assignment Checklist

Check your assignment for the following points:

✔ 1. Does the topic sentence make clear the purpose?
✔ 2. Did you discard or rewrite sentences that are not related to the topic?
✔ 3. Did you organize the paragraph coherently?
✔ 4. Did you supply transitional words to show how the ideas in the paragraph are related?

# 8.2    Revising: Consistency

When you revise a paragraph, you should be sure that you have been consistent in the tense *(pages 117–118)* and voice *(pages 119–120)* of verbs, the person of pronouns *(pages 137–138),* and the tone in which you discuss the topic. Except for the title, the words in italics in the following paragraph show where the writer has been inconsistent.

Present tense
Third person

Shift to
second person

Shift to
past tense

Shifts to
passive voice
and first person

In *The Adventures of Huckleberry Finn,* Mark Twain shows that "good" people are sometimes guilty of using double standards. The woman who generously adopts Huck, for example, the Widow Douglas, forbids him to smoke tobacco because it is a bad habit. Yet the Widow herself regularly takes snuff. *Consider* the two proud frontier families whom Huck gets to know, the Grangerfords and the Shepherdsons. They *attended* the same church on Sundays and *spoke* glowingly of the minister's sermons on brotherly love. Within hours of leaving church, though, the longstanding feud between the families *was resumed. As far as I was concerned, and I am sure old Twain*

Shift to
righteous tone

*would agree if he were around,* the behavior of these
characters was hypocritical. *You should practice what
you preach or stop preaching it!*

Such shifts in writing can obscure your purpose and cause
difficulty for your readers. Consistency makes your writing more
understandable.

## Tense

Use one verb tense consistently unless there is an actual shift
in the time in which the actions occur (*pages 117–118*).

| | |
|---|---|
| INCONSISTENT | The convertible *got* good mileage. Otherwise it *does* not *perform* well. [Tense shifts from past to present.] |
| REVISED | The convertible *got* good mileage. Otherwise, it *did* not *perform* well. [Past tense used consistently.] |
| REVISED | The convertible *gets* good mileage. Otherwise, it *does* not *perform* well. [Present tense used consistently.] |

## Voice

Do not change unnecessarily from the active voice to the
passive voice or from the passive to the active (*pages 119–120*). Be
aware that a change in the voice of the verb also causes a change in
the subject and, thus, a change in focus or emphasis.

| | |
|---|---|
| INCONSISTENT | Mr. Theokas *had* no intention of leaving New Jersey because a new house *had* just *been bought* by him in Hohokus. [Voice shifts from active to passive; subject changes from *Mr. Theokas* to *house*.] |
| REVISED | Mr. Theokas *had* no intention of leaving New Jersey because he *had* just *bought* a new house in Hohokus. [Active voice used consistently.] |

## Person

Be consistent in your use of pronouns (*pages 137–138*). Do not
shift carelessly from a noun to *you* or from *she, he,* or *one* to *you* or to

*I.* If you start in the third person, continue in the third person unless there is an actual change in the person to whom you are referring.

> INCONSISTENT    When *one* learns to drive, *you* should regard it as a serious responsibility. [Pronoun shifts from third person to second person.]

> REVISED    When *one* learns to drive, *he* or *she* should regard it as a serious responsibility. [Third-person pronouns used consistently.]

> REVISED    When *you* learn to drive, *you* should regard it as a serious responsibility. [Second-person pronouns used consistently.]

## Tone

Be consistent in the tone, or attitude, that you convey about your topic. Establish a tone that is appropriate for your topic and your audience and maintain it throughout your paragraph. Do not change your tone from serious to humorous, for example, or from humorous to critical.

> INCONSISTENT
>
> Two elements are necessary if a meeting is to run smoothly. First, the chairperson must take charge and remain in control. Second, the participants must listen carefully. These points are especially important if the group must reach a decision. What's really irritating, though, are those people who whisper and giggle. It's so tempting to yell at them.

> CONSISTENT
>
> Two elements are necessary if a meeting is to run smoothly. First, the chairperson must take charge and remain in control. Second, the participants must listen carefully. These points are especially important if the group must reach a decision. Difficulties arise when people whisper and giggle among themselves. If this behavior interferes with the progress of the meeting, the chairperson must deal with the situation.

**Exercise** **Revising: Consistency** On your paper, revise each group of sentences to make them consistent in tense, voice, person, and tone. Each group may contain more than one error.

1. Much of the Alaska Highway is a deserted, bumpy road. People driving on it should use heavy-duty cars or trucks and should carry spare parts; otherwise, you could get stranded in a broken-down car.

2. Because there are few parking spaces downtown, Laila drives to the train station. Then she parked her car and took a train downtown.

3. Studying architecture and designing buildings were two of Thomas Jefferson's favorite activities. He not only snooped all over France and England to get the hang of European architecture, but he also designed and built his own house.

4. I had a great seat at the basketball game last night. You could see the entire court from my seat, so the game was really enjoyed by me.

5. Riding an old paddleboat down the Mississippi is great. You visit all of the old ports, and sometimes one can steer the boat for a while.

6. Making furniture is becoming more popular. The basic skills are learned in woodworking classes, and then you continue the work at home on your own.

7. If one plans to spend a long time out in the cold, you should dress warmly. Otherwise, frostbite or hypothermia could be suffered.

8. We presented our demand for a new traffic light to the city council last week. We need the light because the traffic on our street is very heavy. Furthermore, it's about time that one receives something for all the dough you fork over to the city.

9. When I use my telescope, many stars and planets are observed. Looking at them was so fascinating that I stayed outside until after midnight.

10. When you come to our concert, you will be pleased because we play music by Telemann and Vivaldi. I know that you are really into their music.

**Assignment  Revising**  On your paper, revise the following paragraph so that it is consistent in tense, voice, person, and tone.

> The Magic Castle is a private restaurant and club located in the hills of Hollywood, California. Admission to the Castle is restricted to member magicians and their guests. Excellent food is served at reasonable prices. The really outstanding aspect of the establishment, though, is the entertainment that it offers its guests. Everywhere that you look in the Castle's magnificent main salon

there are performing magicians. You will see some of these wizards doing card tricks; others will work with coins or metal hoops. I saw one fellow doing some really far-out sleight-of-hand maneuvers with an egg. It made me wish that I knew something about magic. You really wonder how these magicians do it! Anyway, the club has several small salons where various magicians can be seen performing entire acts. There is also a room that had a piano that played itself; it played any tune that I asked it to play. If you ever get a chance to go to the Magic Castle, be sure to grab it!

### Assignment Checklist

Check your assignment for the following points:

✓ 1. Did you use the same verb tense throughout the paragraph?
✓ 2. Did you use pronouns in the same person (first, second, or third) when you referred to the same subject?
✓ 3. Did you maintain a consistent tone in the paragraph?

# 8.3   Revising: Combining Sentences

An effective way to revise sentences is to combine them. Often, you can express your thoughts smoothly by combining two or more sentences into one sentence. The revised sentence often makes clearer the relationship between the ideas in the original sentences.

## 8.3a   Using Coordination

One way to combine sentences is by coordination. **Coordination** is the joining of parts of equal importance. When you coordinate simple sentences, or independent clauses, the result is a compound sentence (*page 90*). If such a sentence also contains a subordinate clause, the result is a compound-complex sentence (*page 91*).

There are three ways to form compound or compound-complex sentences.

**Strategies**

1. *Use a comma and a coordinating conjunction (page 30) or correlative conjunctions (page 31).*

> Caleb is reporting on John Steinbeck, Molly chose Ernest Hemingway, **and** I will be writing about Willa Cather.
>
> **Either** Ms. Wong is an extraordinary teacher, **or** I've suddenly grown smarter.

2. *Use a semicolon and a conjunctive adverb (page 32).* Put a comma after the adverb.

> When the town board met last week, they refused to approve additional funds for recreation; **therefore,** there will be no new soccer field.
>
> Enforcement of the leash law has been strict; **however,** some dog owners prefer paying the fine to leashing their dogs.

3. *Use a semicolon alone.* The relationship between the independent clauses should be close and obvious.

> There is no one to help you; you have only yourself.

The semicolon can be an effective way to show contrast.

> Karen's father owns a bookstore; her mother drives a taxi.

The coordinating words tell exactly how the joined clauses are related. The most common coordinating words and the relationships that they express are summarized in the list that follows.

ADDITION
> and, both . . . and, not only . . . but (also), furthermore, in addition, moreover

CONTRAST OR EXCEPTION
> but, yet, however, instead, nevertheless, still

ALTERNATIVE
> or, nor, either . . . or, neither . . . nor, alternatively, otherwise

RESULT
>  therefore, thus, consequently, accordingly

CAUSE
>  for

Choose your coordinating word or phrase carefully to ensure that your sentence says what you want it to say. Base your choice of words not only on meaning but also on style and emphasis.

You may combine more than two main ideas in a compound sentence if they are appropriately related.

THREE SENTENCES
>  Jeremy plays the cello. Adam plays the clarinet.
>  Louis plays the oboe.

COMPOUND SENTENCE
>  Jeremy plays the cello, Adam plays the clarinet, and Louis plays the oboe.

You can often write a compound sentence in which the clauses have the same subject more effectively as a simple sentence with a compound predicate. Similarly, you can write a compound sentence (or two simple sentences) in which the predicates make similar statements as a simple sentence with a compound subject.

TWO SENTENCES
>  The ambassador from Italy wished to sit next to the President.
>  The consul from France wished to sit there, too.

ONE COMPOUND SENTENCE
>  The ambassador from Italy wished to sit next to the President, and the consul from France wished to sit there, too.

ONE SIMPLE SENTENCE WITH COMPOUND SUBJECT
>  The ambassador from Italy and the consul from France both wished to sit next to the President.

**Exercise 1  Revising: Coordination**  On your paper, combine the following pairs of sentences into one compound or one compound-complex sentence. Use coordinating words that express the relationship indicated in parentheses.

| SAMPLE | Today Albert Contreras is Hollywood's newest star. Yesterday he was just the boy next door. (Contrast) |
|---|---|
| ANSWER | Today Albert Contreras is Hollywood's newest star, but yesterday he was just the boy next door. |

1. The famous movie star Albert Contreras used to live in the next apartment. He was my older brother's best friend. (Addition)

2. He and my brother Clyde were inseparable all through elementary school and high school. They have gone their separate ways now. (Contrast)

3. Clyde had no interest in joining Albert in the pursuit of a career on the stage. Clyde went to the university and got a degree in computer science. (Contrast)

4. After high school, their lives took sharply divergent paths. Despite their previous closeness, they gradually lost contact with each other. (Result)

5. I think that my brother should try to contact Albert. They may never make contact again. (Alternative)

6. Albert became famous in our town many years ago, when he played Wilbur the Pig in the third-grade production of *Charlotte's Web*. People around here like to claim that this role was the beginning of his theatrical career. (Addition)

7. It would seem that Albert was destined to be a performer. He did not make the decision to become an actor until the last year of high school. (Contrast)

8. Albert was always a practical person. He gave himself seven years in which to succeed in his profession. (Result)

9. He would be an established actor in seven years. He would return to school to study mechanical drawing, another interest of his. (Alternative)

10. Albert became moderately successful in only five years. By the time seven years had passed, he was one of the best-known actors on the stage. (Addition)

**Exercise 2 Revising: Coordination** On your paper, rewrite each pair of sentences as a compound or a compound-complex sentence. Include appropriate coordinating words and use correct punctuation.

| | |
|---|---|
| **SAMPLE** | In most arctic areas, the number of polar bears is decreasing. On the shore of Hudson Bay in Churchill, Manitoba, the polar-bear population is increasing. |
| **ANSWER** | In most arctic areas, the number of polar bears is decreasing; however, on the shore of Hudson Bay in Churchill, Manitoba, the polar-bear population is increasing. |

1. Sometimes residents of Churchill get trapped in their houses by bears outside their doors. Conservation officials have given out telephone numbers to call for help in distracting the bears.

2. The town is located at the end of the bears' summer migratory path. The bears stay there from September until winter arrives.

3. During the winter the bears hunt seals on the ice. In the summer they eat berries, seaweed, and small animals.

4. The polar bears prefer to eat seals, which they catch on the ice. They wait for winter at Churchill, where ice forms earliest on the bay.

5. So many polar bears rarely gather in one place. Scientists take the opportunity to study them there.

6. Polar bears can withstand the cold on the ice because they are protected by thick fur. They have a four-inch layer of fat under the skin to shield them further from the cold.

7. Newborn polar bears weigh only about one pound. Full-grown male polar bears can weigh more than half a ton.

8. Polar bears can run as fast as thirty-five miles an hour. They can also swim at a speed of seven or eight miles an hour.

9. Polar bears have become a tourist attraction in Churchill. Towers have been built to provide visitors with good views of the bears.

10. Visitors enjoy watching the polar bears. If no bears are nearby, the visitors get to see other animals, such as snowy owls.

## 8.3b Using Subordination: Clauses

You can join ideas that are unequal in importance by using **subordination.** When one idea in a sentence is less important than another, it is a subordinate idea. You can express subordinate ideas either in subordinate clauses or in phrases.

You can revise sentences by combining them, making one or more into subordinate clauses. When you subordinate one clause to another, you write a complex sentence (*page 91*).

## Adjective Clauses

When two sentences have a noun or a pronoun in common, you can make one sentence an adjective clause (*page 82*) and combine it with the other sentence. Place the more important idea in the independent clause and the subordinate idea in the adjective clause. Connect the clauses with a relative pronoun (*that, which, who, whom, whose*). In the following revised sentences, the adjective clauses are in italics.

TWO SENTENCES

> My cousin recently read a fascinating book. She cannot stop talking about it.

REVISED SENTENCE WITH ADJECTIVE CLAUSE

> My cousin recently read a fascinating book *that she cannot stop talking about.*

TWO SENTENCES

> She was enchanted by the book. It tells a bizarre and interesting story.

REVISED SENTENCE WITH ADJECTIVE CLAUSE

> She was enchanted by the book, *which tells a bizarre and interesting story.*

For rules about punctuating essential and nonessential adjective clauses, see pages 82–83.

## Adverb Clauses

When you can relate two sentences by time, manner, cause, condition, comparison, purpose, or result, you can make one sentence an adverb clause (*pages 84–85*) and combine it with the other sentence. You form an adverb clause by adding a subordinating conjunction to an independent clause. The following list shows the relationships expressed by subordinating conjunctions between the adverb clause and the independent clause in a sentence.

| TIME | after, as, as long as, as soon as, before, since, until, when, whenever, while |
| --- | --- |
| MANNER | as, as if, as though |
| CAUSE | because |
| CONDITION | although, as long as, even if, even though, if, provided that, though, unless, while |
| COMPARISON | as, than |
| PURPOSE OR RESULT | in order that, so that, that |

In the following revised sentences, the adverb clauses are in italics.

TWO SENTENCES

Ms. Sullivan had to catch a plane to Toronto. She left work early.

REVISED SENTENCE WITH ADVERB CLAUSE

*Because Ms. Sullivan had to catch a plane to Toronto,* she left work early. [cause]

THREE SENTENCES

The rest of the family settled into its usual relaxing Sunday afternoon. Walter checked the want ads. He could begin job hunting in the morning.

REVISED SENTENCE WITH ADVERB CLAUSES

*As the rest of the family settled into its usual relaxing Sunday afternoon,* Walter checked the want ads *so that he could begin job hunting in the morning.* [time and purpose]

Choose subordinating conjunctions carefully. Different conjunctions can change the meaning of your sentence. Notice how the meaning of the following sentence changes as the subordinating conjunction is changed.

Before Rona joined the game, the score changed.
Because Rona joined the game, the score changed.
Whenever Rona joined the game, the score changed.

## Noun Clauses

You can also use noun clauses (*pages 86–87*) to subordinate ideas in sentences. To combine sentences by means of a noun clause, you may substitute all or part of one sentence for a pronoun or a noun in the other sentence. In the following revised sentences, the noun clauses are in italics.

TWO SENTENCES
> Phil is concerned. It is clear why. [*It* in the second sentence refers to the entire first sentence.]

REVISED SENTENCE WITH NOUN CLAUSE
> *Why Phil is concerned* is clear. [Noun clause replaces *It* as subject.]

TWO SENTENCES
> The problem is this. His telephone rings late at night. [*This* in the first sentence refers to the entire second sentence.]

REVISED SENTENCE WITH NOUN CLAUSE
> The problem is *that his telephone rings late at night.* [Noun clause replaces *this* as predicate nominative.]

A complex sentence can have more than one kind of subordinate clause.

> The developers *who have been hired by the city* plan to raze the Crown Building *because it is dilapidated.*

**Exercise 3   Revising: Subordination**   On your paper, combine each of the following sets of sentences into one complex sentence. Make one of the sentences the type of subordinate clause indicated in parentheses.

**SAMPLE**   Technology developed for the space program often can be used to learn more about our life on Earth. Scientists have discovered that fact. (Noun clause)

**ANSWER**   Scientists have discovered that technology developed for the space program often can be used to learn more about our life on Earth.

1. Satellites are being used to take pictures of the surface of the earth. The satellites orbit the earth at an altitude of more than five hundred miles. (Adjective clause)

2. The satellite photographs cannot show small items such as buildings or streets. They do show geographical features such as mountains or forests. (Adverb clause)

3. The satellites transform visible light and invisible heat from the earth's surface into electronic signals. The electronic signals are sent to Earth. (Adjective clause)

4. Computers receive the data from the satellites. They transform the electronic signals into pictures. (Adverb clause)

5. All of the United States and 78 percent of the rest of the world have been photographed clearly by satellites from the United States. That is proof of the success of this method. (Noun clause)

6. The process of turning signals into pictures changes the color of things. Forests, for example, show up in red in the pictures. (Adverb clause)

7. The strange coloring does not matter to geologists, environmentalists, and agricultural planners. They review the photographs. (Adjective clause)

8. Geologists examine the photographs for signs of oil deposits or earthquake fault lines. These signs stand out more clearly without such distractions as buildings in the photographs. (Adjective clause)

9. Environmentalists can see clouds of air pollution joining with rain clouds. The environmentalists are trying to determine the effects of air pollution on weather. (Adjective clause)

10. Agricultural planners can judge the number and the health of crops in a wide area. Then they can estimate the current year's food supplies and the amount of planting that will be needed for the next year. (Adverb clause)

**Exercise 4   Revising: Subordination**   On your paper, combine each set of sentences into one complex sentence by making one or more of the sentences into subordinate clauses.

| | |
|---|---|
| **SAMPLE** | Many words are derived from people's names. We use the words every day. |
| **ANSWER** | Many words that we use every day are derived from people's names. |

1. The Earl of Sandwich invented the food named for him. He asked his servant for a piece of meat between two pieces of bread.
2. The begonia was named after Michel Bégon. Bégon found the plant on the island of Santo Domingo.
3. Gabriel Fahrenheit invented a scale for measuring temperature. Scientists honored him by giving the scale his name.
4. A London cloth merchant named Doily designed the material used to make doilies. He wanted an inexpensive but elegant fabric.
5. John Bowler was a London hatmaker. He gave his name to a derby hat. The British call it a bowler.
6. Adolphe Sax invented the saxophone. He was trying to improve the clarinet.
7. Charles Macintosh cemented together two pieces of cloth. He created a waterproof fabric for raincoats. The raincoats now are called mackintoshes.
8. The roads in nineteenth-century Britain needed to be repaired. John McAdam mended them with a mixture of stones and gravel. That mixture is now called macadam.
9. The leotard was named for Jules Léotard. He popularized the snugly fitting elastic garment.
10. Spoonerisms were named after William A. Spooner. It is not surprising. He often mixed up the sounds within a sentence.

## 8.3c   Using Subordination: Phrases

### Participial Phrases

You can use participial phrases (*pages 71–72*) to combine related sentences. The sentence expressing the less important idea becomes a participial phrase. The original sentences need not contain a verb in the same form as the corresponding participial phrase. In the following revised sentences, the participial phrases are in italics.

TWO SENTENCES
> Ira sent an urgent message. It asked for more data.

REVISED SENTENCE WITH PARTICIPIAL PHRASE
> Ira sent an urgent message *asking for more data.* [Subject *It* is deleted; remainder of statement becomes participial phrase.]

THREE SENTENCES

> Jan was asked to reply at once. She sent the information. The information was requested by Ira.

REVISED SENTENCE WITH PARTICIPIAL PHRASES

> Asked to reply at once, Jan sent the information requested by Ira. [*Jan was* deleted from first sentence; remainder of sentence becomes participial phrase. Second *information* is deleted; remainder of sentence becomes participial phrase.]

TWO SENTENCES

> Jan met her obligation. She proceeded with her work.

REVISED SENTENCE WITH PARTICIPIAL PHRASE

> Jan, *having met her obligation,* proceeded with her work.

## Appositives and Appositive Phrases

When two sentences have nouns or pronouns that refer to the same thing, you can sometimes rewrite one of the sentences as an appositive or an appositive phrase (*page 68*) and combine it with the other sentence. In the following revised sentences, the appositive phrases are in italics.

TWO SENTENCES

> The snarled morning traffic into the city is a daily ritual.
>
> It has come to seem normal. [*Traffic* and *it* refer to the same thing, as does the predicate nominative, *ritual.*]

REVISED SENTENCE WITH APPOSITIVE

> The snarled morning traffic, *a daily ritual,* has come to seem normal.

THREE SENTENCES

> Casey Stengel led the New York Yankees to seven world championships between 1949 and 1958. Those were years when the Yankees seemed invincible. Casey Stengel was one of baseball's greatest managers.

REVISED SENTENCE WITH APPOSITIVE PHRASES

> Casey Stengel, *one of baseball's greatest managers,* led the New York Yankees to seven world championships between 1949 and 1958, *years when the Yankees seemed invincible.*

For rules about punctuating essential and nonessential phrases, see pages 68–69.

**Exercise 5   Revising: Subordination**   On your paper, combine each group of sentences into one sentence with one or more participial or appositive phrases. Use the type of phrase indicated in parentheses.

| | |
|---|---|
| **SAMPLE** | The group of tourists had climbed to the overlook. They hoped to see buffalo. The animals wade in the river below. (Participial phrases) |
| **ANSWER** | The group of tourists had climbed to the overlook, hoping to see buffalo wading in the river below. |

1. Ms. Segreda recommended that the company hire another data control technician. Ms. Segreda is the department head. (Appositive phrase)

2. The fantastic pinnacles, mounds, buttes, gullies, and other formations astound a visitor to the South Dakota Bad Lands. The formations were carved by the forces of nature. (Participial phrase)

3. Mount Kilimanjaro is capped by snow. It rises almost four miles above the African countryside around it. (Participial phrase)

4. Joyce Carol Oates is a prolific writer of novels, short stories, criticism, and poetry. She is known for her tales of ordinary people in unpleasant situations. (Appositive phrase)

5. In falconry, the falconer uses a heavy leather glove for protection from the bird's claws. Falconry is a method of hunting small game with trained falcons. (Appositive phrase)

6. Wind farmers throughout the country are using modern windmills to produce energy. The farmers sell the energy to public utility companies. (Participial phrase)

7. The soil here supports very little plant life. The soil is composed mainly of sand and gravel. These are layered with clay, limestone, and sandstone. (Participial phrases)

8. The Marine Society trip is a one-week voyage around the coral reefs of Bermuda. It will offer not only the chance to explore the ecology of the reefs, but also an opportunity to study two fascinating kinds of animal life. One is the humpback whale, and the other is an oceanic bird. (Appositive phrases)

9. My brother wanted to visit San Miguel de Allende, but my sister preferred to explore Teotihuacán. San Miguel is a charming, old Mexican town, and Teotihuacán is the site of Toltec pyramids. (Appositive phrases)

10. London is sinking at the rate of one foot per century. It is in danger of being flooded by the Thames River. The Thames River runs through the middle of the city. (Participial phrases)

**Exercise 6   Revising: Subordination**   On your paper, combine each pair of sentences into one sentence. Change one sentence in each pair into a subordinate clause or a phrase.

> **SAMPLE**   Gymnastic exercises are divided into ten categories. Six categories are for men, and four categories are for women.
>
> **ANSWER**   Gymnastic exercises are divided into ten categories, six categories for men and four for women.

1. Men participate in floor exercises. They perform leaps and hand-springs across a forty-foot square mat.

2. Men also do exercises on a pommel horse. A pommel horse is a padded bar with handles.

3. Men hang from two wooden rings. They do handstands and several types of swings.

4. In another event, men vault over a horse without pommels. The event is the long-horse vault.

5. Men do acrobatic movements on the parallel bars. The parallel bars are two bars that are sixty-five inches from the floor.

6. Men also perform nonstop movements on one horizontal bar. They hold the bar with both hands.

7. Women balance on a beam four inches wide. They run, leap, jump, and even do cartwheels.

8. Women vault over a horse without pommels. This is the second gymnastic event for women.

9. Women do exercises around one bar at a time on the uneven parallel bars. They keep their bodies in constant motion.

10. Women dance, leap, and perform to music. Women compete in floor exercises.

**Assignment    Revising**   On your paper, revise the following paragraph. Use coordination and subordination to combine related sentences so that the paragraph is clear and the sentences are smooth.

Throughout the United States, people are experimenting with job sharing. Job sharing is having two people share one full-time job. Job sharing is beneficial for several reasons. Employers benefit. They get two points of view on all issues. Also, job sharers are working shorter hours. They can be fresher and, consequently, more productive than full-time workers. The employees benefit too. They can share the responsibilities of their jobs with their coworkers. They can still have free time to spend with their families, on studies, or in other activities. Also, they are able to work part time in fields such as teaching and personnel. Those fields usually do not offer part-time work. Finally, the average pay of job sharers is higher than the average pay of regular part-time workers. Because of these benefits, it is clear. Job sharing will become more popular in the future.

**Assignment Checklist**

Check your assignment for the following points:

    ✓ 1. Did you place some related ideas in compound sentences?
    ✓ 2. Did you use appropriate methods of coordination?
    ✓ 3. Did you place subordinate ideas in subordinate clauses and phrases?

# 8.4    Revising Sentences: Variety

Sentences that are varied in form and length work well together. When you revise sentences in a paragraph, check them for variety. Variety in sentences helps to keep your reader interested.

## 8.4a    Variety in Sentence Beginnings

Add variety to your sentences by beginning some of them with a part of the sentence other than the subject. For example, you can often place modifiers at the beginning of a sentence. Here are the most common possibilities.

ADJECTIVE(S)

> *Interesting yet simple,* the melodies of Sir Arthur Sullivan continue to delight audiences.

ADVERB

> *Sometimes* even committed fans of Gilbert and Sullivan forget who wrote the lyrics and who wrote the music.

APPOSITIVE PHRASE

> *Satires on Victorian behavior,* the operettas are lighthearted and witty.

PARTICIPIAL PHRASE (PAST)

> *Built to stage Gilbert and Sullivan's works,* the Savoy Theatre in London has given its name to both the performers and the fans of these operettas.

PARTICIPIAL PHRASE (PRESENT)

> *Working together from 1871 to 1896,* Gilbert and Sullivan wrote more than a dozen operettas.

PREPOSITIONAL PHRASE

> *With their frenzied lyrics,* the songs demand superb breath control.

INFINITIVE PHRASE

> *To portray a Gilbert and Sullivan character effectively,* a performer needs a good sense of humor as much as a good voice.

ADVERB CLAUSE

> *Although the humor was addressed to the "proper" Victorians,* the satire is timeless and the characters universal.

You cannot shift every modifier to the beginning of a sentence. For example, the modifier in the following sentence cannot be shifted to the beginning because the meaning would be changed.

CORRECT    Benny heard the wind tearing through the attic.

INCORRECT    Tearing through the attic, Benny heard the wind.

**Exercise 1   Revising: Variety**   On your paper, rewrite the sentences in which some part can be shifted to the beginning. If no part can be shifted, write *No change.*

> SAMPLE   The textile plant, a victim of advancing technology and declining markets, had silenced its machines decades ago.
>
> ANSWER   A victim of advancing technology and declining markets, the textile plant had silenced its machines decades ago.

1. The railroad tracks and cinderblock buildings of the old plant lay untouched for years, although occasionally someone would complain about the eyesore.
2. The tangle of rusting metal and crumbling bricks decayed silently but steadily, aided by salt air and neglect.
3. The city and the state had ignored the unsightly ruins because they seemed not worth saving.
4. Someone with vision and energy viewed the rotting buildings at last.
5. He imagined a busy, beautiful urban complex rising from the ruins.
6. He approached local and federal agencies, armed with detailed plans, cost estimates, and the support of area residents and workers.
7. The renewal project, having received loans from the appropriate agencies, began.
8. The developer who had the vision directed the renewal project.
9. A new kind of dust spread over the plant, not the dust of decay but the dust of construction.
10. Restored buildings, new shops, and modern apartments soon emerged from the dust.

## 8.4b   Variety in Structure and Length

Variety is also important in the structure and length of your sentences. You can say essentially the same thing in many different ways; choose a way that fits well with the surrounding sentences. In a paragraph you can mix simple, compound, complex, and compound-complex sentences. The following sentences state basically the same idea in a variety of ways.

The Black Hills, which are located in the west-central part of South Dakota, are a popular tourist area. [complex sentence with adjective clause]

Located in the west-central part of South Dakota, the Black Hills are a popular tourist area. [simple sentence with participial phrase]

The Black Hills, a popular tourist area, are located in the west-central part of South Dakota. [simple sentence with appositive phrase]

As you practice writing and revising, you will become increasingly able to sense how an added phrase here or a combined clause there affects the emphasis or the style of your sentences. Before you settle on a final version, rewrite a sentence in different ways to see its effect on the sentences around it.

**Exercise 2  Revising: Variety**  On your paper, revise each sentence to vary its structure.

> **SAMPLE**  Mushrooms, which are unusual plants, have been objects of curiosity and fear for hundreds of years.
>
> **ANSWER**  Because they are unusual plants, mushrooms have been objects of curiosity and fear for hundreds of years.

1. Because mushrooms are the most common nonflowering plants, they can be easily observed.
2. Mushrooms grow in a variety of sizes, which range from microscopic spores to three-foot-wide growths on trees.
3. Most of the mushroom plant grows underground, and we see only the fruit of the plant.
4. Differing greatly from the top part of the plant, the underground part is composed of long, branching strands.
5. Sometimes the underground parts of two plants merge, and a new mushroom forms at their intersection.
6. Because mushrooms can appear overnight, some sixteenth-century observers thought that lightning created them.
7. Mushrooms will grow in wide circles if they can draw enough food from the soil.
8. In a Kansas field, one such ring that has never been disturbed has grown to more than six hundred feet in diameter.

9. In earlier times, people did not understand how mushrooms grow; therefore, they believed that the rings marked the paths of dancing fairies.

10. Mushrooms, which are very strong, can push up heavy pieces of concrete that block their growth.

**Assignment  Revising**  On your paper, revise the following paragraph to vary the lengths and structures of sentences. You may combine some sentences. You do not need to change every sentence.

> The United States Geological Survey was established in 1879. It was created to organize the exploration of the United States. The chief duty of its members was to map the land that they explored. Most of the country has been explored and mapped now. The major duties of the Survey have changed, although the Survey still makes maps. Its members now make studies for government agencies. The agencies use these studies to make decisions about issuing permits for mining, offshore oil drilling, and housing developments. Some members of the Survey work full time on these studies. They would like more time to do their own research projects. In time, perhaps, the Survey's duties will change again so that its members will have more time for research.

**Assignment Checklist**

Check your assignment for the following points:

✔ 1. Did you move some modifiers to the beginnings of sentences?
✔ 2. Did you coordinate some sentences?
✔ 3. Did you convert some sentences to subordinate clauses and phrases and combine them with other sentences?
✔ 4. Did you leave unchanged the structure and the length of some sentences?

# 8.5  Revising Sentences: Parallel Structure

When you revise your sentences, make sure that you use parallel structure where needed. A sentence has **parallel structure** when similar parts of it are written in the same grammatical form.

That is, the conjunctions *and, or, than* and the correlative conjunctions *not only . . . but (also)* and *either . . . or* must join two or more adjectives, prepositional phrases, infinitive phrases, or other elements.

The parallel parts are in italics in the following sentences.

> *Skating on a frozen pond* and *skiing down a white mountainside* are two of the pleasures of winter. [The parts joined by *and* are both in the same form.]

> Roberta was thrilled not only *because of coming in first* but also *because of breaking her own record.* [*Not only* and *but also* connect two phrases beginning with *because of* and followed by a gerund.]

Many times, sentences with faults in parallel structure can be corrected in more than one way.

NOT PARALLEL

> He likes *hiking, camping,* and *to climb mountains.*

REVISED

> He likes *hiking, camping,* and *climbing mountains.* [All of the similar parts are gerunds.]

REVISED

> He likes *to hike, to camp,* and *to climb mountains.* [All of the similar parts are infinitives.]

When you use correlative conjunctions, you must not only use them with parallel sentence elements but also place the two parts of the conjunctions carefully. They must come immediately before the sentence parts that are parallel in form.

NOT PARALLEL

> Janice *not only* **studied** Spanish *but also* **German.**

REVISED

> Janice studied *not only* **Spanish** *but also* **German.**

REVISED

> Janice *not only* **studied** Spanish *but also* **reviewed** German.

If you omit an article, a preposition, a pronoun, or the infinitive *to* from one part of a parallel structure, then you must omit that word from every occurrence of that structure. Similarly, if you include such a word in a parallel structure, you must include it each time you use that structure.

NOT PARALLEL

> On his vacation, Brent wants *to swim, to sail, sleep,* and *sit in the sun.*

REVISED

> On his vacation, Brent wants *to swim, to sail, to sleep,* and *to sit in the sun.*

**Exercise   Revising: Parallel Structure**   On your paper, re-vise the following sentences so that similar parts are parallel.

SAMPLE   Ruth understood replacing the spark plugs and lubri-cating the chassis but not how to adjust the wheel alignment.

ANSWER   Ruth understood how to replace the spark plugs and lubricate the chassis but not how to adjust the wheel alignment.

1. Abe prefers vacuuming rather than to clean the kitchen.
2. Joseph hates to jump into the water, diving from the board, and swimming underwater.
3. Juanita couldn't decide whether to go to Florida or if she wanted to see Mexico on her vacation.
4. The city was encouraged by the surge in retail sales, the invasion of tourists, and how street crime had decreased.
5. The stalls sold handmade quilts, secondhand clothing, and they had some old feathered hats.
6. To put himself to sleep, Harold tried warm milk, restful thoughts, and reading a dull book.
7. Ms. Friedman's dream of succeeding in advertising and that she will become well known in the field is being realized.
8. CAT scanners not only are useful diagnostic devices but also expensive pieces of equipment.
9. Susan Martin will either find a new job here or she has to move to another city.
10. Neither compromising his position on the issue nor his intention to run again, the mayor stood fast.

**Assignment** **Revising**   On your paper, revise the following paragraph so that sentences have parallel structure where necessary.

When Orson Squire Fowler planned his house, he thought carefully about its use and what shape would be most practical. He decided on an octagonal house because it would be cheap to construct, all available sunlight would be caught, and make communication between rooms easy. Because he wanted to share his new design with other home builders, Fowler published a book of designs and that gave instructions. The book made Fowler's octagonal house popular throughout the United States, especially in New York, Ohio, Wisconsin, Minnesota, in Iowa, and Indiana. People built the houses not only for the reasons suggested by Fowler but also because they had their own reasons. Some East Coast residents, for instance, built them because they offered less resistance to the wind from the ocean. The houses went out of style after about ten years, but some modern architects are beginning to experiment again with Fowler's octagonal design.

## Assignment Checklist

Check your assignment for the following points:

✔ 1. Did you make parallel the parts of sentences that serve similar functions?

✔ 2. Did you place correlative conjunctions immediately before the parallel sentence parts?

# 8.6   Revising Sentences: Conciseness

## 8.6a   Avoiding Wordiness

Aim for conciseness, or economy of expression, as you revise your writing. Every word should have a reason for being in your sentences. Wordiness, which is the use of more words than necessary, weakens your writing. By avoiding wordiness and repetition, you will write sentences that are clearer and more effective. The following strategies will guide you in eliminating wordiness.

**Strategies**

1. *Use simple, direct language* rather than long words and flowery expressions. An inflated style is not sophisticated or literary; on the contrary, it can be confusing, immature, and even laughable. The following are examples of the kinds of wordy expressions that you can simplify in your writing.

| WORDY | CONCISE |
|---|---|
| medical facility | hospital |
| during the month of June | in June |
| functionally impaired | broken |
| has the capability of | is able to |
| institution of higher learning | university |
| is desirous of | wants |
| make the purchase of | buy |
| a person in the sciences | scientist |
| a sufficiency of | enough |
| as a result of the fact that | because |
| at the present time | at present, now |
| at this point in time | now |
| due to the fact that | because |
| in point of fact | in fact, actually |
| in this day and age | now |
| in the amount of | for |
| to make a long story short | in short, briefly |

2. *Use the active voice* to make your writing more direct and forceful. Rewrite, whenever possible, passive constructions, especially those that begin with *It is* and *There is*.

> WORDY   It has been agreed by the Town Council that it will have the tennis courts upgraded this year.

> REVISED   The Town Council has agreed to have the tennis courts upgraded this year.

3. *Eliminate redundancy,* the needless repetition of words and ideas. Deliberate repetition, as used in parallel structure, can be effective. Careless repetition, on the other hand, can rob your sentences of clarity and conciseness. In any

sentence, do not use several words that are alike in meaning, and do not use a word that is part of the meaning of another word.

| REDUNDANT | The flaming tanks of chemicals burned for days. [*Flaming* and *burned* are alike in meaning.] |
| REVISED | The tanks of chemicals burned for days. |

| REDUNDANT | Her closing number having received an ovation, the guitarist repeated it again. [*Again* is already implied in the word *repeated*.] |
| REVISED | Her closing number having received an ovation, the guitarist repeated it. |
| REVISED | Her closing number having received an ovation, the guitarist played it again. |

Here are some additional examples of redundant expressions. You should omit the words in italics.

| | |
| --- | --- |
| combine *together* | rebound *back* |
| continue *further* | remote area *far away* |
| cooperate *together* | speed *quickly* |
| descend *down* | sufficiently *enough* |
| each *separate* thing | ten *in number* |
| *exact* same | *true* fact |
| exhale *out* | 4:00 P.M. *in the afternoon* |
| *necessary* requirement | sunset *in the west* |
| pretty *in appearance* | visible *to the eye* |
| previously *before this* | *wrong* misjudgment |

**Exercise 1  Revising: Conciseness**  On your paper, revise the following sentences to make them concise.

| SAMPLE | In point of fact, the musical performer playing the stringed instrument was experiencing a problem in deciphering the musical notations on the page. |
| ANSWER | In fact, the violinist was having a problem reading the notes. |

1. Regina's cousin, an individual who has been trained to travel in outer space, will be sojourning with the members of her family during the month of December.

2. To make a long story short, there are difficulties that are being experienced at present by one of the local grocery establishments with regard to its search for a person who fulfills the requirements for manager in terms of educational background and occupational experience.

3. Due to the fact that each and every one of the motor vehicles has a sticker on it, we are enabled to discern what options are available to us on each vehicle.

4. It is unlikely to a great degree that each and every one of the persons who is desirous of gainful employment at the factory will indeed be successful in acquiring employment at this point in time.

5. The keyboard instrumentalist whose concert Claudia had the opportunity to attend during the week preceding this one gave a performance of a piece of music for which she has developed a definite preference.

6. The beauteous quality of the glowing sunset in the west was such that it exceeded my powers of verbal description.

7. Although it is sometimes the case that Ms. Cruz seems unnecessarily serious, it is also true that there are times when she has the capability of being amusing and entertaining.

8. Because there is some possibility that the storm may continue, it would seem advisable that all persons venturing out of doors take the precaution of wearing foul weather attire.

9. It is a source of amazement to me that a person who works in the profession of chemistry, who, it must be assumed, has developed considerable ability in the intermixing of ingredients, should not possess a sufficiency of ability to produce a drinking tumbler of actual lemonade.

10. It has come to my attention that there is a noticeable trend on the part of all of the various members of our household to devote an increased amount of time to reading activities and to participation in dialogue with one another as a result of the fact that the television set belonging to the household has been functionally impaired.

**Exercise 2  Revising: Conciseness**  On your paper, revise each sentence to eliminate redundancy.

| | |
|---|---|
| **SAMPLE** | In the beginning, when the Cleghorns first moved from their large house in the suburbs, in which they had spent many, many years of their lives, to a small, little apartment in the more urban city, Susan did not believe in her mind that the new residence in which they lived would ever really and truly feel like home. |
| **ANSWER** | When the Cleghorns first moved from their large house in the suburbs, in which they had spent many years, to a small apartment in the city, Susan did not believe that their new residence would ever really feel like home. |

1. The snapshot that I took with my camera was a blurred shot, but it nevertheless still managed to show how handsome in appearance Duane is.

2. Dramatic poems resemble narrative poems in that the poems tell a story and are fairly long in length, but, as in Browning's renowned, famous dramatic poem "My Last Duchess," the story of the poem is told through the speech spoken by the characters in the poem.

3. The reason that a popcorn kernel pops is that the moisture inside the interior of the kernel changes to vaporous steam, the pressure of which finally bursts open the kernel from inside.

4. At 5:00 A.M. in the morning, the physicist working on scientific problems rose up from the stool on which he had been sitting and tiredly, exhaustedly left the scientific laboratory, still not sure with any certainty that the problem was insoluble and could never be answered.

5. The resulting consequences of the years of time that Gloria spent with Daniella together employed at work in the automobile factory that manufactures new cars have been the development of both a beautiful, long-lasting friendship and, in addition, a hateful, long-lasting allergy to automobile exhaust fumes that are expelled from the backs of cars.

6. Since Yukio best prefers to wear the color blue, he chose to select the suit of clothing made of fabric in which two shades of blue were interwoven together.

7. After Mr. Levi fell down and broke the bone in his leg, suffering a fracture, he tried to make every attempt to continue going on being his cheerful good-humored self for the seemingly unending, interminable period of time in which he was necessarily required to wear a cast on his leg.

8. At the time when Dora heard the unmistakable screeching of car brakes that reached her ears, she rushed quickly out the door, descended down in the waiting elevator that stood at her floor, and ran through the downstairs lobby, reaching the street outside just exactly in time to see with her own eyes the pale, light sedan turn the corner of the street.

9. Although the author Herman Melville wrote *Moby Dick, Billy Budd, Typee,* and other novels and books that have now been read and enjoyed by millions of people, Melville did not achieve popular success during the lifetime in which he wrote, and he died in obscurity, unknown and unrecognized.

# 8.6b   Using Reduction

You can reduce many clauses to phrases and reduce phrases to words without significantly changing their meaning. Such reduction can help you to make your sentences more concise. Here are examples of the most important ways to reduce clauses and phrases.

CLAUSE TO PHRASE

> Monty set the clock, but *he did not wind it.*
> Monty set the clock but *did not wind it.*

CLAUSE TO PARTICIPIAL PHRASE

> *Because the pollster wanted opinions on low-calorie snacks,* he questioned shoppers at the mall.
> *Wanting opinions on low-calorie snacks,* the pollster questioned shoppers at the mall.

> Ms. Brady, *who was thrilled to be questioned,* gave interminable responses.
> Ms. Brady, *thrilled to be questioned,* gave interminable responses.

CLAUSE TO GERUND PHRASE

> *After he had typed for more than two hours,* Matthew had a headache.
> *Typing for more than two hours* gave Matthew a headache.

CLAUSE TO INFINITIVE PHRASE

> With no more customers *whom he could serve,* the salesperson went home at 9:00 P.M.

> With no more customers *to serve,* the salesperson went home at 9:00 P.M.

CLAUSE TO PREPOSITIONAL PHRASE

> *After only a year and a half had passed,* the dramatic mail service of the pony express came to an end.

> *After only a year and a half,* the dramatic mail service of the pony express came to an end.

> The telegraph service *that stretched from coast to coast* supplanted the pony express in 1861.

> The telegraph service *from coast to coast* supplanted the pony express in 1861.

CLAUSE TO APPOSITIVE PHRASE

> Andy Warhol, *who is a pop artist,* is famous for his paintings of soup cans.

> Andy Warhol, *a pop artist,* is famous for his paintings of soup cans.

CLAUSE TO WORD

> The firefighters, *who were experienced,* brought the fire under control quickly.

> The *experienced* firefighters brought the fire under control quickly.

Conciseness does not mean the use of the fewest words possible; it means the use of as few words as you need to express your ideas effectively.

**Exercise 3   Revising: Conciseness**   On your paper, revise the following sentences, reducing the expressions in italics.

**SAMPLE**  *As he was leaving school,* Frederick met Mr. Phinney, *who is his guidance counselor.*

**ANSWER**  Leaving school, Frederick met Mr. Phinney, his guidance counselor.

1. Mr. Phinney asked Frederick whether he knew about high school students *who are interning at Community Hospital* and *who are working in the office of their state representative.*

2. The internship program, *which is a relatively new one,* offers juniors and seniors the opportunity to receive school credit and to gain valuable experience.

3. *He had not heard about the program,* and Frederick asked for more information.

4. *Because he is interested in journalism,* Frederick wondered whether there are internships *that are available* on local newspapers.

5. *Because he knew of Frederick's interest in journalism,* Mr. Phinney had already investigated this possibility.

6. After *he had failed to convince three of the local newspapers that they should participate in the internship program,* he finally succeeded with the fourth, *which is a weekly paper.*

7. If, *after they interview Frederick,* the editors find him *to be qualified for the job,* he will spend one day a week at the offices *of the newspaper.*

8. *It is obvious that* Frederick must not expect *that he will begin* by writing stories *that are featured.*

9. *After two months have gone by,* both the newspaper and Mr. Phinney will evaluate the performance *of Frederick,* and Frederick will evaluate the sponsorship *of the newspaper.*

10. *It is not every company that wants to accept a high school intern,* and *it is not every student who wants to be an intern;* however, for students and companies *who are interested,* the relationship can be *a mutually rewarding one.*

## 8.6c Revising Sentences That Lack Coherence and Clarity

Sentences in which you have included too many ideas may lack coherence as well as conciseness. As a result your reader may be unable to follow the relationships among the ideas. When you revise, look for long sentences that may be overloaded with ideas. You can usually make your points more clearly in direct, concise sentences. Apply the following strategies to revise sentences that lack coherence.

## Strategies

1. *Divide the sentence into two or more sentences.* Be sure that the main ideas are in independent clauses and that the less important ideas are in subordinate clauses or phrases.

   NOT COHERENT

   > Maple syrup is still made by the same process used centuries ago in which the sap of the maple tree, after being removed through a spout drilled into the tree, is boiled to remove excess water, and the result is pure, thick maple syrup.

   REVISED

   > Maple syrup is still made by the same process used centuries ago. After being removed through a spout drilled into the tree, the sap is boiled to remove excess water. The result is pure, thick maple syrup.

2. *Subordinate some ideas that have been coordinated.* Subordination is often more precise than coordination. Use subordinate elements to eliminate overuse of the common coordinating words *and* and *but*.

   NOT COHERENT

   > Water is in short supply today, and it has finally come to be regarded as precious and limited.

   REVISED

   > Water, *which is in short supply today,* has finally come to be regarded as precious and limited. [One independent clause changed to a subordinate clause.]

   NOT COHERENT

   > The voters focused on the candidate's past performance rather than on his present promises, and they voted him out of office.

   REVISED

   > The voters, *focusing on the candidate's past performance rather than on his present promises,* voted him out of office. [One independent clause changed to a participial phrase.]

NOT COHERENT

>Mr. Varese was an avid collector of butterflies, and he had his specimens mounted and displayed in his office.

REVISED

>Mr. Varese, *an avid collector of butterflies,* had his specimens mounted and displayed in his office. [One independent clause changed to appositive phrase.]

3. *Rewrite concisely to eliminate unnecessary words or ideas.*

NOT COHERENT

>Looking through the directory that lists names and telephone numbers can be amusing and it can be enlightening because, for example, some of the names can be startling, and many of the categories that are listed for businesses name activities that I never knew existed in this world.

REVISED

>Looking through the telephone directory can be both amusing and enlightening. For example, some of the names are rather startling, and many of the business categories name activities that I never knew existed.

**Exercise 4  Revising: Conciseness**  On your paper, revise the following sentences, which lack coherence. Divide each one into two or more shorter sentences and make other necessary changes. There is more than one way to revise some of the sentences.

SAMPLE
: Did you know that there is a clock that can measure time to a trillionth of a second and can remain accurate to a millionth of a second and that it is being used to measure movements in the earth's crust and that it can therefore help to predict earthquakes?

ANSWER
: Did you know that there is a clock that can measure time to a trillionth of a second and can remain accurate to a millionth of a second? Because this clock can measure movements of the earth's crust, it can help to predict earthquakes.

1. At the county fair, which is an annual event, we went on every ride, sampled all the food, and looked at every exhibit, because we didn't want to miss a thing, even though we go to the fair every year.

2. The National Theater of the Deaf, which tours extensively in this country and abroad, was founded in 1967 and won a Tony Award in 1977 for theatrical excellence, and it offers educational services as well as support for deaf performers, but the prime focus of the theater is on performance.

3. Because salt, which is now a very common substance, was once rare and expensive, spilling it was considered bad luck, and the custom arose of tossing a pinch of spilled salt over the left shoulder with the thumb and forefinger of the right hand to ward off the bad luck.

4. When I was a child, I spent many hours watching my grandfather at his worktable in the basement building objects, like mailboxes in the form of covered wagons and birdhouses that were churches with steeples, that delighted me then and still do now.

5. The all-day seminars to be held at the Community Center from 9:00 to 5:00 on Saturday will offer area residents a wide variety of topics in career and personal development, business matters, and leisure activities, and so bring a lunch and enjoy a day of concentrated discussion and learning.

6. The philodendron plant in the glazed pink pot on the windowsill of the bathroom adjoining the master bedroom had lasted through feline attacks, toddler games, and falls on hard tile floors, as well as frequent periods of neglect, and Marlo had assumed that it would survive anything, but now, after seven years on that windowsill, it was showing signs of giving up.

7. Because the house on the corner of the block on which Sally lived before she moved to her present house had been uninhabited for many years, it had taken on a run-down, gruesome appearance that frightened the neighborhood children, and so Sally had never gone near the house in all the years that she had lived next to it.

8. The prices were high and the quality was low, and in every department the salespeople swooped down on us like crows on a cornfield, and they tried to pressure us into buying things, but we didn't want the things, and in fact we didn't like them.

9. There have been attempts by an accounting firm to settle the rent dispute, but these have failed, and the tenants have gone to court to try to halt the evictions ordered by the management, asking the court to state that they qualify for rent control so that the steep rent increase will be reduced.

10. Representative Gonzalez, besides holding meetings in his district this spring, will be sending some of his aides into each town in the district in a community contact program in order to determine the political issues and personal concerns that are most on the minds of his constituents and to listen to their suggestions on how to deal with these matters.

**Exercise 5   Revising: Conciseness**   On your paper, revise the following sentences to make them concise. Reduce lengthy clauses and phrases, and divide sentences appropriately. Eliminate unnecessary words and ideas.

> **SAMPLE**      The music, which pulsated with a beat, caused a propulsion of persons into the middle of the room in order that they might dance to the music, and the party was getting livelier.
>
> **ANSWER**      The pulsating music propelled people into the middle of the room to dance. The party was getting livelier.

1. James dashed quickly through the vast supermarket, and he completely finished the monthly grocery shopping for February in less than thirty minutes time.
2. Ms. Ciccolo holds the belief that it is more important that a writer have ambition than that a writer have true talent if that writer is to achieve popular success.
3. After due consideration was given to the matter by all of the members of the jury, they reached the decision to believe the theory offered by the prosecutor, namely, that the reason because of which the defendant returned back to the place of residence of the victim was that he felt the need to assure himself of the fact that he had left no traces behind him.
4. David was buoyed up by the exceedingly enthusiastic spirit that was being exhibited by the multitudinous crowds, and so he overcame his reluctance to give expression to the opinions that he held, and he spoke to the crowd with great force and with great effectiveness.
5. Despite the fact that Marina had a hatred for the process of shopping for clothes, she knew that the shopping had to be done, and the only way in which it could be done was to go ahead and to do it.
6. It is certainly obvious that those persons who have been presented

with a natural gift for the art of singing or acting or painting cannot manage to succeed if they squander their talent away wastefully by neglecting to develop it or by misapplying it improperly.

7. The cluster of grouped pine trees has the appearance of clinging on to the cloudy morning mist as if it were unwilling to face the day that is approaching.

8. Since we have been given assistance by a warming trend that has pushed temperatures above the freezing mark even during the month of January, which is ordinarily a fiercely cold month, as you probably know, we have been enabled to reduce down considerably the amount of oil that we have consumed.

9. In order that he might purchase the extremely expensive shoes that he is at the present time wearing on his feet, it was necessary that Raymond spend a goodly sized portion of the monthly wage that he earns from his part-time job working as an orderly in a nearby local medical facility.

10. Each and every one of us has the knowledge of some person who has risen up to the top of a profession or career on account of the fact that that person had a small talent and a great ambition, and so that is without a doubt the way to approach the risky business of trying to get ahead in this world that we live in, and I will work very hard and aim very high.

**Assignment  Revising**  On your paper, revise the following paragraph to make it concise and direct.

Of all the American composers, of which there are many, I think that George Gershwin is, in my opinion, perhaps the most popular of all. Because of the fact that he was so talented, young Gershwin began writing music at the tender age of fifteen. It comes as no surprise to learn that Gershwin's first successful song, which was "Swanee," was written in 1919 when Gershwin was only twenty-one years of age. In the 1920s Gershwin achieved great fame on Broadway with popular musicals. One of the musicals was *Of Thee I Sing,* which was awarded a Pulitzer Prize, and it was the first musical ever to do so. One of his most famous works was called *Porgy and Bess,* and it contained many songs of lasting popularity, songs like "It Ain't Necessarily So" and "Summertime." Gershwin considered *Porgy and Bess* to be a folk opera, and, to this very day, *Porgy and Bess* is considered by many musicians and other people to be the greatest opera written by an American composer. In a surprise that took the world unawares, Gershwin died suddenly in 1937 at the young age of thirty-nine.

## Assignment Checklist

Check your assignment for the following points:

✔ 1. Did you eliminate wordiness by using simple, direct expressions?
✔ 2. Did you change some verbs in the passive voice to the active voice?
✔ 3. Did you eliminate redundant words and ideas?
✔ 4. Did you reduce clauses and phrases where appropriate?
✔ 5. Did you divide and adjust sentences that lack coherence?

# 8.7   Revising and Proofreading

## Completing Your Revision

**Proofreading,** the last stage in the revision process, is the checking of a piece of writing for correct grammar, usage, spelling, and punctuation. When you proofread your writing, check each word and sentence for errors. If you are unsure about the correctness of a word or a sentence construction, assume that it is incorrect. Then look up the information in a dictionary or in this book, or ask your teacher.

You may use the proofreading symbols shown on page 216. After you have completed your revision, make your finished copy.

## An Example of Revising and Proofreading

Here is a first draft of a paragraph that has not been revised or proofread. To the left of the paragraph are notes on revisions that will improve it. After you have read the draft and the notes, read the revised version that follows it, reviewing each change that was made.

FIRST DRAFT

Combine
sentences.

State concisely.

Remove sentence.
State concisely.

Revise for
variety.

Make tense
consistent.

Reduce clause.

Too many
ideas. Revise.

Correct spelling.
Make tone
consistent.

Hidden away in Cambridge, Massachusetts, is a remarkable collection. It combines art and science in a rare manner. The Glass Flower exhibit that is part of the museum of the institution of higher learning known as Harvard is much more than a group of flowers made of glass. Harvard was the first university in America. The vast collection consists in its entirety of 784 separate life-sized models of flowers, plants, and fruits and 3218 enlarged flowers, and it provides specimens for botanical study, and it also provided more than four thousand notable works of art. The models were handcrafted in Germany between the years 1886 and 1936 by the Blaschkas, who were a father-and-son team of artists-naturalists, and this was done at the request of G. L. Goodale, foundor of the museum, who had a very good idea indeed, or at least that is what the bunch of folks who've visited the collection every year think.

REVISED VERSION

Sentences
combined.

Concise
Sentences varied.

Tense consistent.

Clause reduced
to phrase.
Sentence divided.
Spelling
corrected.

Tone consistent.

Hidden away in Cambridge, Massachusetts, is a remarkable collection that combines art and science in a rare manner. The Glass Flower exhibit of the Harvard University Museum is much more than a group of flowers made of glass. Consisting of 784 life-sized models of flowers, plants, and fruits and 3218 enlarged flowers, the vast collection provides specimens for botanical study, on the one hand, and more than four thousand notable works of art, on the other. The models were handcrafted in Germany between 1886 and 1936 by the Blaschkas, a father-and-son team of artists-naturalists, at the request of G. L. Goodale, founder of the museum. According to the thousands of people who visit the collection each year, Mr. Goodale had a very good idea indeed.

**Exercise    Revising: The Paragraph**    On your paper, revise and proofread the following paragraph. Use the notes at the left as a guide.

Eliminate wordiness.

Combine sentences.

Eliminate wordiness.

Divide sentences.
Use active voice.
Use capital.
State concisely.
Correct spelling.

Romeo Montague and Juliet Capulet may have lived, loved, and died in Verona, Italy, but there is no proof to that effect. The Capuleti and Montecchi families did indeed feud over support for the Holy Roman Emperor. The well-documented history of the families reveals this. That this feud tragically affected the lives of a pair of teen-agers is recorded nowhere, at least not until the year of 1531. That was the date in time when Luigi daPorto published a story about a doomed love affair two hundred years earlier, and the basis for Shakespeare's play was probably provided by daPorto's tale. According to the citizens of verona, however, the story is not just literature but it is history, and Juliet's house, balcony, and tomb are proud toorist attractions of the city.

**Assignment    Revising**    On your paper, revise and proofread the following paragraph.

There are a few perils that are associated with the sport of iceboating. Some of these dangers arise as a result of the fact that the boats are not equipped with mechanisms for braking by which they can be slowed or stopped, and as a result of this absense of braking power, an iceboater must take particular care to steer the boat with great exactness. In addition the iceboater must also always be on guard at all times for perilous hazards that may appear at any given moment in or on the ice. Some examples of such hazards include such things as cans, paper, broken glass, holes, cracks, ice-skaters, and other iceboats. In order that protection of some sort is afforded, those who sail iceboats wear helmets for safety. The wearing of goggles is also to be highly recommended. Face masks in addition are adviseable during times when the weather is especially cold and icy. Two pairs of gloves are usually worn on the hands, and several pairs of socks are worn on the feet. The purpose of all of these various layers of clothing is to afford protection from the dangers of spills and also from the dangers of the cold weather. You need such protection for most winter sports. In cases where such precautions as these are indeed taken, the sport of iceboating can be assumed to be a fairly safe one, in addition to being very exciting.

## Assignment Checklist

Check your assignment for the following points:

✔ 1. Did you combine some sentences?
✔ 2. Did you make the tense, voice, person, and tone consistent?
✔ 3. Did you eliminate wordiness?
✔ 4. Did you give sentences parallel structure where necessary?
✔ 5. Did you revise sentences that lack coherence?
✔ 6. Did you proofread for correct grammar, usage, spelling, and punctuation?

## Evaluating a Manuscript: Suggestions for Revising

Situation: You are an assistant editor at a publishing company. A potential author has submitted the introduction to a book about whales. Your editor in chief, who believes that many people would buy a book about whales, would like your company to publish *Whales of the Atlantic Ocean* if the author can improve the quality of her writing. Your editor has asked you to evaluate the author's writing in a report and to revise a segment of it to send to the author as an example of how she should write the rest of the book.

**Writer:** you as assistant editor
**Audience:** author of *Whales of the Atlantic Ocean*
**Topic:** a manuscript about whales
**Purpose:** to evaluate and revise a segment of manuscript

Directions: Follow these steps to evaluate and revise the sample manuscript.

*Step 1.* Read the editor's checklist on the facing page. The list tells you what to watch for as you read the manuscript.

*Step 2.* Read the sample manuscript on the facing page. On your paper, make notes of all the ways in which the author's writing could be improved. The questions to which you answer No on the editor's checklist will guide you.

*Step 3.* Write a brief report evaluating the writing in the sample manuscript. Include some examples of good or bad writing found in the manuscript.

*Step 4.* Revise the sample manuscript to show how the rest of the manuscript should be written. Include your revised sample with your report.

Title: <u>Whales of the Atlantic Ocean</u>

There are many species of whales in the Atlantic Ocean. They vary in size. One of the smallest is the harbor porpoise, which grows to about five feet in length as an adult. The blue whale can grow to eighty-five feet.

Cetaceans share certain features. They are all mammals. They all spend their whole lives in the water. They all have a breathing hole or breathing holes called a blowhole or blowholes on top of they're heads. They have flippers in front and no legs in back. Whales, porposes, and dolphins all belong to a scientific group called cetaceans. They are an endangered species.

There are two suborders of cetaceans, and these are the baleen or whalebone whales, which have plates of whalebone suspended from the roofs of their mouths instead of teeth hanging there, and the toothed whales, which have teeth. They may have as many as two hundred fifty teeth or as few as two. An adult human being has as many as thirty-two teeth. Dolphins and porposes are toothed whales. So is the sperm whale. Whalebone is also called baleen. It is used to strain their food. Their food is called krill. It is made up of small sea organisms. Baleen whales have two blowholes. Toothed whales have only one blowhole. The blue whale is a baleen whale.

**Editor's Checklist**

| | Yes | No |
|---|---|---|
| 1. Does each paragraph have a clear focus? | Yes | No |
| 2. Is each paragraph unified? | Yes | No |
| 3. Is each paragraph coherent? | Yes | No |
| 4. Are the sentences combined for the most effective expression of ideas? | Yes | No |
| 5. Are the sentences varied? | Yes | No |
| 6. If a sentence has coordinate parts, are the parts parallel? | Yes | No |
| 7. Is the writing in the sample consistent in tense, voice, person, and tone? | Yes | No |
| 8. Is the writing concise? | Yes | No |
| 9. Are the sentences clear? | Yes | No |
| 10. Are grammar, usage, spelling, and punctuation correct? | Yes | No |

# Unit Assignments

**Assignment 1**   Select a paragraph that you have written for a previous assignment. Use the information in this unit to revise your paragraph. Then proofread it and make a finished copy.

**Assignment 2**   Find a paragraph in a magazine, newspaper, bulletin, or other printed matter that you think could be improved. Make the revisions that you think would improve it.

**Assignment 3**   Find a piece of writing that is wordy or overwritten. You might look at "Letters to the Editor" or at passages from speeches or lectures to find an example. Revise the passage to make it concise and direct.

**Assignment 4**   Write a paragraph about one of your goals. Give your reasons for setting up this goal or your plans for reaching it. Direct your paragraph to an audience of adults. Revise and proofread your draft.

**Assignment 5**   Write a paragraph explaining your views on a problem in your school or your community. Direct your paragraph to a specific audience and suggest a solution to the problem. Revise and proofread your draft.

## Revising Your Assignments

For help in revising a first draft, consult the Checklist for Revision on the last page of this book.

# Unit Tests

## Test 1

**A.** Number your paper from 1 to 5. Next to each number, write *True* if the sentence is true or *False* if it is false.

1. To make your writing effective, you should use wordy expressions and repeat your ideas for your readers.
2. In a coherent paragraph, each sentence leads logically to the next one.
3. Sentences that are not closely related to your topic sentence should be placed at the end of the paragraph.
4. When you begin a sentence or paragraph in a certain tense, voice, person, or tone, you should finish it in the same way.
5. You can add variety to your sentences by beginning some with a part of the sentence other than the subject.

**B.** Number your paper from 6 to 10. Next to each number, write the letter of the term that correctly completes the sentence. You will not use one of the items.

    a. parallel structure      d. revision
    b. unity      e. proofreading
    c. redundancy      f. subordination

6. __?__ is reorganizing and rewriting your work so that it expresses exactly what you wish to communicate to your reader.
7. Coordination and __?__ are the two ways to combine two or more sentences into one sentence.
8. A sentence has __?__ when similar parts of it are written in the same grammatical form.
9. __?__ is the needless repetition of words and ideas.
10. __?__ is the checking of a piece of writing for correct grammar, usage, spelling, and punctuation.

**C.** Number your paper from 11 to 15. Next to each number, write the letter of the item that correctly answers the question about the following paragraph.

(Continue on the next page.)

(1) Before synthetic dyes were invented at the end of the nineteenth century, dyes were made from natural substances. (2) Dyers used plants, insects, and shells. (3) They produced a variety of colors. (4) They made yellow and brown, the most common dyes, from plants such as saffron and sumac. (5) Dyers could make a red dye from either roots of plants or the dried, crumbled bodies of insects. (6) They also use the eggs of insects to obtain a black dye. (7) Purple was the hardest color to produce. (8) Dyemakers tried various plants, but none produced a deep, permanent purple. (9) By crushing mussel and whelk shells and boiling them for weeks, the dyers produced a beautiful purple, but the process was long and costly, and therefore purple became a royal color, which only high officials could wear. (10) Now that any color can be easily made from synthetic materials, colors are no longer a sign of rank.

11. Which sentence would be improved by the insertion of the transitional words *For example*?
    a. Sentence 3      c. Sentence 6
    b. Sentence 4      d. Sentence 7

12. Which one of the following sentences is the best revision for Sentences 2 and 3?
    a. Dyers used plants, insects, and shells, and they produced a variety of colors.
    b. Using plants, insects, and shells, dyers produced a variety of colors.
    c. A variety of colors was produced from plants, insects, and shells.

13. Which one of the following revisions would give Sentence 5 parallel structure?
    a. Dyers could either produce red dye from roots of plants or the dried, crumbled bodies of insects.
    b. Dyers could produce red dye either from the roots of plants or from the dried, crumbled bodies of insects.
    c. Dyers could produce red dye either from the roots of plants or the dried, crumbled bodies of insects.

14. Which one of the following sentences lacks coherence?
    a. Sentence 1      c. Sentence 8
    b. Sentence 2      d. Sentence 9

15. Which one of the following sentences is inconsistent with the tense of the paragraph?
    a. Sentence 3
    b. Sentence 4
    c. Sentence 6
    d. Sentence 8

## Test 2

Choose one of the Unit Assignments or one suggested by your teacher. Write and revise the assignment as directed and hand it in to your teacher.

# Unit 9

## Three Modes of Writing

---

## Unit Preview

A **mode** of writing is a particular form of writing. There are four modes: exposition, description, narration, and persuasion. You can use each one to achieve a different writing purpose. Use exposition if your purpose is to inform or explain. Use description if your purpose is to convey an impression of a person, a place, or an object. Use narration if your purpose is to tell a story. Use persuasion if your purpose is to convince your reader that your view of an issue is correct. Use a combination of modes if you have more than one writing purpose. In this unit you will study the first three modes. Persuasion is considered separately in Unit 10.

Each of the following passages has a distinct purpose and illustrates a different mode of writing.

Exposition                Individual proprietorship is one of the ways in which a business can be owned. The individual owner controls the business and is personally responsible for all debts from the business.

Description            Mr. O'Brien's workbench is hidden at the back of a basement filled with cartons. The wooden surface of the bench has been scrubbed so often that it is white. Nails are stored by size in six containers at the back of the bench, and small pieces of wood are stacked on the right side of the bench. All of Mr. O'Brien's shiny tools hang in straight rows on the pegboard above the bench.

Narration            At six-thirty on a January morning, it was
dark and cold. Nevertheless, Jo had to leave the
warm farmhouse and hurry to the barn to feed
the animals before she left for school. As she
entered the barn, she encountered an unexpected
sight.

**For Analysis**   On your paper, answer the following questions
about the preceding paragraphs.

1. What topic is the writer of the first paragraph explaining?
2. What general impression of the workbench is created in the
   second paragraph? What does that impression reveal about Mr.
   O'Brien?
3. The narrative paragraph introduces a character and establishes a
   setting. Who and what are they?

In analyzing the passages of exposition, description, and
narration, you have considered some important features of the
three modes of writing. In this unit you will learn how to write
clear explanations, vivid descriptions, and lively narratives. As
you write, you will follow the three steps of the writing process:
prewriting, writing, and revising.

# 9.1   Considering Your Purpose
   and Audience

## Your Purpose

Before you begin to write, you should have your **purpose**
clearly in mind. Do you want to explain, to describe, or to narrate?
For example, you may wish to explain how a calculator works or what
the provisions of a new law are. On the other hand, you may wish to
describe how a farm looks after a snowstorm or how it feels to stand
beside a cool, still pond on a spring morning. You may wish to tell a
story about how you learned mountain-climbing techniques or how
Helen Keller became a lecturer. Once you determine your purpose,

mak... ...ps to accom-
plish ...

writing ... example, in
writing ... usually include descriptions of ...he settings
and th... characters. Similarly, ... ...rrative to
introdu... a piece of expository writing.

## Your Audience

You ... also must consider your **audience**, or readers, ...ore you
begin to wr... Although the audience for much of your writing will
include you... teacher, you should write for a wider audience: your
classmates, your friends, your family, or anyone who might be
interested in your topic. Keep in mind that, in writing for a wider
audience, you may have to explain details that you would not have to
explain to you... teacher.

At times ... will write for a specialized audience. When you
do, emphasize details of interest to that particular audience. For
example, if you are writing an explanation for a science club, you can
include scientific information that is more complex and more detailed
than it would be in an explanation addressed to a general audience.

The purpose of the following paragraph is to explain the league
system in team sports. The writer addresses a general audience.

### Model

> The basic unit of organization in team games is the league.
> . . . A league structure has two key characteristics. First of all, to
> determine a champion, a schedule is made in which each team plays
> every other league member, and a record is kept of victories and
> defeats. The team with the best record wins, so every victory has
> exactly the same value in the league standings, regardless of when it
> was scored or who the opponent was. The second characteristic is a
> strong central government that sets and administers rules about
> team composition and playing conditions.
>
> Leonard Koppett, *Sports Illusion! Sports Reality*

Since he is addressing a general audience, the writer uses
general terms rather than terms that only sports fans would know,

and he explains some practices that would be well known by people familiar with sports.

**Exercise   Prewriting: Purpose**   On your paper, write whether the purpose of each of the following topics would most likely be to explain, to describe, or to narrate.

> **SAMPLE**   The benefits of volcanic eruptions
> **ANSWER**   To explain

1. Scientists' methods of saving the whooping crane *explain*
2. Your great-grandparents' journey to the United States *narrate*
3. The procedure for awarding Nobel prizes *explain*
4. The sky at dawn *describe*
5. How to prepare a canvas for oil painting *explain*
6. The most humorous experience of your life *narrate*
7. An unusual-looking person whom you saw on a bus *describe*
8. What bioluminescence is *explain*
9. An incident that you witnessed yesterday *describe narrate*
10. A rock from the moon *describe*

**Assignment 1   Prewriting**   Choose a topic that interests you. On your paper, list the topic, the purpose for writing, and the audience for the topic. Then, keeping the purpose and the audience in mind, list details that you could use to develop the topic in a single paragraph.

**Assignment 2   Writing / Revising**   Using the topic, purpose, audience, and list of details that you chose in Assignment 1, write a paragraph. When you have finished writing, reread your work as if you were the intended audience. Make any changes that would add to your understanding of the paragraph.

**Assignment 3   Prewriting / Writing**   Choose an event or a celebration in which you participated. Write two versions of what happened: one for a person who is familiar with the event or celebration and one for a person who is not.

## Assignment Checklist

Check your writing assignments for the following points:

✔ 1. Did you include only details that help to accomplish your purpose?
✔ 2. Did you write for your audience?
✔ 3. If you have a specialized audience, did you emphasize details of special interest to this audience?
✔ 4. Did you proofread your work for correct grammar, usage, spelling, and punctuation?

# 9.2   Expository Writing

## 9.2a   Writing a Short Expository Composition

How does a telescope work? What causes colds and flu? What is sharecropping? All of these questions can be answered in short expository compositions. The purpose of **expository writing** is to explain something to your reader or to inform your reader about something.

## Selecting and Limiting a Topic

When your purpose is to explain something in one to five paragraphs, select a topic that can be covered fully in that space. If you are asked to select your own subject, choose one that interests you; then limit the subject by choosing one aspect of it to write about. For example, the complex subject "How to provide first aid in emergencies" can be limited to the manageable topic "How to help a person who is choking on food." Similarly, the subject "The causes of pollution" can be narrowed to the manageable topic "The causes of acid rain." It is better to explain a limited topic thoroughly than it is to discuss a broader or more complex topic superficially.

## Planning the Explanation

Before you begin to write your explanation, make a detailed plan of how you will present the topic to your reader. The following strategies will help you to prepare your plan.

### Strategies

1. *List the points that you want to include in your explanation.* You may need to do research to find all of the information that you require.

2. *Review your list to make sure that you have included all important points and that you have not included any unnecessary information.*

3. *Organize the points in a logical order.* For example, if you want to explain how to do something or how something works, put the steps in chronological order (*page 262*). If you want to explain the causes or the effects of something, put them either in chronological order or in order of importance. When you organize points in order of importance, it is usually best to progress from the least important detail to the most important detail. Whatever method you choose, use it consistently throughout your composition.

4. *Analyze the points to see whether they divide into two or more groups.* If they do, place each group in a separate paragraph when you begin to write your composition.

## Writing the Explanation

Once you have prepared your plan, you are ready to write your explanation. To write a clear explanation, follow these strategies.

### Strategies

1. *Begin each paragraph with a topic sentence (page 252).* In an explanation of more than one paragraph, the first topic sentence should present the topic of the entire explanation.

2. *Use transitional words to move from one sentence or paragraph to another.* Such words and phrases as *then, next,*

*most important,* and *however* make the relationships of your ideas clear to your reader.

3. *Define any terms that your reader may not know.* For example, if you are explaining how different types of sound are blended in a motion picture, you probably will have to define such terms as *dub* and *master.*

4. *Write a concluding sentence.* Your last sentence should indicate to the reader that the explanation has come to an end. In a concluding sentence, you may summarize your explanation or you may comment on the explanation.

The following paragraphs explain to the reader how biofeedback works. The transitional words are printed here in italic type.

**Model**

Overall
topic sentence

Biofeedback is a process that allows people with stress-related illnesses such as high blood pressure to monitor and improve their health by learning to relax. In biofeedback, devices that monitor skin temperature are attached to a patient's arm, leg, or forehead. *Then* the person tries to relax. *As* he or she relaxes completely, the temperature of the area under the devices rises because more blood reaches the area. *When* a machine that is attached to the devices detects the rise in temperature, a buzzer sounds, or the reading on a dial changes. *As long as* the patient is relaxed, the buzzer or dial gives encouragement.

Steps in
chronological
order

Topic sentence
for second
paragraph

*The next part* of the biofeedback process is learning how to relax without the monitoring devices. The patient recalls how he or she felt when the buzzer or dial indicated relaxation and *then* tries to imitate that feeling without having to check the biofeedback machine. *After* succeeding in doing so, the patient tries to maintain the relaxed feeling throughout the day. Stress may cause as much as 75 percent of all illness; *therefore,* biofeedback promises to be an outstanding medical tool.

Concluding
sentence

The writer has divided the explanation of biofeedback into two paragraphs: one paragraph about the part of the process that involves the biofeedback machine and another paragraph about the part that does not. The first paragraph has a topic sentence for the whole explanation, and the second paragraph has its own topic sentence. The transitional words in the passage emphasize the chronological order of the process. In the concluding sentence, the writer comments on the future value of biofeedback.

**Exercise 1   Prewriting: Limiting Topics**   For each of the following general subjects, write on your paper a limited topic that could be developed in an expository composition.

1. Astronomy
2. Social problems
3. Computers
4. City planning
5. Sports
6. Films
7. Politics
8. Ranching

**Exercise 2   Writing: Exposition**   Write an expository paragraph that explains the effect of environmental forces on bridges. The following notes will provide all of the information that you need for the composition. Arrange the notes in an appropriate order before you begin to write.

Wind caused original Tacoma Narrows Bridge in Washington to collapse on November 7, 1940.
Waves and water currents push against and weaken bridge supports.
Water, wind, and earthquakes damage bridges.
Earthquakes put infrequent but strong pressure on bridges.
Engineers try to build bridges that can withstand the damage caused by natural forces, but they are not always successful.
Debris in water hits bridge supports and damages them.
Small earthquakes make bridges sway and may weaken structures.
Wind puts constant strain on bridges.
Wind can cause bridges to move up and down as much as a foot.
Bridges buckled or collapsed in California during strong earthquakes.

## 9.2b   Writing a Review

A **review** is another type of expository writing. A review of a book, a play, a film, or a television program is an explanation of the meaning of the work and the techniques that are used to convey that meaning. It is more than a summary of the work.

The purpose of a review is not simply to state whether you liked or disliked the work, but rather to let your readers know what the work is about and the extent to which it has merit.

As a rule, you should include five kinds of information in a review. The order of the information is often the one suggested here, but you may wish to vary the order in some cases.

1. *Introduction.* In a book review, begin by mentioning the author and the title of the work and by identifying it as a particular type of literature—for example, a biography or a novel. In a review of a play, identify the title and the author. Identify a film or a television program by its title. You may include the name of the director in a film review, particularly if the director is well known. In a review of a play, a film, or a television program, you may mention the principal performers.

2. *Brief Description.* Give your readers an overview of the work. This description should be no more than a few sentences that identify the essential people, situation, and setting. You might describe the autobiography *Blackberry Winter,* by Margaret Mead, in this way: "In this account of her life, Margaret Mead writes of her childhood and college years, her remarkable family and friends, her field trips as an anthropologist, and her views on living and working."

3. *Central Idea.* Continue with a discussion of the central idea of the work. Do not confuse the central idea with "what happens." The central idea of a book is the concept or theme that the author conveys through the information presented or through the story. Plays, television programs, and films also have central ideas. For example, the film *Miracle on 34th Street* tells the story of an elderly gentleman who is hired to play a department store Santa Claus. That is

the basis of the plot; however, the central idea of the film concerns how the characters deal with the question of whether the gentleman is really Santa Claus. Some are cynics, refusing to believe; others are willing to believe in miracles. The film points out that believing is not such a bad thing.

4. *Evaluation.* In the evaluation section of a book review, discuss the extent to which the author has successfully presented the central idea. Present your judgment about the effectiveness of the author's writing. Similarly, in evaluating a film or a television program, consider the effectiveness of the script, the acting, and the photography. This is also an appropriate place to mention some aspect of the work that is particularly memorable. As you can see, an evaluation is much more than an answer to the question "Did you like it?"

5. *Conclusion.* At the end of the review, present your final comment on what you feel the work achieves. Your conclusion should be brief.

The following review of a television documentary includes the elements that are necessary in any review. Notice that the writer uses the present tense in telling about the program.

**Model**

"Last Round-Up of the Elephants," a CBS television documentary about Asian elephants, is educational, interesting, and moving. Jason Robards, the narrator, begins the program with a brief history of the elephant and an explanation of how elephants are losing their forest territory to the people of Asia. Then he describes the ways in which naturalists and the people of the forests are helping to save the elephants from extinction.

The documentary acknowledges that the needs of people must come first: land must be cleared for farms and houses. It argues strongly, however, that the elephants must be protected whenever possible. One way to save the elephants is to capture them and train them to do heavy work. The documentary shows forest dwellers capturing elephants with roping and chasing techniques developed centuries ago. The filmmakers believe that it is even better to allow the elephants to remain free. They show the work of naturalists in Sri Lanka who are moving elephants to safety in national parks.

The filmmakers effectively use cinematic techniques to capture the sympathy of the audience. They show that elephants are devoted to their young and will risk their lives for them. To make the audience feel the elephants' fear when their captors chase them into a pen at night, the cinematographer Dieter Plage moves the camera into a pen at the eye level of the elephants and focuses on terrifying fires burning outside the pen. To help viewers understand the environment and the habits of free elephants, photographers filmed them in all seasons and in all types of terrain. One segment was filmed from the position of the villagers wading through knee-deep mud during the monsoon season in order to push trucks carrying tranquilized elephants into a national preserve. Another segment was filmed from underneath a stampeding elephant by a photographer who was knocked over by the elephant. The final footage of a family of elephants playing in a lake in Sri Lanka provides proof that the efforts of the naturalists and the villagers are worthwhile.

The documentary is written and filmed so effectively that the viewer no longer asks "Should the Asian elephants be saved?" but affirms "The Asian elephants must be saved." The film motivates viewers to support the work to save not only the Asian elephant but other endangered species as well.

In the first paragraph, the writer has combined the introduction and a brief description. There is a separate paragraph for each of the other sections: the central idea, the evaluation, and the conclusion.

## Exercise 3 Prewriting: The Review
Each of the following numbered passages represents one of the five categories of information in a review: introduction, brief description, central idea, evaluation, and conclusion. On your paper, tell which category of a review each passage represents.

1. The fine script, experimental photography, and use of a narrator combine to make *Citizen Kane* a fascinating movie, one that I strongly recommend seeing.

2. One of the key lessons that the reader or viewer of *Hamlet* learns about time is that it is beyond one's control. This concept is presented

as a smaller part of a larger theme: that the destiny of a person is not completely in his or her own hands.

*Richard Reese, Prospect High School*
*Mount Prospect, Illinois*

3. *The Rise of Silas Lapham* is a novel by William Dean Howells.

4. *The Grapes of Wrath* is the story of poor midwestern farmers who were forced to migrate to California.

*Paul Herzing, Oshkosh North High School*
*Oshkosh, Wisconsin*

5. Rather than facing a stage and witnessing numerous entrances and exits, the audience was encompassed by the action of the play. The unusual stage contributed an interesting sparkle to the performance, helping people to feel the outdoor mood of the play. Furthermore, realistic forest sound effects, such as crickets, were used throughout the play.

*Jerry Deck, Santa Cruz High School*
*Santa Cruz, California*

**Assignment 1  Prewriting/Writing/Revising**  Think of a cause or an effect that you would like to explain to a reader. For example, you could explain the effects of air travel on passengers or the causes of the decline of railroads. Do whatever research is necessary to find information. Then write your explanation, making sure that each group of related points is placed in its own paragraph. Using the Assignment Checklist that follows, revise your work.

**Assignment 2  Writing/Revising**  Write a review of a film that you have seen recently in a theater or on television. Include all five parts of a review, making sure that you present both information about the film and your reaction to the film. Then revise your review.

## Assignment Checklist

Check your expository composition for the following points:

  ✔ 1. Did you select a topic that is limited enough so that you can explain it thoroughly?

  ✔ 2. Did you present the points in your explanation in a logical order?

✔ 3. Did you place each group of related points in its own paragraph?

✔ 4. Did you begin each paragraph with a topic sentence?

✔ 5. Did you use transitional words?

✔ 6. Did you write a concluding sentence for your explanation?

✔ 7. Did you proofread your explanation for correct grammar, usage, spelling, and punctuation?

Check your review for the following points:

✔ 8. In your introduction did you mention the author and the title of the work and identify the type of work?

✔ 9. Did you provide a brief description of the work?

✔ 10. Did you explain the central idea of the work?

✔ 11. Did you evaluate the effectiveness of the techniques used to convey the central idea?

✔ 12. In your conclusion did you summarize what the work achieves?

✔ 13. Did you proofread your review for correct grammar, usage, spelling, and punctuation?

# 9.3   Descriptive Writing

The purpose of **descriptive writing** is to communicate to a reader your impression of a person, a place, or an object. You can create a vivid impression by combining careful observation with descriptive techniques that help you to choose the most effective words.

## 9.3a   Selecting Sensory Details

**Sensory details** are the characteristics that you perceive with your five senses: sight, hearing, touch, taste, and smell. To create a sharp impression of a person, a place, or an object, use not only details that you see but also details that you perceive with your other senses. For example, if you describe a farm stand in the fall, you can include not only details about the wooden tables filled with bright orange pumpkins but also details about the rumble of the tractor in the field behind the stand, the cool, smooth feel of the heavy pumpkins, the tart taste of freshly picked apples, and the sweet smell of apple cider.

When you plan a description, you may want to list as many details as possible. Before writing, however, you must select only the most important details to include in your description. Choose the details that show your subject as unique and help to create a sharp, unified impression of your subject.

You may choose details to create a mood—that is, a certain emotional response in the reader. For example, to create a calm mood as you describe a pond, you would emphasize the still water and the rustling of the trees. You would not mention the annoying buzzing of the flies near the pond.

The writer of the following description uses details of sight and touch to show his solitary delight in the beauty of a winter scene.

### Model

> Sitting atop the ridge, I was the highest thing on the horizon. The other mountains loomed below. The magnificent blue sky made my eyes contract to small slits. Sitting with my back propped against my skis, I could feel the snow against my warm blue jeans. To the right I looked down upon a steep drop dotted with pines rising over fifty feet. The snow had the winding scars of other skiers. To the left were the unspoiled mountains. Great expanses of snow shone without even a footprint to mar them. At the foot of these blinding spaces were thousands of pines.
>
> *Paul Sylvester, Grosse Pointe North High School*
> *Grosse Pointe Woods, Michigan*

The writer includes such details of sight as the blue of the sky, the tall pines against the whiteness of the snow, and the "blinding" way in which the snow shines. He surveys the scene from a comfortable spot in which he feels the snow against his "warm blue jeans." The writer's details work together to convey his feeling of pleasure.

The writer of the following paragraph about a person presents details of sight that make both the woman's unusual appearance and her personality clear to the reader.

**Model**

> A woman with shorn white hair is standing at the kitchen window. She is wearing tennis shoes and a shapeless gray sweater over a summery calico dress. She is small and sprightly, like a bantam hen; but, due to a long youthful illness, her shoulders are hunched. Her face is remarkable—not unlike Lincoln's, craggy like that, and tinted by sun and wind; but it is delicate too, finely boned, and her eyes are sherry-colored and timid.
>
> Truman Capote, "A Christmas Memory"

The physical details about the woman's size and facial features and the details about her clothing reveal that she is active and spirited even though she appears frail.

**Exercise 1  Prewriting: Sensory Details**   On your paper, list five of the following items. For each item write at least three precise sensory details. Use all five senses to help you think of the details.

| SAMPLE | An old movie theater |
|---|---|
| ANSWER | Scratchy feel of plush seats |
|  | Smell of popcorn |
|  | Muffled sounds of people talking |

1. An insect
2. A candle
3. A city street
4. A typewriter
5. A beach

6. A tractor
7. A hat
8. A fireplace
9. A basement
10. A lemon

## 9.3b   Using Descriptive Techniques

### Effective Words

If you choose your words carefully, your descriptive writing will be vivid and interesting. Specific nouns and strong verbs give your reader a clear mental image of your subject. For example, in the sentence "The bird flew over the field," *bird* is not a specific noun. It does not indicate whether the reader should visualize a sparrow or a hawk. Similarly, in the sentence "Chris went home," *went* is not a strong verb. Either *walked* or *rushed* would be easier to visualize.

In addition to specific nouns and strong verbs, you will use modifiers—adjectives, adverbs, and participles—in your descriptive writing. A modifier may also be a phrase, such as "turning red from embarrassment." A single, well-chosen modifier is often more effective than several used together. If you find yourself describing a subject with overused, worn-out modifiers, find more interesting synonyms in your dictionary or in a dictionary of synonyms, sometimes called a thesaurus.

Nouns, verbs, and modifiers have not only **denotative meanings,** dictionary definitions, but also **connotative meanings,** the emotions or ideas that we associate with the words. (See Section 16.5 in Unit 16, "Vocabulary Skills.") Two words with nearly the same denotation may have very different connotations. For example, *persistent* and *stubborn* have the same denotation: "refusing to give up." Their connotations, however, are different. We usually associate positive ideas with *persistent,* but we often associate negative ideas with *stubborn.* When you write a description, consider carefully the connotations of the nouns, verbs, and modifiers that you choose.

The writer of the following paragraph uses language effectively as he re-creates a scene for the reader.

## Model

> It was a well-worn path, dark soft leaf-mold earth strewn with broken pieces of sandstone. The trail rounded the shoulder of the canyon and dropped steeply into the bed of the stream. In the shallows the water ran smoothly, glinting in the first morning sun. Small round stones on the bottom were as brown as rust with sun moss. In the sand along the edges of the stream the tall, rich wild mint grew, while in the water itself the cress, old and tough, had gone to heavy seed.
>
> John Steinbeck, "Flight"

In the model paragraph, the noun *sandstone* is more specific than *rock* would have been. It helps the reader to visualize grainy, crumbling, brown stones rather than hard, round gray pebbles.

*Dropped* is a stronger verb than *continued* or *went* would have been; with the vivid modifier *steeply,* it helps the reader to visualize the sudden change in height.

## Similes and Metaphors

Using similes and metaphors is another way to make your descriptions effective. A **simile** is a direct comparison between two unlike things that have one striking characteristic in common. For example, you might describe someone who is unhappy as being "sullen as a wet cat." A simile always contains the word *like* or *as* to emphasize the comparison. Such overused similes as "busy as a bee" and "like a fifth wheel" are called **clichés.** You should avoid using them. In general, you should use similes sparingly.

A **metaphor** is an implied comparison that does not contain the word *like* or *as.* In a metaphor you state that the subject *is* the thing to which it is compared. For example, in the following passage, the writer describes a huge, old-fashioned stove as if it were an ancient castle.

> It was a castle of a stove, a rambling palace of a stove, a cathedral of a stove, with spires and turrets and battlements. A good six feet high and eight feet wide, it was made of heavily nickled iron castings bolted together.
>
> Walker Percy, *The Second Coming*

In comparing the stove to a castle, the writer uses details that reveal the immense size and sturdy construction of the stove.

**Exercise 2   Writing: Effective Words**   On your paper, re-write the following sentences. Replace words that do not create a sharp impression. Instead, use specific nouns, strong verbs, and vivid modifiers.

| | |
|---|---|
| **SAMPLE** | The large animal moved into the water. |
| **ANSWER** | The bulky hippopotamus waded into the swamp. |

1. The street was empty.
2. The woman entered the big room.
3. Plants grew through the cracks in the sidewalk.

4. The boy was awakened by a loud noise.
5. Good smells were present in the house.
6. They went up the stairs into the building.
7. The student read the book.
8. The boat moved across the water.
9. The fire damaged the building.
10. The man used the new machine.

## 9.3c Organizing and Writing Your Description

Your reader will easily understand your description of a person, a place, or an object if it is organized well and written clearly. To organize and write your description, follow these steps.

### Strategies

1. *Begin your description with a topic sentence* that introduces the person, place, or object and, if possible, states your general impression of the subject.

2. *Present your supporting sensory details in a logical order,* using chronological order, spatial order, or order of importance. If you use chronological order, present the details in the order in which they appear. If you use spatial order, present the details in the order in which they exist in space; for example, from left to right, top to bottom, or front to back. If you use order of importance, you may start with the least important detail, continue with stronger details, and end with the most important detail. With each detail your reader is drawn further into your description. On the other hand, you may capture your reader's attention by starting with the strongest detail and continuing with less striking details that reinforce the impression created by the first detail.

3. *Use transitional words and phrases* to emphasize the order of your description. *Then, to the right,* and *finally* are examples of such words.

4. *Place each group of related details in a separate paragraph* if your description contains many details. For example, if you use spatial order to describe a painting, you can place all details about the foreground in one paragraph and all details about the background in another paragraph. Each paragraph should have a topic sentence.

5. *Conclude with a sentence that restates your general impression or indicates the end of your description.*

The writer of the following paragraph arrranged the details in chronological order.

| | |
|---|---|
| Topic sentence | On the train I sat in my swivel armchair and watched the passing scene. The track curved slightly, |
| Sensory details | and I could see the locomotives, the mail car, the baggage car, a coach. And then the black mouth of the tunnel . . . loomed and engulfed us. I sat in an absolute, an impenetrable, an almost palpable dark. There was only a sense of motion and the clickety, |
| Concluding sentence | clackety, click of iron on iron. Then daylight flooded back. |

Berton Roueché, "On the Terrace"

Notice that the writer uses *then* to emphasize the chronological order of the description. Notice, too, that he uses vivid details of sight ("the black mouth of the tunnel"), touch ("a sense of motion"), and sound ("click of iron").

**Exercise 3   Writing: Organizing Details**   Using the following topic sentence and details, write a one-paragraph description of the electric car. Begin by stating a general impression and then arrange the details spatially, progressing from top to bottom.

*Topic sentence:* While I was waiting at the bus stop last Saturday, a bright yellow electric car drove by me and pulled into the lot across the street.

Bottom of car just a few inches off ground
Half the size of a regular car; looked almost like a toy

Windshield that wrapped around almost to back window
Front and back of car sloped sharply; almost met at roof
Wheels small but fat
Roof just a small square of metal

**Exercise 4   Writing: Organizing Details**   Using the following details, write a brief description of a man. Begin by stating a
general impression. Then arrange the details in spatial order or in
increasing order of importance, presenting the most significant
feature last.

Bushy iron-gray hair
Mud-caked work boots
Dark brown eyes sparkling under thick eyebrows
Looked as though he had just emerged from wilderness
Shaggy beard and mustache
Short and stocky
Wide smile
Wore yellow flannel shirt
Carried heavy knapsack with ease

**Assignment 1   Writing/Revising**   Write a description of an
outdoor scene that you see almost every day. Begin with a sentence
that presents a general impression of the place. Include details from
at least three senses to create a specific mood. Then revise your
description.

**Assignment 2   Writing/Revising**   Write a description of
someone whom you would like to know. Organize the details of your
description in order of importance, beginning with the most striking
characteristic of the person and moving to less striking characteristics. Then revise your description.

**Assignment 3   Writing/Revising**   Write a description of
your favorite object from childhood or an object that is important to
you now. Use specific nouns and vivid modifiers to create a clear
image of the object for your reader. Before you make a final copy of
your description, revise it.

## Assignment Checklist

Check your assignments for the following points:

&#10003; 1. Did you include sensory details that show the uniqueness of the object, place, or person that you described?

&#10003; 2. Did you present your sensory details in a logical order?

&#10003; 3. If your description contains many details, did you place each group of related details in a separate paragraph?

&#10003; 4. Did you use specific nouns, strong verbs, and effective modifiers in your descriptions?

&#10003; 5. Did you use words with appropriate connotations?

&#10003; 6. Did you include a topic sentence that introduces your subject?

&#10003; 7. Did you proofread your work for correct grammar, usage, spelling, and punctuation?

# 9.4   Narrative Writing

All **narrative writing** tells a story, either nonfictional or fictional. Nonfictional narratives include biographies and autobiographies. Fictional narratives can be short stories or complete novels.

## 9.4a   Planning a Narrative

### Choosing a Topic

The first step in planning a narrative is choosing an event to narrate. You may decide to narrate a true event. In that case, you will write about actions that really happened and about the real people who performed the actions.

On the other hand, you may choose to write a fictional narrative, for which you will invent the actions, the people, or both. Fictional actions and people do not have to come solely from your imagination. They may be based on your own experiences, which you can narrate as fiction by changing details as you wish. The actions of other people may also serve as a basis for a fictional narrative. For example, if you see a family from another country asking someone for directions, you may imagine what led up to the family's journey away from their homeland.

Whether the event that you choose is nonfictional or fictional, it should be short enough so that you can narrate it completely and clearly in two to seven pages.

## Organizing a Narrative

To plan the structure of your narrative, list in chronological order the actions that you wish to narrate. Include a conflict, a climax, and a conclusion in your list.

The actions of a narrative center on a **conflict,** a situation or a problem that must be resolved at the end. The conflict may be between two people, between a person and a force of nature, or within the mind and feelings of one person. For example, a young person may feel a conflict between having to move to a different community and wishing to stay in the same community.

At the **climax,** or high point, the conflict is greatest. For example, in a story based on the conflict about moving to a new community, the climax may occur when the young person has to enroll in a school in the new community.

After the climax, the actions lead to a **conclusion,** in which the conflict is usually resolved. In the story about moving to a new community, the resolution of the conflict may come when the young person makes friends at the new school.

**Exercise 1   Prewriting: Conflict**   On your paper, describe a conflict and a resolution of the conflict that could develop in each of the following situations.

SAMPLE      A new player tries out for the baseball team.

ANSWER      *Conflict:* The team members resent the new player because they think that the newcomer will take the place of one of them.

*Resolution:* The team members accept the new player, recognizing an outstanding athlete who will help the team greatly.

1. An actor in a play becomes sick on the day of the first performance.
2. A flash flood occurs in a canyon.
3. Two friends visit a new city.

4. Jody plays the drums.

5. Fog surrounds the city.

## 9.4b    Writing a Narrative

When you begin to write your narrative, consider which point of view you will use, how you will begin your narrative, how you will present your characters, and how you will use description.

### Establishing a Point of View

You can write a narrative from a first-person or a third-person point of view. When you use a **first-person point of view,** you are the "I" who presents the actions. You are a participant in the narrative. When you tell a story with a **third-person point of view,** you usually are not a direct participant in the action, and you use *he, she,* and *they* to refer to the main characters when you do not use their names. Use the first person when you write an autobiographical narrative and the third person when you write a biographical narrative. You can write fictional narratives in either the first or the third person.

The following examples illustrate the difference between first-person and third-person narration.

FIRST-PERSON NARRATION

> For years *I* had heard *my* parents talk about the debates at town meetings, but *I* had never attended a meeting. *My* chance to witness—and to participate in—the commotion of a meeting came during the spring that *I* was sixteen.

THIRD-PERSON NARRATION

> For years *he* had heard *his* parents talk about the debates at town meetings, but *he* had never attended a meeting. *His* chance to witness—and to participate in—the commotion of a meeting came during the spring that *he* was sixteen.

Maintain a consistent point of view throughout your narrative. If you begin your narrative in the first person, use that form throughout. Similarly, if you begin a narrative in the third person, use the pronoun *I* only in direct quotations.

## Beginning Your Narrative

In the beginning of a narrative, establish the point of view that you will use. Also, establish the **setting**—the time and location of the actions of the narrative—and introduce the important characters. When possible, suggest the conflict that will develop in the story. Present all of the information in a way that will capture your reader's attention.

## Creating Characters

The characters in a narrative are especially important because they perform most of the actions. If you describe your characters vividly, make their motivations clear, and include interesting dialogue, you will make your narrative come to life for your reader.

**Description.** Your reader will be able to visualize your characters if you describe them precisely. Describe how they look: how tall they are, how heavy they are, and—perhaps—what colors their eyes and hair are. Most people have one or two outstanding features; try to highlight those. Also describe the clothing that your characters are wearing and their typical expressions, gestures, and movements. Such details can help to reveal the personalities of your characters.

**Motivation.** You should make clear what situations and feelings motivate your characters, or cause them to act as they do. For example, if a boy who has spent most of his afternoons with his friends stops spending that time with them, you should explain why. Does he have a job after school? Did something cause him to be annoyed at his friends?

**Dialogue.** Present the conversation of your characters as well as their appearance and their motivations. You can do so in one of two ways. You can present a conversation directly by giving the exact words that the characters say, or you can present the conversation indirectly by summarizing what the characters say. Using **dialogue** —the exact words of your characters—is more lively than reporting speech indirectly; therefore, unless the conversations of the characters are long, you should present the conversations directly.

What characters say reveals their personalities. Dialogue can also reveal your characters' ages, educations, and geographical backgrounds. Because spoken language is more informal than written language, realistic dialogue often will be less formal than the rest of your narrative. For example, it may contain slang or sentence fragments (*page 93*).

Using dialogue helps to bring your characters to life for your reader. Rather than writing "Stavros was proud" or "Grace was confused," you can present the character's words to show more vividly that he was proud or that she was confused. When you write dialogue, you will need to add such explanatory details as "Jan yelled" or "Luis whispered." Such details tell which character is speaking and how he or she is speaking. You also can use dialogue to tell some of the actions and to give information that you would otherwise have to include in the accompanying narration.

In the following dialogue, the writer presents the words of two young men who work in a flower shop. He also uses such explanatory details as "he asked me" and "Teruo almost gasped." Notice the punctuation and paragraphing of the passage.

## Model

I was often in the shop helping Teruo with the customers and the orders. One day Teruo learned that I once worked in the nursery and had experience in flower-growing.

"How do you tell when a flower is fresh or old?" he asked me. "I can't tell one from the other. All I do is follow your instructions and sell the ones you tell me to sell first, but I can't tell one from the other."

I laughed. "You don't need to know that, Teruo," I told him. "When the customers ask you whether the flowers are fresh, say yes firmly. Say, 'Our flowers are always fresh, madam.'"

Teruo picked up a vase of carnations. "These flowers came in four or five days ago, didn't they?" he asked me.

"You're right. Five days ago," I said.

"How long would they keep if a customer bought them today?" Teruo asked.

"I guess in this weather they'll hold a day or two," I said.

"Then they're old!" Teruo almost gasped. "Why, we have fresh ones that will last a week or so."

"Sure, Teruo. And why should you worry about that? You talk right to the customers, and they'll believe you."

Toshio Mori, "Say It with Flowers"

The writer uses the dialogue to reveal the personalities of the two men. The narrator is practical and not altogether honest. Teruo is inexperienced and straightforward.

**Personality.**  The actions of your characters also reveal their personalities. For example, a woman who talks kindly to her neighbors may refuse to help them when they need her. In that case, the character's actions tell more about her personality than her words do. You also may include direct statements about a character's personality. For example, you may write, "Jenny was an adventurous child."

## Using Description

You have already learned that you can use description to bring your characters to life for your reader. You can also describe the settings and objects in your narrative, as well as the way in which actions are performed. Combining vivid description with narration can make your writing more interesting for your reader.

The following passage from a narrative contains effective description.

> The moon was near down to the water when Pepé rode on a winded horse to his home flat. His dog bounced out and circled the horse, yelping with pleasure. Pepé slid off the saddle to the ground. The weathered little shack was silver in the moonlight and the square shadow of it was black to the north and east. Against the east the piling mountains were misty with light; their tops melted into the sky.
>
> John Steinbeck, "Flight"

The writer uses such modifiers as *winded, weathered,* and *misty* to describe the horse, the shack, and the mountains. He contrasts the silver shack with its black shadow. The writer also uses such carefully chosen verbs as *bounced* and *circled* and ends the description with the mountain tops that "melted" into the sky.

## Developing the Action

As you write your narrative, present the actions in chronological order, according to your plan. Place each group of related actions in a paragraph of its own. After you introduce the conflict, work up to the climax, and resolve the situation in the end. Often the end of the story occurs soon after the climax.

The following selection is an example of a longer narrative. Notice how the writer creates and then resolves the conflict.

### Home

What had been wanted was this always, this always to last —the talking softly on this porch, with the snake plant in the jardinière in the southwest corner, and the obstinate slip from Aunt Eppie's magnificent Michigan fern at the left side of the friendly door. Mama, Maud Martha, and Helen rocked slowly in their rocking chairs, and looked at the late afternoon light on the lawn, and at the emphatic iron of the fence and at the poplar tree. These things might soon be theirs no longer. Those shafts and pools of light, the tree, the graceful iron, might soon be viewed possessively by different eyes.

Papa was to have gone that noon, during his lunch hour, to the office of the Home Owners' Loan. If he had not succeeded in getting another extension, they would be leaving this house in which they had lived for more than fourteen years. There was little hope. The Home Owners' Loan was hard. They sat, making their plans.

"We'll be moving into a nice flat somewhere," said Mama. "Somewhere on South Park, or Michigan, or in Washington Park Court." Those flats, as the girls and Mama knew well, were burdens on wages twice the size of Papa's. This was not mentioned now.

"They're much prettier than this old house," said Helen. "I have friends I'd just as soon not bring here."

Yesterday Maud Martha would have attacked her. Tomorrow she might. Today she said nothing. She merely gazed at a little hopping robin in the tree, her tree, and tried to keep the fronts of her eyes dry.

"Well, I do know," said Mama, turning her hands over and over, "that I've been getting tireder and tireder of doing that firing. From October to April there's firing to be done."

"But lately we've been helping, Harry and I," said Maud Martha. "And sometimes in March and April and in October, and even in November, we could build a little fire in the fireplace. Sometimes the weather was just right for that."

She knew from the way they looked at her that this had been a mistake. They did not want to cry.

But she felt that the little line of white, somewhat ridged with smoked purple, and all that cream-shot saffron, would never drift across any western sky except that in back of this house. The rain would drum with as sweet a dullness nowhere but here. The birds on South Park were mechanical birds, no better than the poor caught canaries in those "rich" women's sun parlors.

"It's just going to kill Papa!" burst out Maud Martha. "He loves this house! He *lives* for this house!"

"He lives for us," said Helen. "It's us he loves. He wouldn't want the house, except for us."

"And he'll have us," added Mama, "wherever."

"You know," Helen sighed, "if you want to know the truth, this is a relief. If this hadn't come up, we would have gone on, just dragged on, hanging out here forever."

"It might," allowed Mama, "be an act of God. God may just have reached down and picked up the reins."

"Yes," Maud Martha cracked in, "that's what you always say—that God knows best."

Her mother looked at her quickly, decided the statement was not suspect, looked away.

Helen saw Papa coming. "There's Papa," said Helen.

They could not tell a thing from the way Papa was walking. It was that same dear little staccato walk, one shoulder down, then the other, then repeat, and repeat. They watched his progress. He passed the Kennedys', he passed the vacant lot, he passed Mrs. Blakemore's. They wanted to hurl themselves over the fence, into the street, and shake the truth out of his collar. He opened his gate—the gate—and still his stride and face told them nothing.

"Hello," he said.

Mama got up and followed him through the front door. The girls knew better than to go in too.

Presently Mama's head emerged. Her eyes were lamps turned on.

"It's all right," she exclaimed. "He got it. It's all over. Everything is all right."

The door slammed shut. Mama's footsteps hurried away.

"I think," said Helen, rocking rapidly, "I think I'll give a party. I haven't given a party since I was eleven. I'd like some of my friends to just casually see that we're homeowners."

Gwendolyn Brooks, "Home"

The writer presents the actions of the story in chronological order, building to the climax, when Papa comes home with the important news. She describes the setting and also uses dialogue that is informal enough to sound genuine. The dialogue reveals how the personalities of the characters differ, as do their reactions to the situation. The dialogue also reveals the closeness of the family.

Notice that the writer has provided a one-word title that sums up the central issue in the story but does not reveal too much about what happens. After you have written and revised the first draft of your own narrative, you will want to select a title for it.

**Exercise 2   Writing: Point of View**   The following passage is written in the third person. On your paper, rewrite the passage, changing the point of view from third person to first person.

Humming softly as she drove, Sarah went down West Street and turned into the bank parking lot. Even though it was a hot, dusty day, she was happy. She had finished serving hamburgers for the summer, and once she deposited her last paycheck, she would be free for an entire week before school started. Thoughts of swimming in the cool lake all afternoon made her hurry. She slammed the car door shut and ran into the bank. Because there were no lines, she quickly deposited her check and left the bank.

Back at the car, she reached into her pocket for her keys, but they were not there. She was locked out of the car. Peering through the reflections on the window, she could see the keys dangling in the ignition, where she had left them in her hurry. At first, Sarah panicked. Then she decided not to let the problem ruin her first free day, and soon she had an idea. Using a piece of wire from the gas station across the street, she poked it through the top of the window and used it to pull up the lock. Once again Sarah felt calm and happy as she climbed into her car and began the drive to the lake.

**Assignment 1   Writing / Revising**   Write a narrative about an important event that you want to share with a reader. For example, you could write about your first meeting with a friend or about a time when you completed a difficult task. Construct your narrative so that it has a strong beginning, a climax, and a conclusion. Use dialogue where appropriate. Then, using the Assignment Checklist that follows, revise your narrative.

**Assignment 2** **Writing/Revising** Consider the following situation: you work as an automobile mechanic, a nurse, a police officer, or as any other type of worker that you might like to be. Imagine an exciting event that could happen on the job, and write about that event in a fictional first-person narrative. The narrative should be two or more pages long. Revise your narrative before making a final copy of it.

## Assignment Checklist

Check your assignments for the following points:

1. Did you present the actions of your narrative in chronological order?
2. Did you place each group of related actions in a paragraph of its own?
3. Did you use one point of view consistently?
4. Did you present the main characters and the setting early in your narrative?
5. Did you develop a conflict in your narrative?
6. Did you lead up to a climax in the action?
7. Did you resolve the conflict in your conclusion?
8. Did you use description and dialogue to develop your characters?
9. Did you make clear what motivates your characters?
10. Did you proofread your narrative for correct grammar, usage, spelling, and punctuation?

## A Modern Fable: A Narrative That Includes Description

**Situation:** The Playhouse Film Production Company has decided to make a film based on Aesop's fable of the race between the tortoise and the hare. As writer of the screenplay, you will prepare a script about two marathon runners who have the personality traits of the tortoise and the hare. In your script, as in Aesop's fable, the slower runner will win the race. Before you begin the script for the film, the producer wants you to write a narrative about the race that includes vivid descriptions of the setting and the runners. If the producer approves your narrative, the set designers, casting director, and make-up crew will use it as the basis for their work. As you plan and write your narrative, you will keep in mind the following information.

**Writer:** you as the writer of a screenplay

**Audience:** members of the Playhouse Film Production Company

**Topic:** two runners who compete in a marathon

**Purpose:** to narrate a series of events and to include description

**Directions:** To write your narrative, follow these steps.

*Step 1.* Read Aesop's fable on the facing page. Observe the nature of the two main characters, the setting, and the events of the race.

*Step 2.* Imagine two human characters, the runners in the race, who correspond to the tortoise and the hare. Provide a name for each character. List the

(Continue on page 368.)

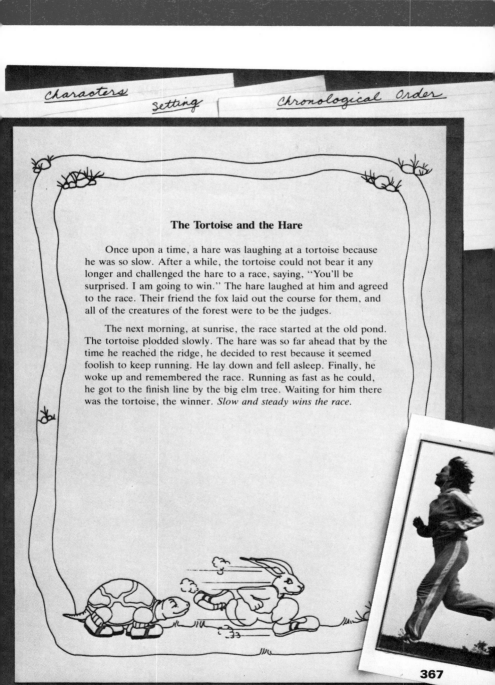

### The Tortoise and the Hare

Once upon a time, a hare was laughing at a tortoise because he was so slow. After a while, the tortoise could not bear it any longer and challenged the hare to a race, saying, "You'll be surprised. I am going to win." The hare laughed at him and agreed to the race. Their friend the fox laid out the course for them, and all of the creatures of the forest were to be the judges.

The next morning, at sunrise, the race started at the old pond. The tortoise plodded slowly. The hare was so far ahead that by the time he reached the ridge, he decided to rest because it seemed foolish to keep running. He lay down and fell asleep. Finally, he woke up and remembered the race. Running as fast as he could, he got to the finish line by the big elm tree. Waiting for him there was the tortoise, the winner. *Slow and steady wins the race.*

significant sensory details that will help to create an impression of each character. Then write a few remarks that indicate the personality and motivation of each character.

*Step 3.* Choose a setting in a community that you know well. Make a list of sensory details that describe the route of the race.

*Step 4.* List the events of the story in chronological order. Begin with the event that causes the slower runner to challenge the faster runner to compete in the marathon, and work up to the climax and conclusion. The climax may occur at a difficult point in the race, perhaps when the faster runner begins to discover that he or she lacks the endurance or the confidence that the slower runner has.

*Step 5.* Using your three lists, write the narrative. In the beginning clearly describe the characters and the setting and introduce the conflict. Include detailed description throughout the narrative.

*Step 6.* Revise your draft as needed.

# Unit Assignments

**Assignment 1**   Select a process to explain to a reader. For example, you could explain how petroleum is found or how runners prepare for a race. Do whatever research is necessary. Then write your explanation, making sure that you define any terms that your reader would not know. When your draft is complete, revise it.

**Assignment 2**   Write a review of a book that you would like your friends to read. Include all five parts of a review, making sure that you present information about the book as well as your evaluation of it. Then revise your review.

**Assignment 3**   Write a description of how a usually busy place looks when no one is there. Use details from several senses, and use words with appropriate connotations for the impression that you wish to create. Present the details in a logical order. Finally, revise your description.

**Assignment 4**   Write a first-person nonfictional narrative about an event in which one of your parents, grandparents, or friends was a participant. Use chronological order, and place each group of related actions in a paragraph of its own.

**Assignment 5**   Recall an interesting or unusual-looking person whom you have seen. Use that person as a character in a third-person fictional narrative. Use description and dialogue to bring that character to life for your reader. Make sure that your narrative has a strong beginning, a climax, and a conclusion. Then revise the narrative.

## Revising Your Assignments

For help in revising expository, descriptive, or narrative writing, consult the Checklist for Revision on the last page of this book.

# Unit Tests

## Test 1

**A.** Number your paper from 1 to 5. Next to each number, write *True* if the sentence is true or *False* if it is false.

1. Related points in a composition should be grouped together in one paragraph.
2. A review is a detailed summary of a book, a play, a film, or a television program.
3. In a description you should include every sensory detail that you can think of.
4. The connotation of a word is its dictionary meaning.
5. The actions of a narrative center on a conflict that must be resolved in the end.

**B.** Number your paper from 6 to 10. Next to each number, write the letter of the term that correctly completes the sentence. You will use all but one of the terms.

| | |
|---|---|
| a. audience | d. mode |
| b. chronological order | e. simile |
| c. climax | f. metaphor |

6. A(n) __?__ of writing is a particular form of writing: exposition, description, narration, or persuasion.
7. Your __?__ is the person or persons to whom your writing is addressed.
8. You write a narrative in __?__.
9. A(n) __?__ uses *like* or *as* to make a comparison between two unlike things that have one striking characteristic in common.
10. At the __?__ of a narrative, the conflict is most intense.

**C.** Number your paper from 11 to 15. Next to each number, write the letter of the item that correctly answers the question.

11. Which of the following is a suitable topic for an expository essay?
    a. The first time I tried to ride a surfboard
    b. How to ride a surfboard
    c. The view of the beach from a surfboard
    d. Mel Daniels's victory in the surfing contest

12. Which of the following is *not* a sensory detail about a cargo ship?
    a. The smoke from the ship billowed over nearby warehouses.
    b. Derricks reached over the side of the ship to pull up brightly colored automobiles.
    c. The ship sails from the dock in New York on the first Wednesday of each month.
    d. The deep sound of the ship's horn reverberated up and down the waterfront.

13. Which of the following sentences contains the most vivid description of Pam's action?
    a. Rushing into the living room, Pam dropped her pile of school books on the large blue armchair.
    b. Pam dropped her books on a chair.
    c. Rushing into the living room, Pam put down her books on a piece of furniture.
    d. Pam put her books on a piece of furniture.

14. Which of the following sentences is certain to be from a first-person narrative?
    a. Andrew put a note on his door so that he would not forget to go to his appointment.
    b. When Mr. Carlisle asked Grace to work late, she replied, "I am sorry, but I have to attend a play rehearsal tonight."
    c. Stuart crossed the finish line first, but I was not far behind.
    d. As soon as Marie heard her aunt's voice, she ran downstairs.

15. Which of the following sentences would be the most effective in a narrative?
    a. As he folded his chessboard, Mark said that the chess game was the longest one he had ever played.
    b. "That was the longest chess game I've ever played," Mark said.
    c. Mark thought that the chess game was long.
    d. "That was the longest chess game I've ever played," Mark said wearily as he folded his chessboard.

# Test 2

Choose one of the Unit Assignments. Write the assignment as directed and hand it in to your teacher.

# Unit 10

*Persuasive*
*Writing*

## Unit Preview

The purpose of **persuasive writing** is to influence the reader, or audience. When you write a persuasive paragraph or composition, you want your audience to accept an idea, to take some sort of action, or both. The following paragraph is an example of persuasive writing.

(1) Although many people complain about modern technology, it has made the world a better place. (2) The function of technology is to provide scientific, efficient ways of doing things. (3) Modern technology makes it possible for farmers to produce increasing amounts of food. (4) Every day, in hospitals around the world, lives are saved through devices made possible by technology. (5) Millions of people earn their livelihoods because of such inventions as the airplane, the automobile, and the computer. (6) Because of technology, people today do not have to labor as hard as people used to. (7) Contrary to the claims of its detractors, modern technology has benefited the world greatly.

**For Analysis**    Reread the paragraph and then follow these directions.

1. On your paper, write the number of the sentence stating the opinion that the writer wants the audience to accept.
2. Explain the purpose of Sentence 2.
3. List the numbers of the sentences in which the writer gives reasons that support his or her opinion.
4. Explain the purpose of Sentence 7.

In analyzing the preceding passage, you have reviewed the structure of a persuasive paragraph. In this unit you will learn how to select reasons to support an opinion. You will also learn how to express your opinion and reasons in a paragraph or in a longer composition that you write to persuade readers to accept your view. As you practice persuasive writing, you will follow the three steps of the composition process: prewriting, writing, and revising.

# 10.1  Selecting a Topic

## 10.1a  Recognizing Opinions

A topic for persuasive writing must be an opinion, not a fact. An **opinion** is the statement of a view that is not shared by everyone. Opinions are subject to disagreement, but facts are not. Factual statements—ideas that are clearly true or can easily be checked—are not suitable as topics because no one needs to be persuaded to accept them. For instance, it would be pointless to try to persuade someone that "a gallon contains eight pints" or that "the novel *Frankenstein* was written by Mary Shelley."

The following statements illustrate the four types of opinions that you can use as topics for persuasive writing.

1. *Opinions That Explain.* These are statements about why something happens, why something is the way it is, or what something means.

> The most important factor in the settling of the American West was the development of the railroads.
> Courage, not cowardice, is the underlying theme of the story.

2. *Opinions That Evaluate.* These are statements that judge the value of something or indicate its good and bad points.

> The band's audition was very poor.
> The cinematography of the movie was excellent.

3. *Opinions That Predict.* These are statements about what will happen in the future.

> Space travel will be available to the general public in the twenty-first century.
>
> The legislature will never approve Governor Hall's program.

4. *Opinions That Advise ("Should" Statements).* These are statements about what people or an organization should do.

> Young people should give careful thought to career planning.
>
> Our nation must strive for energy independence.

Opinions that explain, evaluate, predict, or advise are useful as topics for persuasive writing because they are subject to disagreement. Some people may hold opposite opinions. These are the readers whom you will address in your persuasive paragraph or composition.

**Exercise 1   Prewriting: Opinions**   On your paper, complete the following statements. Each statement should express the type of opinion specified in parentheses.

> SAMPLE      Whenever you feel yourself getting angry, __?__.
> (*Advice*)
>
> ANSWER      Whenever you feel yourself getting angry, you should count slowly to ten and think of something pleasant.

1. The election results were misleading __?__. (*Explanation*)
2. __?__ by the year 2000. (*Prediction*)
3. The made-for-television movie that I saw last night __?__. (*Evaluation*)
4. To succeed in the world of business, __?__. (*Advice*)
5. __?__ is enhanced by our many natural resources. (*Explanation*)
6. The President's speech __?__. (*Evaluation*)
7. __?__ those who fought bravely to protect our liberty. (*Advice*)
8. The Mount St. Helens volcano __?__. (*Prediction*)
9. __?__ to improve your fitness. (*Advice*)
10. The real meaning of the play __?__. (*Explanation*)

# 10.1b Selecting an Opinion as a Writing Topic

Before you begin writing about an opinion, consider whether it is a suitable topic for persuasion. There are three points to keep in mind when you choose a writing topic.

1. *An opinion suitable for persuasive writing is based on more than personal preference.*

   NOT SUITABLE
   > Cantaloupe is more delicious than watermelon.

   This opinion states a personal preference. Everyone has preferences about such things as food, clothing, and music. People's preferences are not likely to be changed by persuasion. Thus, you should not use a personal preference as a topic for persuasive writing.

2. *An opinion suitable for persuasive writing is based on a logical idea rather than on a feeling or a hunch.*

   NOT SUITABLE
   > I have a feeling that we are going to break our losing streak tonight.

   This opinion is based on a feeling. You cannot support such an opinion with reasons that others would accept.

3. *An opinion suitable for persuasive writing is specific and clear.*

   NOT SUITABLE
   > Summer school should be required.

   This opinion is vague and lacking in details. The statement does not tell who should be required to attend summer school or under what circumstances.

The following opinion is suitable as a topic for persuasive writing.

SUITABLE    Passing a road test should be a requirement for renewing one's driver's license.

The opinion is suitable for three reasons: (1) It is not simply a personal preference. (2) It is based on a logical idea, not on a feeling or a hunch. (3) It is clear and specific. If you use the opinion as a writing topic, your readers will know exactly what idea you want them to accept.

**Exercise 2   Prewriting: Suitable Topics**   On your paper, write *Suitable* or *Unsuitable* to indicate whether the opinion could be used as a topic for persuasive writing. If an opinion is unsuitable, indicate whether (1) it states a personal preference, (2) it states a hunch, or (3) it is not specific and clear.

> **SAMPLE**   The most enjoyable type of music is country western.
>
> **ANSWER**   *Unsuitable.* Personal preference

1. The government ought to spend more money on mass transportation.
2. Something is wrong with the economy.
3. Eggs make a tastier breakfast than cereal does.
4. Government employees should receive annual cost-of-living raises.
5. If extracurricular activities are to be reduced, those with the fewest participants should be eliminated first.
6. Careers are a problem.
7. Blue eyes are more attractive than brown eyes.
8. Vocational education should begin at an early age.
9. I have a feeling that the Canadian hockey team will win the gold medal in the next Olympic games.
10. Our major modes of transportation will change entirely in the twenty-first century.

**Exercise 3   Prewriting: Specific Topics**   Rewrite each of the following opinions so that it is specific enough to be used as a topic for persuasive writing. Add whatever details are needed to make each opinion clear and definite.

> **SAMPLE**   Jogging is better than weightlifting.
>
> **ANSWER**   Jogging is a better means of strengthening the heart than weightlifting is.

1. Our local newspaper is poor.
2. Work is important.
3. Something is wrong with the country's tax laws.
4. The sale was a success because of Anita and Lou.
5. Our court system should be improved.

## 10.1c Suiting Your Topic to Your Audience

Before you begin writing, consider how your audience will probably react to your opinion. An opinion that is acceptable to one audience may not be acceptable to another, as the following example shows.

OPINION    Imports of foreign cars ought to be reduced.

| AUDIENCES | REACTIONS |
|---|---|
| Dealers in American-made cars | Will probably agree |
| Dealers in foreign cars | Will probably disagree |
| American car buyers | May agree or disagree |

Ask yourself two questions about your audience's possible reactions to your opinion.

1. *Is my audience already likely to agree with the opinion?* If so, you should restate your topic or select another one that some will disagree with.

   AUDIENCE
   Coaches

   POOR TOPIC
   Athletes should attend team practice every day.

   BETTER TOPIC
   Athletes should not be allowed to attend team practice unless they do well in their studies.

   The second topic is better because some coaches may not agree with the statement.

2. *Is my audience likely to oppose the opinion very strongly?* If so, you may be setting yourself an impossible task. Unless

you hold your opinion so strongly that you do not want to modify it, or unless you enjoy defending an unpopular view, consider replacing the opinion with one that you have a better chance of persuading an audience to accept.

AUDIENCE
> Senators

POOR TOPIC
> Members of Congress should not receive a pay raise.

BETTER TOPIC
> The pay raise for members of Congress should be no larger than the average raise of American workers.

The audience would probably oppose the first opinion but would be likely to consider the second opinion.

**Exercise 4   Prewriting: Audience**    In each of the following pairs, one opinion would probably be unacceptable to the audience and the other opinion would probably be acceptable. On your paper, write the letter of the opinion that the audience might be persuaded to accept.

1. *Audience:* Professional football players
   a. Most of today's professional athletes are vastly overpaid.
   b. Some of today's athletes are vastly overpaid.

2. *Audience:* Newspaper reporters
   a. Television news programs provided more thorough and interesting coverage of the state election results than newspaper articles did.
   b. Newspapers do not necessarily provide a better coverage of events than television newscasts do.

3. *Audience:* Historians
   a. The lessons of history are difficult for students to understand.
   b. History is the least useful subject taught in our schools.

4. *Audience:* Owners of cars with diesel engines
   a. Cars with diesel engines should be outlawed because they create more pollution than do cars with gasoline engines.
   b. Because cars with diesel engines create more pollution than do cars with gasoline engines, they should be fitted with extra pollution-control devices.

5. *Audience:* Lawyers
   a. A lawyer who loses a case should not be paid for his or her services.
   b. A lawyer who wins a case should be paid more than a lawyer who loses a case.

**Assignment 1  Prewriting**  Examine the editorial and opinion pages of a newspaper for five brief statements of opinion. Copy the opinions on your paper. Label each opinion *Explanation, Evaluation, Prediction,* or *Advice.*

**Assignment 2  Prewriting / Writing**  Write two statements of opinion about each of the following subjects. The statements should express the types of opinions specified after each subject.

> **SAMPLE**   Computers: (a) *Evaluation* (b) *Prediction*
> **ANSWER**   a. Computers are only as reliable as the people who program them.
>           b. In the next century, most homes will be equipped with computers to control the use of energy.

1. Airbags in cars: (a) *Evaluation* (b) *Prediction*
2. Water shortage: (a) *Advice* (b) *Explanation*
3. Daylight-saving time: (a) *Prediction* (b) *Evaluation*
4. National conversion to metric system: (a) *Advice* (b) *Prediction*
5. Roller skaters: (a) *Explanation* (b) *Evaluation*

**Assignment 3  Prewriting / Writing**  For each of the following audiences, write one opinion that the audience would probably agree with and one opinion that the audience would probably disagree with.

1. Senior citizens
2. Salespeople
3. Labor-union members
4. Teen-agers
5. Farmers
6. Librarians

**Continuing Assignment  Prewriting / Writing**  Write three opinions that you could use as topics for persuasive writing. For each opinion identify an audience that you want to persuade. Save your paper.

## Assignment Checklist

Check your writing assignments for the following points:

✔ 1. Did you write genuine opinions—that is, statements that are subject to disagreement?

✔ 2. Did you write opinions that explain, evaluate, predict, or advise?

✔ 3. Did you base your opinions on logical ideas rather than on feelings or personal preferences?

✔ 4. Did you make your statements of opinion clear and specific?

✔ 5. Did you take into account the probable reactions of your audiences?

# 10.2  Preparing Support for Your Opinion

Your goal in persuasive writing is to get your audience to accept your opinion. The best way to persuade an audience is to present sound reasons for your opinion.

## 10.2a  Recognizing Facts

The most reliable reasons that you can give your audience are facts. A **fact** is something that is known to be true or that can be shown to be true by observation, measurement, or research. Unlike an opinion, a fact is a statement that you generally do not have to persuade readers to accept. They can confirm a fact for themselves if they have any doubts about it.

Not all sentences that look factual are really statements of fact. A sentence that looks factual may contain an imprecise definition, a careless observation, or incorrect data. Consider the following statements.

A devil's walking stick is a type of shrub.
Sandy is two inches taller than Cindy.

You can show that the first statement is true simply by looking up *devil's walking stick* in a dictionary or encyclopedia. You can show that the second statement is true by measuring the two girls' heights and computing the difference. Thus, each statement can be verified, or shown to be factual.

**Exercise 1  Prewriting: Facts and Opinions**  On your paper, write *Fact* or *Opinion* to indicate whether each statement can easily be verified, or shown to be true.

1. Hypochondriacs are people who constantly think that they are ill.
2. Edgar Allan Poe was America's most talented writer.
3. The problems of the township are the result of bad management.
4. A millimeter equals 0.0394 of an inch.
5. The Circus Maximus, an arena of ancient Rome, had room for nearly 200,000 spectators.
6. Conservation is the best way of handling a shortage of a product or a resource.
7. Following election day in 1948, some newspapers incorrectly reported that Dewey had defeated Truman for President.
8. Every person should learn a second language.
9. Most people who enter the acting profession do so because they like to show off.
10. The circumference of a circle is approximately three and one-seventh times as long as the diameter.

**Exercise 2  Prewriting: Checking Facts**  The following sentences are statements of fact. Three methods of checking each fact are suggested. On your paper, write the letter of the *best* method of checking the fact.

SAMPLE    In most homes in the United States, a television set is on for an average of more than six hours a day.

(a) Check how many hours television is on in your home each day. (b) Look up a magazine article about television viewing habits. (c) Look up *television* in a dictionary.

ANSWER    b

1. Sarah's new car gets forty miles per gallon on the highway.

   (a) Ask Sarah what mileage her car gets. (b) Test-drive the car and record the mileage obtained. (c) Check official mileage-test records for this model of car.

2. Parallel lines never meet.

   (a) Look up *parallel* in the dictionary. (b) Draw two parallel lines and observe whether they meet. (c) Ask your art or drafting teacher.

3. The polio vaccine that Dr. Jonas Salk developed in the 1950s led to the near-elimination of the disease.

   (a) Check the 1950s section of a modern history textbook. (b) Ask the school nurse. (c) Look up *Salk* in a biographical dictionary or encyclopedia.

4. The motorcycle skidded fifty feet on the road before falling into the pond.

   (a) Check the newspaper account of the accident. (b) Ask someone who witnessed the accident. (c) Check the official police report of the accident.

5. Rainfall for the state has been below normal this year.

   (a) Ask homeowners whether their water bills have been higher than usual this year. (b) Check this year's rainfall total in the newspaper and compare it with normal rainfall figures in an almanac. (c) Observe whether plant growth is less than normal.

## 10.2b Recognizing Statements That Combine Fact and Opinion

When you develop evidence to support your **position**—the opinion that you want your audience to accept—do not confuse a factual statement with a partly factual statement. Some statements combine fact and opinion.

FACT AND OPINION COMBINED
> Cheryl believes that *the community's leash laws are too strict.*

This sentence is partly factual. It is a fact that Cheryl believes what she does about the leash laws. You could verify this fact simply by asking Cheryl. However, *what* Cheryl believes—that the community's leash laws are too strict—is not a statement of fact. Some residents of the community feel that the leash laws are adequate or are not strict enough. Thus, the part of the sentence in italic type is a statement of opinion.

Sentences may combine fact and opinion in other ways.

FACT AND OPINION COMBINED
> John does secretarial work for an *outstanding* lawyer.

This example is a statement of fact except for one word. The statement "John does secretarial work for a lawyer" is a fact because it is an observation that can be verified. But the word *outstanding* involves an evaluation and therefore expresses an opinion. You can separate the sentence into two statements.

FACT      John does secretarial work for a lawyer.

OPINION      The lawyer for whom John works is outstanding.

Now consider this example.

FACT AND OPINION COMBINED
> Because car prices are increasing, *more people will use public transportation.*

The first part of the sentence, "car prices are increasing," can easily be checked. Thus, it is factual. The second part, "more people will use public transportation," is an opinion because it predicts what people will do.

As support for an opinion, statements that combine fact and opinion are less effective than statements of fact. The reason is that an opinion is subject to disagreement. In your writing use strictly factual statements as evidence for your position whenever possible.

**Exercise 3**   **Prewriting: Fact and Opinion**   The following sentences combine fact and opinion. On your paper, write each statement of fact in one sentence and each statement of opinion in a second sentence. Label each of your sentences *Fact* or *Opinion.*

SAMPLE      I have four talented sisters and brothers.

ANSWER      *Fact:* I have four sisters and brothers.
                    *Opinion:* They are all talented.

1. The game was lost in the final minutes because our team could not take the pressure.
2. Jim made a face that summed up everyone's feelings about the proposal.
3. The tears that ran down the speaker's face showed his sincerity.
4. The wedding reception, which was held in the banquet hall of the castle, was the finest that the villagers had ever seen.
5. Phoebe danced with Lou, the best dancer in school, thirteen times.

# 10.2c Selecting Facts to Support Your Position

In the following paragraph, each fact supports the position stated at the beginning.

## Model

(1) Position:
Sophomore class
should win prize.

(3) Fact:
Sponsored dances

(4) Fact:
Created Pep Club

(5) Fact:
Surpassed quota

(6) Fact:
Involved in clubs

(7) Fact:
Involved in
sports

(1) The sophomore class of Keller High School deserves the Wilder Trophy this year. (2) The sophomores have done more than any other class to make the school year a success. (3) To begin with, they sponsored the Freshman Welcome Dance and the Valentine's Day Dance, the two best-attended dances of the year. (4) Also, it was the sophomore class that created the Pep Club, which has organized all of the rallies. (5) The sophomore class was the only one to surpass its quota in collecting money for the Service Club drive. (6) Furthermore, over one hundred sophomores have been actively involved in the school's various clubs. (7) Finally, more than 80 percent of the class either play on a school team or attend sports activities regularly. (8) The administration definitely should award this year's Wilder Trophy to the sophomores.

By providing facts about the activities of the sophomore class, the writer supports the position that the class should win the trophy.

In developing the position, the writer had many facts about the class to choose from. However, only some of those facts qualified as **evidence**—data showing that a statement is true or probable. The author chose as evidence the facts that best supported the position.

The following chart illustrates the selection process that the writer might have used to support the position that the sophomore class deserves the Wilder Trophy.

| AVAILABLE FACTS | EVIDENCE |
|---|---|
| More than 80 percent active in sports | Yes |
| Surpassed quota in Service Club drive | Yes |
| Is the largest class in ten years | No |
| Created the Pep Club | Yes |
| Sponsored the best-attended dances | Yes |
| Went on a class trip to Philadelphia | No |
| Over one hundred involved in clubs | Yes |
| Contains many students interested in biology | No |

By selecting facts that furnish evidence for your position, you will support your position effectively.

**Exercise 4  Prewriting: Facts as Evidence**  On your paper, write *Evidence* for each fact that directly supports the position. Write *Not evidence* for each fact that does not support the position.

*Position:* The great Renaissance artist Leonardo da Vinci was a master in many fields.

1. As a military engineer for the Duke of Milan, he planned the rechanneling of rivers.

2. Some of his notebooks have recently been published.

3. Leonardo da Vinci was born near Florence, Italy, in 1452.

4. In the course of his study of anatomy, Leonardo developed theories about blood circulation and the workings of the eye.

5. Between 1478 and 1519, he was a painter, draftsman, sculptor, architect, engineer, scientist, inventor, and teacher.

6. Like other Renaissance painters, he usually chose religious subjects for his paintings.

7. Leonardo designed various machines, including flying machines.
8. He competed with another famous painter, Michelangelo, for an important job.

**Assignment   Prewriting/Writing**   Write four statements of fact, four statements of opinion, and four statements that combine fact and opinion. Write the statements in random order and do *not* label them. Exchange papers with a classmate; each of you will label the other's statements. Then you will check the labels to see whether they are correct. If you and your classmate do not agree about a label, discuss it to see if you can reach agreement.

**Continuing Assignment   Prewriting/Writing**   *Step 1:* Select one of the opinions that you wrote for the Continuing Assignment on page 379. *Step 2:* Write the opinion, as well as the audience that you identified, at the top of another sheet of paper. The opinion will be the statement of position for your argument. *Step 3:* List five reasons that support your position. (Do research as needed.) Label each reason either *Fact* or *Opinion*. Make certain that at least four of the reasons are facts. Save your paper.

## Assignment Checklist

Check your writing assignments for the following points:

- ✔ 1. Did you write factual statements, opinions, and combination statements as needed?
- ✔ 2. When necessary, did you check your facts by research or by observation?

# 10.3  Organizing and Writing an Argument

An **argument** is a series of logically connected sentences that state a position and present reasons to support it. You must organize an argument carefully. A poorly organized argument may confuse, rather than persuade, your audience. The order most often used in persuasive writing includes four steps, or parts. They are labeled in the following persuasive paragraph.

### Model

| | |
|---|---|
| Position statement | The residents of the West Grove Street area should create a community center by renovating the |
| Clarifying remark | old post office. The community center would be a place where all neighborhood people could gather to talk, to play games, to exercise, and to take part in |
| Supporting sentences | sports. At present, the neighborhood has no playing area that is large enough for basketball or volleyball. When young people want to meet, they have no place to go. Many older residents have spoken of wanting a lounge where they could meet for conversation and activities. The community center would provide space for many activities, and it would also be a meeting place for discussing neighborhood issues and for attending films, classes, and lectures. If |
| Concluding sentence | everyone in the neighborhood works to make the community center a reality, the area around West Grove Street will be a much nicer place to live. |

You have seen the form of a simple, one-paragraph argument. In a longer persuasive composition, you need to vary the form, as this section will explain. Even in a longer composition, however, the elements are still the four kinds of statements shown in the model argument.

## 10.3a  Position Statement

When you write an argument, state your position at the beginning so that your audience will know what you intend the argument to show. To express your position effectively, use these strategies.

## Strategies

1. *Phrase your position as a statement, not as a question.* If you phrase your position as a question, your audience may not be able to tell whether you are for or against the idea or action that is being discussed.

   NOT EFFECTIVE
   > Is it fair to charge high school students a special fee for participating in sports?

   EFFECTIVE
   > Charging high school students a special fee for participating in sports is entirely fair.

   EFFECTIVE
   > Charging high school students a special fee for participating in sports is unfair.

2. *Limit your position statement to one opinion.* Different opinions about a subject need to be supported with separate arguments.

   NOT EFFECTIVE
   > Television networks devote too much time to sports coverage, and some of the announcers are biased in their reporting.

   EFFECTIVE
   > Television networks devote too much time to sports coverage.

   EFFECTIVE
   > Some of the sports announcers on television are biased in their reporting.

You have seen that a one-paragraph argument has a single position statement. A longer persuasive composition also has only one position statement, which you must place in the first paragraph. Use a topic sentence for each of the other paragraphs; in these sentences you will probably introduce the evidence to be presented in the paragraph.

**Exercise 1 Prewriting / Revising: Position Statements**
Number your paper from 1 to 10, leaving two lines between
numbers. Write *Yes* or *No* next to each number to indicate whether
the corresponding sentence would be effective as a position statement
for an argument. After each *No* answer, rewrite the sentence,
making it more effective. If necessary, divide the sentence into two
separate statements.

1. What about legislation controlling the flow of illegal aliens into this
   country?
2. Many teen-agers have poor study habits, and some of them have poor
   eating habits too.
3. Some major college sports have become too much like businesses.
4. What if we start giving harder tests to determine a person's eligibility
   for a driver's license?
5. The country needs a more efficient way to conduct a census.
6. It is hard to make friends when you move to a new community.
7. Most of us in the United States and Canada are well off; we have an
   obligation to help developing nations.
8. Should elected politicians be allowed to appoint people to office simply as a means of rewarding them for their help during the election?
9. Weightlifting is the best method of building muscles.
10. Our national debt has become too large, and we ought to start
    electing representatives who have college degrees in economics.

## 10.3b Clarifying Remarks

After stating your position, you may need to clarify it so that
your readers understand exactly what you want to show. If you are
writing a single persuasive paragraph, you should usually limit your
clarifying remark to one sentence. If you are writing a longer
persuasive composition, you may include two or more sentences of
clarifying remarks. In a persuasive composition, place the clarifying
remarks with the position statement in the first paragraph of the
composition. The most common ways of clarifying a position statement are the following.

**Strategies**

1. *Clarify by defining or explaining a key term.*

POSITION STATEMENT
We must find better ways to dispose of toxic waste.

CLARIFYING REMARK
Toxic waste is a poisonous substance, usually a chemical by-product of a manufacturing process.

2. *Clarify by qualifying or limiting the position statement.*

POSITION STATEMENT
The Atlas car is the best buy on the road today.

CLARIFYING REMARK
Although an Atlas costs slightly more than many other cars, it offers far greater value for your money.

3. *Clarify by providing background information.*

POSITION STATEMENT
The Haines bill, now being considered by the state legislature, deserves public support.

CLARIFYING REMARK
Sponsored by Assemblywoman Jill Haines of Fairview, the bill provides for state financing of various mass-transit programs.

4. *Clarify by giving an example or a specific application of the position statement.*

POSITION STATEMENT
We need to re-examine the manner in which the government spends our tax revenues.

CLARIFYING REMARK
In particular, we must devise more effective means of preventing waste and fraud in government spending.

**Exercise 2   Writing: Clarifying Remarks**   On your paper, write the type of clarifying remark specified for each of the following position statements. Use a dictionary, encyclopedia, or other reference work as necessary.

**SAMPLE**   *Position statement:* Movies based on novels do not do as good a job of storytelling as the novels do.

*Type of clarifying remark:* Limit the position statement.

**ANSWER**   *Clarifying remark:* Of course, there have been a few exceptional movies, such as *Gone with the Wind* and *Ben-Hur,* that are just as good as the novels on which they were based.

1. *Position statement:* The development of synthetic fuels should be a major goal of the energy industry.
   *Type of clarifying remark:* Define a key term.
2. *Position statement:* The Lincoln-Douglas debates proved that Abraham Lincoln had the wisdom and skill needed by a President.
   *Type of clarifying remark:* Provide background information.
3. *Position statement:* The average business can benefit greatly from investing in a computer.
   *Type of clarifying remark:* Give an example.
4. *Position statement:* Many of today's young people are dedicated to solving the age-old problems of poverty and injustice.
   *Type of clarifying remark:* Limit the position statement.
5. *Position statement:* Yellow journalism seems to be on the rise again.
   *Type of clarifying remark:* Define a key term.

## 10.3c Supporting Sentences

The sentences that support your position statement form the largest part of your argument. Arrange your supporting sentences in such a way that your audience will understand exactly how you reached your position. Usually you will want to save your strongest supporting sentence for last. Be sure that each sentence you include clearly supports the position statement.

If you have many sentences to support your argument, you will write a persuasive composition rather than a single paragraph. In a persuasive composition, place related supporting sentences in groups, and place each group in a separate paragraph.

Study the following paragraph.

### Model

| | |
|---|---|
| (1) Position statement | (1) Merchants should stand by the products that they sell. (2) They should either replace defective merchandise for the customer or refund the cost of purchase. (3) A business can prosper only if it is conducted in good faith. (4) A store owner rightfully expects customers to pay for their purchases in cash or on approved credit. (5) Stores do not accept counterfeit money or bad checks. (6) Similarly, customers rightfully expect the products that they buy to live up to their advertised performance. (7) They, too, should not have to accept "counterfeit" or "bad" goods. |
| (2) Clarifying remark | |
| (3) First step in reasoning process | |
| (4) (5) Second step in reasoning process | |
| (6) (7) Third step in reasoning process | |

Notice how the supporting sentences in the persuasive paragraph present evidence for the position statement in a logical, step-by-step fashion.

### Exercise 3   Prewriting: Supporting Sentences   *Step 1:* On your paper, copy the position statement and the clarifying remark in the paragraph that follows. *Step 2:* Find but do not copy the one statement that does not support the position statement. *Step 3:* Copy the supporting sentences, arranging them in a logical order, with a strong statement at the end. Save your paper.

*Position statement:* Our city council should act to prevent demolition of the old Victorian homes along Sutter Avenue.

*Clarifying remark:* These homes are scheduled to be demolished next year to make way for a new shopping center.

*Supporting sentences:*   (1) At only a modest cost to the taxpayers, the city could move the homes to a site near the edge of town.   (2) If they are destroyed, the only reminders of our town's past will be a few yellowed photographs hanging in the city hall.   (3) Two of the homes are owned by council members themselves.   (4) If the

Victorian homes are not moved to a new site, we will lose a major link with our past. (5) The houses are the only nineteenth-century structures left in the city. (6) Construction of the shopping center need not result in destruction of the homes, however.

## 10.3d Concluding Sentences

You will strengthen your argument if you provide a conclusion for it. If you are writing a single persuasive paragraph, write one or two concluding sentences. If you are writing a persuasive composition, you may write two or three concluding sentences that constitute your final paragraph.

There are three basic ways to conclude an argument. The example sentences that follow each of the three strategies show one way of concluding the model paragraph on the facing page.

### Strategies

1. *Conclude by restating the position statement in different words.*

   POSITION STATEMENT
   > Stores should stand by the products that they sell.

   RESTATEMENT
   > Thus, stores should accept responsibility for the quality of their merchandise.

2. *Conclude by recommending an action based on the position statement.*

   RECOMMENDATION
   > Customers should insist that stores make good on defective merchandise.

3. *Conclude by stating a personal judgment that is based on your position statement.*

   PERSONAL JUDGMENT
   > If stores lived up to their responsibilities, shopping would be a more pleasant experience than it often is.

Any conclusion that you write must be based on what you have said in your argument.

**Exercise 4    Writing: Concluding Sentences**    Write two different types of concluding sentences for the persuasive paragraph in Exercise 3 on page 392. You may restate the position statement in different words, recommend an action based on it, or offer a personal judgment based on it.

**Assignment 1    Prewriting**    *Step 1:* In a newspaper or magazine, find a persuasive paragraph of seven or more sentences. Cut it out and mount it on a sheet of paper. *Step 2:* Circle the position statement and label it. *Step 3:* Do the same thing for the clarifying remark, if there is one. Also tell what kind of clarification it provides. *Step 4:* Circle and label the supporting sentences. *Step 5:* Do the same thing for the concluding sentence, if there is one. Also tell which kind of conclusion it is.

**Assignment 2    Prewriting/Writing**    Select one set of materials from those that follow; then prepare and write a persuasive paragraph. *Step 1:* Select the position statement that you prefer and copy it. *Step 2:* Underneath the position statement, write a clarifying remark of one of the types specified. *Step 3:* Briefly list several reasons in support of the position statement that you have chosen. Use at least two of the suggested points of evidence. (You may use additional evidence of your own if you wish.) Indicate the most logical order for your points of evidence by numbering them. *Step 4:* Write a concluding sentence of one of the types specified. *Step 5:* Write the paragraph, presenting the supporting sentences in the order indicated on your list.

1. *Position statement:* Americans should (should not) learn to speak a foreign language. *Clarifying remark:* Give an example or provide background information. *Suggested points of evidence:* (a) Foreign languages useful for travel in foreign countries. (b) Most people do not travel to foreign countries. (c) Because many tourists speak English, not necessary to know foreign languages. (d) Fun to learn a foreign language. (e) Interesting to talk to foreign travelers in their

own language. (f) Learning a foreign language improves one's command of English. (g) Time better spent learning science or business skills. *Conclusion:* Restate the position statement or give a personal judgment based on the position statement.

2. *Position statement:* Citizens should (should not) devote two weekends a year to conservation activities. *Clarifying remark:* Define a key term or limit the position statement. *Suggested points of evidence:* (a) Many parks could be cleaned up, and many trees and shrubs could be planted. (b) Experts needed to do useful work. (c) A way of fulfilling one's duty to country. (d) Citizen effort would save tax dollars. (e) Instead, unemployed people could be given full-time work. *Conclusion:* Restate the position statement or recommend an action based on the position statement.

**Assignment 3  Writing**  Write a persuasive composition in which you argue for or against (1) having a national speed limit or (2) raising the minimum driving age to eighteen. *Step 1:* Place your position statement and any clarifying remarks in the first paragraph. *Step 2:* Group related supporting sentences and place each group in a separate paragraph. *Step 3:* Put your concluding sentences in a final paragraph.

**Continuing Assignment  Writing**  Use the position statement and the list of supporting reasons that you wrote for the Continuing Assignment on page 386 as the basis of a persuasive paragraph. *Step 1:* Begin your paragraph with the position statement. *Step 2:* If it is needed, write a second sentence that clarifies your position statement. *Step 3:* Select the strongest reasons from your list and state them in a well-organized series of supporting sentences. *Step 4:* Conclude your argument in a final sentence or two. Save your paper.

### Assignment Checklist

Check your writing assignments for the following points:

✔ 1. Did you write arguments that include all four parts?
✔ 2. Did you write clarifying remarks that will help your readers to understand your argument?

✔ 3. Did you choose effective evidence and present it in a well-organized series of supporting sentences?

✔ 4. Did you write concluding sentences that restate the position statement, recommend an action, or offer a personal judgment?

✔ 5. In Assignment 3, did you write a clear, effective position statement?

✔ 6. In Assignment 3, did you group the sentences in a logical, effective way?

✔ 7. Did you proofread your work for correct grammar, usage, spelling, and punctuation?

# 10.4 Revising Your Argument

When your first draft is complete, revise your argument. As you revise, concentrate on three aspects of your writing: moderation, effectiveness, and sound reasoning.

## 10.4a Moderation

In conversation, opinions are frequently expressed as sweeping statements that may pertain to entire classes of people, objects, or actions. The following opinions are examples of sweeping statements.

*None* of the rules for using the public swimming pool makes any sense.

*All* actors are temperamental.

In persuasive writing, however, you must present evidence to support the opinion expressed in your position statement. The main drawback of a sweeping statement is that a single exception can disprove it. For example, if your reader has met or heard of just one actor who is not temperamental, then he or she will immediately disagree with the statement "All actors are temperamental." A moderate position statement is easier to support than a sweeping statement. A moderate supporting sentence is also more acceptable to readers as evidence.

The following strategies will help you to turn sweeping statements into moderate statements.

### Strategies

1. *Replace superlatives,* modifiers that end in *-est* or modifiers that are preceded by the words *most, least, best,* or *worst.* In place of superlatives, you can use the positive form of the modifier. For example, you can substitute *beautiful* for *most beautiful.* Alternatively, you can insert a phrase such as *one of the* before the superlative. The following examples show how you can alter superlatives.

   SWEEPING STATEMENT
   > Switzerland is *the most picturesque* country in the world.

   MODERATE STATEMENTS
   > Switzerland is *a picturesque* country.
   > Switzerland is *one of the most picturesque* countries in the world.

2. *Change wording to limit sweeping statements.* Such words as *all, always, anytime, completely, constantly, every, everyone, invariably, never, no,* and *none* often appear in sweeping statements. To limit such statements, replace those words with such words and phrases as *many, often, usually, sometimes, frequently, in most cases, for the most part, some, rarely,* and *few.*

   SWEEPING STATEMENT
   > Sue Powell's tennis game is *always* overpowering.

   MODERATE STATEMENT
   > Sue Powell's tennis game is *usually* overpowering.

3. *Add modifiers to limit sweeping statements.* For example, the statement "Wars are caused by economic conditions" actually means "*All* wars are caused by economic conditions." To limit this kind of sweeping statement, add a suitable modifier, such as *some* or *many.* "*Some* wars are caused by economic conditions" is a moderate statement.

**397**

When you write a persuasive paragraph or a persuasive composition, you may have to use more than one of these techniques for making your statements more moderate.

**Exercise 1  Prewriting / Revising: Moderation**  On your paper, write *Sweeping statement* or *Moderate statement* to describe each sentence. Rewrite each sweeping statement to make it more moderate.

1. Having a nice home is every couple's dream.
2. In most cases computer mistakes are caused by inadequate maintenance or human error.
3. Saying something that might hurt someone's feelings is the worst thing that you can do.
4. Rest is always the proper treatment for an injured foot.
5. A dog is the best friend that a child can have.
6. All members of the United States Senate are quite wealthy.
7. Politicians want to be re-elected.
8. Regardless of the circumstances, lateness is never justified.
9. Former athletes often make good sports commentators.
10. Television soap operas have ridiculous plots.

# 10.4b Effectiveness

## Offering Genuine Evidence

Always examine your argument to make sure that you actually have presented evidence. You must do more than merely tell your reader that your position is correct. You must present genuine evidence to show that your position is correct.

The following paragraph seems to offer evidence to support its position statement. Actually, it contains only sentences that repeat the position stated in the first sentence.

INEFFECTIVE ARGUMENT

Position
statement

Most people today do not work as hard as the early pioneers did. The pioneers were extremely hard-working individuals. Their workload was consid-

Position
repeated

erably heavier than ours; the average pioneer had to work much harder than we do. Our workload is mere play when compared to that of the pioneers.

The writer is not likely to persuade the reader simply by repeating the position. The paragraph becomes effective when it contains genuine evidence, as the following revised version does.

EFFECTIVE ARGUMENT

Position
statement

Evidence

Most people today do not work as hard as the early pioneers did. Pioneer men and women, and sometimes even children, regularly worked from sunrise to sunset. Often their work involved heavy manual labor. Today, the average workweek is forty hours or less, and such machines as cranes and tractors are available to do the really backbreaking jobs. Most pioneer families had to rely on their own labor for necessities: they had to hunt and grow their own food, build their own houses, and make their own clothes. They did for themselves what we today usually have others do for us. Although present-day Americans are hard workers, we are not the toilers that the pioneers were. We do not have to be.

## Checking Evidence for Relevance and Completeness

When you present evidence, make sure that you do not include unrelated points that will distract your reader's attention from your position. Make sure, too, that you do not weaken your argument by omitting important pieces of evidence from your argument.

The following argument is not effective because it contains unrelated information and ignores important evidence.

INEFFECTIVE ARGUMENT

Position
statement

The State Water Project Board should approve the county's proposed dam project, which will create a new water supply for the county. Other county

Unrelated
information

Evidence

projects also need approval by state boards. The airport runways need to be resurfaced, and sections of
the sewer system need to be repaired. The proposed
dam project satisfies all county and state environmental standards; therefore, it will not harm the land or
the wildlife in the area. Because 80 percent of the
voters in the county approved construction of the
dam, public financing for the project will be easy to
obtain. By approving the dam project, the board will
perform a real service for the residents of the county.

The information about the other proposed county projects
distracts the reader's attention from the dam project, the real subject
of the argument. Also, because the writer does not explain why the
new dam is needed, the argument is not strong. The following revised
paragraph is more effective.

EFFECTIVE ARGUMENT

Position
statement

Clarifying
remark

More evidence

The State Water Project Board should approve
the county's proposed dam project, which will create
a new water supply for the county. The new water
supply is needed badly because the county population
has doubled in the last ten years. In its annual report, the County Water Commission stated that the
local demand for water already exceeds the supply.
The proposed dam project satisfies all county and
state environmental standards; therefore, it will not
harm the land or the wildlife in the area. Because 80
percent of the voters in the county approved construction of the dam, public financing for the project
will be easy to obtain. By approving the dam project,
the board will perform a real service for the residents
of the county.

The revised argument is effective for three reasons: (1) the
clarifying remark explains why the dam is needed; (2) additional
evidence is provided; (3) no unrelated information is included.

**Exercise 2  Prewriting: Evidence**  On your paper, label each of the lettered statements. Write *Supports* if the statement gives evidence for the position statement. Write *Repeats* if the statement merely repeats the position statement. Write *Not related* if the statement does not relate to the position statement.

1. *Position statement:* Some of the commercials shown on television are an insult to the intelligence of the viewers.
   a. Rather than discuss the merits of their products, sponsors often rely on gimmicks.
   b. Most of the commercials are absurd.
   c. Radio commercials are no better than television commercials.
   d. Many automobile commercials suggest that new cars and beautiful people go together.
   e. Commercials do not interest intelligent people.
   f. Many of the television programs are as insulting as the commercials.
   g. Some commercials work on the principle that people may buy a product if it is shown talking like a person.
   h. The idea behind commercials that use celebrities to endorse products apparently is "What is good enough for them is good enough for everyone."

2. *Position statement:* The minimum wage should be lower for teen-agers than for adults.
   a. Some economists believe that a lower minimum wage for teen-agers would substantially reduce unemployment among teen-agers.
   b. Employers should be allowed to pay teen-agers a lower wage then they pay adults.
   c. Teen-agers usually are not the principal breadwinners in their families and, thus, do not need as high a salary as adults do.
   d. Teen-agers also should be taxed at a lower rate than adults are.
   e. Work experience is more important for some teen-agers than their hourly wage is.

## 10.4c  Sound Reasoning

The final step in revising your argument is identifying and eliminating **fallacies,** or unsound reasoning. Evidence based on false associations between causes and effects and evidence based on the character of a speaker are two fallacies that you should avoid.

## False Association
## Between Causes and Effects

Much of the reasoning that you do involves causes and effects. For example, when you see dark thunderclouds gathering overhead, you conclude that a storm is about to occur. In assuming this, you reason from a cause (clouds) to an effect (storm). You can also reason from an effect to a cause. For example, if you see that the ground and trees are wet in the morning (effect), you can conclude that it rained during the night (cause).

You make a false association between a cause and an effect, however, if you conclude that because one event occurs after another event, the first event must be the cause of the second event.

FALSE ASSOCIATION

> Our school football team had a winning record this year be-
> cause Coach Bell introduced a weightlifting program for the
> players last summer. Before Coach Bell started the program,
> we had four consecutive losing seasons.

In this unsound reasoning, the writer concludes that the weight-lifting program must have been the cause of the team's success. The reasoning contains a fallacy because it ignores the possibility that other events or conditions may have caused the winning season. For example, the team may have had more talented players, may have competed against weaker teams, or may have used better strategies than in previous years. To establish that the weightlifting program was the real cause of the team's improvement, the writer would need to explain the specific ways in which the program helped the players to improve. The writer would also need to account for other possible causes by showing that other factors remained the same.

To revise arguments based on false associations between causes and effects, you must demonstrate how one event or person caused something to happen.

## Argument from Character

In your argument you may decide to present the opinion of an expert on your topic. Such an opinion should be judged by its content, not by the character or the experience of the expert. In the following example, the writer judges an opinion by the character and the experience of the person who holds the opinion. The example shows the fallacy of arguing from character.

ARGUMENT FROM CHARACTER

> According to Major George Washburn, the officer-retirement program should receive greater funding. Major Washburn has served with distinction in two wars. If he says that the retirement program should have more money, then it should have more money.

The fact that Major Washburn served with distinction in two wars does not necessarily mean that his views on the officer-retirement program are correct. His army record, good or bad, has no bearing on the correctness of his views. There is only one way to determine the truth of Major Washburn's position, and that is to examine the position itself. Be sure to examine the content of all opinions presented in your argument.

**Exercise 3   Prewriting: Sound Reasoning**   On your paper, list the number of each group of sentences that contains a fallacy. Identify the fallacy by writing *False association* or *Argument from character*.

1. In his campaign speech, the mayor said that he could clean up and modernize the city parks at a low cost. How can we believe him when he does not even keep his own back yard in good condition?

2. The state received more snow than usual this winter, and temperatures were colder than usual. The frozen moisture in the soil caused the soil to expand. Then the expanding soil caused many roads to crack and buckle.

3. The bus driver said that she would pick up the team at three o'clock. How can we believe someone who was late to her son's baseball game?

4. The transportation director received a pay raise last month. That pay raise caused the bus fares to go up this month.

5. Amy estimated that it will take us three hours to drive to Baltimore. Her estimate cannot be believed, however. Last fall she was wrong about how long it would take us to pack the car with our luggage.

6. Mario used the tape recorder last week, and now the rewind mechanism does not work correctly. Mario must have broken the mechanism.

7. Jack sang well in the school play last week. The director of the Little Theater heard Jack and was so impressed that he offered Jack a role in the musical that he is staging.

8. The building inspector said that the warehouse is not safe. He is correct. There are cracks in the main supports and weak spots in the floors.

9. The company's new president began work in January. The company went bankrupt in July. The new president must have caused the bankruptcy.

10. The field hockey players claim that they need new equipment. They are right, because their sticks are broken, and most of the material on their shin guards has worn away.

**Assignment   Revising**   Rewrite the following paragraph. To revise it, make sweeping statements more moderate, remove supporting sentences that do not relate to the position statement or merely restate it, and correct unsound reasoning.

> Using heat collected by the sun is the best way of heating houses. Bill Messner, who owns a solar heating store, claims that solar heat can be used for much of the year in many parts of the country. Solar heat is the best type of heat. Houses with solar furnaces need only small conventional furnaces as a back-up during extended cloudy periods. Because the use of solar energy reduces the amount of fuel needed for home heating, homeowners spend nothing on heating costs once their solar furnace systems are paid for. The Olson family installed solar heating last fall. That is the only way to explain why their heating bill for the winter was only half as large as it was the year before. Using extra insulation and caulking windows also reduce heating costs. Furthermore, because more than one quarter of the world's fuel is used for heating, the

decreased use of fuel allowed by solar heating could completely solve the energy crisis. All sensible homeowners will help themselves and the world by using solar heating.

**Continuing Assignment Revising** Revise the persuasive paragraph that you wrote for the Continuing Assignment on page 395. Concentrate on moderation, effectiveness, and sound reasoning.

## Assignment Checklist

Check your assignments for the following points:

1. Did you revise sweeping statements to make them more moderate?
2. Did you eliminate supporting sentences that merely repeat the position statement?
3. Did you eliminate points that do not relate to your position statement?
4. Did you add any important pieces of evidence that were missing from your argument?
5. Did you eliminate fallacies from your argument?
6. Did you proofread your argument for correct grammar, usage, spelling, and punctuation?

**Do You Want to Be Your Own Boss?**
**A Persuasive Composition**

Situation:   The American Business Association is offering a prize for the best persuasive composition on either of two topics: "Being Your Own Boss" or "Working for a Boss." As a contestant, you will write either about the benefits of running your own business or about the benefits of working for someone else who is the boss. To help you decide which position to take, you have typed lists of information that show the advantages of each situation. As you write your composition, you will keep in mind the following information.

**Writer:**     you as a contestant
**Audience:**   contest judges
**Topic:**      being, or not being, your own boss
**Purpose:**    to present an opinion persuasively, in a three-paragraph composition

Directions:   To plan and write your persuasive composition, follow these steps.

   *Step 1.* Read the lists on the facing page. Choose the position that is more appealing to you.

   *Step 2.* On a separate piece of paper, expand the list for the position that you have chosen.

   *Step 3.* Using your expanded list, choose the facts that seem to provide the strongest support for your position. If you can think of an example to illustrate each fact, make a note of it.

(Continue on page 408.)

# Unit Assignments

**Assignment 1**   Select one improvement that you think is needed in your school. Write a persuasive paragraph that argues for the improvement. Write the paragraph for a specific audience: the school administration, a parent committee, the teachers, or other students.

**Assignment 2**   Select a movie that you have seen recently, and write one or more paragraphs to persuade a friend to see the movie. Before you begin writing, list the reasons that you think will be persuasive. You will probably consider such elements of the movie as story, cast, acting, photography, and special effects. Use these reasons as evidence in your paragraph.

**Assignment 3**   Write one or more persuasive paragraphs that recommend a candidate for a local, state, or federal office. Write for an audience of voters. Gather as many facts as you can about the candidate and use them as evidence in your composition. If you wish, write your paragraph(s) about a fictional candidate.

**Assignment 4**   Choose an issue—local, state, national, or international—that has been in the news recently. Write one or more persuasive paragraphs that support the side that you oppose. Since you are writing for the side that you oppose, consider yourself the audience for your writing.

**Assignment 5**   Write one or more persuasive paragraphs in which you take a position on whether professional athletes should be allowed to compete in the Olympic games. Write for an audience of sports fans.

## Revising Your Assignments

For help in revising a persuasive paragraph or composition, consult the Checklist for Revision on the last page of this book.

# Unit Tests

## Test 1

**A.** Number your paper from 1 to 5. Next to each number, write *True* if the sentence is true or *False* if it is false.

1. You should judge an opinion by the character of the person who presents it.
2. In persuasive writing, your concluding sentence may recommend an action based on your position.
3. A suitable opinion for persuasive writing is a view that is shared by everyone.
4. In persuasive writing, your task is to convince your readers that your opinion is correct.
5. Before you begin writing an argument, you should ask yourself how your audience will probably react to your opinion.

**B.** Number your paper from 6 to 10. Next to each number, write the letter of the term that correctly completes the sentence. You will use all but one of the items.

    a. clarifying remark    d. position statement
    b. fact    e. argument
    c. fallacies    f. sweeping statements

6. When you revise an argument, you should make __?__ more moderate.
7. A(n) __?__ is a series of logically connected sentences that state a position and present reasons that support it.
8. A(n) __?__ is something that is known to be true or that can be shown to be true by observation, measurement, or research.
9. You should revise your argument to eliminate __?__, or unsound reasoning.
10. Your __?__ tells what you will attempt to show in your argument.

**C.** Number your paper from 11 to 15. Next to each number, write the letter of the item that correctly answers the question.

11. Which of the following is an opinion that advises?
    a. The letter will be delayed if there is a postal strike.
    b. The ZIP code system is complicated.

c. The postal system should be improved so that mail sent between any two cities in the country is delivered in one day.

d. In the United States, 25 billion stamps are issued yearly.

12. Which of the following is a fact?
a. Henrik Ibsen wrote the play *A Doll's House.*

b. *A Doll's House,* written in 1879, is exceptionally moving.

c. This year's production of *A Doll's House* will be a success.

d. You should see *A Doll's House* at the Playhouse.

13. Which of the following is a suitable opinion for persuasive writing?
a. Rock music is better than country music.

b. The buses should run more frequently during rush hours.

c. I have a feeling that I will find a job.

d. Drivers should obey the traffic rules.

14. Which of the following statements combines fact and opinion?
a. The newspaper contains coupons on pages 11 through 16.

b. Newspaper coupons will be used more often if prices increase.

c. People should use newspaper coupons more than they do.

d. Coupons appear regularly on Saturday in our superb newspaper.

15. Which of the following contains an argument from character?
a. Ben's advice to buy the car was wrong. The car stopped running after two weeks.

b. Ben's advice about buying a car cannot be trusted because Ben has never bought a car.

c. Ben is willing to give you advice about buying a car.

d. Ben's advice about buying a car is almost always good.

# Test 2

Choose one of the Unit Assignments. Write the assignment as directed and hand it in to your teacher.

# Unit 11

## _Writing an Essay_

---

## *Unit Preview*

When you write an **essay,** your purpose is to share an idea, an observation, an incident, or an opinion with your reader. In an essay you present your own view of something. Although you may do some reading before you plan and write an essay, it should be about a topic to which you can bring your own experience. Essays are usually two to six pages long.

Every essay has a certain form: an introductory paragraph that presents the topic, body paragraphs in which the topic is developed, and a concluding paragraph. The tone of an essay, however, can range from serious to light.

The following paragraph introduces an essay.

> It was just a house, at least physically, but to my child's mind it was much more. To me it was alive, almost human in its entirety. It was my grandparents' house, reflecting the moods, ideas, and emotions of the two who inhabited it. They made it alive. They were one, a chain unbroken, inextricably linked. They gave each other strength, which was released in joyful exuberance throughout the house. They had kept their home all through the hunger and strife of the Great Depression, through the times when Petaluma was no longer a chicken-farming community. It was their character and love of life and all life had to offer that brought the house alive to me.

> *Deborah Eisenstein, Mira Costa High School*
> *Manhattan Beach, California*

**For Analysis**  On your paper, answer the following questions about the paragraph.

1. What is the topic of the essay that the paragraph introduces?
2. What is the writer's purpose?
3. Is the tone of the essay likely to be serious or humorous?

In analyzing the topic, purpose, and tone of one essay, you have begun to consider various aspects of the essay form. As you plan and write an essay during your study of this unit, you will follow the three steps of the writing process: prewriting, writing, and revising.

# 11.1  Selecting and Limiting a Topic

A well-chosen topic is the basis of a successful essay. You can develop your topic by exposition, description, narration, or persuasion. For example, you might explain why you like acting in plays. You might describe the community in which you live. You might narrate an incident that made you feel proud, or you might attempt to persuade your reader that more career counseling should be available in your school. Often an essay includes two or more modes of writing. For example, in an essay that explains why you like acting in plays, you would probably narrate some of your acting experiences. You might also describe a stage set or a costume for a certain play. Almost always, however, a successful essay has a principal writing purpose. The principal writing purpose of the essay about acting in plays would be to explain.

## Selecting a Topic

When you begin to consider possible topics for your essay, think of subjects that interest you. If you enjoy your topic, you are likely to write an essay that is clear and interesting to your reader. You will probably select your essay topic from two sources: your own experiences and your observations of the world around you. Even if an essay includes some information that you have come across in your reading, it should not be based primarily on research.

You may find that no topic comes to mind quickly. If so, ask yourself the following questions. Examine the way in which possible answers to the questions lead to writing topics.

1. What do I know most about?
   *Possible answer:* Astronomy

2. What do I care about that I would like to share with a reader?
   *Possible answer:* Swimming

3. What have I seen or experienced that I would like to write about?
   *Possible answer:* My trip to Washington, D.C.

4. Have any of my experiences given me an idea about the kind of future that I would like for myself?
   *Possible answer:* Singing in a chorus

5. Who have been the most important people in my life?
   *Possible answer:* My basketball coach

6. What issues and situations do I feel strongly about?
   *Possible answer:* The budget for environmental research

7. What is important in life?
   *Possible answer:* Time spent with family members

## Limiting a Topic

After choosing a topic, consider whether you can develop it fully in two to six pages. Many topics are too general. You can make general topics suitable by limiting them—that is, by making them more specific.

The following examples show how four of the general topics that were found by answering the preceding questions might be limited.

*General topic:* Astronomy
*Limited topic:* The first time that I looked through a telescope

*General topic:* My trip to Washington, D.C.
*Limited topic:* Seeing the *Spirit of St. Louis* in the National Air and Space Museum

*General topic:* Singing in a chorus
*Limited topic:* Why I would like a career in music

*General topic:* The budget for environmental research
*Limited topic:* The budget for research on water pollution should (should not) be increased.

When you decide on a limited topic, you often arrive at a purpose for writing at the same time. Study the following examples of limited topics and principal writing purposes.

*Limited topic:* The first time that I looked through a telescope
*Purpose:* To narrate

*Limited topic:* Seeing the *Spirit of St. Louis* in the National Air and Space Museum
*Purpose:* To describe

*Limited topic:* Why I would like a career in music
*Purpose:* To explain

*Limited topic:* The budget for research on water pollution should (should not) be increased.
*Purpose:* To persuade

A writing purpose serves to focus an essay. As you prepare to write your own essay, remember that every sentence in it must carry out your principal writing purpose.

**Exercise 1  Prewriting: Essay Topics**   Read the following list of topics. On your paper write *Suitable* if the corresponding topic is suitable for an essay. Write *Unsuitable* if the topic is not suitable.

1. My first piano lesson
2. The history of the piano
3. What I learned as a camp counselor
4. The proposed law about jaywalking should be passed.
5. The benefits of scouting
6. The life of John James Audubon
7. The pyramids

8. The development of television
9. Why people enjoy home video games
10. The national park system

**Exercise 2   Prewriting: Limiting Topics**   On your paper, write a limited topic and a principal writing purpose for each of the following general topics.

| | |
|---|---|
| **SAMPLE** | Vacations |
| **ANSWER** | *Limited topic:* My summer on a ranch |
| | *Purpose:* To narrate |

1. Jobs
2. Conserving energy
3. The world in 2000
4. Relatives
5. Music

6. Pen pals
7. White-water rafting
8. Driving
9. Sports
10. Clothing styles

**Assignment   Prewriting**   *Step 1:* List four essay topics. *Step 2:* Limit each topic so that it could be developed adequately in two to six pages. Write the four limited topics on your paper. *Step 3:* List a principal writing purpose for each limited topic.

**Continuing Assignment   Prewriting**   *Step 1:* List five topics for an essay of two to six pages. Choose topics that you would enjoy writing about. *Step 2:* Limit the topics as needed. Copy the limited topics on your paper. *Step 3:* List a principal writing purpose for an essay based on each limited topic. *Step 4:* Put a check mark beside the topic that you like best. Save your paper.

## Assignment Checklist

Check your assignments for the following points:

✔ 1. Did you choose essay topics to which you can bring your own experience?
✔ 2. Did you limit the topics as needed?
✔ 3. Did you list the principal writing purpose for your topics?

# 11.2 Determining Your Audience, Tone, and Style

Just as you must know the purpose of your essay, you should also have clearly in mind the audience for whom you are writing. Then you will be able to adopt a tone and a style that are well suited to your audience and purpose.

## 11.2a Identifying the Audience

When you write, you write for an audience, or reader. Address your writing to anyone who may be interested in what you have to say. There will be times when you will have to write for a special audience, such as an employer or a college admissions committee. Keep that audience in mind as you write. If you write an essay for your local historical society, for example, you can expect the members to be interested in details about your community, not in details about a distant town.

The following passage, which begins an essay, illustrates how details and language can be carefully chosen to appeal to a particular audience. The writer addresses those who do not ride school buses.

**Model**

> It's not easy riding a bus. Now before you nonriders scoff and say that *you* walk seven miles to school, I'd like to say that the plight of the school-bus rider has been so overlooked (or so glossed over) that most people visualize it as a luxurious drive, in heated and spacious comfort, from a warm and covered bus stop to an ideal school. But it's time to dispel all the myths and misrepresentations about riding a bus that have collected over the years.
>
> *Catherine Salton, Ann Arbor Huron High School*
> *Ann Arbor, Michigan*

By identifying a specific audience and writing for that audience, the writer creates an interesting beginning for her essay, in which she humorously describes the inconveniences of traveling in a school bus.

**417**

By addressing her readers as "you," she creates a close relationship with them. The use of "you" is appropriate here, but it would not be in a more formal essay.

**Exercise 1   Prewriting: Audience**   On your paper, list the audience that the writer of the following paragraph is addressing. The paragraph introduces an essay.

> To most viewers *Monday Night Football* is a showcase for the sport of football. To me, however, it is an attempt to create a televised entertainment package that is loosely centered on a football game. The result is a combination of commentators, instant replays, grunts, half time, and football, all of which total about three hours.
>
> (*Adapted*)
> Helen Norton, Mercer Island High School
> Mercer Island, Washington

## 11.2b Selecting the Tone

**Tone** is inseparable from purpose and audience; it is the attitude that a writer conveys about a topic and an audience. Audience, purpose, and tone must work together. For example, in the paragraph from an essay about bus riding, the writer's principal purpose is to explain in an entertaining way, and the tone is appropriately humorous and personal.

You may choose from a wide variety of tones: serious, ironic, affectionate, critical, nostalgic, light, humorous, and so on. In every case, your tone must be appropriate for your topic. It is possible, however, to handle a serious topic lightly or humorously if the writing is skilled and tasteful.

The point of view (*page 358*) that you choose affects the tone of your writing. You can create a close relationship with the reader by using a first-person point of view. The more you reveal your personality to the reader, the closer the relationship is and the more personal the tone is. In contrast, a third-person point of view, which avoids the use of *I*, keeps a distance between you and the reader. By adopting a more distant tone, you emphasize the subject. Whatever tone you adopt, you must maintain it consistently throughout the essay to avoid confusing your reader.

**Exercise 2  Prewriting: Tone**   Each of the following paragraphs introduces an essay. On your paper, write *Serious* or *Light* to identify the tone of each essay.

PARAGRAPH 1

> In the time since the near-meltdown at the Three Mile Island nuclear plant, approximately twenty-five miles from my home, the safety of nuclear energy has become such a widely discussed topic that it is all too easy to forget the local reactions to the accident itself. . . . The bubble terrified me in a way nothing ever had before; for the first time in my life, I was to be the direct victim of a situation over which I had no control and of which I had very little knowledge.

> *Michelle Traina, J. P. McCaskey High School*
> *Lancaster, Pennsylvania*

PARAGRAPH 2

> I used to belong to the Procrastinators' Club of America. Thinking I was immortal, I postponed every possible responsibility, duty, and event in my life until its deadline. My general theory on fulfilling obligations was "There's no time like the future," a slight alteration of an ancient maxim.

> *Julie Breene, Country Day School of the Sacred Heart*
> *Bryn Mawr, Pennsylvania*

## 11.2c  Considering the Style

Two people will express the same thought in different ways. That difference is a difference of style. **Style** in writing is the unique way in which each person puts his or her ideas into words. As you write, you choose particular words, and you put words together in a particular order. Since it is the result of many choices, you can control your style by making the choices purposefully.

## Diction

One aspect of style is **diction,** the choice of words to express your thoughts. When you select one word instead of another, you are controlling your writing style. In choosing a word, you must consider its **connotations,** ideas associated with the word, as well as its **denotations,** or literal meanings. Consider the words *sincere* and *frank,* for example. Both words denote honesty and truthfulness, but *frank* connotes forthrightness of manner, sometimes to the point of bluntness. Be sure that the words you choose have the connotations that you intend. (See also pages 584–585 in Unit 16.)

Also be aware of the level of your diction—that is, its degree of formality. Your diction should be consistent throughout a composition. Consider the three levels of diction.

**Casual.**   A casual level of diction includes many contractions, a number of words labeled by a dictionary as informal or colloquial (such as *slob,* meaning "sloppy person"), and some slang. Because casual diction resembles informal speech, it is usually reserved for writing letters to friends and for writing dialogue in fiction.

**Formal.**   A formal level of diction is at the opposite end of the range. It includes many words that are more common in writing than in speech. The vocabulary is large. Formal diction includes no words labeled by a dictionary as informal or colloquial, no slang, and very few contractions. Formal diction is most appropriate for research papers, the most serious essays (including literary essays), some business reports, and some speeches and persuasive writing.

**Informal.**   Most writing is informal. This level of diction may contain a few contractions and a few words labeled by a dictionary as informal or colloquial. As a rule, you should use such words in informal writing only when no other words convey the meaning as well. The vocabulary of informal diction includes both simple and complex words. In your school writing assignments, you should aim for a level of diction in the range between informal and formal.

## Sentence Length and Complexity

The length and structure of your sentences, the other part of your writing style, should vary from situation to situation. Short, simple sentences create one impression; longer, more sophisticated sentences create another. Generally, informal writing calls for short and medium-length sentences that may be simple, compound, or complex (*pages 90–91*). In the following example, the brevity and simplicity of the sentences suits the nature of the experience that the writer describes.

### Model

> The day crawled out of bed on the wrong side, not ice-cold but cold-cold. I faced the unpleasant job of washing my two cows in the cold, open air at the washrack. My first cow, Indian Creek Hero Renee, behaved very nicely. She even seemed to enjoy her bath. To my second cow, Rose, the bath was a farce from the start.
>
> *Todd Nichols, Saluda High School*
> *Saluda, South Carolina*

In contrast to the style of the preceding paragraph is a more formal style created by longer sentences that have varied and sometimes intricate structures. The shifts, from brief to lengthy and from simple to intricate sentences will occur almost naturally when you write about a topic that can be treated formally. The writer of the following paragraph presents a complex idea.

### Model

> Trapped inside our own bodies and minds, we communicate mainly by words. Words are our symbols of thoughts, ideas, sights, sounds, mundane objects, and deepest feelings. Though a single word may sometimes fail to communicate all that we mean, a combination of powerful words in compelling order can evoke genuine emotions or understanding in almost anyone. The English language is rich and varied, different threads from other languages dead and living running through its cloth, but this language is limited. Other languages constantly express ideas that cannot be translated into English: anyone who tries must lose somewhere the power or grace of the thought or phrase.
>
> *Jayne Williams, Los Gatos High School*
> *Los Gatos, California*

As she explains her insight about language, the writer of this paragraph uses sentences that create a fairly formal style. Two of her sentences are long, and some of her sentences include such structures as subordinate clauses and participial phrases.

**Exercise 3  Writing: Style**   Rewrite the following paragraph, making its style more formal. Be careful to keep your writing clear and direct.

> We had a great week in San Juan. Because we swam at the beach every day, we all got super tans. We stayed at a hotel that used to be a convent. It's in the old part of the city. We got good at using public transportation. Buses in Puerto Rico are called *guaguas*. We also got good at ordering from Spanish menus. Even Dad got over being shy about trying his Spanish with a Cleveland accent.

**Assignment 1  Writing**   Select one of the following topics and its two accompanying audiences. Write two separate paragraphs on the topic, one for the first audience and then one for the second audience. Although you should include essentially the same information in both paragraphs, you should present that information in a different way to each audience.

1. How to keep physically fit
   *Audience A:* Athletes, male and female
   *Audience B:* Nonathletes, male and female
2. The latest fashions in clothing
   *Audience A:* Teen-agers
   *Audience B:* Adults
3. Why we must protect an endangered species (Select a particular animal if you wish.)
   *Audience A:* Hunters
   *Audience B:* Conservationists
4. Why you liked or disliked a particular book, film, or television program
   *Audience A:* Those who have also read or seen it
   *Audience B:* Those who have not read or seen it

✓ **Assignment 2** **Writing** Write two separate paragraphs on one of the following topics. Use a serious tone in one paragraph and a lighter, perhaps humorous, tone in the other. Assume that the paragraphs will be read by your teacher and a few classmates.

1. Eating chicken at a barbecue
2. Driving defensively
3. Choosing a political candidate
4. Avoiding accidents around the home
5. Following a diet

**Assignment 3** **Writing** Write three sentences about something that you would like to see happen. Make one sentence formal, another informal, and the third casual. Then rewrite each of the sentences, using another of the three levels of diction.

**Continuing Assignment** **Prewriting** Use your essay topic and its writing purpose from the Continuing Assignment on page 416. Add the following information to your paper and save the paper for later use.

1. The audience for whom you are writing the essay
2. The tone that is appropriate for that audience, for your topic, and for your purpose. (You may wish to use one or more of the following words to describe the tone: *ironic, affectionate, critical, nostalgic, light, serious, humorous.*)
3. The point of view (first-person or third-person) that you plan to use in the essay
4. The level of diction that you plan to use in the essay

### Assignment Checklist

Check your assignments for the following points:

✓ 1. Did you keep your audience in mind?
✓ 2. Did you choose a tone and a point of view that are appropriate for the topic, purpose, and audience?
✓ 3. Did you consider the style: the level of diction and the length and structure of sentences?
✓ 4. Did you proofread your writing for correct grammar, usage, spelling, and punctuation?

# 11.3   Planning Your Essay

Writing an essay requires careful planning. You must first think through your topic to decide how you can best present it to your reader.

## 11.3a   Listing and Organizing the Ideas

Begin by listing all of the ideas that you might want to include in your essay. You may express the ideas in phrases or in complete sentences. Review your list, eliminating those ideas that do not relate directly to your topic.

Next, organize the ideas on your list. The first step is to divide them into main ideas and supporting details (ideas that further explain a main idea). Then arrange the groups of main ideas and supporting details in a logical order. Your topic will determine the order that you choose. Chronological order, spatial order, and the order of importance are three of the possibilities, just as they are when you organize the details of a single paragraph.

**Chronological Order.**   When you use chronological order, you present details or events in the order in which they occurred. This is the natural organization for a narrative essay.

**Spatial Order.**   When you use spatial order, you present details or objects in the order in which you see them—top to bottom, left to right, or back to front. This order is suitable for a descriptive essay.

**Order of Importance.**   When you use order of importance, you usually list the least important ideas first and build up to the most important ideas. Sometimes, however, you can give the most important idea first for special emphasis. This order works well for listing the points of an expository or persuasive essay.

**Other Methods of Organization.**   Sometimes you write an essay in which you compare and contrast aspects of a topic or explain the causes or effects of something. In such an essay, you use a larger pattern of development that includes one or more of the three basic types of organization that you have just reviewed.

1. *Comparison and Contrast.* You use this pattern of development to make clear the similarities and the differences between two subjects that you are discussing. For example, you might compare and contrast the pleasures of playing a musical instrument and the pleasures of listening to music. You could discuss similarities in one paragraph and differences in another paragraph, or you could discuss similarities and differences one at a time in a point-by-point discussion of the topic. With either method, you could arrange the differences or similarities in the order of their importance.

2. *Cause and Effect.* You use this pattern of development to explain the causes of an event or a situation or to explain its effects. For example, you might discuss the effects of a new business or industry on your community. You could list the effects in chronological order or in order of importance.

**Exercise 1** **Prewriting: Relevant Details** Following are two topics and a list of ideas about each topic. On your paper, write the ideas that are relevant to each topic. Then arrange the ideas in a logical order.

1. *Topic:* The benefits of joining our field hockey team
   a. Value of exercise
   b. Learning teamwork
   c. Rules of the sport
   d. Accepting disappointment
   e. Making new friends
   f. Having fun
   g. Uniforms worn for hockey

2. *Topic:* The satisfactions of growing a vegetable garden
   a. Physical exercise
   b. Working outdoors
   c. Insects and rabbits can destroy a garden
   d. Eating the fruits of my labor
   e. Weeding should be done once a week
   f. Saving money on groceries

# 11.3b  Writing a Thesis Statement

Now write a **thesis statement,** the sentence in the first paragraph that states the topic and the purpose of your essay. Since the thesis statement is the most important sentence of the essay, its meaning must be precise. The following example illustrates how a vague or general thesis statement can be improved.

VAGUE STATEMENT
>Moving can be difficult.

PRECISE THESIS STATEMENT
>When a family has to move to a new community, every member suffers some hardships.

A thesis statement serves both you and your audience. It helps you to focus your essay, making it easier to plan. It helps the reader by making the subject and the direction of the essay clear from the outset.

When you plan an essay, you may find that you need to formulate a preliminary thesis statement early in the prewriting process to guide you as you list your ideas. You may not write the final version of the thesis statement until you are preparing your outline or until you are writing your introductory paragraph.

### Exercise 2    Prewriting/Revising: Thesis Statements

Rate each of the following thesis statements by writing *Precise* or *Vague* on your paper. If a thesis statement is vague, write a more precise statement.

>**SAMPLE**    Exercise builds character.
>
>**ANSWER**    *Vague.* I learned self-discipline when I became a runner.

1. Being in a club is interesting.
2. Being a teen-ager is not easy.
3. Sharing a room with my brother has taught me a good deal about cooperation.
4. My first part-time job taught me the meaning of hard work.
5. Vacations are happy times for families.

# 11.3c Outlining the Essay

After selecting and arranging ideas, prepare an outline, which will be your guide for writing your essay. An outline shows the sequence of ideas in your essay, their importance, and their relation to one another.

Most outlines have Roman-numeral headings for main ideas and capital-letter headings for supporting details. The main ideas are called **main headings,** and the supporting details are called **sub-headings.** You should use at least two capital-letter headings for each Roman-numeral heading that you wish to explain further. Use the Roman numeral *I* for the introduction, and the last Roman numeral for the conclusion.

In a **topic outline,** the most common type, the headings are not written as complete sentences. (See Section 13.4 in Unit 13 for a sample topic outline and for more information about outlining.) In a **sentence outline,** the headings are expressed as complete sentences. Sometimes a **rough outline,** a simple list of main points, is sufficient for a short essay, particularly a narrative or descriptive essay. Usually you write the thesis statement at the top of an outline.

The following example shows how you can organize an essay under a thesis statement in a rough outline. The actual essay appears on pages 431–433.

*Thesis statement:* I clearly remember the night Dad came home after being away from us for a whole year.

1. In the year he was gone, I learned new skills.
2. While he was away, the household atmosphere was like an unfinished portrait.
3. We tried to stay in touch by sending him rolls of photos, food, and numerous tapes.
4. When Mom told me Dad was coming home, I couldn't imagine what he would be like.
5. Mom spent a long time getting ready to meet him.
6. The time spent waiting for him seemed like an eternity.
7. My older brothers ran to meet Dad, but I could not move.
8. Then, when I sat in his lap and asked him to read to me, he cried and held me close.

**Exercise 3   Prewriting: Outlining**   Prepare a topic outline by arranging the following subheadings under the main headings that have been provided. Under each main heading you may vary the order of the subheadings as you wish. The finished outline should include all of the headings.

*Thesis statement:* If I can take driving lessons, it will help me and the rest of my family.

MAIN HEADINGS

       Introduction

       Help others in my family

       Help me to earn money

       Help me to have fun

       Conclusion

SUBHEADINGS

       Driving to visit friends across town

       Getting a morning job distributing newspapers to people with paper routes

       Driving family cats to veterinarian

       Getting Saturday job as delivery person for a store

       Driving to supermarket to do family's shopping

       Driving to football games in nearby towns

       Driving my brothers to meetings

       Driving to school dances

**Assignment   Prewriting**   *Step 1:* List ideas that would be appropriate for a brief essay in which you discuss something that you are thankful for. *Step 2:* Choose the ideas that you wish to use in your essay and then arrange them in what you feel is the strongest, most logical order. *Step 3:* Write an appropriate thesis statement. *Step 4:* Prepare an outline for the essay. You will use the outline as the basis of a brief practice essay that you will write as you study the remaining sections of this unit. Save your paper.

**Continuing Assignment   Prewriting**   *Step 1:* List ideas for the essay topic that you chose for the Continuing Assignment on page 423. *Step 2:* Divide the ideas into main ideas and supporting details, and arrange them in a logical order. *Step 3:* Write a thesis statement. *Step 4:* Using the list of ideas, prepare an outline for the main essay that you will write as you study this unit. Save your paper.

### Assignment Checklist

Check your assignments for the following points:

✔ 1. Did you list ideas related to your topic?
✔ 2. Did you arrange your ideas in a logical order?
✔ 3. Did you write a thesis statement that precisely expresses the topic and the purpose of your essay?
✔ 4. Did you prepare an outline in which the ideas are arranged in an effective, logical order?
✔ 5. Did you place your thesis statement at the top of your outline?

# 11.4 Writing Your First Draft

Once you have planned your essay, you are ready to write your first draft. You should concentrate on putting your ideas on paper in the same order in which they are developed in your outline. Do not spend a long time now trying to choose just the right word. You can make changes in wording when you revise your draft.

## 11.4a Writing the Introductory Paragraph

Because it creates the reader's first impression, the introduction is a very important paragraph in any essay. An introduction should be brief, yet in it you should do three things.

### Strategies

1. *Establish the topic and the purpose of your essay.* In your thesis statement, make clear what you are going to write about and indicate what your principal writing purpose is. You may place your thesis statement anywhere in the introductory paragraph; usually it is placed at the end.

2. *Establish the tone of your essay.* Use the tone that you will continue to use throughout the essay. Your tone should suit your topic, your audience, and your purpose. Also establish the point of view that you will maintain in the rest of the essay.

3. *Capture your reader's interest.* There are several ways of doing so. You can use a quotation or an example, or you can raise a question that you will answer in the body of the essay. You can also preview the essay, briefly mentioning the main points. If you are narrating a personal experience, you can arouse interest simply by making it clear that the experience was unusual, humorous, or important to you.

**Exercise 1 Writing: The Introductory Paragraph** Write an introductory paragraph based on the following thesis statement and main headings from an outline. Use a serious tone and the first-person point of view.

*Thesis statement:* I will benefit from taking a business course during the summer vacation.

   I. Introduction
  II. Skills for getting a job
 III. Information about spending wisely and keeping track of my own money
 IV. Conclusion

## 11.4b Writing the Body Paragraphs

The body paragraphs are the core of an essay. In them you develop the topic that you present in the introductory paragraph. Your main task is to put together sentences that present the ideas in the outline and make clear to the reader how they are related. Sometimes, particularly in a narrative essay, you will need to add details.

## Following the Outline

Before you begin to write the body paragraphs, decide how much attention you want to give to each main heading of the outline. In a single paragraph, you can usually cover a main heading with its subheadings. If there are many subheadings under a main heading, however, you may need to use two or even three paragraphs. Use the main headings in your outline to help you write the topic sentence of each paragraph.

The following narrative essay is based on the rough outline that appears on page 427.

### Model

Home from Vietnam

I don't really know all that happened so many years ago. I recall only disjointed fragments and stories that others have told me. I clearly remember, however, the night Dad came home after being away from us for a whole year.

Dad spent the year in Ton Son-Nhut Air Base, South Vietnam, and Ubon Rachitani Air Base, Thailand. While he was gone, I learned to tie knots in my shoelaces, to work zippers and snaps, and to perform a wealth of other feats.

Even though Mom didn't work that year, the household atmosphere was rather like an unfinished portrait, where the artist has completed the background but not yet put in the subject. The Brobdingnagian clothes hovered among the rafters in my mother's closet, and the overgrown white spiked golf shoes fairly echoed when I put my tiny feet inside them and tried to lift them off the floor. At bedtime the Grinch muttered empty threats about Christmas, which for us meant mailing packages and receiving packages from a stranger.

Most people send letters to someone far away, but that was the least of what we sent to my father. We would send roll upon roll of snapshots. One depicted my brother trying to roll a snowball bigger than his three-year-old self while I tried to catch snowflakes on my tongue; another showed my brother looking at me with a neatly tied bow in his hands while I looked at my hands, which held a tangled piece of string. There were many shots of the family.

In between snapshots we would send food, boxes of cookies, and homemade candy. Once we sent a box of beautiful baklava, which disintegrated into a sodden mass of honey and cardboard upon arrival, forcing my father to write back for identification.

By far the most important things we sent were the tapes. We would record ourselves on them and send one to Dad every ten days. Because I did not know who my father was, making these tapes made me feel small and lost. I never did say much of anything to the man I called Dad; after all, the aggregate of what I knew for certain about him was that he wore a blue, sometimes tan, uniform and had a deep, booming voice.

About a week before Christmas, my mother told us, "Your Daddy's coming home tonight, and you must be very good." I thought, "Dad's coming home tonight. Who is Dad? What will he be like?"

I spent all day imagining how he would look. A huge, hairy man in big combat boots would throw open the door and storm in. An angry man who knew that I didn't recognize him would stamp over the threshold and cut me with steely eyes. Another man would smile blankly at me and ask my name and age. An icily formidable being would silently materialize, and I would scream breathlessly. I wasn't at all sure that I wanted to meet this man called "Dad."

Mom prepared to go to the airport with the precision of an Apollo countdown, first shrouding herself in a mist of hair spray, then gyrating into a back-zippered orange dress and navy blue pumps. Finally, she formed a face with red-brown cheeks, black-rimmed eyes with eyebrows like commas lying down, and a red slash of a mouth that jumped out at me and made me a little afraid. As she gave me a hug, I hated the heavy, lingering, sweet-sticky smell of her perfume and hair spray.

During the quiet eternity that passed between the time my mother left and returned, we tried to dispel the tension that formed like ice on a pool of water. My brother Eric did every last bit of his homework, practiced on his French horn, and read me my pop-up storybook—twice. Kermit, my other brother, took apart, assembled, took apart, and reassembled all of his puzzles and then played with his airplanes until he tired of them.

As the silence threatened to swallow me up in sleep, the door opened. A gust of cold, damp air blew across my face while Eric and Kermit both got up to see the man who was my father. I could not move.

While the man was hefting Eric into the air to see how he had grown, I glanced warily at him from the corner of my eye. He was wearing a tan uniform with short sleeves like those big clothes in the closet, and he was tall, too. His big booming "Hello" almost knocked me over.

Then the man, Kermit, Mom, and Eric all came into the living room, where I was on the floor with my Dr. Seuss book about the Grinch who stole Christmas. After people had made themselves comfortable on the middle-aged, dusty-brown overstuffed sofa and easy chair, the chatter died down and the silence stole in.

Because one glance had aroused my curiosity, I took my book and went to the man in the easy chair. He had black hair, rather straight heavy black eyebrows, and a big straight nose that made him look like my Sam the Eagle puppet. He had funny grayish-yellow eyes with circles under them and a coffee stain on his knee. Quietly he sat looking at me, neither smiling nor frowning. He was not at all as I had imagined him to be, and so far he hadn't bitten my head off. As I carefully climbed into his lap and opened my book, he said nothing. I gravely opened my book, saying, "Read me a. . . . " Looking up, I noticed the tears forming in the corners of his eyes and trickling down his cheeks as he held me close.

*Hope Kerley, Deering High School*
*Portland, Maine*

The writer uses more than one paragraph to cover some of the outline points. For example, Point 3 of the outline on page 427 is covered in three separate paragraphs about photographs, food, and tape recordings.

## Making Transitions

In writing the body paragraphs, pay particular attention to the transitional devices that give coherence to any composition. The first sentence of the second paragraph should follow the thought of the thesis statement in the introductory paragraph. In the same way, the opening sentences of succeeding paragraphs should be linked with the paragraphs that they follow. The other sentences in a paragraph should also follow one another logically.

To make your sentences flow smoothly, use transitional devices in the following ways.

## Strategies

1. *Repeat a key word or phrase from the previous paragraph.* For example, in the first sentence of the fifth paragraph of the model essay, *snapshots* echoes *shots* in the previous sentence.

2. *Use a pronoun to refer to a person or an idea in the previous sentence.* For example, in the second sentence of the second paragraph, *he* refers to *Dad* in the first sentence.

3. *Use transitional words and phrases.* Paragraphs in the model essay begin with such words as *During, As, While,* and *Then.* These words emphasize the chronological order.

**Exercise 2   Writing: Body Paragraphs**   Write two body paragraphs based on the following thesis statement and outline. Use transitional devices to make clear the flow of the ideas within and between the paragraphs.

*Thesis statement:* I found it difficult to decide what to do with my first paycheck from my restaurant job.

   I. Introduction
  II. What I wanted to do with the check
    A. Frame it
    B. Buy presents for my family
    C. Buy something for myself
 III. What I did do with the check
    A. Put half of money in bank
    B. Bought another uniform for work
    C. Bought a new toaster for my family
 IV. Conclusion

# 11.4c  Writing the Concluding Paragraph

The concluding paragraph should make your essay seem complete. Your purpose in writing this paragraph is to help the reader understand the full meaning of your essay. You may use one of four methods to end your essay.

1. *Summary.* You can summarize the main points made in the body of the essay. If you return to the main idea that you presented in the introduction, you should approach the idea from the larger perspective developed in the body of the essay.
2. *Final Idea.* You can present a final idea if you relate it clearly to the rest of your essay. A final idea must follow naturally from your main idea.
3. *Personal Reaction.* You can present your reaction to the topic of your essay. In an essay about a personal experience, you can make clear what the experience meant to you.
4. *Suggested Solution.* If your essay is about a problem or issue, you can suggest a solution. Your solution may be that your audience should take some kind of action.

Occasionally a descriptive or narrative essay does not need a separate concluding paragraph. The description or experience speaks for itself, as in the model essay that you read. In such a case, the final point of the description or the final incident of the experience may serve as the conclusion to the essay.

The following paragraph is the concluding paragraph for an essay about the writer's experience with gardening.

### Model

Despite my knowledge and experience in dealing with problems, the birds, insects, and weather still sometimes take a heavy toll on the garden. I may feel disappointed seeing my labor wasted, but I never lose hope and give up. As human beings have done for centuries, I will continue stubbornly against all odds in my struggle to cultivate the soil and make the earth yield food.

*Alex Trotter, Albert Einstein High School*
*Silver Spring, Maryland*

The writer ends the essay with his personal reaction to his experience. He also explains how he will continue to react to his experience.

**Exercise 3   Prewriting: Concluding Paragraphs**   On your paper, write *Summary, Final idea, Personal reaction,* or *Suggested solution* to describe how the writer develops each of the following paragraphs.

PARAGRAPH 1

     Reading *The Grapes of Wrath* made me believe that our society needs to be improved. I know that a whole society cannot be changed with good intentions alone, but it can be changed with hard work and sacrifices. There are things that we can do through working in helping jobs, voting for new candidates, and donating time and money to make our society a better place in which to live. *The Grapes of Wrath* enabled me to see suffering. My upbringing enables me to see that we can alleviate suffering if we, as Americans, can see beyond our own needs and are willing to make sacrifices for the benefit of all.

*(Adapted)*
*Matt Patchell, Chico High School*
*Chico, California*

PARAGRAPH 2

     After the play ended and the lights came on, I remained seated and reviewed my experience. I decided that I loved plays. I also decided that I would like to be able to give others the same wonderful experience that I had enjoyed. Since then, I have performed in five plays and have discovered that I really enjoy acting. Seeing that play has changed my outlook on life and has given some direction to my life.

*Pamela Williams, Northside High School*
*Atlanta, Georgia*

**Assignment   Writing**   Use your thesis statement and outline for the practice essay about something that you are thankful for (*page 428*). Write the first draft of the essay. In your introductory paragraph, try to capture your reader's interest. Follow your outline as you write the body paragraphs, and conclude the essay with a summary, a final idea, a personal reaction, or a possible solution. Save your paper.

**Continuing Assignment** **Writing** Write the first draft of the main essay that you planned and outlined for the Continuing Assignment on page 428. Follow your outline and, as you write, keep in mind your thesis statement, principal writing purpose, and audience. Save your paper.

## Assignment Checklist

Check your **assignments** for the following points:

✔ 1. Did you **write an introductory** paragraph that includes a thesis statement, sets the tone of your essay, and introduces your topic in a way that should interest your reader?

✔ 2. Did you write body paragraphs that fully develop the ideas and relationships of the outline?

✔ 3. Did you write a concluding paragraph that makes clear the full meaning of your essay?

✔ 4. Did you use transitional devices to make your essay coherent?

✔ 5. Are all the sentences in your essay appropriate for your purpose and your audience?

# 11.5 Revising and Finishing Your Essay

When you have completed the first draft of an essay, you must revise it. When you revise an essay, you review it and rework it. Revising includes far more than correcting spelling and punctuation errors. You must look at your essay as your reader would to see whether the main ideas are understandable. You also must see whether you have used the best words and sentences to present your ideas. That is, you must consider both the content and the style of the essay.

If possible, wait a day or two before you revise your essay. When you reread it then, you will have a fresh outlook, and it will be easier to be critical of your own writing.

## Reviewing the Content

To make sure that each part of your essay says what you want it to say, review the essay for the following points. Use them as a guide to revision.

## Strategies

1. *Introductory Paragraph.* Make sure that you have clearly established your topic and purpose in the thesis statement and that your introduction will capture your reader's interest.

2. *Body Paragraphs.* Check for coherence. Be sure that you have developed your topic clearly and arranged your ideas logically.

3. *Concluding Paragraph.* Review your conclusion to make sure that it will leave your reader with a full understanding of your main idea.

4. *Unity.* Make sure that throughout the essay you have developed the idea presented in the thesis statement. Remove sentences that have little or nothing to do with the topic.

5. *Completeness.* Check to see whether any passages need further details or examples. If necessary, add new material to your sentences or write new sentences.

# Reviewing the Style

After you have reviewed the content of your essay, examine it again for the way in which you expressed your ideas. Check to be sure that the tone of your essay is consistently light or serious throughout the essay. Also make sure that you have maintained one point of view. Finally, as you reread the essay, review its style, using the following guidelines.

## Strategies

1. *Check the length and complexity of your sentences.* Be alert for sentences so complicated that your reader may fail to understand their meaning. You can often divide a long sentence into two more effective sentences. Also look for several short sentences close together; you may want to

combine them. Finally, be sure that the length and complexity of your sentences are appropriate to your topic and your purpose. You may find it helpful to review the section on style that appears earlier in this unit (*pages 419–422*).

2. *Check the level of diction in your writing.* Make sure that you have used a consistent level of diction that falls in the range between informal and formal.

3. *Examine your word choices.* Be sure that you have chosen words with appropriate denotations and connotations. Also be sure that all of your words are correct.

## Proofreading

Proofreading, reading your essay for errors, is the final step in revising. One part of proofreading is checking your essay for correct grammar and usage. For example, be sure that your composition contains no sentence fragments or run-on sentences. The rest of proofreading is checking your work for correct punctuation, capitalization, and spelling.

## Choosing a Title

After revising the first draft of your essay, select a title for it if you have not already done so. Your title should give an idea of what your essay is about, and it should sound interesting. For example, as a title for the model essay about the father's return from Vietnam, "My Father" would not have been specific enough. Keep in mind, too, that a title should not be so unusual that it sounds odd.

## Preparing the Finished Paper

When you have reviewed your essay and made revisions, you can prepare the finished paper. As you copy the paper, keep in mind that neatness and correctness will make a good impression on your reader. Proofread your finished paper to correct errors in copying.

You will find guidelines for preparing a final manuscript on page 217. Use them, with any alterations that your teacher suggests.

**Exercise   Revising: The Essay**   On your paper, rewrite the following brief essay, using these guidelines: (1) Remove details that are not directly related to the thesis statement. (2) Make paragraph divisions so that there is one paragraph for each main point in the essay. (3) Make changes so that the style and point of view are consistent throughout the essay. (4) Replace one incorrect word and revise one sentence that is not consistent with the level of diction of the rest of the essay. (5) Combine short, choppy sentences and make into separate sentences any that are too long.

One of the hardest things that I ever did was to get back on a horse after falling off. I was eight years old and taking riding lessons. One Saturday, the horse that I usually rode was unavailable. Her name was Buttercup. She had thrown a shoe. Anyway, the horse that my instructor gave me instead was named Wildfire, and that name alone should have warned me that there was going to be trouble. Horses often have unusual names.

The rider set her left foot in the stirrup, and Wildfire was off. Before I could get seated, he raced for the fence around the practice ring and, to my surprise, casually jumped right over it, and, of course, I came out of the saddle at just about the same time that Wildfire went over the fence, and I landed in a heap in the dust.

My instructor hastened to my side, brushed off my garments, and led me to another steed. I was terrified of getting on and receiving the same treatment again. I tried to explain that I had lost all interest in these animals, but she pretended not to hear. Like any child faced with that kind of dilettante, I took the only course of action: I cried. The teacher ignored my tears. The teacher gave me a boost. She handed me the reins. Then she slapped the horse into action. Some riders use a crop, a short whip, to start a horse. My tears dried during the second trip around the ring. After the fourth trip, I didn't want to stop. Pride comes from overcoming a fear of an obstacle. I certainly had reason to be proud that day, even if I had a few more things to learn about horseback riding.

**Assignment   Revising**   Revise the first draft of the practice essay that you completed for the Assignment on page 436. Prepare a final copy of the essay.

**Continuing Assignment** **Revising** Revise the first draft of the main essay that you have been writing in the Continuing Assignment throughout this unit. Give attention to both content and style. Copy or type the finished paper and proofread it.

## Assignment Checklist

Check your assignments for the following points:

✔ 1. Did you revise your essay so that it says what you want it to say?

✔ 2. Did you revise your essay so that the relationships between its ideas are clear and coherent?

✔ 3. Did you add details when needed and remove sentences that had little or nothing to do with your topic?

✔ 4. Did you replace any inappropriate words?

✔ 5. Did you revise your sentences to improve their style?

✔ 6. Did you revise your essay to make its tone and point of view consistent?

✔ 7. Did you proofread your final draft for correct grammar, usage, spelling, and punctuation?

✔ 8. Did you choose a suitable title?

✔ 9. Did you prepare the finished paper according to your teacher's guidelines, and did you proofread it carefully?

## Applying to College: Writing an Application Essay

**Situation:**   You have decided to apply for admission to West College. In the application form, the college provides a choice of three essay topics. You will choose one topic and use it to compose an essay of no more than four hundred words. As you write your essay, you will keep in mind the following information.

**Writer:**       you as an applicant to West College
**Audience:**     admissions officers at West College
**Topic:**        one of three topics for a college-application essay
**Purpose:**      to represent yourself well in an essay of no more than four hundred words

**Directions:**   To plan and write your essay, follow these steps.

*Step 1.* Read the three essay topics in the portion of a college-application form that appears on the facing page. Select the topic that most appeals to you. Also read the notes that you made as you read the pamphlet *What Admissions Officers Look for in College-Application Essays.* The notes are also on the facing page.

*Step 2.* At the top of a piece of paper, write your topic. Then list ideas that are related to your topic.

*Step 3.* Choose from your list the ideas that you will use in your essay. Organize the ideas in a logical order.

(Continue on page 444.)

**Application for Admission**
Page 3

Name _____
              Last                  First             Initial

Home Address _____
           Street       City or Town      State      Zip

Freshman Applicants: In the space provided, write a brief essay (of no more than 400 words) that you believe will help the Board of Admissions decide on your application.

**Essay Topics** (*Choose A, B, or C*)

A. An organization or person that has been influential in your life

B. What you expect to gain from attending college

C. An experience from which you learned something important

---

Ideas from *What Admissions Officers Look for in College-Application Essays*

Qualities That Admissions Officers Look For

Sincerity
Straightforwardness
Imagination
Thoughtfulness
Simplicity (not too much detail)

Writing Suggestions

1. Write in your natural voice; avoid stilted language.
2. Keep to the point; do not ramble.
3. If you write about an experience, reflect on it and explain its meaning to you.

*Step 4.* Write a precise thesis statement that presents the main idea and the purpose of your essay.

*Step 5.* Using your organized list of ideas and your thesis statement, prepare an outline of your essay. Under each main idea in the outline, list supporting details or examples.

*Step 6.* Using your outline as a guide, write the first draft of your essay. Be sure that you include an introductory paragraph, body paragraphs in which you develop your topic, and a strong concluding paragraph.

*Step 7.* Review the content and the style of your essay and revise it as needed.

*Step 8.* Prepare the final copy of your essay. Proofread it carefully.

# Unit Assignments

**Assignment 1**   Write two separate paragraphs about the greatest surprise of your life. The first paragraph should be serious in tone, directed at a general audience; the second paragraph should be humorous, directed at an audience of classmates. Make sure that your treatment of the subject will appeal to the audience that you address. Consider the degree of distance that you want to establish between yourself and your readers.

**Assignment 2**   Write a brief essay about what you consider your greatest accomplishment so far. Focus your reader's attention on the experience and its meaning to you. Arrange the details in chronological order.

**Assignment 3**   Write a brief essay in which you discuss your view of love, honor, or humility. Focus the reader's attention on your views rather than on an experience. Adopt an appropriate tone and style, and establish the degree of distance between yourself and your reader that you feel is appropriate for your purpose and topic.

**Assignment 4**   Write a brief essay explaining the benefits of coming from either a large or a small family. Organize the benefits from least to most important. Make sure that the introductory paragraph will stimulate the interest of a general audience.

**Assignment 5**   Write a brief essay in which you try to persuade your audience to accept your view of a current issue. Choose a specific audience, and concentrate on the points that would be most convincing to that audience. Choose the level of diction that would most appeal to your audience. At the top of your paper, specify the audience that you selected.

## Revising Your Assignments

For help in revising an essay, consult the Checklist for Revision on the last page of this book.

# Unit Tests

## Test 1

**A.** Number your paper from 1 to 5. Next to each number, write *True* if the sentence is true or *False* if it is false.

1. An essay is based mainly on research.
2. A topic outline should be written in complete sentences.
3. Each main heading of an outline must be covered in only one paragraph in the body of the essay.
4. In order to revise your essay, you must read the first draft for its content and its style.
5. The first-person point of view helps to establish a closeness between you and your reader.

**B.** Number your paper from 6 to 10. Next to each number, write the letter of the term that correctly completes the sentence. You will use all but one of the items.

a. formal diction      d. thesis statement
b. casual diction      e. style
c. tone                f. essay

6. __?__ is the unique way in which a writer puts ideas into words.
7. __?__ is the attitude of a writer toward a topic and an audience.
8. A(n) __?__ is a short composition in which the writer usually presents a personal experience or a view.
9. __?__ uses no slang, few contractions, and a large vocabulary.
10. The sentence in the first paragraph that states the main idea and the purpose of the essay is called a(n) __?__.

**C.** Number your paper from 11 to 15. Next to each number, write the letter of the item that correctly answers the question.

11. Which of the following sentences has a formal level of diction?
    a. The dance hasn't begun yet.
    b. The dancer mastered the intricate steps.
    c. After the dancers had worked out for an hour, they needed to take a breather.
    d. The dance was a smash hit.

12. Which of the following is *not* a suitable topic for an essay?
    a. The history of the first library built in our community
    b. Why our community needs a new library
    c. My experience in circulating a petition for a new library
    d. The way I react to new books on a shelf

13. The introductory paragraph of an essay should *not* do which of the following?
    a. Present the thesis statement
    c. Establish the tone
    b. Capture the reader's interest
    d. Suggest a final idea

14. Which of the following is the best way to arrange ideas in a brief essay about viewing Buckingham Memorial Fountain in Chicago?
    a. Chronological order
    c. Order of importance
    b. Spatial order
    d. Cause and effect

15. Which of the following is a precise thesis statement?
    a. I have taken driving lessons.
    b. It is hard to save money for a car.
    c. While he taught me to drive, my brother also taught me about the responsibilities of having a license.
    d. My brother taught me to drive.

# Test 2

Choose one of the Unit Assignments. Write the assignment as directed and hand it in to your teacher.

# Unit 12

*Writing About Literature*

---

## Unit Preview

When you write about literature, you enlarge your understanding of it. In an essay about a literary work, you present an interpretation. In an interpretation you go beyond reporting what happens in a work; for example, you may explain how a character changes, or you may explain the meaning of the work as a whole. As in other kinds of writing, you present specific evidence to support your ideas.

The following paragraphs begin an interpretation.

As the main character of the novel *Ethan Frome,* by Edith Wharton, Ethan Frome is a victim of circumstances and cannot control his fate. He is a victim of his moral beliefs as well as the actual events in his life.

Ethan's strong feeling of responsibility is the most important factor in determining his fate. He feels that it is his duty to leave college and go home to take care of his ill mother and the farm after his father dies. Ethan places this heavy burden on himself and, in doing so, ends his youth. After his mother's death, Ethan feels that he has to marry Zeena, who has come to help take care of his mother. When a jealous Zeena tells Ethan that she is going to get rid of her cousin Mattie, Ethan contemplates leaving with Mattie. Again, Ethan's sense of responsibility keeps him from gaining his freedom from the tortuous life he has been living.

The Fromes' financial situation is another one of the circumstances that entrap Ethan in an unhappy life. . . .

*Lori Thornton, San Angelo Central High School*
*San Angelo, Texas*

**For Analysis**  Reread the paragraphs from the essay about the main character in *Ethan Frome*. Then, on your paper, write the answers to the questions that follow.

1. In which sentence does the writer present the topic of the paper? Which sentence in the same paragraph enlarges the topic?
2. What is the writer's first point in the body of the paper?
3. What evidence does the writer give to support the first point?
4. What is the writer's second point?

By analyzing the first paragraphs of the preceding essay, you have observed important characteristics of a literary essay. In this unit you will learn what to look for when you read a literary work. You will also learn how to choose a literary topic, how to gather evidence to support your ideas about the topic, and how to write a literary essay. As you write about literature, you will follow the three steps of the writing process: prewriting, writing, and revising.

## 12.1  The Nature of the Literary Essay

You may have heard someone say, "What a piece of literature means is just a matter of opinion. There is no right or wrong interpretation." It is true that no two readers react in exactly the same way to a work. It does not follow, however, that you can make literature mean anything that you want it to mean. You must base an interpretation on the details, ideas, and characters presented by the author. You can present that interpretation in a literary essay.

### Purpose and Audience

**Purpose.**  Whether it is called a critical essay, an interpretive essay, a literary analysis, or a literary paper, the literary essay has analysis and evaluation as its purposes. A literary essay is different from a report that presents the action of a story or a poem, recounts an author's life, or discusses an aspect of a literary period. In a literary essay, you demonstrate that you have thought about your reading and that you can organize your thoughts and communicate them to your audience. In writing your essay, your purpose will be one or more of the following:

1. To explore the theme, or central meaning, of the work.
2. To show some insight into the techniques that the author uses to create and develop that meaning.
3. To make some judgment about the quality and the impact of the work.

**Audience.**   When you write a literary essay, address an audience that includes anyone who might be interested in your view of the work that you discuss. Assume that most of your readers have read the work, but provide enough information to refresh their memories.

## Tone, Point of View, and Tense

The literary essay observes certain conventions, or customs. The appropriate tone, point of view, and tense are illustrated in the following passage.

### Model

> For centuries women have been forced into roles, whether they wanted to be or not. A sharp and realistic view of women's roles is given in Lillian Hellman's *The Little Foxes*. She shows women's different reactions to being trapped within their roles. The women are presented as real individuals, not as goddesses or evil people.
>
> *Dorothy Arriola, St. Andrew's Priory for Girls*
> *Honolulu, Hawaii*

**Tone.**   The tone of any writing is the attitude that a writer conveys about the topic and the audience. The tone of a literary essay should be serious, in keeping with your approach to the work that you are discussing. The tone of the preceding excerpt is rather formal, appropriate for a literary essay.

**Point of View.**   Use the third-person point of view (*page 358*) in a literary essay. It is not correct to write in the first person, as in "I believe . . ." or "It is my opinion. . . ." The preceding passage illustrates how using the third person avoids a repetitious use of the pronoun *I*.

**Tense.**   Use the present tense when you refer to the characters, the action, or the author's techniques or subject matter. For example, Lillian Hellman "*shows* women's different reactions."

**Exercise 1   Prewriting: The Literary Essay**   Decide whether each of the following sentences is more appropriate for a literary essay or for a report. On your paper, write *Literary essay* or *Report* after each sentence number.

1. Emily Dickinson lived in Amherst, Massachusetts.

2. In *A Hazard of New Fortunes*, William Dean Howells uses realism to present the problems of industrialization in the United States at the end of the nineteenth century.

3. From the beginning to the end of his novel *The Grapes of Wrath*, John Steinbeck paints a portrait of a dispossessed people.

   *Jim Labrenz, Thousand Oaks High School*
   *Thousand Oaks, California*

4. Arthur Miller drew on his experiences during the Great Depression of the 1930s when he wrote *Death of a Salesman*.

5. In *A Farewell to Arms*, Frederic Henry maintains a nonchalant attitude toward the war until he is wounded.

   *Scott Kline, Winston Churchill High School*
   *San Antonio, Texas*

**Exercise 2   Revising: Tone**   The tone of the following passage is not appropriate for a literary essay. Decide what is wrong with the tone; then write an improved version.

> Carl Sandburg's poems are neat to listen to, and he doesn't use flowery words or hard metaphors. They are the kind of poems that you can figure out easily. Many of his poems tell little stories and talk about ordinary folks.

**Exercise 3   Revising: Tense**   The following passage does not use the tense that is customary in a literary essay. Using the appropriate tense, write a revised version of the passage.

> The plot of *The Glass Menagerie*, by Tennessee Williams, revolved around a woman, Amanda, who lived her life through her daughter, Laura. She also spent many years making her son, Tom, feel guilty about ever leaving home and having a life of his own.

**Revising: Point of View**    The point of view in the paragraph from a literary essay is inappropriate. Using an appropriate point of view, write a revised version.

> I have just finished reading "Bartleby the Scrivener," by Herman Melville. Something I noticed that was interesting about the story is the subtle change in the narrator, Bartleby's employer, who is an unnamed Wall Street lawyer. I think that watching Bartleby withdraw from society, and finally from life, makes the narrator change his own view of the world.

**Assignment    Revising**    The following passage fails to observe the conventions of a literary essay. Write a revised version that follows those conventions.

> Most of the characters in *Searching for Caleb,* by Anne Tyler, were members of the Peck family. The main characters were Justine, Duncan, Daniel, and Caleb Peck, the only Pecks who wanted to live away from their family in Baltimore. You won't believe it, but the rest of the Pecks looked alike, talked alike, thought alike, and associated only with one another. Whole chunks of the book explored why four members of the family wanted to move away from the rest. That exploration made the reader realize the importance of freedom and individuality. However, I noticed that the importance of family ties was emphasized too. It was apparent to me that the four Pecks who just took off on their own could relax and enjoy themselves only when they had the best of both worlds.

**Continuing Assignment    Prewriting**    Begin to read a literary work of your choice or one that is assigned by your teacher. You will use this work as the basis of a literary essay of three to five pages.

## Assignment Checklist

Check your revising assignments for the following points:

✔ 1. Did you revise the passage to give it a more serious tone?
✔ 2. Did you rewrite the passage from the third-person point of view?
✔ 3. Did you use the present tense when it was appropriate to do so?

# 12.2 Preparing to Write a Literary Essay

Getting ready to write a literary essay will require almost as much of your attention as the writing itself. First, you will have to read much more carefully than when you read solely for pleasure. Then, as you choose a topic, you will also have to form your interpretation of it. Finally, you will want to find specific incidents or statements that support your interpretation.

## Doing a Careful Reading of the Work

If you know in advance that you will be writing an essay about a literary work, keep the essay in mind as you read. If you are asked to write about a work that you have already read, reread the work thoughtfully.

As you read, ask yourself the following questions. In your literature course, you have probably studied most of the concepts that appear in the questions. If you need to review any of the concepts, consult a literature textbook or a literary handbook.

QUESTIONS TO ASK ABOUT A WORK OF FICTION

What is the main plot of the work?

Who are the central characters?

From what point of view is the story told—first person, third person? Is the point of view omniscient or limited?

What is the setting? Does the work have a certain atmosphere or mood?

What is the central conflict?

What is the climax?

How is the conflict resolved?

What is the theme, or main idea, of the work?

What is distinctive about the writer's style?

QUESTIONS TO ASK ABOUT A POEM

On a literal level, what is the situation in the poem?

What can you deduce about the persona (speaker) in the poem?

What is the persona's reaction, if any, to the situation?

What images does the poem contain? Does one or more of the images seem to be a symbol—that is, does it stand for something larger than itself?

What figurative language—such as metaphors, similes, and personification—does the poem contain? How does figurative language help to convey the meaning?

Is the meaning reinforced by the poet's use of sound, as in rhythm, rhyme, alliteration, and assonance?

What, if anything, does the poem seem to suggest beyond the literal situation? What is the theme of the poem?

## Choosing a Topic and an Approach

If you are not assigned a topic by your teacher, take the time to choose your topic carefully. It should develop logically and naturally from your reactions to the work. You will probably want to choose one of the following approaches to a literary work.

1. *Interpreting the meaning of the work*. By providing evidence from the work, you can explain how the theme is developed. For example, you might explain that the theme of William Faulkner's "The Bear" concerns the meaning of reaching adulthood.

2. *Analyzing a character*. Another approach is showing how a character is changed by his or her experiences—that is, how the character matures or develops. For example, you might explain how Henry Fleming is changed by his battle experiences in Stephen Crane's *The Red Badge of Courage*.

3. *Analyzing a technique*. You can also investigate an aspect of the writer's craft, such as symbolism, imagery, poetic sound, characterization, creation of setting, and so on. For example, you might explain how the sound in Tennyson's "Break, Break, Break" reinforces the meaning.

4. *Comparing an element in two works*. Another approach is a comparison of the same element in two works. For example, you might compare the use of foreshadowing in Poe's "The Fall of the House of Usher" and Hawthorne's "The Birthmark." You could also compare two characters in a single work or in two works.

# Writing a Preliminary
## Thesis Statement

Writing a "working" thesis statement—the statement of what you intend to demonstrate in your essay—will help you focus your attention as you search for evidence to support your interpretation. If you can find such evidence, the statement will become the main idea—and the final thesis statement—of your literary essay. If you cannot find sufficient evidence, you must be willing to revise or abandon that thesis statement.

The following are examples of suitable topics and preliminary thesis statements for literary essays.

TOPIC

The theme of *Huckleberry Finn,* by Mark Twain

PRELIMINARY THESIS STATEMENT

The theme of *Huckleberry Finn* is the conflict between the corrupting influences of society and the natural goodness of human beings.

TOPIC

The use of personification in "Because I could not stop for Death," by Emily Dickinson

PRELIMINARY THESIS STATEMENT

By personifying death as a kindly gentleman in "Because I could not stop for Death," Emily Dickinson presents a fearless view of death.

TOPIC

The character Pearl in *The Scarlet Letter,* by Nathaniel Hawthorne

PRELIMINARY THESIS STATEMENT

Until she is acknowledged by her father, Pearl is depicted as an alien in society; to the Puritans her traits seem peculiar, as do her relationships with the primary elements in her life: nature, other children, and her parents.

**Exercise   Prewriting: Thesis Statements**   On your paper, write *Appropriate* if a sentence is appropriate as the thesis statement for a literary essay and *Not appropriate* if it is not.

1. The theme of Walt Whitman's "I Hear America Singing" is the glorification of the average person engaged in honest labor.
2. The principal character in *A Raisin in the Sun,* by Lorraine Hansberry, is the mother of an inner-city family.
3. "Flight," by John Steinbeck, investigates the meaning of maturity to a young man.
4. In each stanza of "Travel," by Edna St. Vincent Millay, the first and third lines rhyme, as do the second and fourth.
5. In "The Jilting of Granny Weatherall," Katherine Anne Porter effectively uses the narrative technique called "stream of consciousness" to convey to the reader the ideas that rush through the mind of a dying woman.

**Assignment   Prewriting**   Reread a short story or poem that you enjoy. Ask yourself questions about the work in order to choose an essay topic. Then write the topic and a preliminary thesis statement. Save your paper for use in an assignment on page 472.

**Continuing Assignment   Prewriting**   If you have not already done so, finish reading the work that you started for the Continuing Assignment on page 452. After reviewing the explanation of the four kinds of writing topics on page 454, select a topic for your literary essay. Write a preliminary thesis statement. Save your paper for later use.

### Assignment Checklist

Check your assignments for the following points:

  1. Did you limit your topic to one element of the work?
  2. Did you choose a topic that interprets this element of the work?
  3. Did you write a preliminary thesis statement that summarizes your interpretation in one sentence?

# 12.3 Taking Notes

Now you can begin to test your interpretation. Reread the work for any details that you can use to support your preliminary thesis statement. For example, if your topic is the theme of *Huckleberry Finn,* try to find incidents or statements that show civilization corrupting the characters, or characters revealing a natural instinct about what is right and what is wrong.

## Gathering Evidence from the Work

Take notes on the details that you find. Perhaps the simplest and most efficient way to take notes is to use three-by-five-inch or four-by-six-inch note cards. Write only one piece of evidence on each card so that you can easily rearrange them for outlining. Each note card should include a subject heading at the top and, at the bottom, the number of the page on which the evidence appears in the work. When you take notes, record only the essential details of a passage. You need not write in complete sentences or connect one point with another, as the following example shows.

PASSAGE FROM *THE SCARLET LETTER*

> Pearl was born an outcast of the infant world. . . . If spoken to, she would not speak again. If the children gathered about her, as they sometimes did, Pearl would grow positively terrible in her puny wrath, snatching up stones to fling at them, with shrill, incoherent exclamations, that made her mother tremble because they had so much the sound of a witch's anathemas in some unknown tongue. . . . The pine trees, aged, black, and solemn, and flinging groans and other melancholy utterances on the breeze, needed little transformation to figure as Puritan elders; the ugliest weeds of the garden were their children, whom Pearl smote down and uprooted, most unmercifully.

NOTES ON PASSAGE

> *Pearl: outsider to her peers*
> Alienates peers—throws stones, shouts incoherently
> Thinks of them as "ugliest weeds of the garden"
> Pulls up the "weeds" as if they were other children
> pp. 95-96

In your notes you may also include three special types of material: direct quotation, paraphrase, and summary.

**Direct Quotation.**   If you find a particularly memorable statement or description, copy it exactly as it appears in the work and enclose it in quotation marks. The following example is also from *The Scarlet Letter.*

> *Pearl in harmony with nature*
>
> "Pearl set forth at a great pace, and, as Hester smiled to perceive, did actually catch the sunshine, and stood laughing in the midst of it, all brightened by its splendor, and scintillating with the vivacity excited by rapid motion. The light lingered about the lonely child, as if glad of such a playmate, until her mother had drawn almost nigh enough to step into the magic circle too."
> pp. 192-193

**Paraphrase.**   A **paraphrase** is the expression of an author's idea in your own words. A paraphrase may be almost as long as the original passage, but it allows you to write in your own words in order to avoid too long or too frequent direct quotations. The quotation in the last example is paraphrased here.

> *Pearl in harmony with nature*
>
> Pearl moved forward rapidly until she stood in the sunlight. Hester smiled when she saw Pearl's delight in the exercise and in the sun. The sunbeam stayed on Pearl and seemed to play with her until Hester reached its edge.
> pp. 192-193

**Summary.**   A **summary,** like a paraphrase, is the expression of the author's ideas in your own words. However, in a summary, the author's narration and dialogue are condensed to essential details. A summary, unlike ordinary notes, is written in complete sentences. In the following example, a longer passage is summarized in one sentence.

PASSAGE FROM *THE SCARLET LETTER*

> The young minister, on ceasing to speak, had withdrawn a few steps from the group, and stood with his face partially concealed in the heavy folds of the window curtains; while the shadow of his figure,

which the sunlight cast upon the floor, was tremulous with the vehemence of his appeal. Pearl, the wild and flighty little elf, stole softly towards him, and taking his hand in the grasp of both her own, laid her cheek against it; a caress so tender, and withal so unobtrusive, that her mother, who was looking on, asked herself, —"Is that my Pearl?"

SUMMARY

*Pearl's relationship with her parents*

When Pearl's life with Hester is threatened and the minister speaks successfully on their behalf, Pearl thanks him by laying her cheek against his hand and caressing it so lovingly that even her mother is surprised.

p. 117

## Using Secondary Sources

**Secondary sources** are books or essays written by scholars who specialize in interpreting literature. This kind of information can be helpful in giving you another view of the work that you will discuss. You should not regard a secondary source, however, as a replacement for your own reading and interpretation of the work. In fact, many teachers prefer an interpretation to be based solely on a student's own reactions to a work. If you do use secondary sources, you can treat an idea or a quotation from the work as an additional piece of evidence to support your thesis statement.

When reading secondary sources, take notes just as you would for the work itself. At the top right of each note card, place the author's last name, so that you will know the work from which the information came. For each source, be sure to fill out a separate bibliography card (*Section 13.2b in Unit 13*) that lists the author, title, publisher, and place and date of publication. You will need this information when you write footnotes and a bibliography for your essay.

**Exercise 1   Prewriting: Evidence**   Read each of the following preliminary thesis statements and their accompanying evidence. On your paper, list the letters of the sentences that support each statement.

1. *Thesis statement:* Sinclair Lewis uses many details in *Babbitt* to suggest that George Babbitt is a conformist.

   a. Babbitt chooses a car built like those of his neighbors.

   b. Babbitt wants to have the same ideas and political affiliation as his neighbors.

   c. Babbitt lives in Zenith in the 1920s.

   d. Babbitt tries to talk in the way that he thinks a successful real estate salesman should talk.

   e. Babbitt wants to have the right kind of office in the right kind of office building.

2. *Thesis statement:* Throughout "The Voyage," Katherine Mansfield does not explain directly why Fenella and her grandmother are on the voyage; she gives only a few clues to reveal the reason.

   a. Fenella's father is grieving when he sends Fenella on the boat with her grandmother.

   b. Fenella's grandmother carries an umbrella.

   c. Fenella and her grandmother talk to a stewardess on the boat.

   d. Fenella and her grandmother are dressed in black mourning clothes.

   e. The events of the story take place in New Zealand, where Katherine Mansfield spent her childhood.

**Exercise 2    Prewriting: Note Taking**    Take notes on the following passage from page 1 of a secondary source about Katherine Anne Porter. You need not use complete sentences. Give your notes a heading.

> Miss Porter does not actually experiment with forms or techniques, and her style in one story is a good deal like her style in another, though, of course, its tone may and frequently does change. But she represents, as she herself indicates in numerous passages in *The Days Before,* the kind of writer who has something to say rather than the writer who consciously strives for perfection of style or form. The clarity of her style and the precision of her language add greatly to the power of what she has to say, of course, but it is the meaning of human experience as she visualizes it which is of most significance.
>
> Harry J. Mooney, Jr.,
> *The Fiction and Criticism of Katherine Anne Porter*

To prepare the outline of your essay, gather your note cards and follow these steps.

**Strategies**

1. *Sort your note cards into several groups according to their subject headings.* Each group will form one main heading of the outline.

2. *Place the groups of cards in a logical order.* Use order of increasing importance or whatever order will enable you to present your evidence most clearly.

3. *Within the main-heading groups, choose the cards that will form the subheadings of the outline.* Select only those cards that provide strong evidence for your points. Put aside the other cards.

4. *Arrange the cards for the subheadings in a logical order.* Your purpose is to make your discussion of each point easy to follow.

5. *Write the main headings and subheadings in outline form.* Place the thesis statement at the top of the outline.

**Exercise  Prewriting: Outlining**  Use the following list of headings and subheadings to prepare an outline for a paper supporting the thesis statement that is given. You will have to determine which items on the list are main headings and which are subheadings. There is no one correct order for the main headings or for the subheadings under each heading.

> *Thesis statement:* In "The Open Boat," Stephen Crane uses several techniques to emphasize the isolation of the men alone on the sea.
>
> Strange comparisons between items at sea and familiar items on land
> Conclusion
> Gulls
> Waves blocking the sight of almost everything else
> Presentation of sea as dominant sight
> Introduction
> Household items

The time of day revealed by the appearance of the sea

Sharks

Introduction of animals at sea as bad omens

Barnyard items

**Assignment**   **Prewriting**   The first three paragraphs of a literary essay follow. Copy its thesis statement. Underneath it write a topic outline of the three paragraphs. Remember that an introduction needs to be identified but not outlined.

Through the destined darkness, doom, and death of Hawthorne's *The Scarlet Letter* and *The House of the Seven Gables,* many instances of light, hope, and beauty emerge. A luminance is brought by the characters of Phoebe in *The House of the Seven Gables* and Pearl in *The Scarlet Letter* to dominate momentarily, if not eternally, the evil. The personalities and ways of Phoebe and Pearl bring brightness into Hawthorne's melancholy novels.

One example of brightness is the physical beauty of Phoebe and Pearl. Phoebe's beauty is best expressed in Hawthorne's words: "She was very pretty; as graceful as a bird, and graceful much in the same way; as pleasant about the house as a gleam of sunshine falling on the floor through a shadow of twinkling leaves, or as a ray of firelight that dances on the wall while evening is drawing nigh" (291). Pearl, too, is compared to a bird and a gleam of sunshine: "'What little bird of scarlet plumage may this be? Methinks I have seen just such figures, when the sun has been shining through a richly painted window, and tracing out the golden and crimson images across the floor'" (148). Phoebe and Pearl bring light into the two novels, a light that shines through the darkness.

Like their beauty, the personalities of Phoebe and Pearl are also a light and a hope. When humans feel alienated from society, they hold onto or reach for something to give them companionship, security, and hope. Phoebe and Pearl fill this need for Clifford and Hester. Hester holds onto Pearl, for Pearl is "her mother's only treasure" (136). Similarly, Phoebe is important to Clifford because "to him this little figure of the cheeriest household life was just what he required to bring him back into the breathing world" (327). Hester and Clifford are alienated in the dark world, and they find, in the hope that Pearl and Phoebe give, reason for survival.

*Carole Campbell, Hall Senior High School*
*Little Rock, Arkansas*

**Continuing Assignment** **Prewriting** Look over your preliminary thesis statement and the notes that you took for the Continuing Assignments on pages 456 and 461. Revise your thesis statement if necessary. Then prepare a topic outline for your essay.

### Assignment Checklist

Check your assignment for the following points:

✔ 1. Did you identify the thesis statement and copy it at the top of your outline?
✔ 2. Did you prepare a topic outline that shows the relationship of the ideas in the second and third paragraphs?

Check your Continuing Assignment for these points:

✔ 3. Did you write a final thesis statement that you can adequately support with the evidence gathered from the literary work?
✔ 4. Did you sort your note cards according to their subject headings?
✔ 5. Did you prepare a logically organized topic outline that includes all the important points?

## 12.5 Writing the First Draft

Follow the outline as you write your first draft, making adjustments as you write. Your task is to work your evidence into the essay so that the sequence of ideas is logical and the writing is smooth. As you compose the essay, remember that your purpose is to interpret the literary work, not to explain your own philosophy to the reader. Therefore, make sure that all of your comments are directly related to the literary work and are supported by sufficient evidence.

### The Title

Your title should be specific. It must indicate the aspect of the work with which your essay deals: for example, "Contrasts in Melville's *Billy Budd*" or "Themes and Motifs in the Shaving Scene of Melville's *Benito Cereno*."

## The Introductory Paragraph

Your introductory paragraph is an overview of the essay. You should include the author and the title of the work, any brief description of the work that will help the reader to understand your interpretation, and the thesis statement. At the same time, you should also attempt to interest the reader in what you have to say.

### Model

Music can transcend barriers of time and language to convey messages with a beauty all its own. Willa Cather makes use of this quality of music in "Paul's Case," a story about a boy who hates his ugly, ordinary lifestyle and who tries to escape from reality into a world of art and beauty. In the course of the story, Cather refers to several specific operas and classical compositions. They are all works with which Paul comes in contact in his quest for happiness. To readers who are familiar with these works, their mention, taken in context, is very meaningful. Thesis statement The musical references in "Paul's Case" not only give the reader a better understanding of the boy, but also foreshadow Paul's tragic death.

*Sharon Nelson, Cumberland Valley High School*
*Mechanicsburg, Pennsylvania*

## The Body Paragraphs

As you write the body paragraphs, you should consult your outline as you incorporate the specific evidence from your note cards into the body of the essay. Be careful not to use too many quotations. Excessive use of quotations may suggest that you have not thought enough about the ideas in the work to be able to put them into your own words. Instead, the body paragraphs should contain summarized and paraphrased evidence that is related to the thesis statement.

## The Concluding Paragraph

In a concluding paragraph, you close the essay by summarizing what you have shown. You also establish how and why the aspect of the work that you discussed in the essay is important to the work as a whole. The following paragraph concludes an essay in which the writer compares the characters Tom Sawyer and Huckleberry Finn.

**Model**

> The most memorable achievement of Mark Twain's entire career was the inspired creation of the characters of Tom Sawyer and Huckleberry Finn. By using Tom as a foil for Huck, Twain emphasizes the shrewdness, practicality, and humanity that characterize the humorless yet humorous Huckleberry Finn. Although Tom will always live in the minds of readers as an amusing and adventurous young boy, he will never be associated with the tolerance and sensitivity that are peculiar to Huck Finn.

> *Kathryn Olmsted, Pacific High School*
> *San Bernardino, California*

## Quotations

**Short Prose Quotations.**   When you decide to quote a particularly memorable passage from the work that you are interpreting, you should copy it in the essay exactly as it appears in the work. The proper way of incorporating the quotation in the essay depends on its length. Short quotations of no more than four lines are written or typed as part of the paragraph. They are enclosed by quotation marks and followed by the number of the page on which the quoted passage appears in the original work. Notice that the final punctuation mark comes after the page reference.

> Moreover, in describing Pearl's many facets, Hawthorne refers to her attractiveness as a "wild-flower prettiness" (90).

**Long Prose Quotations.**   Quotations of five or more lines are made easier to read by setting them off from the text; they are indented five spaces on both sides and single-spaced. For quotations that are set off in this manner, it is not necessary to use quotation marks. You may shorten a long quotation by using ellipsis points ( . . . ) to indicate the omitted words. Use three points in the middle of a sentence, and use three points plus a period at the end of a sentence. As with short quotations, give the page number at the end. The following passage is long enough to be set off from the text of a literary essay. In this kind of quotation, the page reference follows the final punctuation mark.

> Her Pearl! For so had Hester called her; not as a name expressive of her aspect, which had nothing of the calm, white, unimpassioned lustre that would be indicated by the comparison. But she had named the infant "Pearl," as being of great price. . . . God . . . had given her a lovely child . . . to connect her parent for ever with the race and descent of mortals, and to be finally a blessed soul in heaven! (89)

When you shorten a quotation, you sometimes need to supply words that are not part of the original text but are needed for sense. Enclose such words and phrases in brackets. Bracketed words are used in two quotations on page 470 of the model essay.

**Poetry Quotations.**    Quotations of up to three lines of a poem may be enclosed in quotation marks and run in with the text. The ends of lines are indicated by a slash (/) with a space before and after it, as in the following example.

> In examining a seashell, Holmes finds a moral lesson: "Build thee more stately mansions, O my soul, / As the swift seasons roll!"

When four or more lines of a poem are quoted, they are single-spaced and set off from the text just as a prose quotation is. No quotation marks are used.

## Documentation

To **document** an essay is to supply information about the original works from which you copied the quotations in the essay. As you have just seen, you must follow each quotation with a reference, in parentheses, to the page on which it appears in the original work. In an essay about a long poem, use line numbers instead; in an essay about a Shakespearean play, use the numbers of the act, scene, and line (as V.iii.75–78). Then, in a bibliography page (*Section 13.5 in Unit 13*) at the end of the essay, list the complete publication information in a standard entry, as follows.

> Hawthorne, Nathaniel. *The Scarlet Letter*. New York: Simon and Schuster, 1972.

Your teacher may prefer you to use another way of citing the work from which your quotations come. The first time you quote from the work, place an explanatory footnote at the bottom of the page or on a separate footnotes page. In either case, the correct form is as follows.

[1] Nathaniel Hawthorne, *The Scarlet Letter* (New York: Simon and Schuster, 1972), p. 115. All subsequent references are to this edition.

The remaining quotations in the essay are followed by page numbers in parentheses; the standard bibliography page is optional.

The preceding information applies only to literary essays that are based entirely on the original work. If an essay also includes references to secondary sources (*page 459*), a footnote must appear for the first reference to the original work; other references to the work may be included with the text. References to quotations or ideas from the secondary sources appear as footnotes, and the bibliography includes entries for each secondary source and for the original work. For additional information about documenting a paper, see Section 13.5 in Unit 13. When you document any kind of literary essay, follow your teacher's directions.

## A Model Literary Essay

The literary essay referred to in this unit is given on the following pages as a model for reference and study.

### Model

The Puritan Elf in Hawthorne's *The Scarlet Letter*

Many writers have created characters who seem different from their society, detached from the usual world. Such a person is Nathaniel Hawthorne's Pearl in *The Scarlet Letter*. Until she is acknowledged by her father, Pearl is depicted as an alien in society; to the Puritans her traits seem peculiar, as do her relationships with the primary elements in her life: nature, other children, and her parents.

One of Pearl's most important relationships is with nature. Hawthorne describes her as an "elfish child" (162) and an "airy sprite" (92). In describing Pearl's many facets, Hawthorne

refers to her attractiveness as a "wild-flower prettiness" (90).
Hawthorne also likens her to a bird, "a bird of bright plumage"
(256) or "a floating sea-bird" (248). Indeed, the imagery that is
applied to Pearl depicts her as a wild creature of nature.

The Puritans believed that no one can thrive by nature alone;
yet it is apparent that the wild Pearl feels a strong allegiance to her
natural surroundings, the forest being both her nursery and her
second home. Thus, by Puritan standards, Pearl is not a normal
child, and she becomes a stranger to society.

Pearl is obviously in harmony with nature. Her friends consist
of the forest and its inhabitants. She plays with flowers, berries, and
leaves; she adorns her hair and clothing with this foliage, transform-
ing herself into a nymph-child. During the process of her decoration,
Pearl seldom disturbs the woodland members: "The small denizens
of the wilderness hardly took pains to move out of her path. . . .
these wild things which [the mother-forest] nourished, all recognized
a kindred wildness in the human child" (215-216). One particular
element, the sun, seems especially allied with Pearl, for it tends to
follow her wherever she goes: "Through the dim medium of the
forest-gloom [Pearl was] all glorified with a ray of sunshine that was
attracted thitherward as by a certain sympathy" (219).

A contrasting relationship can be seen between Pearl and
other children. The Puritan children recognize that Pearl is not one
of them, and they consider her and her mother, Hester, outsiders.
"Mother and daughter stood together in the same circle of seclusion
from human society . . . " (95). Pearl often watches her peers, yet
she never attempts to make acquaintances. When the children advance toward her, she throws stones at them and mutters incoherent
exclamations. When amusing herself outdoors, Pearl envisions the
weeds as her peers and uproots them unmercifully, illustrating the
hostility with which she regards the children.

Perhaps Pearl's most complex relationship is with her parents.
Pearl is brought up entirely by Hester. The very name that Hester
bequeaths to her child suggests her feelings:

> Her Pearl! For so had Hester called her; not as a name
> expressive of her aspect, which had nothing of the calm,
> white, unimpassioned lustre that would be indicated by the
> comparison. But she had named the infant "Pearl," as
> being of great price. . . . God . . . had given her a lovely
> child . . . to connect her parent for ever with the race and
> descent of mortals, and to be finally a blessed soul in
> heaven! (89)

Although Pearl is Hester's "only treasure" (89), she is also her mother's cause for sorrow, especially when Hester sees in her child a wild, desperate mood. Moreover, Pearl has an obsession with her mother's scarlet letter *A* and constantly questions the meaning behind it. Much to Hester's despair, Pearl imitates the symbol, crafting her *A* out of green eel grass. It is as if Pearl's purpose is to "make out its hidden import" (186).

Pearl's relationship with her father, Arthur Dimmesdale, is quite different. She repeatedly seeks recognition from him. Even as a mere infant in her mother's arms, Pearl demonstrates her feelings of kinship when she stretches her arm toward Dimmesdale. When Pearl's life with Hester is threatened and the minister speaks successfully on their behalf, Pearl thanks him by laying her cheek against his hand and caressing it so lovingly that even her own mother is surprised. Furthermore, when mother and daughter encounter Dimmesdale on the scaffold in the dead of night, Pearl attempts to extract from the minister a promise that he will stand with her mother and her on the scaffold the following day at noon. However, the paternal recognition that Pearl seeks is not to be had yet.

Pearl changes swiftly, however, in a climactic scene on the scaffold, where Dimmesdale finally confesses. When Pearl complies with her father's wishes and kisses him, it is a sign that she is finally acknowledged publicly. With that one kiss, the wild infant cries. Each tear that "fell upon her father's cheek" (269) represents one more step away from wildness and perversity.

It is through Dimmesdale's ultimate confession that Pearl and society are reconciled. Now she has a name, a social status in the Puritan community. Her wildness, her capriciousness, and her elfish charm have been pushed aside in favor of the new Pearl, the Pearl who has ceased to be an outcast.

Bibliography

Hawthorne, Nathaniel. *The Scarlet Letter*. New York: Simon and Schuster, 1972.

(*Adapted*)
*Martha F. Chang, Madison High School*
*Madison, New Jersey*

**Exercise** **Prewriting: The Bibliography Entry** Given the following information about a book, write a bibliography entry for it. Use the bibliography entry on page 468 as a guide.

Title: *My Ántonia*

Author: Willa Cather
Date of publication: 1926
Publisher: Houghton Mifflin
Place of publication: Boston

**Assignment** **Writing** Take out the paper on which you wrote a topic and thesis statement for a literary essay about a short story or poem (*page 456*). Write an introductory paragraph for the essay. Be sure to give the author and title of the work and to include your thesis statement. Save your paper.

**Continuing Assignment** **Writing** Using the note cards and the outline that you prepared for the Continuing Assignments on pages 461 and 465, write the first draft of your literary essay.

### Assignment Checklist

Check your assignments for the following points:

✓ 1. Did you include the author and the title of the work that you are discussing?
✓ 2. Did you include a clear thesis statement in your introductory paragraph?

Check your Continuing Assignment for these additional points:

✓ 3. Did you give your essay a title that indicates the aspect of the work that you are analyzing?
✓ 4. Did you present your evidence clearly in the body of the essay?
✓ 5. Did you write a concluding paragraph that summarizes what the essay has shown?
✓ 6. Did you use the proper form for quotations, and did you document them correctly?

# 12.6 Revising and Finishing Your Essay

If possible, begin your revision a day or so after you have finished writing your first draft. In this way you will have a more objective view of your writing. Revising is far more than proofreading. It is the reworking and polishing of the entire essay, both the content and the style. You will probably need to rewrite some passages and attach them to the appropriate portion of the first draft. In a thorough revision, you should observe the following guidelines.

## Strategies

1. *Check the draft against the outline.* Be sure that you covered all points in the right order. Add any needed sentences.

2. *Make sure that each piece of evidence supports your thesis statement.* Omit sentences with unnecessary information.

3. *Make sure that the ideas flow coherently.* Rearrange them if they do not, using transitional words as needed.

4. *Change wording where necessary* to make it more precise or to make the sentence structure smoother.

5. *Make sure that the tone of your essay is consistent.* It should be serious and formal.

6. *Make sure that you have used the third-person point of view consistently.*

7. *Make sure that you have used the present tense* when you refer to characters, the action, and the author's techniques or subject matter.

8. *Proofread the essay.* Correct any errors in grammar, usage, spelling, and punctuation. In particular, make sure that you copied the quotations and page references accurately.

When you are satisfied that your essay is as good as you can make it, you have a final draft. Copy it on 8½-by-11-inch paper, following accepted manuscript guidelines (*page 217*). Proofread your finished paper carefully.

**Exercise** **Revising: The Literary Essay** The parts of the following paragraph that are in italic type need revision. Three possible ways of revising each part are listed. On your paper, write the letter of the revision that will most improve the paragraph.

(1) *It appears to me that in the opening scenes of Shakespeare's* Henry IV, Part I, *young Prince Hal neglects all of his responsibilities to his father and to his country.* Instead, he loafs in a tavern with his

companion Falstaff.   (2) *Falstaff has a remarkable ability to play with words.*   (3) *In soliloquies and in talks with his father and Falstaff, Hal indicated that he intended to surprise everyone with a sudden reformation of his character.*   (4) *He talks about his reform.* He uses images of money, sunlight, and jewels.   (5) Each of the images *happens* throughout the play.

1. a. Rewrite sentence: *In the opening scenes of Shakespeare's* Henry IV, Part I, *young Prince Hal neglects all of his responsibilities to his father and to his country.*

   b. Remove sentence.

   c. Rewrite sentence: *It appears to me that young Prince Hal neglects all of his responsibilities to his father and to his country in the opening scenes of* Henry IV, Part I.

2. a. Combine with previous sentence: *Instead, he loafs in a tavern with his friend Falstaff, who has a great ability to play with words.*

   b. Rewrite sentence: *Falstaff's ability to play with words is remarkable.*

   c. Remove sentence.

3. a. Remove sentence.

   b. Rewrite sentence: *In soliloquies and in talks with his father and Falstaff, Hal indicates that he intends to surprise everyone with a sudden reformation of his character.*

   c. Rewrite sentence: *Hal indicated that he intended to surprise everyone with a sudden reformation of his character.*

4. a. Rewrite sentence: *He talked about his reform.*

   b. Remove sentence.

   c. Combine with following sentence: *When he talks about his reform, he uses images of money, sunlight, and jewels.*

5. a. Change word: *recurs*

   b. Change word: *exists*

   c. Change word: *was written*

**Assignment   Revising**   Rewrite the following portion of a first draft. Revise it with respect to these four points: tense, tone, point of view, and the form used for quotations.

> To be a tragic hero, a character must have a potential for greatness but be destroyed by a tragic flaw in his or her personality. I think Macbeth was certainly a tragic hero.
>
> In many ways, Macbeth was an admirable figure. The first act established that he was a great and respected general, who had

earned the trust both of his men and of his king. He also had a powerful love for his wife, Lady Macbeth, as well as for his comrades. And I can't help but admire his sense of morality; he knew that his actions were wrong, and he was plagued by guilt. At the end of Act I, his soliloquy revealed this self-awareness: "we but teach / Bloody instructions, which, being taught, return / To plague th' inventor. This even-handed justice / Commends th' ingredients of our poison'd chalice / To our own lips" (I.vii.7-12).

But as I mentioned earlier, Macbeth's good qualities were outweighed by the powerful tragic flaw that destroyed him: ambition. The temptation of power was too great. He couldn't resist Lady Macbeth's own ambitious arguments. Macbeth committed a series of murders that would lead to the throne, for he believed

> For mine own good
> All causes shall give way. (III.iv.135-136)

**Continuing Assignment** **Revising** Revise the first draft that you prepared for the Continuing Assignment on page 472. Then copy the finished paper and proofread it carefully. Submit your outline with the finished paper.

## Assignment Checklist

Check your assignments for the following points:

✓ 1. Did you revise the first draft to make the tense, tone, and point of view consistent?
✓ 2. When necessary, did you correct the form used for quotations?

Check your Continuing Assignment for these additional points:

✓ 3. Did you add any needed sentences?
✓ 4. Did you omit any unnecessary sentences?
✓ 5. Did you revise the draft to make it more coherent?
✓ 6. Did you revise the draft to improve word choices and the phrasing of sentences?
✓ 7. Did you proofread the final draft for correct grammar, usage, spelling, and punctuation?
✓ 8. Did you prepare the finished paper according to your teacher's guidelines and proofread it carefully?

## Metaphor and Meaning: Writing About Poetry

Situation: *The Anthology,* a student literary magazine, is
running a contest and will publish the three best short essays
about a poem by Emily Dickinson. Each essay should be no
more than five hundred words long. As a contestant, you will
write an essay about the relationship of metaphor and meaning in the poem "'Hope' is the thing with feathers." As you
write your essay, keep in mind the following information.

**Writer:**    you as a contestant

**Audience:**    contest judges and readers of the magazine

**Topic:**    metaphor and meaning in the Dickinson poem

**Purpose:**    to analyze the poem in a literary essay of no
more than five hundred words

Directions: To plan and write your essay, follow these steps.

Step 1. Read the poem, which appears on the facing
page. Look up any words that you do not know.
Identify the metaphor that is developed in the
poem and decide how it develops the meaning of
the work.

Step 2. Using your observations about the use of metaphor in the poem, write a preliminary thesis
statement for your essay.

Step 3. List evidence from the poem that supports your
preliminary thesis statement. Include each instance in which metaphor contributes to the
meaning of the poem. Make sure that you have
listed the evidence in the order in which it appears in the poem. Your list will be a rough outline for you to follow as you write your essay.

*Step 4.* Write a specific title for your essay.

*Step 5.* Write the first draft of your essay. Include an introductory paragraph with a thesis statement (revised if necessary), one or more body paragraphs, and a concluding paragraph. Write in the third person and use the present tense. Be sure to copy quotations correctly.

*Step 6.* Revise your first draft. Then prepare a final copy of your essay and proofread it carefully.

---

### "Hope" is the thing with feathers

"Hope" is the thing with feathers—
That perches in the soul—
And sings the tune without the words—
And never stops—at all—

And sweetest—in the Gale—is heard—    5
And sore must be the storm—
That could abash the little Bird
That kept so many warm—

I've heard it in the chillest land—    10
And on the strangest Sea—
Yet, never, in Extremity,
It asked a crumb—of Me.

*Emily Dickinson*

# Unit Assignments

**Assignment 1**   Analyze the theme of a literary work that is concerned with social problems. For example, you might choose *The Grapes of Wrath,* by John Steinbeck; *The Jungle,* by Upton Sinclair; or "The Unknown Citizen," by W. H. Auden. In your thesis statement, set forth the principal problem with which the work is concerned. Give adequate examples in your essay.

**Assignment 2**   Explain the theme of Emily Dickinson's "This is my letter to the world," Robert Frost's "Birches," or another work by either of these poets. In your essay consider the techniques that the poet uses to develop the theme.

**Assignment 3**   Compare and contrast the views of American life presented in *Our Town,* by Thornton Wilder, and *Main Street,* by Sinclair Lewis. Include in your study a consideration of each author's purpose.

**Assignment 4**   Analyze Ernest Hemingway's use of symbols in *The Old Man and the Sea.* You should explain how the symbols relate to the theme.

**Assignment 5**   Compare and contrast the themes in two poems by Edna St. Vincent Millay or two poems by Gwendolyn Brooks. Be sure to present quotations from both works.

**Assignment 6**   Compare and contrast Natty Bumppo, the hero of *The Deerslayer,* by James Fenimore Cooper, and the hero of a twentieth-century novel.

**Assignment 7**   Analyze Edgar Allan Poe's use of poetic sound in "Annabel Lee," "The Raven," or "To Helen."

**Assignment 8**   Analyze a character's reaching maturity in "The Bear," by William Faulkner, or in another work.

**Assignment 9**  Discuss the view of society presented in "Paul's Case" or "The Sculptor's Funeral," by Willa Cather.

**Assignment 10**  Explain the theme of "O Captain! My Captain!" by Walt Whitman.

## Revising Your Assignments

For help in revising a literary essay, consult the Checklist for Revision on the last page of this book.

# Unit Tests

## Test 1

**A.**  Number your paper from 1 to 5. Next to each number, write *True* if the sentence is true or *False* if it is false.

1. An author's life is a suitable topic for a literary essay.
2. The purpose of a literary essay is analysis and evaluation.
3. In a literary essay, prose quotations of five or more lines are set off from the text.
4. A literary essay must be based on secondary sources.
5. In writing a literary essay, you consistently use the past tense.

**B.**  Number your paper from 6 to 10. Next to each number, write the letter of the item that correctly completes the sentence. You will use all but one of the items.

a. thesis statement     d. direct quotation

b. documentation     e. summary

c. literary essay     f. tone

6. In a __?__, you must base your interpretation on the incidents, ideas, and characters presented by the author.
7. __?__ for a literary essay supplies information about the works from which you took quotations or ideas.
8. In a literary essay, a __?__ may be used for expressing a particularly memorable passage from the work being discussed.
9. The body paragraphs should consist of evidence that is clearly related to the __?__.
10. The __?__ of a literary essay should be serious and formal.

**C.**  Number your paper from 11 to 15. Next to each number, write the letter of the item that correctly answers the question.

11. Which of the following is a suitable topic for a literary essay?
    a. What happens in *A Tale of Two Cities*
    b. How Poe maintains suspense in "The Tell-Tale Heart"
    c. Kate Chopin's childhood
    d. Colonial literature

12. Which of the following sentences is appropriate for a literary essay?
    a. Three characters take turns narrating the actions of *Absalom, Absalom!*
    b. I believe that the need for simplicity is the theme of *Walden.*
    c. *Our Town* presented the stories of families in a town.
    d. In *The Prairie* Natty Bumppo is not too crazy about civilization; therefore, he hides out in the wilderness whenever he can.

13. Which of the following topics would involve an analysis of a character in a literary work?
    a. The use of humor in "A Good Man Is Hard to Find"
    b. The importance of money in "The Necklace"
    c. Paul in "Paul's Case"
    d. References to the sense of smell in *The Sound and The Fury*

14. Which of the following topics would involve an analysis of a technique used in a literary work?
    a. Ophelia in *Hamlet*
    b. Interaction among the characters in "The Open Boat"
    c. The theme of "An Occurrence at Owl Creek Bridge"
    d. The repetition of sound in "O What Is That Sound?"

15. Which of the following is an appropriate thesis statement for a literary essay?
    a. I always enjoy reading "Ozymandias," by the nineteenth-century poet Percy Bysshe Shelley.
    b. The theme of "Ozymandias" is the irony of greatness in history.
    c. Percy Bysshe Shelley also wrote "Ode to the West Wind."
    d. The main character in the poem is Ozymandias, at one time a ruler in Egypt.

# Test 2

Choose one of the Unit Assignments. Write the assignment as directed and hand it in to your teacher.

# Unit 13

# Writing a Research Paper

---

## Unit Preview

**Research** is a process of investigation. A research paper is a formal presentation in two thousand to twenty-five hundred words (seven to ten typed pages) of your findings. Your paper begins with an introduction that includes a **thesis statement,** a statement that indicates what you intend to prove in the paper. The body of the research paper contains the information that supports or proves your thesis statement.

The following paragraphs are from the beginning of a research paper about the use of computers in schools:

Introduction

Thesis statement

Body paragraph

An increasing number of schools are using computerized instruction, which can range from exercises that reinforce lessons taught by the teacher to complete lessons taught and tested by a computer. Computerized instruction is valuable for several reasons: it provides individualized instruction; it teaches students about the technology that they may use in future jobs; and it saves the teacher hours usually spent in presenting and grading exercises.

The most complete individualized computer instruction is provided in New York City by Mr. Leachim, a computer that can speak and can understand speech. Mr. Leachim stores information about the grades, test scores, families, and interests of the students it teaches. Then Mr. Leachim uses its knowledge to tailor lessons and exercises for each student.

**For Analysis**   On your paper, answer the following questions about the preceding paragraphs from the research paper on computerized instruction.

1. What does the writer intend to prove in this research paper?
2. What is the topic of the second paragraph?

In this unit you will follow the development of a research paper about a women's labor movement in Lowell, Massachusetts, from the selection and narrowing of the topic, through the research, to the preparation of the final paper. You will also work through the process of preparing and writing your own research paper.

# 13.1  Planning Your Research Paper

## 13.1a  Selecting and Limiting a Topic

Selecting a topic of interest to you is the first step in writing your research paper. You may be assigned a general subject, such as American life in the nineteenth and twentieth centuries, or you may choose a topic of your own. When selecting a topic, keep in mind the resources of the library that you will be using. Do not choose a topic on which the library will have little or no information.

To arrive at your topic, start with a general subject and keep limiting it until you reach a specific topic. For example, you can limit the general subject of American life in the nineteenth and twentieth centuries to the following subjects:

| | | |
|---|---|---|
| Family life | Environment | Technology |
| Cities | Farm life | Television |
| Education | Industrialization | Transportation |

Each of these subjects is still too broad for a research paper. The following examples demonstrate how you can further limit a subject to a specific topic for research:

| | |
|---|---|
| SUBJECT | Education |
| TOPICS | Preschool education, Computer-assisted instruction, School sports |
| SUBJECT | Environment |
| TOPICS | Pollutants, Recycling, Environmental legislation |
| SUBJECT | Industrialization |
| TOPICS | Women workers, Early factories, Labor unions |
| SUBJECT | Television |
| TOPICS | Nielsen ratings, Educational television, Producing news programs |

**Exercise 1   Prewriting: Research-Paper Topics**   On your paper, write three possible research-paper topics for each of five of the following subjects.

| | |
|---|---|
| **SAMPLE** | Music |
| **ANSWER** | Electronic music, The music of Aaron Copland, Rock opera |

| | | |
|---|---|---|
| 1. Advertising | 9. Education | 17. Inventions |
| 2. Aging | 10. Fashion | 18. Marine biology |
| 3. Architecture | 11. Folk art | 19. Meteorology |
| 4. Business | 12. Genealogy | 20. Modern art |
| 5. Careers | 13. Geology | 21. The Old West |
| 6. Comic books | 14. Heroes | 22. Photography |
| 7. Conservation | 15. Hobbies | 23. Sports |
| 8. Crafts | 16. Holidays | 24. Theater |

## 13.1b Writing a Preliminary Thesis Statement

Once you have a topic for your research paper, limit it further by writing a preliminary thesis statement. The **thesis statement** is a sentence in which you state your position on the topic; it makes clear the purpose of your paper. A thesis statement can be supported or proved by research findings. You will begin your research with the purpose expressed in your preliminary thesis statement. You may have to change your preliminary thesis statement after you have learned more from your research, but the preliminary statement is a starting point for your investigation.

The following examples show the progression from a general subject to a topic to a thesis statement.

*General subject:* Education
*Topic:* Preschool education
*Thesis statement:* Preschool education helps students to perform better throughout their school careers.

*General subject:* Environment
*Topic:* Environmental legislation
*Thesis statement:* Much of the legislation that prohibits fishing in polluted waters has not been effective.

*General subject:* Industrialization
*Topic:* Women workers
*Thesis statement:* Adverse conditions forced women to start a labor movement in Lowell, Massachusetts, in the nineteenth century.

*General subject:* Television
*Topic:* Educational television
*Thesis statement:* Many educational television programs are intended to make learning fun for children.

Follow this procedure in moving from your topic to a preliminary thesis statement.

### Procedure

1. *Read one or two general articles on your topic* in a magazine, a textbook, an encyclopedia, or another source.

2. *Note at least two ideas, questions, comparisons, or suggestions in your reading that help you to focus the topic.*

3. *Formulate a specific idea that you can support or prove by research.* Write it as your preliminary thesis statement.

As you develop your preliminary thesis statement, keep the following points in mind:

1. A thesis statement establishes your position on the topic.
2. The position in your thesis statement can be supported or proved by research findings. Therefore, a thesis statement should *not* be one of the following:
    a. A well-known fact that can be shown to be true, such as "American astronauts were the first to be on the moon."
    b. A biased opinion that cannot be proved, such as "The Rocky Mountains provide the best outdoor recreation in North America."
    c. A biographical statement, such as "Emily Dickinson lived her entire life in Amherst, Massachusetts."
    d. A personal statement on which you can write entirely from your own knowledge or experience, such as "I have been writing computer programs for two years."

**Exercise 2  Prewriting: Thesis Statements**  On your paper, tell why the following sentences are not satisfactory thesis statements. Revise five of them to make them good thesis statements.

| | |
|---|---|
| **SAMPLE** | Dinosaurs are extinct. |
| **ANSWER** | The statement is a well-known fact. |
| | *Revised:* There were at least three major factors that brought about the extinction of dinosaurs. |

1. Movies are better now than ever.
2. Albert Schweitzer lived a long life.
3. I have successfully trained dogs to herd sheep.
4. Everyone should learn a foreign language.
5. William Fulbright had a long career in the Senate.
6. Big business in the United States is too powerful.
7. I have observed firsthand the dangers of coal mining.

8. Many important machines were invented in the 1900s.
9. Sunspots are areas of strong magnetic force.
10. Mariposa lilies are the most beautiful flowers.

**Exercise 3 Prewriting: Thesis Statements** On your paper, limit five of the following subjects to make them suitable topics for research papers. Then write a thesis statement for each of the five topics.

> **SAMPLE** Medicine
>
> **ANSWER** *Topic:* Paramedics
> *Thesis statement:* Paramedical workers can often take the place of a doctor.

1. Newspaper journalism
2. American artists
3. The New Deal
4. The Great Depression
5. The Constitution
6. Professional sports
7. Prison reform
8. Theories of education
9. Career education
10. Jazz

## 13.1c Making a Rough Outline

Before you begin your research, make a research plan in the form of a rough outline, a simple listing of main headings. After you have read articles in preparation for writing the preliminary thesis statement, you can probably identify the main ideas that will support your thesis statement. These ideas will be the headings in your rough outline. This outline may change after you have gathered information, but now, along with your preliminary thesis statement, it will guide your research. You will develop a complete outline after you have finished your research.

The following rough outline is the research plan for the paper on the women factory workers in Lowell, Massachusetts. It supports the ideas in the thesis statement developed earlier (*page 485*): Adverse conditions forced women to start a labor movement in Lowell, Massachusetts, in the nineteenth century.

> I. Establishment of mills in the United States
> II. The Lowell experience
> III. Organization of workers
> IV. Other movements for women

**Exercise 4   Prewriting: Rough Outlines**   On your paper, write the following three thesis statements. Under each one list the headings that belong with it. Then arrange the headings so that they form a rough outline for each topic.

1. One-way and two-way radios have many uses—from business to research to recreation.
2. Broadcasting the early, dramatic radio programs was a complex production that involved the work of many people.
3. Scientists understood the technology needed to make radios long before the first radio broadcast took place.

> Experimental broadcasts in 1910
> Scriptwriters
> Entertainment
> Source of two-way communication
> Discovery of electromagnetic current in 1800
> Announcers
> Technicians
> Information
> Explanation of electromagnetic theory in 1864
> Directors
> Invention of vacuum tubes to amplify sound in 1900
> Operation of remote control devices
> Transmission of signals across the Atlantic Ocean in 1901
> Orchestras
> First voice communication in 1906
> Aids in forecasting weather
> Special-effects people
> First transmission of signals in 1895 by Marconi
> Live audience
> Issuance of first license to radio station in 1920

**Assignment   Prewriting**   Make a list of five subjects that interest you and that are suitable for research. Limit three of them, and write preliminary thesis statements for those three.

**Continuing Assignment   Prewriting**   *Step 1:* Select a topic for your research paper. It may be based on an assignment or it may be a topic of your own choosing. *Step 2:* Limit your topic. Write a preliminary thesis statement that tells what you plan to prove. *Step 3:* Make a rough outline of the major points that you plan to cover in your paper. Save your preliminary thesis statement and rough outline.

## Assignment Checklist

Check your assignments for the following points:

✓ 1. Did you select topics that you can research?
✓ 2. Did you limit the topics so that they can be covered thoroughly in two thousand to twenty-five hundred words?
✓ 3. Did you write preliminary thesis statements in which you establish your position on the topics?

Check your Continuing Assignment for this additional point:

✓ 4. Did you make a rough outline of the ideas that you think you will use to support your thesis statement?

# 13.2  Doing the Research

## 13.2a  Using a Library

You will do most of your research in a library. Because libraries differ in the amount of material that they provide, it is important that you use the best library available to you.

Now that you have a limited topic and a rough outline to direct your research, use all of the library resources that will help you to locate material related to your topic.

## The Card Catalog

Begin your search for information in the card catalog. The **card catalog** is made up of cards, filed alphabetically, for every book in the library. Most books are listed in three ways: by author, by title, and by subject. Each catalog card contains the name(s) of the author(s), the complete title, the subject, the publisher, the publication date, the number of pages in the book, and the **call number** of the book—a number that enables you to find the book on the shelf. If the book contains illustrations, maps, bibliographies, or any other special features, these are indicated on the card.

The following are examples of catalog cards:

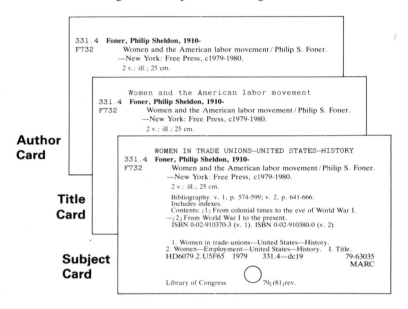

**Author Card**

**Title Card**

**Subject Card**

For common subjects, such as television, comedy, baseball, and transportation, you will probably find subject cards when you look up the subject. When you look up other subjects, you may find a cross-reference card directing you to another subject heading in the catalog. For example, the cross-reference "Labor Unions" directs you to "*See* Trade Unions." Books on the subject will be listed under that heading.

The card catalog will tell you what books in the library might be useful in your research. To find the books, you will need the call numbers. Nonfiction books are arranged on the shelves according to their call numbers. The call numbers follow the system of classification used by the library, either the Dewey decimal system or the Library of Congress classification.

School libraries and many town libraries use the Dewey decimal system. The Dewey decimal system divides all branches of knowledge into ten parts according to hundreds, 000 through 900. These parts are then further divided into more specific areas of knowledge.

**The Dewey Decimal System**

| | | | |
|---|---|---|---|
| 000–099 | General Works | 500–599 | Science |
| 100–199 | Philosophy | 600–699 | Technology |
| 200–299 | Religion | 700–799 | Fine Arts |
| 300–399 | Social Sciences | 800–899 | Literature |
| 400–499 | Language | 900–999 | History |

Many college and university libraries and some city libraries use the Library of Congress classification, which divides all fields of knowledge into twenty groups.

**The Library of Congress Classification**

| | | | |
|---|---|---|---|
| A | General Works | M | Music |
| B | Philosophy, Psychology, and Religion | N | Fine Arts |
| | | P | Language and Literature |
| C | History—Auxiliary Sciences | | |
| D | History (except American) | Q | Science |
| E, F | American History | R | Medicine |
| G | Geography, Anthropology, and Recreation | S | Agriculture |
| | | T | Technology |
| H | Social Sciences | U | Military Science |
| J | Political Science | V | Naval Science |
| K | Law | Z | Bibliography |
| L | Education | | |

## General Reference Works

Knowing how to use reference works will help you to find certain kinds of information. Some reference works give you information, and others tell you where to find information.

For basic, general information, the most common sources are encyclopedias. You can use an encyclopedia to get an overview of your topic when you begin your research. The articles are arranged alphabetically by subject and give reliable, general information. At the end of an article, or in the index volume, you may find a listing of related topics that appear elsewhere in the encyclopedia. General encyclopedias, such as *Collier's Encyclopedia* and *The World Book Encyclopedia,* are available in most libraries.

Special-interest encyclopedias can also help you to begin your research. The following are examples of specialized encyclopedias that you may find in a large library.

> *Encyclopedia of World Art*
> *Grzimek's Animal Life Encyclopedia*
> *Van Nostrand's Scientific Encyclopedia*

There are also reference works for a variety of subjects such as history, science, or business. You should be aware of the following types of references:

> Almanacs and Yearbooks—annual publications composed of various lists, charts, and tables of useful information in many fields
> Atlases—bound collections of maps
> Gazetteers—geographical dictionaries or indexes of places

The following are among the many sources where you can find biographical information:

> *Who's Who in America*
> *Who's Who in the World*
> *Biographical Directory of the American Congress, 1774–1971*
> *Current Biography*

## Periodical Indexes

The most useful reference works for finding information in other sources are indexes to periodical literature. These indexes list articles that have appeared in magazines, newspapers, and other publications.

Magazines and newspapers provide current information on changing attitudes and new developments before these ideas are included in books. If your topic requires current information, use periodical indexes to begin your research. Most periodical indexes are published monthly or quarterly with cumulative annual volumes. At the front of each index is a list of abbreviations for the periodicals listed in the index. Authors and subjects are arranged in one alphabetical listing.

The *Readers' Guide to Periodical Literature* is an index to popular and nontechnical magazines. Other indexes list articles in scholarly publications and specialized magazines.

You might consult the following indexes in a large library for periodical articles that deal with your research topic:

> *Art Index*
> *General Science Index*
> *Social Sciences Index*
> *The New York Times Index*

Entries in periodical indexes are similar in form to the following one from the *Readers' Guide:*

**LOWELL, Mass.**
Working ladies of Lowell. B.A. Weisberger. biblog il Am Heritage 12:42-5+ F '61

The entry contains the following information:

| | |
|---|---|
| TITLE | "Working ladies of Lowell" |
| AUTHOR | B. A. Weisberger |
| PERIODICAL | *American Heritage*, volume 12 |
| PAGES | 42 to 45; continued later in magazine |
| DATE | February 1961 |

When using an index to periodical literature, look up your topic and related topics. Write down the name, date, and volume of each magazine or newspaper and the name, author, and page number of each article that you find. Ask the librarian whether the library has back issues of the periodicals that you want. In some libraries back issues are allowed to circulate; in other libraries periodicals are used only in the library reference areas. If you must use periodicals in the library, allow plenty of time for library research.

## The Vertical File

The **vertical file** is a large file cabinet that contains material that is not kept on shelves. You will find pictures, pamphlets, newspaper clippings, and government pamphlets stored in folders arranged alphabetically by subject.

**Exercise 1** **Prewriting: Library Resources** On your paper, write the letter of the source or sources that you might use to find general information on each topic in the numbered list.

> a. *The New York Times Index*
> b. *Encyclopedia of World Art*
> c. *Grzimek's Animal Life Encyclopedia*
> d. *Readers' Guide to Periodical Literature*
> e. *General Science Index*
> f. *Current Biography*

> **SAMPLE** the use of lasers in surgery
> **ANSWER** a, d, e

1. Maxie Anderson's accomplishments as a balloonist
2. The 1960 Presidential election
3. Disease-resistant corn
4. Michelangelo's sculpture
5. Changing temperature patterns on Earth
6. The 1982 World Series
7. Jamie Wyeth's paintings
8. The migration of swallows
9. The seven species of bears
10. Fashions in the 1960s and the 1970s

## 13.2b Making a Working Bibliography

The first step in your library research is to prepare a working bibliography. A **bibliography** is a list of the books, magazines, and other sources used in preparing a research paper. The **working bibliography** is the list that you make at the beginning of your research of the sources that you intend to use. Your working bibliography will help you to determine how much information is available on your topic. Make a working bibliography by consulting the card catalog, indexes to periodical literature, and other appropriate reference works. If there is not enough information on your topic, change your topic to something that you can research adequately in your library.

## Bibliography Cards

Record on note cards (three-by-five-inch index cards) the books, articles, pamphlets, and other sources that you find. Recording this information will help you in two ways. First, you will be able to locate sources more easily when you are ready to take notes. Second, you will have all the necessary information when you write the footnotes and the bibliography. Make a separate card for each source, and include on the card the call number of the book and the library where you found the book. Record the author, title, and publication information in the correct forms, which follow:

A BOOK WITH ONE AUTHOR

> Litwack, Leon. *The American Labor Movement.* Englewood Cliffs, New Jersey: Prentice-Hall, Inc., 1962.

A BOOK WITH TWO AUTHORS

> Brownlee, W. Elliot, and Mary H. Brownlee. *Women in the American Economy: A Documentary History, 1675 to 1927.* New Haven, Connecticut: Yale University Press, 1976.

A BOOK COMPILED BY AN EDITOR

> Eisler, Benita, ed. *The Lowell Offering: Writings by New England Mill Women (1840–1845).* New York: J. B. Lippincott Company, 1977.

AN ARTICLE IN A COLLECTION

> Livermore, Thomas L. "Relations Between Labor and Capital." In *The People Shall Judge: American History and Its Great Arguments.* Ed. by the staff, Social Sciences. Chicago: The University of Chicago Press, 1949.

AN ARTICLE IN A MAGAZINE
> Ginger, Ray. "Labor in a Massachusetts Cotton Mill, 1853
> –1860." *Business History Review,* Mar. 1954, pp.
> 67–91.

A FILMSTRIP OR A TAPE
> *Women Who Work.* Guidance Associates, 1976.

A NEWSPAPER ARTICLE
> "Growing Acceptance for the Coalition of Union Women."
> *New York Times,* 19 Oct. 1977, Sec. D, p. 3, col. 1.

AN ARTICLE IN AN ENCYCLOPEDIA
> "Labor Force." *International Encyclopedia of the Social Sciences.* 1968 ed.

A PAMPHLET
> U.S. Department of Labor. *A Look at Hours Worked Under
> the Fair Labor Standards Act.* Washington, D.C.: U.S.
> Government Printing Office, 1980.

Here is a sample bibliography card:

## Bibliography Card

| | |
|---|---|
| Author<br>Title | Foner, Philip S. Women and the<br>American Labor Movement:<br>From Colonial Times to<br>the Eve of World War I. |
| Place of publication | New York : The Free Press, |
| Publisher<br>Date of publication | 1979. |
| Call number<br>Library | 331.4   Public Library<br>F732 |

**Exercise 2   Prewriting: Bibliography Entries**   On your paper or on note cards, write bibliography listings based on the following information.

| AUTHOR | TITLE | PUBLICATION FACTS |
|---|---|---|
| *Books* | | |
| 1. Morton Grosser | *Gossamer Odyssey* | Houghton Mifflin Company Boston, Massachusetts 1981 |
| 2. Irene Wood Bell and Jeanne E. Wieckert | *Basic Media Skills Through Games* | Libraries Unlimited, Inc. New York, New York 1979 |
| *Article in a Book* | | |
| 3. Lionel Casson | "Where Did Ancient Traders Sail?" | *Mysteries of the Past* Joseph Thorndike, editor American Heritage Publishing Company New York, New York 1977 |
| *Article in a Periodical* | | |
| 4. Not given | "Master of Inconsistency" | *Newsweek* June 29, 1981 pp. 74–76 |
| 5. Gayla Grier Smith | "Is Critical Care Nursing Right for You?" | *Nursing 80* June 1980 pp. 97–105 |
| 6. Not given | "The Price of Cleaner Air" | *New York Times* 27 July 1981 Sec. A, p. 14 cols. 1–2 |
| 7. Arlen J. Large | "Big Windmills Are Becoming Marketable" | *Wall Street Journal* 7 April 1981 Sec. 2, p. 56, cols. 1–3 |
| *Article in a Reference Book* | | |
| 8. Not given | "Acoustics" | *Encyclopedia Americana* 1981 |
| 9. Not given | "Richard Erskine Leakey" | *Who's Who in America* 1952 |

*Pamphlet or Government Document*

| | | |
|---|---|---|
| 10. Not given | *Consumer's Guide to Food Labels* | General Services Administration U.S. Government Printing Office Washington, D.C. 1978 pp. 1–4 |

**Assignment   Prewriting**   Prepare a working bibliography of at least five sources for research on one of the following topics:

1. Cave paintings in North America
2. Solar energy
3. The Supreme Court
4. Wildlife conservation

**Continuing   Assignment   Prewriting**   Prepare a working bibliography for the topic that you selected and limited in the Continuing Assignment on page 488. Use the card catalog, periodical indexes, other reference works, and the vertical file. Make a bibliography card for each source that you can consult for your research. Save your working bibliography.

## Assignment Checklist

Check your assignments for the following points:

  ✔ 1. Did you use the card catalog, periodical indexes, reference works, and the vertical file to make a working bibliography?
  ✔ 2. Did you make a separate card for each source?
  ✔ 3. Does each card include complete bibliography information, the call number of the book, and the name of the library where it is located?
  ✔ 4. Did you write the bibliography information in the correct form?

# 13.3  Taking Notes

The next step in your research is to locate the sources in your working bibliography. Then, take notes on information that will help you to support your thesis statement.

## 13.3a Evaluating Sources

Take time to evaluate each source before you decide to take notes from it. Follow these strategies to evaluate a source.

### Strategies

1. *Examine the table of contents and the index* of a book to see if the book contains information directly related to your topic.

2. *Check the publication date of books and articles.* If your topic is in a field of rapid growth or change, your thesis statement will require current information as support. Older books and articles may contain inaccurate, incomplete, or obsolete information.

3. *Skim chapters or articles for supporting information,* while keeping your preliminary thesis statement in mind.

**Exercise 1 Prewriting: Evaluating Sources** On your paper, tell whether each source would provide useful information in support of the given thesis statement. Give a reason for each answer.

> **SAMPLE** *Thesis Statement:* The modern Olympics were organized in 1896 to promote learning and world peace.
>
> *Sources:*
>
> a. "Athens 1896," *The Story of the Olympic Games: 776 B.C. to 1968*
>
> b. "Boxing," *Olympic Sports Official Album: Montreal 1976*
>
> **ANSWER** a. Useful. The founding of the modern Olympics would be included in *The Story of the Olympic Games.* Also, an entire chapter is devoted to the events of 1896.
>
> b. Not useful. The subject "boxing" is not related to the founding of the modern Olympics. Also, the book is about an Olympic meet that is too recent.

1. *Thesis statement:* The octopus is not as dangerous as people generally think it is.

   *Sources:*

   a. *Field Guide to Freshwater Fishes of North America*

   b. "Danger," Chapter 11 of *Kingdom of the Octopus*

   c. *Collier's Encyclopedia*

   d. "Unusual Foods from the Sea" in *Food Talk* magazine

   e. *Grzimek's Animal Life Encyclopedia*

   f. *Glossary of Oceanographic Terms*

   g. "Eyes and Skin of Octopus" in *Endeavour* magazine

2. *Thesis statement:* The designs on North American Indian pottery differ according to the region in which they were produced.

   *Sources:*

   a. "Pottery" in *North American Indian Arts*

   b. "Southwestern Pottery Region" in *North American Indian Arts*

   c. "Textiles" in *North American Indian Arts*

   d. *American Indian Art: Form and Tradition*

   e. *Indians of Today*

   f. "Pottery from the Tigua Pueblo" in *Art News* magazine

   g. "Word Is Out: Buy American Pottery" in *Vogue* magazine

   h. "Indian Arts for Indian Students" in *Design* magazine

## 13.3b  How to Take Notes

When you have determined that information in a source is useful for your paper, you are ready to take notes on it. Take notes on three-by-five-inch or four-by-six-inch index cards. The following strategies will help you to organize your note taking so that the information that you need will be easy to find when you write your paper.

### Strategies

1. *Keep your preliminary thesis statement and your rough outline before you.*

2. *Read carefully through a source for understanding.* Read

through each source a second time, recording facts, ideas, statistics, quotations, or other information that will help support your thesis statement.

3. *On the top line of each card, write a subject heading to identify the subject of the note.* Some subject headings will correspond to the headings on your rough outline; others will be more specific. These subject headings will be useful when you develop your detailed outline. They will form some of the major headings and subheadings.

4. *Write the last name of the author and an abbreviated title* (or just the title if the author is not known) at the upper right of each card.

5. *Write only one idea on each card.* This method will allow you to rearrange your cards when organizing your information later on.

6. *Write on only the front of the card.* You might later overlook information on the back of a card. If you need more room, use a second card.

7. *Write the number of the page(s) from which you took the information.* You will need the page numbers for footnotes.

You will take notes according to one of the following methods: direct quotation, paraphrase, summary, or a combination of these methods. Choose the method best suited to your sources.

## Direct Quotation

A **direct quotation** reproduces the exact words of your source. Use a direct quotation when the author makes a point in a significant or unusual way. In such cases, a direct quotation may be the strongest way to support your point. Copy the words exactly and put quotation marks around the passage. If you leave out any words from the quoted passage, use an ellipsis (three spaced periods) to indicate that words have been omitted. See Unit 5, pages 207–208.

### Direct Quotation

Subject heading ———
Author (editor) ——
Abbreviated title ——

*Factory System*     *Foner, Factory Girls*

Note ——

"Wages were set at a level which would be high enough to induce young women to leave the farms and stay away from competing employment, such as household manufactures and domestic service, but low enough to offer an advantage for employing females rather than males...."

Page reference ——

p. xix

## Paraphrase

A **paraphrase** is a restatement in your own words of the ideas in a passage. Paraphrase material that you want to use but do not need in the exact words of the writer. Keep the author's meaning without using the author's words.

The following passage from *The Lowell Offering*, edited by Benita Eisler, is the basis of the paraphrase that follows it.

> From the farms of Massachusetts, Vermont, New Hampshire, and Maine, came robust young women, lured by the highest wages offered to female employees anywhere in America—from $1.85 to $3.00 a week, depending on skill and speed. This seemingly generous scale represented a considerable saving for the mill owners, since male mill workers were paid twice as much.

### Paraphrase

Subject heading ———
Author (editor) ——
Abbreviated title ——

*Factory System*     *Eisler, Lowell Offering*

Note ——

Women from New England farms were attracted by the highest wages paid to women workers in America. Their wages depended on how fast and how skillfully they worked. The wages that seemed generous to women were a bargain for owners because men were paid more.

Page reference ——

p. 15

## Summary

A **summary** is a condensed version of a passage. Write a summary in your own words, giving just the main points and essential details. On your note cards, summarize longer passages that contain views, interpretations, or statistics that support your points.

The following passage from *The Factory Girls,* edited by Philip S. Foner, is the basis of the summary note that follows it.

> These new periodicals carried their share of genteel poetry, stories, and advice on general conduct. But they also spoke out vigorously in defense of the factory operatives and supported all of their efforts to organize to improve their conditions. Moreover, through their columns the young women began at once to demolish the myth concerning the so-called Beauty of Factory Life. They did this in letters, articles, and even poetry describing the actual conditions in the mills. Liberal papers like the *Manchester Democrat* also opened their columns to letters and articles from factory operatives that described the real conditions they faced in the mills.

### Summary

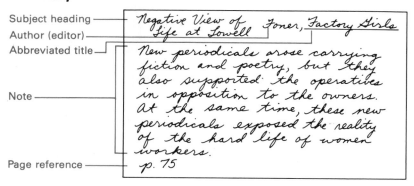

Subject heading — Negative View of *Life at Lowell* — Foner, *Factory Girls*

Author (editor) —

Abbreviated title —

Note — New periodicals arose carrying fiction and poetry, but they also supported the operatives in opposition to the owners. At the same time, these new periodicals exposed the reality of the hard life of women workers.

Page reference — p. 75

**Exercise 2   Prewriting: Taking Notes**   You are writing a research paper about the varieties of color and form in snow crystals. You want to take notes on the information in the following passage. Using the subject heading "Color," write one note that is a direct quotation.

> Snow is remarkably varied. For example, consider hue. There is the glistening white of wet spring snow and the dull powdery white of new-fallen dry snow, the glitter of sequin crystals following

a bitterly cold night, and the forlorn grime of snow soiled by city dirt and country dust. Snow can be gray and invisible against the horizon on an overcast day, or it may turn violet-blue as the rays of incoming light are filtered out except for the blue end of the spectrum.

Ruth Kirk, *Snow,* page 17

**Exercise 3   Prewriting: Taking Notes**   Make a second note card with the subject heading "Color," based on the passage in Exercise 2. Write a paraphrase of a sentence that you did not quote directly for Exercise 2.

**Exercise 4   Prewriting: Taking Notes**   You are writing a research paper on the features that help animals to survive in their environments. Write a note card with the subject heading "Giraffe's legs—disadvantages" that summarizes the following passage.

When the giraffe wishes to drink or lick salt from the ground, its attitude appears to be extremely awkward. It becomes obvious that the giraffe's neck in relation to its forelegs is shorter than that of most ruminants [animals that chew cud]. Thus it must either bend its knees or splay its legs apart. It has to learn how to do this. Very young giraffes get themselves into all sorts of complicated positions with one leg bent and one leg straight before they master the technique. It never likes to adopt this lowered position as it is then most vulnerable to predators. Usually it makes a few preliminary bobs up and down with its head before actually lowering it completely, and then, while drinking, it will suddenly look up to see if anything is attempting to surprise it. It can rise very suddenly by snapping its head back and simultaneously straightening or pulling its legs under it.

C. A. Spinage, *The Book of the Giraffe,* page 126

**Assignment   Prewriting**   Find a short article in a magazine. Read the article and write three note cards based on it. Make one note a direct quotation, one a paraphrase, and one a summary. Give each note card a subject heading.

**Continuing Assignment   Prewriting**   In the Continuing Assignment on page 498, you prepared a working bibliography. Using the sources in your working bibliography, take notes for each part of your rough outline. Use the type of note that is most appropriate for the information that you are recording. Save your note cards.

### Assignment Checklist

Check your assignments for the following points:

- ✓ 1. Did you accurately record information from your sources on note cards?
- ✓ 2. Did you include on each card a subject heading, the author's last name, an abbreviated title, and a page reference?
- ✓ 3. Did you copy quotations exactly?
- ✓ 4. Did you enclose all direct quotations in quotation marks?
- ✓ 5. Did you write the paraphrase in your own words?
- ✓ 6. Did you write summaries that cover the key points of a section?

# 13.4  Organizing Your Information

## Revising Your Preliminary Thesis Statement

The next step in the process of writing a research paper is to compare your preliminary thesis statement with your notes. Now that you have more information, you may find it necessary to revise your preliminary thesis statement so that it accurately reflects the information that you are about to present.

The thesis statement is the most important sentence in the paper because you develop your entire paper from it. The following example shows the revision of the preliminary thesis statement for a paper on the women factory workers of Lowell, Massachusetts.

*Preliminary thesis statement:* Adverse conditions forced women to start a labor movement in Lowell, Massachusetts, in the nineteenth century.

*Revised thesis statement:* In the early part of the nineteenth century, the living and working conditions in the town of Lowell, Massachusetts, united women in a labor movement.

## Making a Detailed Outline

Your next step is to organize your ideas into a detailed topic outline like the one on page 507. Use the following procedure.

### Procedure

1. *Read through all your note cards.* Separate the cards according to their subject headings. You will probably find several cards with the same or similar subject headings. Keep related cards together.

2. *Use the subject headings on your groups of note cards to determine the main headings on your outline.* Look again at your rough outline. Now that you have more information, you may change some of the headings, eliminating those that do not support your revised thesis statement and adding others that do. Then, depending on your topic and your purpose, arrange the headings in a suitable order, for example, chronological order, order of importance, cause and effect, or comparison and contrast.

3. *Use your note cards to help you add supporting details.* Eliminate those note cards that do not support your points. Separate the remaining cards again according to those subject headings that will support your points. These will be subheadings on your outline.

4. *Use a Roman numeral for each main heading.* Use *I* for the introduction and use the last Roman numeral for the conclusion. Use a capital letter for each subheading. If you list further details under the subheadings, give those details Arabic numerals.

5. *Write corresponding headings in the same grammatical form.* For example, if the heading for *A* is a phrase, the headings for *B, C,* and *D* should be the same kind of phrase. (An outline that is written in complete sentences is called a sentence outline. Your teacher may ask you to prepare this kind of outline instead.)

6. *Subdivide a topic into two or more sections.* Do not have an *A* without a *B,* for example, or a *1* without a *2.* If you

cannot subdivide a topic into at least two parts, then the larger topic may not need to be divided at all.

When you have finished organizing your information, you should have a thesis statement and an outline like those that follow. The outline is a revision of the outline for the model research paper about the women factory workers in Lowell on pages 526–534. As you compare the revised outline with the original rough outline (page 487), you will see that changes have been made. New topics have been added and the organization has been changed because after researching the topic, the writer has new information to include.

*Thesis Statement:* In the early part of the nineteenth century, the living and working conditions in the mill town of Lowell, Massachusetts, united women in a labor movement.

   I. Introduction
  II. Establishment of factory system
     A. Francis Cabot Lowell's mills
     B. Opposition to industrialization
     C. Plan of Boston Associates
       1. Women workers
       2. Boarding houses
     D. Development of Lowell, Massachusetts
 III. Positive effects of life at Lowell
     A. Financial independence
     B. Educational opportunities
       1. Courses and lectures
       2. Literary magazine
     C. Solidarity
       1. Interdependence
       2. Shared experiences
 IV. Negative view of life at Lowell
     A. Long hours and hard work
     B. Worsening conditions
       1. Increased speed of machines
       2. Use of additional machines
       3. Rewards for overseers only
  V. Unified action by women
     A. Strikes
     B. Political activity
       1. Petitioning legislature
       2. Lobbying for change
 VI. Conclusion

## Taking Additional Notes

The outline enables you to visualize the sequence of your ideas and the amount of development that you have for each major point. You do not need to give equal development to each topic on your outline, but you may find that some of the topics need more support. If so, do additional research to find the necessary information. The more time you spend arranging and supporting your ideas at this stage, the less time it will take you to write and revise your paper.

**Exercise 1 Prewriting: Outlining** On your paper, make an outline for each thesis statement and set of note-card headings and subheadings. Use the given headings as major topics and the sub-headings as details. Arrange the topics in a logical order.

1. *Thesis statement:* Although the Incas had no written language to record their history, other sources have provided information about them.

   HEADINGS

   Writings
   Symbols
   Objects

   SUBHEADINGS

   Buildings
   Figures painted on pottery
   Artifacts from graves
   Accounts written by Spaniards
   Marks on lima beans
   Items from rubbish piles
   Accounts written by Incas who learned Spanish

2. *Thesis statement:* Prominent people, technological advances, and popular activities have been the causes of changes in types of clothing and fashion.

   HEADINGS

   Influence of foreign travelers
   Invention of new machines

Influence of sports
Development of synthetic fibers
Influence of nobility

SUBHEADINGS

Blue jeans to Europe from United States
Cheap clothing from mass production
Silk clothing to Europe from Far East
Jogging outfits in United States
Uniform clothing from mass production
Fox-hunting outfits in England
Styles in seventeenth-century France to copy Louis XIV
Padded clothing to imitate image of Queen Victoria of England

**Exercise 2   Prewriting: Outlining**   On your paper, write a topic outline that develops the thesis statement. Use the note cards provided on the following pages. The outline format that follows the thesis statement shows the number of main headings, subheadings, and details that you will need. Provide for an introduction and a conclusion, and take the other three main headings from the subject headings of the note cards. Supply the subheadings and details from the information in the notes.

*Thesis statement:* Activities of people in or near national parks are damaging the parks' natural resources.

    I. Introduction
   II.  _?_
         A.  _?_
              1.  _?_
              2.  _?_
         B.  _?_
         C.  _?_
  III.  _?_
         A.  _?_
         B.  _?_
         C.  _?_
   IV.  _?_
    V. Conclusion

**Note Card 1**

> Pollution                    Ash and May,
>                             <u>Petrified Forest</u>
>
> In the streams in the Petrified
> Forest National Park, "the silt
> mixes with sewage and
> industrial pollutants and
> the water is unfit."
> p. 31

**Note Card 2**

> Pollution            Pierce, <u>Yosemite</u>
> In Yosemite National Park, as in
> most national parks, most
> tourists arrive in automobiles.
> The air pollution and noise
> from the cars are causing
> problems in the park.
> p. 5

**Note Card 3**

> Pollution                    Bryan,
>                   <u>Preserving Wilderness</u>
> In Great Smoky Mountain National
> Park, some people want helicopter
> and plane transportation
> for tourists, but those
> would add to the noise
> and spoil the wilderness.
> p. 21

**Note Card 4**

Carelessness                    Bach, Yellowstone
   of visitors                        Backcountry

One hundred careful hikers
cause no harm, but one
hiker who litters or steps
on delicate ground plants
can cause serious damage.
p. 7

**Note Card 5**

Carelessness                    Beazley,
   of visitors                    Book of Forest

Ninety percent of wilderness fires
are started by people. "This
kind of fire accounts for
the loss of more than four
million acres each year in
the United States alone."
p. 46

**Note Card 6**

Thievery                        Ash and May,
                               Petrified Forest

Every year, twenty-five
pounds of petrified wood
is stolen from the Petrified
Forest National Park.

p. 25

**Assignment    Prewriting**    List five categories or groups that are part of a subject with which you are familiar, such as animals, games, music, musical instruments, or sports. Arrange the groups in a logical order, such as importance, type, size, popularity, or whatever best suits your subject. Under èach group list its subdivisions, making an outline. Write a sentence that summarizes and focuses the information in your outline.

**Continuing Assignment    Prewriting**    *Step 1:* Read through the note cards that you prepared for the Continuing Assignment on page 504. If necessary, revise your thesis statement. *Step 2:* Separate your note cards according to subject headings. Use your rough outline and your note cards to write a detailed topic outline for your paper. *Step 3:* Examine your note cards and your revised outline. If any parts of the outline do not have sufficient support, find additional sources and take notes to complete your research.

### Assignment Checklist

Check your prewriting assignment for the following points:

  ✔ 1. Did you arrange your five groups in a logical order for your subject?

  ✔ 2. Did you list at least two subdivisions under each group that you listed?

  ✔ 3. Does your summarizing sentence make a statement about the information on your outline?

Check your Continuing Assignment for these points:

  ✔ 4. Did you revise your thesis statement as a result of your research?

  ✔ 5. Did you separate your note cards into groups according to subject headings?

  ✔ 6. Did you write a topic outline that is well organized and includes all major and supporting points?

  ✔ 7. Did you take more notes if you did not have enough supporting information for any point?

# 13.5 Drafting and Documenting Your Paper

## 13.5a Writing Your First Draft

With a detailed outline and with note cards arranged according to the outline headings, you are ready to write your first draft. As you write, treat each Roman-numeral section on your outline as a unit to be written in one sitting. You will be better able to focus on the topic if you handle only one section at a time.

When you write the first draft, keep in mind that it is a rough draft. Although you should write the first draft carefully, you do not need to worry too much at this point about your word choice or sentence structure. You can improve your writing when you rewrite your paper. It is important in your first draft to write down all of your major points and supporting information in proper sequence.

Use only one side of the paper for your first draft, and write on every other line. This method will allow you to revise more easily. Number the pages of your draft as you write.

**The Introduction.** Write an introductory paragraph that explains the purpose and scope of your paper. Include the thesis statement. Give enough background information so that your reader will understand the thesis statement. You can use the introduction to state the importance of the topic, to describe the approach taken in the paper, to define important terms, and, of course, to gain the interest of your reader.

**The Body.** The body is the main part of a research paper. In it you provide the information that supports or proves your thesis statement.

Write the body of your paper by developing each heading on your outline. Use the information on your note cards to support and develop your own ideas; do not just string together your notes.

If you include direct quotations, copy them exactly. Use transitional words to incorporate them into your paper. Show the importance of the quotations to your readers by using them to illustrate or support a point.

**The Conclusion.**   In the concluding paragraph, review your main points and show that you have supported or proved your thesis statement. All of the supporting points in the paper should lead to the conclusion.

## 13.5b  Documentation

As you write your first draft, you must document the ideas that you incorporate from your notes. **Documentation** is the process by which you acknowledge the sources of the information used in your research paper. Documentation takes two forms: footnotes and bibliography.

### Footnotes

A **footnote** acknowledges the author and publication from which you have borrowed information. Each time you use information that is not your own, you must footnote it. To do so, place a superscript, or raised number, in the text above the line at the end of the information. In a corresponding note, you will give the author and the publication information. Number footnotes consecutively throughout the paper. The following rules will help you to know when to use a footnote.

**Rule**   Footnote your source when you quote an author's exact words. Use direct quotations only when the author's style is important or when the source adds authority to your paper.

> Lowell's partners chose "the most appropriate memorial: expansion of their flourishing enterprise on a new site, to be named Lowell in his honor."[1]

**Rule**   Footnote your source when you use an idea that is the author's, even though you have not used the author's exact words.

> Though the early strikes did not improve working conditions, they showed that the bond, the women's solidarity, extended to militant action against the mill owners and agents.[2]

**Rule**  Footnote your source when you give figures or statistics.

> The population of Lowell grew from 200 in 1820 to 17,633 in 1836, and to over 30,000 in 1845.[3]

Do not footnote commonly known information (information that appears in several sources) even though that information is new to you. Although you want to give credit to your sources, you also want to avoid having too many footnotes in your paper. It is important that you document your sources to avoid **plagiarism,** that is, using someone else's words or ideas as if they were your own.

**Footnote Forms.**  Footnote forms vary according to the type of source. Use the following forms unless your teacher gives you other styles to use. Notice that you do not have to include the word *The* at the beginning of the name of a magazine, newspaper, or encyclopedia. Also, you do not need to include the subtitle if a source has one.

A BOOK WITH ONE AUTHOR
> [1]Leon Litwack, *The American Labor Movement* (Englewood Cliffs, New Jersey: Prentice-Hall, Inc., 1962), p. 26.

A BOOK WITH TWO AUTHORS
> [2]W. Elliot Brownlee and Mary H. Brownlee, *Women in the American Economy* (New Haven, Connecticut: Yale University Press, 1979), p. 109.

A BOOK COMPILED BY AN EDITOR
> [3]Benita Eisler, ed., *The Lowell Offering* (New York: J. B. Lippincott Company, 1977), p. 13.

AN ARTICLE IN A COLLECTION
> [4]Thomas L. Livermore, "Relations Between Labor and Capital," in *The People Shall Judge,* ed. by the staff, Social Sciences (Chicago: The University of Chicago Press, 1949), p. 67.

AN ARTICLE IN A MAGAZINE
> [5]Ray Ginger, "Labor in a Massachusetts Cotton Mill, 1853-1860," *Business History Review,* Mar. 1954, p. 67.

A FILMSTRIP OR A TAPE
> [6]*Women Who Work,* Guidance Associates, 1976.

A NEWSPAPER ARTICLE

> [7]"Growing Acceptance for the Coalition of Union Women," *New York Times,* 19 Oct. 1977, Sec. D, p. 3, col. 1.

AN ARTICLE IN AN ENCYCLOPEDIA

> [8]"Labor Force," *International Encyclopedia of the Social Sciences,* 1968 ed.

A PAMPHLET

> [9]U.S. Department of Labor, *A Look at Hours Worked Under the Fair Labor Standards Act* (Washington, D.C.: U.S. Government Printing Office, 1980), p. 6.

You can refer to a particular source more than once in your paper. Once you have given complete information in a footnote, do not repeat the full note. In later references to the same source, identify only the author (or title if no author is given) and the page number, as shown here:

> [10]Eisler, p. 15.

If more than one book by the same author is cited in the paper, include a shortened form of the title to identify the appropriate work.

> [11]Foner, *Factory Girls,* p. 93.

**Footnote Placement.**   You may place footnotes in one of two positions. You may group the footnotes that go with each page of a research paper at the bottom of the page. When you use this arrangement, leave three lines blank between the text and the single-spaced footnotes.

You may instead place all the footnotes for a research paper on a separate page at the end of the paper. When you choose this method, write or type *Notes* at the top of the page, and place it just before the bibliography. This system simplifies the copying of the final draft of the report. Double-space footnotes when you place them on a separate page, and indent the first line of each one. Your teacher will instruct you in which form to use.

## Bibliography

The **bibliography,** the last page of your research paper, lists all the works acknowledged in the footnotes. Compile the bibliography by arranging in alphabetical order the bibliography cards for the works that you have used. Write or type an entry for each work. See page 534 for a sample bibliography page.

In preparing your bibliography, follow this procedure.

### Procedure

1. *Begin the first line of an entry at the left margin,* but indent the succeeding lines five spaces.

2. *Separate the items in the entry with periods.*

3. *Include the subtitle if a source has one.*

4. *Give the author's name in the first entry* if there are two works by the same author. In the second entry, substitute ten hyphens for the author's name, put a period after the last hyphen, and write the rest of the entry.

5. *Do not number the entries.*

**Exercise 1   Writing: Footnotes**   On your paper, write footnotes for the following information. Use the item numbers as footnote numbers. Be sure to use correct punctuation.

| AUTHOR | TITLE | PUBLICATION FACTS |
|--------|-------|-------------------|
| *Books* | | |
| 1. Dan McDonagh | *Martha Graham: a Biography* | New York, New York Praeger Publishing Co. 1973 p. 129 |
| 2. Margaret Lloyd | *The Borzoi Book of Modern Dance* | New York, New York Dance Horizons, Inc. 1974 p. 55 |
| 3. Louis Horst and Carroll Russell | *Modern Dance Forms in Relation to Other Modern Arts* | Impulse Publications San Francisco, California, 1961 p. 61 |

*Articles in a Collection*

4. Martha Graham      "Graham 1937"      *Martha Graham*
                                          Merle Armitage, editor
                                          New York, New York
                                          Dance Horizons, Inc.
                                          1966
                                          p. 83

*Magazines*

5. Tobi Tobias        "Self-Fulfilling    *New York,*
                      Prophecies"         March 16, 1981
                                          p. 46

6. Nicolas            "Choreography       *Dance Magazine,*
   Arcomano           and Copyright"      June 1980
                                          p. 62

*Newspapers*

7. Not given          "Martha Graham      *New York Times*
                      Hailed by Nation;   15 October 1976
                      Given Freedom       Section A
                      Medal by Ford"      p. 12, col. 4

*Reference Book*

8. Not given          "Martha Graham"     *Current Biography
                                          Yearbook,* 1961

**Exercise 2   Writing: Second-Entry Footnotes**   Write a second-entry footnote for sources 1 through 5 in Exercise 1.

**Exercise 3   Writing: Bibliography**   Prepare a bibliography page for the information in Exercise 1. Be sure to use correct punctuation and to alphabetize the entries.

**Assignment   Writing**   Using the outline that you prepared in Exercise 2, page 509, write a first draft of two paragraphs for the body of a paper. Use the note cards given for that exercise. Include one direct quotation.

**Continuing Assignment   Writing**   *Step 1:* Using the outline and the note cards that you prepared in the Continuing Assignments on pages 504 and 512, write a first draft of your research paper. Begin with an introduction that includes your thesis statement. Then write one section of your paper at a time. Write a conclusion that summarizes your main points. *Step 2:* Write your footnotes on a separate page, unless your teacher tells you otherwise. *Step 3:* Prepare a bibliography.

### Assignment Checklist

Check your assignments for the following points:

  ✔ 1. Is the main idea of each paragraph clear?
  ✔ 2. Did you use the supporting information listed under the appropriate heading on your outline?
  ✔ 3. Did you use direct quotations in the paragraphs?
  ✔ 4. Did you place a superscript after each direct quotation?

Check your Continuing Assignment for these additional points:

  ✔ 5. Did you write an introduction that includes your thesis statement?
  ✔ 6. Did you follow your outline, presenting your information in an orderly fashion?
  ✔ 7. Did you write accurate footnotes for the words and ideas that you borrowed from sources?
  ✔ 8. Did you write a conclusion that summarizes the points that you have made in the body of the paper?
  ✔ 9. Did you prepare the bibliography correctly?

## 13.6 Revising and Finishing Your Paper

When you have completed a first draft, set it aside for a while, if possible, before you revise it. Time away from your draft will better enable you to see where improvement is needed. Revising is your opportunity to make your paper better organized, more precise and convincing, more readable, and, of course, correct.

## 13.6a  A Guide to Revising

You will need to read your first draft slowly and carefully several times to revise it. Read the draft once for each of the following points and make the necessary changes.

**Organization.**   Check your draft against your outline to make sure that you have covered all the points in the right order. If you see a better way to organize the material, do not hesitate to depart from the outline and move or change sections of your paper. If you move a section that contains footnoted material, be sure that you also make the necessary change in the footnote order. Also, make the corresponding change on your outline. The outline that you pass in should reflect the final organization of the paper.

**Unity and Completeness.**   Check each section for unity. Each supporting detail should clearly relate to the point being made in the section. Each point should help to develop and prove the thesis statement. Remove or rewrite any sentence or detail that does not clearly relate to the point being made.

On the other hand, be sure that you have included enough information to support each point. Your reader will understand your ideas if you use facts, examples, and quotations to explain them.

**Transitions.**   Make your paper coherent by using transitions. When you wrote the first draft, you concentrated on writing one section at a time. As you revise the paper, add appropriate transitions to lead the reader from one idea to the next. Use the following strategies to make smooth transitions.

**Strategies**

1. *Use transitional words and phrases.*

   To show time: *after, at the same time, finally, later, meanwhile, next, soon, then, until*

   To present examples: *for example, for instance, one, another, to illustrate*

   To show results: *as a result, consequently, for this reason, therefore*

   To indicate logical relationships: *accordingly, also, because, however, in addition, in fact, nevertheless, yet*

2. *Use a pronoun that refers to a person or idea just mentioned in the preceding sentence or paragraph.*

> For the first time, *large numbers of women* worked outside the home in nondomestic labor. *They* earned an income, which made *them* financially independent of their families.

3. *Repeat a key word or an idea from the last sentence of a paragraph in the first sentence of the next paragraph.*

> For the workers this meant *worse conditions* and lower wages.
>
> As *conditions* at Lowell *worsened,* the women took action.

**Words and Sentences.**   When you revise, check to see that you have used the best words to express your ideas precisely. If you have used specialized terms, define them.

Express your ideas in the most effective sentences that you can write. Be careful to eliminate wordiness. Your sentences should be concise but clear. Combine short, choppy sentences into a more effective single sentence. If you find long, confusing sentences, separate them into shorter, clear sentences. Vary sentence structure and sentence length so that your writing flows smoothly. Be sure that you have been consistent in your use of person and verb tense.

**Proofreading.**   Finally, read your draft once more, correcting errors in grammar, usage, spelling, punctuation, and capitalization. Make sure that your footnotes and bibliography are correct.

When you have revised your first draft to your satisfaction, you have a final draft. Select a title that reflects the topic, while creating interest for your reader. You are now ready to type or write your finished paper.

**Exercise 1   Revising: Sentences**   The following excerpt from a research paper needs revision. On your paper, write the letter of the suggested revision for the numbered sentence that you think would best improve the draft. If you think that a sentence is effective as it stands, write the letter that indicates *Make no change.*

(1) When trains were developed in the 1800s, they first were used to haul freight over long distances.   (2) The trains were not designed to transport people.   (3) The trains were not equipped with passenger cars.   (4) When the first passenger cars were built, they were simply stagecoaches put on wheels, and, like stagecoach passengers, some of the train passengers were seated on the roof, where they were exposed to sparks from the engine and to strong winds.   (5) Some railroad companies continued to use that type of passenger car, and others tried to develop more comfortable cars.

(6) The first of the new passenger cars in the United States were only a slight advance on the old cars.   (7) They were long, single-compartment cars with rows of wooden seats on each side and an aisle down the middle.   (8) Each car seated fifty or sixty people. (9) The ride in these passenger cars was not a comfortable ride because the seats were made of wood that was hard to sit on and because the train started and stopped with violent jerks.   (10) Also, heat came only from stoves at each end of the car; consequently, "in winter those near the stoves roasted and those in the middle of the car froze."[1]   (11) Peddlers also provided additional relief by selling drinks of water and some food.   (12) Occasionally, peddlers would pass through the trains with hot bricks to help warm the feet of those in the middle of the car.   (13) These peddlers were like those at baseball games who also sell food and drinks.   (14) Not even the comforts offered by the peddlers could make riding in those rough cars pleasant.

[1]Oliver Jensen, *The American Heritage History of Railroads in America* (New York: American Heritage Publishing Co., Inc., 1975), p. 22.

1. Sentence 1
   a. Add a footnote number.
   b. Make no change.
   c. Eliminate sentence.

2. Sentences 2 and 3
   a. Make no change.
   b. Eliminate Sentence 3.
   c. Combine Sentences 2 and 3 to read, "Because the trains were not designed to transport people, they were not equipped with passenger cars."

3. Sentence 4

   a. Place the transitional word "Therefore" at the beginning of the sentence.

   b. Make no change.

   c. Separate into two sentences as follows: "When the first passenger cars were built, they were simply stagecoaches put on wheels. Like stagecoach passengers, some of the train passengers were seated on the roof, where they were exposed to sparks from the engine and to strong winds."

4. Sentence 5

   a. Replace with "Railroad companies in the United States soon developed new types of cars for passengers, but it was a long time before these cars were comfortable."

   b. Replace with "New types of passenger cars were developed in the United States."

   c. Make no change.

5. Sentence 6

   a. Make no change.

   b. Replace "advance" with "improvement."

   c. Replace with "The old cars were only slightly advanced upon by the first of the new United States passenger cars."

6. Sentence 9

   a. Eliminate sentence.

   b. Replace with "The ride in those cars was still not comfortable."

   c. Replace with "The ride in these cars was not comfortable because the seats were hard and because the train started and stopped with violent jerks."

7. Sentence 10

   a. Eliminate footnote number.

   b. Make no change.

   c. Paraphrase the quotation.

8. Sentences 11 and 12

   a. Make no change.

   b. Reverse positions of Sentence 11 and Sentence 12.

   c. Eliminate sentence 11.

9. Sentence 13
   a. Eliminate sentence.
   b. Replace with "Peddlers at baseball games also pass through aisles to sell food and drink."
   c. Make no change.

10. Sentence 14
   a. Place the transitional word "However" at the beginning of the sentence.
   b. Place the transitional word "Consequently" at the beginning of the sentence.
   c. Make no change.

**Exercise 2  Revising: Footnotes**  Number your paper from 1 to 5. Beside the numbers, tell what is wrong with the following footnotes. Each footnote contains one error or omission.

> **SAMPLE**  [1]Dora R. Evers and S. Norman Feingold, *Your Future in Exotic Occupations* (New York: 1972), p. 76.
>
> **ANSWER**  The name of the publishing company is missing.

[1]*Exploring the Galaxies,* Simon Mitton (New York: Charles Scribner's Sons, 1976), p. 98.

[2]William Winterbotham, "Variety and Harmony in Pennsylvania," ed. Arthur Mann, in *Immigrants in American Life* (Boston: Houghton Mifflin Company, 1974), p. 22.

[3]Donal Henahon, *New York Times*, 9 Aug. 1981, Sec. B, p. 1., col. 1.

[4]Goldstein, David Henry, "Typesetting: From Master Craft to Computer Application," *Graphic Arts Monthly,* June 1981, p. 36.

[5]"The Resale Business in Phone Lines." *Business Week,* 13 July 1981, p. 68.

**Exercise 3  Revising: Bibliography Entries**  On your paper, tell what is wrong with the following bibliography entries. Each entry has one error or omission.

| | |
|---|---|
| **SAMPLE** | Ickis, Marguerite. *The Standard Book of Quilt Making and Collecting.* Dover Publications, Inc.: New York, 1959. |
| **ANSWER** | The name of the city where the book was published should precede the name of the publishing company. |

1. "Bold Hand at the Guthrie's Helm." 27 July 1981, p. 74.

2. "James Turrell: The Art of Deception." *Art in America,* May 1981.

3. *The Oxford Companion to World Sports and Games.* John Arlott, ed. New York: Oxford University Press, 1975.

4. Pevsner, Nikolaus. *Pioneers of Modern Design.* Middlesex, England: Penguin Books.

5. Sandberg, Larry, and Weissman, Dick. *The Folk Music Sourcebook.* New York: Alfred A. Knopf, 1976.

## 13.6b The Finished Paper

Unless your teacher gives you other instructions, your finished paper should include the following parts arranged in this order:

1. Title page
2. Outline
3. The written or typed paper
4. Notes (if you put your footnotes on a separate page)
5. Bibliography

If possible, type your research paper. If you cannot type it, write it as legibly as you can. Your paper should make a good impression. Follow the guidelines in Unit 5, page 217, for the preparation of a finished paper.

To prepare a title page, center the title about halfway down the page. Capitalize the first word and all words except articles, conjunctions, and prepositions of fewer than five letters. Do not underline the title or put quotation marks around it. Center the word *by* under the title and center your name under that. In the lower right quarter, write your teacher's name, the name of the course, and the date.

Following is the model research paper on women factory workers in Lowell. The outline for the paper is on page 507.

Women in a Labor Movement

by

Charles Norton

Ms. Sweeney

American History

December 13, 19___

A labor movement consists of workers banding together to achieve political and economic goals.  In the early part of the nineteenth century, the living and working conditions in the mill town of Lowell, Massachusetts, united women in a labor movement.  This movement was unusual because, for the first time, a group of women had both the independence and the solidarity to work toward political and economic goals.  It was the first time that women played a significant part in a labor movement.

This women's labor movement arose as part of the industrialization of America.  The movement toward industrialization in America was in progress by the end of the eighteenth century.  Francis Cabot Lowell, a New England industrialist, was most responsible for the development of the textile industry in America.  He was the first to set up a textile mill in which both the spinning and the weaving could be done.

At the time there was much opposition to the development of manufacturing in America. People were afraid that industrial growth would be accompanied by the use of child labor and by the development of slums like those in English manufacturing cities. Lowell and his partners, the Boston Associates, devised a plan to increase industrialization without creating the problems that people feared. They planned a factory system that seemed to please everyone.

According to their plan, children would not be employed, because the machinery was too complicated to be run by children. Therefore, families would not flock to the mill towns; and hastily built housing, which would soon develop into slums, would not be needed to accommodate the families. Instead, young women, mostly from rural New England, would be hired to run the machinery. This plan provided the mill owners with a cheap labor force without the use of child labor. The employment of women was, clearly, an economical move for mill owners. "Wages would be set at a level which would be high enough to induce young women to leave the farm . . . but low enough to offer an advantage for employing females rather than males. . . ."[1]

In addition to wages, Lowell's new factory system provided for other conditions, both to attract the women

to the mills and to satisfy their parents that their
working and living situation was proper.  The Boston
Associates created a system of boarding houses, and the
women who worked in the mills had to live in one of these
houses.  Each boarding house was run by a matron, who was
paid by the company.  Strict rules were set down to govern
the activities of the women.  For example, the doors were
locked at ten o'clock, and attendance at religious
services was required.

The system was so successful that, after Lowell's
death, his partners chose "the most appropriate memorial:
expansion of their flourishing enterprise on a new site,
to be named Lowell in his honor."[2]  Accordingly, the
Merrimack Manufacturing Company was set up in 1822, and
the first factory began operation in Lowell in 1823.
Between 1823 and 1839, nine textile companies were
established.  The population of Lowell grew from 200 in
1820 to 17,633 in 1836, and to over 30,000 in 1845.[3]

The expanded Lowell system gave women opportunities
and experiences that were otherwise unavailable to them.
For the first time, large numbers of women worked outside
the home in nondomestic labor.  They earned an income,
which made them financially independent of their families.
Even though many sent a portion of their income home to
help their families, they had money left to save or to

spend as they chose. This financial independence was a new and welcome experience for the women.

The Lowell system also made educational and cultural opportunities available to the women. After working hours, they could take advantage of libraries, lectures, courses, and concerts. Furthermore, many of the women wrote about their experiences and had their works published in such publications as the Lowell Offering, a literary magazine that contained stories, poems, and essays. These activities offset the long hours and hard work in the mills, and most women used these opportunities for self-improvement or entertainment. Because the women found education and entertainment as well as work at Lowell, they developed their lives around the mill. They relied less upon their families and became socially as well as financially independent.

Both kinds of independence were very important to the women. In one contribution to the Lowell Offering, Josephine L. Baker explained to the readers why mill workers accepted their working conditions, which were often tedious.

> The time we do have is our own. The money we earn
> comes promptly; more so than in any other situation;
> and our work, though laborious, is the same from day
> to day; we know what it is, and when finished we feel
> perfectly free. . . . There are lectures, evening
> schools, and libraries, to which all may have
> access.[4]

The friendships that the women formed played a significant part in this movement. Eliza J. Cate, also writing in the Lowell Offering, attests to the companionship experienced by the women who lived in the boarding houses and worked together in the mills.[5] The women's writings in the Lowell Offering further indicate that these friendships deepened into strong bonds. The women at the mills supported one another as they adjusted to life in Lowell, and they depended on one another when they were sick. These relationships created a solidarity that enabled women to work together for their own goals.

In spite of the independence and friendships of the women, living and working in Lowell was not as ideal as it may have seemed. Before long, the length of the working day was increased to twelve or fourteen hours. Sarah Bagley, an outspoken critic of the mill system, pointed out that few workers went to the mill voluntarily; necessity sent them to work in the mills to earn money for themselves or their families.[6] The women, who had little time left for themselves, began to express their discontent with the low wages and long hours.

Some periodicals, unlike the Lowell Offering, published articles that emphasized the long hours and hard work, not the advantages of life at Lowell. Other articles expressed unfavorable views of mill life and conditions. For example, in an article in The Voice of

Industry, December 3, 1847, one writer pointed out that
the view of Lowell as a place where women could work and
study after hours was false. The workers, she emphasized,
were exhausted from thirteen hours of labor: "The great
mass are there to toil and toil only. . . . The old
homestead must be redeemed, a poor sick mother or an aged
and infirm father needs their little savings. . . ."[7]

The workers had good reason for their discontent. As
time went on, working conditions became worse, not better.
When the price of cloth declined because of competition
and expansion in the textile industry, owners attempted to
increase their profits at the expense of the workers.
They used three methods of increasing production:
increasing the operating speed of the machines, assigning
additional machines to each worker, and rewarding the
overseer (not the workers) for greater production. For
the workers this meant worse conditions and lower wages.

As conditions at Lowell worsened, the women took
action. The first strike in Lowell occurred in 1834 over
a cut in wages. The bond that had developed through
living and working together now supported the women as
they worked together to achieve better working conditions.
They proclaimed, "Union is power. Our present object is
to have union and exertion, and we remain in possession of
our unquestionable rights."[8] The strike was cut short
when the factory owners threatened to bring in other

531

_____ a full-fledged

labor movement.

Notes

[1]Philip S. Foner, ed., The Factory Girls (Urbana,
Ill.: University of Illinois Press, 1977), p. xix.

[2]Benita Eisler, ed., The Lowell Offering (New York:
J.B. Lippincott Company, 1977), p. 13.

[3]Foner, Factory Girls, pp. xvii–xviii.

[4]Josephine L. Baker, "A Second Peep at Factory Life,"
in The Lowell Offering, ed. Benita Eisler (New York: J.B.
Lippincott Company, 1977), p. 82.

[5]Eliza J. Cate, "Leisure Hours of the Mill Girls," in
The Lowell Offering, ed. Benita Eisler (New York: J.B.
Lippincott Company, 1977), pp. 99–112.

[6]Foner, Factory Girls, p. 160.

[7]Foner, Factory Girls, p. 93.

[8]Philip S. Foner, Women and the American Labor
Movement (New York: The Free Press, 1979), p. 34.

[9]Foner, Labor Movement, p. 35.

[10]Thomas Dublin, Women at Work (New York: Columbia
University Press, 1979), pp. 86–87.

[11]Howard Zinn, A People's History of the United States
(New York: Harper & Row, Publishers, 1981), p. 225.

workers to replace the strikers.  During the next strike

in Lowell, which occurred in October 1836, the workers

formed the Factory Girls Association and claimed 2500

members.  The association raised a fund for "those who

have not the means to pay their board."[9]  Though the early

strikes did not improve working conditions, they showed

that the bond, the women's solidarity, extended to

militant action against the mill owners and agents.[10]

The movement for shorter hours and higher wages led

to the formation of the Lowell Female Labor Reform

Association (FLRA) in January 1845.  The Female Labor

Reform Association shifted the focus from strikes to

political activity.  Members sent petitions to the

Massachusetts legislature asking that a ten-hour day be

made the law.  The legislature held public hearings on

mill conditions at which the women testified.  Later, when

a legislative committee visited the mills and reported no

problems, the FLRA denounced the report.  The FLRA then

lobbied in the legislature to remove the chairman of the

committee.[11]

Between 1823, when the first mill was established in

Bibliography

Baker, Josephine L.  "A Second Peep at Factory Life."  In
The Lowell Offering.  Ed. Benita Eisler.  New York:
J.B. Lippincott Company, 1977, pp. 99–112.

Cate, Eliza J.  "Leisure Hours of the Mill Girls."  In The
Lowell Offering.  Ed. Benita Eisler, New York: J.B.
Lippincott Company, 1977, pp. 77–82.

Dublin, Thomas.  Women at Work: The Transformation of Work
and Community in Lowell, Massachusetts, 1826–1860.
New York: Columbia University Press, 1979.

Eisler, Benita, ed.  The Lowell Offering: Writings by New
England Mill Women (1840–1845).  New York: J.B.
Lippincott Company, 1977.

Foner, Philip S., ed.  The Factory Girls.  Urbana, Ill.:
University of Illinois Press, 1977.

—————.  Women and the American Labor Movement: From
Colonial Times to the Eve of World War I.  New York:
The Free Press, 1979.

Zinn, Howard.  A People's History of the United States.
New York: Harper & Row, Publishers, 1981.

**Exercise 4   Revising: Analysis of a Research Paper**   On your paper, answer the following questions about the model research paper.

1. The thesis statement says that the living and working conditions in Lowell had the effect of uniting women in a labor movement. What specific causes and effects does the author use to show the development of this movement? Make a list of each cause and its effects.

2. What ideas from the introduction are restated in the conclusion?

3. Write the topic sentence of a paragraph that is supported with examples. List those examples.

4. List five examples of transitional words used between sentences or between paragraphs.

5. List three examples of transitions that repeat a word or an idea from a previous paragraph in a new paragraph. Write the sentences and underline the repeated words or ideas.

**Assignment** **Revising** Revise the first draft of the paragraphs that you wrote in the Assignment on page 518. Be sure that the paragraphs are clear and complete and that you have made a transition between them.

**Continuing Assignment** **Revising** *Step 1:* Revise the draft that you prepared in the Continuing Assignment on page 518. Revise your draft as many times as necessary to improve your paper. *Step 2:* Prepare your finished research paper. Follow the manuscript form given on page 217, or follow your teacher's specific guidelines. Make a final copy of your notes and bibliography. Be sure to proofread your finished paper for correct grammar, spelling, punctuation, and capitalization.

Check your assignments for the following points:

1. Did you develop each paragraph sufficiently?
2. Are the paragraphs unified?
3. Did you make clear transitions between paragraphs?

Check your Continuing Assignment for these additional points:

4. Did you check your draft against your outline for organization?
5. Do all the points in the paper contribute to the proof of the thesis statement?
6. Is each point clearly stated and developed?
7. Is your paper unified?
8. Did you connect your ideas with transitions?
9. Did you check your paper for complete and accurate documentation?
10. Is your finished paper neat and free of errors?

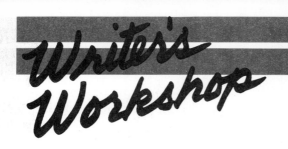

## Surviving in Space: A Research Paper

**Situation:** The science museum in your town plans to set up an exhibit on survival in space. The planners of the exhibit have hired the consulting firm for which you work to compile background information for the exhibit. You have been asked to do research and write a paper about the developments in space suits that have helped astronauts to survive in space. As you plan and write the paper, you will keep in mind the following information.

**Writer:** you as a research consultant

**Audience:** planners of the exhibit at the science museum

**Topic:** the development of space suits

**Purpose:** to organize your research notes and to write the first two paragraphs of the paper.

**Directions:** To plan and write your paper, follow these steps.

*Step 1.* Read the note cards on the following page, which you made from sources that you found in the library.

*Step 2.* In doing research, you developed the following preliminary thesis statement: "The first space suits limited the motion of the astronauts; however, as a result of technological developments, the new suits allow the astronauts to move and work freely in space." Using your thesis statement and your note cards as guides, write a topic outline for your paper. (Follow the model on page 507.) Use chronological order to organize the information in your outline. The headings on your note cards may be used as headings and sub-

(Continue on page 538.)

**New Space Suit — Construction**
"Space Suits"
After the Skylab program
(early 1970s) and before first
shuttle flight (1981), new fiber
glass space suit was
developed.

p. 2

---

**First Space Suit — Construction**
Webbon, _Survival_
Project Mercury space suit (1958)
was actually two suits.
— inner suit made of rubber
(to contain gas)
— outer suit made of heavy
synthetic canvaslike
material — like workers'
overalls
p. 52

---

**First Space Suit — Limitations**
Webbon, _Survival_
"It did not have to provide much
mobility because the Mercury
astronauts remained seated in the
capsule at all times. Since the
suit was not meant to be used
outside the capsule, it did not
have to protect the astronauts
from temperature extremes and
other hazards of space."
p. 52

---

**Purpose of Space Suit**
Treacher, _Conquest_
— fundamental purpose of space
suit, to provide human being
with artificial atmosphere
in space
— suit also must protect astronaut
from other hazards: exposure to
sunlight, extremes of temperature,
bombardment by meteors

p. 4

---

**First Space Suit — Attachments**
Webbon, _Survival_
— helmet and gloves mechanically
attached after astronaut entered
suit through small opening
— a hose supplied oxygen for
breathing: a second hose
removed carbon dioxide from
suit

p. 52

---

**New Space Suit — Attachments**
"Space Suits"
"We are developing new portable
life-support systems and space
suits which are self-contained
so that cooling and carbon
dioxide control systems do not
need to be supplied continually
with new material from the
outside." Angela Wiesel, NASA
scientist and researcher
p. 4

---

**New Space Suit — Construction**
Webbon, _Survival_
— new space suit has torso made
of fiber glass instead of
rubber and fabric
— comes in separate pieces and can
be put together according to what
is needed; basic torso can have
lightweight arms and legs when
used close to Earth; shielding
can be added when at higher
altitudes.
p. 57

Astronaut Allen te

headings in your outline. Use two or three details under each subheading, and make sure that the details under each heading are appropriate for that heading.

*Step 3.* Write the introductory paragraph of the paper. Begin with a sentence that states the thesis that you intend to prove. In the rest of the paragraph, include a one- or two-sentence overview of the contents of the paper and, as background information for your reader, an explanation of what a space suit must do to be effective.

*Step 4.* Write the next paragraph of the paper, a paragraph discussing the first space suit. Refer to your note cards and topic outline as you write the paragraph. Use a direct quotation if it seems appropriate.

*Step 5.* At the bottom of the page on which a direct quotation appears, write a footnote. Be sure that you write a complete footnote entry for each direct quotation. (See pages 515–516 for the correct forms for footnote entries.)

*Step 6.* Prepare a bibliography page for the following sources that you used in this section of the paper. (See pages 495–496 for the forms for bibliography entries.)

## Sources for Your Paper

1. The book *The Conquest of Space: A Survey of Progress,* which was written by R. Gordon Treacher and Denise Hobson and published by Platinum Press. It was published in Chicago in 1981, and it contains 251 pages.
2. The article "Survival in Space," which was written by Bruce Webbon and published in *Natural History.* It appeared on pages 55–57. It was published in December 1981.
3. The pamphlet "Space Suits of the Eighties," which was published in Washington, D.C., by the U.S. Government Printing Office. It was published in March 1982.

# Unit Assignments

**Assignment 1**   Limit the following topics. Write a preliminary thesis statement and make a rough outline for a research paper on one of them.

1. A historic or contemporary person from your town
2. A historic event that took place in or near your town
3. The country from which your relatives or ancestors came

**Assignment 2**   Prepare a working bibliography for the topic for which you developed a thesis statement and rough outline in Assignment 1.

**Assignment 3**   Take notes on the topic for which you have prepared a working bibliography in Assignment 2. Organize your notes and make an outline. Present your findings in one of the following ways:

1. Give an oral report using your outline and notes. After you have given your report, submit a written bibliography, your outline, and your note cards.
2. Write a research paper. Be sure to include footnotes and a bibliography.

**Assignment 4**   Prepare a research paper on an aspect of conservation. For example, you might discuss the necessity of saving the oceans or investigate the possibility of desalinization as a source of fresh water. Arrange your findings in order of importance.

**Assignment 5**   Prepare a research paper about the contributions of members of a minority group to an aspect of culture in the United States.

## Revising Your Assignments

For help in revising a research paper, consult the Checklist for Revision on the last page of this book.

# Unit Tests

## Test 1

**A.** Number your paper from 1 to 5. Next to each number, write *True* if the sentence is true or *False* if it is false.

1. Each book in a library is represented by a single card in the card catalog.
2. Your first draft is written with a detailed outline and with note cards arranged according to the outline headings.
3. One step in your research is to take notes on information that will support your thesis statement.
4. After your research is completed, you make a rough outline.
5. Footnotes and a bibliography are two forms of documentation for the research paper.

**B.** Number your paper from 6 to 10. Next to each number, write the letter of the term that correctly completes the sentence. You will use all but one of the items.

a. card catalog
b. bibliography
c. vertical file

d. thesis statement
e. plagiarism
f. footnote

6. An alphabetical list of the books, magazines, and other sources used in preparing a research paper is called a __?__.
7. After you limit a topic and prepare a rough outline to direct your research, you use the __?__ in the library to begin your research.
8. You must document your sources in a research paper to avoid __?__, or using someone else's words or ideas as if they were your own.
9. A __?__ acknowledges the author and the publication from which you borrowed information.
10. The sentence in which you state your position is called a __?__.

**C.** Number your paper from 11 to 15. Next to each number, write the letter of the item that correctly answers the question.

11. Which of the following is specific enough for a research-paper topic?
   a. Clothing styles
   b. Renaissance fashions for men
   c. History of dress
   d. Clothing materials

12. Which of the following is a satisfactory thesis statement for a research paper?
    a. *Habitat* in Montreal is an experimental project designed to solve specific problems in urban housing.
    b. Walter Gropius founded the Bauhaus school of architecture.
    c. Several years ago I saw the Eiffel Tower in Paris.
    d. The most spectacular cathedral in Europe is Notre Dame in Paris.

13. Which of the following is *not* included on your note cards?
    a. Subject heading
    b. Page reference
    c. Publication information
    d. Author and abbreviated title

14. Which of the following would you locate in the periodical index in order to research facts to support your thesis statement?
    a. A photograph of a gasohol factory
    b. Books about alternative fuel
    c. A description of gasohol
    d. A newspaper article about gasohol

15. Which of the following would you do when you revise your research paper for proper organization?
    a. Check for errors in grammar, usage, spelling, punctuation, and capitalization.
    b. Check whether supporting details develop and prove the thesis statement.
    c. Check your draft against your outline.
    d. Check whether key words or ideas are repeated from one paragraph to the next.

## Test 2

Choose one of the Unit Assignments or a topic suggested by your teacher. Write the assignment as directed and hand it in to your teacher.

# Writing
# Business
# Letters

---

## Unit Preview

There will be many occasions when you will have to write a business letter. Whatever your reason for writing, your letter will be effective if it is complete, concise, and courteous.

The letter on the following page contains all of the information necessary to the person who will receive it.

**For Analysis** On your paper, answer the following questions about the letter from Margie Chin.

1. What is the purpose of the letter?
2. What information is being requested?
3. Why is the information needed?
4. Where should the information be sent?

In this unit you will learn how to write standard business letters: the order letter, the request letter, and the adjustment letter. In addition, you will learn how to write a letter applying for a job, how to write a résumé, and how to write a letter expressing your opinion. In writing these letters, you will practice the three steps of the writing process: prewriting, writing, and revising.

```
      62 Overlea Avenue
      Tulsa, Oklahoma 74126
      April 3, 19___

      Tulsa Inter-Tribal Cultural Center
      17 Everett Place
      Tulsa, Oklahoma 74126

      Dear Sir or Madam:

      I am president of the Tulsa High School Honor
      Society. Each year we invite a representative
      of the arts to speak at our induction
      ceremonies. This year's ceremony will be held
      on May 18.

      We would be pleased if you could provide a
      guest speaker to discuss the goals and
      achievements of the Center, the purpose of its
      founding, and the exhibits and events that are
      open to the public. In addition, we would enjoy
      a brief program of Indian songs and dances. We
      would allot forty-five minutes of our program
      to the speaker and the performers.

      Would representatives of the Center be willing
      to take part in our ceremonies? We can offer an
      honorarium of fifty dollars. Because we must
      complete our plans soon, may I hear from you by
      April 15. Thank you very much.

      Very truly yours,

      Margie Chin
      Margie Chin
```

# 14.1  Standard Business Letters

## Parts of a Business Letter

All business letters, regardless of their purpose, consist of the following parts.

**Heading.**    The heading is your address and the date. Place it at the upper right or upper left of your stationery, depending on which letter style you are using *(pages 544–545).* Spell out the name of your state, or abbreviate it by using the standard abbreviation or the Postal Service abbreviation.

**Inside Address.**   The inside address is the name and address of the person or the organization to whom you are writing. Include titles such as *Dr., Mr.,* or *Ms.* with a person's name. In the last line of the inside address, write the name of the state in the same form as you did in the heading.

**Salutation.**   Capitalize the first word and all the nouns in the salutation, or greeting. Place a colon after the salutation. Use *Dear Sir or Madam* when addressing someone whose name you do not know.

**Body.**   The body consists of the paragraphs of the letter itself. Leave an extra line of space between the salutation and the first paragraph and between all other paragraphs.

**Complimentary Close.**   Capitalize only the first word of the complimentary close. Place a comma at the end of the close. *Yours truly, Very truly yours, Sincerely yours,* and *Yours sincerely* are acceptable complimentary closes.

**Signature.**   Write your name in full below the complimentary close. If your letter is handwritten, print your name under your signature. If your letter is typed, type your name under your signature.

## Styles of Business Letters

The two styles of business letters are the block style and the modified block style. In the **block style,** all parts of the letter start at the left margin. Paragraphs are not indented. Use the block style only when you are typing a letter. The letter on page 543 is written in block style.

In the **modified block style,** place the heading, the complimentary close, and the signature on the right. You may either indent paragraphs or start them at the left, as in the block style. The modified block style can be used when handwriting or typing letters.

Regardless of the style that you use, be sure to leave sufficient margins above, below, and on both sides of your letter by centering it on the paper.

Follow these strategies for writing brief, clear, and accurate business letters.

## Strategies

1. *Use unlined paper measuring 8½ inches by 11 inches.*

2. *Type your letter, if possible.* If you cannot, then use black or blue ink. Never use pencil.

3. *Make sure that the heading and the inside address are complete and accurate.*

4. *Include in the body of the letter all information necessary to achieve your purpose.*

5. *Avoid slang and contractions.* Do not write in a tone that is casual or informal.

6. *Reread your letter carefully to see that there are no errors in typing, grammar, usage, spelling, or punctuation.* If you find errors, rewrite or retype your letter.

## The Request Letter

You write a request letter, or an inquiry letter, when you need specific information on a particular subject or when you need a brochure or a catalogue. Like all business letters, the request letter should be brief, but it must also contain all necessary information. Study the example on the following page.

When writing a request letter, follow the general strategies for business letters on this page. In addition, follow these specific strategies.

## Strategies

1. *Make your requests reasonable and specific.* For example, do not write to the United States Postal Service and ask for all of the information that they have on stamps.

102 Kenton Street
Lincolnwood, Illinois 60646
December 2, 19___

Mr. William F. Stifel, President
American Kennel Club
51 Madison Avenue
New York, New York 10010

Dear Mr. Stifel:

    I am writing a class report on the popularity of certain breeds of dogs. It would help me very much if you could provide me with figures on the popularity of specific breeds in the United States during the last fifty years. I am particularly interested in statistics for collies, German shepherds, and poodles.

    Also, if you have any literature on the development of new breeds of dogs and their certification by the American Kennel Club, I would appreciate having it.

    If there is a fee for this information, please inform me.

    Thank you very much.

          Sincerely yours,

          *Robert McCarthy*
          Robert McCarthy

  2. *Offer to pay for any printed material if you are not certain that it is free.*

## The Order Letter

    When you order merchandise through the mail, you must sometimes write an order letter. Make sure that your letter contains complete, accurate information about quantity, size, color, cost, and catalogue number. Study the example.

1301 Briarwood Street
Oak Ridge, Tennessee 37830
April 10, 19___

Brooksport Frames, Inc.
128 Voss Farm Road
Ames, Iowa 50011

Dear Sir or Madam:

I would like to order the following items from your spring and summer catalogue.

| Code | Quantity | Description | Price |
|------|----------|-------------|-------|
| U-1641 | 1 | Diamond glass cutter | $13.50 |
| U-1886 | 1 | Glass pliers | 7.75 |
| U-4631 | 1 | Mat-cutting system | 18.98 |
| U-3662 | 1 | Package of spare blades | 1.55 |
| | | | $41.78 |
| | | Shipping and handling | 4.15 |
| | | Total | $45.93 |

Please send the above items to

Ms. Lenore Lawrence
611 Putnam Lane
Stamford, Connecticut 06902

If for any reason the order cannot be filled by May 1, please cancel my order and refund my payment.

I have enclosed a money order for forty-five dollars and ninety-three cents ($45.93).

Sincerely,

*Vince Hanak*

Vince Hanak

Enclosure: money order #606-4

When writing an order letter, follow the general strategies for business letters on page 545. In addition, follow these strategies.

### Strategies

1. *List the source of the advertisement or the catalogue year, season, and number from which you are ordering.*

2. *Double-check your arithmetic.* Be sure to include postage and handling costs if necessary.

3. *Explain how you intend to pay for the merchandise.* Do not send cash through the mail. Use a money order or a check instead.

4. *State whether you must have the merchandise by a certain date.*

5. *List substitutes, if any, that you would accept in place of the merchandise that you are ordering.*

6. *Type or write the word* Enclosure *in the lower left corner of your letter* if you have enclosed a check or a money order. State the item that is enclosed.

## The Adjustment Letter

Write an adjustment letter whenever an order that you place is not filled correctly or when merchandise that you purchase is defective. In an adjustment letter, you must explain the problem clearly and courteously and suggest a solution. Study the example.

When writing an adjustment letter, follow the general strategies on page 545. In addition, follow these specific strategies.

### Strategies

1. *State the problem accurately and clearly.* Try to explain the problem in the first paragraph of your letter.

2. *Suggest a solution.* Ask politely for a refund or a replacement.

208 Park Lane
Siloam Springs, Arkansas 72761
September 23, 19___


Magnolia Publications, Inc.
6 Gwynn Oak Street
Baltimore, Maryland 21207

Dear Sir or Madam:

On May 8, I ordered a one-year gift subscription to your magazine, Southern Expressions, to be sent to Mr. Gregory Linski, 1313 Killian Drive, Hurst, Texas 76053. I enclosed a money order for $15.00.

To date, Mr. Linski has not received any issues of the magazine. The subscription was to have begun with the July issue. Would you please look into the matter and see that Mr. Linski receives all issues, starting with the July issue.

I would appreciate a letter from you informing me when delivery has started.

Thank you very much.

Yours truly,

Debbie Tamura
Debbie Tamura

3. *Keep a copy of your letter until the adjustment that you request has been made.* You may need it for reference if your requested adjustment is not made promptly.

**Exercise 1   Writing: A Request Letter**   Use the following information to write a request letter in modified block style. Then reread your letter and revise it.

Your name is Joseph McDaniel, and you live at 1540 Newton Avenue, Philadelphia, Pennsylvania 19147. The eighteen members of your outing club have decided to go on a white-water rafting trip. As secretary of the club, you have been asked to request information about the trip from New England Rafters, 400 Main Street, Kennebunkport, Maine 04046. You will need to ask about the cost of the trip, the destination and length of the trip, and the supplies, clothing, and all equipment that will be needed. The club wants to go on the trip during the last week in June. You are writing the letter on April 17, 19—.

**Exercise 2   Writing: An Adjustment Letter**   Use the following information to write an adjustment letter in block style. After completing the first draft, revise your letter.

> Your name is Marie Washington. You live at 56 Cheshire Street, Apt. 302, Flagstaff, Arizona 86003. For your father's birthday, you ordered an automobile emergency kit from Auto Accessories, 5702 Stanton Street, St. Paul, Minnesota 55122. When the package arrived, the flashlight in the kit was broken. Because it is October 23, there is still time to have a new flashlight sent before your father's birthday on December 1.

**Assignment 1   Writing**   On an unlined sheet of paper, write a request letter in modified block style to a local museum of science and natural history that holds arts and crafts classes during the summer. Write for information about a class in lapidary art. You want to know what age group the class is organized for, whether it is for beginning or advanced students, when and where classes will meet, what materials you will need, and how much the course will cost. Make up a name and address for the museum, but use your own return address.

**Assignment 2   Writing**   On an unlined sheet of paper, write an order letter in modified block style to Jason's, 11 Federal Street, Minneapolis, Minnesota 55403. From their Christmas catalogue, order these items: one brown wallet for $17.50, item number L-973; one pair of silver-colored earrings, clip-on style, for $10.00, item number J-226; and one green-and-white plaid scarf for $12.98, item number S-198. Include $3.50 for postage and handling. Use your own return address.

### Assignment Checklist

Check your assignments for the following points:

✔ 1. Did you include all of the necessary parts of the business letter?

✔ 2. Does the body of your letter contain all of the necessary information?

✔ 3. Did you use the modified block style?

✔ 4. Did you state your request or order briefly, clearly, and courteously?

✔ 5. Did you specify terms of payment in your order letter?

✔ 6. Did you proofread your letter for correct grammar, usage, spelling, and punctuation?

# 14.2 Applying for a Job

When applying for a job, you need to write a letter of application and a résumé. Both are necesary to give a prospective employer an accurate impression of you and your qualifications.

## Application Letter

The purpose of your application letter is to get an appointment for an interview. To improve your chances, be certain that your letter contains the following information.

**Reason for Writing.**   In the first paragraph, state what position you are seeking and tell how you learned of it. Do not simply say that you are interested in any and all positions that happen to be open.

**Experience.**   In the second paragraph, make a brief reference to whatever experience that you have that qualifies you for the job. You need not present this information in detail here. You will be more explicit in your résumé *(pages 553–554)*.

**Closing.**   State courteously that you would like to have a personal interview at the employer's convenience. Tell where and when you can be reached to arrange an appointment.

Study the letter of application on the following page.

```
                              2030 Gentilly Drive
                              Medford, Oregon 97501
                              June 8, 19__

Dr. Hugh Stephens
1618 St. Charles Avenue
Medford, Oregon 97501

Dear Dr. Stephens:

        I am responding to your advertisement
in the Banner of June 6 for a summer
companion for two children, ages six and
eight.  I would like to be considered for
that position.

        You will note from my enclosed
résumé that I have experience working
with children as a lifeguard and as a
supervisor of recreational activities.

        I believe that my background and
experience qualify me for the position
advertised.  I will be pleased to meet
with you for an interview at your
convenience.  My phone number is
555-7694.  I can be reached any afternoon
after three o'clock.

        Thank you for your consideration.
I look forward to hearing from you.

                         Sincerely yours,

                         Angela Berard
                         Angela Berard
Enclosure
```

When writing a job-application letter, follow the general strategies for business letters on page 545. In addition, follow these specific strategies.

## Strategies

1. *Express confidence in your ability to do the job, but do not boast.*

2. *Read your letter aloud for tone* to make sure that you do not

```
                    Angela Berard
                    2030 Gentilly Drive
                    Medford, Oregon 97501
                    Telephone: 555-7694


Position        Day-care companion to
Wanted          school-age children

Experience      Vandergriff Park, July-August, 19__
                Planned and supervised recreational
                activities for children ages 5-10

                Oak Cliffs YWCA, June-August, 19__
                Lifeguard at YWCA pool

Education       Attending Marquis High School

                Completed defensive driving course
                in driver education

References       Mr. Charles Biggs, Coach
                Marquis High School
                6832 Vineland Street
                Medford, Oregon 97501
                Telephone: 555-6110

                Ms. Alice Wrightson, Director
                Parks and Recreational Department
                1300 Broadway
                Medford, Oregon 97501
                Telephone: 555-1045
```

sound arrogant, flippant, or too casual. If you wish, have a family member or a teacher read your letter.

3. *Include additional information about yourself in an enclosed résumé.*

## Writing a Résumé

Enclose a résumé with your letter of application. A **résumé,** sometimes called a data sheet, is a summary of your qualifications. Its purpose is to present your qualifications in a clear, well-organized form. Always include the following information in your résumé: position wanted, experience, education, and references.

The sample résumé on the preceding page has side headings to point out the categories of information.

Use the following strategies when writing a résumé.

## Strategies

1. *Type your résumé.* Make sure that it is neat and free of errors.

2. *Limit your résumé to one or two pages.*

3. *List your most recent work experience first.* Include the dates that you were employed, the names of persons who employed you, and the places where you were employed.

4. *Include only the personal information about yourself that is relevant* to the job that you are seeking. Do not include your age, height, weight, status of health, or information about your family background.

5. *List two, preferably three, references, with an address or telephone number for each.* One of your references should be a character reference. Do not include family members or friends your own age. Do not list anyone without first obtaining his or her permission.

**Exercise 1   Writing: An Application Letter**   Using the following information, write a job-application letter. Use the modified block style. Proofread and revise your completed letter.

Your name is Eric H. Maleson. You live at 1572 Middlefield Road, Palo Alto, California 94306. Your telephone number is 555-2506. You are completing your junior year at Palo Alto High School. You want a summer job as a file clerk in a law office, and in the future you want to be a lawyer. You have a Saturday-morning job at the law firm Massey and Bailen, where you file case materials and type labels. You can be reached at home after 3:30 on weekday afternoons. You are writing your letter on February 25, 19—, to Mr. Philip Post, Personnel Director of Abbot and Williams. That law firm is located at 5 Mary Street, Mountain View, California 94300.

**Exercise 2   Writing: A Résumé**   Using the following information, write a résumé for Susan Nageli. Use side headings to categorize the information. Proofread the finished résumé and correct any mistakes.

Your name is Susan R. Nageli. In June 19—, you will complete your junior year at Meyers High School in East Lansing, Michigan. You live at 58 Circle Street, Apt. 2, East Lansing, Michigan 48824. Your phone number is 555-1629.

You would like a summer job as a lab assistant. You feel that you are qualified for the job because you have taken a biology class during each semester this year. Your biology teacher, Ms. Patricia Adams, will supply a reference for you. She can be reached at Meyers High School, 506 South Street, East Lansing, Michigan 48824, 555-8369.

Every day after school you work for Mr. Jack Forsley, the head of the biology department at Meyers High School. Your duties are to prepare specimens for the labs and to wash glassware. You have done this work from last January to the present.

Last summer, you worked at Martin's Family Restaurant, 5 Plymouth Street, East Lansing, Michigan 48824, 555-9876. Your duties were to clear tables, to load and unload the dishwasher, and to put away the dishes. Mr. Paul Martin, the owner, was your supervisor.

An old family friend, Mr. Harold Reiff, has agreed to serve as a reference. He lives at 7 Arrow Place, East Lansing, Michigan 48824, 555-6141.

**Assignment 1   Writing**   Find a help-wanted ad that interests you in the classified section of your local newspaper. Write a letter applying for the job. Prepare a résumé to accompany your letter.

**Assignment 2   Writing**   Your guidance counselor has told you that the Hospital Volunteers Association at one of the local hospitals needs young people to entertain children in the children's ward. The association needs people who can be clowns, who can perform juggling acts, or who can act as puppeteers or as mimes. Write a letter of application to the association at your local hospital. Prepare a résumé to accompany your letter.

## Assignment Checklist

Check your assignments for the following points:

✓ 1. Did you begin your letter by stating what position you are seeking?

✓ 2. Did you tell where and when you can be reached?

✓ 3. Did you read your letter for appropriate tone?

✓ 4. Did you include side headings in your résumé?

✓ 5. Did you list your most recent work experience first in your résumé?

✓ 6. Did you list at least two references, with addresses and phone numbers, in your résumé?

✓ 7. Did you proofread your letter and your résumé for correct grammar, usage, spelling, and punctuation?

# 14.3  Expressing an Opinion

Occasionally there may be local or national issues on which you wish to express your opinion. One effective way to do so is by writing a letter to your school paper, your local newspaper, a national magazine, or a radio or television network.

To make your letter effective, follow these steps.

1. Begin your letter by giving a brief summary of the situation or issue about which you are writing. Then state your opinion briefly and clearly.

2. Support your opinions with logical and, when possible, factual statements. Once you have made your point, do not wander from it; do not include irrelevant statements.

3. Conclude your letter by summarizing your main points or, when appropriate, by suggesting a course of action that you think should be followed.

A reasonable tone is also important in making your letter effective. Anger, sarcasm, or accusations will offend readers and therefore will not persuade them to accept your point of view. If your letter is restrained, courteous, and tactful, you will be more likely to persuade others to accept your opinion.

The following letter to the editor of a newspaper is brief, restrained, and well organized.

73 Elmer Street., Apt. 306
Canton, Ohio 44721
August 22, 19___

The Canton Bugle
11 West Ninth Street
Canton, Ohio 44721

To the Editor:

I am writing in response to the article in yesterday's Bugle concerning the plan by the Canton Music Hall to phase out its Saturday afternoon free concerts for young people. The management of the Music Hall cites rising costs as its reason for dropping this series, which it concedes has always been popular.

Given today's economy, I have no doubt that the cost of this series has increased appreciably over the years. Additional heating, lighting, and maintenance costs are incurred by opening the building in the afternoon, when ordinarily it would be closed.

Attendance figures should show that this series has always been popular with the young people from Canton and from neighboring communities. Surely many of these young people would have few, if any, other opportunities to hear live concerts of classical music free of charge.

Therefore, I suggest that, instead of dropping this popular series, the Music Hall seek ways to underwrite the costs. Local businesses and private donations from the community could subsidize the series. The management could also ask those attending to donate whatever they can. I urge the Music Hall to explore all of these possibilities in an effort to continue to make this series available.

Sincerely yours,

*Mark Eismann*

Mark Eismann
555-0995

Use the following strategies when writing letters of opinion.

**Strategies**

1. *Keep your letter brief.* Many newpapers indicate the pre-ferred length for letters, usually two hundred words or less.

2. *Use the salutation* To the Editor *in letters to newpapers and magazines.*

3. *Sign your letter.* Also include your address and telephone number so that the newspaper can verify that you wrote the letter. Your address and phone number will not be printed with your letter.

4. *Write promptly.* Editors often will not publish letters on subjects that are no longer current.

For further information on writing to express an opinion, see Unit 10, "Persuasive Writing."

**Exercise   Revising: An Opinion Letter**   On your paper, re-vise the following letter of opinion. Eliminate unrelated statements and expressions of anger or sarcasm. Make sure that the beginning and the conclusion contain clear summaries of the writer's opinion.

> 73 Inman Street, Apt. 564
> Duluth, Minnesota 55810
> November 16, 19—

The *City News*
125 Hennepin Avenue
Duluth, Minnesota 55810

To the Editor:

In last week's edition of *City News,* there was an article about a proposal to cut back bus service in the city. The city council is incredibly stupid even to suggest cuts that will hurt city residents.

The city may save money by cutting service, but city residents will have to pay with their own money and time. How are people supposed to get to work and to school? Should they have to walk ten miles through snow in winter? I certainly cannot afford to buy a car. The cut will hurt everyone. People will also be hurt by cuts made in the hours that the library is open. Both of the cuts that are proposed are unfair.

I hope that you pay attention to my position.

Yours truly,
Ruth Mitchell

**Assignment 1** **Writing** You have just read a magazine article about outstanding vacation areas in the United States. Your state was not mentioned. Write a letter to the editor of the magazine, explaining why you think your state should have been included. Use the modified block style. Make up a name and address for the magazine, but use your own return address.

**Assignment 2** **Writing** Your favorite television program has just been canceled because of low ratings. Write to the president of the network and explain why you think that the network should reconsider its decision. Make up a name and address for the network, but use your own return address.

**Assignment 3** **Writing** Select a letter to the editor from the editorial page of your local newspaper. Write a letter to the editor in which you offer support for or arguments against the points it contains.

## Assignment Checklist

Check your assignments for the following points:

1. Did you state your opinion briefly, clearly, and courteously?
2. Did you stick to the point?
3. Did you summarize your main points or suggest a course of action?
4. Did you maintain a reasonable tone?
5. Did you include your name, address, and telephone number?
6. Did you proofread your letter for correct grammar, usage, spelling, and punctuation?

*Writer's Workshop*

## Applying for a Job

**Situation:** This is your first year living in Waco, Texas. Summer is approaching, and you would like to have a job similar to the one that you had last summer in Lingleville, Texas. Your guidance counselor has told you that there are lifeguard jobs available with the Department of Parks and Recreation. The counselor has suggested that you submit a résumé and a letter of application to Mr. Clarence Briggs, 14 Grove Avenue, Waco, Texas 76707.

**Writer:** you as a summer-job applicant

**Audience:** Director of the Department of Parks and Recreation

**Topic:** your qualifications for the job

**Purpose:** to present your qualifications in a résumé and in a letter of application

**Directions:** To write your résumé and job-application letter, follow these steps.

*Step 1:* Read the notes on the facing page, which you have made about all of your previous work experience, qualifications, and references.

*Step 2:* Decide which notes are appropriate for inclusion in your résumé.

*Step 3:* Organize into a résumé those notes that you decided are appropriate. Rewrite the notes into acceptable form. Use side headings in your résumé.

*Step 4:* Reread the notes to see which ones contain information that you would include in a job-application letter.

*Step 5:* Write a job-application letter from those notes. Mention your enclosed résumé.

## Work Experience

- coached swimming team (members aged 10-12) at Lingleville Junior High to regional championship
- was lifeguard at Lingleville Recreation Dept. previous two summers
- mowed lawns for neighbors last summer
- worked in stockroom of the Majestic supermarket after school for two years

## Qualifications and References

- am familiar with swimming-pool maintenance
- have Red Cross certification as Senior Lifesaver
- am member of school debating team
- can teach lifesaving classes
- like working with young children
- no absences from school for illness
- have references:

Ms. Amanda Richards,
   Guidance Counselor
Lingleville High School
14 Buell Street
Lingleville, Texas 76461
   555-9020

Mr. Lawrence R. Ewing,
   Faculty Advisor
Lingleville High School
14 Buell Street
Lingleville, Texas 76461
   555-9020

Mr. Joel Coyle,
   Senior Lifeguard
Lingleville Recreation Dept.
Lingleville, Texas 76461
   555-1813

- available all summer, all hours
- telephone number 555-0144

# Unit Assignments

**Assignment 1**  Write a request letter to a local health or sports club for information about joining the club. Make sure that your letter is brief, yet specific. Reread and revise your letter to correct any errors.

**Assignment 2**  Write an order letter to a music publisher for a rare piece of sheet music not available in stores. Provide complete information about the item that you are ordering. Specify the method of payment. Then revise your letter.

**Assignment 3**  Write an adjustment letter to a mail-order service that has sent you the wrong product. Explain the problem and suggest a solution. Then reread your letter and eliminate any errors.

**Assignment 4**  Think of the job that you would most like to have. Write a job-application letter to the person who would be your employer for that job. Also write a résumé that shows that you have the appropriate experience and education for the job. Reread and revise your letter and your résumé.

**Assignment 5**  Think of an issue in your school or community about which you have a strong opinion. Write an opinion letter about that issue to someone who is responsible for making a decision about it. Express your point of view clearly and courteously. Reread and revise your letter to correct any errors in content, spelling, punctuation, and tone.

**Assignment 6**  As the head of your school's concert committee, write a request letter to a musical group that plays at local events. Ask for information about the days that they are available next month, about the rates that they charge, and about the facilities that they need. Then reread and revise your letter.

**Assignment 7**  Find a newspaper article about a bill or an issue on which the United States Senate will vote soon. Write an opinion letter to one of your Senators. Express your point of view on how the senator should vote. Then revise your letter to correct any errors.

**Assignment 8**   A day camp near your home had advertised for counselors for this summer. Write a job-application letter to the director of the camp. In addition, prepare a résumé that shows you have the experience and education necessary for the job. Reread and revise your letter and your résumé.

## Revising Your Assignments

For help in revising a letter, consult the Checklist for Revision on the last page of this book.

# Unit Tests

## Test 1

**A.** Number your paper from 1 to 5. Next to each number. write *True* if the sentence is true or *False* if it is false.

1. Use slang and contractions throughout your business letters.
2. Capitalize only the first word of a complimentary close.
3. The purpose of a job-application letter is to get an appointment for an interview.
4. Your résumé should be at least two pages long.
5. The tone of an opinion letter should be restrained and courteous.

**B.** Number your paper from 6 to 10. Next to each number, write the letter of the term that correctly completes the sentence. You will use all but one of the terms.

    a. adjustment letter    d. opinion letter

    b. block style          e. inside address

    c. résumé            f. modified block style

6. The __?__ is the name and address of the person to whom you are writing.
7. In the __?__, all parts of the letter start at the left margin.
8. You write a(n) __?__ when an order that you placed was not filled correctly or when merchandise that you purchased was defective.
9. A(n) __?__ is a summary of your qualifications for a job.
10. A(n) __?__ expresses your view of a local or national issue.

**C.** Number your paper from 11 to 15. Next to each number, write the letter of the item that correctly answers the question.

11. Which of the following would be a reasonable request to send in a letter?
    a. A request to the California Tourist Bureau for information on all of the tourist attractions in the state.
    b. A request to the Chamber of Commerce in the town of Stowe, Vermont, for information on the inns in the town.
    c. A request to a bookstore for information on the books that it stocks.
    d. A request to the District Attorney for information on the laws in your state.

12. Which of the following statements would be appropriate in an adjustment letter?
    a. I cannot believe that your stupid salesperson made a mistake.
    b. Anyone can see that this shirt is not the color that I ordered.
    c. Please send me a new glass to replace the broken one.
    d. I demand that you refund my money immediately.

13. Which of the following statements does *not* belong in a job-application letter?
    a. I am interested in applying for the cashier's position that was advertised in Sunday's *Town Crier*.
    b. I can be reached at 555-4901 any afternoon after four o'clock.
    c. My birth date is February 23, 1970.
    d. While working in my father's store, I learned how to operate a cash register.

14. Which of the following could be listed in the experience section of your résumé?
    a. That you are a student at West High School.
    b. That you would like to be a day-camp counselor.
    c. That your neighbor Mr. Pyros will provide a reference for you.
    d. That you did babysitting last summer.

15. Which of the following would be an appropriate reason for writing an opinion letter?
    a. You would like information about the city's air pollution laws.
    b. You would like to object to a new air-pollution law that a city commissioner has proposed.
    c. You would like information on pollution-control devices on new cars.
    d. You would like a refund on a defective pollution-control device for your car.

## Test 2

Choose one of the Unit Assignments. Write the assignment as directed and hand it in to your teacher.

# Part Three

## Related Skills

Unit 15  Spelling Skills                568
Unit 16  Vocabulary Skills             578
Unit 17  Public Speaking Skills        588
Unit 18  Test-Taking Skills            606

In many situations you will use skills that are related to writing. Spelling and vocabulary skills are necessary for all of your school assignments, and they are equally important for correspondence with friends, prospective employers, and others. You may be called on to present a speech not only for one of your classes but possibly for a club or organization to which you belong. You can benefit from good test-taking strategies in school now and also later if you take tests for college or job applications.

By studying the information and strategies in Part Three, you will develop skills that will be useful for your school work and for your outside activities. Some of the skills will help you to improve your writing, and others will help you to apply your writing abilities to a variety of tasks.

# Unit 15

## *Spelling Skills*

## 15.1 How to Study Spelling Words

Follow these five steps to help you learn to spell.

**Procedure**

1. *Look at the word and study its letters.*

2. *Pronounce the word* to yourself and think about the letters in it and the sounds that they have.

3. *Write the word.* As you write it, think about any difficult letter combinations in the word.

4. *Check your spelling* to see whether it is correct.

5. *Study the word* until you have memorized its spelling.

## 15.2 Spelling Rules

### 15.2a Making Nouns Plural

Study the following rules for forming the plurals of nouns. Learning these rules will enable you to spell the plurals of nouns correctly when you write.

**Rule**  Form the plural of most common and proper nouns by adding -*s* to the noun.

| | | | |
|---|---|---|---|
| elbow | million | Riley | Viking |
| elbows | millions | the Rileys | the Vikings |

**Rule**  Form the plural of common and proper nouns that end with *s, x, z, ch,* or *sh* by adding -*es* to the noun.

| | | | |
|---|---|---|---|
| chorus | reflex | Dominguez | MacLeish |
| choruses | reflexes | the Dominguezes | the MacLeishes |

**Rule**  Form the plural of a common noun that ends with *y* preceded by a consonant by changing the *y* to *i* and adding -*es*.

| | | | |
|---|---|---|---|
| beauty | courtesy | energy | secretary |
| beauties | courtesies | energies | secretaries |

**Rule**  Form the plural of a common noun that ends with *y* preceded by a vowel by adding -*s*.

| | | | |
|---|---|---|---|
| alley | delay | journey | paisley |
| alleys | delays | journeys | paisleys |

**Rule**  Form the plural of most proper nouns that end with *y* by adding -*s*.

| | | |
|---|---|---|
| | Frank and Joanna Brody | Roy |
| | the Brodys | the two Roys |
| BUT | The Rocky Mountains | |
| | The Rockies | |

**Rule**  Form the plural of most nouns that end with *f* or *fe* by changing the *f* to *v* and adding -*es*.

| | | | |
|---|---|---|---|
| | elf | life | sheaf |
| | elves | lives | sheaves |
| BUT | belief | clef | safe |
| | beliefs | clefs | safes |

**569**

**Rule**   If a noun ends in *o* preceded by a vowel, add *-s* to form the plural.

| | | | |
|---|---|---|---|
| curio | duo | igloo | stereo |
| curios | duos | igloos | stereos |

**Rule**   If a noun ends in *o* preceded by a consonant, form the plural by adding *-s* or *-es*. Certain nouns are correct with either *-s* or *-es*. Check your dictionary when you are uncertain of plural forms.

| | | |
|---|---|---|
| ADD *-s* | auto | cello |
| | autos | cellos |
| ADD *-es* | hero | tomato |
| | heroes | tomatoes |
| ADD *-s* OR *-es* | commando | mosquito |
| | commandos | mosquitos |
| | commandoes | mosquitoes |

**Rule**   Form the plural of a letter, symbol, number, or word that has been italicized (or underlined) for special attention (*page 211*) by adding an apostrophe and *-s* (*'s*). Do not underline the plural ending.

| | | |
|---|---|---|
| *A* | *10* | *maybe* |
| *A*'s | *10*'s | *maybe*'s |

Certain nouns are spelled differently when they are plural.

| | | | |
|---|---|---|---|
| foot | ox | tooth | woman |
| feet | oxen | teeth | women |

Some common nouns and many proper nouns have the same spelling for both singular and plural.

| | | | |
|---|---|---|---|
| bison | swine | Siamese | Viennese |

**Rule**   Form the plural of a compound noun that is written as one word by changing the last word in the compound to its plural form. Form the plural of a compound noun that is hyphenated or written as two or more words by making the most important word plural.

| doorman | aide-de-camp | governor general |
|---------|--------------|------------------|
| doormen | aides-de-camp | governors general |

## 15.2b Adding Endings

The following rules for adding endings other than the plural (*-s* and *-es*) will help you to remember how to spell many words.

### Doubling the Final Consonant

Double the final consonant of a word *only* if you are adding an ending that begins with a vowel.

**Rule** Double the final consonant of words that have only one syllable and that end with a single consonant preceded by a single vowel.

| beg | ship | whip |
|-----|------|------|
| begged | shipper | whipping |

**Rule** Double the final consonant of words that have more than one syllable, that end with a single consonant preceded by a single vowel, and that have the stress on the last syllable.

| confer | control | propel |
|--------|---------|--------|
| conferring | controlled | propeller |

**Note:** When you add endings that begin with *e* or *i* to words that end in *c* preceded by a single vowel, do not double the final consonant but add *-k* before the ending to keep the hard *c* sound.

| frolic | panic | picnic |
|--------|-------|--------|
| frolicking | panicked | picnickers |

Use the questions on the following page to decide whether to double the final consonant when you add an ending to a word.

| | | Yes | No |
|---|---|---|---|
| 1. Does the ending begin with a vowel? | | ? | ? |
| 2. Does the word end with one consonant preceded by one vowel? | | ? | ? |
| 3. Does the word have only one syllable? | | ? | ? |
| 4. Does the word have more than one syllable, and is the greatest stress on the last syllable? | | ? | ? |

If you answer *Yes* to three of these questions, double the final consonant of the word before you add the ending.

## Dropping the Final e

**Rule**   When you add an ending that begins with a vowel to a word that ends with silent *e*, drop the final *e*.

| arrange | exaggerate | hesitate |
|---|---|---|
| arranging | exaggeration | hesitated |

**Rule**   Keep the final *e* when you add an ending that begins with a consonant to a word that ends with silent *e*.

| | hope | separate | whole |
|---|---|---|---|
| | hopeful | separateness | wholeness |
| BUT | abridge | wise | |
| | abridgment | wisdom | |

**Rule**   Keep the final *e* when you add an ending that begins with *a* or *o* to a word that ends in *ce* or *ge* to preserve the soft sound.

| change | outrage | peace |
|---|---|---|
| changeable | outrageous | peaceable |

## Changing Final y to i

**Rule**   If a word ends with *y* preceded by a consonant, change the *y* to *i* before adding any ending except *-ing*.

| defy | hasty | mystery | accompany |
|---|---|---|---|
| defiance | hastily | mysterious | accompanying |

**Rule** If a word ends with *y* preceded by a vowel, do not change the *y* to *i* before adding an ending.

|       | annoy     | convey   | defray    | gray   |
|-------|-----------|----------|-----------|--------|
|       | annoyance | conveyor | defraying | grayer |
| BUT   | day       | gay      |           |        |
|       | daily     | gaily    |           |        |

**Assignment** **Adding Endings** On your paper, write the correct spelling of each word with the indicated ending added. Then write a sentence using each new word that you have formed.

1. ceremony (-ial)
2. patch (plural)
3. fascinate (-ed)
4. turkey (plural)
5. bargain (-ing)
6. display (-ed)
7. monotone (-ous)
8. forget (-able)
9. 200 (plural)
10. necessary (-ly)
11. box (-ful)
12. accept (-ance)
13. waltz (plural)
14. mimic (-ing)
15. trace (-able)
16. wolf (plural)

# 15.3  Spelling Patterns

## The *ie/ei* Pattern

The following rules will help you to decide whether to spell a word with *ei* or with *ie*.

**Rule** Use *ie* if this vowel combination has a long *e* sound (as in *fiend*) unless the letter *c* immediately precedes the vowel combination.

| achieve | hygiene | mien    |
|---------|---------|---------|
| diesel  | stymie  | conceit |

**Rule** Use *ei* if this vowel combination does not have a long *e* sound (as in *weight*).

| foreign | forfeit | height |
|---------|---------|--------|

**Rule**   Use *ei* after *c*.

   ceiling     deceive      perceive

**Rule**   Use *ei* if this vowel combination has a long *a* sound (as in *freight*).

   beige     feign     neigh

**Rule**   If the two vowels are pronounced separately in the word, spell them in the order of their pronunciation.

   ambient     being     happier

## The "Seed" Sound Pattern

The "seed" ending sound has three spellings: *-sede*, *-ceed*, and *-cede*. The spelling *s-e-e-d* does not occur as a suffix in any word.

1. Only one word ends in *-sede*: *supersede*.
2. Three words end in *-ceed*: *exceed, proceed,* and *succeed*.
3. All other "seed" words end in *-cede*: *accede, intercede, secede,* and so on.

# 15.4  Pronunciation and Spelling

Certain kinds of pronunciation errors commonly cause spelling problems. If you are unsure of the pronunciation of a word, check your dictionary. Note the letter combinations that make up the sounds in the word. Say the word silently until you are sure of the pronunciation.

**Extra Sounds or Omitted Sounds.**   Sometimes people misspell words like *attacked* and *arctic* because they mispronounce them, either by adding a sound that the word does not have or by leaving out a sound. The following list contains some words that are often misspelled. Pay special attention to the underlined letters to be sure that you neither add nor omit sounds in those parts of the words when you pronounce or spell them.

| | | |
|---|---|---|
| ath<u>le</u>te | co<u>lu</u>mn | mathematics |
| Antar<u>c</u>tic | gene<u>ra</u>lly | miniature |
| artisti<u>ca</u>lly | grie<u>vo</u>us | nu<u>cle</u>ar |

**Transposed Letters.** Sometimes people write letters in the wrong order because they pronounce them in the wrong order. Such errors often occur in the words in the following list. Be sure that you pronounce and spell the underlined letters in the proper order.

| | | |
|---|---|---|
| anon<u>ym</u>ous | per<u>sp</u>iration | rep<u>re</u>sent |
| demo<u>cr</u>acy | <u>re</u>altor | stub<u>bo</u>rn |

**Homophones and Commonly Confused Words.** Words that have the same pronunciation but different spellings and meanings, such as *profit* and *prophet*, are called **homophones**. Some other words, such as *exalt* and *exult*, are not homophones, but they are similar enough in sound and spelling to create confusion. Be sure that you know the spelling and meaning of each word in the following list. (See also Usage Notes, pages 156–177.)

| | |
|---|---|
| cache, cash | maize, maze |
| cede, seed | palate, palette, pallet |
| dew, do, due | refuge, refugee |
| dual, duel | splatter, splutter |
| empress, impress | summary, summery |
| extant, extent | thrash, thresh |

# 15.5 Other Spelling Aids

In addition to learning all the preceding spelling rules and patterns, you can improve your spelling in other ways. Here are some suggestions that will help.

## Strategies

1. *Develop your own methods of word study.* Knowing the rules and patterns of spelling will help.

2. *Keep a list of troublesome words.* Study your list frequently.

3. *Create memory aids,* called mnemonic (nĭ-MŎN′ĭk) devices, for difficult words. For example:

> **Earnest** put his *ear* to the *nest.*
> Put a *c* in *send* to make **descend.**
> *O be die* begins **obedience.**

4. *Pay attention to how words sound and look.*

5. *Always check in your dictionary when you are unsure of the spelling of a word.*

## Other Spellings of Some Sounds

If you do not know how to spell a word, you may have difficulty locating it in your dictionary. You will have to guess the spelling of the word and then check other possible spellings until you find the correct one. You already know which letters usually stand for the various sounds in English. The following list suggests where to look for a word when it does not begin the way that you expect.

| CONSONANT SOUNDS | OTHER SPELLINGS |
|---|---|
| *f,* as in *f*eat | *ph,* as in *ph*armacy |
| *j,* as in *j*ury | *g,* as in *g*enial |
| *k,* as in *k*een | *c* or *ch,* as in *c*onfide and *ch*lorine |
| *n,* as in *n*erve | *gn, kn,* or *pn,* as in *gn*ash, *kn*ave, and *pn*eumatic |
| *r,* as in *r*ival | *wr,* as in *wr*eath |
| *s,* as in *s*kim | *ps* or *c,* as in *ps*eudonym and *c*inema |

| VOWEL SOUNDS | OTHER SPELLINGS |
|---|---|
| *a,* as in *a*ble | *ei,* as in *ei*ghty |
| *i,* as in *i*deal | *ei,* as in *Ei*nstein |
| *u,* as in *u*rge | *e* or *ea,* as in *e*rmine and *ea*rth |

# 15.6  Frequently Misspelled Words

Certain words are misspelled so often that many writers consider them problem words. You have already studied some troublesome words earlier in this unit. The following list gives twenty-five more for you to master.

| | | |
|---|---|---|
| analyze | grammar | pleasant |
| anxious | humorous | possess |
| awkward | interfere | pursue |
| bureau | knowledge | recommendation |
| campaign | magazine | repetition |
| consistent | pamphlet | sincerely |
| despair | perhaps | tragedy |
| discipline | persuade | typical |
| especially | | |

**Assignment 1  Improving Your Spelling**  With a classmate, take turns giving each other a test on the words listed on this page. In your notebook, make a list of the words that you misspelled on the test. Whenever you are unsure of the spelling of a word that you encounter, add that word to your list. Develop a mnemonic device for each word on your list, and study the words and the devices frequently to improve your spelling.

**Assignment 2  Learning New Words**  Choose ten words that you often misspell. List them in your notebook, and create a mnemonic device for each word. When you have mastered the correct spelling, use each word as often as you can in your writing.

# Unit 16

*Vocabulary Skills*

Words can confound, delight, please, shock, enrage, and terrify. They have the power to bewilder, to mystify, to tantalize, to satisfy. They can solve problems or cause dissension. They can be used to create myths and to describe nature. They can be used to record the past and to establish expectations for the future.

In this unit you will discover how to learn words, how to choose words that convey precise meaning, and how certain words have become part of our language.

## 16.1 How to Learn New Words

The following process will help you to learn new words so that you can enrich your vocabulary and enhance the effectiveness of what you write and what you say.

In your notebook, make a list of words that you want to add to your vocabulary. Look up the meanings in your dictionary, and add the meanings to your list. Study these words and their meanings as often as you can. Use the words frequently in your writing and in your conversation. When you come across these words in your reading, study the context in which they are used.

As you become more confident in your use of these words, you will find that your list has become a reliable vocabulary resource. Add to your list and continue to use it in developing effective vocabulary skills.

# 16.2 Using Context to Get Meaning

When you encounter an unfamiliar word in your reading, you may be able to determine its meaning without consulting your dictionary if you examine the **context,** the passage in which the word appears. The following strategies suggest ways in which you can use context to help you to determine meaning.

**Strategies**

1. *Use the general sense of the passage* along with your own knowledge and experience of what is described to help you decide on a likely meaning.

2. *Read carefully and look for synonyms or restated definitions of the unfamiliar word.*

3. *Use any examples that may appear after the unfamiliar word* to help you determine its meaning.

4. *Notice whether the unfamiliar word is compared to or contrasted with a word or an idea that you know.* If so, use that known idea to help you determine the meaning of the unfamiliar word.

# 16.3 Getting Meanings from Word Parts

If you know the meanings of a few roots, prefixes, and suffixes, you can often use them to determine the meanings of unfamiliar words.

**Roots.** Because many words in English have Latin or Greek origins, you can expand your vocabulary by learning the meanings of some Latin and Greek roots. Recognizing a single **root,** the central or basic element of a word, can help you to figure out the meanings of a number of English words. For example, you may recognize the common root -*gen*- (meaning "born") in the words *genetic, genealogy,* and *general.* This information can help you to understand the meaning of these words. If you read the sentence "Scientists are working to determine the *genesis* of the disease," you can use the context plus your knowledge of the root *-gen-* to conclude that *genesis* means "beginning" or "origin."

The spelling of the root may change slightly when it becomes part of an English word. Roots may be combined with prefixes and suffixes, as well as with other word roots, to make other words.

Even when you know the meanings of some word roots, you must consider the rest of the word and the context. Just as two words may have the same spelling but different meanings (homographs), two or more roots may have the same spelling but different meanings. For example, the two roots spelled *-leg-* in the following list of Latin roots are spelled the same way, but their meanings differ.

The hyphens before and after each root in the following lists indicate that the root may appear at the beginning, in the middle, or at the end of a word.

### COMMON LATIN ROOTS

| | *Root* | *Meaning(s)* | *Examples* |
|---|---|---|---|
| 1. | -cred- | trust, believe | credit, incredible |
| 2. | -fin- | limit, end | final, infinite |
| 3. | -frag- (-frac-) | break | fragment, fraction |
| 4. | -leg- | law | legal, legitimate |
| | -leg- (-lect-, | gather, read | legend, elect |
| | -les-, -lig-) | | lesson, intelligent |
| 5. | -pend- (-pens-) | hang | depend, suspense |
| 6. | -reg- (-rect-) | guide, direct | regulation, correct |
| 7. | -scan- (-scen-) | climb | ascend, descendant |
| 8. | -sent- (-sens-) | sense, feel | sentiment, sensible |
| 9. | -uni- | one, single | unicorn, uniform |
| 10. | -verb- | word | proverb, verbal |

### COMMON GREEK ROOTS

| | *Root* | *Meaning(s)* | *Examples* |
|---|---|---|---|
| 1. | -chrom- | color | chromatic, chromosome |
| 2. | -chron- | time | chronic, synchronize |
| 3. | -cosm- | well-ordered | cosmic, cosmetics |
| 4. | -derm- | skin, hide | dermatology, taxidermy |
| 5. | -orth- | straight, correct | orthography, orthodox |
| 6. | -pan- | every, all | panacea, panorama |
| 7. | -path- | suffering | sympathy, pathetic |
| 8. | -poly- | many | polychrome, polygon |
| 9. | -scop- | look at, see | telescope, microscope |

**Prefixes and Suffixes.** A **prefix** is a letter or a group of letters placed before a word or before a root to make another word. A **suffix** is a letter or a group of letters placed at the end of a word or at the end of a root to change its function and, sometimes, to change its meaning. When you add a prefix to a word or root, the spelling does not change. However, when you add a suffix to a word or root, the spelling may change. Sometimes, several suffixes are added to the end of a word to make another word; for example, *sensationalism* is made up of *sense* plus *-ation* plus *-al* plus *-ism*.

Knowing the meanings of prefixes, suffixes, and roots can help you to figure out the meanings of unfamiliar words. For example, if you know that *dis-* (*dif-*) means "apart," that *-ion* means "act of," and that *-sent-* means "to feel," you can figure out the meaning of *dissension* ("disagreement").

PREFIXES

| | Prefix | Meaning(s) | Examples |
|---|---|---|---|
| 1. | a- | on, in, at | ashore, abroad |
| | a- | up, out, off | awake, arise |
| 2. | ab- (a-, abs-) | away from, from | abstain, abrupt |
| 3. | ad- (a-, ab-, ac-, af-, ag-, al-, an-, ap-, ar-, as-, at-) | to, toward | adapt, affiliate |
| 4. | an- (a-) | not, without | anarchy, atypical |
| 5. | ana- (an-) | upward, according to | analogy, anagram |
| | ana- (an-) | back, backward | anachronism |
| 6. | be- | make | becalm, belittle |
| | be- | thoroughly | beloved, besmirch |
| 7. | en- (em-) | put or go into or on, give, cause to become or resemble | enthrone, empower |
| | en- (em-) | in, into, within | energy, empathy |
| 8. | mal- (male-) | bad, badly, wrongly | malformed |
| 9. | out- | surpassing, outside of | outshine, outboard |
| 10. | sub- (suc-, suf-, sug-, sup-, sur-, sus-) | under, down, less than, slightly | submarine, succumb, suffocate |

SUFFIXES

| Suffix | Meaning(s) | Examples |
|---|---|---|
| *These suffixes are used to make verbs:* | | |
| 1. -ate | make, apply, do | originate, regulate |
| 2. -en | cause to be or become | fasten, weaken |
| 3. -fy | make or form into | unify, justify |
| 4. -ize, (-ise) | make, make into, cause, cause to be | sterilize, advertise |
| *These suffixes are used to make nouns:* | | |
| 1. -an | one belonging to | human, veteran |
| 2. -ant (-ent) | state or condition of, one who | variant, resident |
| 3. -hood | condition, state of | brotherhood |
| 4. -ory | place or instrument for | conservatory, directory |
| 5. -sis | condition, state of | osmosis, paralysis |
| 6. -some | a group of | threesome |
| 7. -ism | condition, state of | barbarism, realism |
| 8. -y | condition, state of, result of | injury, jealousy |
| *These suffixes are used to make adjectives or adverbs:* | | |
| 1. -er | more | whiter, slower |
| 2. -ly | like | sisterly, miserly |
| -ly | in the given manner | gradually, partly |
| 3. -ward (-wards) | in the direction of | homeward |
| 4. -wise | in a certain manner, direction, position | likewise, clockwise |

**Assignment   Roots, Prefixes, and Suffixes**   The words in the following list contain some roots, prefixes, and suffixes from the lists on pages 580–582. Use what you already know and what you have recently learned about those word parts to determine the meanings of the words. Check the meanings in your dictionary. Then, for each word, write a sentence that clearly shows your understanding of the meaning of the word.

**SAMPLE**   unorthodox

**ANSWER**   Geneva's unorthodox ideas often cause arguments.

1. discredit
2. regulatory
3. enfeeble
4. suspensefully
5. codify
6. sensory
7. mobilize
8. anachronism
9. fragility
10. descendant
11. verbally
12. lecture
13. accredit
14. embolden
15. polychromatic

## 16.4 Word Origins

Some historical events and literary figures are so well known that their names have acquired meanings of their own. The following list of words, now commonly used in English, come from history, geography, literature, and mythology.

**bedlam.** In England, the Hospital of St. Mary of Bethlehem was commonly called *Bedlam* by the local people. When the hospital was converted into an asylum for the insane, the word *bedlam* came to describe any noisy, disorderly, confused situation.

**cashmere.** Wool from goats found in the Kashmir region of northwest India is used to make this soft fabric.

**denim.** A fabric called serge was manufactured in the French city of Nîmes and was consequently called *serge de Nîmes* (serge from Nîmes). This name was shortened to *de Nîmes* and then to *denim*.

**derrick.** A hangman in England in the 1600s was named Derick. From his name and occupation comes the word for tall framework supporting heavy equipment.

**diesel.** Rudolf Diesel invented this kind of internal-combustion engine.

**hector.** In Homer's *Iliad*, Hector was a hero. In England during the 1600s, however, a street gang named after the hero Hector behaved in a rowdy manner. Consequently, the verb *hector* came to mean "to bully, intimidate, browbeat."

**jeans.** The fabric used to make these pants was first made in Genoa, called *Gênes* in French.

**mentor.** This word, meaning "wise and trusted counselor," comes from the name of the trusted friend who took care of Odysseus' son when Odysseus left on his travels.

**odyssey.** For ten years after the Trojan War, Odysseus (Ulysses) was compelled to wander the world before he could return home. Hence, an *odyssey* is a long journey.

**sardine**. This small fish was first caught near the island of Sardinia.

**suede**. Gloves of this soft leather originally were made in Sweden, which is *Suède* in French.

**tangerine**. These small, sweet, reddish oranges were first imported from *Tangier,* a seaport in Morocco.

# 16.5  How to Choose the Best Word

To be sure that you use the most appropriate word in a given situation, you need to learn about synonyms and about the difference between denotation and connotation.

## Synonyms

Over the centuries, the English language has incorporated words from many languages, resulting in a large vocabulary, rich in **synonyms,** or words with similar meanings. The verb *puzzle,* for example, has the following synonyms: perplex, mystify, bewilder, confound, and baffle.

There is often some slight difference in meaning that makes one word more appropriate than another in a specific situation. These differences in meaning are often called shades of meaning. Consider the word *puzzle* and five of its synonyms to see the shades of meaning that synonyms can have.

The verb *puzzle* usually means to present an intricate, difficult, but solvable problem. *Perplex* stresses uncertainty or anxiety over reaching a decision or a solution. *Mystify* means to puzzle by purposely obscuring or concealing facts. *Bewilder* emphasizes not only perplexity, but extreme confusion of the mind. *Confound* strongly implies astonishment. *Baffle* means to outwit or frustrate by puzzling.

As skilled writers you need to be aware of shades of meaning and to use the synonym that is most effective in conveying precise meaning in any given situation.

## Connotations and Denotations

Most words have two kinds of meanings: **denotations,** the definitions exactly as found in a dictionary, and **connotations,** the ideas and feelings associated with the words. In the following examples, note the stronger connotation of *outrage* compared to the connotation of *offend*.

> It **offended** me when Ned didn't say "Please."
>
> The committee members were **outraged** when they learned that the senator had ignored their requests.

Also, the connotation of the same word can change with the context in which the word is used. Consider the difference in the meaning of the word *wreck* when it is used in two different contexts. Suppose a friend inquires about your car, an old car that you are proud of and have tinkered with for months. You may slap the fender of the car and say, "Do you mean this old wreck?" Obviously, in that sentence, *wreck* would not have the same meaning as it would if you were filing an accident report for an insurance claim in which you used the word *wreck*.

The connotations of the words that you use in your writing must match your intended meaning. Appropriate words add strength and descriptive power to whatever you write.

**Assignment** **Using New Words** From each of the following sets of three words, choose the one word that has the strongest connotation and write a sentence using it. Use your dictionary to be sure that you have chosen the right word. Be prepared to explain the connotations of the other words also.

> SAMPLE   costly, valuable, priceless
>
> ANSWER   The museum hired three guards to protect the **priceless** antiques.

1. argue, debate, discuss
2. save, hoard, accumulate
3. frank, blunt, honest
4. glad, joyous, cheerful
5. look, examine, probe

# 16.6   Using the Dictionary

If you wish to find the meaning, the pronunciation, or other information about a word, you need to know how to use your dictionary.

To find a word in the dictionary, first use the **guide words,** at the tops of the pages, to help you find the right page. Then find the **entry word,** in boldface type, in alphabetical order on the page.

## Parts of a Dictionary Entry

The **entry** includes all the information that is given about the word: syllabication, pronunciation, part(s) of speech, definitions, and etymology. Entry words of more than one syllable are divided by dots or hyphens. This syllabication indicates where to divide a word at the end of a line of writing.

**Pronunciations.**   The pronunciation usually follows the entry word and appears within brackets, parentheses, or bars. Light and heavy accent marks show which syllables are stressed. Most dictionaries contain a complete **pronunciation key** near the front of the dictionary and a shorter key at the bottom of each page or each pair of facing pages. Use the key to interpret the pronunciation symbols. Because pronunciation keys vary, become familiar with the particular system that your dictionary uses.

**Definitions.**   The most important information in a dictionary is the definitions, or meanings, of words. When an entry word has multiple definitions, each definition is numbered. Read all of the definitions before selecting one that is appropriate for a context.

**Parts of Speech.**   Dictionaries identify the part(s) of speech of a word. The following abbreviations are used in most dictionaries and usually appear after the pronunciation.

| | | | |
|---|---|---|---|
| *n.* | noun | *adj.* | adjective |
| *pron.* | pronoun | *adv.* | adverb |
| *v.* or *vb.* | verb | *prep.* | preposition |
| *vt.* or *v. tr.* | transitive verb | *conj.* | conjunction |
| *vi.* or *v. intr.* | intransitive verb | *interj.* | interjection |

**Synonyms.**   Because the English language contains so many synonyms, dictionaries often list synonyms for an entry word and explain their connotations. Some dictionaries also list **antonyms,** words that mean the opposite of a given word.

**Homographs.**   Words that are spelled alike but have different origins and different meanings are called **homographs.** Such words may also have different pronunciations and syllabications. In most dictionaries homographs are listed as separate entry words and are identified by **superscripts,** small raised numerals placed before or after the entry word. When homographs are listed in your dictionary, read all the definitions of each entry to find the meaning that is appropriate to the context in which the word is used. For example, for the entry word *league,* you will find **league**[1], meaning "an organization or association" and **league**[2], meaning "a unit of distance equal to three statute miles." You would have to read both entries to know the meaning of *league* in the sentence "At two hours after midnight appeared the land, at a distance of two **leagues**" (from Christopher Columbus's *Journal of the First Voyage*).

**Etymologies.**   The **etymology** of a word is its origin and historical development. It is usually given in brackets or parentheses after the pronunciation or at the end of the entry. Often the etymology gives additional insight into the meaning of a word.

**Labels.**   When appropriate, dictionary entries include usage labels, such as Nonstandard, Informal or Colloquial, Regional or Dialect, or Slang. Such labels are a guide to the correct use of words.

**Assignment** **Improving Your Vocabulary**   From the following list, choose ten words that are not already part of your everyday vocabulary. Write the words in your notebook in alphabetical order, leaving room for a definition and a sentence. Look up each word in your dictionary to learn its meaning and pronunciation. Then, in your notebook, write a brief definition and a sentence using the word. Study the words from time to time, and use them in your speaking and writing whenever appropriate. When you have learned these words, make a new list and study them in the same way.

| | | |
|---|---|---|
| 1. tedious | 8. compulsory | 15. barbarous |
| 2. inexorable | 9. magnanimity | 16. cosmopolitan |
| 3. kindred | 10. envisage | 17. melancholy |
| 4. acquiesce | 11. hypocrisy | 18. conciliatory |
| 5. conjecture | 12. pecuniary | 19. ubiquitous |
| 6. ingenious | 13. ornate | 20. phenomenon |
| 7. mediocre | 14. jeopardy | |

# Unit 17

*Public*
*Speaking Skills*

Whenever you address a group of listeners, you are engaging in public speaking. Regardless of the occasion or the circumstances, you want to interest your listeners and hold their attention. You want to communicate facts and ideas in a clear and understandable way. In this unit you will learn how to organize and deliver informative and persuasive speeches.

## 17.1 Kinds of Speeches

A speech may be **formal,** such as an inaugural address, or **informal,** such as a report to your homeroom class on the progress of a committee. Speeches also may be either **impromptu** or **prepared**. Your response to a classmate's suggestion for raising funds for a club activity is an example of an impromptu speech. When you gather and organize your material ahead of time, as for a campaign speech or for an oral report, the result is a prepared speech.

Your purpose in speaking is to inform your listeners, to persuade them, or to entertain them. You may have more than one purpose for the same speech. For example, you may want to persuade people to vote for a particular candidate and, at the same time, inform them about the candidate's record. Although all three kinds of speeches are described here, this unit concentrates on informative and persuasive speeches only.

**Speaking to Inform.**    Your principal purpose in an informative speech is to increase your listeners' knowledge of the subject. An appropriate subject is one about which you can provide information that will be both new and interesting to your audience. Here are two examples:

> You review a television documentary on World War I for your history class.
>
> You show new members of the swim team the required warm-up drill and explain why each step is important.

**Speaking to Persuade.**    Your principal purpose in a persuasive speech is to form or change your listeners' attitudes or opinions. In addition, you may want to cause them to take some action. Your subject for this kind of speech would be some issue on which your listeners may have different opinions. Your audience would include people whose views may differ from yours, for you would not need to persuade them if they agreed with you already. Two examples follow:

> You urge the school board to buy computers as you present the advantages of computer-assisted instruction.
>
> You encourage the members of your scout troop to ask other troops in the area to help set up a community recycling center.

**Speaking to Entertain.**    Your principal purpose in an entertaining speech is to give your listeners enjoyment. The subject matter of such a speech is light rather than serious, as in these examples:

> You thank your coach at a victory banquet.
>
> You describe to your garden club your misfortune when you planted gourd seeds, instead of squash seeds.

## 17.2  Preparing Your Speech

You will find it easier to plan and prepare a speech if you proceed with one step at a time. The steps for planning and giving any speech are briefly described here. Later in this unit, you will follow these steps in preparing informative and persuasive speeches.

**Selecting and Limiting Your Topic.**    A good speech topic, like a good composition topic, must be narrow enough for you to cover adequately in the time allowed. Photography, for instance, is too broad a topic for a satisfactory speech. Narrow the subject to a topic such as how filters can help you take better pictures, why your school should set up a darkroom, or why some of your candid shots should never have been taken.

To limit your topic, think about your general purpose and your specific purpose. Your **general purpose** for making a speech is to inform, to persuade, or to entertain your listeners, or a combination of these purposes. Your **specific purpose** states exactly what you want to inform your listeners about, or what you want to persuade them to do, or how you want to amuse them.

From your specific purpose and limited topic, you develop a **thesis statement** (*page 426*), in which you tell your audience what you are going to talk about. For example, your thesis statement might be "There are four ways that filters can help you to take better pictures."

**Gathering Information.** You now proceed to gather information to develop your topic. You may need to consult reference books, magazine or newspaper articles, or radio and television broadcasts to supplement your own knowledge and experience. You may also consult people with special knowledge about your topic. Most important, you should analyze your information and develop your own ideas about the topic.

**Organizing Your Speech.** As you organize the material for your speech, decide what main ideas you will cover. Make an outline (*page 427*) that includes main headings, subheadings, and supporting details. Like a written report, your speech should have an introduction, a body, and a conclusion. Later in this unit, you will learn about specific ways to organize informative and persuasive speeches.

**Preparing and Delivering Your Speech.** To ensure a smooth and effective delivery, you should use note cards. Make notes of the main headings and the supporting ideas in your speech. Adequate rehearsal, using your note cards, will help you to relax and to focus on your voice, posture, and other elements of delivery that will make your speech clear and interesting.

**Assignment 1** **Limiting Topics** Write three limited speech topics for each of the following broad subjects.

| | | |
|---|---|---|
| 1. Mass transit | 3. Used cars | 5. Nutrition |
| 2. Inflation | 4. Sources of energy | 6. Driver education |

**Assignment 2  Purpose and Audience**  For each of the broad subjects in Assignment 1, select one of your three limited speech topics. On your paper, list the general purpose and the specific purpose for each of these six topics. Write a thesis statement and describe an appropriate audience for each topic.

# 17.3  Speeches to Inform

The purpose of an informative speech is to increase your listeners' knowledge about your topic. You want to plan, organize, and deliver your speech in such a way that your listeners will understand and remember the information that you give them.

Many people, including teachers, newscasters, judges, and coaches, make informative speeches frequently as part of their jobs. Informative speeches include travel talks, public lectures, classroom instruction, book and entertainment reviews, and demonstrations. Reports and announcements are also examples of informative speeches.

## 17.3a  What to Include in an Informative Speech

An important part of your informative speech is the material that supports your main ideas. This information should be primarily factual and objective, rather than based on your personal opinion. Nevertheless, you do need to analyze and interpret the material that you select for your speech.

In deciding what to include in your speech, consider the time limit and the amount of information that your listeners can absorb during that time. Rather than trying to cover too much information in a relatively short time, limit yourself to the most significant points. Give your listeners only as much information as they are likely to retain and appreciate.

## Kinds of Information

The following kinds of material are particularly appropriate in informative speeches:

1. *Explanations.* To explain a new concept to your listeners, begin with material that they are familiar with and, from that, develop the new material step by step. You can explain what something is, how something functions, or why something happens as it does.
2. *Definitions.* When a word is difficult to understand or is used in an unusual way, define it for your listeners.
3. *Examples.* An example is a case or a sample that you can use to represent a category or to illustrate a general rule.
4. *Illustrations.* An illustration is an extended example with details included. Illustrations may involve personal experiences, stories, reports of events, or demonstrations.
5. *Quotations.* A quotation is a statement that was originally spoken or written by another person. You may quote from many sources: books, magazines, newspapers, poems, plays, speeches, documents, laws, conversations, and so forth.
6. *Statistics.* Statistics are facts in the form of numbers. Although statistics give authority to your points, you should use them sparingly so that they can have the greatest impact on your listeners.
7. *Questions.* To stimulate thoughts and ideas about your topic, you may ask your listeners a rhetorical question. A rhetorical question is one that is both asked and answered by the speaker.
8. *Restatements or Summaries.* Sometimes, within the body of your speech, you may want to remind your listeners of information that you have discussed earlier.

You can test the appropriateness of your supporting material by asking yourself the following questions:

1. Is the supporting material directly related to the main ideas of my speech?
2. Have I included enough supporting material from a variety of sources?

3. Is my supporting material clear and accurate?
4. Is it consistent with the rest of the content of my speech?
5. Do I explain the supporting material so that my listeners will understand it?
6. Is my supporting material integrated into the body of my speech so that the speech flows smoothly and logically?
7. Did I remember to cite the sources of the supporting material?

## Visual Aids

Use visual aids whenever they are appropriate. Your audience will often understand new information better if they can see it at the same time that they are hearing it.

Visual aids include scale models, slides, maps, sketches, photographs, charts, and posters. Keep the following points in mind when you use visual aids in any kind of speech.

### Strategies

1. *Use a visual aid only if it is an integral part of your speech,* not merely to attract the attention of your audience.

2. *Make sure that the visual aid is large enough to be seen distinctly by all members of the audience.*

3. *Avoid blocking the audience's view of the aid.*

4. *Remember to face your listeners, not the visual aid.*

5. *Limit the visual aid to a supporting role in your speech.* Do not use it as a substitute for effective speaking.

## 17.3b How to Organize an Informative Speech

The three main parts of your speech—the introduction, the body, and the conclusion—should be related in such a way that the speech as a whole is easy for your listeners to understand and remember. Because the body contains most of the informative material, you should develop this central part of your speech first.

## The Body of Your Speech

As you decide what main points you want to bring out in your speech, make a rough outline of the major points (*page 487*): Then develop a detailed outline (*page 506*) with main headings, subheadings, and supporting information. The nature of the topic and your knowledge of the audience determine the method by which you organize the body of your speech.

**Methods of Organization.**   When you arrange the main headings of your speech outline, use the pattern that is most appropriate for your topic. You can organize an informative speech in a number of ways, including the following:

Use the **topical pattern** when you can divide your topic into distinct parts. For example:

> There are three kinds of rocks: igneous, metamorphic, and sedimentary.

Use the **chronological pattern** when your topic includes a set of steps or a time sequence, as in this example:

> We can trace the growth of our municipal zoo from the time it was founded in 1936 to the present.

Use the **spatial pattern** when your topic involves physical or geographical relationships. Consider the following:

> Let us imagine a trip along the Rio Grande from its origin in Colorado to where it empties into the Gulf of Mexico.

Use the **problem-solution pattern** when you are describing a problem and suggesting solutions, as in this example:

> The problem of pedestrian safety can be approached in several ways.

Use the **cause-and-effect pattern** when your speech topic deals with the reasons behind events or with the results of actions or changes. Consider the following:

> An adequate amount of calcium in the diet has important benefits to your health.

Use the **comparison-and-contrast pattern** when you point out similarities and differences between situations, persons, or concepts. Here is an example:

> The British Parliament is similar to the United States Congress in many ways.

## The Introduction to Your Speech

After organizing the body of your speech, you can plan an introduction that will prepare your listeners for the material that you are going to present. The following strategies can help you develop an effective introduction.

### Strategies

1. *Gain the interest and attention of your listeners.* You may ask a provocative question or make a startling statement. You may use a quotation or offer a humorous anecdote. You might refer to a personal experience or relate the topic to your listeners' experience as a way of arousing interest.

2. *Present your thesis statement.* Tell your listeners exactly what you plan to talk about.

3. *Indicate how your speech is organized.* Give your listeners some clue to the organizational pattern that your speech will follow.

4. *Establish a good relationship with your listeners.* Convey to your audience the feeling that you are confident and relaxed and that you know about your subject. Your audience will respond by listening attentively to your speech and by being receptive to what you have to say.

## The Conclusion of Your Speech

As you bring your speech to a close, you have your last opportunity to ensure that your listeners understand the information that you are presenting. Give them an overview, or summary, of the topic so that they can see it as a whole. Refer to your major points and important information. In some cases, you may want to tell your listeners where they can obtain additional information.

If you end your speech in a strong and interesting way, you will help your listeners remember what you have told them.

## 17.3c How to Word an Informative Speech

You should think carefully about your audience when you decide how to word your speech. Your language should be simple enough for your listeners to understand easily, but not so simple that they become bored. Take time to define words and specialized terms, keeping in mind that your listeners do not have the same knowledge of your topic as you have.

Avoid trite and overused words and expressions. Instead, use colorful and descriptive words that catch and hold your listeners' attention. Words that convey a picture to the listener's mind, such as *bounced* or *trudged* rather than *went,* will make your speech more vivid and interesting.

Use transitional words and phrases to make your speech flow smoothly. Transitional words can connect different ideas in your speech and show your listeners the relationship between them. Here are some frequently used transitional words:

| | |
|---|---|
| therefore | on the other hand |
| consequently | as a result |
| instead | in addition |
| nevertheless | another question |

In addition to using transitional words and phrases, you should include key words and phrases that act as **signals.** You need to let listeners know that you are about to state the purpose of your speech or that you are about to summarize. You can also signal that you are about to tell them how your speech is organized and what the main ideas are. Remember that a listener, unlike a reader, cannot refer to the material afterward to see how it is structured, what the main

points a
followir

I

co
fo

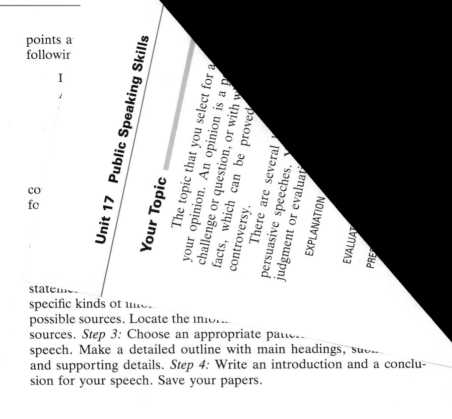

**Your Topic**

The topic that you select for a
your opinion. An opinion is a p
challenge or question, or with w
facts, which can be proved
controversy.
There are several
persuasive speeches.
judgment or evaluat

EXPLANATION

EVALUAT

PRE

stateme
specific kinds of info...
possible sources. Locate the info...
sources. *Step 3:* Choose an appropriate patte...
speech. Make a detailed outline with main headings, sub...
and supporting details. *Step 4:* Write an introduction and a conclusion for your speech. Save your papers.

## 17.4 Speeches to Persuade

The purpose of a persuasive speech is to change an opinion.
You want your listeners to accept a new idea, to take some sort of
action, or both.

Almost everyone has occasion to speak persuasively to others,
whether the speaker is a lawyer defending a client or a student trying
to persuade a teacher to change a test date.

In planning a persuasive speech, consider both your topic and
your audience.

persuasive speech should reflect
osition or a view that others may
hich others agree or disagree. Unlike
or checked, an opinion is open to

kinds of opinions that you can express in
ou may explain your opinion, express your
on, make a prediction, or propose a policy.

The popularity of movies declined because of the invention of television.

ON    The play was not well acted.

ICTION    By early in the next century, medical computers may make doctors obsolete.

POLICY    The legislature should pass this water pollution bill.

## Your Audience

In planning a persuasive speech, it is particularly important to consider your audience. Consider carefully the background, experiences, and needs of your listeners. Think about how they might respond to your persuasive speech. You are trying to influence their opinions and possibly their actions; therefore, you must appeal to their interests and concerns and win their confidence.

In planning a persuasive speech, keep in mind that your listeners are more likely to change their views or actions if you can convince them of the following:

1.  The change is consistent with their beliefs, attitudes, and values. For example, if you know that your listeners donate time and money to charitable organizations, they may be willing to donate time and money to a charitable cause that you propose.
2.  The change will require small efforts, rather than large ones. It is easier to persuade your listeners to sign a petition that you pass among them than it is to get them to write letters to the governor.

3. The change meets their needs. If you know that your listeners seek tax reductions, for instance, you might persuade them to approve a zoning change by showing how the change would bring more tax money into the community.
4. You suggest the change gradually. Your listeners are more likely to be persuaded if you give more neutral information first. Begin by giving reasons, examples, and explanations before encouraging your listeners to take action.

## 17.4a What to Include in a Persuasive Speech

In many instances, you can strengthen your position and your reasons by supporting them with facts. The reasons that you use to build your argument may be opinions, facts, or opinions supported by facts.

OPINION

A quiet bus is more pleasant to ride on.

FACT

In our society, each municipality has the right to control its zoning and to make decisions about land use.

OPINION SUPPORTED BY FACT

Most corporate retirement plans do not provide enough money to cover unanticipated expenses. [You would need to support this opinion with statistics from typical corporate retirement plans.]

Supporting material that may be appropriate in a persuasive speech includes the same kinds of material that you would use in an informative speech. (See also pages 380–385 and 389–392 in Unit 10, "Persuasive Writing.")

Include in your persuasive speech only material that clearly supports your position. Do not include extraneous material that might confuse your listeners or distract them from the purpose of your speech.

## 17.4b How to Organize a Persuasive Speech

Once you have chosen a topic that is suitable for your audience, you are ready to begin organizing your persuasive speech. Like an informative speech, a persuasive speech has an introduction, a body, and a conclusion. Because the body conveys your primary message, you should organize and develop that part of your speech first.

### The Body of Your Speech

In order to persuade your listeners, you have to show why you consider your position correct. When you present reasons or evidence to support your opinion, you are presenting an **argument,** a series of logically connected statements. The first statement expresses your position, the view that you want your listeners to accept. In the supporting material, you give the reasons for your audience to accept your position.

| | |
|---|---|
| POSITION | We should elect Gina Margoles student body president. |
| REASON | Gina has shown leadership ability in clubs and on committees. |
| REASON | Gina has been a member of the student senate. |
| REASON | Gina has devoted a great deal of time to school activities, often volunteering for difficult tasks. |
| REASON | Gina communicates well with both students and faculty. |
| REASON | Gina has good ideas that she can implement as student body president. |
| POSITION | Admission fees at the municipal art gallery should be optional. |
| REASON | All taxpayers support the gallery through their taxes. |
| REASON | Businesses and individuals generously support the museum through tax-deductible contributions and membership fees. |

REASON      Persons willing and able to pay could contribute as much or as little as they wish.

REASON      Access to art inspires latent interests and talents in citizens of all ages and income brackets.

There are a number of ways in which you can organize your persuasive speech. Here are five methods:

1. *Direct Request for Action.* When you use this method, you ask your listeners to do something, giving reasons for them to do what you propose.
2. *Order of Importance.* In this method you arrange your reasons according to their importance. You may start with the most important reason and follow it with less important ones, or you may begin by offering less important reasons and build to the most important one.
3. *Developmental Approach.* When you use this method, you review the background of the situation or problem in order to show that your solution is valid. When appropriate, you may refer to unsuccessful past efforts at a solution.
4. *Comparison and Contrast.* You may wish to organize your argument by comparing your position with similar successful solutions or by contrasting it with other proposals that you consider less workable.
5. *Collaborative Approach.* You can organize your persuasive speech around views that you think your audience may already hold. Each time your listeners agree with your supporting statements, you have moved them closer to accepting your position.

## The Introduction to Your Speech

Your introduction should arouse your listeners' interest and focus their attention on your topic. Depending on the method of organization that you are using in the body, you may or may not choose to state your position in the introduction.

In planning your introduction, remember that you want your listeners to be willing to listen to you regardless of whether they agree with your views.

In some cases you may gain your listeners' attention with a startling statement, a question, a quotation, an anecdote, or a request for action. However you choose to begin your persuasive speech, be sure that the introduction is closely related to your topic and is suitable to both your audience and the occasion.

## The Conclusion of Your Speech

The conclusion of a persuasive speech brings to a climax all the material that has preceded it. Your goal is to summarize your argument and to make a strong final impression that will move your listeners to accept your position. You may make a plea for action or issue a challenge to your listeners.

Depending on your topic and method of organization, the conclusion of a persuasive speech can be either dramatic or subtle. In either case an effective conclusion must be directly related to the body of your speech.

## 17.4c How to Word a Persuasive Speech

In making a persuasive speech, speak in words that your listeners will understand. Be sure to define any terms that may be unfamiliar or used in unusual ways. If your listeners do not fully understand your proposal or your supporting reasons, they are not likely to be persuaded.

Guard against using expressions that are emotionally charged or that unfairly attack an opposing view. Your speech will be most effective if you state your argument calmly and objectively.

In any kind of speech, avoid trite or overused expressions. Vivid, colorful, concrete words help to hold your listeners' attention and make a lasting impression.

**Assignment   Organizing a Persuasive Speech**   *Step 1:* Choose a topic for a ten-minute persuasive speech. On your paper, write a specific topic and a statement of your position. *Step 2:* Make a rough outline, listing the major reasons that support your position. *Step 3:* Choose an appropriate method for organizing your speech.

Make a detailed outline with main headings, subheadings, and supporting material. *Step 4:* Locate facts that you need to support your opinion, and add them to your outline. *Step 5:* Write an introduction and a conclusion for your speech. Save your papers.

## 17.5 Delivering Informative and Persuasive Speeches

The effectiveness of your speech depends in large part upon the effectiveness of your delivery. Good preparation will help you communicate your message and reduce your nervousness.

### 17.5a Preparing to Deliver Your Speech

There are two ways to deliver informative or persuasive speeches, depending upon the circumstances and your own preference. One way is to speak extemporaneously, using note cards. The other way is to read from a prepared manuscript.

**Using Note Cards.** Delivering a speech from note cards requires careful preparation. Write on your note cards key words and phrases to remind you of what you want to say. Keep these notes brief; do not write in full sentences.

You can keep your notes well organized if you make one card for each main heading in your outline, with its subheadings and supporting material. Often, however, you will need to use more than one card for a main heading, especially when you have many supporting details. Do not put more than one main heading on a single note card.

Because you will just be glancing at your note cards, be sure that you write clearly and do not crowd your notes. You may find it helpful to use different colored inks to distinguish between main points, subheadings, and supporting material. Number the cards so that you can keep them in the correct order.

Using note cards has certain advantages over reading a speech. When you use note cards, you are more likely to speak naturally and to put your audience at ease. You will also be able to maintain more eye contact with your listeners and to avoid distracting them by shuffling papers.

Giving a speech from notes allows you to be more flexible. Because you have not fixed the exact wording, you can adapt what you say according to the feelings and reactions that you sense in your listeners.

**Writing Out Your Speech.**   When you write out your speech and read it from a manuscript, you have less flexibility and less eye contact with your audience. However, you may find certain advantages, as well. In some situations, especially formal ones, this type of delivery allows you to give your speech word for word as you have planned it.

When you plan to deliver a written speech, triple space your manuscript for ease of reading, and practice reading it aloud. Make notes in the margins or between paragraphs to remind yourself when to pause, what words to emphasize, and when to change your vocal inflection. Remember, also, to look up from time to time to establish eye contact with your listeners.

**Rehearsing Your Speech.**   Your speech will proceed much more smoothly if you rehearse it adequately. Rehearsing allows you to become very familiar with the content of your speech; therefore, you will be more relaxed in your delivery. You will speak more naturally and be able to maintain eye contact with your listeners.

Rehearse your speech aloud several times, using your note cards or manuscript. If your notes are unclear or incomplete, make appropriate changes on your cards. Time your speech to be sure that it conforms to your time limit. If possible, ask a friend or a family member to listen to your speech and make suggestions. You may also want to use a tape recorder if one is available.

## 17.5b  Presenting Your Speech

The way in which you deliver informative or persuasive speeches can increase your listeners' interest and help them to concentrate and understand the content. Your voice, your facial expression, the amount of eye contact between you and your audience, your gestures, and even your posture can contribute to your effectiveness in imparting information or winning people to your point of view.

**Voice.**   Speak slowly enough for your words to be clearly understood. Speak loudly enough to be heard by everyone in the room. Because you are speaking to an audience, you need to speak more distinctly than you would in everyday conversation. Pause occasionally for emphasis, to signal a transition to a new idea, or to let your listeners consider an important point. Vary the rate, tone, pitch, and volume of your voice to add emphasis and greater interest.

**Facial Expression.**   Occasionally you can smile, frown, or wrinkle your brow, just as you would when talking to friends. By your expression you can show concern, surprise, delight, puzzlement, determination, or any emotion that you feel as you talk. If you think about your topic and let yourself react naturally, your facial expressions will reinforce what you are saying.

**Eye Contact.**   As you speak, look around the room. Catch the eye of one listener, then another. Avoid staring at your notes, at the floor or back wall, or at just one person in the audience. Because you want your message to reach all the people in the room, you must look at all of them. With your eyes show that you care about your listeners and about their response.

**Gestures and Posture.**   Feel free to move about and to use your hands and body in a natural, relaxed way. Movements that look rehearsed or artificial can distract your listeners. Point, shrug, nod, and use other gestures as you would in everyday conversation.

Your posture, too, should be natural. Stand straight but not stiffly. Do not lean on a desk or lectern or sway from side to side.

**Assignment   Delivering Your Speech**   Examine your notes, outlines, introductions, and conclusions from the Assignments on pages 597 and 602. Decide whether you want to deliver the informative speech or the persuasive speech. Prepare note cards for your speech. Rehearse your speech several times and make any needed improvements in your notes. Then deliver your ten-minute speech to your English class.

# Unit 18

## Test-Taking Skills

If you plan to attend college, you will be among the thousands of students required to take a standardized test to gain admission. Most colleges require scores from the Scholastic Aptitude Test (SAT), given by the College Entrance Examination Board. Others require scores from the American College Testing Program (ACT). Although the information in this unit is based on the verbal-skills and written-English sections of the SAT, it will also be helpful if you plan to take the ACT.

Preparing for the SAT takes time. Cramming will not be very helpful to you. The best ways to prepare are to complete all class assignments conscientiously and to read widely. Only through reading can you enlarge your vocabulary and develop your reading comprehension.

## 18.1 Verbal Skills

The verbal section of the SAT has four types of items: antonyms, analogies, sentence completion, and reading comprehension. These items measure the extent of your vocabulary and your ability to understand what you read.

### 18.1a Antonyms

Each antonym item on the test has a word in capital letters followed by five answer choices. You must select the word that means most nearly the *opposite* of the given word. Most antonym items follow the format shown below.

ASCEND: (A) answer (B) attend (C) decant (D) descend (E) unbend

The word most nearly opposite in meaning to *ascend* is answer (D), *descend*.

Follow these strategies when answering antonym questions.

## Strategies

1. *Consider all of the choices before deciding which one is the best possible answer.* Remember that few words have exact opposites; choose the word that is *most nearly* opposite.

2. *Remember that you are looking for* antonyms, *not synonyms.* A synonym may be listed as a possible answer, but do not let it distract you.

3. *Remember that words may have more than one meaning.* If, for example, you do not realize that *magazine* means "a storage place for ammunition," as well as "a periodical," you may miss a test item.

4. *Use your knowledge of prefixes, suffixes, and Greek and Latin roots to help you figure out the meaning of unfamiliar words.* See Unit 16, "Vocabulary Skills."

**Assignment 1  Antonyms**  Write the antonym of each word given in capital letters. Use a dictionary, if necessary, to check your choices after you have finished.

1. TEMPORARY: (A) calm (B) contemptuous (C) extemporaneous (D) permanent (E) tempestuous
2. REGRESS: (A) irregular (B) progress (C) recess (D) retrogress (E) withdraw
3. RATIONAL: (A) abundant (B) placid (C) proportional (D) seasonal (E) unreasonable
4. INSIGNIFICANT: (A) autographed (B) ignorant (C) important (D) meaningless (E) vigilant

5. TERMINATE: (A) complete (B) exterminate
   (C) facilitate (D) inaugurate (E) intern
6. AFFLUENT: (A) afflicted (B) effluent (C) fluid
   (D) indigent (E) wealthy
7. DIVERGE: (A) converge (B) divulge (C) emerge
   (D) multiply (E) submerge
8. JEOPARDY: (A) danger (B) facility (C) geography
   (D) pleasantry (E) safety
9. MALIGNANT: (A) apolegetic (B) benign (C) malicious
   (D) sinister (E) unmitigated
10. LEGIBLE: (A) illegal (B) illegitimate (C) ineligible
    (D) legless (E) unreadable

# 18.1b Analogies

Analogies test your ability to understand the relationship between two words and your ability to recognize a similar or parallel relationship between two other words. In analogies, you must first establish the relationship that exists between two given words. Then, from a list of choices, you select another pair of words with the same relationship. Most analogies follow the format shown here.

CEDAR : TREE :: (A) boy : man (B) elm : oak (C) limb : trunk
(D) maple : forest (E) salmon : fish

When reading analogies, substitute "is to" for the single colons. Substitute "as" for the double colon. You should read the preceding example as "Cedar *is to* tree *as* boy *is to* man," and so forth.

To find the correct choice in the example, first determine how *cedar* and *tree* are related. Cedar is a kind of tree. Look for a similar relationship among the answer choices. The correct answer is *(E) salmon : fish*. Salmon is a kind of fish.

Follow these strategies when answering analogy questions.

**Strategies**

1. *Determine the relationship that exists between the first pair of words.* In a sentence or phrase, say to yourself what that relationship is.

*2. Read all of the answer choices before selecting one.*

**Assignment 2** **Analogies** On your paper, write the letter of the pair of words having the same relationship as the words in capital letters.

1. PUNCTUAL : PROMPT :: (A) late : later (B) postpone : defer
   (C) punctuate : abbreviate (D) stingy : generous
   (E) tardy : early

2. PAIR : PEAR :: (A) hoarse : horse (B) married : single
   (C) pare : peer (D) repair : appear (E) vegetable : fruit

3. HANGAR : PLANE :: (A) dirigible : zeppelin
   (B) field : helicopter (C) garage : car (D) ship : dock
   (E) track : train

4. MILK : QUART :: (A) beans : pod (B) butter : pound
   (C) cream : coffee (D) dollar : money (E) water : pump

5. APRIL : MAY :: (A) fall : spring (B) January : December
   (C) June : July (D) November : September
   (E) showers : flowers

6. ALIGN : ALINE :: (A) auto : place (B) birds : fence
   (C) brake : bumper (D) catsup : ketchup
   (E) wheels : headlights

7. HERD : CATTLE :: (A) snake : cobra (B) pride : lion
   (C) rat : mouse (D) bird : canary (E) pig : porcine

8. SMALLEST : SMALL :: (A) best : well (B) large : larger
   (C) lest : less (D) long : longest

9. HOE : GARDENER :: (A) cow: farmer (B) place : carpenter
   (C) shovel : plow (D) song : chorus (E) ski : skier

10. CONFEDERATE : PARTNER :: (A) gray : blue
    (B) outsider : insider (C) predicament : plight
    (D) senior : teammate (E) Southerner : Northerner

## 18.1c Sentence Completion

In sentence-completion questions, you must complete a sentence by supplying a missing word or words consistent with the rest of the sentence. In order to do so, you must first understand the ideas expressed in the sentence. Generally, sentence-completion questions do not require any special knowledge beyond an understanding of all of the words in the sentence itself and in the answer choices. Thus your skill in determining meaning from context is crucial (*page 579*). Study the following example.

> Fortunately, during television newscasts describing the __?__ problems of the world, we see, intermittently, commercials that provide __?__ to our own personal problems.
>
> (A) tragic..comfort (B) belligerent..peace
> (C) insoluble..solutions (D) catastrophic..advice
> (E) recurring..continuity

In answering the preceding example, you eliminate choices (A), (B), and (D); for in each case the second word would be inappropriate for the second blank in the sentence. It is not possible to provide comfort, peace, or advice to our own personal problems. You would also eliminate answer (E) because one provides continuity *in* something, not *to* something. The correct answer, therefore, is (C) because both words make sense in their respective blanks.

Follow these strategies when answering sentence-completion questions.

### Strategies

1. *Read the entire sentence through before trying to supply the missing word or words.*

2. *Make sure that both answers make sense in a sentence that has two blanks.*

3. *Check your answers by reading the complete sentence silently with the word(s) in place.*

**Assignment 3   Sentence Completion**   On your paper, write the letter of the word or words that correctly complete the sentence. Use a dictionary, if necessary.

1. When Lincoln said, "You can fool all of the people some of the time," he knew that not only the __?__ are fooled by propaganda.
   (A) poor (B) hungry (C) gullible (D) academicians
   (E) intelligentsia

2. Swarms of mosquitoes can be __?__ in those areas where __?__ puddles were left by the heavy spring rains.

   (A) seen..no (B) heard..oily (C) eliminated..huge

   (D) caught..small (E) expected..stagnant

3. Liquids that are __?__ should be kept in a tightly stoppered bottle.

   (A) volatile (B) effusive (C) expensive (D) rare

   (E) herbivorous

4. After the __?__ of his family's farm, he was distressed by the __?__ of the city.

   (A) odors..smoke (B) chaos..noise (C) animals..cars

   (D) tranquility..commotion (E) vegetables..supermarkets

5. The audience considered the dancer's performance to be __?__, but the newspaper critic cited several __?__.

   (A) awkward..falls (B) graceful..jumps (C) powerful..awards

   (D) flawless..mistakes (E) listless..missteps

6. In a time of inflation our rich country can expect the __?__ of scarcity amid plenty.

   (A) paradox (B) deflation (C) elimination (D) combination

   (E) preponderance

7. Such __?__ is inappropriate and in bad taste during a solemn ceremony.

   (A) levity (B) serenity (C) generosity (D) profundity

   (E) deliberation

8. The citizens became __?__ as the neighboring country __?__ troops along their common border.

   (A) tired..paraded (B) amazed..displayed

   (C) vituperative..exercised (D) knowledgeable..increased

   (E) apprehensive..stationed

## 18.1d Reading Comprehension

Reading-comprehension items test your understanding of what is directly or indirectly stated. They may also test your ability to interpret and to analyze what you read. Reading passages vary in length, but they always contain all of the information that you need to answer the questions that follow.

Follow these strategies when answering reading-comprehension questions.

### Strategies

1. *Read the passage closely and attentively.* Try to get a sense of the ideas and the organization of the passage, but do not waste time underlining or making marginal notes.

2. *Read the questions first if the passage is on a subject unfamiliar to you.* For example, if the passage is on physics, about which you may know little, reading the questions first may help you to follow the information more easily and to look for important points.

3. *Read all possible answers before selecting one.*

4. *Select your answer solely on the basis of what is in the passage,* not on your personal knowledge or opinion.

5. *Skip a passage that is too difficult for you and go on to the next one.* Come back to it if time allows.

Study the following example of a reading passage and its questions.

Although she was blind and deaf before the age of two, Helen Keller had many more wonderful experiences than most persons with full sight and hearing. She once wrote, "My hand is to me what your hearing and sight together are to you. In large measure we travel the same highways, read the same books, speak the same language; yet our experiences are different."

In the years after being received by President Cleveland in the White House, Helen Keller returned often to Washington to meet many Presidents and, reportedly, even made the staid Calvin Coolidge smile. She traveled around the world, visiting Europe, Australia, New Zealand, Egypt, South Africa, South America, and many other places. It was through her hands that she was able to experience so much.

In *Out of the Dark,* Keller wrote that her hands enabled her to read the faces and hands of people she met. She could distinguish a Southern drawl from a Yankee twang by touching spots on the speakers' throats. Hands were for her as easy to recognize as faces, and they revealed more openly the secrets of the character. One quiet, apologetic man had a fist of iron; a braggart had a hand that was timid; a bishop had a jovial hand; and a humorist had a hand of lead. Mark Twain's hands were full of drolleries and whims that changed to sympathy and companionship while you held them. Twain said that Helen Keller was the most marvelous woman who had existed on the earth since Joan of Arc. With her hands she probably saw more than you and I ever will.

1. The author of this passage especially commented on the fact that Helen Keller made President Coolidge smile because

   (A) Keller was a comedian.

   (B) Keller could not speak.

   (C) Keller had made many presidents laugh.

   (D) Coolidge had just lost an election.

   (E) Coolidge was reputed to be averse to levity.

2. Helen Keller was recognized in many countries throughout the world because she

   (A) wrote books.          (D) knew many presidents.
   (B) traveled widely.       (E) was an ambassador.
   (C) was like Joan of Arc.

3. Mark Twain knew that Helen Keller was a marvelous woman because he

   (A) read *Out of the Dark.*

   (B) knew her personally.

   (C) was told so by her family.

   (D) heard about her from President Cleveland.

   (E) heard about her in many foreign countries that he visited.

4. Helen Keller could sense a person's character most readily through his or her

   (A) walk          (D) hands
   (B) voice         (E) handwriting
   (C) face

If you have read carefully, following the strategies on page 612, you know that the answers are 1. (E), 2. (B), 3. (B), and 4. (D).

**Assignment 4   Reading Comprehension**   Read the essay on pages 431-433 in Unit 11, "Writing an Essay." Then on your paper, write the letter of the correct answers to the following questions.

1. The author was reluctant to approach her father when he returned because

   (A) she felt shy around someone who seemed like a stranger.

   (B) she was angry with her father for going away.

   (C) she thought that he would not know who she was.

   (D) her brothers would not let her near him.

   (E) her mother had told her to wait in her room.

2. The father had been away from home for over a year because he

   (A) was the ambassador to Thailand.

   (B) was serving in the military.

   (C) was hospitalized in another city.

   (D) was a foreign correspondent in South Vietnam.

   (E) was playing in a series of golf tournaments.

3. The most important item that the author and her family sent to her father was

   (A) cookies and homemade candy.

   (B) local newspapers.

   (C) tape recordings.

   (D) cans of golf balls.

   (E) new shirts and socks.

# 18.2  Standard Written English

The SAT also has a section called the Test of Standard Written English (TSWE). This test is not used as a college admission test; it is used, after you have gained admission, to determine which English course you should take. The TSWE is divided into two sections: Usage and Sentence Correction.

**Usage.**   The questions in Usage require you to identify writing that does not follow the conventions of standard usage. Examples may include incorrect verb usage, lack of parallel structure, incorrect pronoun usage, incorrect use of idiomatic expressions, and so forth. The usage questions follow the format shown here.

Leave us not grant the award solely for the candidate's looks.
   A        B                 C           D

No error.
   E

Look carefully at each lettered part and decide if it is correct or incorrect. Sometimes a sentence will have no error. No sentence ever has more than one error. The preceding example does have an error: choice A. The appropriate form is *Let us.*

**Sentence Correction.**  The examples in this portion of the test reflect errors in logic or in the structure of a sentence. You are instructed to choose the *best* way of stating an underlined portion of a sentence. If more than one answer seems correct, choose the one that is most effective in the context. In this kind of test, choice (A) is always the same as the underlined portion and means "Make no change." Study the following example.

At the age of three, my father first gave me swimming lessons.
(A) At the age of three,
(B) At the age of three
(C) Upon reaching the age of three,
(D) When I was three years old,
(E) Because I was going to be three years old,

Read the entire sentence; then study closely the underlined portion to determine how it is incorrect. In the example the underlined portion is a misplaced modifier. It implies that the father was three years old. Next, read all of the answer choices carefully before selecting one. The correct answer is (D).

**Preparing for the TSWE.**  Cramming will not help you to prepare for this test. However, there are things that you can do to improve your chances of performing well. First, read works by skilled writers so that you become accustomed to accepted usage. Second, review the units in Part One of this book. Finally, revise all of your written assignments as often as necessary to be sure that you have no errors in usage.

**Assignment 1   Grammar and Usage**   On your paper, write the letter of the error in each sentence. Write (E) if there is no error.

1. The <u>nurse said</u> to my <u>mother,</u> "<u>Theirs</u> nothing to worry <u>about.</u>"
        A              B      C                         D
   <u>No error.</u>
     E

2. <u>Being that</u> his name was the <u>only one</u> on the ballot, he <u>expected</u> to
     A                       B                    C
   <u>be elected.</u> <u>No error.</u>
     D       E

3. <u>It will</u> be <u>all right</u> for you <u>to take</u> the <u>examination</u> on Tuesday.
   A       B              C          D
   <u>No error.</u>
     E

4. Mario was the <u>shortest twin;</u> <u>yet</u> he could <u>easily outskate</u> José on <u>both</u>
              A      B            C            D
   roller skates and ice skates. <u>No error.</u>
                              E

5. Among <u>Laura's records</u> you can find <u>all kinds</u> of <u>music: jazz,</u> rock,
            A                     B       C
   <u>classical, and etc.</u> <u>No error.</u>
        D          E

**Assignment 2   Sentence Correction**   On your paper, write the letter of the correct answer for each item.

1. My teacher did not like <u>me writing my name in red ink</u> on my books.
   (A) me writing my name in red ink
   (B) me writing in red ink my name
   (C) me to write in red ink my own name
   (D) my writing my name in red ink
   (E) myself writing my name in red ink

2. She completed her research; <u>then her dissertation was written.</u>
   (A) then her dissertation was written
   (B) then she wrote her dissertation
   (C) at which point in time she prepared a dissertation

(D) then following this she wrote her dissertation

(E) then a dissertation was written by her

3. Do you know if it <u>was he whom</u> they elected president?

   (A) was he whom
   (B) was he who
   (C) was him who
   (D) was him whom
   (E) were he whom

4. <u>By climbing a tree, Diane could see the parade better.</u>

   (A) By climbing a tree, Diane could see the parade better.

   (B) Diane could see the parade, climbing a tree, better.

   (C) Diane could be able to see the parade better if she climbed a tree.

   (D) By climbing a tree, the parade could be seen better by Diane.

   (E) By climbing a tree, Diane could be able to see better the parade.

5. <u>In the skies again in 1986 we shall be in a position to see Halley's Comet.</u>

   (A) In the skies again in 1986 we shall be in a position to see Halley's Comet.

   (B) In the skies again we shall be in a position to see Halley's Comet in 1986.

   (C) Halley's Comet will again be visible in 1986.

   (D) Returning in 1986, we shall again be able to see Halley's Comet.

   (E) Once more we shall be able to see Halley's Comet when it reappears in 1986.

# Index

Abbreviations: in business letters, 544; capitalization of, 185, 188; periods after, 191

Absolute phrases: defined, 72

Abstract nouns: defined, 5

Action verbs: defined, 13; objects after, 51–54; representing physical or mental activities, 13

Active voice, 119–120, 314

Adjective clauses: agreement of subjects and verbs in, 132; defined, 82; essential, 82; with implied introductory word, 82; nonessential, 83; relative adverbs in, 82; relative pronouns in, 82, 145–146; subordinating with, 298

Adjective phrases: defined, 66

Adjectives: answering *Which? What kind? How many?*, 18; articles, 18–19; clauses used as, 82–83; comma with, 19, 192–193; defined, 18; demonstrative pronouns used as, 21; indefinite pronouns used as, 21; infinitives and infinitive phrases used as, 76; interrogative pronouns used as, 21; after linking verbs, 19; nouns used as, 20; as objective complements, 54; participles and participial phrases used as, 70–72; placement of, 19; possessive nouns used as, 20; predicate, 56; prepositional phrases used as, 28–29, 66; pronouns used as, 20–21; proper, 19–20, 187; relative pronouns used as, 21; in a series, 192–193

Adjustment letter, 548–549

Adverb clauses: comma after, 194; defined, 84; subordinating conjunctions in, 84–85; subordinating with, 298–299

Adverb phrases: defined, 67

Adverbs: answering *How? When? Where? How often? To what extent?*, 23–24; clauses used as, 84–85; defined, 23; distinguished from prepositions, 29; infinitives and infinitive phrases used as, 76; modifying adjectives, 24–25; modifying adverbs, 25; modifying verbs, 24; *not, never,* 24; nouns used as, 24; placement of, 24–25; prepositional phrases used as, 28–29, 67; used for emphasis, 24

Agreement of pronouns and antecedents, 134–138: antecedents joined by *and,* 134; antecedents joined by *or, nor,* 135; collective nouns as antecedents, 136; in gender, 136–137; indefinite pronouns as antecedents, 135–136; intensive pronouns, 138; in number, 134–136; in person, 137–138; personal pronouns, 134–137; plural antecedents, 134; reflexive pronouns, 138; singular antecedents, 134

Agreement of subjects and verbs, 123–133: in adjective clauses, 132; auxiliary verbs, 124; collective nouns, 128; compound subjects, 125–126; *every a, many a,* 132; *I* and *you,* 124; indefinite pronouns, 126–127; intervening words and phrases, 124; inverted word order, 131; nouns ending in *s,* 128; *one of those,* 133; plural subjects, 123–124; predicate nominatives, 132; singular subjects, 123–124; titles and names, 129; verb phrases, 124; words of amount and time, 130

Almanacs, 492

Analogies, in test taking, 608–609

Antecedent: agreement of pronoun with, 134–138; defined, 8, 134; reference of pronoun to, 148–149

Antonyms: in dictionary, 586; in test taking, 606–607

Apostrophe: in contractions, 204;

in plural of letters, numbers, etc., 204, 570; in possessives, 203–204

Application letter, 551–553

Appositive phrases: commas with, 68–69; defined, 68; essential, 68; nonessential, 68–69; subordinating with, 303–304; *we* and *us* in, 146–148

Appositives: commas with, 68–69; defined, 68; essential, 68; nonessential, 68–69; subordinating with, 303–304

Arabic numerals: in outline, 506; in writing numbers, 213

Argument: defined, 386; effectiveness of, 398–400; fallacies in, 401–403; moderation in, 396–397; in persuasive speech, 600; revising, 396–403; strategies for concluding, 393–394

Articles: definite, 19; indefinite, 18–19; in titles, 186, 211

Atlases, 492

Audience: defined, 239; for essay, 417–418; identifying, 239–240, 338–339; for literary essay, 450; for persuasive speech, 598–599; suiting topic to, 377–378

Author card, 490

Auxiliary verbs: agreement with subjects, 124; defined, 14; list, 14; with past participle, 108, 109; with present participle, 108, 109; in verb phrases, 14, 124

*Be:* as auxiliary verb, 14, 108, 109; as linking verb, 13, 55; partial conjugation of, 122

Bibliography: for literary essay, 468–469; procedure for, 517; for research paper, 494–496, 517

Bibliography cards: for literary essay, 459; for research paper, 495–496

Biographical sources, 492

Body: of business letter, 544; of essay, 430–434; of informative speech, 593, 594; of literary

essay, 466; of paragraph, 255–258; of persuasive speech, 600–601; of research paper, 513

Brackets, 209–210, 468

Business letters, 542–565: adjustment letters, 548–549; application letters, 551–553; block style, 544; body, 544; complimentary close, 544; heading, 543–544; inside address, 544; modified block style, 544; opinion letters, 556–558; order letters, 546–548; request (inquiry) letters, 545–546; salutation, 544; signature, 544; strategies for writing, 545–546, 548–549, 552–553, 558

Call number, 490, 495

Capitalization: of the abbreviations *A.D.*, *B.C.*, *A.M.*, *P.M.*, 188; of abbreviations after names of persons, 185; of abbreviations in titles of persons, 185; of compass points, 185; of family-relationship words, 184; of first word in direct quotation, 183; of first word in line of poem, 184; of first word in sentence, 183; of initials, 184; of interrupted quotation, 183–184; of names of days, months, holidays, special events, 186; of names of gods of mythology, 185; of names of heavenly bodies, 186; of names of historical events, periods, awards, documents, 186; of names of nationalities, peoples, languages, 186; of names of organizations, 187; of names of people, 184; of names of school subjects, 187; of names of structures, 187; of names of trains, ships, etc., 187; of personal and official titles, 185; of place names, 185; of Postal Service abbreviations, 188; of the pronoun *I,* 187; of proper adjectives, 19–20, 187; of proper

nouns, 4, 184–187; of titles of books, newspapers, poems, etc., 186; of trade names, 187
Capital letters, in outline, 427, 462, 506
Card catalog, 489–490
Case. *See* Pronoun case.
Cause and effect: distinguished, 271; in essay, 425; false association between, 402; in informative speech, 594; in paragraph development, 271–272; words suited to, 271
Characters: in literary analysis, 454; in narrative writing, 359–361
Chronological order: defined, 262; in descriptive writing, 353; in essay, 424; in expository writing, 341, 342; in informative speech, 594; in narrative writing, 361–362, 364; in paragraph development, 262; transitional words used in, 262
Clarity. *See* Coherence.
Classification: definition of, 267; in paragraph development, 267–268
Clauses, 79–87: adjective, 82–83, 132; adverb, 84–85; defined, 79; elliptical, 85; independent, 79–80; infinitive, 76, 140–141; noun, 86–87; reducing to phrases, 318–319; subordinate, 80–87; subordinating with, 297–300
Clichés, 352
Climax, in narratives, 357, 364
Coherence: defined, 261; in paragraphs, 249, 261–275, 285–287; in sentences, 320–322
Collective nouns: agreement of verbs with, 128; defined, 4
Colloquial language, 106
Colon, 198–199, 202, 544
Comma: with adjectives in a series, 192–193; after adverb clauses, 194; to avoid confusion, 194; with clauses in a series, 193; after closing of letter, 195, 544; with compound comparisons, 153; after conjunctive adverbs, 197; before coordinating conjunctions, 194, 294; in dates and addresses, 195; with direct address, 194; after greeting of social letter, 195; with independent clauses, 79, 90, 194; after interjections, 35, 194; with modifiers in a series, 192–193; with nonessential appositives, 69, 195; with nonessential clauses, 83, 195; with nonessential phrases, 69, 195; with parenthetical expressions, 194; after participial phrases, 194; with phrases in a series, 193; after prepositional phrases, 194; with quotation marks, 202; in run-on sentence, 96; to separate sentence parts, 194–195; in a series, 192–193
Common nouns: defined, 4
Comparative degree, 151–152
Comparison and contrast: distinguished, 269; in essay, 425; in literary essay, 454; in paragraph development, 269–270; transitional expressions, 269
Comparison of modifiers: compound, 153; correct use of, 151–152; degrees of, 151; double, 152; with *-er, -est,* 151; illogical, 153–154; incomplete, 152–153; irregular, 152; with *less, least,* 152; with *more, most,* 152
Complements: defined, 51; direct objects, 51–52, 54; indirect objects, 52; after linking verbs, 55–56; objective, 54; subject, 55–56
Complete predicate: defined, 47
Complete sentence: defined, 93
Complete subject: defined, 47
Complex sentence: defined, 91
Complimentary close, in business letter, 195, 544
Compound comparison, of modifiers, 153
Compound-complex sentence: defined, 91; in sentence revision, 293–295
Compound adjective complement, 54
Compound nouns: defined, 4;

forming possessive, 204; spelling plurals, 570–571

Compound objects: defined, 52

Compound predicate: defined, 46

Compound preposition: defined, 28; list, 28

Compound sentence: defined, 90; punctuating, 79, 90, 194, 197, 202, 294; in sentence revision, 293–295

Compound subject: agreement of verb with, 125–126; defined, 45

Conciseness, 313–319

Concluding paragraph: of essay, 434–435; of informative speech, 595–596; of literary essay, 466–467; of persuasive speech, 602; of research paper, 514

Concluding sentence: defined, 256; in descriptive writing, 354; in expository writing, 342, 343; in persuasive writing, 393–394

Concrete nouns: defined, 4

Conflict, in narratives, 357

Conjugation, of verbs, 111–112, 122

Conjunctions: conjunctive adverbs as, 32; coordinating, 30; correlative, 31; defined, 30; subordinating, 31; in titles, 186

Conjunctive adverbs: comma after, 197; defined, 32; list, 32; with independent clauses, 79–80, 90, 194, 197

Connotation, 351, 420, 584–585

Context, and meaning, 579

Contractions, 204

Coordinating conjunctions: comma with, 79, 90, 194, 294; defined, 30; with independent clauses, 79, 90, 294–295; list, 30; relationships expressed by, 294–295

Coordination: defined, 293; reversing sentences by, 291–295

Correlative conjunctions: defined, 31; list, 31; in parallel structure, 310; relationships expressed by, 294

Cross-reference card, 490

Dangling modifier, 155–156

Dash, 207

Data, analyzing, 231

Declarative sentence: defined, 44; placement of subject and predicate in, 48; punctuating, 44, 191

Definite articles: defined, 19

Definitions: in dictionary, 586; in expository writing, 342; in informative speech, 596; in persuasive writing, 390

Degrees of comparison, 151

Demonstrative pronouns: as adjectives, 21; defined, 9

Denotation, 351, 420, 584–585

Dependent clauses. *See* Subordinate clauses.

Descriptions: effective words in, 350–352; in narrative writing, 359, 361; purpose of, 348; sensory details in, 348–350; similes and metaphors in, 352; strategies for writing, 353–354

Descriptive writing, 336, 348–354. *See also* Descriptions.

Details, in paragraph development, 255–256

Dewey decimal system, 490–491

Dialect, American, viii–xxiii

Dialogue: in narrative writing, 359–360, 362, 364; punctuating, 200

Diction, levels of, 420

Dictionary: antonyms in, 586; definitions, 586; entry, parts of, 586; entry word, 586; etymologies in, 587; guide words, 586; homographs in, 586–587; labels in, 587; parts of speech in, 586; pronunciation key, 586; superscripts in, 586–587; synonyms in, 586; and vocabulary, 585–587

Direct objects: compound, 53; defined, 51

Direct quotations: capitalization in, 183–184; of five or more lines, 201; in literary essay, 458, 467–468; of more than one paragraph, 201; of poetry, in literary essay, 468; of prose, in literary essay, 467–468; punctuating, 200–201; in research paper, 501–502, 514. *See also* Dialogue.

Documentation: of literary essay, 468–469; of research paper, 514–517

Double comparison, of modifiers, 152

Ellipsis points, 207–208

Elliptical clauses: defined, 85

Emphatic forms, of verbs, 116

Encyclopedias, 491–492

Entry word, in dictionary, 586

Essays, 412–447: audience for, 417–418; body paragraphs in, 430–434; capturing reader's interest, 430; complexity of sentences in, 420–422; concluding paragraph in, 434–435; defined, 412; diction in, 420; introductory paragraph in, 429–430; listing ideas for, 424; organizing ideas for, 424–425; outlining, 427, 431; point of view in, 418–419; proofreading, 439; purpose of, 412, 429; selecting and limiting a topic for, 413–415; strategies for revising, 437–439; style in, 419–422; thesis statement in, 426, 429; title for, 439; tone of, 418–419; transitions in, 433–434. *See also* Literary essays.

Essential clauses, 82, 195

Essential phrases, 68, 195

Etymologies, 587

Evidence: in literary essay, 457–459; in persuasive writing, 385, 398–400

Examples: in paragraph development, 255–256; in persuasive writing, 390

Exclamation point, 35, 44, 191, 202

Exclamatory sentence: defined, 44; placement of subject and predicate in, 48; punctuating, 44, 191

Explanations: selecting and limiting

a topic for, 340; strategies for planning, 341; strategies for writing, 341–342

Expository writing, 336, 340–346. *See also* Explanations.

Facts: combined with opinions, 382–383; defined, 380; as evidence, 384–385; in paragraph development, 255–256; in persuasive speech, 599; recognizing, 380–381; as support for opinions, 380–381, 382–383, 384–385

Fallacies, in reasoning, 401–403

First-person narration, 358

Footnotes: defined, 514; forms for, 515–516; placement of, 516

Future perfect tense, 114

Future tense, 113

Gazetteers, 492

Gender: agreement of pronouns and antecedents in, 136–137; defined, 9

Gerund phrases: defined, 73; function of, 73–74

Gerunds: defined, 73; functions of, 73; modified by possessive pronouns, 143

Greek roots, common, 580

Guide words, in dictionary, 586

Heading, in business letter, 543–544

Helping verbs. *See* Auxiliary verbs.

Historical present, 112

Homographs, 586–587

Homophones, 575

Hyphen, 205–207

Idioms, 106

Imperative mood, 121

Imperative sentence: defined, 44;

punctuating, 44, 191; subject implied, 48

Incomplete comparison, of modifiers, 152–153

Indefinite articles: defined, 18–19

Indefinite pronouns: as adjectives, 21; agreement of verbs with, 126–127; as antecedents, 135–136; defined, 11; list, 11, 126; plural, 127; singular, 126–127; singular or plural, 127; as subjects, 126–127

Independent clauses: comma with, 79, 90, 194; conjunctive adverb with, 79–80, 90, 197, 294; coordinating conjunctions with, 79, 90, 194, 294; defined, 79; semicolon with, 79, 197, 294

Indexes, to periodical articles, 492–493

Indicative mood, 121

Indirect objects: compound, 53; defined, 52

Indirect quotations, 200

Infinitive clauses: defined, 76; pronoun as subject or object of, 140–141

Infinitive phrases: defined, 76; functions of, 76

Infinitives: defined, 75; forming, 75; functions of, 75; without *to,* 76

Informative speeches, 591–597

Inside address, 544

Intensive pronouns: agreement with antecedent, 138; defined, 10

Interjections: comma after, 35, 194; defined, 35; exclamation point after, 35, 191

Interrogative pronouns: as adjectives, 21; case of, 144–145; defined, 10; in subordinate clauses, 87

Interrogative sentence: defined, 44; placement of subject and predicate in, 48; punctuating, 44, 191

Intransitive verbs, 16–17, 120

Introductory paragraph: of essay, 429–430; of informative speech, 595; of literary essay, 466; of persuasive speech, 601–602; of

research paper, 513

Inverted word order: agreement of subjects and verbs in, 131; placement of subjects and predicates in, 48

Irregular verbs, 109–110

Italics, 211–212

Jargon, 106

Language history: American English, viii–xxiii

Latin roots, common, 580

Letters. *See* Business letters.

Library, using, 489–494

Library of Congress classification, 490–491

Linking verbs: adjectives after, 19, 56; defined, 13; list, 13, 54; nouns after, 13, 56; pronouns after, 13, 56; subject complements after, 55–56

Lists: of points for explanation, 341; prewriting, 233–234, 235–236

Literary essays, 448–473. *See also* Essays.

Main headings, in outline, 427, 431, 462, 487, 506

Main verb, 14

Manuscript form, 217

Mechanics, 182–223: defined, 182. *See also* Capitalization; Italics; Numbers, in writing; Punctuation.

Metaphors, 352

Misplaced modifiers, 154–155, 307

Modes, of writing: defined, 336; description, 336, 348–354; exposition, 336, 340–346; narration, 336–337, 356–364; persuasion, 336. *See also* Argument, Descriptions, Essays, Explanations, Literary essays, Narratives, Persuasive writing.

Modifiers: adjective clauses, 82–83, 298; adjectives, 18–19; adverb clauses, 84, 298–299; adverbs, 23–25; at beginning of sentence, 307; comparison of, 151–154; correct use of, 151–156; dangling, 155–156; infinitive and infinitive phrases, 76; misplaced, 154–155, 307; participles and participial phrases, 70–72; placement of, 154–156; prepositional phrases, 28–29, 66–67

Mood, of verb, 120–121

Narratives: actions in, 361–362; choosing a topic for, 356–357; chronological order in, 361–362, 364; climax in, 357, 364; conclusion of, 357; conflict in, 357; creating characters for, 359–361; descriptions in, 359, 361; dialogue in, 359–361, 362, 364; organizing, 357; point of view in, 358; setting for, 359, 364; titles for, 364

Narrative writing, 336–337, 356–364. *See also* Narratives.

Nominative case, 140

Nonessential clauses, 83

Nonessential phrases, 69, 195

Nonstandard language, 106

Note cards: for research paper, 500–501, 502, 503; for speech, 603–604

Note taking: direct quotations in, 501–502; for literary essay, 457–459; paraphrase in, 502; for research paper, 499–503; strategies for, 501; summary in, 503

Noun clauses: defined, 86; functions of, 87; with omitted introductory word, 87; subordinating with, 300

Nouns: abstract, 5; as adjectives, 20; as adverbs, 24; clauses used as, 86–87; collective, 4; 128; common, 4; compound, 4, 204, 570–571; concrete, 4–5; defined, 3; ending in *s,* 128; effective use of, 7; gerunds and gerund phrases used as, 73–74; infinitives and infinitive phrases used as, 76; kinds, 4–5; after linking verbs, 13; plural, 123–124, 568–571; possessive, 20, 203–204; proper, 4, 184–187; specific, 7

Number: agreement of pronouns and antecedents in, 134–135; agreement of subjects and verbs in, 123–133; defined, 9; of nouns, 123; of personal pronouns, 9; of pronouns, 124; of subjects, 125–130; of verbs, 124, 125–130

Numbers, in writing: with *and,* 213; at beginning of sentence, 213; in dates, street numbers, room numbers, etc., 213–214; in expressions of time, 213

Objective case, 140–141

Objective complement: defined, 54

Objects: compound, 52–53; defined, 51; direct, 51–52, 54; indirect, 52; of prepositions, defined, 28

Opinion letter, 556–558

Opinions: combined with facts, 382–383; defined, 373; in persuasive speech, 599; in persuasive writing, 373–376, 377–378, 380–381, 382–383, 388; support for, 380–381, 382–383, 384–385; as topics for persuasive writing, 375–378

Order letter, 546–548

Order of importance: defined, 265; in descriptive writing, 353; in essay, 424; in expository writing, 341; in paragraph development, 265–266; transitional words used in, 265

Origins, of words, 583–584, 587

Outlining: an essay, 427, 431; a literary essay, 462–463; procedure for, 506–507; a research paper, 486, 506–507; strategies for, 463

Paragraphs, 248–283: body of, 255–258; cause and effect in, 271–272; chronological order in, 262; classification, 267–268; coherence in, 249, 261–275; combined methods of organization in, 275–276; comparison and contrast in, 269–270; concluding sentence, 249, 256–257; defined, 248; details in, 255–256; developing, 249–257; examples in, 255–256; facts in, 255–256; limiting topics for, 249–251; order of importance in, 265–266; organizing, 261–272; 275–276; reasons in, 255–256; separate, in descriptive writing, 354; spatial order in, 263–264; supporting sentences, 248–249, 255–256; topic sentence, 248, 252–254, 257–258; transitional words and phrases in, 249, 262, 263–264, 265–266, 269–270

Parallel structure, 310–312

Paraphrase, 458, 502

Parentheses, 209

Participial phrases: defined, 71; placement of, 71–72; subordinating with, 302–303

Participles, as adjectives: with auxiliary verbs, 70; defined, 70; past, 70–71; present, 70, 71; in verb phrases, 71

Passive voice, 119–120

Parts of speech, 2–41. *See also* Adjectives, Adverbs, Conjunctions, Interjections, Nouns, Prepositions, Pronouns, Verbs.

Part-of-speech labels, in dictionary, 586

Past perfect tense, 114

Past tense, 113

Period, 44, 190–191, 202

Periodical indexes, 492–493

Personal pronouns: agreement with antecedents, 134–137; case, 139–143; chart, 9; defined, 9; gender of, 9, 136–137; number of, 9, 134–136; person of, 9, 137–138; plural, 9, 134–136;

possessive, 9, 20–21, 142–143; singular, 9, 134–136

Person, of pronouns: agreement in, 137–138; consistency of, 290–291; defined, 9

Persuasive writing, 372–411

Phrases, 64–76: absolute, 72; appositive, 68–69; defined, 65; essential, 68, 195; gerund, 73–74; infinitive, 76; kinds, 65–76; nonessential, 69, 195; participial, 70–72; prepositional, 28–29, 66–67; as sentence fragments, 94; subordinating with, 302–304; verbal, 69–76

Plagiarism, 515

Point of view: in essay, 418–419, 430; in literary essay, 450; in narrative writing, 358

Position: defined, 382; in persuasive speech, 600–601; in persuasive writing, 382–383, 384–385; in research paper, 486; strategies for clarifying, 389–390; strategies for stating, 387–388

Positive degree, 151–152

Possessive case, 142-143

Possessive nouns, 20, 203–204

Possessive pronouns: as adjectives, 20–21, 143; defined, 9; replacing and referring to nouns, 142–143

Predicate: complete, 47; compound, 46; placement of, 48; simple, 46

Predicate adjective: defined, 56

Predicate nominative: defined, 56

Prefixes, defined, 581; hyphen after, 206; list of common, 581; and meaning, 581

Prepositional phrases: as adjectives, 28–29, 66; as adverbs, 28–29, 67; defined, 28, 66; modifiers in, 28, 66; objects in, 28, 66

Prepositions: compound, 28; defined, 27; distinguished from adverbs, 29; lists, 27, 28; objects of, 28; in titles, 186

Present perfect tense, 114

Present tense, 112–113

Prewriting, 226–247: defined, 226; developing ideas, 233–235;

finding ideas, 227–231; focusing ideas, 238–240; lists, 233–234, 235–236

Principal parts, of verb, 107–110

Progressive forms, of verb, 115–116

Pronominal adjectives. *See* Possessive pronouns.

Pronoun case: defined, 139; of interrogative pronouns, 144–145; nominative, 140; objective, 140–141; of personal pronouns, 139–143; possessive, 142–143; of relative pronouns, 145–146

Pronoun reference, 148–149

Pronouns: as adjectives, 20–21, 143; agreement with antecedents, 134–138; antecedent of, defined, 8, 134; in appositive phrases, 146–147; case, 139–146; in comparisons, 146; in compound constructions, 141; correct use of, 134–149; defined, 8; demonstrative, 9; indefinite, 11, 135–136; interrogative, 10, 144–145; intensive, 10, 138; kinds, 8–11; personal, 9; plural, 134; possessive, 9, 142–143; reference to antecedents, 148–149; reflexive, 10, 138; relative, 11, 145–146; singular, 134

Pronunciation: key, 576, 586; and spelling, 574–575, 576

Proofreading: defined, 326; an essay, 439; a research paper, 421; symbols, 216

Proper adjectives: capitalization of, 19–20, 187; creating with suffixes, 20; defined, 19

Proper nouns: capitalization of, 4, 184–187; defined, 4; forming plural, 569; forming possessive, 203

Public speaking, 588–605. *See also* Speeches.

Punctuation: apostrophe, 203–205, 570; brackets, 209–210, 468; colon, 198–199, 202, 544; comma, 35, 69, 79, 83, 90, 153, 192–195, 197, 202, 294, 544; dash, 207; ellipsis points,
207–208; exclamation point, 35, 44, 191; hyphen, 205–207; parentheses, 209; period, 44, 190–191, 202; question mark, 44, 191, 202; quotation marks, 200–202; semicolon, 79, 197, 202

Purpose, in speaking: general, 588–589; specific, 590

Purpose, in writing: defined, 238; of descriptive writing, 348; determining, 238–239, 337–338; of essay, 412, 429; of expository writing, 340; of literary essay, 449–450; of persuasive writing, 372

Question mark, 44, 191, 202

Quotation marks, 200–202

Quotations. *See* Direct quotations.

Readers' Guide to Periodical Literature, 493

Reading: comprehension, in test taking, 611–612; for literary essay, 453–454

Reasoning, sound, 401–403

Reasons: in paragraph development, 255–256; in persuasive speech, 600–601

Reduction, revising by, 318–319

Redundancy, eliminating, 314–315

Reference works, general, 491–492

Reflexive pronouns: agreement with antecedent, 138; defined, 10

Regular verbs, 108

Relative adverbs, 82

Relative pronouns: as adjectives, 21; case of, 145–146; defined, 11; list, 11, 87; in subordinate clauses, 80–81, 82, 87

Request (inquiry) letter, 545–546

Research paper, 482–541: bibliography for, 494–496; defined, 482; direct quotations in, 501–502, 514; documenting, 514–517; drafting, 513–514; finished form for, 525–534;

footnotes in, 514–516; organizing information for, 505–508; outlining, 487; research for, 489–494; revising, 519–521; selecting and limiting topic for, 483–485; taking notes for, 498–503; thesis statement for, 485–486

Résumé, writing a, 553–554

Review, writing a, 344–346

Revising, 284–335: an argument, 396–403; for completeness, 520; for consistency, 289; by coordination, 291–295; defined, 284; an essay, 437–439; a literary essay, 472–473; for organization, 520; for paragraph unity and coherence, 285–287; for parallel sentence structure, 310–312; by reduction, 318–319; a research paper, 519–521; for sentence coherence, 320–322, 521; for sentence conciseness, 313–319, 521; for sentence variety, 306–309, 521; by subordination, 297–304; for transitions, 520–521; for unity, 520

Roman numerals, in outline, 427, 462, 506

Roots: defined, 579; Greek, 580; Latin, 580; and meaning, 579–580

Rough outline, 427, 486

Run-on sentence: defined, 96

Salutation: of business letter, 199, 544; of social letter, 195

SAT (Scholastic Aptitude Test): preparing for, 606–613; strategies for analogy questions, 608–609; strategies for antonym questions, 607; strategies for reading-comprehension questions, 612; strategies for sentence-completion questions, 610

Secondary sources, 459, 469

Semicolon, 79, 197, 202

Sensory details, 348–350

Sentence: capitalization of, 183; coherence in, 320–322, 521; complements, 51–56; complete, 93–97; completion, in test taking, 609–610; complex, 91; compound, 90; compound-complex, 91; conciseness in, 313–319, 521; correction, in test taking, 615; declarative, 44; defined, 43; exclamatory, 44; fragment, 93–95; imperative, 44; interrogative, 44; length and complexity, in essays, 420–422; parallel structure in, 310–312; purpose, 43–44; run-on, 96–97; sample, 90; structure, 42–63; subject and predicate, 45–48; supporting, 255–256; topic, defined, 252; variety, 306–309, 521

Sentence combining, 64–65, 72–73, 74–75, 77, 83–84, 86, 91–93, 93–96, 293–306

Sentence fragment, 93–95

Sentence outline, 427

Setting, 359, 364

Signature, in business letter, 544

Similes, 352

Simple predicate: defined, 46

Simple sentence: defined, 90

Simple subject: defined, 45

Single quotation marks, 202

Slang, 106

Sources, evaluating, 499; secondary, 459, 469

Spatial order: defined, 263; in descriptive writing, 353; in essay, 424; in informative speech, 594; in paragraph development, 263–264; transitional words used in, 263

Speeches: information for, 590, 591–593, 599; informative, 591–597; kinds, 588–589; organizing, 590; persuasive, 597–602; preparing and delivering, 590, 603–604; presenting, 604–605; purpose for, 588–589, 590; selecting and limiting topics for, 589–590; thesis statements for, 590

Spelling, 568–577: *-cede, ceed,*

-*sede,* 574; changing final *y* to *i,* 572–573; doubling final consonant, 571–572; dropping final *e,* 572–573; homophones, 575; *ie/ei,* 573–574; patterns, 573–574; plurals, 568–571; procedure for studying, 568; pronunciation and, 574–575, 576; rules, 568–573; strategies for, 575–576; words commonly confused, 575; words frequently misspelled, 576–577

Style, in essays, 419–422

Subheadings, in outline, 427, 431, 462

Subject card, 490

Subject complement: defined, 55

Subject, of composition, explaining, 235–236

Subject, of sentence: agreement of verb with, 123–133; complete, 47; compound, 45; placement of, 48; simple, 45; understood, 45

Subjunctive mood, 121–122

Subordinate clauses: as adjectives, 82–83; as adverbs, 84–85; defined, 80; interrogative pronouns in, 87; kinds, 82–87; as nouns, 86–87; reducing, 318–319; relative adverbs in, 82; relative pronouns in, 82, 145–146; revising with, 298–299; as sentence fragments, 95; subordinating conjunctions in, 80–81, 84–85, 87

Subordinating conjunctions: defined, 31; list, 84; relationships expressed by, 31–32; in sentence revision, 299; in subordinate clauses, 80–81, 84–85, 87

Subordination: defined, 297; revising sentences by, 297–304

Suffixes: defined, 581; list of common, 582; and meaning, 581, 582

Summary, 458–459, 503

Superlative degree, 151–152

Superscripts: in dictionary, 587; in footnotes, 515

Supporting sentences: examples in, 255; facts in, 255; in persuasive writing, 391–392; reasons in, 255

Synonyms, 584, 586

Tense: consistency of, 117–118, 290; future, 113; future perfect, 114; historical present, 112; in literary essay, 451; past, 113; past perfect, 114; present, 112–113; present perfect, 114; sequence of, 117–118; shifts in, 118

Tests, taking. *See* SAT, TSWE.

Thesis statement: for essay, 426, 429; for literary essay, 455, 461, 466; for research paper, 485–486, 505

Third-person narration, 358

Title card, 490

Titles: agreement of verbs with, 129; capitalization of, 186; correct manuscript form, 217; italics with, 211; for literary essay, 465; quotation marks with, 201

Tone, of essay, 418–419, 430, 450

Topic: defined, 238; for essay, 413–415; limiting, 249–251, 340; for literary essay, 454; for narrative, 357; opinion as, 375–378; for persuasive speech, 598; for persuasive writing, 373–378; procedure for finding, 238; for research paper, 483–484

Topic outline, 427

Topic sentence: defined, 252; in descriptive writing, 353; in essay, 430; in expository writing, 341, 342; implied, 253–254; placement of, 255–257

Transitional words and phrases, 249, 262, 263–264, 265–266, 269–270, 341–342, 353, 434, 596

Transitive verbs, 16–17, 120

TSWE (Test of Standard Written English), preparing for, 614–617

Unity, paragraph, 285–287

Usage: alphabetical notes, 156–177; correct, 107–156

Usage labels, in dictionary, 587

Variety: in sentence beginnings, 306–307; in sentence structure and length, 308–309

Verbal phrases: absolute, 72; gerund, 73–74; infinitive, 76; participial, 71–72

Verbals, defined, 69; gerunds, 73; infinitives, 75; participles, 70–71

Verb phrase, 14, 124

Verbs: action, 13, 16, 51–54; active voice, 119–120, 314; agreement with subject, 123–133; auxiliary, 14, 108, 109; changes in form, 17; characteristics of, 16–17; conjugation, 111–112, 122; consistency of tenses, 117–118, 290; correct use of, 107–133; defined, 13; emphatic forms, 116; imperative mood, 121; indicative mood, 121; intransitive, 16–17, 120; irregular, 109–110; kinds, 13–14; linking, 13–14, 16, 54, 55–56; mood, 120–121; objective complements after, 54; objects after, 51–53; passive voice, 119–120; principal parts, 107–110; progressive forms, 115–116; regular, 108; sequence of tenses, 117–118; subject complements after, 55–56; subjunctive mood, 121–122; tenses, 111–114; transitive, 16–17, 120; voice, 119–120

Vertical file, in library, 494

Visual aids, in informative speeches, 593

Vocabulary, 578–587: choosing the best word, 584–585; connotation and denotation, 584–585; context and meaning, 579; dictionary and, 585–587; origins of words, 583–584; prefixes and meaning, 581; roots and meaning, 579–580; suffixes and meaning, 581, 582; synonyms, 584

Voice, of verb, 119–120, 290

Writer's notebook: defined, 227; strategies for beginning, 227–229

# Acknowledgments (continued)

The Publisher also wishes to thank all the students whose names appear in this textbook for granting permission to use their writing as models. The editors and the Publisher have been solely responsible for selecting the student writing used as models.

The editors have made every effort to obtain permission to use student writing. In two instances, however, it was not possible to locate student writers.

From "On the Terrace" by Berton Roueché, from *A Reporter at Large* in *The New Yorker,* September 15, 1980. © 1980 Berton Roueché. Originally in *The New Yorker.* From "An Occurrence at Owl Creek Bridge" from the *Collected Writings of Ambrose Bierce* by Ambrose Bierce. Reprinted by permission of the Citadel Press, Secaucus, N.J. From "The Great Lover" from *The Collected Poems of Rupert Brooke* by Rupert Brooke. Copyright © 1915. Reprinted by permission of Dodd, Mead, & Company, Inc. Sidgwick & Jackson Ltd., and The Canadian Publishers, McClelland and Stewart Limited, Toronto. "Home" from *The World of Gwendolyn Brooks* by Gwendolyn Brooks. Copyright 1953 by Gwendolyn Brooks Blakely. Reprinted by permission of Harper & Row, Publishers, Inc. From "A Christmas Memory" from *Selected Writings of Truman Capote* by Truman Capote. Copyright 1956. Reprinted by permission of Random House, Inc. From "Babe Ruth Comes to New York" by Robert W. Creamer from *The Yankees: The Four Fabulous Eras of Baseball's Most Famous Team* by Dave Anderson, Murray Chass, Robert W. Creamer, and Harold Rosenthal. Copyright 1979. Reprinted by permission of Random House, Inc. "'Hope' is the thing with feathers" by Emily Dickinson. Reprinted by permission of the publishers and the Trustees of Amherst College from *The Poems of Emily Dickinson,* edited by Thomas H. Johnson, Cambridge, Mass: The Belknap Press of Harvard University Press, Copyright © 1951, © 1955, 1979 by the President and Fellows of Harvard College. From *The Lowell Offering: Writings by New England Mill Women (1810-1845),* edited by Benita Eisler. (J.B. Lippincott Co.) Copyright © 1977 by Benita Eisler. Reprinted by permission of Harper & Row, Publishers, Inc., Cantrell-Colas, Inc, and Benita Eisler. From *The Factory Girls,* edited by Philip S. Foner. Copyright © 1977 by the Board of Trustees of the University of Illinois. Reprinted by permission of the University of Illinois Press. From *Snow* by Ruth Kirk. Copyright © 1977 by Ruth Kirk. Reprinted by permission of William Morrow & Company, and Paul R. Reynolds, Inc. From *Sports Illusion! Sports Reality* by Leonard Koppett. Copyright 1981 by Leonard Koppett. Reprinted by permission of Houghton Mifflin Company. From *Don't Touch That Dial! Radio Programming in American Life, 1920-1960* by J. Fred MacDonald. Copyright © 1979 by J. Fred MacDonald. Reprinted by permission of Nelson-Hall, Inc. From "The Way to Rainy Mountain" by N. Scott Momaday. First published in *The Reporter,* 26 January, 1967. Reprinted from *The Way to Rainy Mountain,* © 1969, The University of New Mexico Press. Reprinted by permission. From *The Fiction and Criticism of Katherine Anne Porter* by Harry J. Mooney, Jr. Reprinted by permission of the University of Pittsburgh Press. © 1957 by the University of Pittsburgh Press. From "Say It with Flowers" from *Yokohama, California* by Toshio Mori. Reprinted by permission of the Caxton Printers, Ltd., Caldwell, Idaho. From "By the North Gate" from *By the North Gate* by Joyce Carol

## Credits

Cover concept, book design, and art production: Ligature Publishing Services, Inc.

*Photos*
Carl Corey: cover xxiv–1, 566–567
James L. Ballard: 224–225, 243, 279, 331, 367, 407, 443, 477, 537, 561.
Pages viii, xii, xiv, xvi, xvii: Historical Pictures Service, Chicago     Page 279: Jane Burton/Bruce Coleman Incorporated     Page 537: NASA/Photos.

# Checklist for Revision

As a guide in revising your writing, consider the following questions:

✔ 1. Did you cover your topic thoroughly?

✔ 2. Did you remove any information not directly related to your topic?

✔ 3. Did you include a topic sentence or a thesis statement?

✔ 4. Did you present your information in a logical order?

✔ 5. Did you use transitional words and phrases to emphasize the order of your ideas?

✔ 6. Did you write an appropriate conclusion?

✔ 7. Did you use words and details that are suitable for your audience?

✔ 8. Did you achieve your purpose for writing?

✔ 9. Did you vary the length and structure of your sentences?

✔ 10. Did you use accurate and precise words?

✔ 11. Did you use the correct forms for research papers and letters?

✔ 12. Did you avoid using sentence fragments, run-on sentences, and other incorrect sentence structures?

✔ 13. Did you use correct usage, spelling, punctuation, and capitalization?

✔ 14. Did you carefully proofread your finished copy?